- **NEW** "Understand, Analyze, and Evaluate" questions encourage students to think critically about historical information.
- **NEW** "Looking Ahead" and "Recall and Reflect" questions guide students through mastery of the key events and main ideas.
- **NEW** CONNECT online activities place students in a more active environment.
- Connect History builds advanced thinking and writing skills through "Critical Missions" scenarios that place students in a pivotal moment in time and ask them to develop a historical argument.
- **Debating the Past, Patterns of Popular Culture and America in the World** features throughout the book provide insights into complex historical topics, social and cultural history, and the global context, respectively.

Better grades

Research shows that students' grades improve when using Connect History and LearnSmart. Imagine being able to document this type of grade improvement through easily-run reports:

Final analysis indicates more B students improve their learning and earn A's, and more C students get B's

The distribution shows the aggregate of letter grades assigned by instructors. A Chi Square test was performed to determine if final course grades were distributed differently across the two groups (control and experimental). The test indicated a significant difference, $X2\ (4) = 11.667, p = .020$ (an alpha level of .05 was adopted for this statistical test).

Listen to instructors:

- *My class that is **using Connect scored higher than any other class in my 25 years of teaching.**" ~ University of Colorado Denver*
- *"The students really love Connect. They also got the **best test scores on their first exam that I have ever seen in my teaching career.**" ~ Georgia Southern University*

The Unfinished Nation: the digital and print program that Connects students to Success!

THE UNFINISHED NATION

A Concise History of the
American People
Volume 2: From 1865

Seventh Edition

ALAN BRINKLEY
Columbia University

Connect
Learn
Succeed™

THE UNFINISHED NATION: A CONCISE HISTORY OF THE AMERICAN PEOPLE, VOLUME 2,
SEVENTH EDITION

Published by McGraw-Hill, a business unit of The McGraw-Hill Companies, Inc., 1221 Avenue of the Americas,
New York, NY 10020. Copyright © 2014 by The McGraw-Hill Companies, Inc. All rights reserved. Printed
in the United States of America. Previous editions © 2010, 2008, and 2004. No part of this publication may
be reproduced or distributed in any form or by any means, or stored in a database or retrieval system, without
the prior written consent of The McGraw-Hill Companies, Inc., including, but not limited to, in any network
or other electronic storage or transmission, or broadcast for distance learning.

Some ancillaries, including electronic and print components, may not be available to customers outside the
United States.

This book is printed on acid-free paper.

1 2 3 4 5 6 7 8 9 0 DOC/DOC 1 0 9 8 7 6 5 4 3

ISBN 978-0-07-741230-2

MHID 0-07-741230-3

Senior Vice President, Products & Markets:
Kurt L. Strand
Vice President, General Manager, Products &
Markets: *Michael Ryan*
Vice President, Content Production & Technology
Services: *Kimberly Meriwether David*
Managing Director: *Gina Boedeker*
Director: *Matthew Busbridge*
Brand Coordinator: *Kaelyn Schulz*
Director of Development: *Rhona Robbin*
Managing Development Editor: *Nancy Crochiere*
Development Editor: *Briana Porco*
Marketing Manager: *Stacy Best*

Content Project Manager: *April R. Southwood*
Buyer: *Nicole Baumgartner*
Senior Designer: *David W. Hash*
Cover/Interior Designer: *John Joran*
Cover Image: *Construction worker connecting steel
girders,* © *Bettmann/CORBIS; Chrysler Building,
New York, USA,* © *Paul Giamou/Getty Images*
Lead Content Licensing Specialist: *Carrie K. Burger*
Photo Research: *PhotoSearch*
Compositor: *Aptara®, Inc.*
Typeface: *10/12 Adobe Caslon Pro Regular*
Printer: *R. R. Donnelley*

All credits appearing on page or at the end of the book are considered to be an extension of the copyright page.

ix: © *PoodlesRock/Corbis; xii:* © *PoodlesRock/Corbis; xiii: Everett Collection; xiv: Photo by Instituto Nazionale
Luce/Alinari/Getty Images; xv:* © *Bettmann/Corbis; xix: Photo Courtesy of U.S. Army/U.S. Coast Guard photograph
by Petty Officer 2nd Class Kyle Niemi.*

Library of Congress Cataloging-in-Publication Data for the Main Title

Brinkley, Alan.
   The unfinished nation : a concise history of the American people / Alan Brinkley, Columbia University. —
Seventh edition.
      pages cm
   Includes bibliographical references and index.
   ISBN 978–0–07–340698–5 — ISBN 0–07–340698–8 (hard copy : acid-free paper) 1. United States–History.
I. Title.
   E178.1.B827 2014
   973–dc23

2012043288

The Internet addresses listed in the text were accurate at the time of publication. The inclusion of a website
does not indicate an endorsement by the authors or McGraw-Hill, and McGraw-Hill does not guarantee the
accuracy of the information presented at these sites.

www.mhhe.com

BRIEF CONTENTS

ABOUT THE AUTHOR

ALAN BRINKLEY is the Allan Nevins Professor of History at Columbia University. He served as University Provost at Columbia from 2003 to 2009. He is the author of *Voices of Protest: Huey Long, Father Coughlin, and the Great Depression*, which won the 1983 National Book Award; *American History: Connecting with the Past*; *The End of Reform: New Deal Liberalism in Recession and War*; *Liberalism and Its Discontents*; *Franklin D. Roosevelt*; and *The Publisher: Henry Luce and His American Century*. He is the chair of the board of the national Humanities Center, the chair of the board of the Century Foundation, and a trustee of Oxford University Press. He is a member of the Academy of Arts and Sciences. In 1998–1999, he was the Harmsworth Professor of History at Oxford University, and in 2011–2012, the Pitt Professor at the University of Cambridge. He won the Joseph R. Levenson Memorial Teaching Award at Harvard and the Great Teacher Award at Columbia. He was educated at Princeton and Harvard.

CONTENTS

18 | THE AGE OF THE CITY 417

22 THE NEW ERA 532

25 THE GLOBAL CRISIS, 1921–1941 599

26 AMERICA IN A WORLD AT WAR 615

27 THE COLD WAR 641

30 | THE CRISIS OF AUTHORITY 722

THE title *The Unfinished Nation* is meant to suggest several things. It is a reminder of America's exceptional diversity—of the degree to which, despite all the many efforts to build a single, uniform definition of the meaning of the American nationhood, that meaning remains contested. It is a reference to the centrality of change in American history—to the ways in which the nation has continually transformed itself and to how it continues to do so in our own time. And it is also a description of the writing of American history itself—of the ways in which historians are engaged in a continuing, ever unfinished, process of asking new questions.

Like any history, *The Unfinished Nation* is a product of its time and reflects the views of the past that historians of recent generations have developed. The writing of our nation's history—like our nation itself—changes constantly. It is not, of course, the past that changes; rather, there are shifts in the way historians, and the publics they serve, ask and answer questions about the past. There are now, as there have always been, critics of changes in historical understanding who argue that history is a collection of facts and should not be subject to "interpretation" or "revision." But historians insist that history is not and cannot be simply a collection of facts. Names and dates and a record of events are only the beginning of historical understanding. It is up to the writers and readers of history to try to interpret the evidence before them; and in doing so, they will inevitably bring to the task their own questions, concerns, and experiences.

Our history requires us to examine the many different peoples and ideas that have shaped American society. But it also requires us to understand that the United States is a nation whose people share many things: a common political system, a connection to an integrated national (and now international) economy, and a familiarity with a shared and enormously powerful mass culture. To understand the American past, it is necessary to understand both the forces that divide Americans and the forces that draw them together.

It is a daunting task to attempt to convey the remarkable history of the United States in a single book, and the seventh edition of *The Unfinished Nation* has, as have all previous editions, been carefully written and edited to keep the book as concise and readable as possible. In this edition, I have added significant additions throughout the book on the history of conservatism, which has become an important part of American life. I have also added new material on the U.S. Constitution; coverage of the early Africans in America before slavery; revised sections on the middle colonies; a description of the changing way Americans voted in the nineteenth century; and additional material on the emergence of "containment" as a core of American foreign policy and the conservative opposition to it. And I have provided new material on the recent past, including the 2012 election.

In addition to these changes, the seventh edition of *The Unfinished Nation* now contains a new set of primary source features titled "Consider the Source." My hope is that these features will prompt students to not only consider the way that historians read historical documents but also to think carefully about the many sources of information they encounter daily. All content is now reinforced and supplemented by a rich set of online practice and assessment resources, housed within the Connect platform. It is not only the writing of history that changes with time—the tools and technologies through which information is delivered change as well.

As always, I want to thank the students, teachers, and other readers of this book who have offered comments, criticism, and corrections. Suggestions can be sent to me at Department of History, Columbia University, New York, NY 10027; or by email to ab65@columbia.edu.

ALAN BRINKLEY

ACKNOWLEDGMENTS

WE are grateful to the many advisers and reviewers who generously offered comments, suggestions, and ideas at various stages in the development of this project. Our thanks go to:

Academic Reviewers

Tramaine Anderson, *Tarrant County College, Northeast*

Darlene Antezana, *Prince George's Community College*

Maj. Paul Belmont, *U.S. Military Academy, West Point*

Peter Belser, *Ivy Tech Community College*

Robert Bender, *Eastern New Mexico University, Roswell*

Devan Bissonette, *Excelsior College*

Blanche Brick, *Blinn College*

Brian Cervantez, *Tarrant County College Northwest*

Keith D. Dickson, *Old Dominion University*

Angela S. Edwards, *Florence-Darlington Technical College*

Ron Enders, *Ashland Community College*

Amy Essington, *California State University, Long Beach*

Glen Findley, *Odessa College*

Brandon Franke, *Blinn College*

Mary E. Frederickson, *Miami University of Ohio*

Joy Giguere, *Ivy Tech Community College*

Donn Hall, *Ivy Tech Community College*

Andrew Hollinger, *Tarrant Community College Northeast*

Brian Johnson, *Tarrant County College South*

Philbert Martin, *San Jacinto College South*

Linda McCabe, *Tarrant County College, Northeast*

Maureen A. McCormick, *Florida State College at Jacksonville*

Wesley Moody, *Florida State College*

Rebekkah Morrow, *Western Oklahoma State College*

Matt Schaffer, *Florence Darlington Technical College*

Rebecca Seaman, *Elizabeth City State University*

Eddie Weller, *San Jacinto College, South*

Ann K. Wentworth, *Excelsior College*

Geoffrey Willbanks, *Tyler Junior College*

Cary Wintz, *Texas Southern University*

Connect Board of Advisors

Michael Downs, *University of Texas— Arlington*

Jim Halverson, *Judson University*

Reid Holland, *Midlands Technical College*

Stephen Katz, *Rider University*

David Komito, *Eastern Oregon University*

Wendy Sarti, *Oakton Community College*

Linda Scherr, *Mercer County Community College*

Eloy Zarate, *Pasadena City College*

Symposium and Digiposium Attendees

Gisela Ables, *Houston Community College*

Sal Anselmo, *Delgado Community College*

Mario A. J. Bennekin, *Georgia Perimeter College*

C. J. Bibus, *Wharton County Junior College*

Olwyn M. Blouet, *Virginia State University*

Michael Botson, *Houston Community College*

Cathy Briggs, *Northwest Vista College*

Brad Cartwright, *University of Texas—El Paso*

Roger Chan, *Washington State University*

June Cheatham, *Richland College*

Karl Clark, *Coastal Bend College*

Bernard Comeau, *Tacoma Community College*

Kevin Davis, *North Central Texas College*

Michael Downs, *Tarrant County College*

Laura Dunn, *Brevard Community College*

Arthur Durand, *Metropolitan Community College*

Amy Forss, *Metropolitan Community College*

Jim Good, *Lone Star College*

R. David Goodman, *Pratt Institute*

Wendy Gunderson, *Colin County Community College*

Debbie Hargis, *Odessa College*

John Hosler, *Morgan State University*

James Jones, *Prairie View A&M University*

Philip Kaplan, *University of North Florida*

Carol A. Keller, *San Antonio College*

Greg Kelm, *Dallas Baptist University*

Michael Kinney, *Calhoun Community College*

Meredith R. Martin, *Collin College*

Linda McCabe, *North Lake College*

Sandy Norman, *Florida Atlantic University*

Michelle Novak, *Houston Community College*
Jessica Patton, *Tarrant County College*
Robert Risko, *Trinity Valley Community College*
Esther Robinson, *Lone Star College*
Geri Ryder, *Ocean County College*
Linda Scherr, *Mercer County Community College*
Jeffrey Smith, *Lindenwood University*
Rachel Standish, *San Joaquin Delta College*
Roger Ward, *Colin County Community College*
Don Whatley, *Blinn College*
Geoffrey Willbanks, *Tyler Junior College*
Scott M. Williams, *Weatherford College*
Carlton Wilson, *North Carolina*
Chad Wooley, *Tarrant County College*

Focus Group Participants

Simon Baatz, *John Jay College*
Manu Bhagavan, *Hunter College*
David Dzurec, *University of Scranton*

Mark Jones, *Central Connecticut State University*
Stephen Katz, *Philadelphia University*
Jessica Kovler, *John Jay College*
David Lansing, *Ocean County College*
Benjamin Lapp, *Montclair State University*
Julian Madison, *Southern Connecticut State University*
David Marshall, *Suffolk Community College*
George Monahan, *Suffolk Community College*
Tracy Musacchio, *John Jay College*
Mikal Nash, *Essex County College*
Veena Oldenburg, *Baruch College*
Edward Paulino, *John Jay College*
Craig Pilant, *County College of Morris*
Susan Schmidt Horning, *Saint John's University*
Donna Scimeca, *College of Staten Island*
Matthew Vaz, *City College of New York*
Christian Warren, *Brooklyn College*

Special thanks to Volker Janssen for his contributions to the "Consider the Source" feature, and Major Adrienne Harrison for her detailed review of the history of the middle colonies.

EXPERIENCE SUCCESS IN HISTORY

The Unfinished Nation makes history relevant to students through a series of engaging features:

New > CONSIDER THE SOURCE FEATURES

These features guide students through careful analysis of historical documents, and prompt them to closely examine the ideas expressed, as well as the historical circumstances. Among the classic sources included are Benjamin Franklin's testimony against the Stamp Act, the Gettysburg Address, a radio address from FDR, and Eisenhower's farewell speech on the Military Industrial Complex.

> **CONSIDER THE SOURCE**
>
> **BARTOLOME DE LAS CASAS, "OF THE ISLAND OF HISPANIOLA" (1542)**
>
> GOD has created all these murderless people to be quite the simplest...
>
> **UNDERSTAND, ANALYZE, & EVALUATE**
>
> 1. How did Bartolome de Las Casas characterize the natives? How do you think they would have responded to this description?
> 2. What metaphor did Las Casas use to describe the natives and where does this metaphor come from?
> 3. What role did Las Casas expect the Spaniards to play on Hispaniola? What did they do instead?

New > CRITICAL THINKING QUESTIONS

"Looking Ahead" and "Recall and Reflect" prompts bookend each chapter, encouraging students to move beyond memorization of facts and names to explore the importance and significance of the chapter themes. In addition, "Understand, Analyze, and Evaluate" questions at the end of each essay cue students to think critically about the featured content.

> **LOOKING AHEAD**
>
> 1. How did the English colonies in t... differ from one another in purpc
> 2. How "English" were the colonies
> 3. What did the English want from settlement in North America?

> **UNDERSTAND, ANALYZE, & EVALUATE**
>
> 1. What do historians say is the relationship between racism and slavery?
> 2. What are the economic ... forward by historians t... system of slave labor th... America? Do these arg... fully for the developme...

> **RECALL AND REFLECT**
>
> 1. How did patterns of family life and attitudes toward women differ in the northern and southern colonies?
> 2. How did the lives of African slaves change over the course of the first century of slavery?
> 3. Who emigrated to North America in the seventeenth century, and why did they come?
> 4. What was the intellectual culture of colonial America, as expressed in literature, philosophy, science, education, and law?
> 5. How and why did life in the English colonies diverge from life in England?

DEBATING THE PAST FEATURES

Twenty-two essays introduce students to the contested quality of much of the American past, and they provide a sense of the evolving nature of historical scholarship. From examining specific differences in historical understandings of the Constitution, to exploring the character of slavery and the causes of the Great Depression, these essays familiarize students with the interpretive character of historical understanding.

> **DEBATING THE PAST**
>
>
>
> **THE ORIGINS OF SLAVERY**
>
> THE debate among historians over how and why white Americans created a system of slave labor in the seventeenth century—and how and why only African Americans should be slaves—has been an unusually lively one. At its center is a debate over whether slavery was a result of white racism, or whether racism was a result of slavery.
>
> In 1950, Oscar and Mary Handlin published an influential article comparing slavery to other systems of "unfreedom" in the colonies. What separated slavery from other conditions of servitude, they argued, was that it was restricted to people of African descent, that it was permanent, and that it passed from one generation to the next. The unique characteristics of slavery, the Handlins argued, were part of an effort by colonial legislatures to increase the available labor force. White laborers needed an incentive to come to America; black laborers, forcibly imported from Africa, did not.
>
> Winthrop Jordan was one of a number of historians who later challenged the Handlins' thesis and argued that white racism, more than economic interests, produced African slavery. In *White Over Black* (1968) and other works, Jordan argued that Europeans had long viewed people of color as inferior beings. Those attitudes migrated with white Europeans to the New World, and white racism shaped the treatment of Africans in America from the beginning. Even without the
>
> economic incentives the Handlins described, in other words, whites would have been likely to oppress blacks in the New World.
>
> Peter Wood's *Black Majesty* (1974), a study of seventeenth-century South Carolina, was one of a number of works that moved the debate back toward social and economic conditions. Wood demonstrated that blacks and whites often worked together on relatively equal terms in the early years of settlement. But as rice cultivation expanded, it became more difficult to find white laborers willing to do the arduous work. The increase in the forcible importation of African slaves was a response to this growing demand for labor. It was also a response to fears among whites that without slavery it would be difficult to control a labor force brought to America against its will. Edmund Morgan's *American Slavery, American Freedom* (1975) argued similarly that the southern labor system was at first relatively flexible and later grew more rigid. In colonial Virginia, he claimed, white settlers did not at first intend to create a system of permanent bondage. But as the tobacco economy grew and created a high demand for cheap labor, white landowners began to feel uneasy about their reliance on a large group of dependent white workers. Such workers were difficult to recruit and control. Slavery, therefore, was less a result of racism than of the desire for whites to find a reliable and stable labor force.
>
> Robin Blackburn's *The Making of New World Slavery* (1996) argues particularly strenuously that while race was a factor in making the enslavement of Africans easier
>
> for whites to justify to themselves, the real reasons for the emergence of slavery were hardheaded economic decisions by ambitious entrepreneurs who realized very early that a slave-labor system in the labor-intensive agricultural world of the American South and the Caribbean was more profitable than a free labor system. Slavery served the interests of a powerful combination of groups: planters, merchants, industrialists, and consumers. The most important reason for the creation and continuation of the system, therefore, was not racism but the pursuit of profits. Slavery was not, Blackburn concludes, an
>
> antiquated remnant of an older world. It was a recognizably modern labor system that served the needs of an emerging market economy.
>
> **UNDERSTAND, ANALYZE, & EVALUATE**
>
> 1. What do historians say is the relationship between racism and slavery?
> 2. What are the economic arguments put forward by historians to explain the system of slave labor that developed in America? Do these arguments account fully for the development of slavery?

LONDON'S VIRGINIA.

(The Granger Collection, NYC)

AMERICA IN THE WORLD FEATURES

These fifteen essays focus on specific parallels between American history and those of other nations, and demonstrate the importance of the many global influences on the American story. Topics such as the global industrial revolution, the abolition of slavery, and the origins of the Cold War provide concrete examples of the connections between the history of the United States and the history of other nations.

PATTERNS OF POPULAR CULTURE FEATURES

These nine essays bring fads, crazes, hang-outs, hobbies, and entertainment into the story of American history, encouraging students to expand their definition of what constitutes history, and to think about how we can best understand the living experience of past lives.

The book's **Online Learning Center** at www.mhhe.com/unfinishednation7e includes an instructor's manual, computerized test bank, and PowerPoint presentations.

Design your ideal course materials with **McGraw-Hill Create™**, www.mcgrawhillcreate.com! Rearrange or omit chapters, combine material from other sources, and upload your syllabus or any other content you have written to make the perfect resource for your students. Register today at **www.mcgrawhillcreate.com**, and get a complimentary review copy in print or electronically.

McGraw-Hill Campus® is a new one-stop teaching and learning experience available to users of any learning management system. This institutional service allows faculty and students to enjoy **single sign-on (SSO) access to all McGraw-Hill Higher Education materials**, including the award-winning McGraw-Hill Connect platform, from directly within the institution's web site. With this program enabled, faculty and students will never need to create another account to access McGraw-Hill products and services.

McGraw-Hill Tegrity® is a service that makes class time available all the time by automatically capturing every lecture in a searchable format for students to review. With a simple one-click start-and-stop process, you capture all computer screens and corresponding audio. Students can replay any part of any class with easy-to-use, browser-based viewing on a PC or Mac. Help turn all of your students' study time into learning moments immediately supported by your lecture. To learn more about Tegrity, watch a 2-minute demo at http://tegritycampus.mhhe.com.

CourseSmart offers thousands of the most commonly adopted textbooks across hundreds of courses from a wide variety of higher education publishers. It is the only place for faculty to review and compare the full text of a textbook online, providing immediate access without the environmental impact of requesting a printed exam copy. At CourseSmart, students can save up to 50 percent off the cost of a printed book, reduce their impact on the environment, and gain access to powerful web tools for learning, including full text search, notes and highlighting, and e-mail tools for sharing notes among classmates. Learn more at www.coursesmart.com.

THE
UNFINISHED
NATION

15 RECONSTRUCTION AND THE NEW SOUTH

THE PROBLEMS OF PEACEMAKING

RADICAL RECONSTRUCTION

THE SOUTH IN RECONSTRUCTION

THE GRANT ADMINISTRATION

THE ABANDONMENT OF RECONSTRUCTION

THE NEW SOUTH

LOOKING AHEAD

1. What were the various plans for Reconstruction proposed by Lincoln, Johnson, and Congress? Which plan was enacted and why?

2. What were the effects of Reconstruction for blacks and whites in the South?

3. What were the political achievements and failures of the Grant administration?

FEW PERIODS IN THE HISTORY of the United States have produced as much bitterness or created such enduring controversy as the era of Reconstruction—the years following the Civil War during which Americans attempted to reunite their shattered nation. To many white Southerners, Reconstruction was a vicious and destructive experience—a period when vindictive Northerners inflicted humiliation and revenge on the defeated South. Northern defenders of Reconstruction, in contrast, argued that their policies were the only way to prevent unrepentant Confederates from restoring Southern society to what it had been before the war.

To most African Americans at the time, and to many people of all races since, Reconstruction was notable for other reasons. Neither a vicious tyranny, as white Southerners charged, nor a thoroughgoing reform, as many Northerners hoped, it was, rather, a small but important first step in the effort to secure civil rights and economic power for the former slaves. Reconstruction did not provide African Americans with either the legal protections or the material resources to ensure anything like real equality. Most black men and women had little power to resist their oppression for many decades.

And yet for all its shortcomings, Reconstruction did help African Americans create new institutions and some important legal precedents that helped them survive and that ultimately, well into the twentieth century, became the basis of later efforts to win greater freedom and equality.

1863

Lincoln announces
Reconstruction plan

1864

Lincoln vetoes
Wade-Davis Bill

1865

Lincoln assassinated;
Johnson is president

Freedmen's Bureau

Joint Committee on
Reconstruction

1866

Republicans gain in
congressional elections

1867

Congressional
Reconstruction begins

1868

Johnson impeached and
acquitted

14th Amendment
ratified

1869

Congress passes 15th
Amendment

Grant elected president

1872

Grant reelected

1873

Panic and depression

1875

"Whiskey ring" scandal

1877

Hayes wins disputed
election

Compromise of 1877
ends Reconstruction

1883

Supreme Court
upholds segregation

1890s

Jim Crow laws in South

1895

Atlanta Compromise

1896

Plessy v. Ferguson

THE PROBLEMS OF PEACEMAKING

Although it was clear in 1865 that the war was almost over, the path to actual peace was not yet clear. Abraham Lincoln could not negotiate a treaty with the defeated government; he continued to insist that the Confederacy had no legal right to exist. Yet neither could he simply readmit the Southern states into the Union.

THE AFTERMATH OF WAR AND EMANCIPATION

The South after the Civil War was a desolate place. Towns had been gutted, plantations burned, fields neglected, bridges and railroads destroyed. Many white Southerners—stripped of their slaves through emancipation and of capital invested in now worthless Confederate bonds and currency—had almost no personal property. More than 258,000 Confederate soldiers had died in the war, and thousands more returned home wounded or sick. Some white Southerners faced starvation and homelessness.

If conditions were bad for Southern whites, they were far worse for Southern blacks—the three and a half million men and women now emerging from bondage. As soon as the war ended, hundreds of thousands of them left their plantations in search of a new life in freedom. But most had nowhere to go, and few had any possessions except the clothes they wore.

COMPETING NOTIONS OF FREEDOM

For blacks and whites alike, Reconstruction became a struggle to define the meaning of the war and, above all, the meaning of freedom. But the former slaves and the defeated whites had very different conceptions of what freedom meant.

Some African Americans believed the only way to secure freedom was land reform—to have the government take land away from whites, who owned virtually all of it, and give it to black people, who owned virtually none. Others asked only for legal equality, confident that they could advance successfully in American society once the formal obstacles to their advancement disappeared. But whatever their demands, virtually all former slaves were united in their desire for independence from white control. Throughout the South, African Americans separated themselves from white institutions—pulling out of white-controlled churches and establishing their own, creating their own clubs and societies, and in some cases starting their own schools.

For most white Southerners, freedom meant something very different. It meant the ability to control their own destinies without interference from the North or the federal government. And in the immediate aftermath of the war, this meant trying to restore their society to its antebellum form. When these white Southerners fought for what they considered freedom, they were fighting above all to preserve local and regional autonomy and white supremacy.

In the war's immediate aftermath, the federal government's contribution to solving the question of the South's future was modest. Federal troops remained to preserve order and protect the freedmen. And in March 1865, Congress established the Freedmen's Bureau, an agency of the army directed by General Oliver O. Howard. The Freedmen's Bureau distributed food to millions of former slaves. It established schools, staffed by missionaries and teachers sent by Freedmen's Aid Societies and other private and church groups in the North. It even made a modest effort to settle blacks on lands of their own. But the Freedmen's Bureau was not a permanent solution. With authority to operate for only

RICHMOND, 1865 By the time Union forces captured Richmond in early 1865, the Confederate capital had been under siege for months and much of the city lay in ruins, as this photograph reveals. On April 4, President Lincoln, accompanied by his son Tad, visited Richmond. As he walked through the streets of the shattered city, hundreds of former slaves emerged from the rubble to watch him pass. "No triumphal march of a conqueror could have equalled in moral sublimity the humble manner in which he entered Richmond," a black soldier serving with the Union army wrote. "It was a great deliverer among the delivered. No wonder tears came to his eyes." (Library of Congress)

one year, it was, in any case, far too small to deal effectively with the enormous problems facing Southern society. In the meantime, other proposals for reconstructing the defeated South were emerging.

PLANS FOR RECONSTRUCTION

Control of Reconstruction rested in the hands of the Republicans, who were divided in their approach to the issue. Conservatives within the party insisted that the South accept abolition, but they proposed few other conditions for the readmission of the seceded states. The Radicals, led by Representative Thaddeus Stevens of Pennsylvania and Senator Charles Sumner of Massachusetts, urged a much harsher course, including

A MONUMENT TO THE CONFEDERATE DEAD   This monument in the town square of Greenwood, South Carolina, was typical of many such memorials erected all across the South. They served to commemorate the soldiers who had died in the struggle, but also to remind white Southerners of what was by the 1870s already widely known and romanticized as the "Lost Cause." (Museum of the Confederacy, Richmond, Virginia)

disenfranchising large numbers of Southern whites, protecting black civil rights, confiscating the property of wealthy whites who had aided the Confederacy, and distributing the land among the freedmen. Republican Moderates rejected the most stringent demands of the Radicals but supported extracting at least some concessions from the South on black rights.

President Lincoln favored a lenient Reconstruction policy, believing that Southern Unionists (mostly former Whigs) could become the nucleus of new, loyal state governments in the South. Lincoln announced his Reconstruction plan in December 1863, more than a year before the war ended. It offered a general amnesty to white Southerners—other than high officials of the Confederacy—who would pledge an oath of loyalty to the government and accept the abolition of slavery. When 10 percent of a state's total number of voters in 1860 took the oath, those loyal voters could set up a state government. Lincoln also proposed extending suffrage to African Americans who were educated, owned property, or had served in the Union army. Three Southern states—Louisiana, Arkansas, and Tennessee, all under Union occupation—reestablished loyal governments under the Lincoln formula in 1864.

Outraged at the mildness of Lincoln's program, the Radical Republicans refused to admit representatives from the three "reconstructed" states to Congress. In July 1864, they pushed their own plan through Congress: the Wade-Davis Bill. It called for the president to appoint a provisional governor for each conquered state. When a majority of the white males of a state pledged their allegiance to the Union, the governor could summon a state constitutional convention, whose delegates were to be elected by voters who had never borne arms against the United States. The new state constitutions would be required to abolish slavery, disenfranchise Confederate civil and military leaders, and repudiate debts accumulated by the state governments during the war. Only then would Congress readmit the states to the Union. Like the president's proposal, the Wade-Davis Bill left the question of political rights for blacks up to the states.

Congress passed the bill a few days before it adjourned in 1864, but Lincoln disposed of it with a pocket veto that enraged the Radical leaders, forcing the pragmatic Lincoln to recognize he would have to accept at least some of the Radical demands.

THE DEATH OF LINCOLN

What plan the president might have produced no one can say. On the night of April 14, 1865, Lincoln and his wife attended a play at Ford's Theater in Washington. John Wilkes Booth, an actor fervently committed to the Southern cause, entered the presidential box from the rear and shot Lincoln in the head. Early the next morning, the president died.

The circumstances of Lincoln's death earned him immediate martyrdom. They also produced something close to hysteria throughout the North, especially because it quickly became clear that Booth had been the leader of a conspiracy. One of his associates shot and wounded Secretary of State William Seward on the night of the assassination, and another abandoned at the last moment a plan to murder Vice President Andrew Johnson. Booth himself escaped on horseback into the Maryland countryside, where, on April 26, he was cornered by Union troops and shot to death in a blazing barn. Eight other people were convicted by a military tribunal of participating in the conspiracy. Four were hanged.

RECONSTRUCTION

DEBATE over the nature of Reconstruction has been unusually intense. Indeed, few issues in American history have raised such deep and enduring passions.

Beginning in the late nineteenth century and continuing well into the twentieth, a relatively uniform and highly critical view of Reconstruction prevailed among historians. William A. Dunning's *Reconstruction, Political and Economic* (1907) was the principal scholarly expression of this view. Dunning portrayed Reconstruction as a corrupt and oppressive outrage imposed on a prostrate South by a vindictive group of Northern Republican Radicals. Unscrupulous carpetbaggers flooded the South and plundered the region. Ignorant and unfit African Americans were thrust into political offices. Reconstruction governments were awash in

THE FREEDMEN'S BUREAU   For four years after the Civil War, the Freedmen's Bureau served newly freed slaves, helping them to get housing, food, education, and other services. This image shows African American men and women waiting for rations, most of them old and sick. (The New York Public Library/Art Resource, NY)

corruption and compiled enormous levels of debt. The Dunning interpretation dominated several generations of historical scholarship and helped shape such popular images of Reconstruction as those in the novel and film *Gone with the Wind*.

W. E. B. Du Bois, the great African American scholar, offered one of the first alternative views in *Black Reconstruction* (1935). To Du Bois, Reconstruction was an effort by freed blacks (and their white allies) to create a more democratic society in the South, and it was responsible for many valuable social innovations. In the early 1960s, John Hope Franklin and Kenneth Stampp, building on a generation of work by other scholars, published new histories of Reconstruction that also radically revised the Dunning interpretation. Reconstruction, they argued, was a genuine, if inadequate, effort to solve the problem of race in the South. Congressional Radicals were not saints, but they were genuinely concerned with protecting the rights of former slaves. Reconstruction had brought important, if temporary, progress to the South and had created no more corruption there than was evident in the North at the same time. What was tragic about Reconstruction, the revisionists claimed, was not what it did to Southern whites but what it failed to do for Southern blacks. It was, in the end, too weak and too short-lived to guarantee African Americans genuine equality.

In more recent years, some historians have begun to question the assessment of the first revisionists that, in the end, Reconstruction accomplished relatively little. Leon Litwack argued in *Been in the Storm So Long* (1979) that former slaves used the protections Reconstruction offered them to carve out a certain level of independence for themselves within Southern society: strengthening churches, reuniting families, and resisting the efforts of white planters to revive the gang labor system.

Eric Foner's *Reconstruction: America's Unfinished Revolution* (1988) and *Forever Free* (2005) also emphasized how far African Americans moved toward freedom and independence in a short time and how important they were in shaping the execution of Reconstruction policies. Reconstruction, he argues, "can only be judged a failure" as an effort to secure "blacks' rights as citizens and free laborers." But it "closed off even more oppressive alternatives. . . . The post-Reconstruction labor system embodied neither a return to the closely supervised gang labor of antebellum days, nor the complete dispossession and immobilization of the black labor force and coercive apprenticeship systems envisioned by white Southerners in 1865 and 1866. . . . The doors of economic opportunity that had opened could never be completely closed." •

UNDERSTAND, ANALYZE, & EVALUATE

1. According to the essay, *The Birth of a Nation* and *Gone with the Wind* are popular depictions of Reconstruction that reflect Dunning's interpretation of the era. Can you find other popular depictions that reflect other interpretations of Reconstruction?

2. A new view of Reconstruction began to emerge in the 1960s, the end of the civil rights movement. Why do you think the civil rights movement might have encouraged historians and others to reexamine Reconstruction?

ABRAHAM LINCOLN   This haunting photograph of Abraham Lincoln, showing clearly the weariness and aging that four years as a war president had created, was taken in Washington only four days before his assassination in 1865. (Library of Congress)

To many Northerners, however, the murder of the president seemed evidence of an even greater conspiracy—masterminded and directed by the unrepentant leaders of the defeated South. Militant Republicans exploited such suspicions relentlessly in the ensuing months.

JOHNSON AND "RESTORATION"

Leadership of the Moderates and Conservatives fell to Lincoln's successor, Andrew Johnson of Tennessee. A Democrat until he had joined the Union ticket in 1864, he became president at a time of growing partisan passions.

Johnson revealed his plan for Reconstruction—or "Restoration," as he preferred to call it—soon after he took office and implemented it during the summer of 1865 when Congress was in recess. Like Lincoln, he offered some form of amnesty to Southerners who would take an oath of allegiance. In most other respects, however, his plan resembled the Wade-Davis Bill. The new president appointed a provisional governor in each state and charged him with inviting qualified voters to elect delegates to a constitutional convention. To win readmission to Congress, a state had to revoke its ordinance of secession, abolish slavery and ratify the Thirteenth Amendment, and repudiate Confederate and state war debts.

By the end of 1865, all the seceded states had formed new governments—some under Lincoln's plan, others under Johnson's—and awaited congressional approval of them. But Radicals in Congress vowed not to recognize the Johnson governments, for, by now, Northern opinion had become more hostile toward the South. Delegates to the Southern conventions had angered much of the North by their apparent reluctance to abolish slavery and by their refusal to grant suffrage to any blacks. Southern states had also seemed to defy the North by electing prominent Confederate leaders to represent them in Congress, such as Alexander Stephens of Georgia, who had been vice president of the Confederacy.

RADICAL RECONSTRUCTION

Reconstruction under Johnson's plan—often known as "presidential Reconstruction"—continued only until Congress reconvened in December 1865. At that point, Congress refused to seat the representatives of the "restored" states and created a new Joint Committee on Reconstruction to frame a policy of its own. The period of "congressional," or "Radical," Reconstruction had begun.

THE BLACK CODES

Meanwhile, events in the South were driving Northern opinion in still more radical directions. Throughout the South in 1865 and early 1866, state legislatures enacted sets of laws known as the Black Codes, which authorized local officials to apprehend unemployed blacks, fine them for vagrancy, and hire them out to private employers to satisfy the fines. Some codes forbade blacks to own or lease farms or to take any jobs other than as plantation workers or domestic servants, jobs formerly held by slaves.

Congress first responded to the Black Codes by passing an act extending the life and expanding the powers of the Freedmen's Bureau so that it could nullify work agreements forced on freedmen under the Black Codes. Then, in April 1866, Congress passed the first Civil Rights Act, which declared blacks to be citizens of the United States and gave the federal government power to intervene in state affairs to protect the rights of citizens. Johnson vetoed both bills, but Congress overrode him on each of them.

THE FOURTEENTH AMENDMENT

In April 1866, the Joint Committee on Reconstruction proposed the Fourteenth Amendment to the Constitution. Congress approved it in early summer and sent it to the states for ratification. It offered the first constitutional definition of American citizenship. Everyone born in the United States, and everyone naturalized, was automatically a citizen and entitled to all the "privileges and immunities" guaranteed by the Constitution, including equal protection of the laws by both the state and national governments. There could be no other requirements for citizenship. The amendment also imposed penalties on states that denied suffrage to any adult male inhabitants. (Supporters of woman suffrage were dismayed by the addition of the word "male" to the amendment.) Finally, it prohibited former members of Congress or other former federal officials who had aided the Confederacy from holding any state or federal office unless two-thirds of Congress voted to pardon them.

Congressional Radicals offered to readmit to the Union any state whose legislature ratified the Fourteenth Amendment. Only Tennessee did so. All the other former

Confederate states, along with Delaware and Kentucky, refused, leaving the amendment temporarily without the necessary approval of three-fourths of the states.

But by now, the Radicals were growing more confident and determined. Bloody race riots in New Orleans and other Southern cities were among the events that strengthened their hand. In the 1866 congressional elections, Johnson actively campaigned for Conservative candidates, but he did his own cause more harm than good with his intemperate speeches. The voters returned an overwhelming majority of Republicans, most of them Radicals, to Congress. In the Senate, there were now 42 Republicans to 11 Democrats; in the House, 143 Republicans to 49 Democrats. Congressional Republicans were now strong enough to enact a plan of their own even over the president's objections.

The Congressional Plan

The Radicals passed three Reconstruction bills early in 1867 and overrode Johnson's vetoes of all of them. These bills finally established, nearly two years after the end of the war, a coherent plan for Reconstruction.

Under the congressional plan, Tennessee, which had ratified the Fourteenth Amendment, was promptly readmitted. But Congress rejected the Lincoln-Johnson governments of the other ten Confederate states and, instead, combined those states into five military districts. A military commander governed each district and had orders to register qualified voters (defined as all adult black males and those white males who had not participated in the rebellion). Once registered, voters would elect conventions to prepare new state constitutions, which had to include provisions for black suffrage. Once voters ratified the new constitutions, they could elect state governments. Congress had to approve a state's constitution, and the state legislature had to ratify the Fourteenth Amendment. Once enough states ratified the amendment to make it part of the Constitution, the former Confederate states could be restored to the Union.

By 1868, seven of the ten remaining former Confederate states had fulfilled these conditions and were readmitted to the Union. Conservative whites held up the return of Virginia and Texas until 1869 and Mississippi until 1870. By then, Congress had added an additional requirement for readmission—ratification of another constitutional amendment, the Fifteenth, which forbade the states and the federal government to deny suffrage to any citizen on account of "race, color, or previous condition of servitude." Ratification by the states was completed in 1870.

To stop Johnson from interfering with their plans, the congressional Radicals passed two remarkable laws of dubious constitutionality in 1867. One, the Tenure of Office Act, forbade the president to remove civil officials, including members of his own cabinet, without the consent of the Senate. The principal purpose of the law was to protect the job of Secretary of War Edwin M. Stanton, who was cooperating with the Radicals. The other law, the Command of the Army Act, prohibited the president from issuing military orders except through the commanding general of the army (General Grant), who could not be relieved or assigned elsewhere without the consent of the Senate.

The congressional Radicals also took action to stop the Supreme Court from interfering with their plans. In 1866, the Court had declared in the case of *Ex parte Milligan* that

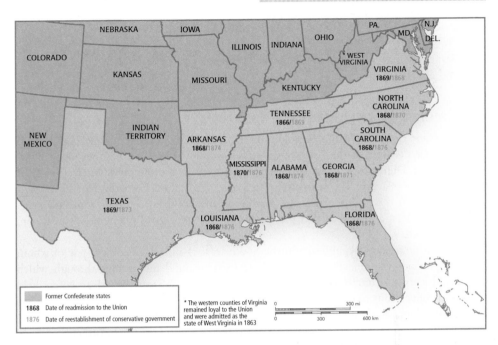

RECONSTRUCTION, 1866–1877 This map shows the former Confederate states and provides the date when each was readmitted to the Union as well as a subsequent date when each state managed to return political power to traditional white, conservative elites—a process white Southerners liked to call "redemption." • *What had to happen for a state to be readmitted to the Union? What had to happen before a state could experience "redemption"?*

military tribunals were unconstitutional in places where civil courts were functioning. Radicals in Congress immediately proposed several bills that would require two-thirds of the justices to support any decision overruling a law of Congress, would deny the Court jurisdiction in Reconstruction cases, would reduce its membership to three, and would even abolish it. The justices apparently took notice. Over the next two years, the Court refused to accept jurisdiction in any cases involving Reconstruction.

THE IMPEACHMENT OF ANDREW JOHNSON

President Johnson had long since ceased to be a serious obstacle to the passage of Radical legislation, but he was still the official charged with administering the Reconstruction programs. As such, the Radicals believed, he remained a major impediment to their plans. Early in 1867, they began looking for a way to remove him from office, and a search for grounds for impeachment began. Republicans found them, they believed, when Johnson dismissed Secretary of War Stanton despite Congress's refusal to agree. Elated Radicals in the House quickly impeached the president and sent the case to the Senate for trial.

The trial lasted throughout April and May 1868. The Radicals put heavy pressure on all the Republican senators, but the Moderates vacillated. On the first three charges to come to a vote, seven Republicans joined the Democrats and independents to support acquittal. The vote was 35 to 19, one vote short of the constitutionally required two-thirds majority. After that, the Radicals dropped the impeachment effort.

THE SOUTH IN RECONSTRUCTION

Reconstruction may not have accomplished what its framers intended, but it did have profound effects on the South.

THE RECONSTRUCTION GOVERNMENTS

Critics labeled Southern white Republicans with the derogatory terms "scalawags" and "carpetbaggers." Many of the "scalawags" were former Whigs who had never felt comfortable in the Democratic Party or farmers who lived in remote areas where there had been little or no slavery. The "carpetbaggers" were white men from the North, most of them veterans of the Union army who looked on the South as a more promising frontier than the West and had settled there at war's end as hopeful planters, businessmen, or professionals.

The most numerous Republicans in the South were the black freedmen, few of whom had any previous experience in politics. They tried to build institutions through which they could learn to exercise their power. In several states, African American voters held their own conventions to chart their future course. Their newfound religious independence from white churches also helped give them unity and self-confidence.

African Americans played significant roles in the politics of the Reconstruction South. They served as delegates to the constitutional conventions and held public offices of practically every kind. Between 1869 and 1901, twenty blacks served in the United States House of Representatives, two in the Senate. They served, too, in state legislatures and in various other state offices. Southern whites complained loudly about "Negro rule," but in the South as a whole, the percentage of black officeholders was small—and always far lower than the percentage of blacks in the population.

The record of the Reconstruction governments is mixed. Critics at the time and later denounced them for corruption and financial extravagance, and there is some truth to both charges. But the corruption in the South, real as it was, was hardly unique to the Reconstruction governments. Corruption had been rife in some antebellum and Confederate governments, and it was at least as rampant in the Northern states. And the large state expenditures of the Reconstruction years were huge only in comparison with the meager budgets of the antebellum era. They represented an effort to provide the South with desperately needed services that antebellum governments had never provided.

EDUCATION

Perhaps the most important accomplishment of the Reconstruction governments was a dramatic improvement in Southern education. Much of the impetus for educational reform in the South came from outside groups—the Freedmen's Bureau, Northern private philanthropic organizations, the many Northern white women who traveled to the South to teach in freedmen's schools—and from African Americans themselves. Over the opposition of many Southern whites, who feared that education would give blacks "false notions of equality," these reformers established a large network of schools for former slaves—4,000 schools by 1870, staffed by 9,000 teachers (half of them black), teaching 200,000 students. In the 1870s, Reconstruction governments began to build a comprehensive public school system. By 1876, more than half of all white children and about 40 percent of all black children were attending schools in the South (although almost all such schools were racially segregated). Several black "academies," offering more advanced education, also began operating. Gradually, these academies grew into an important network of black colleges and universities.

LANDOWNERSHIP AND TENANCY

The most ambitious goal of the Freedmen's Bureau, and of some Republican Radicals in Congress, was to reform landownership in the South. The effort failed. By June 1865, the bureau had settled nearly 10,000 black families on their own land—most of it drawn from abandoned plantations in areas occupied by the Union armies. By the end of that year, however, Southern plantation owners were returning and demanding the restoration of their property. President Johnson supported their demands, and the government eventually returned most of the confiscated lands to their original white owners.

Even so, the distribution of landownership in the South changed considerably in the postwar years. Among whites, there was a striking decline in landownership, from 80 percent before the war to 67 percent by the end of Reconstruction. Some whites lost their land because of unpaid debt or increased taxes; others left the marginal lands they had owned to move to more fertile areas, where they rented. Among blacks, during the same period, the proportion of landowners rose from virtually none to more than 20 percent.

Still, most blacks, and a growing minority of whites, did not own their own land during Reconstruction and, instead, worked for others in one form or another. Many black agricultural laborers—perhaps 25 percent of the total—simply worked for wages. Most, however, became tenants of white landowners—that is, they worked their own plots of land and paid their landlords either a fixed rent or a share of their crops (hence the term "sharecropping"). As tenants and sharecroppers, blacks enjoyed at least a physical independence from their landlords and had the sense of working their own land, even if in most cases they could never hope to buy it. But tenantry also benefited landlords in some ways, relieving them of the cost of purchasing slaves and of responsibility for the physical well-being of their workers.

INCOMES AND CREDIT

In some respects, the postwar years were a period of remarkable economic progress for African Americans in the South. The per capita income of blacks (when the material benefits of slavery are counted as income) rose 46 percent between 1857 and 1879, while the per capita income of whites declined 35 percent. African Americans were also able to work less than they had under slavery. Women and children were less likely to labor in the fields, and adult men tended to work shorter days. In all, the black labor force worked about one-third fewer hours during Reconstruction than it had been compelled to work under slavery—a reduction that brought the working schedule of blacks roughly into accord with that of white farm laborers.

But other developments limited these gains. While the black share of profits was increasing, the total profits of Southern agriculture were declining. Nor did the income redistribution of the postwar years lift many blacks out of poverty. Black per capita income rose from about one-quarter of white per capita income (which was itself low) to about one-half in the first few years after the war. After this initial increase, however, it rose hardly at all.

Blacks and poor whites alike found themselves virtually imprisoned by the crop-lien system. Few of the traditional institutions of credit in the South—the "factors" and

SOUTHERN BLACKS ASK FOR HELP, 1865

WE, the undersigned members of a Convention of colored citizens of the State of Virginia, would respectfully represent that, although we have been held as slaves, and denied all recognition as a constituent of your nationality for almost the entire period of the duration of your Government, and that by your *permission* we have been denied either home or country, and deprived of the dearest rights of human nature; yet when you and our immediate oppressors met in deadly conflict upon the field of battle—the one to destroy and the other to save your Government and nationality, we, with scarce an exception, in our inmost souls espoused your cause, and watched, and prayed, and waited, and labored for your success. . . .

When the contest waxed long, and the result hung doubtfully, you appealed to us for help, and how well we answered is written in the rosters of the two hundred thousand colored troops now enrolled in your Service; and as to our undying devotion to your cause, let the uniform acclamation of escaped prisoners, "whenever we saw a black face we felt sure of a friend," answer.

Well, the war is over, the rebellion is "put down," and we are *declared* free! Four fifths of our enemies are paroled or amnestied, and the other fifth are being pardoned, and the President has, in his efforts at the reconstruction of the civil government of the States, late in rebellion, left us entirely at the mercy of these subjugated but unconverted rebels, in *everything* save the privilege of bringing us, our wives and little ones, to the auction block. *We know* these men—know them well—and we assure you that, with the majority of them, loyalty is only "lip deep," and that their professions of loyalty are used as a cover to the cherished design of getting restored to their former relations with the Federal Government, and then, by all sorts of "unfriendly legislation," to render the freedom you have given us

banks—returned after the war. In their stead emerged a new credit system, centered in large part on local country stores—some of them owned by planters, others owned by independent merchants. Blacks and whites, landowners and tenants—all depended on these stores. And since farmers did not have the same steady cash flow as other workers, customers usually had to rely on credit from these merchants to purchase what they needed. Most local stores had no competition and thus could set interest rates as high as 50 or 60 percent. Farmers had to give the merchants a lien (or claim) on their crops as collateral for the loans (thus the term "crop-lien system," generally used to describe Southern farming in this period). Farmers who suffered a few bad years in a row, as many did, could become trapped in a cycle of debt from which they could never escape.

As a result of this burdensome credit system, some blacks who had acquired land during the early years of Reconstruction, and many poor whites who had owned land for years, gradually lost it as they fell into debt. Southern farmers also became almost wholly dependent on cash crops—and most of all on cotton—because only such marketable commodities seemed to offer any possibility of escape from debt. The relentless planting of more Intolerable than the slavery they intended for us.

We warn you in time that our only safety is in keeping them under Governors of the *military persuasion* until you have so amended the Federal Constitution that it will prohibit the States from making any distinction between citizens on account of race or color. In one word, the only salvation for us besides the power of the Government, is in the *possession of the ballot.* Give us this, and we will protect ourselves. . . . But, 'tis said we are ignorant. Admit it. Yet who denies we *know* a traitor from a loyal man, a gentleman from a rowdy, a friend from an enemy? . . . All we ask is an *equal chance* with the white *traitors* varnished and japanned with the oath of amnesty. Can you deny us this and still keep faith with us? . . .

We are "sheep in the midst of wolves," and nothing but the military arm of the Government prevents us and all the *truly* loyal white men from being driven from the land of our birth. Do not then, we beseech you, give to one of these "wayward sisters" the rights they abandoned and forfeited when they rebelled until you have secured our rights by the aforementioned amendment to the Constitution.

UNDERSTAND, ANALYZE, & EVALUATE

1. What did the authors of this petition emphasize in the first two paragraphs, and why did they feel this was important?
2. Why did the authors emphasize that they had been "declared" free? What dangers to their prospect of freedom did they observe?
3. What federal legal responses did they propose? Can you recognize these suggestions in the constitutional changes that came with Reconstruction?

Source: "Proceedings of the Convention of the Colored People of Virginia, Held in the City of Alexandria, August 2, 3, 4, 5, 1865" (Alexandria, Va., 1865), in W. L. Fleming (ed.), *Documentary History of Reconstruction* (Cleveland, Ohio, 1906), vol. 1, pp. 195–196; located in "Southern Blacks Ask for Help (1865)," in Thomas A. Bailey and David M. Kennedy (eds.), *The American Spirit*, vol. 1, 7th ed. (Lexington, Mass., 1991), pp. 466–467.

cotton contributed to soil exhaustion, which undermined the Southern agricultural economy over time.

THE AFRICAN AMERICAN FAMILY IN FREEDOM

A major reason for the rapid departure of so many blacks from plantations was the desire to find lost relatives and reunite families. Thousands of African Americans wandered through the South looking for husbands, wives, children, or other relatives from whom they had been separated. Former slaves rushed to have their marriages, previously without legal standing, sanctified by church and law.

Within the black family, the definition of male and female roles quickly came to resemble that within white families. Many women and children ceased working in the fields. Such work, they believed, was a badge of slavery. Instead, many women restricted themselves largely to domestic tasks. Still, economic necessity often compelled black women to engage in income-producing activities: working as domestic servants, taking in laundry, or helping their husbands in the fields. By the end of Reconstruction, half of all black women over the age of sixteen were working for wages.

A VISIT FROM THE OLD MISTRESS   Winslow Homer's 1876 painting of an imagined visit by a Southern white woman to a group of her former slaves was an effort to convey something of the tension in relations between the races in the South during Reconstruction. The women, once intimately involved in one another's lives, look at one another guardedly, carefully maintaining the space between them. White Southerners attacked the painting for portraying white and black women on a relatively equal footing. Some black Southerners criticized it for depicting poor rural African Americans instead of the more prosperous professional blacks who were emerging in Southern cities. "There were plenty of well-dressed negroes if he would but look for them," one wrote. (Smithsonian American Art Museum, Washington, DC/Art Resource, NY)

THE GRANT ADMINISTRATION

American voters in 1868 yearned for a strong, stable figure to guide them through the troubled years of Reconstruction. They turned trustingly to General Ulysses S. Grant.

THE SOLDIER PRESIDENT

Grant could have had the nomination of either party in 1868. But believing that Republican Reconstruction policies were more popular in the North, he accepted the Republican nomination. The Democrats nominated former governor Horatio Seymour of New York. The campaign was a bitter one, and Grant's triumph was surprisingly narrow. Without the 500,000 new black Republican voters in the South, he would have had a minority of the popular vote.

Grant entered the White House with no political experience, and his performance was clumsy and ineffectual from the start. Except for Hamilton Fish, whom Grant appointed secretary of state, most members of the cabinet were ill-equipped for their tasks. Grant relied chiefly on established party leaders—the group most ardently devoted to patronage, and his administration used the spoils system even more blatantly than most of its predecessors. Grant also alienated the many Northerners who were growing disillusioned with the Radical Reconstruction policies, which the president continued to support. Some Republicans suspected, correctly, that there was also corruption in the Grant administration itself.

By the end of Grant's first term, therefore, members of a substantial faction of the party—who referred to themselves as Liberal Republicans—had come to oppose what they called "Grantism." In 1872, hoping to prevent Grant's reelection, they bolted the party and nominated their own presidential candidate: Horace Greeley, veteran editor and publisher of the *New York Tribune*. The Democrats, somewhat reluctantly, named Greeley their candidate as well, hoping that the alliance with the Liberals would enable them to defeat Grant. But the effort was in vain. Grant won a substantial victory, polling 286 electoral votes to Greeley's 66.

GRANT THE TRAPEZE ARTIST This cartoon by eminent cartoonist Joseph Keppler shows President Ulysses S. Grant swinging on a trapeze holding on to the "whiskey ring" and the "navy ring" (references to two of the many scandals that plagued his presidency). Using a strap labeled "corruption," he holds aloft some of the most notorious figures in those scandals. The cartoon was published in 1880, when Grant was attempting to win the Republican nomination to run for another term as president. (Library of Congress)

The Grant Scandals

During the 1872 campaign, the first of a series of political scandals came to light that would plague Grant and the Republicans for the next four years. It involved the French-owned Crédit Mobilier construction company, which had helped build the Union Pacific Railroad. The heads of Crédit Mobilier had used their positions as Union Pacific stockholders to steer large fraudulent contracts to their construction company, thus bilking the Union Pacific of millions. To prevent investigations, the directors had given Crédit Mobilier stock to key members of Congress. But in 1872, Congress did conduct an investigation, which revealed that some highly placed Republicans—including Schuyler Colfax, now Grant's vice president—had accepted stock.

One dreary episode followed another in Grant's second term. Benjamin H. Bristow, Grant's third Treasury secretary, discovered that some of his officials and a group of distillers operating as a "whiskey ring" were cheating the government out of taxes by filing false reports. Then a House investigation revealed that William W. Belknap, secretary of war, had accepted bribes to retain an Indian-post trader in office (the so-called Indian ring). Other, lesser scandals also added to the growing impression that "Grantism" had brought rampant corruption to government.

The Greenback Question

Compounding Grant's problems was a financial crisis, known as the Panic of 1873. It began with the failure of a leading investment banking firm, Jay Cooke and Company, which had invested too heavily in postwar railroad building. There had been panics before—in 1819, 1837, and 1857—but this was the worst one yet.

Debtors now pressured the government to redeem federal war bonds with greenbacks, which would increase the amount of money in circulation. But Grant and most Republicans wanted a "sound" currency—based solidly on gold reserves—which would favor the interests of banks and other creditors. There was approximately $356 million in paper currency issued during the Civil War that was still in circulation. In 1873, the Treasury issued more in response to the panic. But in 1875, Republican leaders in Congress passed the Specie Resumption Act, which provided that after January 1, 1879, greenback dollars would be redeemed by the government and replaced with new certificates, firmly pegged to the price of gold. The law satisfied creditors, who had worried that debts would be repaid in paper currency of uncertain value. But "resumption" made things more difficult for debtors, because the gold-based money supply could not easily expand.

In 1875, the "Greenbackers" formed their own political organization: the National Greenback Party. It failed to gain widespread support, but the money issue was to remain one of the most controversial and enduring issues in late-nineteenth-century American politics.

Republican Diplomacy

The Johnson and Grant administrations achieved their greatest successes in foreign affairs as a result of the work not of the presidents themselves but of two outstanding secretaries of state: William H. Seward and Hamilton Fish.

An ardent expansionist, Seward acted with as much daring as the demands of Reconstruction politics and the Republican hatred of President Johnson would permit. He accepted a Russian offer to buy Alaska for $7.2 million, despite criticism from many who derided the purchase as "Seward's Folly." In 1867, Seward also engineered the American annexation of the tiny Midway Islands, west of Hawaii.

Hamilton Fish's first major challenge was resolving the long-standing controversy over the American claims that Britain had violated neutrality laws during the Civil War by permitting English shipyards to build ships (among them the *Alabama*) for the Confederacy. American demands that England pay for the damage these vessels had caused became known as the "*Alabama* claims." In 1871, after a number of failed efforts, Fish forged an agreement, the Treaty of Washington, which provided for international arbitration.

THE ABANDONMENT OF RECONSTRUCTION

As the North grew increasingly preoccupied with its own political and economic problems, interest in Reconstruction began to wane. By the time Grant left office, Democrats had taken back seven of the governments of the former Confederate states. For three other states—South Carolina, Louisiana, and Florida—the end of Reconstruction had to wait for the withdrawal of the last federal troops in 1877.

THE SOUTHERN STATES "REDEEMED"

In the states where whites constituted a majority—the states of the upper South—overthrowing Republican control was relatively simple. By 1872, all but a handful of Southern whites had regained suffrage. Now a clear majority, they needed only to organize and elect their candidates.

In other states, where blacks were a majority or where the populations of the two races were almost equal, whites used intimidation and violence to undermine the Reconstruction regimes. Secret societies—the Ku Klux Klan, the Knights of the White Camellia, and others—used terrorism to frighten or physically bar blacks from voting. Paramilitary organizations—the Red Shirts and White Leagues—armed themselves to "police" elections and worked to force all white males to join the Democratic Party. Strongest of all, however, was the simple weapon of economic pressure. Some planters refused to rent land to Republican blacks; storekeepers refused to extend them credit; employers refused to give them work.

The Republican Congress responded to this wave of repression with the Enforcement Acts of 1870 and 1871 (better known as the Ku Klux Klan Acts), which prohibited states from discriminating against voters on the basis of race and gave the national government the authority to prosecute crimes by individuals under federal law. The laws also authorized the president to use federal troops to protect civil rights—a provision President Grant used in 1871 in nine counties of South Carolina. The Enforcement Acts, although seldom enforced, discouraged Klan violence, which declined by 1872.

WANING NORTHERN COMMITMENT

But this Northern commitment to civil rights did not last long. After the adoption of the Fifteenth Amendment in 1870, some reformers convinced themselves that their long campaign on behalf of black people was now over, that with the vote blacks ought to be able to take care of themselves. Former Radical leaders such as Charles Sumner and Horace

Greeley now began calling themselves Liberals, cooperating with the Democrats, and denouncing what they viewed as black-and-carpetbag misgovernment. Within the South itself, many white Republicans now moved into the Democratic Party.

The Panic of 1873 further undermined support for Reconstruction. In the congressional elections of 1874, the Democrats won control of the House of Representatives for the first time since 1861. Grant reduced the use of military force to prop up the Republican regimes in the South.

THE COMPROMISE OF 1877

Grant had hoped to run for another term in 1876, but most Republican leaders—shaken by recent Democratic successes and scandals by the White House—resisted. Instead, they settled on Rutherford B. Hayes, three-time governor of Ohio and a champion of civil service reform. The Democrats united behind Samuel J. Tilden, the reform governor of New York, who had been instrumental in overthrowing the corrupt Tweed Ring of New York City's Tammany Hall.

Although the campaign was a bitter one, few differences of principle distinguished the candidates from one another. The election produced an apparent Democratic victory. Tilden carried the South and several large Northern states, and his popular margin over Hayes was nearly 300,000 votes. But disputed returns from Louisiana, South Carolina, Florida, and Oregon, whose electoral votes totaled 20, threw the election in doubt. Hayes could still win if he managed to receive all 20 disputed votes.

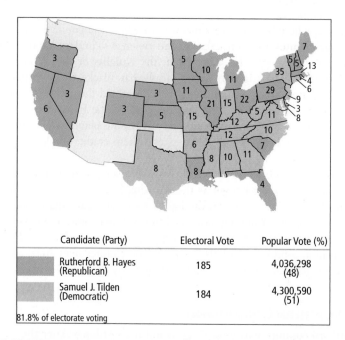

Candidate (Party)	Electoral Vote	Popular Vote (%)
Rutherford B. Hayes (Republican)	185	4,036,298 (48)
Samuel J. Tilden (Democratic)	184	4,300,590 (51)

81.8% of electorate voting

THE ELECTION OF 1876   The election of 1876 was one of the most controversial in American history. As in the elections of 1824, 1888, and 2000, the winner of the popular vote—Samuel J. Tilden—was not the winner of the electoral college, which he lost by one vote. The final decision as to who would be president was not made until the day before the official inauguration in March. • *How did the Republicans turn this apparent defeat into a victory?*

The Constitution had established no method to determine the validity of disputed returns. The decision clearly lay with Congress, but it was not clear with which house or through what method. (The Senate was Republican, and the House was Democratic.) Members of each party naturally supported a solution that would yield them the victory. Finally, late in January 1877, Congress tried to break the deadlock by creating a special electoral commission composed of five senators, five representatives, and five justices of the Supreme Court. The congressional delegation consisted of five Republicans and five Democrats. The Court delegation would include two Republicans, two Democrats, and the only independent, Justice David Davis. But when the Illinois legislature elected Davis to the United States Senate, the justice resigned from the commission. His seat went instead to a Republican justice. The commission voted along straight party lines, 8 to 7, awarding every disputed vote to Hayes.

Behind this seemingly partisan victory, however, lay a series of elaborate compromises among leaders of both parties. When a Democratic filibuster threatened to derail the commission's report, Republican Senate leaders met secretly with Southern Democratic leaders. As the price of their cooperation, the Southern Democrats exacted several pledges from the Republicans: the appointment of at least one Southerner to the Hayes cabinet, control of federal patronage in their areas, generous internal improvements, federal aid for the Texas and Pacific Railroad, and most important, withdrawal of the remaining federal troops from the South.

In his inaugural address, Hayes announced that the South's most pressing need was the restoration of "wise, honest, and peaceful local self-government," and he soon withdrew the troops and let white Democrats take over the remaining Southern state governments. That produced charges that he was paying off the South for acquiescing in his election. But the election had already created such bitterness that not even Hayes's promise to serve only one term could mollify his critics.

The president and his party hoped to build up a "new Republican" organization in the South committed to modest support for black rights. But although many white Southern leaders sympathized with Republican economic policies, resentment of Reconstruction was so deep that supporting the party became politically impossible. The "solid" Democratic South, which would survive until the mid-twentieth century, was taking shape.

THE LEGACY OF RECONSTRUCTION

Reconstruction made important contributions to the efforts of former slaves to achieve dignity and equality in American life. There was a significant redistribution of income and a more limited but not unimportant redistribution of landownership. Perhaps most important, African Americans themselves managed to carve out a society and culture of their own and to create or strengthen their own institutions.

Reconstruction was not as disastrous for Southern white elites as most believed at the time. Within little more than a decade after a devastating war, the white South had regained control of its own institutions and, to a great extent, restored its traditional ruling class to power. The federal government imposed no drastic economic reforms on the region and, indeed, few lasting political changes of any kind other than the abolition of slavery.

Reconstruction was notable, finally, for its limitations. For in those years, the United States failed in its first serious effort to resolve its oldest and deepest social problem—the problem of race. The experience so disillusioned white Americans that it would be nearly a century before they would try again to combat racial injustice.

Given the odds confronting them, however, African Americans had reason for considerable pride in the gains they were able to make during Reconstruction. And future generations could be grateful for two great charters of freedom—the Fourteenth and Fifteenth Amendments to the Constitution—which, although widely ignored at the time, would one day serve as the basis for a "Second Reconstruction" that would renew the drive to bring freedom to all Americans.

THE NEW SOUTH

The Compromise of 1877 was supposed to be the first step toward developing a stable, permanent Republican Party in the South. In that respect at least, it failed. In the years following the end of Reconstruction, white southerners established the Democratic Party as the only viable political organization for the region's whites. Even so, the South did change in some of the ways the framers of the Compromise had hoped.

THE "REDEEMERS"

Many white southerners rejoiced at the restoration of what they liked to call "home rule." But in reality, political power in the region was soon more restricted than at any time since the Civil War. Once again, most of the South fell under the control of a powerful, conservative oligarchy, whose members were known variously as the "Redeemers" or the "Bourbons."

In some places, this post-Reconstruction ruling class was much the same as the ruling class of the antebellum period. In Alabama, for example, the old planter elite retained much of its former power. In other areas, however, the Redeemers constituted a genuinely new ruling class of merchants, industrialists, railroad developers, and financiers. Some of them were former planters, some of them northern immigrants, some of them ambitious, upwardly mobile white southerners from the region's lower social tiers. They combined a defense of "home rule" and social conservatism with a commitment to economic development.

The various Bourbon governments of the New South behaved in many respects quite similarly. Virtually all the new Democratic regimes lowered taxes, reduced spending, and drastically diminished state services. One state after another eliminated or reduced its support for public school systems.

INDUSTRIALIZATION AND THE NEW SOUTH

Many white southern leaders in the post-Reconstruction era hoped to see their region develop a vigorous industrial economy, a "New South." Henry Grady, editor of the *Atlanta Constitution,* and other New South advocates seldom challenged white supremacy, but they did promote the virtues of thrift, industry, and progress—qualities that prewar southerners had often denounced in northern society.

Southern industry did expand dramatically in the years after Reconstruction, most visibly in textile manufacturing. In the past, southern planters had usually shipped their cotton to manufacturers in the North or in Europe. Now textile factories appeared in the South itself—many of them drawn to the region from New England by the abundance of water power, the ready supply of cheap labor, the low taxes, and the accommodating conservative governments. The tobacco processing industry similarly established an important foothold in the region. In the lower South, and particularly in Birmingham, Alabama, the iron (and, later, steel) industry grew rapidly.

Railroad development also increased substantially in the post-Reconstruction years. Between 1880 and 1890, trackage in the South more than doubled. And in 1886, the South changed the gauge (width) of its trackage to correspond with the standards of the North. No longer would it be necessary for cargoes heading into the South to be transferred from one train to another at the borders of the region.

Yet southern industry developed within strict limits, and its effects on the region were never even remotely comparable to the effects of industrialization on the North. The southern share of national manufacturing doubled in the last twenty years of the century, but it was still only 10 percent of the total. Similarly, the region's per capita income increased 21 percent in the same period, but average income in the South was still only 40 percent of that in the North; in 1860 it had been more than 60 percent. And even in those industries where development had been most rapid—textiles, iron, railroads—much of the capital had come from, and many of the profits thus flowed to, the North.

The growth of southern industry required the region to recruit a substantial industrial workforce for the first time. From the beginning, a high percentage of the factory workers were women. Heavy male casualties in the Civil War had helped create a large population of unmarried women who desperately needed employment. Hours were long (often as much as twelve hours a day), and wages were far below the northern equivalent; indeed, one of the greatest attractions of the South to industrialists was that employers were able to pay workers there as little as one-half of what northern workers received. Life in most mill towns was rigidly controlled by the owners and managers of the factories, who rigorously suppressed attempts at protest or union organization. Company stores sold goods to workers at inflated prices and issued credit at exorbitant rates (much as country stores did in agrarian areas), and mill owners ensured that no competing merchants were able to establish themselves in the community.

Some industries, such as textiles, offered virtually no opportunities to African American workers. Others—tobacco, iron, and lumber, for example—did provide some employment for blacks. Some mill towns, therefore, were places where the black and white cultures came into close contact, increasing the determination of white leaders to take additional measures to protect white supremacy.

Tenants and Sharecroppers

The most important economic problem in the post-Reconstruction South was the impoverished state of agriculture. The 1870s and 1880s saw an acceleration of the process that had begun in the immediate postwar years: the imposition of systems of tenantry and debt peonage on much of the region; the reliance on a few cash crops rather than on a diversified agricultural system; and increasing absentee ownership of valuable farmlands. During Reconstruction, perhaps a third or more of the farmers in the South were tenants; by 1900, the figure had increased to 70 percent.

African Americans and the New South

The "New South creed" was not the property of whites alone. Many African Americans were attracted to the vision of progress and self-improvement as well. Some former slaves (and, as the decades passed, their offspring) succeeded in elevating themselves into the

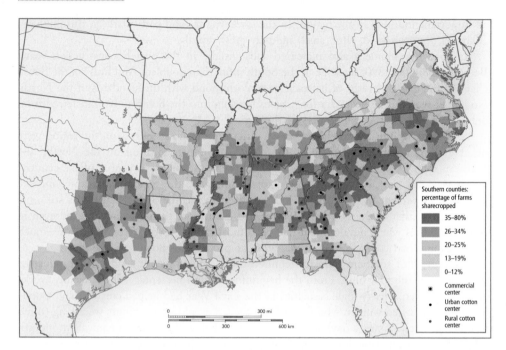

THE CROP-LIEN SYSTEM IN 1880 In the years after the Civil War, more and more southern farmers—white and black—became tenants or sharecroppers on land owned by others. This map shows the percentage of farms that were within the so-called crop-lien system, the system by which people worked their lands for someone else, who had a claim (or "lien") on a part of the farmers' crops. Note the high density of sharecropping and tenant farming in the most fertile areas of the Deep South, the same areas where slaveholding had been most dominant before the Civil War. • *How did the crop-lien system contribute to the shift in southern agriculture toward one-crop farming?*

middle class, acquired property, established small businesses, or entered professions. Believing strongly that education was vital to the future of their people, they expanded the network of black colleges and institutes that had taken root during Reconstruction into an important educational system.

The chief spokesman for this commitment to education was Booker T. Washington, founder and president of the Tuskegee Institute in Alabama. Born into slavery, Washington had worked his way out of poverty after acquiring an education (at Virginia's Hampton Institute). He urged other blacks to follow the same road to self-improvement.

Washington's message was both cautious and hopeful. African Americans should attend school, learn skills, and establish a solid footing in agriculture and the trades. Industrial, not classical, education should be their goal. Blacks should, moreover, refine their speech, improve their dress, and adopt habits of thrift and personal cleanliness; they should, in short, adopt the standards of the white middle class. Only thus, he claimed, could they win the respect of the white population.

In a famous speech in Georgia in 1895, Washington outlined a controversial philosophy of race relations that became widely known as the Atlanta Compromise. Blacks, he said, should forgo agitation for political rights and concentrate on self-improvement and preparation for equality. Washington offered a powerful challenge to those whites who wanted to discourage African Americans from acquiring an education or winning any economic gains. But his message was also intended to assure whites that blacks would not challenge the emerging system of segregation.

THE BIRTH OF JIM CROW

Few white southerners had ever accepted the idea of racial equality. That the former slaves acquired any legal and political rights at all after emancipation was in large part the result of their own efforts and critical federal support. That outside support all but vanished after 1877, when federal troops withdrew and the Supreme Court stripped the Fourteenth and Fifteenth Amendments of much of their significance. In the so-called civil rights cases of 1883, the Court ruled that the Fourteenth Amendment prohibited state governments from discriminating against people because of race but did not restrict private organizations or individuals from doing so.

Eventually, the Court also validated state legislation that institutionalized the separation of the races. In *Plessy v. Ferguson* (1896), a case involving a Louisiana law that required segregated seating on railroads, the Court held that separate accommodations did not deprive blacks of equal rights if the accommodations were equal. In *Cumming v. County Board of Education* (1899), the Court ruled that communities could establish schools for whites only, even if there were no comparable schools for blacks.

Even before these dubious decisions, white southerners were working to separate the races to the greatest extent possible, and were particularly determined to strip African Americans of the right to vote. In some states, disenfranchisement had begun almost as soon as Reconstruction ended. But in other areas, black voting continued for some time after Reconstruction—largely because conservative whites believed they could control the black electorate and use it to beat back the attempts of poor white farmers to take control of the Democratic Party.

TUSKEGEE INSTITUTE, 1881 From these modest beginnings, Booker T. Washington's Tuskegee Institute in Alabama became the preeminent academy offering technical and industrial training to black men. It deliberately de-emphasized the traditional liberal arts curricula of most colleges. Washington considered such training less important than developing practical skills. (© Bettmann/Corbis)

In the 1890s, however, franchise restrictions became much more rigid. During those years, some small white farmers began to demand complete black disenfranchisement—because they objected to the black vote being used against them by the Bourbons. At the same time, many members of the conservative elite began to fear that poor whites might unite politically with poor blacks to challenge them.

In devising laws to disenfranchise black males, the southern states had to find ways to evade the Fifteenth Amendment, which prohibited states from denying anyone the right to vote because of race. Two devices emerged before 1900 to accomplish this goal: the poll tax or some form of property qualification (few blacks were prosperous enough to meet such requirements) or the "literacy" or "understanding" test, which required voters to demonstrate an ability to read and to interpret the Constitution. Even those African Americans who could read had a hard time passing the difficult test white officials gave them. (The laws affected poor white voters as well as blacks.) By the late 1890s, the black vote had decreased by 62 percent, the white vote by 26 percent.

Laws restricting the franchise and segregating schools were only part of a network of state and local statutes—known as the Jim Crow laws—that by the first years of the twentieth century had institutionalized an elaborate system of segregation reaching into almost every area of southern life. Blacks and whites could not ride together in the same railroad cars, sit in the same waiting rooms, use the same washrooms, eat in the same restaurants, or sit in the same theaters. Blacks had no access to many public parks, beaches, or picnic areas; they could not be patients in many hospitals. Much of the new legal structure did no more than confirm what had already been widespread social practice in the South. But the Jim Crow laws also stripped blacks of many of the modest social, economic, and political gains they had made in the late nineteenth century.

More than legal efforts were involved in this process. The 1890s witnessed a dramatic increase in white violence against blacks, which, along with the Jim Crow laws, served to inhibit black agitation for equal rights. The worst such violence—lynching of blacks by white mobs—reached appalling levels. In the nation as a whole in the 1890s, there was an average of 187 lynchings each year, more than 80 percent of them in the South. The vast majority of victims were black. Those who participated in lynchings often saw their actions as a legitimate form of law enforcement, and some victims of lynchings had in fact committed crimes. But lynchings were also a means by which whites controlled the black population through terror and intimidation.

The rise of lynchings shocked the conscience of many white Americans in a way that other forms of racial injustice did not. In 1892, Ida B. Wells, a committed black journalist, published a series of impassioned articles after the lynching of three of her hometown friends in Memphis, Tennessee; her articles launched what became an international antilynching movement. The movement gradually attracted substantial support from whites in both the North and South (particularly from white women). Its goal was a federal antilynching law, which would allow the national government to do what state and local governments in the South were generally unwilling to do: punish those responsible for lynchings.

But the substantial southern white opposition to lynchings stood as an exception to the general white support for suppression of African Americans. Indeed, just as in the antebellum period, the shared commitment to white supremacy helped dilute class animosities between poorer whites and the Bourbon oligarchies. Economic issues tended to play a secondary role to race in southern politics, distracting people from the glaring social inequalities that afflicted blacks and whites alike.

A LYNCH MOB, 1893 A large, almost festive crowd gathers to watch the lynching of a black man accused of the murder of a three-year-old white girl. Lynchings remained frequent in the South until as late as the 1930s, but they reached their peak in the 1890s and the first years of the twentieth century. Lynchings such as this one—publicized well in advance and attracting whole families who traveled great distances to see them—were relatively infrequent. Most lynchings were the work of smaller groups, operating with less visibility. (Library of Congress)

CONCLUSION

Reconstruction was a profoundly important moment in American history. Despite the bitter political battles in Washington and throughout the South, culminating in the unsuccessful effort to remove President Andrew Johnson from office, the most important result of the effort to reunite the nation after its long and bloody war was a reshaping of the lives of ordinary people in all regions.

In the North, Reconstruction solidified the power of the Republican Party. The rapid expansion of the northern economy continued and accelerated, drawing more and more of its residents into a burgeoning commercial world.

In the South, Reconstruction fundamentally rearranged the relationship between the region's white and black citizens. Only for a while did Reconstruction permit African Americans to participate actively and effectively in southern politics. After a few years of widespread black voting and significant black officeholding, the forces of white supremacy ushered most African Americans to the margins of the southern political world, where they would mostly remain until the 1960s.

In other ways, however, the lives of southern blacks changed dramatically and permanently. Overwhelmingly, they left the plantations. Some sought work in towns and cities. Others left the region altogether. But the great majority began farming on small farms of their own—not as landowners, except in rare cases, but as tenants and sharecroppers on land owned by whites. The result was a form of economic bondage, driven by debt, only scarcely less oppressive than the legal bondage of slavery. Within this system, however, African Americans managed to carve out a much larger sphere of social and cultural activity than they had ever been able to create under slavery. Black churches proliferated in great numbers. African American schools emerged in some communities, and black colleges began to operate in the region. Some former slaves owned businesses and flourished.

Strenuous efforts by "New South" advocates to advance industry and commerce in the region produced significant results in a few areas. But the South on the whole remained what it had always been: a largely rural society with a sharply defined class structure. It also maintained a deep commitment among its white citizens to the subordination of African Americans—a commitment solidified in the 1890s and the early twentieth century when white southerners erected an elaborate legal system of segregation (the Jim Crow laws). The promise of the great Reconstruction amendments to the Constitution—the Fourteenth and Fifteenth—remained largely unfulfilled in the South as the century drew to its close.

RECALL AND REFLECT

1. What were the principal questions facing the nation at the end of the Civil War?
2. What were the achievements of Reconstruction? Where did it fail and why?
3. What new problems arose in the South as the North's interest in Reconstruction waned?
4. What was the Compromise of 1877, and how did it affect Reconstruction?
5. How did the New South differ from the South before the Civil War?

16 | THE CONQUEST OF THE FAR WEST

THE SOCIETIES OF THE FAR WEST

THE CHANGING WESTERN ECONOMY

THE ROMANCE OF THE WEST

THE DISPERSAL OF THE TRIBES

THE RISE AND DECLINE OF THE WESTERN FARMER

LOOKING AHEAD

1. What various ethnic and racial groups populated the American West, and how were the cultural characteristics of these groups reflected in the West?

2. How did the arrival and settlement of substantial numbers of Anglo-Americans transform the society and economy of the West?

3. What role did the federal government play in shaping the development of the West?

BY THE MID-1840s, WHITE AMERICAN migrants, along with many others, from the eastern regions of the nation had settled in the West in substantial numbers. Farmers, ranchers, and miners all found opportunity in the western lands. By the end of the Civil War, the West had become legendary in the eastern states. No longer the Great American Desert, it was now the "frontier": an empty land awaiting settlement and civilization; a place of wealth, adventure, opportunity, and untrammeled individualism.

In fact, the real West of the mid-nineteenth century bore little resemblance to its popular image. It was a diverse land, with many different regions, climates, and stores of natural resources. And it was extensively populated. The English-speaking migrants of the late nineteenth century did not find an empty, desolate land. They found Indians, Mexicans, African Americans, French and British Canadians, Asians, and others, some of whose families had been living in the West for generations.

TIME LINE

THE SOCIETIES OF THE FAR WEST

The Far West was in fact many lands. It contained both the most arid regions and some of the wettest and lushest areas of the United States. It contained the flattest plains and the highest mountains. It also contained many peoples.

THE WESTERN TRIBES

The Indian tribes made up the largest and most important western population group before the great white migration. Some were members of eastern tribes who had been forcibly resettled west of the Mississippi. But most were members of indigenous tribes.

More than 300,000 Indians (among them the Serrano, Chumash, Pomo, Maidu, Yurok, and Chinook) had lived on the Pacific Coast before the arrival of Spanish settlers. They supported themselves through a combination of fishing, foraging, and simple agriculture. The Pueblos of the Southwest had long lived largely as farmers and had established permanent settlements there.

The most widespread Indian groups in the West were the Plains Indians. They were, in fact, made up of many different tribal and language groups. Some lived more or less sedentary lives as farmers, but many subsisted largely through hunting buffalo. Riding small but powerful horses, the tribes moved through the grasslands following the herds, constructing tepees as temporary dwellings. The buffalo, or bison, provided the economic basis for the Plains Indians' way of life. The flesh of the large animal was their principal source of food, and its skin supplied materials for clothing, shoes, tepees, blankets, robes, and utensils. "Buffalo chips"—dried manure—provided fuel; buffalo bones became knives and arrow tips; buffalo tendons formed the strings of bows.

The Plains warriors proved to be the most formidable foes the white settlers had encountered. But the tribes were usually unable to unite against white aggression. At times, tribal warriors faced white forces who were being assisted by guides and even fighters from rival tribes. Some tribes, however, were able to overcome their divisions and unite effectively. By the mid-nineteenth century, for example, the Sioux, Arapaho, and Cheyenne had forged a powerful alliance that dominated the northern plains. That proved no protection, however, against the greatest danger to the tribes: ecological and economic decline. Indians were highly vulnerable to eastern infectious diseases, such as the smallpox epidemics that decimated the Pawnee in Nebraska in the 1840s. And the tribes were, of course, at a considerable disadvantage in any long-term battle with an economically and industrially advanced people.

Hispanic New Mexico

For centuries, much of the Far West had been part of the Spanish Empire and, later, the Mexican Republic. When the United States acquired its new lands there in the 1840s, it also acquired many Mexican residents.

In New Mexico, the centers of Spanish-speaking society were farming and trading communities established in the seventeenth century. Descendants of the original Spanish settlers (and more recent migrants from Mexico) engaged primarily in cattle and sheep ranching. When the United States acquired title to New Mexico in the aftermath of the Mexican War, General Stephen Kearny—who had commanded the American troops in the region—tried to establish a territorial government out of the approximately 1,000 Anglo-Americans in the region, ignoring the more than 50,000 Hispanics. There were widespread fears among Hispanics and Indians that the new American rulers would confiscate their lands. In 1847, before the new government had established itself, Taos Indians rebelled, killing the new governor and other Anglo-American officials before being subdued by United States Army forces. New Mexico remained under military rule for three years, until the United States finally organized a territorial government there in 1850. The United States Army finally broke the power of the Navajo, Apache, and other tribes in the region. The defeat of the tribes led to substantial Hispanic migration into other areas of the Southwest and as far north as Colorado.

The Anglo-American presence in the Southwest grew rapidly once the railroads established lines into the region in the 1880s and early 1890s. With the railroads came extensive new ranching, farming, and mining. This expansion of economic activity attracted a new wave of Mexican immigrants, who moved across the border in search of work. The English-speaking proprietors of the new enterprises restricted most Mexicans to the lowest-paying and least stable jobs.

Hispanic California and Texas

In California, Spanish settlement began in the eighteenth century with a string of Catholic missions along the Pacific Coast. The missionaries and the soldiers who accompanied them gathered most of the coastal Indians into their communities, some forcibly and others by persuasion. In the 1830s, after the new Mexican government began reducing the power of the church, the mission society largely collapsed. In its place emerged a secular Mexican aristocracy, which controlled a chain of large estates in the fertile lands west of the Sierra mountains. For them, the acquisition of California by the United States was disastrous. So vast were the numbers of English-speaking immigrants that the *californios* (as the

Hispanic residents of the region were known) had little power to resist the onslaught. English-speaking prospectors organized to exclude them, sometimes violently, from the mines during the gold rush. Many *californios* also lost their lands—either through corrupt business deals or through outright seizure.

Increasingly, Mexicans and Mexican Americans became part of the lower end of the state's working class, clustered in *barrios* in Los Angeles or elsewhere or laboring as migrant farmworkers. Even small Hispanic landowners who managed to hang on to their farms found themselves unable to raise livestock, as once-communal grazing lands fell under the control of powerful Anglo ranchers.

A similar pattern occurred in Texas after it joined the United States. Many Mexican landowners lost their land—some as a result of fraud and coercion, others because even the most substantial Mexican ranchers could not compete with the emerging Anglo-American ranching kingdoms. In 1859, angry Mexicans, led by the rancher Juan Cortina, raided the jail in Brownsville and freed all the Mexican prisoners inside. But such resistance had little long-term effect. As in California, Mexicans in southern Texas became an increasingly impoverished working class, relegated largely to unskilled farm or industrial labor.

THE CHINESE MIGRATION

At the same time that ambitious or impoverished Europeans were crossing the Atlantic in search of opportunities in the New World, many Chinese were crossing the Pacific in hopes of better lives. Not all came to the United States. Many Chinese—some as "coolies" (indentured servants whose condition was close to slavery)—moved to Hawaii, Australia, Latin America, South Africa, and even the Caribbean.

A few Chinese traveled to the American West even before the gold rush, but after 1848 the flow increased dramatically. By 1880, more than 200,000 Chinese had settled in the United States. Almost all came as free laborers. For a time, white Americans welcomed the Chinese as a conscientious, hardworking people. Very quickly, however, white opinion turned hostile—in part because the Chinese were so industrious and successful that some white Americans began considering them rivals.

In the early 1850s, large numbers of Chinese immigrants joined the hunt for gold. Many of them were well-organized, hardworking prospectors, and for a time some of them enjoyed considerable success. But opportunities for the Chinese to prosper in the mines were fleeting. In 1852, the California legislature began trying to exclude the Chinese from gold mining by enacting a "foreign miners" tax. Gradually, the effect of the discriminatory laws, the hostility of white miners, and the declining profitability of the surface mines drove most Chinese out of prospecting.

As mining declined as a source of wealth and jobs for the Chinese, railroad employment grew. Beginning in 1865, over 12,000 Chinese found work building the transcontinental railroad, forming 90 percent of the labor force of the Central Pacific. The company preferred them to white laborers because they worked hard, made few demands, and accepted relatively low wages.

Work on the Central Pacific was arduous and often dangerous. In the winter, many Chinese tunneled into snowbanks at night to create warm sleeping areas for themselves, even though such tunnels frequently collapsed, suffocating those inside. In the spring of 1866, 5,000 Chinese railroad workers rebelled against the terrible conditions and went on strike to demand higher wages and a shorter workday. The company isolated them, surrounded them with strike-breakers, and starved them into submission.

A CHINESE FAMILY IN SAN FRANCISCO This portrait of Chun Duck Chin and his seven-year-old son Chun Jan Yut was taken in a studio in San Francisco in the 1870s. Both father and son appear to have dressed up for the occasion, in traditional Chinese garb, and the studio—which likely took many such portraits of Chinese families—provided a formal Chinese backdrop. The son is holding what appears to be a chicken, perhaps to impress relatives in China with the family's prosperity. (National Archives)

In 1869, the transcontinental railroad was completed, and thousands of Chinese lost their jobs. Some moved into agricultural work, usually in menial positions. Increasingly, however, the Chinese flocked to cities. By far the largest single Chinese community was in San Francisco. Much of community life there, and in other "Chinatowns" throughout the West, revolved around organizations, somewhat like benevolent societies, that filled many of the roles that political machines often served in immigrant communities in eastern cities. Often led by prominent merchants (in San Francisco, the leading merchants—known as the "Six Companies"—often worked together to advance their interests in the city and state), these organizations became, in effect, employment brokers, unions, arbitrators of disputes, defenders against outside persecution, and dispensers of social services. They also organized the elaborate festivals and celebrations that were such a conspicuous and important part of life in Chinatowns.

Other Chinese organizations were secret societies, known as "tongs." Some of the tongs were violent criminal organizations, involved in the opium trade and prostitution. Few people outside the Chinese communities were aware of their existence, except when rival tongs engaged in violent conflict (or "tong wars").

In San Francisco and other western cities, the Chinese usually occupied the lower rungs of the employment ladder. Many worked as common laborers, servants, and unskilled factory hands. Some established their own small businesses, especially laundries. There were few commercial laundries in China, but they could be started in America with very little capital and required only limited command of English. By the 1890s, Chinese constituted over two-thirds of all the laundry workers in California.

During the earliest Chinese migrations to California, virtually all the relatively small number of women who made the journey did so because they had been sold into prostitution. As late as 1880, nearly half the Chinese women in California were prostitutes. Gradually, however, the number of Chinese women increased, and Chinese men in America became more likely to seek companionship in families.

Anti-Chinese Sentiments

As Chinese communities grew larger and more conspicuous, anti-Chinese sentiment among white residents intensified. Anti-Chinese activities, some of them violent, reflected the resentment of many white workers toward Chinese laborers for accepting low wages and thus undercutting union members. As the political value of attacking the Chinese grew in California, the Democratic Party took up the call. So did the Workingmen's Party of California—created in 1878 by Denis Kearney, an Irish immigrant—which gained significant political power in the state largely because of its hostility to the Chinese. By the mid-1880s, anti-Chinese agitation and violence had spread up and down the Pacific Coast and into other areas of the West.

In 1882, Congress responded to the political pressure and the growing violence by passing the Chinese Exclusion Act, which banned Chinese immigration into the United States for ten years and barred Chinese already in the country from becoming naturalized citizens. Congress renewed the law for another ten years in 1892 and made it permanent in 1902. It had a dramatic effect on the Chinese population, which declined by more than 40 percent in the forty years after the act's passage.

Migration from the East

The scale of post–Civil War white migration to the American West dwarfed everything that had preceded it. In previous decades, the settlers had come in thousands. Now they came in millions. Most of the new settlers were from the established Anglo-American societies of the eastern United States, but substantial numbers—over 2 million between 1870 and 1900—were foreign-born immigrants from Europe: Scandinavians, Germans, Irish, Russians, Czechs, and others.

They came to the West for many reasons. Settlers were attracted by gold and silver deposits, by the short-grass pasture for cattle and sheep, and ultimately by the sod of the plains and the meadowlands of the mountains. The completion of the great transcontinental railroad line in 1869, and the construction of the many subsidiary lines that spread out from it, encouraged settlement. So did the land policies of the federal government. The Homestead Act of 1862 permitted settlers to buy plots of 160 acres for a small fee if they occupied the land they purchased for five years and improved it.

Supporters of the Homestead Act believed it would create new markets and new outposts of commercial agriculture for the nation's growing economy. But a unit of 160 acres, while ample in much of the East, was too small for the grazing and grain farming of the Great Plains. Eventually, the federal government provided some relief. The Timber Culture Act (1873) permitted homesteaders to receive grants of 160 additional acres if they planted 40 acres of trees on them. The Desert Land Act (1877) allowed claimants to buy 640 acres at $1.25 an acre, provided they irrigated part of their holdings within three years. These and other laws ultimately made it possible for individuals to acquire as much as 1,280 acres of land at little cost.

Political organization followed on the heels of settlement. By the mid-1860s, territorial governments were in operation in the new provinces of Nevada, Colorado, Dakota, Arizona, Idaho, Montana, and Wyoming. Statehood rapidly followed. Nevada became a state in 1864, Nebraska in 1867, and Colorado in 1876. In 1889, North and South Dakota, Montana, and Washington won admission; Wyoming and Idaho entered the next year. Congress denied Utah statehood until its Mormon leaders convinced the government in 1896 that polygamy (the practice of men taking several wives) had been abandoned. At the turn of the century, only Arizona, New Mexico, and Oklahoma remained outside the Union.

THE CHANGING WESTERN ECONOMY

The great wave of Anglo-American and European settlement transformed the economy of the Far West and tied the region firmly to the growing industrial economy of the East.

LABOR IN THE WEST

As commercial activity increased, many farmers, ranchers, and miners found it necessary to recruit a paid labor force—not an easy task for people far away from major population centers. This labor shortage led to higher wages for some workers than were typical in the East. But working conditions were often arduous, and job security was almost nonexistent. Once a railroad was built, a crop harvested, a herd sent to market, a mine played out, hundreds and even thousands of workers could find themselves suddenly unemployed.

The western working class was highly multiracial. English-speaking whites worked alongside African Americans and immigrants from southern and eastern Europe, as they did in the East. Even more, they worked with Chinese, Filipinos, Mexicans, and Indians. But the workforce was highly stratified along racial lines. In almost every area of the western economy, white workers (whatever their ethnicity) occupied the upper tiers of employment: management and skilled labor. The lower tiers—unskilled work in the mines, on the railroads, or in agriculture—were filled overwhelmingly by nonwhites.

The western economy was, however, no more a single entity than the economy of the East. In the late nineteenth century, the region produced three major industries, each with distinctive history and characteristics: mining, ranching, and commercial farming.

THE ARRIVAL OF THE MINERS

The first economic boom in the Far West was the result of mining. The mining boom began around 1860 and flourished until the 1890s. Then it abruptly declined.

At first it was news of a gold or silver strike that would start a stampede. The California gold rush of 1849 was the first and most famous gold rush. But it was followed by others. Individual prospectors would pan for gold, extracting the first shallow deposits of ore largely by hand, a method known as placer mining. After these surface deposits dwindled, corporations moved in to engage in lode or quartz mining, which dug deeper beneath the surface. Then, as those deposits dwindled, commercial mining declined, and ranchers and farmers moved in and established a more permanent economy.

The first great mineral strikes (other than the California gold rush) occurred just before the Civil War. In 1858, gold was discovered in the Pike's Peak district of what would soon be the territory of Colorado; the following year, 50,000 prospectors stormed in. Denver and other mining camps blossomed into "cities" overnight. Almost as rapidly as they had developed, the booms ended. Later, the discovery of silver near Leadville supplied a new source of mineral wealth.

While the Colorado rush of 1859 was still in progress, news of another strike drew miners to Nevada. Gold had been found in the Washoe district. Even more plentiful and more valuable was the silver found in the great Comstock Lode (first discovered in 1858 by Henry Comstock) and other Washoe veins. The first prospectors to reach the Washoe fields came from California, and from the beginning, Californians dominated the settlement and development of Nevada. A remote desert without railroad transportation, the territory produced no supplies of its own, and everything had to be shipped from California to Virginia City, Carson City, and other roaring camp towns. When the first placer (or surface) deposits ran out, Californian and eastern capitalists bought the claims of the pioneer prospectors and began to use the more difficult process of quartz mining, which enabled them to retrieve silver from deeper veins. For a few years, these outside owners reaped tremendous profits: from 1860 to 1880, the Nevada lodes yielded bullion worth $306 million. After that, the mines quickly played out.

The next important mineral discoveries came in 1874, when gold was found in the Black Hills of southwestern Dakota Territory. Prospectors swarmed into the remote area. Like the others, the boom flared for a time, until surface resources faded and corporations took over—above all, the enormous Homestake Mining Company—and came to dominate the fields. The Dakotas, like other boom areas of the mineral empire, ultimately developed a largely agricultural economy.

The gold and silver discoveries generated the most popular excitement. But less glamorous natural resources proved more important to western development. The great Anaconda copper mine, launched by William Clark in 1881, marked the beginning of an industry that would remain important to Montana for many decades. In other areas, mining operations had significant success with lead, tin, quartz, and zinc.

Men greatly outnumbered women in the mining towns, and younger men in particular had difficulty finding female companions of comparable age. Those women who did gravitate to the new communities often came with their husbands. Single women, or women whose husbands were earning no money, did work for wages at times, as cooks, laundresses, and tavernkeepers. And in the sexually imbalanced mining communities, there was always a ready market for prostitutes.

The thousands of people who flocked to the mining towns in search of quick wealth and failed to find it often remained as wage laborers in corporate mines after the boom period, working in almost uniformly terrible conditions. In the 1870s, one worker in every thirty was disabled in the mines, and one in every eighty was killed. That rate fell later in the nineteenth century, but mining remained one of the most dangerous and arduous working environments in the United States.

The Cattle Kingdom

A second important element of the changing economy of the Far West was cattle ranching. The open range—the vast grasslands of the public domain—provided a huge area on the Great Plains where cattle raisers could graze their herds.

The western cattle industry was Mexican and Texan by ancestry. Long before citizens of the United States entered the Southwest, Mexican ranchers had developed the techniques and equipment that the cattlemen and cowboys of the Great Plains later employed: branding, roundups, roping, and the gear of the herders—their lariats, saddles, leather chaps, and spurs. Americans in Texas, with the largest herds of cattle in the country, adopted these methods and carried them to the northernmost ranges of the cattle kingdom. From Texas, too, came the small, muscular horses (broncos and mustangs) that enabled cowboys to control the herds.

At the end of the Civil War, an estimated 5 million cattle roamed the Texas ranges. Eastern markets offered good prices for steers. The challenge facing the cattle industry lay in getting the animals from the range to the railroad centers. Early in 1866, some Texas cattle ranchers began driving their combined herds, up to 260,000 steers, north to Sedalia, Missouri, on the Missouri Pacific Railroad. The caravan suffered heavy losses. But the drive proved that cattle could be driven to distant markets and pastured along the trail. This earliest of the "long drives" established the first, tentative link between the isolated cattle breeders of west Texas and the booming urban markets of the East.

Market facilities soon grew up at Abilene, Kansas, on the Kansas Pacific Railroad, and for years the town reigned as the railhead of the cattle kingdom. But by the mid-1870s, agricultural development in western Kansas had eaten away at the open-range land. Cattlemen had to develop other trails and other market outlets. As the railroads reached farther west, other locations began to rival Abilene as major centers of stock herding: Dodge City and Wichita in Kansas, Ogallala and Sidney in Nebraska, Cheyenne and Laramie in Wyoming, and Miles City and Glendive in Montana.

There had always been an element of risk and speculation in the open-range cattle business. Rustlers and Indians frequently seized large numbers of animals. But as the settlement of the plains increased, new forms of competition arose. Sheep breeders from California and Oregon brought their flocks onto the range to compete for grass. Farmers ("nesters") from the East threw fences around their claims, blocking trails and breaking up the open range. A series of "range wars"—between sheepmen and cattlemen, ranchers and farmers—erupted out of the tensions among these competing groups.

Accounts of the lofty profits to be made in the cattle business tempted eastern, English, and Scottish capital to the plains. Increasingly, the structure of the cattle economy became corporate; in one year, twenty corporations with a combined capital of $12 million were chartered in Wyoming. The result of this frenzied, speculative expansion was that the ranges, already shrunk by the railroads and the farmers, became overstocked. There was not enough grass to support the crowding herds or sustain the long drives. Two severe winters, in 1885–1886 and 1886–1887, and a searing summer between them scorched the plains. Hundreds of thousands of cattle died. Streams and grass dried up. Princely ranches and costly investments disappeared in a season.

The open-range industry never recovered, and the long drive finally disappeared for good. Railroads displaced the trail as the route to market for livestock. But some established cattle ranches survived, grew, and prospered, eventually producing more beef than ever.

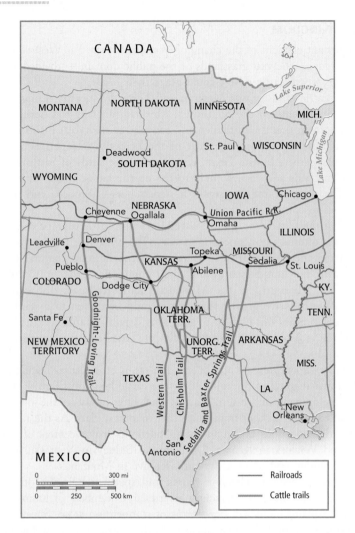

THE CATTLE KINGDOM, ca. 1866–1887 Cattle ranching and cattle drives are among the most romanticized features of the nineteenth-century West. But they were also hardheaded businesses, made possible by the growing eastern market for beef and the availability of reasonably inexpensive transportation—thanks to the dense network of trails and railroads—to take cattle to the urban markets. • *Why was the open range necessary for the great cattle drives, and what eventually ended the cattle trails?*

THE ROMANCE OF THE WEST

The rapidly developing West occupied a special place in the Anglo-American imagination. Many white Americans continued to consider it a romantic place, a wilderness where individuals could experience true freedom.

The Western Landscape and the Cowboy

Part of the attraction of the West was its spectacular natural landscape. Painters of the new "Rocky Mountain school"—of whom the best known were Albert Bierstadt and Thomas Moran—celebrated the new West in grandiose canvases, some of which toured the eastern and Midwestern states and attracted enormous crowds, eager for a vision of the Great West.

Gradually, paintings and photographs inspired a growing wave of tourism among people eager to see the natural wonders of the region. In the 1880s and 1890s, resort hotels began to spring up near some of the region's most spectacular landscapes.

Even more appealing was the rugged, free-spirited lifestyle that many Americans associated with the West. Many nineteenth-century Americans came especially to idealize the figure of the cowboy. Western novels such as Owen Wister's *The Virginian* (1902) romanticized the cowboy's supposed freedom from traditional social constraints, his affinity with nature, even his supposed propensity for violence. Wister's character—one of the most enduring in popular American literature—was a semi-educated man whose natural decency, courage, and compassion made him a powerful symbol of the supposed virtues of the "frontier." But *The Virginian* was only the most famous example of a type of literature that soon swept throughout the United States. Novels and stories about the West, and about the lives of cowboys in particular, appeared in boys' magazines, pulp novels, theater, and serious literature.

Among the reasons for the widespread admiration of the cowboy were the remarkably popular Wild West shows that traveled throughout the United States and Europe. Most successful were the shows of Buffalo Bill Cody, a former Pony Express rider and Indian fighter, and the hero of popular dime novels for children. Cody's Wild West show, which spawned dozens of imitators, exploited his own fame and romanticized the life of the cowboy through reenactments of Indian battles and displays of horsemanship and riflery (many of them by the famous sharpshooter Annie Oakley). Buffalo Bill and his imitators

PROMOTING THE WEST Buffalo Bill's Wild West show was popular all over the United States, and indeed through much of the world. He was so familiar a figure that many of his posters contained only his picture with the words "He is Coming." This more conventional poster announces a visit of the show to Brooklyn. (Culver Pictures, Inc.)

confirmed the popular image of the West as a place of romance and glamour and helped keep that image alive for later generations.

THE IDEA OF THE FRONTIER

It was not simply the particular character of the new West that resonated in the nation's imagination. It was also that many Americans considered it the last frontier. Since the earliest moments of European settlement in America, the image of uncharted territory to the west had always comforted and inspired those who dreamed of starting life anew.

Mark Twain gave voice to this romantic vision of the frontier in a series of novels and memoirs. In *The Adventures of Tom Sawyer* (1876) and *The Adventures of Huckleberry Finn* (1885), he produced characters who repudiated the constraints of organized society and attempted to escape into a more natural world. (For Huck Finn, the vehicle of escape was a small raft on the Mississippi.) This yearning for freedom reflected a larger vision of the West as the last refuge from the constraints of civilization.

One of the most beloved and successful artists of the nineteenth century was Frederic Remington, a painter and sculptor whose works came to represent the romance of the West. He portrayed the cowboy as a natural aristocrat, much like Wister's *The Virginian*, living in a natural world in which all the normal supporting structures of "civilization" were missing.

Theodore Roosevelt also contributed to the romanticizing of the West. He traveled to the Dakota badlands in the mid-1880s to recover from the sudden death of his young wife. In the 1890s, he published a four-volume history, *The Winning of the West*, with a heroic account of the spread of white civilization into the frontier.

Perhaps the most influential statement of the romantic vision of the frontier came from the historian Frederick Jackson Turner, in a memorable paper he delivered in Chicago in 1893 titled "The Significance of the Frontier in American History." In it he boldly claimed that the experience of western expansion had stimulated individualism, nationalism, and democracy; kept opportunities for advancement alive; and made Americans the distinctive people that they were. "Now," Turner concluded portentously, "the frontier has gone and with its going has closed the first period of American history."

In accepting the idea of the "passing of the frontier," many Americans were acknowledging the end of one of their most cherished myths. As long as it had been possible for them to see the West as an empty, open land, it was possible to believe that there were constantly revitalizing opportunities in American life. But by the end of the nineteenth century, there was a vague and ominous sense of opportunities foreclosed.

THE DISPERSAL OF THE TRIBES

Having imagined the West as a "virgin land" awaiting civilization by white people, many Americans tried to force the region to match their image of it. That meant, above all, ensuring that the Indian tribes would not be obstacles to the spread of white society.

WHITE TRIBAL POLICIES

The traditional policy of the federal government was to regard the tribes simultaneously as independent nations (with which the United States could negotiate treaties) and as

HELD UP BY BUFFALO Once among the most numerous creatures in North America, the buffalo became almost extinct as a result of indiscriminate slaughter by white settlers and travelers, who often fired at herds from moving trains simply for the sport of it. This scene was painted around 1880 by N. H. Trotter. (National Museum of American History, Smithsonian Institution)

wards of the president (who would exercise paternalistic authority over the Indians). The concept of Indian sovereignty had supported the government's attempt before 1860 to erect a permanent frontier between whites and Indians. But the belief in tribal sovereignty and the treaties or agreements with the Indians were not strong enough to withstand the desire of white settlers for Indian lands.

By the early 1850s, the government created a new reservations policy known as "concentration." In 1851, the government assigned each tribe its own defined reservation, confirmed by individual treaties—treaties often illegitimately negotiated with unauthorized "representatives" chosen by whites, people known sarcastically as "treaty chiefs." The new arrangement had many benefits for whites and few for the Indians. It divided the tribes from one another and made them easier to control. It allowed the government to force tribes into scattered locations and to take over the most desirable lands for white settlement. But "concentration" did not survive as the basis of Indian policy for long.

In 1867, Congress established the Indian Peace Commission, composed of both soldiers and civilians, to recommend a new and presumably permanent Indian policy. The commission recommended that the government move all the Plains tribes into two large reservations—one in Indian Territory (Oklahoma), the other in the Dakotas. At a series of meetings with the tribes, government agents cajoled, bribed, and tricked their representatives into agreeing to treaties establishing the new reservations.

But this "solution" worked little better than previous ones. Part of the problem was the corrupt or incompetent agents of the Bureau of Indian Affairs who administered the reservations. But the problem was also a result of the relentless slaughtering by whites of

THE FRONTIER AND THE WEST

THE emergence of the history of the American West as an important field of scholarship can be traced to a paper Frederick Jackson Turner delivered to the American Historical Association in 1893: "The Significance of the Frontier in American History." Turner stated his thesis simply. The settlement of the West by white Americans—"the existence of an area of free land, its continuous recession, and the advance of American settlement westward"—was the central story of the nation's history. The process of westward expansion had transformed a desolate and savage land into modern civilization and had continually renewed American ideas of democracy and individualism.

In the first half of the twentieth century, virtually everyone who wrote about the West echoed at least part of Turner's argument. Ray Allen Billington's *Westward Expansion* (1949) was almost wholly consistent with the Turnerian model. In *The Great Plains* (1931) and *The Great Frontier* (1952),

SAN FERNANDO VALLEY, 1991 Once a sparsely populated farming region of the "New West," the San Fernando Valley—like much of the rest of what used to be considered the "frontier"—became a densely settled and highly urbanized area with a population today of over 1.7 million. (© Nik Wheeler/Corbis)

Walter Prescott Webb similarly emphasized the bravery and ingenuity of white settlers in the Southwest.

Serious efforts to displace the Turner thesis as the explanation of western American history began after World War II. In *Virgin Land* (1950), Henry Nash Smith examined many of the same heroic images of the West that Turner and his disciples had presented; but he treated those images less as descriptions of reality than as myths. Earl Pomeroy challenged Turner's notion of the West as a place of individualism, innovation, and democratic renewal. "Conservatism, inheritance, and continuity bulked at least as large," he claimed. Howard Lamar, in *Dakota Territory, 1861–1889* (1956) and *The Far Southwest* (1966), emphasized the highly diverse character of the West.

The western historians who emerged in the late 1970s launched an even more emphatic attack on the Turner thesis and the idea of the "frontier." "New western historians" such as Richard White, Patricia Nelson Limerick, William Cronon, Donald Worster, Peggy Pascoe, and many others challenged the Turnerians on a number of points.

Turner saw the nineteenth-century West as "free land" awaiting the expansion of Anglo-American settlement and American democracy. The more recent western historians reject the concept of an empty "frontier," emphasizing instead the elaborate and highly developed civilizations that already existed in the region. White, English-speaking Americans, they have argued, did not so much "settle" the West as conquer it. And they continued to share the region not only with the Indians and Hispanics who preceded them there, but also with African Americans, Asians, Latin Americans, and others who flowed into the West at the same time they did.

The Turnerian West was a place of heroism, triumph, and above all progress, dominated by the feats of brave white men. The West that the new western historians describe was a less triumphant (and less masculine) place in which bravery and success coexisted with oppression, greed, and failure; in which decaying ghost towns, bleak Indian reservations, impoverished barrios, and ecologically devastated landscapes have been as characteristic of western development as great ranches, rich farms, and prosperous cities.

To Turner and his disciples, the nineteenth-century West was a place where rugged individualism flourished and replenished American democracy. The new scholars point out that the region was inextricably tied to a national and international capitalist economy. Westerners depended on government-subsidized railroads for access to markets, federal troops for protection from Indians, and (later) government-funded dams and canals for irrigating their fields and sustaining their towns.

And while Turner defined the West as a process—a process of settlement that came to an end with the "closing of the frontier" in the late nineteenth century—the new historians see the West as a region. Its distinctive history did not end in 1890 but continues into our own time.   •

UNDERSTAND, ANALYZE, & EVALUATE

1. How and why did the portrayal of the West by the newer western historians differ from the West that Turner described?
2. Why did the newer western historians challenge Turner's views, and why has their depiction of the West, in turn, provoked such controversy?

the buffalo herds that supported the tribes' way of life. After the Civil War, professional and amateur hunters—even casual visitors shooting from passing trains—swarmed over the plains, slaughtering the huge animals. Some Indian tribes (notably the Blackfeet) also began killing large numbers of buffalo to sell in the booming new market. In 1865, there had been at least 15 million buffalo; a decade later, fewer than 1,000 of the great beasts survived. By destroying the buffalo herds, whites were destroying the Indians' source of food and supplies and their ability to resist white advance.

THE INDIAN WARS

Whites and Indians fought incessantly from the 1850s to the 1880s, as Indians struggled against the growing threats to their civilizations. Indian warriors attacked wagon trains, stagecoaches, and isolated ranches, often in retaliation for earlier attacks on them by whites. As the United States Army became more deeply involved in the fighting, the tribes began to focus more of their attacks on white soldiers.

At times, this small-scale fighting escalated. During the Civil War, the eastern Sioux in Minnesota, cramped on a small reservation and exploited by corrupt white agents, suddenly rebelled. Led by Little Crow, they killed more than 700 whites before being subdued. Thirty-eight of the Indians were hanged, and the tribe was exiled to the Dakotas.

At the same time, fighting flared up in eastern Colorado, where the Arapaho and Cheyenne were coming into conflict with white miners settling in the region. Bands of Indians attacked stagecoach lines and settlements in an effort to regain territory they had lost. In response to these incidents, whites called up a large territorial militia. The governor urged all friendly Indians to congregate at army posts for protection before the army began its campaign. One Arapaho and Cheyenne band under Black Kettle, apparently in response to the invitation, camped near Fort Lyon on Sand Creek in November 1864. Some members of the party were warriors, but Black Kettle believed he was under official protection and exhibited no hostile intention. Nevertheless, Colonel J. M. Chivington led a volunteer militia force—largely consisting of unemployed miners, many of whom were apparently drunk—to the unsuspecting camp and massacred 133 people, 105 of them women and children. Black Kettle himself escaped the Sand Creek massacre. But four years later, in 1868, he and Cheyenne soldiers went to war with the whites. The Indians were caught on the Washita River, near the Texas border, by Colonel George A. Custer. White troops killed the chief and his people.

At the end of the Civil War, white troops stepped up their wars against the western Indians on several fronts. The most serious and sustained conflict was in Montana, where the army was attempting to build a road, the Bozeman Trail, to connect Fort Laramie, Wyoming, to the new mining centers. The western Sioux resented this intrusion into the heart of their buffalo range. Led by one of their great chiefs, Red Cloud, they so harried the soldiers and the construction party that the road could not be used.

But it was not only the United States military that harassed the tribes. It was also unofficial violence by white vigilantes who engaged in what became known as "Indian hunting." Sometimes the killing was in response to Indian raids on white communities. But considerable numbers of whites were committed to the goal of literal "elimination" of the tribes whatever their behavior, a goal that rested on the belief in the essential inhumanity of Indians and the impossibility of white coexistence with them. In California, civilians killed close to 5,000 Indians between 1850 and 1880—one of many factors (disease and poverty being the more important) that reduced the Indian population of the state from 150,000 before the Civil War to 30,000 in 1870.

The treaties negotiated in 1867 brought a temporary lull to many of the conflicts. But new forces soon shattered the peace again. In the early 1870s, more waves of white settlers, mostly miners, began to penetrate the lands in Dakota Territory supposedly guaranteed to the tribes in 1867. Indian resistance flared anew. In the northern plains, the Sioux rose up in 1875 and left their reservation. When white officials ordered them to return, bands of warriors gathered in Montana and united under two great leaders: Crazy Horse and Sitting Bull. Three army columns set out to round them up and force them back onto the reservation. With the expedition, as colonel of the famous Seventh Cavalry, was the colorful and controversial George A. Custer. At the Battle of the Little Bighorn in southern Montana in 1876, an unprecedentedly large army, perhaps 2,500 tribal warriors, surprised Custer and part of his regiment, surrounded them, and killed every man.

But the Indians did not have the political organization or the supplies to keep their troops united. Soon the warriors drifted off in bands to elude pursuit or search for food, and the army ran them down and returned them to Dakota. The power of the Sioux quickly collapsed. They accepted defeat and life on reservations.

One of the most dramatic episodes in Indian history occurred in Idaho in 1877. The Nez Percé were a small and relatively peaceful tribe, some of whose members had managed to live unmolested in Oregon into the 1870s without ever signing a treaty with the United States. But under pressure from white settlers, the U.S. government forced them to move onto a reservation. With no realistic prospect of resisting, the Indians began the journey to the reservation; but on the way, several younger Indians, drunk and angry, killed four white settlers.

The leader of the band, Chief Joseph, persuaded his followers to flee from the inevitable retribution. American troops pursued and attacked them, only to be driven off in a battle at White Bird Canyon. After that, the Nez Percé scattered in several directions and became part of a remarkable chase. Joseph moved with 200 warriors and 350 women, children, and old people in an effort to reach Canada. Pursued by four columns of American soldiers, the Indians covered 1,321 miles in seventy-five days, repelling or evading the army time and again. They were finally caught just short of the Canadian boundary. Some escaped and slipped across the border; but Joseph and most of his followers, weary and discouraged, finally gave up. "Hear me, my chiefs," Joseph said after meeting with the American general Nelson Miles, "I am tired. My heart is sick and sad. From where the sun now stands, I will fight no more forever."

The last Indians to maintain organized resistance against the whites were the Chiricahua Apache. The two ablest chiefs of this fierce tribe were Mangas Colorados and Cochise. Mangas was murdered during the Civil War by white soldiers who tricked him into surrendering. In 1872 Cochise agreed to peace in exchange for a reservation that included some of the tribe's traditional land. But Cochise died in 1874, and his successor, Geronimo, fought on for more than a decade longer, establishing bases in the mountains of Arizona and Mexico and leading warriors in intermittent raids against white outposts. With each raid, however, the number of warring Apache dwindled, as some warriors died and others drifted away to the reservation. By 1886, Geronimo's band consisted of only about 30 people, including women and children, while his white pursuers numbered perhaps 10,000. Geronimo recognized the odds and surrendered.

The Apache Wars, the most violent of all the Indian conflicts, produced brutality on both sides. But it was the whites who committed the most flagrant atrocities. That did not end

CHIEF GARFIELD George Curtis, one of the most accomplished photographers of tribal life in the early twentieth century, made this portrait of a Jicarilla Apache chief in 1904. By then, the Jicarilla were living in a reservation in northern New Mexico, and white officials had assigned all members of the tribe Spanish or English names. The man depicted here, the head chief, had chosen the name Garfield himself. (© Stapleton Collection/Corbis)

with the conclusion of the Apache Wars. Another tragic encounter occurred in 1890 as a result of a religious revival among the Sioux—a revival that itself symbolized the catastrophic effects of the white assaults on Indian civilization. As other tribes had done in trying times in the past, many of these Indians turned to a prophet who led them in a religious revival.

This time the prophet was Wovoka, a Paiute who inspired a fervent spiritual awakening that began in Nevada and spread quickly to the plains. Wovoka predicted the imminent coming of a messiah. The new revival's most conspicuous feature was a mass, emotional "Ghost Dance," which inspired ecstatic, mystical visions—including images of the retreat of white people from the plains and a restoration of the great buffalo herds. White agents on the Sioux reservation, bewildered and fearful, warned the army that dances might be the prelude to hostilities.

On December 29, 1890, the Seventh Cavalry tried to round up a group of about 350 cold and starving Sioux at Wounded Knee, South Dakota. Fighting broke out in which about 40 white soldiers and up to 200 Indians died. An Indian may have fired the first shot, but the battle soon turned into a one-sided massacre, as the white soldiers turned their new machine guns on the Indians and mowed them down in the snow.

THE DAWES ACT

Even before the Ghost Dance and the Wounded Knee tragedies, the federal government had moved to destroy forever the tribal structure that was the cornerstone of Indian culture. Reversing its policy of nearly fifty years, Congress abolished the practice by which tribes owned reservation lands communally. The new policy required Indians to become landowners and farmers, to abandon their collective society and culture and become part of white civilization. Some supporters of the new policy believed they were acting for the good of the Indians, whom they considered a "vanishing race" in need of rescue by and assimilation into white society.

The Dawes Severalty Act of 1887 provided for the gradual elimination of most tribal ownership of land and the allotment of tracts to individual owners: 160 acres to the head of a family, 80 acres to a single adult or orphan, 40 acres to each dependent child. Adult owners were given United States citizenship, but unlike other citizens, they could not gain full title to their property for twenty-five years (supposedly to prevent them from selling the land to speculators).

In applying the Dawes Act, the Bureau of Indian Affairs relentlessly promoted the idea of assimilation that lay behind it. Not only did agents of the bureau try to move Indian families onto their own plots of land; but also they took many Indian children away from their families and sent them to boarding schools run by whites. They moved as well to stop Indian religious rituals and encouraged the spread of Christianity and the creation of Christian churches on the reservations.

Few Indians were prepared for this wrenching change. In any case, white administration of the Dawes Act was so corrupt and inept that ultimately the government simply abandoned most efforts to enforce it. Much of the reservation land, therefore, was never distributed to individual owners.

THE RISE AND DECLINE OF THE WESTERN FARMER

The arrival of the miners, the empire building of the cattle ranchers, the dispersal of the Indian tribes—all served as a prelude to the decisive phase of white settlement of the Far West. Even before the Civil War, farmers had begun moving into the plains region, challenging the dominance of the ranchers and the Indians. By the 1870s, what was once a trickle had become a deluge. Farmers poured into the plains and beyond, enclosed land that had once been hunting territory for Indians and open range for cattle, and established a new agricultural region.

For a time in the late 1870s and early 1880s, the new western farmers flourished, enjoying the fruits of an agricultural economic boom. Beginning in the mid-1880s, however, the boom turned to bust, and the western agricultural economy began a long, steady decline.

FARMING ON THE PLAINS

Many factors combined to produce the surge of post–Civil War western agricultural settlement, but the most important was the railroads. Before the war, the Great Plains had been accessible only through a difficult journey by wagon. But beginning in the 1860s, a great new network of railroad lines made huge areas of settlement accessible for the first time.

WALTER BARON VON RICHTHOFEN, *CATTLE RAISING ON THE PLAINS IN NORTH AMERICA*, 1885

THE immense profits which have been universally realized in the Western cattle business for the past, and which will be increased in the future, owing to the more economical methods pursued, so long as ranges can be purchased at present prices, may seem incredible to many of my readers, who, no doubt, have considered the stories of the fortunes realized as myths. Yet it is true that many men who started only a few years ago with comparatively few cattle, are now wealthy, and, in some cases, millionaires. They certainly did not find the gold upon the prairies, nor did they have any source of revenue beyond the increase of their cattle. The agencies producing this immense wealth are very natural and apparent.

The climate of the West is the healthiest on the earth; the pure, high mountain air and dry atmosphere are the natural remedies, or rather preventives, against sickness among cattle in general, and against all epidemic diseases in particular; for "nowhere in the Western states do we find any traces of pleuro-pneumonia, foot or mouth, and such like contagious diseases."

The pure, clear water of the mountain rivers affords to cattle another health preserver, and the fine nutritious and bountiful grasses, and in winter the naturally cured hay, furnish to them the healthiest natural food.

Formerly these pastures cost nothing, and at present only a trifle . . . so that the interest on the investment in purchasing land is of little importance in the estimate of the cost of keeping a herd. In fact, ownership of land is now indispensable for a herd-owner. This land in less than ten years will be a considerable factor in the profits of the cattle business, as the value of pastures will constantly-increase.

The principal cost of raising cattle is only the herding and watching the cattle by herders, without any cost for sheltering or feeding. In time even these expenses will be reduced, as now already herds are kept in large fenced ranges, and many of the herders are dispensed with.

The losses of cattle, as shown by statistics, are larger among Eastern and European herds, which are sheltered in stables and fed the whole year round, than

The building of the transcontinental train line—completed in 1869 when the two lines met at Promontory Point, Utah—was a dramatic and monumental achievement. But the construction of subsidiary lines in the following years proved of greater importance to the West. State governments, imitating Washington, subsidized railroad development by offering direct financial aid, favorable loans, and more than 50 million acres of land (on top of the 130 million acres the federal government had already provided). Although built and operated by private corporations, the railroads were in many respects public projects.

The railroad companies also actively promoted settlement. The companies set rates so low for settlers that almost anyone could afford the trip west. And they sold much of their land at very low prices and with liberal credit to prospective settlers.

Contributing further to the great surge of white agricultural expansion was a pronounced but temporary change in the climate of the Great Plains. For several years in succession, beginning in the 1870s, rainfall in the plains states was well above average. White Americans now rejected the old idea that the region was the "Great American Desert."

among the shelterless herds of the West. The losses in the West . . . are practically reduced by long experience to a certain percentage, which enables the stockmen to calculate infallibly the profits and losses of their business.

This annual loss is found to average 2 to 3 per cent. We may safely put the loss in the extreme Northern states at about 3 per cent, and in the more Southern and temperate districts at 2 or less per cent. The annual cost of herding the cattle . . . is about $.70 per head; adding the other expenses, such as taxes, loss of interest on the purchase-money of land, etc., we find that the entire annual expense is less than $1.50 per head.

Now let me illustrate the profits realized from one Texas cow, worth $30.00. In ten years she will have eight calves, which, if they are all steers, will have produced at the end of fourteen years $320, or a profit of $272.00. The cow herself still remains, and is worth about her original cost for the butcher. These figures are made without reference to any increase in the value of cattle or beef, and without reference to any improvement of the stock by crossing it with better blood. . . .

Ten years ago an Irish servant-girl wanted money due her, amounting to $150, from a cattle-raiser who lived in Montana. Cattle had been dull, and he could not dispose of any of his herd, but agreed to her to brand fifteen cows in her name, give her the increase, and carry them with his herd, free of cost, until she was ready to sell, he to have the first privilege of purchase. She accepted, held on to her purchase, and last May sold out her master for $25,000.

UNDERSTAND, ANALYZE, & EVALUATE

1. How did Von Richthofen describe the land and natural resources for cattle ranching in the North American plains? Why did Von Richthofen stress the importance of landownership?
2. Does Von Richthofen strike you as a cautious businessman? What might explain the confidence he showed in his projections?
3. Why do you think the author concluded with the example of the Irish servant girl?

Source: Walter Baron Von Richthofen, *Cattle Raising on the Plains of North America* (1885; repr., Norman: University of Oklahoma Press, 1964), pp. 70–73, 80; located in Marilynn S. Johnson (ed.), *Violence in the West: The Johnson County Range War and the Ludlow Massacre: A Brief History with Documents* (Boston: Bedford St. Martin's, 2009), pp. 37–39.

But even under the most favorable conditions, farming on the plains presented special problems. First was the problem of fencing. Farmers had to enclose their land, but materials for traditional wood or stone fences were unavailable. In the mid-1870s, however, two Illinois farmers, Joseph H. Glidden and I. L. Ellwood, solved this problem by developing and marketing barbed wire, which became standard equipment on the plains and revolutionized fencing practices all over the world.

The second problem was water. Water was scarce even when rainfall was above average. After 1887, a series of dry seasons began, and lands that had been fertile now returned to semidesert. Some farmers dealt with the problem by using deep wells pumped by steel windmills, by turning to "dryland farming" (a system of tillage designed to conserve moisture in the soil by covering it with a dust blanket), or by planting drought-resistant crops. In many areas of the plains, however, only large-scale irrigation could save the endangered farms. But irrigation projects of the necessary magnitude required government assistance, and neither the federal nor the state governments were prepared to fund the projects.

Most of the people who moved into the region had previously been farmers in the Midwest, the East, or Europe. In the booming years of the early 1880s, with land values rising, the new farmers had no problem obtaining extensive and easy credit. But the arid years of the late 1880s—during which crop prices fell while production became more expensive—changed the farmers' prospects. Tens of thousands of farmers could not pay their debts and were forced to abandon their farms. There was, in effect, a reverse migration: white settlers moving back east, sometimes turning once-flourishing communities into desolate ghost towns. Those who remained continued to suffer from falling prices (for example, wheat, which had sold for $1.60 a bushel at the end of the Civil War, dropped to 49 cents in the 1890s) and persistent indebtedness.

Commercial Agriculture

By the late nineteenth century, the sturdy, independent farmer of popular myth was being replaced by the commercial farmer—attempting to do in the agricultural economy what industrialists were doing in the manufacturing economy. Commercial farmers specialized in cash crops that were sold in national or world markets. They did not often make their own household supplies or grow their own food but bought them from merchants. This kind of farming, when it was successful, raised farmers' living standards. But it also made them dependent on bankers and interest rates, railroads and freight rates, national and European markets, world supply and demand. And unlike the capitalists of the industrial order, they could not regulate their production or influence the prices of what they sold.

Between 1865 and 1900, farm output increased dramatically, not only in the United States but in Brazil, Argentina, Canada, Australia, New Zealand, Russia, and elsewhere. Beginning in the 1880s, worldwide overproduction led to a drop in prices for most agricultural goods and hence to great economic distress for many of the more than 6 million American farm families. By the 1890s, 27 percent of the farms in the country were mortgaged; by 1910, 33 percent. In 1880, 25 percent of all farms had been operated by tenants; by 1910, the proportion had grown to 37 percent. Commercial farming made some people fabulously wealthy. But the farm economy as a whole was suffering a significant decline relative to the rest of the nation.

The Farmers' Grievances

American farmers were painfully aware that something was wrong. But few people yet understood the implications of national and world overproduction. Instead, they concentrated their attention and anger on more immediate, more comprehensible—and no less real—problems: inequitable freight rates, high interest charges, and an inadequate currency.

The farmers' first and most burning grievance was against the railroads. In many cases, the railroads charged higher rates for farm goods than for other goods, and higher rates in the South and West than in the Northeast. Railroads also controlled elevator and warehouse facilities in buying centers and charged arbitrary storage rates.

Farmers also resented the institutions controlling credit—banks, loan companies, insurance corporations. Since sources of credit in the West and South were few, farmers had to take loans on whatever terms they could get, often at interest rates ranging from 10 to 25 percent. Many farmers had to pay these loans back in years when prices were dropping and currency was becoming scarce. As a result, expansion of the currency became an increasingly important issue to farmers.

A third grievance concerned prices. A farmer could plant a large crop at a moment when its price was high and find that by the time of the harvest the price had declined. Farmers' fortunes rose and fell in response to unpredictable forces. But many farmers became convinced (often with some reason) that "middlemen"—speculators, bankers, regional and local agents—were conspiring with one another to fix prices so as to benefit themselves at the growers' expense. Many farmers also came to believe (again, not entirely without reason) that manufacturers in the East were colluding to keep the prices of farm goods low and the prices of industrial goods high. Although farmers sold their crops in a competitive world market, they bought manufactured goods in a domestic market protected by tariffs and dominated by trusts and corporations.

THE AGRARIAN MALAISE

These economic difficulties helped produce social and cultural resentments. Among them was the isolation of farm life. Farm families in some parts of the country were virtually cut off from the outside world. During the winter months, the loneliness and boredom could become nearly unbearable. Many farmers lacked access to adequate education for their children. They had few or no proper medical facilities. There were few recreational or cultural activities. Older farmers felt the sting of watching their children leave the farm for the city. They felt the humiliation of being ridiculed as "hayseeds" by the new urban culture that was coming to dominate American life.

This sense of isolation and obsolescence led to a growing malaise among many farmers, a discontent that helped create a great national political movement in the 1890s. It found reflection, too, in some of the literature that emerged from rural America. Writers in the late nineteenth century might romanticize the rugged life of the cowboy and the western miner. For the farmers, however, the image of the agricultural world was different. Hamlin Garland, for example, reflected the growing disillusionment in a series of novels and short stories. In the introduction to his novel *Jason Edwards* (1891), he wrote that in the past, the agrarian frontier had seemed to be "the Golden West, the land of wealth and freedom and happiness." Now, however, the bright promise had faded. The trials of rural life were crushing the human spirit. "So this is the reality of the dream!" a character in *Jason Edwards* exclaims, "A shanty on a barren plain, hot and lone as a desert. My God!" Once, sturdy yeoman farmers had viewed themselves as the backbone of American life. Now they were becoming painfully aware that their position was declining in relation to the rising urban-industrial society to the east.

CONCLUSION

To many Americans in the late nineteenth century, the West seemed an untamed "frontier" in which hardy pioneers were creating a new society. The reality of the West in these years, however, was very different from this enduring image. White Americans moved into the vast regions west of the Mississippi at a remarkable rate in the years after the Civil War, and many of them indeed settled in lands far from any civilization they had ever known. But the West was not an empty place. It contained a large population of Indians, with whom the white settlers sometimes lived uneasily and with whom they sometimes battled; but almost always in the end, the Indians were pushed aside and (with help from the federal government) relocated onto lands whites did not want. There were significant numbers of Mexicans in some areas, small populations of Asians in others, and African Americans moving in from the South in search of land and freedom. The West was not a barren frontier but a place of many cultures.

The West was also closely and increasingly tied to the emerging capitalist-industrial economy of the East. The miners who flooded into California, Colorado, Nevada, the Dakotas, and elsewhere were responding to the demand in the East for gold and silver, but even more for iron ore, copper, lead, zinc, and quartz. Cattle and sheep ranchers produced meat, wool, and leather for eastern consumers and manufacturers. Farmers grew crops for sale in national and international commodities markets. The West certainly looked different from the East. But the growth of the West was very much a part of the growth of the rest of the nation. And the culture of the West, despite the romantic images of pioneering individuals embraced by easterners and westerners alike, was at its heart as much a culture of economic growth and capitalist ambition as was that of the rest of the nation.

RECALL AND REFLECT

1. How did the ethnic, racial, and cultural prejudice affect western society?
2. What were the three major industries involved in the development of the West, and how did these industries transform the western economy?
3. What was the romantic image of the West, and how was this image expressed in art, literature, and popular culture?
4. How did actions and policies of the federal government affect the fate of Indians in the West?

17 INDUSTRIAL SUPREMACY

SOURCES OF INDUSTRIAL GROWTH

CAPITALIST CONSERVATISM AND ITS CRITICS

THE ORDEAL OF THE WORKER

LOOKING AHEAD

1. What factors drove America's industrial expansion in the late nineteenth and early twentieth centuries?

2. Who were the critics of America's new industrial economy, what were their criticisms, and what solutions did they propose?

3. How did the conditions and characteristics of the workforce change during this period of rapid industrialization?

"TWENTY-FIVE YEARS AFTER THE DEATH of Lincoln, America had become, in the quantity and value of her products, the first manufacturing nation of the world. What England had accomplished in a hundred years, the United States had achieved in half the time." So wrote the historians Charles and Mary Beard in the 1920s, expressing the amazement many Americans felt when they considered the remarkable expansion of their industrial economy in the late nineteenth century.

In fact, America's rise to industrial supremacy was not as sudden as such observers suggested. The nation had been building a manufacturing economy since early in the nineteenth century. But Americans were clearly correct in observing that the accomplishments of the last three decades of the nineteenth century overshadowed all the earlier progress.

The remarkable growth did much to increase the wealth and improve the lives of many Americans. But such benefits were very unequally shared. While industrial titans and a growing middle class were enjoying a prosperity without precedent in the nation's history, workers, farmers, and others were experiencing an often painful ordeal that slowly edged the United States toward a great economic and political crisis.

TIME LINE

SOURCES OF INDUSTRIAL GROWTH

Many factors contributed to the growth of American industry: abundant raw materials, a large and growing labor supply, a surge in technological innovation, the emergence of a talented and often ruthless group of entrepreneurs, a federal government eager to assist the growth of business, and an expanding domestic market for the products of manufacturing.

INDUSTRIAL TECHNOLOGIES

The rapid emergence of new technologies, together with the discovery of new materials and productive processes, was one of the principal sources of late-nineteenth-century industrial growth. Some of the most important innovations were in communications. In 1866, Cyrus W. Field laid a transatlantic telegraph cable to Europe. During the next decade, Alexander Graham Bell developed the first telephone with commercial capacity. By 1900, there were 1.35 million telephones, and by 1920, 13.3 million. And the Italian inventor Guglielmo Marconi was taking the first steps toward the development of radio in the 1890s; the technology he developed quickly found its way to the United States. Other inventions that speeded the pace of business organization were the typewriter (by Christopher L. Sholes in 1868), the cash register (by James Ritty in 1879), and the calculating, or adding, machine (by William S. Burroughs in 1891).

Among the most revolutionary innovations was the introduction in the 1870s of electricity as a source of light and power. The pioneers of electric lighting included Charles F. Brush, who devised the arc lamp for street illumination, and Thomas A. Edison, who invented the incandescent lamp (or lightbulb). Edison and others designed improved generators and built large power plants to furnish electricity to whole cities. By the turn of the century, electric power was becoming commonplace in street railway systems, in the elevators of urban skyscrapers, in factories, and increasingly in offices and homes.

Particularly important to trade and industry was the development of new high-efficiency steam engines capable of powering larger ships at faster speeds than ever before. The new high-speed freighters, for example, made it cheaper for Britain to buy wheat grown in Canada and the United States than to grow it at home. The introduction of refrigerated ships in the 1870s made it possible to transport meat from North America, and even Australia and Asia, to Europe.

THE TECHNOLOGY OF IRON AND STEEL PRODUCTION

Iron production had developed slowly in the United States through most of the nineteenth century, mostly driven by the demand for iron rails; steel production had developed hardly at all by the end of the Civil War. In the 1870s and 1880s, however, iron production soared as railroads added 40,000 new miles of track, and steel production made great strides toward its eventual dominance in the metals industry.

An Englishman, Henry Bessemer, and an American, William Kelly, developed, almost simultaneously, a process for converting iron into the much more durable and versatile steel. (The process, which took Bessemer's name, consisted of blowing air through molten iron to burn out the impurities and create a much stronger metal.) The Bessemer process also relied on the discovery by the British metallurgist Robert Mushet that ingredients could be added during conversion to transform iron into steel, giving it additional strength. In 1868, the New Jersey ironmaster Abram S. Hewitt introduced from Europe another method of making steel—the open-hearth process. These techniques made possible the production of steel in great quantities and large dimensions, for use in the manufacture of locomotives, rails, and girders for the construction of tall buildings.

The steel industry emerged first in western Pennsylvania and eastern Ohio, partly because iron ore could be found there in abundance. It was also because the new forms of steel production created a demand for new kinds of fuel—and particularly for the anthracite (or hard) coal that was plentiful in Pennsylvania. Later, new techniques made it possible to use bituminous (or soft) coal, also easily mined in western Pennsylvania. As a result, Pittsburgh quickly became the center of the steel world. But the industry was growing fast and new sources of ore soon emerged. The upper peninsula of Michigan, the Mesabi Range in Minnesota, and the area around Birmingham, Alabama, became important ore-producing centers, and new centers of steel production grew up near them: Cleveland, Detroit, Chicago, and Birmingham, among others.

Until the Civil War, iron and steel furnaces were mostly made of stone and usually built against the side of a hill to reduce construction demands. By the 1870s, however, furnaces were redesigned as cylindrical iron shells lined with brick. These massive new furnaces were 75 feet tall and higher and could produce over 500 tons a week.

As the steel industry spread, new transportation systems emerged to serve it. Steel production in the Great Lakes region produced steam freighters that could carry ore on the lakes. Shippers used new steam engines to speed the unloading of ore. The demand for vessels capable of transporting oil and the development of new and more powerful steam engines led to the design of larger and heavier freighters.

There was an even closer relationship between the emerging steel companies and the railroads. Steel manufacturers provided rails and parts for cars; railroads were both markets for and transporters of manufactured steel. But the relationship soon became more

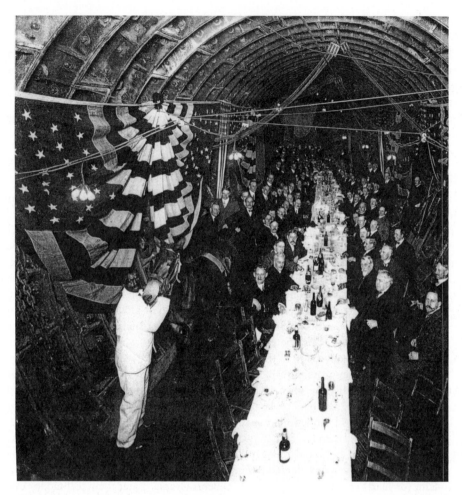

CELEBRATING A TUNNEL   The new industrial economy made possible many great feats that only decades before would have been unthinkable. In this striking photograph, the engineers and financiers who planned and paid for this underwater tunnel between Manhattan and New Jersey attend a banquet to celebrate its successful completion in 1907. (Culver Pictures)

intimate than that. The Pennsylvania Railroad, for example, created the Pennsylvania Steel Company.

The steel industry's need for lubrication for its machines helped create another important new industry in the late nineteenth century—oil. (Not until later did oil become important primarily for its potential as a fuel.) The existence of petroleum reserves in western Pennsylvania had been common knowledge for some time. The Pennsylvania businessman George Bissell showed that the substance could be burned in lamps and that it could also yield such products as paraffin, naphtha, and lubricating oil. Bissell raised money to begin drilling; and in 1859, Edwin L. Drake, one of Bissell's employees, established the first oil well near Titusville, Pennsylvania, which soon produced 500 barrels of oil a month. Demand for petroleum grew quickly, and promoters soon developed other oil fields in Pennsylvania, Ohio, and West Virginia.

THE AUTOMOBILE AND THE AIRPLANE

Among the most important technological innovations was the invention of the automobile. Two technologies led to its development. First was the creation of gasoline (or petrol), the product of an extraction process developed in the late nineteenth century in the United States by which lubricating oil and fuel oil were removed separately from crude oil. The second technology was the development of a self-contained engine. As early as the 1870s, designers in France, Germany, and Austria had begun to develop an "internal combustion engine," which used the expanding power of burning gas to drive pistons. A German, Nicolaus August Otto, created a gas-powered "four-stroke" engine in the mid-1860s, which was a precursor to automobile engines. But he did not develop a way to untether it from gas lines to be used portably in machines. One of Otto's former employees, Gottfried Daimler, later perfected an engine that could be used in automobiles.

The American automobile industry developed rapidly in the aftermath of these European breakthroughs. Charles and Frank Duryea built the first gasoline-driven motor vehicle in America in 1893. Three years later, Henry Ford produced the first of the famous cars that would bear his name. In 1895, there were only four automobiles on the American highways. By 1917, there were nearly 5 million.

The search for a means of human flight, as old as civilization, had been almost entirely futile until the late nineteenth century, when engineers, scientists, and tinkerers in both the United States and Europe began to experiment with a wide range of aeronautic devices. Balloonists began to consider ways to make dirigibles useful vehicles of transportation. Others experimented with kites and gliders.

Two brothers in Ohio, Wilbur and Orville Wright, began to construct a glider in 1899 that could be propelled through the air by an internal combustion engine. Four years later, Orville made a celebrated test flight near Kitty Hawk, North Carolina, in which an airplane took off by itself and traveled 120 feet in 12 seconds under its own power before settling back to earth. By the fall of 1904, they had improved the plane to the point where they were able to fly over 23 miles, and in the following year they began to take a few passengers on their flights with them.

Although the first working airplane was built in the United States, aviation technology was slow to gain a foothold in America. Most of the early progress in airplane design occurred in France, where there was substantial government funding for research and development. The U.S. government created the National Advisory Committee on Aeronautics in 1915, twelve years after the Wright brothers' flight, and American airplanes became a significant presence in Europe during World War I. But the prospects for commercial flight seemed dim until the 1920s, when Charles Lindbergh's famous solo flight from New York to Paris electrified the nation and the world.

RESEARCH AND DEVELOPMENT

New industrial technologies persuaded many businesses to build their own research operations. The corporate research-and-development laboratories coincided with a decline in government support for research, helping corporations attract skilled researchers. It also decentralized the sources of research funding and ensured that inquiry would move in many directions, and not just along paths determined by the government.

A rift began to emerge between scientists and engineers. Engineers—both inside and outside of universities—became increasingly tied up with the research-and-development agendas of corporations. Many scientists continued to scorn this "commercialization" of knowledge and preferred to stick to basic research that had no immediate practical applications. But many American scientists were more closely connected to practical challenges than were their European counterparts, and some joined engineers in corporate research-and-development laboratories, which over time began to sponsor both practical and basic research.

THE SCIENCE OF PRODUCTION

Central to the growth of the automobile and other industries were changes in the techniques of production. By the turn of the century, many industrialists were embracing the new principles of "scientific management," often known as "Taylorism" after its leading theoretician, Frederick Winslow Taylor. Taylor and his many admirers argued that scientific management made human labor compatible with the demands of the machine age. He persuaded employers to take control of the workplace. Taylor also urged employers to reorganize the production process by subdividing tasks. This sped up production and made workers more interchangeable, thus diminishing a manager's dependence on any particular employee. If properly managed by trained experts, he claimed, workers using modern machines could perform simple tasks at much greater speed, greatly increasing productive efficiency.

AUTOMOBILE PRODUCTION   Workers labor to finish and paint automobile bodies in a Fisher Body plant in 1918, just after the end of World War I. By then, General Motors had emerged as the giant of the industry, and Fisher Body was one of many companies it had bought to consolidate its control over the entire production process. (General Motors Corporation. Used with permission of GM Media Archives.)

The most important change in industrial technology was the emergence of mass production and, along with it, the moving assembly line, which Henry Ford introduced in his automobile plants in 1914. The assembly line was a particular place—a factory through which automobiles moved as they were assembled by workers who specialized on particular tasks. It was also a concept. The concept stressed the complete interchangeability of parts. General Motors adopted the same philosophy. Automobile production relied on other technologies, too, in particular the intensive use of electricity—to drive the assembly line, to light the factories, and to run the critical ventilating systems that kept dust from interfering with the machines. The revolutionary assembly-line technique enabled Ford to raise wages and reduce hours while cutting the base price of his Model T from $950 in 1914 to $290 in 1929. It became a standard for many other industries.

RAILROAD EXPANSION AND THE CORPORATION

The principal agent of industrial development in the late nineteenth century was still the expansion of the railroads. Railroads gave industrialists access to distant markets and remote sources of raw materials. The nation's largest businesses created new forms of corporate organization. And they were America's biggest investors, stimulating economic growth through their own enormous expenditures on construction and equipment.

Total railroad trackage increased from 30,000 miles in 1860 to 193,000 in 1900. Subsidies from federal, state, and local governments (along with foreign loans and investments) were vital to this expansion. Equally important was the emergence of great railroad "combinations" (mergers), many of them dominated by one or two individuals.

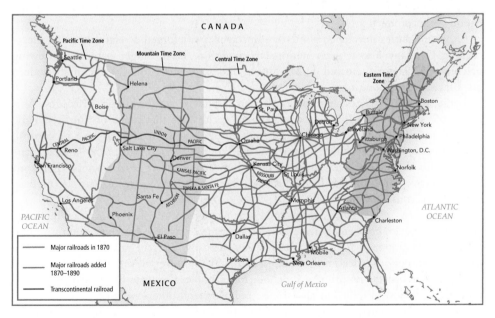

RAILROADS, 1870–1890 This map illustrates the rapid expansion of railroads in the late nineteenth century. In 1870, there was already a dense network of rail lines in the Northeast and Midwest, illustrated here by the green lines. The red lines show the further expansion of rail coverage between 1870 and 1890, much of it in the South and the areas west of the Mississippi River. • *Why were railroads so essential to the nation's economic growth in these years?*

The achievements (and excesses) of these tycoons—Cornelius Vanderbilt, James J. Hill, Collis R. Huntington, and others—became symbols to much of the nation of concentrated economic power. But railroad development was less significant for the individual barons it created than for its contribution to the growth of a new institution: the modern corporation.

There had been various forms of corporations in America since colonial times, but the modern corporation emerged as a major force only after the Civil War. By then, railroad magnates and other industrialists realized that their great ventures could not be financed by any single person.

Under the laws of incorporation passed in many states in the 1830s and 1840s, business organizations could raise money by selling stock to members of the public; after the Civil War, one industry after another began doing so. What made these stocks appealing was that investors now had only "limited liability"—they risked only the amount of their investments and were not liable for any debts the corporation might accumulate beyond that point. The ability to sell stock to a broad public made it possible for entrepreneurs to gather vast sums of capital and undertake great projects.

The Pennsylvania and other railroads were among the first to adopt the new corporate form of organization. But incorporation quickly spread beyond the railroad industry. Andrew Carnegie, a Scottish immigrant, worked his way up from modest beginnings and, in 1873, opened his own steelworks in Pittsburgh. Soon he dominated the industry. With his associate Henry Clay Frick, he bought up coal mines and leased part of the Mesabi iron range in Minnesota, operated a fleet of ore ships on the Great Lakes, and acquired railroads. He financed his vast undertakings not only out of his own profits but also out of the sale of stock. Then, in 1901, he sold out for $450 million to the banker J. Pierpont Morgan, who merged the Carnegie interests with others to create the giant United States Steel Corporation—a $14 billion enterprise that controlled almost two-thirds of the nation's steel production.

Other industries developed similarly. Gustavus Swift forged a relatively small meat-packing company into a great national corporation. Isaac Singer patented a sewing machine in 1851 and created I. M. Singer and Company—one of the first modern manufacturing corporations.

Large, national business enterprises needed systematic administrative structures. As a result, corporate leaders introduced managerial techniques that relied on the systematic division of responsibilities. Companies built carefully designed hierarchies of control, strict cost-accounting procedures, and a new breed of business executives: the "middle managers," who formed a layer of command between workers and owners. Efficient administrative capabilities helped make possible another major feature of the modern corporation: consolidation.

Businessmen created large consolidated organizations primarily through two methods. "Horizontal integration" combined a number of firms engaged in the same enterprise into a single corporation, such as the consolidation of many different railroad lines into one company. Through "vertical integration," a company took over all the different businesses on which it relied for its primary function, for example, Carnegie Steel, which came to control not only steel mills but also mines, railroads, and other enterprises.

The most celebrated corporate empire of the late nineteenth century was John D. Rockefeller's Standard Oil. Shortly after the Civil War, Rockefeller launched a refining company in Cleveland and immediately began trying to eliminate his competition. Allying himself with other wealthy capitalists, he formed the Standard Oil Company of Ohio in

1870, which in a few years had acquired twenty of the twenty-five refineries in Cleveland, as well as plants in Pittsburgh, Philadelphia, New York, and Baltimore.

So far, Rockefeller had expanded only horizontally—buying many refineries. But soon he began expanding vertically as well. He built his own barrel factories, terminal warehouses, and pipelines. Standard Oil owned its own freight cars and developed its own marketing organization. By the 1880s, Rockefeller had established such dominance within the petroleum industry that to much of the nation he served as a leading symbol of monopoly.

Rockefeller and other industrialists saw consolidation as a way to cope with what they believed was the greatest curse of the modern economy: "cutthroat competition." Most businessmen claimed to believe in free enterprise and a competitive marketplace, but in fact they feared that substantial competition could spell instability and ruin for all.

As the movement toward consolidation accelerated, new vehicles emerged to facilitate it. The railroads began with so-called pool arrangements—informal agreements among various companies to stabilize rates and divide markets (arrangements that would, in later years, be known as cartels). But the pool arrangements were too weak and could not ensure cost stability.

The failure of the pools led to new techniques of consolidation. The next effort to stabilize prices was the creation of the "trust"—pioneered by Standard Oil in the early 1880s and the banker J. P. Morgan. Under a trust agreement, stockholders in individual corporations transferred their stocks to a small group of trustees in exchange for shares in the trust itself. Owners of trust certificates often had no direct control over the decisions of the trustees; they simply received a share of the profits of the combination. The trustees themselves, on the other hand, might literally own only a few companies but could exercise effective control over many.

In 1889, the state of New Jersey helped produce a third form of consolidation by changing its laws of incorporation to permit companies to buy up rivals. Other states soon followed. Once actual corporate mergers were permitted, the original "trusts" became unnecessary. Rockefeller, for example, quickly relocated Standard Oil to New Jersey and created what became known as a "holding company"—a central corporate body that would buy up the stock of various members of the Standard Oil trust and establish direct, formal ownership of them.

By the end of the nineteenth century, 1 percent of the corporations in America were able to control more than 33 percent of the manufacturing. A system of economic organization was emerging that lodged enormous power in the hands of very few men—the great bankers of New York such as Morgan, industrial titans such as Rockefeller (who himself gained control of a major bank), and others.

The industrial giants of the era clearly contributed to substantial economic growth. They were also creating the basis for one of the greatest public controversies of their era: a raging debate over concentrated economic and political power that continued well into the twentieth century.

CAPITALIST CONSERVATISM AND ITS CRITICS

The inequality of the roaring capitalism of the late nineteenth century was not without its critics. Farmers, workers, middle-class businessmen, and many others considered the new capitalism to be a threat to their own destinies. But the industrial titans built a powerful defense for the new corporate economy.

ANDREW CARNEGIE EXPLAINS THE GOSPEL OF WEALTH, 1889

THE problem of our age is the proper administration of wealth, that the ties of brotherhood may still bind together the rich and poor in harmonious relationship. The conditions of human life have not only been changed, but revolutionized, within the past few hundred years. In former days there was little difference between the dwelling, dress, food, and environment of the chief and those of his retainers. The Indians are today where civilized man then was. . . . The contrast between the palace of the millionaire and the cottage of the laborer with us to-day measures the change which has come with civilization. This change, however, is not to be deplored, but welcomed as highly beneficial. It is well, nay, essential, for the progress of the race that the houses of some should be homes for all that is highest and best in literature and the arts,—and for all the refinements of civilization, rather than that none should be so. Much better this great irregularity than universal squalor. . . . The "good old times" were not good old times. Neither master nor servant was as well situated then as to-day. A relapse to old conditions would be disastrous to both—not the least so to him who serves—and would sweep away civilization with it. But whether the change be for good or ill, it is upon us, beyond our power to alter, and, therefore, to be accepted and made the best of. It is a waste of time to criticize the inevitable.

It is easy to see how the change has come. . . . In the manufacture of products we have the whole story. . . . To-day the world obtains commodities of excellent quality at prices which even the preceding generation would have deemed incredible. The poor enjoy what the rich could not before afford. What were the luxuries have become the necessaries of life. The laborer has now more comforts than the farmer had a few generations ago. The farmer has more luxuries than the landlord had, and is more richly clad and better housed. The landlord has books and pictures rarer and appointments more artistic than the king could then obtain.

The price we pay for this salutary change is, no doubt, great. . . . Under the law of competition, the employer of thousands is forced into the strictest economies, among which the rates paid to labor figure prominently, and often there is friction between the employer and the employed, between capital and labor, between rich and poor. Human society loses homogeneity.

The price which society pays for the law of competition, like the price it pays for cheap comforts and luxuries, is also great; but the advantages of this law are also greater still than its cost—for it is to this law that we owe our wonderful material development, which brings improved conditions in its train. But, whether the law be benign or not, we must say of it, as we say of the change in the conditions of men to which we have referred: It is here; we cannot evade it; no substitutes for it have been found; and while the law may be sometimes hard for the individual, it is best for the race, because it insures the survival of the fittest in every department.

What is the proper mode of administering wealth after the laws upon which civilization is founded have thrown it into the hands of the few? . . .

There remains . . . only one mode of using great fortunes; in this we have the true antidote for the temporary unequal distribution of wealth, the reconciliation of the rich and the poor—a reign of harmony. . . . It is founded upon the present most intense Individualism, and the race is prepared to put it in practice by degrees whenever it pleases.

Under its sway we shall have an ideal State, in which the surplus wealth of the few will become, in the best sense, the property of the many, because administered for the common good; and this wealth, passing through the hands of the few, can be made a much more potent force for the elevation of our race than if distributed in small sums to the people themselves. Even the poorest can be made to see this, and to agree that great sums gathered by some of their fellow-citizens and spent for public purposes, from which the masses reap the principal benefit, are more valuable to them than if scattered among themselves in trifling amounts through the course of many years. . . .

Poor and restricted are our opportunities in this life, narrow our horizon, our best work most imperfect; but rich men should be thankful for one inestimable boon. They have it in their power during their lives to busy themselves in organizing benefactions from which the masses of their fellows will derive lasting advantage, and thus dignify their own lives. The highest life is probably to be reached, not by such imitation of the life of Christ as Count Tolstoi' gives us, but, while animated by Christ's spirit, by recognizing the changed conditions of this age, and adopting modes of expressing this spirit suitable to the changed conditions under which we live, still laboring for the good of our fellows, which was the essence of his life and teaching, but laboring in a different manner.

This, then, is held to be the duty of the man of wealth: To set an example of modest, unostentatious living, shunning display or extravagance; to provide moderately for the legitimate wants of those dependent upon him; and, after doing so, to consider all surplus revenues which come to him simply as trust funds, which he is called upon to administer, and strictly bound as a matter of duty to administer in the manner which, in his judgment, is best calculated to produce the most beneficial results for the community—the man of wealth thus becoming the mere trustee and agent for his poorer brethren, bringing to their service his superior wisdom, experience, and ability to administer, doing for them better than they would or could do for themselves. . . .

[T]he best means of benefiting the community is to place within its reach the ladders upon which the aspiring can rise—free libraries, parks, and means of recreation, by which men are helped in body and mind; works of art, certain to give pleasure and improve the public taste; and public institutions of various kinds, which will improve the general condition of the people; in this manner returning their surplus wealth to the mass of their fellows in the forms best calculated to do them lasting good.

Thus is the problem of rich and poor to be solved. The laws of accumulation will be left free, the laws of distribution free. Individualism will continue, but the millionaire will be but a trustee for the poor, intrusted for a season with a great part of the increased wealth of the community, but administering it for the community far better than it could or would have done for itself. . . .

Such, in my opinion, is the true gospel concerning wealth, obedience to which is destined some day to solve the problem of the rich and the poor, and to bring "Peace on earth, among men good will."

UNDERSTAND, ANALYZE, & EVALUATE

1. What did Carnegie think of the inequality of wealth in industrial America? What were the wealthy supposed to do in this inequality of wealth, and what role did Andrew Carnegie envision for the poor?

2. What was the price of this new inequality? What was its benefit and how did this relate to Social Darwinism?

Source: Andrew Carnegie, "Wealth." *North American Review* (1889); located in: Michael P. Johnson, *Reading the American Past: Selected Historical Documents, vol. 2: From 1865.* 5th ed. (Boston: Bedford St. Martin's, 2012), pp. 52–55.

THE NOVELS OF HORATIO ALGER

A young boy, perhaps an orphan, makes his way through life on the rough streets of the city by selling newspapers or peddling matches. One day, his energy and determination catch the eye of a wealthy man, who gives him a chance to improve himself. Through honesty, charm, hard work, and aggressiveness, the boy rises in the world to become a successful man.

That, in a nutshell, is the story that Horatio Alger presented to his vast public in novel after novel—over 100 of them in all—for over forty years. During his lifetime, Americans bought millions of copies of his novels. After his death in 1899, his books (and others written in his name) continued to sell at an astonishing rate. Even today, when the books themselves are largely forgotten, the name Horatio Alger has come to represent the idea of individual advancement through (in a phrase Alger coined) "pluck and luck."

Alger was born in 1832 into a middle-class New England family, attended Harvard, and spent a short time as a Unitarian minister. In the mid-1850s, he turned to writing stories and books, and he continued to do so for the rest of his life. His most famous novel, *Ragged Dick*, was published in 1868. Almost all of his books were fables of a young man's rise "from rags to riches." The purpose of his writing, he claimed, was twofold. He wanted to "exert a salutary influence upon the class of whom [he] was writing, by setting before them inspiring examples of what energy, ambition, and an honest purpose may achieve." He also wanted to show his largely middle-class readers "the life and experiences of the friendless and vagrant children to be found in all our cities."

Most Americans of the late nineteenth and early twentieth centuries were attracted to Alger's stories because the stories helped them believe in one of the most cherished national myths: that with willpower and hard work, individuals could rise in the world. That belief was all the more important in the late nineteenth century when large-scale corporate industrialization was making it increasingly difficult for individuals to control their own fates.

Alger placed great emphasis on the moral qualities of his heroes; their success was a reward for their virtue. But many of his readers

SURVIVAL OF THE FITTEST

The new rationale for capitalism was based on the belief of individualism—an ideology that would remain at the heart of American conservatism for many decades. Wealthy capitalists defended their wealth by saying that they had earned their wealth and power through their own hard work and their acquisitiveness and thrift. Those who failed had only themselves to blame—a result of ignorance, stupidity, or laziness.

Conservative social theories helped support the belief that through "survival of the fittest" wealthy capitalists deserved their success. Among them was the theory of "Social Darwinism." Darwin's theories argued that the fittest forms of life survived over thousands

BOUND TO RISE

ALGER

A NEWSBOY'S STORY Alger's novels were even more popular after his death in 1899 than they had been in his lifetime. This reprint of one of his many rags-to-riches stories—about a New York newsboy's rise to wealth and success—was typical of his work. (Private Collection)

not just the opportunities for advancement it sometimes created, but also its cruelty. That was one reason that in almost all his books, his heroes triumphed not just because of their own virtues or efforts, but because of some amazing stroke of luck. To Alger, at least, the modern age did not guarantee success through hard work alone; there had to be some providential assistance as well. Over time, however, Alger's admirers ignored his own misgivings about industrialism and portrayed his books purely as celebrations of (and justifications for) laissez-faire capitalism and the accumulation of wealth.

An example of the transformation of Alger into a symbol of individual achievement is the Horatio Alger Award, established in 1947 by the American Schools and Colleges Association to honor "living individuals who by their own efforts [have] pulled themselves up by their bootstraps in the American tradition." Among its recipients have been Presidents Dwight D. Eisenhower and Ronald Reagan, evangelist Billy Graham, and Supreme Court Justice Clarence Thomas. •

ignored the moral message and clung simply to the image of sudden and dramatic success. After the author's death, his publishers abridged many of Alger's works, eliminating the parts of his stories where the heroes do good deeds and focusing solely on the success of Alger's heroes in rising in the world.

Alger himself had very mixed feelings about the new industrial order he described. His books were meant to reveal

UNDERSTAND, ANALYZE, & EVALUATE

1. How do Alger's novels both defend industrial capitalism and criticize it?
2. According to the essay, Alger placed great emphasis on the moral qualities of his heroes, but his publishers later eliminated that aspect of the novels. Why?

of years because of their biological fitness. Social Darwinism argued that individuals rose or fell in society because of their innate "fitness." (Darwin himself, along with most scientists, debunked Social Darwinism, but many Americans embraced it nevertheless.) The English philosopher and biologist Herbert Spencer introduced the theory of Social Darwinism in his book *Principles of Biology* (1864). Society, he argued, benefited from the elimination of the unfit and the survival of the strong and talented. William Graham Sumner, a sociologist at Yale, borrowed from Spencer's theory and created a theory of his own in his famous 1906 book *Folkways*. Those who failed, he argued in an essay 1913, were unfit for success: "Before the tribunal of nature a man has no more right to life than a rattlesnake; he has no more right to liberty than any wild beast; his right to pursuit of happiness is nothing but a license to maintain the struggle for existence." Wealthy corporate leaders were attracted to the ideas of Spencer and Sumner. Their success confirmed their own virtues and "fitness."

Capitalists argued that they earned their wealth through the virtues of competition and the free market. But critics of the industrial and financial titans claimed that they earned their wealth not because of the innate fitness of those who succeeded, but because they replaced the natural workings of the marketplace by building great monopolies that would protect them from competition.

THE GOSPEL OF WEALTH

Some businessmen attempted to temper the harsh philosophy of Social Darwinism with a gentler, if in some ways equally self-serving, idea: the "gospel of wealth." People of great wealth, they argued, had not only great power but also a great responsibility to use their riches to advance social progress. Elaborating on this creed in his 1901 book *The Gospel of Wealth*, Andrew Carnegie wrote that people of wealth should consider all revenues in excess of their own needs to be "trust funds" used for the good of the community. Carnegie was only one of many industrialists who devoted large parts of their fortunes to philanthropic works.

The idea of private wealth as a public blessing existed alongside another popular concept: the notion of great wealth as something available to all. Russell H. Conwell, a Baptist minister, became one of the most prominent spokesmen for the idea by delivering one lecture, "Acres of Diamonds," more than 6,000 times between 1880 and 1900. Conwell told a series of stories, which he claimed were true, of individuals who had found opportunities for extraordinary wealth in their own backyards. (One such story involved a modest farmer who discovered a vast diamond mine in his own fields.) Most of the millionaires in the country, Conwell claimed (inaccurately), had begun on the lowest rung of the economic ladder and had worked their way to success.

But the most famous promoter of the success story was Horatio Alger. He was originally a minister in a small town in Massachusetts but was driven from his pulpit as a result of sexual scandals. He moved to New York, where he wrote over 100 celebrated novels—all of them tributes to social mobility and the ability of Americans to rise from "rags to riches."

If Alger's rags-to-riches tales captured the aspiration of many men, Louisa May Alcott's enormously popular novels helped give voice to the often unstated ambitions of many women. Alcott was the daughter of a noted New England reformer, but her family nevertheless experienced considerable hardship. After serving as a nurse in the Civil War and writing a series of popular adventure novels (under a pen name that disguised her gender), she became a major literary figure with the publication of *Little Women* in 1869 and two sequels over the next twenty years. The main character in these novels, Jo March, struggles to build a life for herself that is not defined by conventional women's roles and ambitions. She spurns a conventional marriage and eventually weds a professor who appears to support her literary ambitions. "Girls write to ask who the little women marry, as if that was the only end and aim of a woman's life," Alcott wrote a friend. "I won't marry Jo to Laurie [the attractive, wealthy neighbor who proposes to her] to please any one." Alcott's female characters, in some ways like Alger's male ones, are remarkable for their independence and drive. Jo March is willful, rebellious, stubborn, ambitious, and often selfish—far from the posed, romantic, submissive women in most popular sentimental novels of Alcott's time aimed at female audiences.

ALTERNATIVE VISIONS

Alongside the celebrations of competition and the justifications for great wealth stood a group of alternative philosophies, challenging the corporate ethos and, at times, capitalism itself.

One such philosophy came from the sociologist Lester Frank Ward. In *Dynamic Sociology* (1883) and other books, he argued that civilization was not governed by natural selection but by human intelligence, which could shape society as it wished. Sumner believed that state intervention to remodel the environment was futile, but Ward thought that an active government engaged in positive planning was society's best hope.

Other Americans adopted more radical approaches to reform. Some dissenters found a home in the Socialist Labor Party, founded in the 1870s and led for many years by Daniel De Leon, an immigrant from the West Indies. Although De Leon attracted a following in the industrial cities, the party never became a major political force and never polled more than 82,000 votes. A dissident faction of De Leon's party, eager to forge stronger ties with organized labor, broke away and in 1901 formed the more enduring American Socialist Party.

Other radicals gained a wider following. Among them was the California writer and activist Henry George. His angrily eloquent *Progress and Poverty*, published in 1879, became one of the best-selling nonfiction works in American publishing history. George blamed social problems on the ability of a few monopolists to grow wealthy as a result of rising land values. An increase in the value of land, he claimed, was not a result of any effort by the owner, but an "unearned increment," produced by the growth of society around the land. Such profits were rightfully the property of the community. And so George proposed a "single tax" on land, to replace all other taxes, which would return the increment to the people. The tax, he argued, would destroy monopolies, distribute wealth more equally, and eliminate poverty.

Rivaling George in popularity was Edward Bellamy, whose utopian novel *Looking Backward,* published in 1888, sold more than 1 million copies. It described the experiences of a young Bostonian who went into a hypnotic sleep in 1887 and awoke in the year 2000 to find a new social order in which want, politics, and vice were unknown. The new society had emerged through a peaceful, evolutionary process: the large trusts of the late nineteenth century had continued to grow in size and to combine with one another until ultimately they formed a single, great trust, controlled by the government, which distributed the abundance of the industrial economy equally among all the people. "Fraternal cooperation" had replaced competition. Class divisions had disappeared. Bellamy labeled the philosophy behind this vision "nationalism."

THE PROBLEMS OF MONOPOLY

Relatively few Americans shared the views of those who questioned capitalism itself. But as time went on, a growing number of people were becoming deeply concerned about the growth of monopoly.

By the end of the century, a wide range of groups had begun to assail monopoly and economic concentration. In the absence of competition, they argued, monopolistic industries could charge whatever prices they wished. Railroads, in particular, charged very high rates along some routes because they knew their customers had no choice but to pay them.

"MODERN COLOSSUS OF (RAIL) ROADS" Cornelius Vanderbilt, known as the "Commodore," accumulated one of America's great fortunes by consolidating several large railroad companies in the 1860s. His name became a synonym not only for enormous wealth but also (in the eyes of many Americans) for excessive corporate power—as suggested in this cartoon, showing him standing astride his empire and manipulating its parts. (Culver Pictures, Inc.)

Beginning in 1873, the economy fluctuated erratically, producing severe recessions every five or six years, each worse than the last.

THE ORDEAL OF THE WORKER

Most workers in the late nineteenth century experienced a real rise in their standard of living. But they did so at the cost of arduous and often dangerous working conditions, diminishing control over their own work, and a growing sense of powerlessness.

THE IMMIGRANT WORKFORCE

The industrial workforce expanded dramatically in the late nineteenth century as a result of massive migration into industrial cities. Rural Americans continued to flow into factory towns and cities—people disillusioned with or bankrupted by life on the farm. There was also a great wave of immigration from abroad (primarily from Europe, but also from Asia, Canada, Mexico, and other areas) in the decades following the Civil War—an influx greater than that of any previous era. The 25 million immigrants who arrived in the United States between 1865 and 1915 were more than four times the number who had arrived in the previous fifty years.

In the 1870s and 1880s, most of the immigrants came from England, Ireland, and northern Europe. By the end of the century, however, the major sources of immigrants had shifted, with large numbers of southern and eastern Europeans (Italians, Poles, Russians, Greeks, Slavs, and others) moving into the country and into the industrial workforce.

The new immigrants came to America in part to escape poverty and oppression in their homelands. But they were also attracted by expectations of new opportunities. Railroads lured immigrants into their western landholdings by distributing misleading advertisements overseas. Industrial employers actively recruited immigrant workers under the Labor Contract Law, which—until its repeal in 1885—permitted them to pay for the passage of workers in advance and deduct the amount later from their wages. Even after the repeal of the law, employers continued to encourage the immigration of unskilled laborers, often with the assistance of foreign-born labor brokers, such as the Greek and Italian *padrones*, who recruited work gangs of their fellow nationals.

The arrival of these new groups heightened ethnic tensions within the working class. Low-paid Poles, Greeks, and French Canadians began to displace higher-paid British and Irish workers in the textile factories of New England. Italians, Slavs, and Poles emerged as a major source of labor for the mining industry. Chinese and Mexicans competed with Anglo-Americans and African Americans in mining, farmwork, and factory labor in California, Colorado, and Texas.

WAGES AND WORKING CONDITIONS

At the turn of the century, the average income of the American worker was $400 to $500 a year—below the $600 figure that many believed was required to maintain a reasonable level of comfort. Nor did workers have much job security. All were vulnerable to the boom-and-bust cycle of the industrial economy and the instability caused by technological advances. Even those who kept their jobs could find their wages suddenly and substantially cut in hard times. Few workers, in other words, were ever very far from poverty.

Many first-generation workers, accustomed to the patterns of agrarian life, had trouble adjusting to the nature of modern industrial labor: routine, repetitive tasks on a strict and monotonous schedule. Skilled artisans, whose once-valued tasks were now performed by machines, found the new system impersonal and demeaning. Most factory laborers worked ten-hour days, six days a week; in the steel industry they worked twelve hours a day. Industrial accidents were frequent.

The decreasing need for skilled work in factories induced many employers to increase the use of women and children, whom they could hire for lower wages than adult males. By 1900, 20 percent of all manufacturing workers were women. Women worked in all areas of industry, even in some of the most arduous jobs. Most women, however, worked in a few industries where unskilled and semiskilled machine labor (as opposed to heavy manual labor) prevailed. The textile industry remained the largest single industrial employer of women. (Domestic service remained the most common female occupation overall.) Women worked for wages well below the minimum necessary for survival (and well below the wages paid to men working the same jobs).

At least 1.7 million children under sixteen years of age were employed in factories and fields; 10 percent of all girls aged ten to fifteen, and 20 percent of all boys, held jobs. Under public pressure, thirty-eight states passed child labor laws in the late nineteenth century. But 60 percent of child workers were employed in agriculture, which was typically exempt from the laws. For children employed in factories, the laws merely set a minimum age of twelve years and a maximum workday of ten hours, standards that employers often ignored in any case.

EMERGING UNIONIZATION

Laborers attempted to fight back against such conditions by creating national unions. By the end of the century, however, their efforts had met with little success.

There had been craft unions in America, representing small groups of skilled workers, since well before the Civil War. But most unions could not hope to exert significant power in the economy. And during the turbulent recession years of the 1870s, unions faced the additional problem of widespread public hostility. When labor disputes with employers turned bitter and violent, as they occasionally did, much of the public instinctively blamed the workers for the trouble, rarely the employers. Particularly alarming to middle-class Americans was the emergence of the "Molly Maguires" in the anthracite coal region of western Pennsylvania. This militant labor organization sometimes used violence and even murder in its battle with coal operators.

Excitement over the Molly Maguires paled beside the near hysteria that gripped the country during the railroad strike of 1877, which began when the eastern railroads announced a 10 percent wage cut and soon expanded into something approaching a class war. Strikers disrupted rail service from Baltimore to St. Louis, destroyed equipment, and rioted in the streets of Pittsburgh and other cities. State militias were called out, and in July President Hayes ordered federal troops to suppress the disorders. In Baltimore, eleven demonstrators died and forty were wounded in a conflict between workers and militiamen. In Philadelphia, the state militia killed twenty people when the troops opened fire on thousands of workers and their families who were attempting to block the railroad crossings. In all, over 100 people died before the strike finally collapsed several weeks after it had begun. The great railroad strike was America's first major national labor conflict.

THE KNIGHTS OF LABOR

In the first major effort to create a genuinely national labor organization, the Noble Order of the Knights of Labor was founded in 1869 under the leadership of Uriah S. Stephens. Membership was open to all who "toiled," a definition that included all workers, most business and professional people, and virtually all women—whether they worked in factories, as domestic servants, or in their own homes. Only lawyers, bankers, liquor dealers, and professional gamblers were excluded. The Knights of Labor championed an eight-hour workday and the abolition of child labor, but they were more interested in long-range reform of the economy. The Knights hoped to replace the "wage system" with a new "cooperative system," in which workers would themselves control their workplaces.

For several years, the Knights remained a secret fraternal organization. But in the late 1870s, under the leadership of Terence V. Powderly, the order moved into the open and entered a period of spectacular expansion. By 1886, it claimed a total membership of over 700,000. Local unions or assemblies associated with the Knights launched a series of railroad and other strikes in the 1880s in defiance of Powderly's wishes. Their failure helped discredit the organization. By 1890, membership of the Knights had shrunk to 100,000. A few years later, the organization disappeared altogether.

The AFL

Even before the Knights began to decline, a rival association appeared. In 1881, representatives of a number of craft unions formed the Federation of Organized Trade and Labor Unions of the United States and Canada. Five years later, this body took the name it has borne ever since, the American Federation of Labor (AFL).

Rejecting the Knights' idea of one big union for everybody, the federation was an association of essentially autonomous craft unions that represented mainly skilled workers. Samuel Gompers, the powerful leader of the AFL, concentrated on labor's immediate objectives: wages, hours, and working conditions. As one of its first objectives, the AFL demanded a national eight-hour workday and called for a general strike if the goal was not achieved by May 1, 1886. On that day, strikes and demonstrations for a shorter workday took place all over the country.

In Chicago, a center of labor and radical strength, a strike was already in progress at the McCormick Harvester Company. City police had been harassing the strikers, and labor and radical leaders called a protest meeting at Haymarket Square on May 1. When the police ordered the crowd to disperse, someone threw a bomb that killed seven policemen and injured sixty-seven others. The police, who had killed four strikers the day before, fired into the crowd and killed four more people. Conservative, property-conscious Americans— frightened and outraged—demanded retribution. Chicago officials finally rounded up eight anarchists and charged them with murder, on the grounds that their statements had incited whoever had hurled the bomb. All eight scapegoats were found guilty after a remarkably injudicious trial. Seven were sentenced to death. One of them committed suicide, four were executed, and two had their sentences commuted to life imprisonment.

To most middle-class Americans, the Haymarket bombing was an alarming symbol of social chaos and radicalism. "Anarchism" now became in the public mind a code word for terrorism and violence, even though most anarchists were relatively peaceful. For the next thirty years, the specter of anarchism remained one of the most frightening concepts in the American imagination. It was a constant obstacle to the goals of the AFL and other labor organizations, and it did particular damage to the Knights of Labor. However much they tried to distance themselves from radicals, labor leaders were always vulnerable to accusations of anarchism, as the violent strikes of the 1890s occasionally illustrated.

The Homestead Strike

The Amalgamated Association of Iron and Steel Workers was the most powerful trade union in the country. Its members were skilled workers, in great demand by employers, and they had long been able to exercise significant power in the workplace. In the mid-1880s, however, demand for skilled workers declined as new production methods changed the steelmaking process. In the streamlined Carnegie system, which was coming to dominate the steel industry, the union was able to maintain a foothold in only one of the corporation's three major factories—the Homestead plant near Pittsburgh.

By 1890, Carnegie and his chief lieutenant, Henry Clay Frick, had decided that the Amalgamated "had to go." Over the next two years, they repeatedly cut wages at Homestead. At first, the union acquiesced, aware that it was not strong enough to wage a successful strike. But in 1892, when the company stopped even discussing its decisions with the union and gave it two days to accept another wage cut, the Amalgamated called for a strike.

Frick abruptly shut down the plant and called in 300 guards from the Pinkerton Detective Agency, well known as strikebreakers, to enable the company to hire nonunion workers. They approached the plant by river, on barges, on July 6, 1892. The strikers poured gasoline on the water, set it on fire, and then met the Pinkertons at the docks with guns and dynamite. After several hours of fighting, which killed three guards and ten strikers and injured many others, the Pinkertons surrendered and were escorted roughly out of town.

But the workers' victory was temporary. The governor of Pennsylvania, at the company's request, sent the state's entire National Guard contingent, some 8,000 men, to Homestead. Production resumed, with strikebreakers now protected by troops. And public opinion turned against the strikers when a radical made an attempt to assassinate Frick. Slowly, workers drifted back to their jobs, and finally—four months after the strike began—the Amalgamated surrendered. By 1900, every major steel plant in the Northeast had broken with the Amalgamated. Its membership shrank from a high of 24,000 in 1891 (two-thirds of all eligible steelworkers) to fewer than 7,000 a decade later.

THE PULLMAN STRIKE

A dispute of greater magnitude, if less violence, was the Pullman strike in 1894. The Pullman Palace Car Company manufactured railroad sleeping and parlor cars at a plant near Chicago. There the company constructed a 600-acre town, Pullman, and rented its trim, orderly houses to the employees. George M. Pullman, owner of the company, saw the town as a model—a solution to the problems of industrial workers. But many residents chafed at the regimentation (and the high rents). In the winter of 1893–1894, the Pullman Company slashed wages by about 25 percent, citing its own declining revenues in the depression, without reducing the rent it charged its employees. Workers went on strike and persuaded the militant American Railway Union, led by Eugene V. Debs, to support them by refusing to handle Pullman cars and equipment. Within a few days, thousands of railroad workers in twenty-seven states and territories were on strike, and transportation from Chicago to the Pacific Coast was paralyzed.

Unlike most elected politicians, the governor of Illinois, John Peter Altgeld, was a man with demonstrated sympathies for workers and their grievances. He refused to call out the militia to protect employers. Bypassing Altgeld, railroad operators asked the federal government to send regular army troops to Illinois, using the pretext that the strike was preventing the movement of mail on the trains. In July 1894, President Grover Cleveland ordered 2,000 troops to the Chicago area. A federal court issued an injunction forbidding the union to continue the strike. When Debs and his associates defied it, they were arrested and imprisoned. With federal troops protecting the hiring of new workers and with the union leaders in a federal jail, the strike quickly collapsed.

THE PULLMAN STRIKE   This image portrays the Great Pullman Strike of 1894. It shows striking workers setting fire to the freight cars that they themselves had built. (The Granger Colletion, NYC)

SOURCES OF LABOR WEAKNESS

In the last decades of the nineteenth century, labor made few real gains despite militant organizing efforts. Industrial wages rose hardly at all. Labor leaders won a few legislative victories—the abolition of the Contract Labor Law, the establishment of an eight-hour day for government employees, compensation for some workers injured on the job, and others. But many such laws were not enforced. Widespread strikes and protests, and many other working-class forms of resistance, large and small, led to few real gains. The end of the century found most workers with less political power and less control of the workplace than they had had forty years before.

Workers failed to make greater gains for many reasons. The principal labor organizations represented only a small percentage of the industrial workforce; the AFL, the most important, excluded unskilled workers, and along with them most women, blacks, and recent immigrants. Divisions within the workforce, such as tensions among different ethnic and racial groups, contributed further to union weakness.

Another source of labor weakness was the shifting nature of the workforce. Many immigrant workers came to America intending to earn some money and then return home. The assumption that they had no long-range future in the country eroded their willingness to organize. Other workers were in constant motion, moving from one job to another, one town to another, seldom in a single place long enough to establish any institutional ties or exert any real power.

Above all, perhaps, workers made few gains in the late nineteenth century because they faced corporate organizations of vast wealth and power, which were generally determined to crush any efforts by workers to challenge their prerogatives. And as the Homestead and Pullman strikes suggest, the corporations usually had the support of local, state, and federal authorities, who were willing to send in troops to "preserve order" and crush labor uprisings on demand.

Despite the creation of new labor unions and a wave of strikes and protests, workers in the late nineteenth century failed on the whole to create successful organizations or to protect their interests. In the battle for power within the emerging industrial economy, almost all the advantages seemed to lie with capital.

CONCLUSION

In the four decades after the Civil War, the United States propelled itself into the forefront of the industrializing nations of the world. Large areas of the nation remained overwhelmingly rural, to be sure. But even so, America's economy, and along with it the nation's society and culture, was being profoundly transformed.

New technologies, new forms of corporate management, and new supplies of labor helped make possible the rapid growth of the nation's industries and the construction of its railroads. The factory system contributed to the growth of the nation's cities. Immigration provided a steady supply of new workers for the growing industrial economy. The result was a steady increase in national wealth, rising living standards for much of the population, and the creation of great new fortunes.

But industrialization did not spread its fruits evenly. Large areas of the country, most notably the South, and large groups in the population, most notably minorities, women, and recent immigrants, profited relatively little from economic growth. Industrial workers experienced arduous conditions of labor. Small merchants and manufacturers found themselves overmatched by great new combinations.

Industrialists strove to create a rationale for their power and to persuade the public that everyone had something to gain from it. But many Americans remained skeptical of modern capitalism, and some—workers struggling to form unions, reformers denouncing trusts, socialists envisioning a new world, and many others—created broad and powerful critiques of the new economic order. Industrialization brought both progress and pain to late-nineteenth-century America. Controversies over its effects defined the era and would continue to define the first decades of the twentieth century.

RECALL AND REFLECT

1. Who were some of the business and industrial titans of the late nineteenth century, and what did they contribute to America's industrial growth?
2. What changes took place in corporate organization in the late nineteenth century, and how did these changes affect the nation's economy?
3. What was the Gospel of Wealth?
4. How did Social Darwinism attempt to justify the social consequences of industrial capitalism?
5. How did workers respond to the expansion of industrialization and the new industrial economy?

18 | THE AGE OF THE CITY

THE NEW URBAN GROWTH
THE URBAN LANDSCAPE
STRAINS OF URBAN LIFE
THE RISE OF MASS CONSUMPTION
LEISURE IN THE CONSUMER SOCIETY
HIGH CULTURE IN THE URBAN AGE

LOOKING AHEAD

1. What were some of the problems that resulted from rapid urbanization, and how did urban governments respond to these problems?

2. How did the sources of immigration to America shift in the late nineteenth century, and what was the native response to the change?

3. How did the rise of mass consumption affect leisure and entertainment?

THE FACE OF AMERICAN SOCIETY was transformed in countless ways by the growth of industry and commerce. But no change was more profound than the growing size and influence of cities. Having begun its life as a primarily agrarian republic, the United States in the late nineteenth century was becoming an urban nation.

1869

First intercollegiate
football game

1870

NYC opens first
elevated railroads

1871

Boston and Chicago
fires

1872

Boss Tweed convicted

1876

Baseball's National
League founded

1882

Congress restricts
Chinese immigration

1884

First "skyscraper" in
Chicago

1890

Riis's *How the Other
Half Lives*

1891

Basketball invented

1894

Immigration
Restriction League
formed

1895

Crane's *The Red Badge of
Courage*

1897

Boston opens first
subway in America

1901

Baseball's American
League founded

1903

First World Series

1906

San Francisco
earthquake and fire

Sinclair's *The Jungle*

1910

NCAA founded

THE NEW URBAN GROWTH

Although the great movement of people to the city was not unique to the United States, Americans found urbanization particularly jarring. The urban population increased sevenfold in the half century after the Civil War. And in 1920, the census revealed that for the first time, a majority of the American people lived in "urban" areas—defined as communities of 2,500 people or more.

Natural increase accounted for only a small part of the urban growth. Urban families experienced a high rate of infant mortality, a declining fertility rate, and a high death rate from disease. Without immigration, cities would have grown relatively slowly.

THE MIGRATIONS

In the late nineteenth century, Americans left the declining agricultural regions of the East at a dramatic rate. Some moved to the newly developing farmlands of the West. But almost as many moved to the growing cities of the East and the Midwest.

Among those leaving rural America for industrial cities in the 1880s were black men and women trying to escape the poverty, debt, violence, and oppression they faced in the rural South. They were also seeking new opportunities in cities. Factory jobs for African Americans were rare and professional opportunities almost nonexistent. Urban blacks tended to work in service occupations as cooks, janitors, domestic servants, and so on. Because many such jobs were considered women's work, black women often outnumbered black men in the cities.

The most important source of urban population growth, however, was the great number of new immigrants from abroad. Some came from Canada, Latin America, and—particularly on the West Coast—China and Japan. But the greatest number came from Europe. After 1880, the flow of new arrivals began to include large numbers of people from southern and eastern Europe. By the 1890s, more than half of all immigrants came from these regions.

In earlier years, most new immigrants from Europe (particularly Germans and Scandinavians) had arrived with at least some money and education. Most of them arrived at one of the major port cities on the Atlantic Coast (the greatest number landing at New York's famous immigrant depot on Ellis Island) and then headed west. But the new immigrants of the late nineteenth century generally lacked the capital to buy farmland and lacked the education to establish themselves in professions. So, like similarly poor Irish immigrants before the Civil War, they settled overwhelmingly in industrial cities, where they worked largely in unskilled jobs.

THE ETHNIC CITY

By 1890, most of the population of the major cities consisted of immigrants: 87 percent of the population in Chicago, 80 percent in New York, 84 percent in Milwaukee and Detroit. Equally striking was the diversity of new immigrant populations. In other

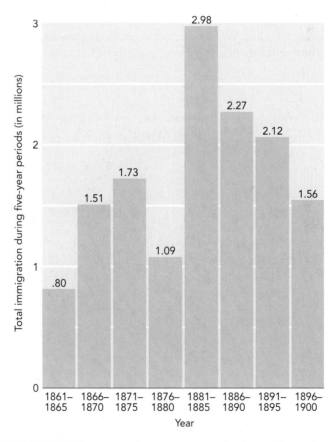

TOTAL IMMIGRATION, 1861–1900   Over 10 million immigrants from abroad entered the United States in the last forty years of the nineteenth century, with particularly high numbers arriving in the 1880s and 1890s. This chart shows the pattern of immigration in five-year intervals. • *What external events might help explain some of the rises and falls in the rates of immigration in these years?*

countries experiencing heavy immigration in this period, most of the new arrivals were coming from one or two sources. But in the United States, no single national group dominated.

Most of the new arrivals were rural people, and for many of them the adjustment to city life was painful. To help ease the transition, some immigrant groups formed close-knit ethnic communities within the cities, in neighborhoods often called "immigrant ghettoes." Ethnic neighborhoods offered newcomers much that was familiar, including newspapers and theaters in their native languages, stores selling their native foods, and church and fraternal organizations that provided links to their national pasts. Many immigrants also maintained close ties with their native countries. They stayed in touch with relatives who had remained behind, and perhaps as many as a third in the early years returned to their homelands after a relatively short time. Others helped bring the rest of their families to America.

The cultural cohesiveness of the ethnic communities clearly eased the pain of separation from the immigrants' native lands. What role it played in helping immigrants become absorbed into American economic life is a more difficult question to answer. Some ethnic groups (Jews and Germans, in particular) advanced economically more rapidly than others (for example, the Irish). One explanation is that by huddling together in ethnic neighborhoods, immigrant groups tended to reinforce the cultural values of their previous societies. When those values were particularly well suited to economic advancement—for example, the high value Jews placed on education—ethnic identification may have helped members of a group to improve their lots. When other values predominated—maintaining community solidarity, strengthening family ties, preserving order—progress could be less rapid.

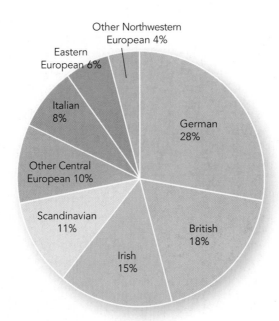

SOURCES OF IMMIGRATION FROM EUROPE, 1860-1900   This pie chart shows the sources of European immigration in the late nineteenth century. The largest number of immigrants continued to come from traditional sources (Britain, Ireland, Germany, Scandinavia), but the beginnings of what in the early twentieth century would become a major influx of immigrants from new sources—southern and eastern Europe in particular—are already visible here. Immigration from other sources—Mexico, South and Central America, and Asia—was also significant during this period. • *Why would these newer sources of European and other kinds of immigration create controversy among older-stock Americans?*

But other factors were at least as important in determining how well immigrants fared. Immigrants who aroused strong racial prejudice among native-born whites found it very difficult to advance, whatever their talents. Those white immigrants who arrived with a valuable skill or with some capital did better than those who did not. And over time, those who lived in cities where people of their own nationality came to predominate—for example, the Irish in New York and Boston or the Germans in Milwaukee—gained an advantage as they learned to exert their political power.

ASSIMILATION AND EXCLUSION

Despite the many differences among the various immigrant communities, virtually all groups had certain things in common. Most immigrants shared the experience of living in cities. Most were young; the majority of newcomers were between fifteen and forty-five years old. And in most communities of the foreign-born, ethnic ties had to compete against the desire for assimilation.

Many of the new arrivals had come with romantic visions of the New World. And however disillusioning they might have found their first contact with the United States, they usually retained the dream of becoming true "Americans." Second-generation immigrants were especially likely to attempt to break with the old ways. Young women, in particular, sometimes rebelled against parents who tried to arrange (or prevent) marriages or who opposed women entering the workplace.

Old stock Americans encouraged assimilation in countless ways. Public schools taught children in English, and employers often insisted that workers speak English on the job. Most nonethnic stores sold mainly American products, forcing immigrants to adapt their diets, clothing, and lifestyles to American norms. Church leaders were often native-born Americans or more assimilated immigrants who encouraged their parishioners to adopt American ways. Some even embraced reforms to make their religion more compatible with the norms of the new country. Reform Judaism, imported from Germany in the late nineteenth century, was an effort by American Jewish leaders (as it had been by German ones) to make their faith less "foreign" to the dominant culture.

The vast numbers of new immigrants, and the way many of them clung to old ways and created distinctive communities, provoked fear and resentment among some native-born Americans in much the same way that earlier arrivals had done. In 1887, Henry Bowers, a self-educated lawyer, founded the American Protective Association, a group committed to stopping immigration. By 1894, membership in the organization reportedly reached 500,000, with chapters throughout the Northeast and Midwest. That same year, five Harvard alumni founded a more genteel organization—the Immigration Restriction League—in Boston. They proposed screening immigrants through literacy tests and other standards, to separate the "desirable" from the "undesirable."

The government responded to popular concern about immigration even earlier. In 1882, Congress excluded the Chinese, denied entry to "undesirables"—convicts, paupers, the mentally incompetent—and placed a tax of 50 cents on each person admitted. Later legislation of the 1890s enlarged the list of those barred from immigrating.

But these laws kept out only a small number of aliens, and more ambitious restriction proposals made little progress in Congress, for immigration provided a cheap and plentiful labor supply to the rapidly growing economy, and many argued that America's industrial (and indeed agricultural) development would be impossible without it.

GLOBAL MIGRATIONS

THE great waves of immigration that transformed American society in the nineteenth and early twentieth centuries were not unique to the United States. They were part of a great, global movement of peoples—unprecedented in history—that affected every continent in the world and that have continued to this day. These great migrations were the product of two related forces: population growth and industrialization.

The population of Europe grew faster in the second half of the nineteenth century than it had ever grown before and than it has ever grown since—almost doubling between 1850 and the beginning of World War I. The population growth was a result of growing economies able to support more people and of more efficient and productive agriculture that helped end debilitating famines. But the rapid growth nevertheless strained the resources of many parts of Europe and affected, in particular, rural people, who were now too numerous to live off the available land. Many decided to move to other parts of the world where land was more plentiful.

At the same time, industrialization drew millions of people out of the countryside and into cities—sometimes into cities in their own countries but often to industrial cities in other, more economically advanced nations. Historians of migration speak of "push" factors (pressures on people to leave their homes) and "pull" factors (the lure of new lands) in

explaining population movements. The "push" for many nineteenth-century migrants was poverty and inadequate land at home; for others it was political and religious oppression. The "pull" was the availability of land or industrial jobs in other regions or lands—and, for some, the prospect of greater freedom abroad. Faster, cheaper, and easier transportation—railroads, steamships, and much later airplanes—also aided large-scale immigration.

(Bodleian Library, University of Oxford)

THE URBAN LANDSCAPE

The city was a place of remarkable contrasts. It had homes of almost unimaginable size and grandeur and hovels of indescribable squalor. It had conveniences unknown to earlier generations and problems that seemed beyond the capacity of society to solve.

From 1800 to the start of World War I, 50 million Europeans migrated to new lands overseas—people from almost all areas of Europe, but in the later years of the century (when migration reached its peak) mostly from poor rural areas in southern and eastern Europe. Italy, Russia, and Poland were among the biggest sources of late-nineteenth-century migrants. Almost two-thirds of these immigrants came to the United States. But nearly 20 million Europeans migrated to other lands. Migrants from England and Ireland (among others) moved in large numbers to those areas of the British Empire with vast, seemingly open lands: Canada, Australia, New Zealand, and South Africa. Large numbers of Italians moved to Argentina and other parts of South America. Many of these migrants moved to open land in these countries and established themselves as farmers, using the new mechanical farming devices made possible by industrialization. In many places—Australia, New Zealand, Argentina, South Africa, and the United States—immigrants evicted the native residents of their territories and created societies of their own. Many others settled in the industrial cities that were growing up in all these regions and formed distinctive ethnic and national communities within them.

But it was not only Europeans who were transplanting themselves in these years. Tremendous numbers of migrants—usually poor, desperate people—left Asia, Africa, and the Pacific Islands in search of better lives. Most of them could not afford the journey abroad on their own. They moved instead as indentured servants (in much the same way many English migrants moved to America in the seventeenth century), agreeing to a term of servitude in their new land in exchange for food, shelter, and transportation. Recruiters of indentured servants fanned out across China, Japan, areas of Africa and the Pacific Islands, and above all, India. French and British recruiters brought hundreds of thousands of Indian migrants to work in plantations in their own Asian and African colonies. Chinese laborers were recruited to work on plantations in Cuba and Hawaii; mines in Malaya, Peru, South Africa, and Australia; and railroad projects in Canada, Peru, and the United States. African indentured servants moved in large numbers to the Caribbean, and Pacific Islanders tended to move to other islands or to Australia.

The immigration of European peoples to new lands was largely voluntary and brought most migrants to the United States, where indentured servitude was illegal (although sometimes imposed on workers through labor contracts). But the migration of non-European peoples often involved an important element of coercion and brought relatively small numbers of people to the United States. This non-European migration was a function of the growth of European empires, and it was made possible by the imperial system—by its labor recruiters, by its naval resources, by its law, and by its economic needs. Together, these various forms of migration produced one of the greatest population movements in the history of the world and transformed not just the United States but much of the globe. •

UNDERSTAND, ANALYZE, & EVALUATE

1. What were some of the "push" and "pull" factors that motivated the migration of both Europeans and non-Europeans?
2. Why did more Europeans than non-Europeans migrate to the United States?

THE CREATION OF PUBLIC SPACE

There were a few early American cities that were planned from the beginning—Philadelphia and Washington most prominently. By the mid-nineteenth century, reformers, planners, architects, and others began to call for more ordered visions of many other cities.

1765 – FIRST AVENUE, SEATTLE, WASHINGTON.

SEATTLE IN THE EARLY TWENTIETH CENTURY   The late nineteenth and early twentieth centuries were times of tremendous urban growth in many areas of the United States. This postcard of downtown Seattle shows a dense and bustling city, almost all of whose buildings are relatively new. (© PoodlesRock/Corbis)

Among the most important urban innovations of the mid-nineteenth century were great city parks, which reflected the desire of urban leaders to provide an antidote to the congestion of the city landscape. Parks, they argued, would allow city residents a healthy, restorative escape from the strains of urban life by reacquainting them with the natural world. This notion of the park as refuge was most effectively promoted by the landscape designers Frederick Law Olmsted and Calvert Vaux, who together in the late 1850s designed New York's Central Park. They deliberately created a public space that would look as little like the city as possible. Instead of the ordered, formal spaces common in some European cities, they created a space that seemed entirely natural. Central Park was from the start one of the most popular and admired public spaces in the world.

At the same time that cities were creating great parks, they were also creating great public buildings: libraries, art galleries, natural history museums, theaters, and concert and opera halls. New York's Metropolitan Museum of Art was the largest and best known of many great museums taking shape in the late nineteenth century, but giant museums grew up quickly in many cities—Boston, Philadelphia, Chicago, and many others. In one city after another, new and lavish public libraries appeared, as if to confirm the city's role as a center of learning and knowledge.

Wealthy residents were the principal force behind the creation of the great art museums, concert halls, opera houses, and, at times, even parks. As their own material and social aspirations grew, they wanted the public life of the city to provide them with amenities to match their expectations. Becoming an important patron of a major cultural institution was an especially effective route to social distinction.

As both the size and aspirations of great cities increased, urban leaders launched monumental projects to remake them. Some cities began to clear away older neighborhoods and streets and create grand, monumental avenues lined with new and more impressive buildings. A particularly important event in inspiring such efforts was the 1893 Columbian Exposition in Chicago, a world's fair constructed to honor the 400th anniversary of Columbus's first voyage to America. At the center of the wildly popular exposition was a cluster of neoclassical buildings—the "Great White City"—arranged symmetrically around a formal lagoon. It became the inspiration for the "city beautiful" movement, led by the architect of the Great White City, Daniel Burnham. The movement strove to impose a similar order and symmetry on the disordered life of cities around the country. Only rarely, however, were planners able to overcome the obstacles of private landowners and complicated urban politics to realize more than a small portion of their dreams.

The effort to remake the city did not focus only on redesigning the existing landscapes. It occasionally led to the creation of entirely new ones. In one of the largest public works projects ever undertaken in America to that point, the city of Boston gradually filled in a large area of marshy tidal land in the late 1880s to create the neighborhood known as "Back Bay." Boston was not alone. Chicago reclaimed large areas from Lake Michigan and at one point raised the street level for the entire city to help avoid the problems the marshy land created. In New York and other cities, the response to limited space was not so much to create new land as to annex adjacent territory. A great wave of annexations expanded the boundaries of many American cities in the 1890s and beyond, most notably New York City's 1898 annexation of Brooklyn, which was itself a large and important city.

THE SEARCH FOR HOUSING

One of the greatest urban problems was to provide housing for the thousands of new residents pouring into the cities every day. For the prosperous, housing was seldom a worry. The availability of cheap labor reduced the cost of building and permitted anyone with even a moderate income to afford a house. Some of the richest urban residents lived in palatial mansions located in exclusive neighborhoods in the heart of the city—Fifth Avenue in New York, Back Bay and Beacon Hill in Boston, Society Hill in Philadelphia, Lake Shore Drive in Chicago, Nob Hill in San Francisco, and many others.

Many of the moderately well-to-do city dwellers took advantage of less expensive land on the edges of cities and settled in new suburbs, linked to the downtowns by trains or streetcars. Chicago in the 1870s, for example, connected nearly 100 residential suburbs to the downtown by railroad. Real estate developers worked to create suburban communities that would appeal to many city dwellers' nostalgia for the countryside, promoting them with lawns, trees, and houses designed to look manorial.

Most urban residents, however, could not afford either to own a house in the city or to move to the suburbs. Instead, they stayed in the city centers and rented. Landlords tried to squeeze as many rent-paying residents as possible into the smallest available space. In Manhattan, for example, the average population density in 1894 was 143 people per acre—a rate far higher than that of any other American or European city then or since. In the cities of the South—Charleston, New Orleans, Richmond—poor African Americans lived in crumbling former slave quarters. In Boston, immigrants moved into cheap three-story wooden houses ("triple-deckers"). In Baltimore and Philadelphia, the new arrivals crowded into narrow brick row houses. And in New York and many other cities, they lived in tenements.

The word "tenement" had originally referred simply to a multiple-family rental building, but by the late nineteenth century it had become a term for slum dwellings only. The first tenements, built in 1850, had been hailed as a great improvement in

THE OTHER HALF   This harsh photograph shows young homeless boys sleeping in an alley. Many such young people found themselves homeless in the rapidly growing city. (© Bettmann/Corbis)

housing for the poor. But most were, in fact, miserable places, with many windowless rooms and little or no plumbing or heating. Jacob Riis, a Danish immigrant and New York newspaper photographer, shocked many middle-class Americans with his sensational (and, some claimed, sensationalized) descriptions and pictures of tenement life in his 1890 book *How the Other Half Lives.* But the solution reformers often adopted was simply to raze slum dwellings without building any new housing to replace them.

URBAN TECHNOLOGIES: TRANSPORTATION AND CONSTRUCTION

Urban growth posed monumental transportation challenges. Sheer numbers of people mandated the development of mass transportation. Streetcars drawn on tracks by horses had been introduced into some cities even before the Civil War. But the horsecars were not fast enough, so many communities developed new forms of mass transit. In 1870, New York opened its first elevated railway, whose noisy, steam-powered trains moved rapidly above the city streets on massive iron structures. New York, Chicago, San Francisco, Boston, and other cities also experimented with cable cars, towed by continuously moving underground cables. Richmond, Virginia, introduced the first electric trolley line in 1888, and in 1897, Boston opened the first American subway. At the same time, cities were developing new techniques of road and bridge building. One of the great technological marvels of the 1880s was the completion of the Brooklyn Bridge in New York—a dramatic steel-cable suspension span designed by John A. Roebling.

Cities grew upward as well as outward. In Chicago, the 1884 construction of the first modern "skyscraper"—by later standards a relatively modest ten-story building—launched a new era in urban architecture. Critical to the creation of the skyscraper was a new technology of construction, which emerged as a result of several related developments. New kinds of steel girders could support much greater tension than the metals of the past. The invention and development of the passenger elevator made much taller buildings possible. And the search for ways to protect cities from the ravages of great fires, which caused such terrible destruction in wood-frame cities of the late nineteenth century, led to steel-frame construction which, among other things, made cities more fireproof. Once the technology existed to permit the construction of tall buildings, there were few obstacles to building taller and taller structures. The early Chicago skyscrapers paved the way for some of the great construction achievements later in the twentieth century: the Chrysler Building and the Empire State Building in New York, the Lasalle Building in Chicago, and ultimately the vast numbers of steel and glass skyscrapers of the post-1945 cities around the world.

STRAINS OF URBAN LIFE

Increasing urban congestion and the absence of adequate public services produced serious hazards. Crime, fire, disease, and indigence all placed strains on the capacities of metropolitan institutions, and both governments and private agencies were for a time poorly equipped to respond.

FIRE AND DISEASE

In one major city after another, fires destroyed large downtown areas. Chicago and Boston suffered "great fires" in 1871, and other cities experienced similar disasters. The terrible experience of the great fires encouraged the construction of fireproof buildings and the development of professional fire departments. They also forced cities to rebuild at a time when new technological and architectural innovations were available. Some of the high-rise downtowns of American cities arose out of the rubble of great fires.

An even greater hazard than fire was disease, especially in poor neighborhoods with inadequate sanitation facilities. An epidemic that began in a poor neighborhood could (and often did) spread easily into other neighborhoods as well. Few municipal officials recognized the relationship of improper sewage disposal and water contamination to such epidemic diseases as typhoid fever and cholera; many cities lacked adequate systems for disposing of human waste until well into the twentieth century. Flush toilets and sewer systems began to appear in the 1870s, but they could not solve the problem as long as sewage continued to flow into open ditches or streams, polluting cities' water supplies.

ENVIRONMENTAL DEGRADATION

Modern notions of environmental science were unknown to most Americans in these years. But the environmental degradation of many American cities was a visible and disturbing fact of life. The frequency of great fires, the dangers of disease and plague, the crowding of working-class neighborhoods—all exemplified the environmental costs of industrialization and rapid urbanization.

Poor disposal of human and industrial waste was common in almost all large cities. The presence of domestic animals—horses, cows, pigs, and other animals—also contributed to the contamination of drinking water and other environmental problems.

Air quality in many cities was poor as well. Few Americans had the severe problems that London experienced in the late nineteenth century with its seemingly perpetual "fogs" created by the burning of soft coal. But air pollution from factories and from stoves and furnaces in offices, homes, and other buildings was constant and at times severe. The incidence of respiratory infection and related diseases was much higher in cities than it was in rural areas, and it accelerated rapidly in the late nineteenth century.

By the early twentieth century, reformers, actively crusading to improve the environmental conditions of cities, were beginning to achieve some notable successes. By 1910, most large American cities had constructed sewage disposal systems, often at great cost, to protect the drinking water of their inhabitants and to prevent the great bacterial plagues that impure water had helped create in the past—such as the yellow fever epidemic in Memphis that killed 5,000 people.

In 1912, the federal government created the Public Health Service, which was charged with preventing such occupational diseases as tuberculosis, anemia, and carbon dioxide poisoning, which were common in the garment industry and other trades. It attempted to create common health standards for all factories; but since the agency had few powers of enforcement, it had limited impact. The creation of the Occupational Safety and Health Administration in 1970, which gave government the authority to require employers to create safe and healthy workplaces, was a legacy of the Public Health Service's early work.

URBAN POVERTY, CRIME, AND VIOLENCE

Above all, perhaps, urban expansion spawned widespread and often desperate poverty. Public agencies and private philanthropic organizations offered some relief. But they were generally poorly funded and, in any case, dominated by middle-class people who believed that too much assistance would breed dependency. Most tried to restrict aid to the "deserving poor"—those who truly could not help themselves. Charitable organizations conducted elaborate "investigations" to separate the "deserving" from the "undeserving." Other charitable societies—for example, the Salvation Army, which began operating in America in 1879—concentrated more on religious revivalism than on relief of the homeless and hungry.

Middle-class people grew particularly alarmed over the rising number of poor children in the cities, some of them orphans or runaways. They attracted greater attention from reformers than any other group—although that attention produced no lasting solutions to their problems.

Poverty and crowding bred crime and violence. The American murder rate rose rapidly in the late nineteenth century, from 25 murders for every million people in 1880 to over 100 by the end of the century. That reflected in part a very high level of violence in some nonurban areas: the American South, where lynching and homicide were particularly high, and the West, where the rootlessness and instability of new communities (cow towns, mining camps, and the like) created much violence. But the big cities contributed their share to the increase as well. Native-born Americans liked to believe that crime was a result of the violent proclivities of immigrant groups, and they cited the rise of gangs and criminal organizations in various ethnic communities. But native-born Americans in the cities were as likely to commit crimes as immigrants. The rising crime rates encouraged many cities to develop larger and more professional police forces. But police forces themselves could spawn corruption and brutality.

Some members of the middle class, fearful of urban insurrections, felt the need for even more substantial forms of protection. Urban National Guard groups built imposing armories on the outskirts of affluent neighborhoods and stored large supplies of weapons and ammunition in preparation for uprisings that, in fact, virtually never occurred.

The city was a place of strong allure and great excitement. Yet it was also a place of alienating impersonality and, to some, of degradation and exploitation. Theodore Dreiser's novel *Sister Carrie* (1900) exposed one troubling aspect of urban life: the plight of single women (like Dreiser's heroine, Carrie) who found themselves without any means of support. Carrie first took an exhausting and ill-paying job in a Chicago shoe factory, then drifted into a life of "sin," exploited by predatory men.

THE MACHINE AND THE BOSS

Newly arrived immigrants were much in need of institutions to help them adjust to American urban life. For many residents of the inner cities, the principal source of assistance was the political "machine."

The urban machine owed its existence to the power vacuum that the chaotic growth of cities had created and to the potential voting power of large immigrant communities. Out of that combination emerged the "urban bosses." The principal function of the political boss was simple: to win votes for his organization. That meant winning the loyalty of his constituents. To do so, a boss might provide them with occasional relief— a basket of groceries or a bag of coal. He might step in to save those arrested for petty crimes from jail. When he could, he found work for the unemployed. Above all, he rewarded many of his followers with patronage: with jobs in city government or in the police (which the machine's elected officials often controlled); with jobs building or operating the new transit systems; and with opportunities to rise in the political organization itself.

Machines were also vehicles for making money. Politicians enriched themselves and their allies through various forms of graft and corruption. A politician might discover in advance where a new road or streetcar line was to be built, buy land near it, and sell it at a profit when property values rose as a result of the construction. There was also covert graft. Officials received kickbacks from contractors in exchange for contracts to build public projects, and they sold franchises for the operation of public utilities. The most famously corrupt city boss was William M. Tweed, boss of New York City's Tammany Hall in the 1860s and 1870s, whose extravagant use of public funds and kickbacks landed him in jail in 1872.

The urban machine was not without competition. Reform groups frequently mobilized public outrage at the corruption of the bosses and often succeeded in driving machine politicians from office. But the reform organizations typically lacked the permanence of the machine.

THE RISE OF MASS CONSUMPTION

In the last decades of the nineteenth century, a distinctive middle-class culture began to exert influence over the whole of American life. Other groups in society advanced less rapidly, or not at all, but the rise of the new urban consumer culture began to shape a new image of the nation.

CONSIDER THE SOURCE

JOHN WANAMAKER, THE FOUR CARDINAL POINTS OF THE DEPARTMENT STORE, 1911

FOUR CARDINAL POINTS

By which we will hereafter steer our craft

FULL GUARANTEE   CASH PAYMENT

ONE PRICE   CASH RETURNED

Explanation and Elaboration of the New Plan

FIRST POINT—"CASH"—Houses doing a credit business must provide for losses on bad debts, interest on long-standing accounts, capital locked up, etc. To bear such losses themselves would drive them out of business. Therefore a per cent is added to the price of each article sold to cover this leakage, and cash buyers, whether they know it or not, really pay the bad debts and the interest on the long credits of the other customers. Under the cash payment system one pays only for what he gets, and contributes nothing to a "Sinking Fund."

By this radical change we shall lose some of our customers, no doubt, but we will gain ten where we lose one, the advantages being so great to all who can avail themselves of them. So we say CASH THROUGHOUT. Bring money for Clothing and we will supply it at prices possible under no other plan.

SECOND POINT—"ONE PRICE"—The fairness of this feature of our plan all will praise. It is simply treating all alike—exacting nothing from indisposition to bargain or ignorance, and, at the same time, conceding all that shrewdness on the shrewdest customer's part could possibly extort, because the "One Price" which we mark on our goods shall invariably be Not the "First" Price, but the Last and Lowest Price.

Not the "Top" Price, but the Very Bottom Price.

THIRD POINT—"FULL GUARANTEE"—A printed guarantee, bearing the signature of our firm will accompany each garment as a warrantee. This binds us in every sense, and will be honored as quickly as a good draft of the Government of the United States. This is a sample of the full guarantee, and tells its own story—Guarantee.

WE HEREBY GUARANTEE

First—That the prices of our goods shall be as low as the same quality of material and manufacture are sold anywhere in the United States.

Patterns of Income and Consumption

Incomes rose for almost everyone in the industrial era, although highly unevenly. One result of the new economy was the creation of vast fortunes, but perhaps the most important result for society as a whole was the growth and increasing prosperity of the middle class. Clerks, accountants, middle managers, and other "white-collar" workers saw their salaries rise by an average of a third between 1890 and 1910. Doctors, lawyers, and other professionals experienced a particularly dramatic increase in both the prestige and the profitability of their professions. Working-class incomes rose in those years as well, although from a much lower base and more slowly. The iron and steel industries saw workers' hourly wages increase by a third between 1890 and 1910; but industries with large female workforces—shoes, textiles, and paper—saw more modest increases, as did almost

Second—That prices are precisely the same to everybody for same quality, on same day of purchase.

Third—That the quality of goods is as represented on printed labels.

Fourth—That the full amount of cash paid will be refunded, if customers find the articles unsatisfactory, and return them unworn and uninjured within ten days of date of purchase.

FOURTH POINT—"CASH RETURNED"—This is simply a concession on our part to our customers, to secure them full confidence in dealing for goods they know very little about, and we thus prevent any occasion for dissatisfaction from any and every cause whatsoever. If the garment is not exactly what you thought, if your taste changes, if the "home folks" prefer another color or another shape, if you find you can buy the same material and style elsewhere for less money, if you conclude you don't need it after you get home, if the season changes suddenly and you wish you had not bought it, bring it back unworn and uninjured, and the full amount of money you paid will be returned on the spot. What more can we do for our customers than this, when we make our clothing so that they can draw the money value with it equally as well as with a check on the banks?

The ADVANTAGES incident to a system having for its cardinal points these which we have now explained, are simply innumerable. Saving of time and temper, perfect security, absence of all huckstering, etc., etc.

But above all this . . .

All of these "By-ways" lead direct to CHEAPNESS; and this without lowering the quality or style of our celebrated make of MEN'S AND BOY'S CLOTHING.

UNDERSTAND, ANALYZE, & EVALUATE

1. What were the benefits of Wanamaker's four cardinal points for consumers? What were the benefits for Wanamaker? Judging by Wanamaker's new way of doing business, what must business practices and customer service have looked like before?
2. Why might these assurances have been particularly important for a large department store? Why might it have been essential for the urban consumer market?

Source: *Golden Book of the Wanamaker Stores, Jubilee Year, 1861–1911* (Philadelphia: John Wanamaker, 1911), pp. 152–154. This advertisement was originally published in 1874. Located in Regina Lee Blaszczyk and Philip B. Scranton (eds.), *Major Problems in American Business History* (Boston: Houghton Mifflin Company, 2006), pp. 298–299.

all industries in the South. Wages for African Americans, Mexicans, and Asians also rose more slowly than those for white workers.

Rising incomes created new markets for consumer goods, which were now available to a mass market for the first time, as a result of technological innovations and new merchandising techniques. An example of such changes was the emergence of ready-made clothing. In the early nineteenth century, most Americans had made their own clothing. The invention of the sewing machine and the Civil War demand for uniforms spurred the manufacture of clothing and helped create an enormous industry devoted to producing ready-made garments. By the end of the century, almost all Americans bought their clothing from stores. Partly as a result, much larger numbers of people became concerned with personal style. Interest in women's fashion, for example, had once been a luxury reserved for the relatively affluent. Now middle-class and even working-class women could strive to develop a distinctive style of dress.

Buying and preparing food also became a critical part of the new consumerism. The development and mass production of tin cans in the 1880s created a large new industry devoted to packaging and selling canned food and condensed milk. Refrigerated railroad cars made it possible for perishable foods to be transported over long distances without spoiling. Artificially frozen ice enabled many households to afford iceboxes. The changes brought improved diets and better health. Life expectancy rose six years in the first two decades of the twentieth century.

CHAIN STORES, MAIL-ORDER HOUSES, AND DEPARTMENT STORES

Changes in marketing also altered the way Americans bought goods. New "chain stores" could usually offer a wider array of goods at lower prices than the small local stores with

THE MONTGOMERY WARD DEPARTMENT STORE This 1880 advertisement for the Montgomery Ward department store in downtown Chicago has stripped away the outside walls to reveal the vast array of goods inside what the poster calls "the enormous establishment." (Chicago History Museum, ICHi-01622)

which they competed. The Atlantic and Pacific Tea Company (the A&P) began a national network of grocery stores in the 1870s. F. W. Woolworth built a chain of dry goods stores. Sears and Roebuck established a large market for its mail-order merchandise by distributing an enormous catalog each year.

In larger cities, the emergence of great department stores helped make shopping more alluring and glamorous. Marshall Field in Chicago created one of the first American department stores—a place deliberately designed to produce a sense of wonder and excitement. Similar stores emerged in New York, Brooklyn, Boston, Philadelphia, and other cities.

WOMEN AS CONSUMERS

The rise of mass consumption had particularly dramatic effects on American women. Women's clothing styles changed much more rapidly than men's, which encouraged more frequent purchases. Women generally bought and prepared food for their families, so the availability of new food products changed not only how people ate but also how women shopped and cooked.

The consumer economy produced new employment opportunities for women as salesclerks and waitresses. And it spawned the creation of a new movement in which women played a vital role: the consumer protection movement. The National Consumers League (NCL), formed in the 1890s under the leadership of Florence Kelley, attempted to mobilize the power of women as consumers to force retailers and manufacturers to improve wages and working conditions. The NCL encouraged women to buy only products with the League's "white label," which indicated that the product was made under fair working conditions.

LEISURE IN THE CONSUMER SOCIETY

Closely related to the rise of consumption was a growing interest in leisure time. Members of the urban middle and professional classes had large blocks of time during which they were not at work—evenings, weekends, even paid vacations. Working hours in many factories declined, from an average of nearly seventy hours a week in 1860 to under sixty in 1900. Even farmers found that the mechanization of agriculture gave them more free time. As many people's lives became more compartmentalized, with clear distinctions between work and leisure, many Americans began to search for new forms of recreation and entertainment.

REDEFINING LEISURE

In earlier eras, relatively few Americans had considered leisure a valuable thing. Many equated it with laziness or sloth. In the late nineteenth century, however, the beginnings of a redefinition of leisure appeared. The economist Simon Patten articulated this new view of leisure in *The Theory of Prosperity* (1902), *The New Basis of Civilization* (1910), and other works. He challenged the centuries-old assumption that the normal condition of civilization was a scarcity of goods. In earlier times, Patten argued, fear of scarcity had caused people to place a high value on thrift, self-denial, and restraint. But in modern industrial societies, new economies could create enough wealth to satisfy not just the needs but also the desires of all.

As Americans became more accustomed to leisure as a normal part of life, they began to look for new experiences and entertainments. Mass entertainment occasionally bridged differences of class, race, and gender. But it could also be sharply divided. Saloons and some sporting events tended to be male preserves. Shopping and going to tea rooms and luncheonettes were more characteristic of female leisure. Theaters, pubs, and clubs were often specific to particular ethnic communities or particular work groups. When the classes did meet in public spaces—as they did, for example, in city parks— there was often considerable conflict over what constituted appropriate public behavior. Elites in New York City, for example, tried to prohibit anything but quiet, "genteel" activities in Central Park, while working-class people wanted to use the public spaces for sports and entertainments.

Spectator Sports

Among the most important responses to the search for entertainment was the rise of organized spectator sports, especially baseball. A game much like baseball—known as "rounders" and derived from cricket—had enjoyed limited popularity in Great Britain in the early nineteenth century. Versions of the game began to appear in America in the early 1830s. By the end of the Civil War, interest in the game had grown rapidly. (See "Patterns of Popular Culture," pp. 324–325.) More than 200 amateur or semiprofessional teams and clubs existed, many of which joined a national association and proclaimed a set of standard rules. As the game grew in popularity, it offered opportunities for profit. The first salaried team, the Cincinnati Red Stockings, was formed in 1869. Other cities fielded professional teams, and in 1876 the teams banded together in the National League. A rival league, the American Association, appeared and collapsed, but in 1901 the American League emerged to replace it. And in 1903, the first modern World Series was played, in which the American League's Boston Red Sox beat the National League's Pittsburgh Pirates. By then, baseball had become an important business and a national preoccupation.

Baseball had great appeal to working-class males. The second most popular game, football, appealed at first to a more elite segment of the male population, in part because it originated in colleges and universities. The first intercollegiate football game in America occurred between Princeton and Rutgers in 1869. Early intercollegiate football bore only an indirect relation to the modern game; it was more similar to present-day rugby. By the late 1870s, however, the game was becoming standardized and was taking on the outlines of its modern form.

Basketball was invented in 1891 in Springfield, Massachusetts, by Dr. James A. Naismith, a Canadian working as an athletic director for a local college. Boxing, which had long been a disreputable activity concentrated primarily among the urban lower classes, became by the 1880s a more popular and, in some places, more reputable sport.

Participation in the major sports was almost exclusively the province of men, but several sports emerged in which women became involved. Golf and tennis both experienced a rapid increase among relatively wealthy men and women. Bicycling and croquet also enjoyed widespread popularity in the 1890s among women as well as men. Women's colleges introduced their students to more strenuous sports as well—track, crew, swimming, and (beginning in the late 1890s) basketball.

Music, Theater, and Movies

Other forms of popular entertainment also developed in the cities. Many ethnic communities maintained their own theaters—many of them created by immigrants. Many ethnic theaters presented plays in the languages of the immigrant communities. Urban theaters in the heart of the cities attracted a much broader audience. They introduced new and distinctively American entertainment forms: the musical comedy, which evolved gradually from the comic operettas of Europe; and vaudeville, a form of theater adapted from French models, which remained the most popular urban entertainment into the first decades of the twentieth century. It consisted of a variety of acts (musicians, comedians, magicians, jugglers, and others) and was, at least in the beginning, inexpensive to produce. As the economic potential of vaudeville grew, some promoters—most prominently Florenz Ziegfeld of New York—staged much more elaborate spectacles.

Vaudeville was also one of the few entertainment media open to black performers, who brought to it elements of the minstrel shows they had earlier developed for black audiences in the late nineteenth century. Some minstrel singers (including the most famous, Al Jolson) were white performers wearing heavy makeup (or "blackface"), but most were black. Entertainers of both races performed music based on the gospel and folk tunes of the plantation and on the jazz and ragtime of black urban communities. Performers of both races also tailored their acts to prevailing white prejudices, ridiculing African Americans by acting out demeaning stereotypes.

The most important form of mass entertainment was the movies. Thomas Edison and others had created the technology of the motion picture in the 1880s. Soon after that, short films became available to individual viewers watching peepshows in pool halls, penny arcades, and amusement parks. Soon, larger projectors made it possible to display the images on big screens, which permitted substantial audiences to see films in theaters. By 1900, Americans were becoming attracted in large numbers to these early movies—usually plotless films of trains or waterfalls or other spectacles. The great D. W. Griffith carried the motion picture into a new era with his silent epics—*The Birth of a Nation* (1915), *Intolerance* (1916), and others—which introduced serious (if notoriously racist) plots and elaborate productions to filmmaking. Motion pictures were the first truly mass entertainment medium.

Patterns of Public and Private Leisure

Particularly striking about popular entertainment in the late nineteenth and early twentieth centuries was its public quality. Many Americans spent their leisure time in places where they would find not only entertainment but also other people. Thousands of working-class New Yorkers spent evenings in dance halls, vaudeville houses, and concert halls. More-affluent New Yorkers enjoyed afternoons in Central Park, where a principal attraction was seeing other people (and being seen by them). Moviegoers were attracted not just by the movies themselves but by the energy of the audiences at lavish new "movie palaces," just as sports fans were drawn by the crowds as well as by the games.

Perhaps the most striking example of popular public entertainment in the early twentieth century was Coney Island, the famous and self-consciously fabulous amusement park and resort on a popular beach in Brooklyn. Luna Park, the greatest of the Coney Island attractions, opened in 1903 and provided rides, stunts, and lavish reproductions of exotic places and spectacular adventures: Japanese gardens, Venetian canals with gondoliers, a Chinese theater, a simulated trip to the moon, and reenactments of such disasters as

POSTCARD FROM LUNA PARK   Visitors to Coney Island sent postcards to friends and relatives by the millions, and those cards were among the most effective promotional devices for the amusement parks. This one shows the brightly lit entrance to Luna Park, Coney Island's most popular attraction for many years. (© Lake County Museum/Corbis)

burning buildings and earthquakes. A year later, a competing company opened Dreamland, which tried to outdo even Luna Park with a 375-foot tower, a three-ring circus, chariot races, and a Lilliputian village from *Gulliver's Travels*. The popularity of Coney Island in these years was phenomenal. Thousands of people flocked to the large resort hotels that lined the beaches. Many thousands more made day trips out from the city by train and (after 1920) subway. In 1904, the average daily attendance at Luna Park alone was 90,000 people.

Most people found Coney Island appealing in part because it provided an escape from the genteel standards that governed so much of American life at the time. In the amusement parks of Coney Island, decorum was often forgotten, and people delighted in finding themselves in situations that in any other setting would have seemed embarrassing or improper: women's skirts blown above their heads with hot air; people pummeled with water and rubber paddles by clowns; hints of sexual freedom as strangers were forced to come into physical contact with one another on rides and amusements.

Not all popular entertainment, however, involved public events. Many Americans amused themselves privately by reading novels and poetry. The so-called dime novels, cheaply bound and widely circulated, became popular after the Civil War, with detective stories, tales of the Wild West, sagas of scientific adventure, and novels of "moral uplift." Publishers also distributed sentimental novels of romance, which developed a large audience among women, as did books about animals and about young children growing up. Louisa May Alcott's *Little Women,* most of whose readers were women, sold more than 2 million copies.

The Technologies of Mass Communication

American publishing and journalism experienced dramatic change in the decades following the Civil War. Between 1870 and 1910, the circulation of daily newspapers increased nearly ninefold (from under 3 million to more than 24 million), a rate three times as great as the rate of population increase. And while standards varied widely from one paper to another, American journalism was developing the beginnings of a professional identity. Salaries of reporters increased; many newspapers began separating the reporting of news from the expression of opinion; and newspapers themselves became important businesses.

This transformation was to a large degree a result of new technologies of communication. The emergence of national press services, for example, was a product of the telegraph, which made it possible to supply papers with news and features from around the nation and the world. By the turn of the century, important newspaper chains had emerged as well, linked together by their own internal wire services. The most powerful was owned by William Randolph Hearst, who by 1914 controlled nine newspapers and two magazines. New printing technologies were making possible more elaborate layouts, the publication of color pictures, and, by the end of the century, the printing of photographs. These advances not only helped publishers make their own stories more vivid; they also made it possible for them to attract more advertisers.

THE TELEPHONE

The most important new technology of communication in the late nineteenth century was the telephone, which Alexander Graham Bell had first demonstrated in 1876. In its first years, the telephone was a relatively impractical tool. Those who subscribed to telephone service had to have direct wire links to everyone else they wished to call. In 1878, the first "switchboard" opened in New Haven, Connecticut, opening the way for more practical uses of the telephone. Once there was a switchboard, a telephone subscriber needed only a line to the central telephone office from which connections could be made to any other subscriber. A new occupation—the "telephone operator"—was born. The Bell System, which controlled all American telephone service, hired young white women to work as operators, hoping that a pleasant female voice would make the experience of using the telephone (and the inconvenience of the frequent technological problems that accompanied it) more appealing, or less irritating, to customers. Telephone signals were very weak at first, and callers could seldom reach anyone more than a few miles away. In an effort to increase the range of telephones, engineers created the "repeater," which periodically strengthened the signal as it moved over distances. By 1914, the repeaters had improved to the point that it was now practical to envision a transcontinental line.

In its early years, the telephone was an almost entirely commercial instrument. Of the nearly 7,400 telephone customers in the New York–New Jersey area in 1891, 6,000 were businesses and organizations. Even the residential telephones tended to belong to doctors or business managers.

The growing reach of the telephone in the early years of the twentieth century made the Bell System (formally named American Telephone and Telegraph, or AT&T) one of the most powerful corporations in America and a genuine monopoly. Central to its success was an early decision by executives that the company would exclusively build and own all telephone instruments and then lease them to subscribers. That made it possible for AT&T to control both the equipment and the telephone service itself, and to exclude any competitors in either field. It also gave AT&T effective control over the local telephone companies allied with it and made the nation's telephone system into an effective cartel.

HIGH CULTURE IN THE URBAN AGE

In addition to the important changes in popular culture that accompanied the rise of cities and industry, there were profound changes in the realm of "high culture." The distinction between "highbrow" and "lowbrow" culture was largely new to the industrial era. In the early nineteenth century, most cultural activities had targeted people of all classes. By the late nineteenth century, however, elites were developing a cultural and intellectual life quite separate from the popular amusements of the urban masses.

LITERATURE AND ART IN URBAN AMERICA

One of the strongest impulses in American literature was the effort to recreate urban social reality. This trend toward realism found an early voice in Stephen Crane, who—although perhaps best known for his novel of the Civil War, *The Red Badge of Courage* (1895)—created a sensation in 1893 when he published *Maggie: A Girl of the Streets*, a grim picture of urban poverty and slum life. Theodore Dreiser, Frank Norris, and Upton Sinclair were similarly drawn to social issues as themes. Kate Chopin, a southern writer who explored the oppressive features of traditional marriage, encountered widespread public abuse after the publication of her shocking 1899 novel, *The Awakening*, which described a young wife and mother who abandoned her family in search of personal fulfillment. William Dean Howells, in *The Rise of Silas Lapham* and other works, described what he considered the shallowness and corruption in ordinary American lifestyles.

American art through most of the nineteenth century had been overshadowed by that of Europe. By 1900, however, a number of American artists broke from Old World traditions and experimented with new styles. Winslow Homer was vigorously American in his paintings of New England maritime life and other native subjects. James McNeil Whistler was one of the first Western artists to introduce Oriental themes into American and European art.

By the first years of the new century, some American artists were turning decisively away from the traditional academic style (a style perhaps most identified in America by the brilliant portraitist John Singer Sargent). Members of the so-called Ashcan school produced work startling in its naturalism and stark in its portrayal of the social realities of the era. John Sloan portrayed the dreariness of American urban slums; George Bellows caught the vigor and violence of his time in paintings and drawings of prizefights; Edward Hopper explored the starkness and loneliness of the modern city. The Ashcan artists were also among the first Americans to appreciate expressionism and abstraction; and they showed their interest in new forms in 1913, when they helped stage the famous "Armory Show" in New York City, which displayed works of the French postimpressionists and of some American moderns.

THE IMPACT OF DARWINISM

One of the most profound intellectual developments in the late nineteenth century was the widespread acceptance of the theory of evolution, associated most prominently with the English naturalist Charles Darwin. Darwin argued that the human species had evolved from earlier forms of life through a process of "natural selection." History, Darwin suggested, was not the working out of a divine plan. It was a random process dominated by the fiercest or luckiest competitors.

The theory of evolution met widespread resistance at first from educators, theologians, and even many scientists. By the end of the century, however, the evolutionists had converted most members of the urban professional and educated classes. Even many middle-class Protestant religious leaders had accepted the doctrine, making significant alterations in theology to accommodate it. The rise of Darwinism, however, contributed to something unseen by most urban Americans at the time: a deep schism between the new, cosmopolitan culture of the city and the more traditional, provincial culture of some rural areas. Thus the late nineteenth century saw not only the rise of a liberal Protestantism in tune with new scientific discoveries but also the beginning of an organized Protestant fundamentalism.

Darwinism helped spawn other new intellectual currents. There was the Social Darwinism of William Graham Sumner and others, which industrialists used so enthusiastically to justify their favored position in American life (see pp. 406–408). But there were also more sophisticated philosophies, among them a doctrine that became known as "pragmatism." William James, a Harvard psychologist (and brother of the novelist Henry James), was the most prominent publicist of the new theory, although earlier intellectuals such as Charles S. Peirce and later ones such as John Dewey were also important to its development and dissemination. According to the pragmatists, modern society should rely for guidance not on inherited ideals and moral principles but on the

EDWARD HOPPER, *AUTOMAT* Edward Hopper was one of a growing group of American painters in the early twentieth century who chose to chronicle not the world of wealth and power, the characteristic subject of earlier artists, but the harsh, gritty world of the modern city. Hopper's work was distinctive for its evocation of the loneliness of urban life. This 1927 painting of a scene in an "automat" in New York City is characteristic of his work. (Des Moines Art Center Permanent Collection. Purchased with funds from the Edmundson Art Foundation, Inc., 1958.2.)

test of scientific inquiry. No idea or institution (not even religious faith) was valid, they claimed, unless it "worked," unless it stood the test of experience.

A similar concern for scientific inquiry was influencing the social sciences. Sociologists such as Edward A. Ross and Lester Frank Ward urged applying the scientific method to the solution of social and political problems. Historians such as Frederick Jackson Turner and Charles Beard argued that economic factors more than spiritual ideals had been the governing force in historical development. John Dewey proposed a new approach to education that placed less emphasis on the rote learning of traditional knowledge and more on flexible, democratic schooling.

The implications of Darwinism also promoted the growth of anthropology and encouraged some scholars to begin examining other cultures in new ways. Some white Americans began to look at Indian society, for example, as a coherent culture with its own norms and values that were worthy of respect and preservation, even though they were different from those of white society.

TOWARD UNIVERSAL SCHOOLING

The growing demand for specialized skills and scientific knowledge naturally created a growing, and changing, demand for education. The late nineteenth century, therefore, was a time of rapid expansion and reform of American schools and universities.

Free public primary and secondary education spread rapidly. By 1900, compulsory school attendance laws existed in thirty-one states and territories. Education was still far from universal. Rural areas lagged far behind urban-industrial ones in funding public education. In the South, many African Americans had no access to schools at all. But for many white men and women, educational opportunities were expanding rapidly.

Educational reformers tried to extend educational opportunities to the Indian tribes as well, in an effort to "civilize" them and help them adapt to white society. In the 1870s, reformers recruited small groups of Indians to attend Hampton Institute (a primarily black college). In 1879, they organized the Carlisle Indian Industrial School in Pennsylvania. Like many black colleges, Carlisle emphasized practical "industrial" education. Ultimately, however, these reform efforts failed, in part because they were unpopular with their intended beneficiaries.

UNIVERSITIES AND THE GROWTH OF SCIENCE AND TECHNOLOGY

Colleges and universities also proliferated rapidly in the late nineteenth century. The Morrill Land Grant Act of 1862, by which the federal government had donated public land to states for the establishment of colleges, led to the creation of sixty-nine "land-grant" institutions in the last decades of the century—among them the state university systems of California, Illinois, Minnesota, and Wisconsin. Other universities, including Chicago, Columbia, Harvard, Northwestern, Princeton, Syracuse, and Yale, benefited from millions of dollars contributed by business and financial titans such as Rockefeller and Carnegie. Other philanthropists founded new universities or reorganized older ones to perpetuate their family names—for example, Vanderbilt, Johns Hopkins, Cornell, Duke, Tulane, and Stanford.

These and other universities played a vital role in the economic development of the United States in the late nineteenth century and beyond. The land-grant institutions were specifically mandated to advance knowledge in "agriculture and mechanics." From the beginning, therefore, they were committed not just to abstract knowledge but to making discoveries that would be of practical use to farmers and manufacturers. As they evolved into great state universities, they retained that tradition and became the source of many of the great discoveries that helped American industry and commerce to advance. Private universities emerged that served many of the same purposes: the Massachusetts Institute of Technology, founded in 1865, soon became the nation's premier engineering school; Johns Hopkins University in Baltimore, founded in 1876, did much to advance medical scholarship, as did the Rockefeller Institute for Medical Research in New York (later Rockefeller University) and the Carnegie Institution. By the early twentieth century, older and more traditional universities were beginning to form relationships with the private sector and the government, doing research that did not just advance knowledge for its own sake but that was directly applicable to practical problems of the time.

MEDICAL SCIENCE

Both the culture of and the scientific basis for medical care were changing rapidly in the early twentieth century. Most doctors were beginning to accept the new medical assumption that there were underlying causes to particular symptoms—that a symptom was not itself a disease. They were also beginning to make use of new or improved technologies—the X-ray, improved microscopes, and other diagnostic devices—that made it possible to classify, and distinguish among, different diseases. Laboratory tests could now identify infections such as typhoid and dysentery. These technologies were a critical first step toward the effective treatment of diseases. At about the same time, pharmaceutical research began to produce some important new medicines. Aspirin was first synthesized in 1899. Other researchers experimented with chemicals that might destroy diseases in the blood, an effort that eventually led to the various forms of chemotherapy that are still widely used in treating cancer. In 1906, an American surgeon, G. W. Crile, became the first physician to use blood transfusion in treatment, which revolutionized surgery. In the past, patients often lost so much blood during operations that extensive surgery could be fatal for that reason alone. With transfusions, it became possible to conduct much longer and more elaborate operations.

The widespread acceptance by the end of the nineteenth century of the germ theory of disease had important implications. Physicians quickly discovered that exposure to germs did not by itself necessarily cause disease, and they began looking for the other factors that determined who got sick and who did not. Among the factors they eventually discovered were general health, previous medical history, diet and nutrition, and eventually genetic predisposition. The awareness of the importance of infection in spreading disease also encouraged doctors to sterilize their instruments, use surgical gloves, and otherwise purify the medical environment of patients.

By the early twentieth century, American physicians and surgeons were generally recognized as among the best in the world, and American medical education was beginning to attract students from many other countries. These improvements in medical knowledge and training, along with improvements in sanitation and public health, did much to reduce infection and mortality in most American communities.

EDUCATION FOR WOMEN

The post–Civil War era saw an important expansion of educational opportunities for women, although such opportunities continued to lag far behind those available to men and were almost entirely denied to black women.

Most public high schools accepted women readily, but opportunities for higher education were fewer. At the end of the Civil War, only three American colleges were coeducational. After the war, many of the land-grant colleges and universities in the Midwest and such private universities as Cornell and Wesleyan began to admit women along with men. But coeducation was less crucial to women's education in this period than was the creation of a network of women's colleges. Mount Holyoke in central Massachusetts had begun its life in 1836 as a "seminary" for women; it became a full-fledged college in the 1880s, at about the same time that entirely new female institutions were emerging: Vassar, Wellesley, Smith, Bryn Mawr, Wells, and Goucher. A few of the larger private universities created separate colleges for women on their campuses (Barnard at Columbia and Radcliffe at Harvard, for example).

The female college was part of an important phenomenon in the history of modern American women: the emergence of distinctive women's communities outside the family. Most faculty members and many administrators were women (usually unmarried). And college life produced a spirit of sorority and commitment among educated women that had important effects in later years. Most female college graduates ultimately married, but they married at a more advanced age than their noncollege counterparts. A significant minority, perhaps over 25 percent, did not marry at all, but devoted themselves to careers. The growth of female higher education clearly became for some women a liberating experience, persuading them that they had roles other than those of wives and mothers to perform in their rapidly changing urban-industrial society.

CONCLUSION

The extraordinary growth of American cities in the last decades of the nineteenth century led to both great achievements and enormous problems. Cities became centers of learning, art, and commerce and produced great advances in technology, transportation, architecture, and communications. They provided their residents—and their many visitors—with varied and dazzling experiences, so much so that people increasingly left the countryside to move to the city.

But cities were also places of congestion, filth, disease, and corruption. With populations expanding too rapidly for services to keep up, most American cities in this era struggled with makeshift techniques to solve the basic problems of providing water, disposing of sewage, building roads, running public transportation, fighting fire, stopping crime, and preventing or curing disease. City governments, many of them dominated by political machines and ruled by party bosses, were often models of inefficiency and corruption—although in their informal way they also provided substantial services to the working-class and immigrant constituencies who needed them most. Yet they also managed to oversee great public projects: the building of parks, museums, opera houses, and theaters, usually in partnership with private developers.

The city brought together races, ethnic groups, and classes of extraordinary variety—from the families of great wealth that the new industrial age was creating to the vast working class, much of it consisting of immigrants, who crowded into densely packed neighborhoods divided by nationality. The city also spawned temples of consumerism: shops, boutiques, and, above all, the great department stores. And it created forums for public recreation and entertainment: parks, theaters, athletic fields, amusement parks, and, later, movie palaces.

Urban life created anxiety among those who lived within the cities and among those who observed them from afar. But in fact, American cities adapted reasonably successfully over time to the great demands their growth made of them and learned to govern themselves if not entirely honestly and efficiently, at least adequately to allow them to survive and grow.

RECALL AND REFLECT

1. What groups of people were most likely to move to the cities of late-nineteenth-century America, and why?
2. What was the relationship between immigration and urbanization in the late nineteenth century?
3. How did the new consumer economy affect roles and expectations for women?
4. What was Darwinism, and what was its impact on American intellectual life?

19 FROM CRISIS TO EMPIRE

LOOKING AHEAD

1. What were the major social and economic problems that beset the United States in the late nineteenth century, and how did the two major political parties respond to these problems?
2. What was Populism, what were its goals, and to what degree were these goals achieved?
3. How did the United States become an imperial power?

THE UNITED STATES APPROACHED the end of the nineteenth century as a fundamentally different nation from what it had been at the beginning of the Civil War. With rapid change came cascading social and political problems—problems that the weak and conservative governments of the time showed little inclination or ability to address.

A catastrophic economic depression that began in 1893 and rapidly intensified created devastating hardship for millions of Americans. Farmers responded by creating an agrarian political movement known as Populism. American workers, facing massive unemployment, staged large and occasionally violent strikes. Not since the Civil War had American politics been so polarized and impassioned. The election of 1896, which pitted the agrarian hero William Jennings Bryan against the solid, conservative William McKinley, was dramatic but anticlimactic. Supported by the mighty Republican Party and many eastern groups who looked with suspicion and unease at the agricultural demands coming from the West, McKinley easily triumphed.

McKinley did little in his first term in office to resolve the problems and grievances of his time, but the economy revived nevertheless. Having largely ignored the depression, however, McKinley focused on another great national cause: the plight of Cuba in its war with Spain. In the spring of 1898, the United States declared war on Spain and entered the conflict in Cuba—a brief but bloody war that ended with an American victory four months later. The conflict had begun as a way to support Cuban independence from the Spanish, but a group of fervent and influential imperialists worked to convert the war into an occasion for acquiring overseas possessions. Despite a powerful anti-imperialist movement, the acquisition of the former Spanish colonies proceeded—only to draw Americans into yet another imperial war, this one in the Philippines, where the Americans, not the Spanish, were the targets of local enmity.

THE POLITICS OF EQUILIBRIUM

The enormous social and economic changes of the late nineteenth century strained not only the nation's traditional social arrangements but its political institutions as well. Searching for stability and social justice, Americans looked to the government for leadership. Yet American government during much of this period was ill equipped to confront these new challenges. As a result, problems and grievances festered and grew without any natural outlet.

THE PARTY SYSTEM

The most striking feature of late-nineteenth-century politics was the remarkable stability of the party system. From the end of Reconstruction until the late 1890s, the electorate was divided almost precisely evenly between the Republicans and the Democrats. Sixteen states were solidly and consistently Republican, and fourteen states (most in the South) were solidly and consistently Democratic. Only a handful of states were usually in doubt, and they generally decided the results of national elections, often on the basis of voter turnout. The Republican Party captured the presidency in all but two of the

TIME LINE

1867
National Grange founded

1875
Reciprocity Treaty with Hawaii

1876
Hayes elected president

1880
Garfield elected president

1881
Garfield assassinated; Arthur becomes president

1884
Cleveland elected president

1887
Interstate Commerce Act

1888
Benjamin Harrison elected president

U.S. gains base at Pearl Harbor

1890
Sherman Antitrust Act

Sherman Silver Purchase Act

McKinley Tariff

1892
Cleveland elected president again

People's Party formed

1893
Revolution in Hawaii

Economic depression begins

Sherman Silver Purchase Act repealed

1894
Coxey's Army marches on Washington

1895
Venezuelan boundary dispute

1896
McKinley elected president

1898
War with Spain

Treaty of Paris

1898–1902
Philippines revolt

U.S. annexes Hawaii, Puerto Rico, Philippines

1899
Open Door notes

1900
Boxer Rebellion

McKinley reelected

1901
Platt Amendment

elections of the era, but in the five presidential elections beginning in 1876, the average popular-vote margin separating the Democratic and Republican candidates was 1.5 percent. The congressional balance was similarly stable, with the Republicans generally controlling the Senate and the Democrats generally controlling the House.

Despite the relatively modest differences, most eligible Americans had strong loyalties to their chosen party. Voter turnout in presidential elections between 1860 and 1900 averaged over 78 percent of all eligible voters. Large groups of potential voters were disenfranchised in these years: women in most states and almost all blacks and many poor whites in the South. But for adult white males, there were few franchise restrictions.

What explains this extraordinary loyalty to the two political parties? It was not, certainly, that the parties took distinct positions on important public issues. They did so rarely. Party loyalties reflected other factors. Region was perhaps the most important. To white southerners, loyalty to the Democratic Party—the vehicle by which they had triumphed over Reconstruction and preserved white supremacy—was a matter of unquestioned faith. Republican loyalties were equally intense in the North. To many, the party of Lincoln remained a bulwark against slavery and treason.

Religious and ethnic differences also shaped party loyalties. The Democratic Party attracted most of the Catholic voters, recent immigrants, and poorer workers. The Republican Party appealed to northern Protestants, citizens of old stock, and much of the middle class. Among the few substantive issues on which the parties took clearly different stands were immigration matters. Republicans tended to support immigration restriction and to favor temperance legislation, which many believed would help discipline immigrant communities. Catholics and immigrants viewed such proposals as assaults on them and their cultures, and the Democratic Party followed their lead.

Party identification, then, was usually more a reflection of cultural inclinations than a calculation of economic interest. Individuals might affiliate with a party because their parents had done so or because it was the party of their region, their church, or their ethnic group.

THE NATIONAL GOVERNMENT

One reason the parties managed to avoid most substantive issues was that the federal government did relatively little. The government in Washington was responsible for delivering the mail, maintaining a military, conducting foreign policy, and collecting tariffs and taxes. It had few other responsibilities and few institutions capable of undertaking additional responsibilities even if it had chosen to do so.

There was one significant exception. From the end of the Civil War to the early twentieth century, the federal government administered a system of annual pensions for retired Union Civil War veterans and their widows. At its peak, this pension system was making payments to a majority of the male citizens (black and white) of the North and to many women as well. Some reformers hoped to make the system permanent and universal. But when the Civil War generation died out, the pension system died with it.

In most other respects, the United States in the late nineteenth century was a society without a modern national government. The most powerful institutions were the two political parties (and the bosses and machines that dominated them) and the federal courts.

PRESIDENTS AND PATRONAGE

Presidents in the late nineteenth century had great symbolic importance, but they were unable to do very much except distribute government appointments. A new president and his tiny staff had to make almost 100,000 appointments.

Even so, it sometimes proved impossible for a president to avoid factional conflict, as the presidency of Rutherford B. Hayes demonstrated. By the end of his term, two groups—the Stalwarts, led by Roscoe Conkling of New York, and the Half-Breeds, captained by James G. Blaine of Maine—were competing for control of the Republican Party. Rhetorically, the Stalwarts favored traditional, professional machine politics, while the Half-Breeds favored reform. In fact, both groups were mainly interested in a larger share of patronage. Hayes tried to satisfy both and ended up satisfying neither.

The battle over patronage overshadowed all else during Hayes's unhappy presidency. His one important, substantive initiative—an effort to create a civil service system—attracted no support from either party. And his early announcement that he would not seek reelection only weakened him further.

The Republicans managed to retain the presidency in 1880 in part because they agreed on a ticket that included a Stalwart and a Half-Breed. They nominated James A. Garfield, a veteran congressman from Ohio and a Half-Breed, for president and Chester A. Arthur of New York, a Stalwart, for vice president. The Democrats nominated General Winfield Scott Hancock, a minor Civil War commander with no national following. Benefiting from the end of the recession of 1879, Garfield won a decisive electoral victory, although his popular-vote margin was thin.

Garfield began his presidency by defying the Stalwarts and supporting civil service reform. He soon found himself embroiled in an ugly public quarrel with Conkling and the Stalwarts. The dispute was never resolved. On July 2, 1881, only four months after his inauguration, Garfield was shot twice while standing in the Washington railroad station by an apparently deranged gunman (and unsuccessful office seeker) who shouted, "I am a Stalwart and Arthur is president now!" Garfield lingered for nearly three months but finally died.

Garfield's successor, Chester A. Arthur, had spent his political lifetime as a devoted, skilled, and open spoilsman and a close ally of the New York political boss Roscoe Conkling. But on becoming president, he tried—like Hayes and Garfield before him—to follow an independent course and even to promote reform. To the dismay of the Stalwarts, Arthur kept most of Garfield's appointees in office and supported civil service reform. In 1883, Congress passed the first national civil service measure, the Pendleton Act, which required that some federal jobs be filled by competitive written examinations rather than by patronage. Relatively few offices fell under civil service at first, but its reach steadily extended.

CLEVELAND, HARRISON, AND THE TARIFF

In the unsavory election of 1884, the Republican candidate for president was Senator James G. Blaine of Maine—known to his admirers as the "Plumed Knight" but to many others as a symbol of seamy party politics. A group of disgruntled "liberal Republicans," known by their critics as the "mugwumps," announced that they would bolt the party and support an honest Democrat. Rising to the bait, the Democrats nominated Grover Cleveland, the reform governor of New York.

In a campaign filled with personal invective, what may have decided the election was the last-minute introduction of a religious controversy. Shortly before the election, a delegation of Protestant ministers called on Blaine in New York City; their spokesman, Dr. Samuel

Burchard, referred to the Democrats as the party of "rum, Romanism, and rebellion." Blaine was slow to repudiate Burchard's indiscretion, and Democrats quickly spread the news that Blaine had tolerated a slander on the Catholic Church. Cleveland's narrow victory probably resulted from an unusually heavy Catholic vote for the Democrats in New York.

Grover Cleveland was respected, if not often liked, for his stern and righteous opposition to politicians, grafters, pressure groups, and Tammany Hall. He embodied an era in which few Americans believed the federal government could, or should, do very much. Cleveland had always doubted the wisdom of protective tariffs (taxes on imported goods designed to protect domestic producers). The existing high rates, he believed, were responsible for the annual surplus in federal revenues, which was tempting Congress to pass "reckless" and "extravagant" legislation, which he frequently vetoed. In December 1887, therefore, he asked Congress to reduce the tariff rates. Democrats in the House approved a tariff reduction, but Senate Republicans defiantly passed a bill of their own, actually raising the rates. The resulting deadlock made the tariff an issue in the election of 1888.

The Democrats renominated Cleveland and supported tariff reductions. Endorsing protection, Republicans settled on former senator Benjamin Harrison of Indiana, who was obscure but respectable (and the grandson of President William Henry Harrison). It was one of the most corrupt elections in American history. Cleveland won the popular vote by 100,000, but Harrison won an electoral majority of 233 to 168.

NEW PUBLIC ISSUES

Benjamin Harrison's record as president was little more substantial than that of his grandfather, who had died a month after taking office. Harrison had few visible convictions, and he made no effort to influence Congress. And yet during Harrison's passive administration, public opinion was beginning to force the government to confront some of the pressing social and economic issues of the day, most notably the power of trusts.

By the mid-1880s, fifteen western and southern states had adopted laws prohibiting combinations that restrained competition. But corporations found it easy to escape limitations by incorporating in states, such as New Jersey and Delaware, that offered them special privileges. If antitrust legislation was to be effective, its supporters believed, it would have to come from the national government. In July 1890, both houses of Congress passed the Sherman Antitrust Act, almost without dissent. For over a decade after its passage, the Sherman Act—indifferently enforced and steadily weakened by the courts—had no impact. As of 1901, the Justice Department had instituted many antitrust suits against unions, but only fourteen against business combinations.

The Republicans were more interested in the issue they believed had won them the 1888 election: the tariff. Representative William McKinley of Ohio and Senator Nelson W. Aldrich of Rhode Island drafted the highest protective measure ever proposed to Congress. Known as the McKinley Tariff, it became law in October 1890. But Republican leaders apparently misinterpreted public sentiment. Many voters saw the high tariff as a way to enrich producers and starve consumers. The party suffered a stunning reversal in the 1890 congressional election. The Republicans' substantial Senate majority was slashed to 8; in the House, the party retained only 88 of the 323 seats. For the first time since 1878, the Democrats won a majority of both houses of Congress. Nor were the Republicans able to recover over the next two years. In the presidential election of 1892, Benjamin Harrison once again supported protection; Grover Cleveland, renominated by the Democrats, once again opposed it. A new third party, the People's Party, with James B. Weaver as its candidate, advocated substantial economic reform. Cleveland won 277 electoral votes to Harrison's 145 and had a popular margin of 380,000. Weaver ran far behind.

The policies of Cleveland's second term were much like those of his first. Again, he supported a tariff reduction, which the House approved but the Senate weakened. Cleveland denounced the result but allowed it to become law as the Wilson-Gorman Tariff.

Public pressure had been growing since the 1880s for other reforms, among them regulation of the railroads. Farm organizations in the Midwest (most notably the Grangers) had persuaded several state legislatures to pass regulatory legislation in the early 1870s. But in 1886, the Supreme Court—in *Wabash, St. Louis, and Pacific Railway Co. v. Illinois,* known as the *Wabash* case—ruled one of the Granger Laws in Illinois unconstitutional. According to the Court, the law was an attempt to control interstate commerce and thus infringed on the exclusive power of Congress. Later, the courts limited the powers of the states to regulate commerce even within their own boundaries.

Effective railroad regulation, it was now clear, could come only from the federal government. Congress responded to public pressure in 1887 with the Interstate Commerce Act, which banned discrimination in rates between long and short hauls, required that railroads publish their rate schedules and file them with the government, and declared that all interstate rail rates must be "reasonable and just." A five-person agency, the Interstate Commerce Commission (ICC) was to administer the act. But it had to rely on the courts to enforce its rulings. For almost twenty years after its passage, the Interstate Commerce Act—which was, like the Sherman Act, haphazardly enforced and narrowly interpreted by the courts—had little practical effect.

THE AGRARIAN REVOLT

No group watched the performance of the federal government in the 1880s with greater dismay than American farmers, who helped produce one of the most powerful movements of political protest in American history: what became known as Populism.

THE GRANGERS

Farmers had been making efforts to organize politically for several decades before the 1880s. The first major farm organization was the National Grange of the Patrons of Husbandry, founded in 1867. From it emerged a network of local organizations that tried to teach new scientific agricultural techniques to their members. When the depression of 1873 caused a sharp decline in farm prices, membership rapidly increased and the direction of the organization changed. Granges in the Midwest began to organize marketing cooperatives and to promote political action to curb monopolistic practices by railroads and warehouses. At their peak, Grange supporters controlled the legislatures in most of the midwestern states. The result was the Granger Laws of the early 1870s, by which many states imposed strict regulations on railroad rates and practices. But the destruction of the new regulations by the courts, combined with the political inexperience of many Grange leaders and the return of prosperity in the late 1870s, produced a dramatic decline in the power of the association.

THE FARMERS' ALLIANCES

As early as 1875, farmers in parts of the South were banding together in so-called Farmers' Alliances just as the Granges were weakening. By 1880, the Southern Alliance had more than 4 million members; a comparable Northwestern Alliance was taking root in the plains states and the Midwest, largely replacing the Grange.

Like the Granges, the Alliances formed cooperatives and other marketing mechanisms. They established stores, banks, processing plants, and other facilities to free their members from dependence on the hated "furnishing merchants" who kept so many farmers in debt. Some Alliance leaders, however, saw the movement in larger terms: as an effort to build a society in which economic competition might give way to cooperation. Alliance lecturers traveled throughout rural areas, lambasting the concentrated power of great corporations and financial institutions.

Although the Alliances quickly became far more widespread than the Granges had ever been, they suffered from similar problems. Their cooperatives did not always work well, partly because of mismanagement and partly because of the strength of opposing market forces. These economic frustrations helped push the movement into a new phase at the end of the 1880s: the creation of a national political organization.

In 1889, the Southern and Northwestern Alliances agreed to a loose merger. The next year the Alliances held a national convention at Ocala, Florida, and issued the so-called Ocala Demands, which were, in effect, a party platform. In the 1890 off-year elections, candidates supported by the Alliances won partial or complete control of the legislatures in twelve states. They also won six governorships, three seats in the U.S. Senate, and approximately fifty in the U.S. House of Representatives. Many of the successful Alliance candidates were Democrats who had benefited—often passively—from Alliance endorsements. But dissident farmers drew enough encouragement from the results to contemplate further political action.

Alliance leaders discussed plans for a third party at meetings in Cincinnati in May 1891 and St. Louis in February 1892. Then, in July 1892, 1,300 exultant delegates poured into Omaha, Nebraska, to proclaim the creation of the new party, approve an official set of principles, and nominate candidates for the presidency and vice presidency. The new organization's official name was the People's Party, but the movement was more commonly referred to as Populism.

The election of 1892 demonstrated the potential power of the new movement. The Populist presidential candidate—James B. Weaver of Iowa, a former Greenbacker—polled more than 1 million votes. Nearly 1,500 Populist candidates won election to seats in state legislatures. The party elected three governors, five senators, and ten congressmen. It could also claim the support of many Republicans and Democrats in Congress who had been elected by appealing to Populist sentiment.

THE POPULIST CONSTITUENCY

Already, however, there were signs of the limits of Populist strength. Populism had great appeal to farmers, particularly to small farmers with little long-range economic security. But Populism failed to move much beyond that group. Its leaders made energetic efforts to include labor within the coalition by courting the Knights of Labor and adding a labor plank to its platform. But Populism never attracted significant labor support, in part because the economic interests of labor and the interests of farmers were often at odds.

In the South, white Populists struggled with the question of whether to accept African Americans into the party. There was an important black component to the movement—a network of "Colored Alliances" that by 1890 numbered over 1.25 million members. But most white Populists accepted the assistance of African Americans only as long as it was clear that whites would remain indisputably in control. When southern conservatives began to attack the Populists for undermining white supremacy, the interracial character of the movement quickly faded.

POPULIST IDEAS

The Populists spelled out their program first in the Ocala Demands of 1890 and then, more clearly, in the Omaha platform of 1892. They proposed a system of "subtreasuries," a network of government-owned warehouses where farmers could deposit their crops, to allow them to borrow money from the government at low rates of interest until the price of their goods went up. In addition, the Populists called for the abolition of national banks (which they believed were dangerous institutions of concentrated power), the end of absentee ownership of land, the direct election of United States senators (which would weaken the power of conservative state legislatures), and other devices to improve the ability of the people to influence the political process. They called as well for regulation and (after 1892) government ownership of railroads, telephones, and telegraphs. And they demanded a system of government-operated postal savings banks, a graduated income tax, the inflation of the currency, and, later, the remonetization of silver.

Some Populists were anti-Semitic, anti-intellectual, anti-eastern, and antiurban. But bigotry was not the dominant force behind Populism. It was, rather, a serious and usually responsible effort to find solutions to real problems. Populists emphatically rejected the laissez-faire orthodoxies of their time, including the idea that the rights of ownership are absolute. They raised one of the most overt and powerful challenges of the era to the direction in which American industrial capitalism was moving.

THE CRISIS OF THE 1890s

The agrarian protest was only one of many indications of the national political crisis emerging in the 1890s. There was a severe depression, widespread labor unrest and violence, and the continuing failure of either major party to respond to the growing distress. Grover Cleveland, who took office for the second time just as the economy was collapsing, remained rigidly conservative, convinced that any government action would be a violation of principle.

THE PANIC OF 1893

The Panic of 1893 launched the most severe depression the nation had ever experienced. It began in March 1893, when the Philadelphia and Reading Railroad, unable to meet payments on loans, declared bankruptcy. Two months later, the National Cordage Company failed as well. Together, these two corporate failures triggered a stock market collapse. And since many of the major New York banks were heavy investors in the market, a wave of bank failures soon began. That caused a contraction of credit, which meant that many of the new, aggressive, and loan-dependent businesses soon went bankrupt.

The depression reflected, among other things, the degree to which all parts of the American economy were now interconnected. And it showed how dependent the economy was on the health of the railroads, which remained the nation's most powerful corporate and financial institutions. When the railroads suffered, as they did beginning in 1893, everything suffered.

POPULISM

THE scholarly debates over Populism reflect a larger debate over the nature of popular mass movements. To some historians, mass uprisings seem dangerous and potentially antidemocratic; and to them, the Populist movement has usually appeared ominous. To others, such insurgency is evidence of a healthy democratic resistance to oppression; and to them, Populism has generally seemed more appealing.

The latter view shaped the first, and for many years the only, general history of Populism: John D. Hicks's *The Populist Revolt* (1931). Hicks portrayed Populism as an expression of the healthy democratic sentiments of the West. Populists were reacting rationally and constructively to the harsh impact of eastern industrial growth on agrarian society and were proposing potentially valuable reforms to restrict the power of the new financial titans. Populism was, he wrote, "the last phase of a long and perhaps a losing struggle—the struggle to save agricultural America from the devouring jaws of industrial America."

(Kansas Historical Society (FK2.D2.56#1))

Once the panic began, it spread with startling speed. Within six months, more than 8,000 businesses, 156 railroads, and 400 banks failed. Already low agricultural prices tumbled further. Up to 1 million workers, 20 percent of the labor force, lost their jobs. The depression was unprecedented not only in its severity but also in its persistence. Although conditions improved slightly beginning in 1895, prosperity did not fully return until 1901.

The depression produced widespread social unrest, especially among the enormous numbers of unemployed workers. In 1894, Jacob S. Coxey, an Ohio businessman and

In the early 1950s, scholars sensitive to the nature of European fascism and contemporary communism took a more suspicious view of mass popular politics and thus a more hostile view of Populism. The leading figure in this reinterpretation was Richard Hofstadter. In *The Age of Reform* (1955), he conceded that the Populists had genuine grievances and advanced some sensible reforms. But he concentrated on revealing what he called the "soft" and "dark" sides of the movement. Populism, Hofstadter claimed, rested on a romanticized and obsolete vision of the role of farmers in American society and was permeated with bigotry and ignorance.

Hofstadter's harsh portrait inspired a series of spirited challenges. Norman Pollack, beginning in 1962, argued that the agrarian revolt rested not on nostalgic and romantic concepts but on a sophisticated and even radical vision of reform. A year later, Walter T. K. Nugent attempted to show that Populists were not bigoted, that they not only tolerated but also welcomed Jews and other minorities into their party. And in 1976, Lawrence Goodwyn published *Democratic Promise,* which described Populism as a "cooperative crusade" battling against the "coercive potential of the emerging corporate state."

At the same time that historians were debating the meaning of Populism, they were also arguing over who the Populists were. Hicks, Hofstadter, and Goodwyn, for all their many disagreements, shared a belief that Populists were victims of economic distress—usually one-crop farmers in economically marginal regions victimized by drought and debt. Others, however, have suggested that this description is inadequate, if not wrong. Sheldon Hackney maintained in 1969 that Populists in Alabama were not only economically troubled but also socially rootless, "only tenuously connected to society by economic function, by personal relationships, by stable community membership, by political participation, or by psychological identification with the South's distinctive myths." Peter Argersinger, Stanley Parsons, James Turner, and others have similarly suggested that Populists tended to be people who were socially and even geographically isolated. Steven Hahn's 1983 study *The Roots of Southern Populism* described the poor farmers of "upcountry" Georgia as people almost entirely unconnected to the modern capitalist economy. They were reacting to a real economic threat to their way of life: the intrusion into their world of a new commercial order from which they were unlikely to benefit.

There has, finally, been continuing debate over the legacy of Populism. Michael Kazin, in *The Populist Persuasion* (1994), is one of a number of scholars who have argued that a Populist tradition has survived throughout much of the twentieth century, influencing movements as different as those led by Huey Long in the 1930s, George Wallace in the 1960s, Ross Perot in the 1990s, and the "Tea Parties" of the 2010s. •

UNDERSTAND, ANALYZE, & EVALUATE

1. What have been historians' principal interpretations of Populism?
2. Where can you find evidence of the Populist legacy in politics today?

Populist, began advocating a massive public works program to create jobs for the unemployed. When it became clear that Congress was ignoring his proposals, Coxey organized a march of the unemployed (known as "Coxey's Army") to Washington to present his demands to the government. Congress continued to ignore them.

To many middle-class Americans, the labor turmoil of the time—the Homestead and Pullman strikes, for example (see pp. 413–414)—was a sign of a dangerous instability, even perhaps a revolution. Labor radicalism—some of it real, more of it imagined by the frightened middle class—heightened the general sense of crisis among the public.

COXEY'S ARMY Jacob S. Coxey leads his "army" of unemployed men through the town of Allegheny, Pennsylvania, in 1894, en route to Washington, where he hoped to pressure Congress to approve his plans for a massive public works program to put people back to work. (Culver Pictures, Inc.)

THE SILVER QUESTION

The financial panic weakened the government's monetary system. President Cleveland believed that the instability of the currency was the primary cause of the depression. The "money question," therefore, became one of the burning issues of the era.

The debate centered on what would form the basis of the dollar, what would lie behind it and give it value. Today, the value of the dollar rests on little more than public confidence in the government. But in the nineteenth century, many people believed that currency was worthless if there was not something concrete behind it—precious metal (specie), which holders of paper money could collect if they presented their currency to a bank or to the Treasury.

During most of its existence as a nation, the United States had recognized two metals— gold and silver—as a basis for the dollar, a system known as "bimetallism." In the 1870s, however, that had changed. The official ratio of the value of silver to the value of gold for purposes of creating currency (the "mint ratio") was 16 to 1: sixteen ounces of silver equaled one ounce of gold. But the actual commercial value of silver (the "market ratio") was much higher than that. Owners of silver could get more by selling it for manufacture into jewelry and other objects than they could by taking it to the mint for conversion to coins. So they stopped taking it to the mint, and the mint stopped coining silver.

In 1873, Congress passed a law that seemed simply to recognize the existing situation by officially discontinuing silver coinage. Few objected at the time. But later in the 1870s, the market value of silver fell well below the official mint ratio of 16 to 1. Silver was suddenly available for coinage again, and it soon became clear that Congress had foreclosed a potential method of expanding the currency. Before long, many Americans concluded that a conspiracy of big bankers had been responsible for the "demonetization" of silver and referred to the law as the "Crime of '73."

Two groups of Americans were especially determined to undo the Crime of '73. One consisted of the silver-mine owners, now understandably eager to have the government take their surplus silver and pay them much more than the market price. The other group consisted of discontented farmers, who wanted an increase in the quantity of money—an inflation of the currency—as a means of raising the prices of farm products and easing payment of the farmers' debts. The inflationists demanded that the government return at once to the "free and unlimited coinage of silver" at the old ratio of 16 to 1. Congress responded weakly to these demands with the Sherman Silver Purchase Act of 1890, which required the government to purchase silver and pay for it in gold. But the government allowed only existing silver coinage. It did not allow any newly minted silver money.

At the same time, the nation's gold reserves were steadily dropping. President Cleveland believed that the chief cause of the weakening gold reserves was the Sherman Silver Purchase Act. Early in his second administration, therefore, Congress responded to his request and repealed the Sherman Act—although only after a bitter and divisive battle that helped create a permanent split in the Democratic Party.

"A CROSS OF GOLD"

Republicans, watching the failure of the Democrats to deal effectively with the depression, were confident of success in 1896. Party leaders, led by the Ohio boss Marcus A. Hanna, settled on former congressman William McKinley, author of the 1890 tariff act and now governor of Ohio, as the party's presidential candidate. The tariff, they believed, should be the key issue in the campaign. But they also opposed the free coinage of silver, except by agreement with the leading commercial nations (which everyone realized was unlikely). Thirty-four delegates from the mountain and plains states walked out of the convention in protest and joined the Democratic Party.

The Democratic Convention of 1896 was unusually tumultuous. Southern and western delegates, eager for a way to compete with the Populists, were determined to seize control of the party from conservative easterners, incorporate some Populist demands—among them free silver—into the Democratic platform, and nominate a pro-silver candidate.

Defenders of the gold standard seemed to dominate the debate, until William Jennings Bryan, a handsome, thirty-six-year-old congressman from Nebraska, mounted the podium to address the convention. His great voice echoed through the hall as he delivered what became one of the most famous political speeches in American history. The closing passage sent his audience into something close to a frenzy: "Having behind us the producing masses of this nation and the world, supported by the commercial interests, the laboring interests and the toilers everywhere, we will answer their demand for a gold standard by saying to them: 'You shall not press down upon the brow of labor this crown of thorns; you shall not crucify mankind upon a cross of gold.'" It became known as the "Cross of Gold" speech.

In the glow of Bryan's speech, the convention voted to adopt a pro-silver platform. And the following day, Bryan (as he had eagerly and not entirely secretly hoped) was nominated for president on the fifth ballot.

The choice of Bryan and the Democratic platform created a quandary for the Populists. They had expected both major parties to adopt conservative programs and nominate conservative candidates, leaving the Populists to represent the growing forces of protest. But now the Democrats had stolen much of their thunder. The Populists faced the choice of naming their own candidate and splitting the protest vote or endorsing Bryan and losing their identity as a party. Many Populists argued that "fusion" with the Democrats would

BEARING THE CROSS OF GOLD   The cartoonist Grant Hamilton created this image of William Jennings Bryan shortly after he made his famous "Cross of Gold" speech at the Democratic National Convention, which subsequently nominated him for president. The cartoon highlights two of the most powerful images in Bryan's speech—a "crown of thorns" and a "cross of gold," both biblical references and both designed to represent the oppression that the gold standard imposed on working people. (The Granger Collection, NYC)

destroy their party. But the majority concluded that there was no viable alternative. Amid considerable acrimony, the convention voted to support Bryan.

THE CONSERVATIVE VICTORY

The campaign of 1896 produced panic among conservatives. The business and financial community, frightened beyond reason at the prospect of a Bryan victory, contributed lavishly to the Republican campaign. From his home in Canton, Ohio, McKinley conducted a

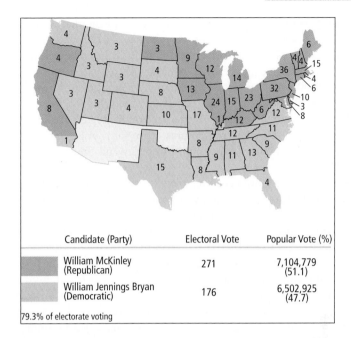

Candidate (Party)	Electoral Vote	Popular Vote (%)
William McKinley (Republican)	271	7,104,779 (51.1)
William Jennings Bryan (Democratic)	176	6,502,925 (47.7)

79.3% of electorate voting

THE ELECTION OF 1896 The results of the presidential election of 1896 are, as this map shows, striking for the regional differentiation they reveal. William McKinley won the election by a comfortable but not enormous margin, but his victory was not broad-based. He carried all the states of the Northeast and the industrial Midwest, along with California and Oregon, but virtually nothing else. Bryan carried the entire South and almost all of the agrarian West. • *What campaign issues in 1896 helped account for the regional character of the results?*

traditional "front-porch" campaign by receiving pilgrimages of the Republican faithful, organized and paid for by Hanna.

Bryan showed no such restraint. He became the first presidential candidate in American history to stump every section of the country systematically. He traveled 18,000 miles and addressed an estimated 5 million people.

On election day, McKinley polled 271 electoral votes to Bryan's 176 and received 51.1 percent of the popular vote to Bryan's 47.7. Bryan carried the areas of the South and West where miners or struggling staple farmers predominated. The Democratic program, like that of the Populists, had been too narrow to win a national election.

For the Populists and their allies, the election results were a disaster. They had gambled everything on their fusion with the Democratic Party and lost. Within months of the election, the People's Party began to dissolve.

McKINLEY AND RECOVERY

The administration of William McKinley saw a return to relative calm. One reason was the exhaustion of dissent. Another reason was the shrewd character of the McKinley administration itself, committed as it was to reassuring stability. Most important, however, was the gradual easing of the economic crisis, a development that undercut many of those who were agitating for change.

McKinley and his allies committed themselves fully to only one issue: the need for higher tariff rates. Within weeks of his inauguration, the administration won approval of the Dingley Tariff, raising duties to the highest point in American history. The administration dealt more gingerly with the explosive silver question (an issue that McKinley himself had never considered very important). He sent a commission to Europe to explore the possibility of a silver agreement with Great Britain and France. As he and everyone else anticipated, the effort produced no agreement. The Republicans then enacted the Currency, or Gold Standard, Act of 1900, which confirmed the nation's commitment to the gold standard.

And so the "battle of the standards" ended in victory for the forces of conservatism. Economic developments at the time seemed to vindicate the Republicans. Prosperity began to return in 1898. Foreign crop failures drove farm prices upward, and American business entered another cycle of expansion. Prosperity and the gold standard, it seemed, were closely allied.

But while the free-silver movement had failed, it had raised an important question for the American economy. In the quarter century before 1900, the countries of the Western world had experienced a spectacular growth in productive facilities and population. Yet the supply of money had not kept pace with economic progress. Had it not been for a dramatic increase in the gold supply in the late 1890s (a result of new techniques for extracting gold from low-content ores and the discovery of huge new gold deposits in Alaska, South Africa, and Australia), Populist predictions of financial disaster might in fact have proved correct. In 1898, two and a half times as much gold was produced as in 1890, and the currency supply was soon inflated far beyond anything Bryan and the free-silver forces had anticipated.

By then, however, Bryan—like many other Americans—was becoming engaged with another major issue: the nation's growing involvement in world affairs and its increasing flirtation with imperialism.

STIRRINGS OF IMPERIALISM

For over two decades after the Civil War, the United States expanded hardly at all. By the 1890s, however, some Americans were ready—indeed, eager—to resume the course of Manifest Destiny that had inspired their ancestors to wrest an empire from Mexico.

THE NEW MANIFEST DESTINY

Several developments helped shift American attention to lands across the seas. The experience of subjugating the Indian tribes had established a precedent for exerting colonial control over dependent peoples. The supposed "closing of the frontier" produced fears that natural resources would soon dwindle. The depression of the 1890s encouraged some businessmen to look for new markets abroad. The bitter social protests of the time—the Populist movement, the free-silver crusade, bloody labor disputes—led some politicians to urge a more aggressive foreign policy as an outlet for frustrations that would otherwise destabilize domestic life.

Americans were well aware of the imperialist fever that was raging through Europe, leading the major powers to partition much of Africa among themselves and to turn eager eyes on the Far East and the feeble Chinese Empire. Some Americans feared that their nation would soon be left out of all these potential markets. Scholars and others found a philosophic justification for expansionism in Charles Darwin's theories. They contended that nations or "races," like biological species, struggled constantly for existence and that only the fittest could survive. For strong nations to dominate weak ones was, therefore, in accordance with the laws of nature.

The ablest and most effective apostle of imperialism was Alfred Thayer Mahan, a captain and, later, admiral in the United States Navy. Mahan's thesis, presented in *The Influence of Sea Power upon History* (1890) and other works, was simple: countries with sea power were the great nations of history. Effective sea power required, among other things, colonies. Mahan believed that the United States should, at the least, acquire defensive bases in the Caribbean and the Pacific and take possession of Hawaii and other Pacific islands. He feared that the United States did not have a large enough navy to play the great role he envisioned. But during the 1870s and 1880s, the government launched a shipbuilding program that by 1898 had moved the United States to fifth place among the world's naval powers, and by 1900 to third place.

HAWAII AND SAMOA

The islands of Hawaii in the mid-Pacific had been an important way station for American ships in the China trade since the early nineteenth century. By the 1880s, officers of the expanding United States Navy were looking covetously at Pearl Harbor on the island of Oahu as a possible permanent base for U.S. ships. The growing number of Americans who had taken up residence on the islands also pressed for an increased American presence in Hawaii.

Settled by Polynesian people beginning in about 1500 B.C., Hawaii had developed an agricultural and fishing society in which different islands (and different communities on the same islands), each with its own chieftain, lived more or less self-sufficiently. When the first Americans arrived in Hawaii in the 1790s on merchant ships from New England, there were perhaps half a million people living there. Battles among rival communities were frequent, as ambitious chieftains tried to consolidate power over their neighbors. In 1810, after a series of such battles, King Kamehameha I established his dominance, welcomed American traders, and helped them develop a thriving trade between Hawaii and China. But Americans soon wanted more than trade. Missionaries began settling there in the early nineteenth century; and in the 1830s, William Hooper, a Boston trader, became the first of many Americans to buy land and establish a sugar plantation on the islands.

The arrival of these merchants, missionaries, and planters was devastating to traditional Hawaiian society. The newcomers inadvertently brought infectious diseases to which the Hawaiians, like the American Indians before them, were tragically vulnerable. By the mid-nineteenth century, more than half the native population had died. The Americans brought other incursions as well. Missionaries worked to replace native religion with Christianity. Other white settlers introduced liquor, firearms, and a commercial economy, all of which eroded the traditional character of Hawaiian society. By the 1840s, American planters had spread throughout the islands; and an American settler, G. P. Judd, had become prime minister of Hawaii under King Kamehameha III, who had agreed to establish a constitutional monarchy. Judd governed Hawaii for over a decade.

In 1887, the United States negotiated a treaty with Hawaii that permitted it to open a naval base at Pearl Harbor. By then, growing sugar for export to America had become the basis of the Hawaiian economy—as a result of an 1875 agreement allowing Hawaiian sugar to enter the United States duty-free. The American-dominated sugar plantation system displaced native Hawaiians from their lands and relied heavily on Asian immigrants, whom the Americans considered more reliable and more docile than the natives.

IMPERIALISM

EMPIRES were not, of course, new to the nineteenth century, when the United States acquired its first overseas colonies. They had existed since the early moments of recorded history, and they have continued into our own time.

But in the second half of the nineteenth century, the construction of empires took on a new form, and the word "imperialism" emerged for the first time to describe it. In many places, European powers now created colonies not by sending large numbers of migrants to settle and populate new lands, but instead by creating military, political, and business structures that allowed them to dominate and profit from the existing populations. This new imperialism changed the character of the colonizing nations, enriching them greatly and producing new classes of people whose lives were shaped by the demands of imperial business and administration. It changed the character of colonized societies even more, drawing them into the vast nexus of global industrial capitalism and introducing Western customs, institutions, and technologies to the subject peoples.

As the popularity of empire grew in the West, efforts to justify it grew as well. Champions of imperialism argued that the acquisition of colonies was essential for the health, even the survival, of their own industrializing nations. Colonies were sources of raw materials vital to industrial production; they were markets for manufactured goods; and they were suppliers of cheap labor. Defenders of empire also argued that imperialism was good for the colonized people. Many saw colonization as an opportunity to export Christianity to "heathen" lands, and new missionary movements emerged in Europe and America in response. More secular apologists argued that imperialism helped bring colonized people into the modern world.

The invention of steamships, railroads, telegraphs, and other modern vehicles of transportation and communication; the construction of canals (particularly the Suez Canal, completed in 1869, and the Panama Canal, completed in 1914); the creation of new military technologies (repeating rifles, machine guns, and modern artillery)—all contributed to the ability of Western nations to reach, conquer, and control distant lands.

The greatest imperial power of the nineteenth century was Great Britain. By 1800, despite its recent loss of the colonies that became the United States, it already possessed vast territory in North America, the Caribbean, and the Pacific. In the second half of the nineteenth century, Britain greatly expanded its empire. Its most important acquisition was India, one of the largest and most populous countries in the world and a nation in which Great Britain had long exerted informal authority. In 1857, when native Indians revolted against British influence, British forces brutally crushed the rebellion and established formal colonial control over India. British officials, backed by substantial military power, now governed India through a large civil service staffed mostly by people from England and Scotland but with some Indians serving in minor positions. The British invested heavily in railroads, telegraphs, canals, harbors, and agricultural improvements, to enhance the economic opportunities available to them. They created schools for Indian children in an effort to draw them into British culture and make them supporters of the imperial system.

The British also extended their empire into Africa and other parts of Asia. The

THE BRITISH RAJ The Drum Corps of the Royal Fusiliers in India poses here for a formal portrait, taken in 1877. Although the drummers are British, an Indian associate is included at top left. This blending of the dominant British with subordinate Indians was characteristic of the administration of the British Empire in India—a government known as the "raj," from the Indian word for "rule." (Time & Life Pictures/Getty Images)

great imperial champion Cecil Rhodes expanded a small existing British colony at Capetown into a substantial colony that included much of what is now South Africa. In 1895, he added new British territories to the north, which he named Rhodesia (and which today are Zimbabwe and Zambia). Others spread British authority into Kenya, Uganda, Nigeria, and much of Egypt. British imperialists also extended the empire into East Asia, with the acquisition of Singapore, Hong Kong, Burma, and Malaya; and they built a substantial presence—although not formal colonial rule—in China.

Other European states, watching the vast expansion of the British Empire, quickly jumped into the race for colonies. France created colonies in Indochina (Vietnam and Laos), Algeria, west Africa, and Madagascar. Belgium moved into the Congo in west Africa. Germany established colonies in the Cameroons, Tanganyika, and other parts of Africa, and in the Pacific islands north of Australia. Dutch, Italian, Portuguese, Spanish, Russian, and Japanese imperialists created colonies as well in Africa, Asia, and the

Pacific—driven both by a calculation of their own commercial interests and by the frenzied competition that had developed among rival imperial powers. In 1898, the United States was drawn into the imperial race, in part inadvertently as an unanticipated result of the Spanish-American War. But the drive to acquire colonies resulted as well from the deliberate efforts of home-grown proponents of empire (among them Theodore Roosevelt), who believed that in the modern industrial-imperial world, a nation without colonies would have difficulty remaining, or becoming, a true great power. •

UNDERSTAND, ANALYZE, & EVALUATE

1. What motivated the European nations' drive for empire in the late nineteenth century?
2. Why was Great Britain so successful in acquiring its vast empire?
3. How do the imperial efforts and ambitions of the United States at the end of the nineteenth century compare with those of European powers?

Native Hawaiians did not accept their subordination without protest. In 1891, they elevated a powerful nationalist to the throne: Queen Liliuokalani, who set out to challenge the growing American control of the islands. But she remained in power only two years. In 1890, the United States had eliminated the exemption from American tariffs in Hawaiian sugar trade. The result was devastating to the economy of the islands, and American planters concluded that the only way for them to recover was to become part of the United States (and, hence, exempt from its tariffs). In 1893, they staged a revolution and called on the United States for protection. After the American minister ordered marines from a warship in Honolulu harbor to go ashore to aid the American rebels, the queen yielded her authority.

A provisional government, dominated by Americans, immediately sent a delegation to Washington to negotiate a treaty of annexation. Debate over the treaty continued until 1898, when Congress finally approved the agreement.

Three thousand miles south of Hawaii, the Samoan islands had also long served as a way station for American ships in the Pacific trade. As American commerce with Asia increased, business groups in the United States regarded Samoa with new interest, and the American navy began eyeing the Samoan harbor at Pago Pago. In 1878, the Hayes administration extracted a treaty from Samoan leaders for an American naval station at Pago Pago.

Great Britain and Germany were also interested in the islands, and they, too, secured treaty rights from the native princes. For the next ten years, the three powers jockeyed for dominance in Samoa, finally agreeing to create a tripartite protectorate over Samoa, with the native chiefs exercising only nominal authority. The three-way arrangement failed to halt the rivalries of its members, and in 1899, the United States and Germany divided the islands between them, compensating Britain with territories elsewhere in the Pacific. The United States retained the harbor at Pago Pago.

WAR WITH SPAIN

Imperial ambitions had thus begun to stir within the United States well before the late 1890s. But a war with Spain in 1898 turned those stirrings into overt expansionism.

CONTROVERSY OVER CUBA

The Spanish-American War emerged out of Cuban resistance to Spanish rule which had been a source of tension since at least 1868. Many Americans had sympathized with the Cubans during that long struggle, but the United States did not intervene.

In 1895, the Cubans rose up again. This rebellion produced a ferocity on both sides that horrified Americans. The Cubans deliberately devastated the island to force the Spaniards to leave. The Spanish, commanded by General Valeriano Weyler (known in the American press as "Butcher Weyler"), confined civilians in concentration camps, where they died by the thousands from disease and malnutrition. The Spanish had used equally savage methods during the earlier struggle in Cuba without shocking American sensibilities. But the revolt of 1895 was reported more fully and sensationally by the American press, which helped create the impression that the Spaniards were committing all the atrocities, when in fact there was considerable brutality on both sides.

The conflict in Cuba came at a particularly opportune moment for the publishers of some American newspapers: Joseph Pulitzer with his *New York World* and William Randolph Hearst with his *New York Journal.* In the 1890s, Hearst and Pulitzer were engaged in a ruthless circulation war, and they both sent batteries of reporters and illustrators to Cuba with orders to provide accounts of Spanish atrocities. A growing population of Cuban émigrés in the United States—centered in Florida, New York, Philadelphia, and Trenton, New Jersey—gave extensive support to the Cuban Revolutionary Party (whose headquarters were in New York) and helped publicize its leader, José Martí, who was killed in Cuba in 1895. Later, Cuban Americans formed other clubs and associations to support the cause of *Cuba Libre* (Free Cuba).

The mounting storm of indignation against Spain did not persuade President Cleveland to support intervention. But when McKinley became president in 1897, he formally protested Spain's "uncivilized and inhuman" conduct, causing the Spanish government (fearful of American intervention) to recall Weyler, modify the concentration policy, and grant the island a qualified autonomy.

Whatever chances there were for a peaceful settlement vanished as a result of two dramatic incidents in February 1898. The first occurred when a Cuban agent stole a private letter written by Enrique Dupuy de Lôme, the Spanish minister in Washington, and turned it over to the American press. The letter described McKinley as a weak man and "a bidder for the admiration of the crowd." This was no more than many Americans, including some Republicans, were saying about their president. (Theodore Roosevelt described McKinley as having "no more backbone than a chocolate eclair.") But coming from a foreigner, it created intense popular anger. Dupuy de Lôme promptly resigned.

While excitement over the Dupuy de Lôme letter was still high, the American battleship *Maine* blew up in Havana harbor with a loss of more than 260 people. Many Americans assumed that the Spanish had sunk the ship, particularly when a naval court of inquiry hastily and inaccurately reported that an external explosion by a submarine mine had caused the disaster. (Later evidence suggested that the disaster was actually the result of an accidental explosion inside one of the engine rooms.) War hysteria swept the country, and Congress unanimously appropriated $50 million for military preparations.

McKinley still hoped to avoid a war. But others in his administration (including Assistant Secretary of the Navy Theodore Roosevelt) were clamoring for war. In March 1898, at the president's request, Spain agreed to stop the fighting and eliminate its concentration camps but refused to negotiate with the rebels and reserved the right to resume hostilities at its discretion. That satisfied neither public opinion nor Congress. A few days later, McKinley asked for and, on April 25, received a congressional declaration of war.

"A SPLENDID LITTLE WAR"

Secretary of State John Hay called the Spanish-American conflict "a splendid little war," an opinion that most Americans—with the exception of many of the enlisted men who fought in it—seemed to share. Declared in April, it was over in August, in part because Cuban rebels had already greatly weakened the Spanish resistance, making the American intervention in many respects little more than a "mopping-up" exercise. Only 460 Americans were killed in battle or died of wounds, although some 5,200 others perished of disease: malaria, dysentery, and typhoid, among others. Casualties among Cuban insurgents, who continued to bear the brunt of the fighting, were much higher.

THE YELLOW PRESS AND THE WRECK OF THE *MAINE* No evidence was ever found tying the Spanish to the explosion in Havana harbor that destroyed the American battleship *Maine* in February 1898. Indeed, most evidence indicated that the blast came from inside the ship, a fact that suggests an accident rather than sabotage. Nevertheless, the newspapers of Joseph Pulitzer and William Randolph Hearst ran sensational stories about the incident that were designed to arouse public sentiment in support of war. This front page from Pulitzer's *New York World* is an example of the lurid coverage the event received. Circulation figures at the top of the page indicate, too, how successful the coverage was in selling newspapers. (The Granger Collection, NYC)

The American war effort was not without difficulties. United States soldiers faced serious supply problems: a shortage of modern rifles and ammunition, uniforms too heavy for the warm Caribbean weather, inadequate medical services, and skimpy, almost indigestible food. The regular army numbered only 28,000 troops and officers, most of whom had experience in quelling Indian outbreaks but none in larger-scale warfare. That meant that, as in the Civil War, the United States had to rely heavily on National Guard units, organized by local communities and commanded for the most part by local leaders without military experience.

A significant proportion of the American invasion force consisted of black soldiers. Some were volunteer troops put together by African American communities. Others were members of the four black regiments in the regular army, who had been stationed on the frontier to defend white settlements against Indians and were now transferred east to fight in Cuba. As the black soldiers traveled through the South toward the training camps, some resisted the rigid segregation to which they were subjected. African American soldiers in Georgia deliberately made use of a "whites only" park; in Florida, they beat a soda-fountain operator for refusing to serve them; in Tampa, white provocations and black retaliation led to a nightlong riot that left thirty wounded.

Racial tensions continued in Cuba. African Americans played crucial roles in some of the important battles of the war (including the famous charge at San Juan Hill) and won many medals. Nearly half the Cuban insurgents fighting with the Americans were themselves black, including one of the leading insurgent generals, Antonio Maceo. The sight of black Cuban soldiers fighting alongside whites as equals gave African Americans a stronger sense of the injustice of their own position.

Seizing the Philippines

By an accident of history, the assistant secretary of the navy during the Cuban revolution was Theodore Roosevelt, an ardent Anglophile eager to see the United States join the British and other nations as imperial powers. Roosevelt was, in fact, a relatively minor figure in the Navy Department, but he was determined to expand his power. British friends had persuaded him that the war in Cuba gave the United States a rare opportunity to expand the American empire. Roosevelt responded by sending the Navy's Pacific fleet to the Philippines, with orders to attack as soon as America declared war. On May 1, 1898, Commodore George Dewey led the fleet into Manila Harbor, quickly destroyed the aging Spanish fleet, and forced the Spanish government to surrender Manila with hardly a shot fired. He became the first American hero of the war.

The Battle for Cuba

Cuba remained the principal focus of American military efforts. At first, the American commanders planned a long period of training before actually sending troops into combat. But when a Spanish fleet under Admiral Pascual Cervera slipped past the American navy into Santiago harbor on the southern coast of Cuba, plans changed quickly. The American Atlantic fleet quickly bottled Cervera up in the harbor. And the U.S. Army's commanding general, Nelson A. Miles, hastily altered his strategy and left Tampa in June with a force of 17,000 to attack Santiago.

General William R. Shafter, the American commander, moved toward Santiago, which he planned to surround and capture. On the way he met and defeated Spanish forces at Las Guasimos and, a week later, in two simultaneous battles, El Caney and San Juan Hill. At the center of the fighting (and on the front pages of the newspapers) during many of these engagements was a cavalry unit known as the Rough Riders. Nominally commanded by General Leonard Wood, its real leader was Colonel Theodore Roosevelt, who had resigned from the Navy Department to get into the war and who had struggled with an almost desperate fury to get his regiment into the fighting. His passion to join the war undoubtedly reflected the decision of his beloved father, Theodore Roosevelt, Sr., not to fight in the Civil War, a source of private shame within his family that his son sought to erase.

Roosevelt rapidly emerged as a hero of the conflict. His fame rested in large part on his role in leading a bold, if perhaps reckless, charge up Kettle Hill (a minor part of the

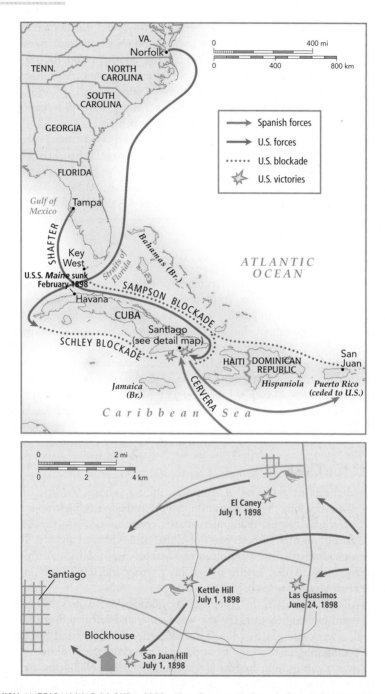

THE SPANISH-AMERICAN WAR IN CUBA, 1898 The military conflict between the United States and Spain in Cuba was a brief affair. The Cuban rebels and an American naval blockade had already brought the Spanish to the brink of defeat. The arrival of American troops was simply the final blow. In the space of about a week, U.S. troops won four decisive battles in the area around Santiago in southeast Cuba—one of them (the Battle of Kettle Hill) the scene of Theodore Roosevelt's famous charge up the adjacent San Juan Hill. This map shows the extent of the American naval blockade, the path of American troops from Florida to Cuba, and the location of the actual fighting. • *What were the implications of the war in Cuba for Puerto Rico?*

AFRICAN AMERICAN CAVALRY Substantial numbers of African Americans fought in the United States Army during the Spanish-American War. Although confined to all-black units, they engaged in combat alongside white units and fought bravely and effectively. This photograph shows a troop of African American cavalry in formation in Cuba. (© Corbis)

larger battle for the adjacent San Juan Hill) directly into the face of Spanish guns. Roosevelt himself emerged unscathed, but nearly a hundred of his soldiers were killed or wounded. He remembered the battle as "the great day of my life."

Although Shafter was now in position to assault Santiago, his army was so weakened by sickness that he feared he might have to abandon his position. But unknown to the Americans, the Spanish government had by now decided that Santiago was lost and had ordered Cervera to evacuate. On July 3, Cervera tried to escape the harbor. The waiting American squadron destroyed his entire fleet. On July 16, the commander of Spanish ground forces in Santiago surrendered. At about the same time, an American army landed in Puerto Rico and occupied it against virtually no opposition. On August 12, an armistice ended the war. Under the terms of the armistice, Spain recognized the independence of Cuba, ceded Puerto Rico and the Pacific island of Guam to the United States, and accepted continued American occupation of Manila pending the final disposition of the Philippines.

PUERTO RICO AND THE UNITED STATES

The island of Puerto Rico had been a part of the Spanish Empire since 1508. By the early seventeenth century, the native people of the island, the Arawaks, had largely disappeared as a result of infectious diseases, Spanish brutality, and poverty. Puerto Rican society developed, therefore, with a Spanish ruling class and a large African workforce for the coffee and sugar plantations that came to dominate its economy.

Puerto Rican resistance to Spanish rule began to emerge in the nineteenth century. The resistance prompted some reforms: the abolition of slavery in 1873, representation in the Spanish parliament, and other changes. Demands for independence continued to grow, and in 1898, Spain granted the island a degree of independence. But before the changes had any chance to take effect, control of Puerto Rico shifted to the United States. American military forces occupied the island during the Spanish-American War, and they remained in control until 1900, when the Foraker Act ended military rule and established

PLATFORM OF THE AMERICAN ANTI-IMPERIALIST LEAGUE, 1899

WE hold that the policy known as imperialism is hostile to liberty and tends toward militarism, an evil from which it has been our glory to be free. We regret that it has become necessary in the land of Washington and Lincoln to reaffirm that all men, of whatever race or color, are entitled to life, liberty, and the pursuit of happiness. We maintain that governments derive their just powers from the consent of the governed. We insist that the subjugation of any people is "criminal aggression" and open disloyalty to the distinctive principles of our Government.

We earnestly condemn the policy of the present National Administration in the Philippines. It seeks to extinguish the spirit of 1776 in those islands. We deplore the sacrifice of our soldiers and sailors, whose bravery deserves admiration even in an unjust war. We denounce the slaughter of the Filipinos as a needless horror. We protest against the extension of American sovereignty by Spanish methods.

We demand the immediate cessation of the war against liberty, begun by Spain and continued by us. We urge that Congress be promptly convened to announce to the Filipinos our purpose to concede to them the independence for which they have so long fought and which of right is theirs.

The United States have always protested against the doctrine of international law which permits the subjugation of the weak by the strong. A self-governing state cannot accept sovereignty over an unwilling people. The United States cannot act upon the ancient heresy that might makes right.

Imperialists assume that with the destruction of self-government in the Philippines by American hands, all opposition here will cease. This is a grievous error. Much as we abhor the war of "criminal aggression" in the Philippines, greatly as we regret that the blood of the Filipinos is on American hands, we more deeply resent the betrayal of American institutions at home. The real firing line is not in the suburbs of Manila.

---

a formal colonial government. Agitation for independence continued, and in 1917, Congress passed the Jones Act, which declared Puerto Rico to be United States territory and made all Puerto Ricans American citizens.

The Puerto Rican sugar industry flourished as it took advantage of the American market that was now open to it without tariffs. As in Hawaii, Americans from the mainland began establishing large sugar plantations on the island and hired natives to work them. The growing emphasis on sugar as a cash crop, and the transformation of many Puerto Rican farmers into paid laborers, led to a reduction in the growing of food for the island and greater reliance on imported goods. When international sugar prices were high, Puerto Rico did well. When they dropped, the island's economy sagged, pushing the many plantation workers—already poor—into destitution.

THE DEBATE OVER THE PHILIPPINES

Although the annexation of Puerto Rico produced relatively little controversy, the annexation of the Philippines created an impassioned debate. Controlling a nearby Caribbean island fit reasonably comfortably into the United States' sense of itself as the dominant power in

The foe is of our own household. The attempt of 1861 was to divide the country. That of 1899 is to destroy its fundamental principles and noblest ideals.

Whether the ruthless slaughter of the Filipinos shall end next month or next year is but an incident in a contest that must go on until the Declaration of Independence and the Constitution of the United States are rescued from the hands of their betrayers. Those who dispute about standards of value while the Republic is undermined will be listened to as little as those who would wrangle about the small economies of the household while the house is on fire. The training of a great people for a century, the aspiration for liberty of a vast immigration are forces that will hurl aside those who in the delirium of conquest seek to destroy the character of our institutions.

We deny that the obligation of all citizens to support their Government in times of grave national peril applies to the present situation. If an Administration may with impunity ignore the issues upon which it was chosen, deliberately create a condition of war anywhere on the face of the globe, debauch the civil service for spoils to promote the adventure, organize a truth-suppressing censorship and demand of all citizens a suspension of judgment and their unanimous support while it chooses to continue the fighting, representative government itself is imperiled.

We propose to contribute to the defeat of any person or party that stands for the forcible subjugation of any people. We shall oppose for reelection all who in the White House or in Congress betray American liberty in pursuit of un-American gains. We still hope that both of our great political parties will support and defend the Declaration of Independence in the closing campaign of the century. . . .

UNDERSTAND, ANALYZE, & EVALUATE

1. On what grounds did the Anti-imperialist League oppose U.S. expansion, and where were these principles ratified?
2. What were the costs of imperial expansion for the United States and what losses were Filipinos to incur?
3. How did the prospect of an American empire affect the nation's democratic principles?

Source: "Platform of the American AntiImperialist League," in *Speeches, Correspondence, ard Political Papers of Carl Schurz*, vol. 6, ed. Frederick Bancroft (New York: G.P. Putnam's Sons, 1913), p. 77, note 1.

the Western Hemisphere. But to many Americans, controlling a large and densely populated territory thousands of miles away seemed very different and more ominous.

McKinley claimed to be reluctant to support annexation. But, according to his own accounts, he came to believe there were no acceptable alternatives. Returning the Philippines to Spain would be "cowardly and dishonorable," he claimed. Turning them over to another imperialist power (France, Germany, or Britain) would be "bad business and discreditable." Granting them independence would be irresponsible because the Filipinos were "unfit for self government." The only solution was "to take them all and to educate the Filipinos, and uplift and Christianize them, and by God's grace do the very best we could by them."

The Treaty of Paris, signed in December 1898, confirmed the terms of the armistice and brought a formal end to the war. American negotiators had startled the Spanish by demanding that they also cede the Philippines to the United States, but an American offer of $20 million for the islands softened their resistance. They accepted all the American terms.

In the United States Senate, however, resistance was fierce. During debate over ratification of the treaty, a powerful anti-imperialist movement arose to oppose acquisition of the

Philippines. The anti-imperialists included some of the nation's wealthiest and most power-ful figures: Andrew Carnegie, Mark Twain, Samuel Gompers, Senator John Sherman, and others. Some anti-imperialists believed that imperialism was immoral, a repudiation of America's commitment to human freedom. Others feared "polluting" the American popula-tion by introducing "inferior" Asian races into it. Industrial workers feared being undercut by a flood of cheap laborers from the new colonies. Conservatives worried about the large standing army and entangling foreign alliances that they believed imperialism would require and that they feared would threaten American liberties. Sugar growers and other anti-imperialists feared unwelcome competition from the new territories. The Anti-Imperialist League, established late in 1898 by upper-class Bostonians, New Yorkers, and others to fight against annexation, waged a vigorous campaign against ratification of the Paris treaty.

But favoring ratification was an equally varied group. There were the exuberant imperial-ists such as Theodore Roosevelt, who saw the acquisition of empire as a way to reinvigorate the nation. Some businessmen saw opportunities to dominate the Asian trade. Most Republicans saw partisan advantages in acquiring valuable new territories through a war fought and won by a Republican administration. Perhaps the strongest argument in favor of annexation, however, was that the United States already possessed the islands.

When anti-imperialists warned of the danger of acquiring heavily populated territories whose people might have to become citizens, the imperialists had a ready answer: the nation's long-standing policies toward Indians—treating them as dependents rather than as citizens—had created a precedent for annexing land without absorbing people.

The fate of the treaty remained in doubt for weeks, until it received the unexpected support of William Jennings Bryan, a fervent anti-imperialist. He backed ratification because he hoped to move the issue out of the Senate and make it the subject of a national referendum in 1900, when he expected to be the Democratic presidential candidate again. Bryan persuaded a number of anti-imperialist Democrats to support the treaty so as to set up the 1900 debate. The Senate ratified it finally on February 6, 1899.

But Bryan miscalculated. If the election of 1900 was in fact a referendum on the Philippines, as Bryan expected, it proved beyond a doubt that the nation had decided in favor of imperialism. Once again Bryan ran against McKinley; and once again McKinley won—even more decisively than in 1896. It was not only the issue of the colonies, how-ever, that ensured McKinley's victory. The Republicans were the beneficiaries of growing prosperity—and also of the colorful personality of their vice presidential candidate, Theodore Roosevelt, the hero of San Juan Hill.

THE REPUBLIC AS EMPIRE

The new American empire was small by the standards of the great imperial powers of Europe. But it embroiled the United States in the politics of both Europe and the Far East in ways the nation had always tried to avoid in the past. It drew Americans into a brutal war in the Philippines.

GOVERNING THE COLONIES

Three American dependencies—Hawaii, Alaska, and Puerto Rico—presented relatively few problems. They received territorial status (and their residents American citizenship) relatively quickly: Hawaii in 1900, Alaska in 1912, and Puerto Rico in 1917. The navy took control of the Pacific islands of Guam and Tutuila. The United States simply left alone some of the smallest, least populated Pacific islands now under its control. Cuba was a thornier problem. American military forces, commanded by General Leonard Wood, remained there until 1902 to prepare the island for independence. Americans built roads, schools, and hospitals; reorganized the legal, financial, and administrative systems; and introduced medical and sanitation reforms. But the United States also laid the basis for years of American economic domination of the island.

When Cuba drew up a constitution that made no reference to the United States, Congress responded by passing the Platt Amendment in 1901 and pressuring Cuba into incorporating its terms into its constitution. The Platt Amendment barred Cuba from making treaties with other nations; gave the United States the right to intervene in Cuba to preserve independence, life, and property; and required Cuba to permit American naval stations on its territory. The amendment left Cuba with only nominal political independence.

American capital made the new nation an American economic appendage as well. American investors poured into Cuba, buying up plantations, factories, railroads, and refineries. Resistance to "Yankee imperialism" produced intermittent revolts against the Cuban government—revolts that at times prompted U.S. military intervention. American troops occupied the island from 1906 to 1909 after one such rebellion; they returned again in 1912 to suppress a revolt by black plantation workers. As in Puerto Rico and Hawaii, sugar production—spurred by access to the American market—increasingly dominated the island's economy and subjected it to the same cycle of booms and busts that plagued other sugar-producing appendages of the United States economy.

THE PHILIPPINE WAR

Like other imperial powers, the United States soon discovered that subjugating another people was not an easy task. The American experience in the Philippines began with a long and bloody war.

The conflict in the Philippines is the least remembered of all American wars. It was also one of the longest. It lasted from 1898 to 1902, and it was one of the most vicious. It involved 200,000 American troops and resulted in 4,300 American deaths. The number of Filipinos killed in the conflict has long been a matter of dispute, but it seems likely that at least 50,000 natives (and perhaps many more) died. The American occupiers faced brutal guerrilla tactics in the Philippines, and they soon found themselves drawn into the same pattern of brutality that had outraged so many Americans when Weyler had used them in the Caribbean.

The Filipinos had rebelled against Spanish rule before 1898, and as soon as they realized the Americans had come to stay, they rebelled against them as well. Ably led by Emilio Aguinaldo, who claimed to head the legitimate government of the nation, Filipinos harried the American army of occupation from island to island for more than three years. At first, American commanders believed the rebels had only a small popular following. But by early 1900, General Arthur MacArthur, an American commander in the islands (and father of General Douglas MacArthur), was writing: "I have been reluctantly compelled to believe that the Filipino masses are loyal to Aguinaldo and the government which he heads."

To MacArthur and others, that realization was not a reason to moderate American tactics or conciliate the rebels, but rather to adopt much more severe measures. Gradually, the American military effort became more systematically vicious and brutal. Captured Filipino guerrillas were treated not as prisoners of war but as murderers. Many were summarily executed. On some islands, entire communities were evacuated—the residents

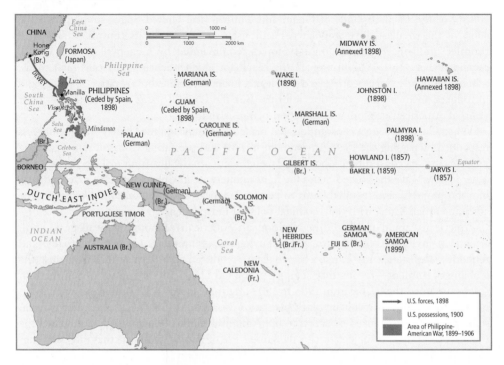

THE AMERICAN SOUTH PACIFIC EMPIRE, 1900 Except for Puerto Rico, all of the colonial acquisitions of the United States in the wake of the Spanish-American War occurred in the Pacific. The new attraction of imperialism persuaded the United States to annex Hawaii in 1898. The war itself gave America control of the Philippines, Guam, and other, smaller Spanish possessions in the Pacific. When added to the small, scattered islands that the United States had acquired as naval bases earlier in the nineteenth century, these new possessions gave the nation a far-flung Pacific empire, even if one whose total territory and population remained small by the standards of the other great empires of the age. • *What was the reaction in the United States to the acquisition of this new empire?*

forced into concentration camps while American troops destroyed their villages. A spirit of savagery grew among some American soldiers, who came to view the Filipinos as almost subhuman and, at times, seemed to take pleasure in arbitrarily killing them.

By 1902, reports of the brutality and of the American casualties had soured the American public on the war. But by then, the rebellion had largely exhausted itself and the occupiers had established control over most of the islands. The key to their victory was the March 1901 capture of Aguinaldo, who later signed a document urging his followers to stop fighting and declared his own allegiance to the United States. Fighting continued intermittently until as late as 1906, but American possession of the Philippines was now secure. In the summer of 1901, the military transferred authority over the islands to William Howard Taft, who became their first civilian governor and gave the Filipinos broad local autonomy. The Americans also built roads, schools, bridges, and sewers; instituted major administrative and financial reforms; and established a public health system. Filipino self-rule gradually increased, and on July 4, 1946, the islands finally gained their independence.

THE OPEN DOOR

The American acquisition of the Philippines increased the already strong U.S. interest in Asia. Americans were particularly concerned about the future of China, which was now

FILIPINO PRISONERS   American troops guard captured Filipino guerrillas in Manila. The suppression of the Filipino insurrection was a much longer and costlier military undertaking than the Spanish-American War, by which the United States first gained possession of the islands. By mid-1900, there were 70,000 American troops in the Philippines, under the command of General Arthur MacArthur (whose son, Douglas, won fame in the Philippines during World War II). (Library of Congress)

so enfeebled that it provided a tempting target for exploitation by stronger countries. By 1900, England, France, Germany, Russia, and Japan were beginning to carve up China among themselves, pressuring the Chinese government for "concessions" that gave them effective control over various regions of China. In some cases, they simply seized Chinese territory and claimed it as their own. Many Americans feared that the process would soon cut them out of the China trade altogether.

Eager for a way to advance American interests in China without risking war, McKinley issued a statement in September 1898 saying the United States wanted access to China but no special advantages there. "Asking only the open door for ourselves, we are ready to accord the open door to others." The next year, Secretary of State John Hay translated those words into policy when he addressed identical messages—which became known as the "Open Door notes"—to England, Germany, Russia, France, Japan, and Italy. He asked that each nation with a "sphere of influence" in China allow other nations to trade freely and equally in its sphere. The principles Hay outlined would allow the United States to trade freely with China without fear of interference.

Europe and Japan received the Open Door proposals coolly. Russia openly rejected them; the other powers claimed to accept them in principle but to be unable to act unless all the other powers agreed. Hay refused to consider this a rebuff. He boldly announced that all the powers had accepted the principles of the Open Door in "final and definitive" form and that the United States expected them to observe those principles.

No sooner had the diplomatic maneuvering over the Open Door ended than the Boxers, a secret Chinese martial-arts society with highly nationalist convictions (and a somewhat mystical vision of their invulnerability to bullets), launched a revolt against foreigners in China. The Boxer Rebellion spread widely across eastern China, attacking Westerners wherever they could find them—including many Christian missionaries. But the climax of the revolt was a siege of the entire Western foreign diplomatic corps, which took refuge in the British embassy in Beijing. The imperial powers (including the United States) sent an international expeditionary force into China to rescue the diplomats. In August 1900, it fought its way into Peking and broke the siege.

The Boxer Rebellion became an important event for the role of the United States in China. McKinley and Hay had agreed to American participation in quelling the Boxer Rebellion in order to secure a voice in the settlement of the uprising and prevent the partition of China by the European powers. Hay now won support for his Open Door approach from England and Germany and induced the other participating powers to accept compensation from the Chinese for the damages the Boxer Rebellion had caused. Chinese territorial integrity survived at least in name, and the United States retained access to its lucrative China trade.

A MODERN MILITARY SYSTEM

The war with Spain had revealed glaring deficiencies in the American military system. Had the United States been fighting a more powerful foe, disaster might have resulted. After the war, McKinley appointed Elihu Root, an able corporate lawyer in New York, as secretary of war to supervise a major overhaul of the armed forces.

Root's reforms enlarged the regular army from 25,000 to a maximum of 100,000. They established federal army standards for the National Guard, ensuring that never again would the nation fight a war with volunteer regiments trained and equipped differently than those in the regular army. They sparked the creation of a system of officer training schools, including the Army Staff College (later the Command and General Staff School) at Fort Leavenworth, Kansas, and the Army War College in Washington. And in 1903, a general staff (named the Joint Chiefs of Staff) was established to act as military advisers to the secretary of war. As a result of the new reforms, the United States entered the twentieth century with something resembling a modern military system.

CONCLUSION

For nearly three decades after the end of Reconstruction, American politics remained locked in a rigid stalemate. The electorate was almost evenly divided, and the two major parties differed on only a few issues. A series of dull, respectable presidents presided over this political system as unwitting symbols of its stability and passivity.

Beneath the calm surface of national politics, however, social issues were creating deep tensions: battles between employers and workers, growing resentment among American farmers facing declining prosperity, outrage at what many voters considered corruption in government and excessive power in the hands of corporate titans. When a great depression began in 1893, these social tensions exploded.

The most visible sign of the challenge to the political stalemate was the Populist movement, an uprising of American farmers demanding far-reaching changes in politics and the economy. In 1892, they created their own political party, the People's Party, which for a few years showed impressive strength. But in the climactic election of 1896, in which the Populist hero William Jennings Bryan became the presidential nominee of both the Democratic Party and the People's Party, the Republicans won a substantial victory—and, in the process, helped create a great electoral realignment that left the Republicans with a clear majority for the next three decades.

The crises of the 1890s coincided with, and helped strengthen, the United States' growing involvement in the world. In 1898, the United States intervened in a colonial war between Spain and Cuba, won a quick and easy military victory, and signed a treaty with Spain that ceded significant territory to the Americans. A vigorous anti-imperialist movement failed to stop the imperial drive. But taking the colonies proved easier than holding them. In the Philippines, American forces became bogged down in a brutal four-year war with Filipino rebels. The conflict soured much of the American public, and the annexation of colonies in 1898 proved to be both the beginning and the end of American territorial imperialism.

RECALL AND REFLECT

1. How and why did the federal government attempt to regulate interstate commerce in the late nineteenth century?
2. What efforts did farmers undertake to deal with the economic problems they faced in the late nineteenth century?
3. What was the "silver question"? Why was it so important to so many Americans? How did the major political parties deal with this question?
4. How did the Spanish-American War change America's relationship to the rest of the world?
5. What were the main arguments of those who supported U.S. imperialism and those who opposed the nation's imperial ambitions and efforts?

20 THE PROGRESSIVES

LOOKING AHEAD

1. What role did women and women's organizations play in the reforms of the progressive era? How did progressive era reforms affect women?

2. What changes to politics and government did progressive reformers advocate at the local, state, and federal levels? How did government change as a result of their reform efforts?

3. How did Woodrow Wilson's progressivism differ from that of Theodore Roosevelt? In what ways was it similar to Roosevelt's?

WELL BEFORE THE END OF the nineteenth century, many Americans had become convinced that rapid industrialization and urbanization had created a growing crisis. The nation's most pressing need, they claimed, was to impose order and justice on a society that seemed to be approaching chaos. By the early years of the twentieth century, this outlook had acquired a name: progressivism.

Not even those who called themselves progressives could agree on what the term meant, for it was a phenomenon of great scope and diversity. But despite, or perhaps because of, its great diversity, progressivism created a remarkable period of political and social innovation. From the late nineteenth century until at least the end of World War I, progressive reformers brought into public debate such issues as the role of women in society, racial equality, the rights of labor, and the impact of immigration and cultural diversity.

Progressivism began as a series of local movements and encompassed many different efforts to improve the working of society. Slowly but steadily, these efforts became national efforts.

Ultimately it was the presidency, not the Congress, that became the most important vehicle of national reform—first under the dynamic leadership of Theodore Roosevelt and then under the disciplined, moralistic leadership of Woodrow Wilson. By the time America entered World War I in 1917, the federal government—which had exercised limited powers prior to the twentieth century—had greatly expanded its role in American life.

THE PROGRESSIVE IMPULSE

Progressives believed, as their name implies, in the idea of progress. They were optimistic that society was capable of improvement and that continued growth and advancement were the nation's destiny. But progressives believed, too, that growth and progress could not continue to occur recklessly, as they had in the late nineteenth century. The "natural laws" of the marketplace, and the doctrines of laissez-faire and Social Darwinism that dominated those laws, were not sufficient. Direct, purposeful human intervention was essential to ordering and bettering society.

Progressives did not always agree on the form their interventions should take, and the result was a variety of reform impulses. One powerful impulse was the spirit of "antimonopoly," the fear of concentrated power and the urge to limit and disperse authority and wealth. Another progressive impulse was a belief in the importance of social cohesion: the belief that individuals are part of a great web of social relationships, that each person's welfare is dependent on the welfare of society as a whole. Still another impulse was a deep faith in knowledge—in the possibilities of applying to society the principles of natural and social sciences. Most progressives believed, too, that a modernized government could—and must—play an important role in the process of improving and stabilizing society.

TIME LINE

1873
Women's Christian Temperance Union (WCTU) founded

1889
Jane Addams opens Hull House in Chicago

1893
Anti-Saloon League founded

1900
Galveston, Texas, establishes commission government

1901
McKinley assassinated; Theodore Roosevelt becomes president

1902
Northern Securities antitrust case

1906
Hepburn Railroad Regulation Act

Meat Inspection Act

1907
Financial panic and recession

1908
Taft elected president

1909
NAACP formed

Pinchot-Ballinger dispute

1911
Triangle Shirtwaist Company fire

1912
Roosevelt forms Progressive Party

Woodrow Wilson elected president

1913
Sixteenth Amendment (income tax)

Seventeenth Amendment (direct popular election of U.S. senators)

Federal Reserve Act

1914
Federal Trade Commission Act

Clayton Antitrust Act

1919
Eighteenth Amendment (prohibition)

1920
Nineteenth Amendment (woman suffrage)

The Muckrakers and the Social Gospel

Among the first people to articulate the new spirit of national reform were crusading journalists who began to direct public attention toward social, economic, and political injustices. Known as the "muckrakers," after Theodore Roosevelt accused them of raking up muck through their writings, they were committed to exposing scandal, corruption, and injustice.

Their first major targets were the trusts and, particularly, the railroads, which the muckrakers considered powerful and deeply corrupt. Exposés of the great corporate organizations began to appear as early as the 1860s, when Charles Francis Adams, Jr., and others uncovered corruption among the railroad barons. Decades later, journalist Ida Tarbell produced a scorching study of the Standard Oil trust. By the turn of the century, many muckrakers were turning their attention to government and particularly to the urban political machines. Among the most influential was Lincoln Steffens, a reporter for *McClure's* magazine. His portraits of "machine government" and "boss rule" in cities, written in a tone of studied moral outrage, helped arouse sentiment for urban political reform. By presenting social problems to the public with indignation and moral fervor, they helped inspire other Americans to take action.

Growing outrage at social and economic injustice committed many reformers to the pursuit of social justice. ("Social justice" is a term widely used around the world to promote a kind of justice that goes beyond the individual but, instead, seeks justice for society as a whole. Advocates of social justice are likely to believe in a more egalitarian society.) That impulse helped create the rise of what became known as the "Social Gospel," the effort to make faith into a tool of social reform. The Social Gospel movement was chiefly concerned with redeeming the nation's cities.

THE BOSSES OF THE SENATE (1889), BY JOSEPH KEPPLER   Keppler was a popular political cartoonist of the late nineteenth century who shared the growing concern about the power of the trusts—portrayed here as bloated, almost reptilian figures standing menacingly over the members of the U.S. Senate, to whose chamber the "people's entrance" is "closed." (The Granger Collection, NYC)

The Salvation Army, which began in England but soon spread to the United States, was one example of the fusion of religion with reform. A Christian social welfare organization with a vaguely military structure, it had recruited 3,000 "officers" and 20,000 "privates" by 1900 and was offering both material aid and spiritual service to the urban poor. In addition, many ministers, priests, and rabbis left traditional parish work to serve in the troubled cities. Charles Sheldon's book *In His Steps* (1898), the story of a young minister who abandoned a comfortable post to work among the needy, sold more than 15 million copies. The Social Gospel was never the dominant element in the movement for urban reform. But the engagement of religion with reform helped bring to progressivism a powerful moral commitment to redeem the lives of even the least favored citizens.

THE SETTLEMENT HOUSE MOVEMENT

An element of much progressive thought was the belief in the influence of the environment on individual development. Nothing produced greater distress, many urban reformers believed, than crowded immigrant neighborhoods. One response to the problems of such communities, borrowed from England, was the "settlement house." The most famous was Hull House, which opened in 1889 in Chicago as a result of the efforts of the social worker Jane Addams. It became a model for more than 400 similar institutions throughout the nation. Staffed by members of the educated middle class, settlement houses sought to help immigrant families adapt to the language and customs of their new country.

Young college women (mostly unmarried) were important participants in the settlement house movement. Working in a settlement house, a protected site that served mostly women, was consistent with the widespread assumption that women needed to be sheltered from difficult environments. The clean and well-tended buildings that settlement houses created were not only a model for immigrant women, but also an appropriate site for elite women as well.

The settlement houses also helped create another important institution of reform: the profession of social work. A growing number of programs for the professional training of social workers began to appear in the nation's leading universities, partly in response to the activities of the settlement houses.

THE ALLURE OF EXPERTISE

As the emergence of the social work profession suggests, progressives involved in humanitarian efforts placed a high value on knowledge and expertise. Even nonscientific problems, they believed, could be analyzed and solved scientifically. Many reformers came to believe that only enlightened experts and well-designed bureaucracies could create the stability and order America needed.

Some even spoke of the creation of a new civilization, in which the expertise of scientists and engineers could be brought to bear on the problems of the economy and society. The social scientist Thorstein Veblen, for example, proposed a new economic system in which power would reside in the hands of highly trained engineers. Only they, he argued, could fully understand the "machine process" by which modern society must be governed.

THE PROFESSIONS

The late nineteenth century saw a dramatic expansion in the number of Americans engaged in administrative and professional tasks. Industries needed managers, technicians, and accountants as well as workers. Cities required commercial, medical, legal, and educational services.

New technology required scientists and engineers, who, in turn, required institutions and instructors to train them. By the turn of the century, those performing these services had come to constitute a distinct social group—what some historians have called a "new middle class."

By the early twentieth century, millions within this new middle class were building organizations and establishing standards to secure their position in society. Most of all, they created the modern, organized professions. The idea of professionalism had been a frail one in America even as late as 1880, but as the demand for professional services increased, so did the pressures for reform.

Among the first to respond was the medical profession. In 1901, doctors who considered themselves trained professionals reorganized the American Medical Association (AMA) into a national professional society. By 1920, nearly two-thirds of all American doctors were members. The AMA quickly called for strict, scientific standards for admission to the practice of medicine. State governments responded by passing new laws requiring the licensing of all physicians. By 1900, medical education at a few medical schools—notably Johns Hopkins in Baltimore (founded in 1893)—compared favorably with those in the leading institutions of Europe.

By 1916, lawyers in all forty-eight states had established professional bar associations. The nation's law schools accordingly expanded greatly. Businessmen supported the creation of schools of business administration and set up their own national organizations: the National Association of Manufacturers in 1895 and the United States Chamber of Commerce in 1912. Farmers responded to the new order by forming, through the National Farm Bureau Federation, a network of agricultural organizations designed to spread scientific farming methods.

The professions removed the untrained and incompetent. But the admission requirements also protected those already in the professions from excessive competition and lent prestige and status to the professional level. Some professions used their entrance requirements to exclude African Americans, women, immigrants, and other "undesirables" from their ranks. Others used them simply to keep the numbers down, to ensure that demand would remain high.

WOMEN AND THE PROFESSIONS

American women found themselves excluded from most of the emerging professions. But a substantial number of middle-class women—particularly those emerging from the new women's colleges and from the coeducational state universities—entered professional careers nevertheless.

A few women managed to establish themselves as physicians, lawyers, engineers, scientists, and corporate managers. Most, however, turned by necessity to those professional outlets that society considered suitable for women: settlement houses, social work, and, most important, teaching. Indeed, in the late nineteenth century, perhaps 90 percent of all professional women were teachers. For educated black women, in particular, the existence of segregated schools in the South created a substantial market for African American teachers.

Women also dominated other professional activities. Nursing had become primarily a women's field during and after the Civil War. By the early twentieth century, it was adopting professional standards. And many women entered academia—often earning advanced degrees at such predominantly male institutions as the University of Chicago, MIT, or Columbia, and then finding professional opportunities in the new and expanding women's colleges.

WOMEN AND REFORM

The prominence of women in reform movements is one of the most striking features of progressivism. In many states in the early twentieth century, women could not vote. They almost never held public office. They had footholds in only a few (and usually primarily female) professions and lived in a culture in which most people, male and female, believed that women were not suited for the public world. What, then, explains the prominent role so many women played in the reform activities of the period?

THE "NEW WOMAN"

The phenomenon of the "new woman" was a product of social and economic changes in both the private and public spheres. By the end of the nineteenth century, almost all income-producing activity had moved out of the home and into the factory or the office. At the same time, many women were having fewer children, and their children were beginning school at earlier ages and spending more time there. For wives and mothers who did not work for wages, the home was less of an all-consuming place. Hence, more and more women began looking for activities outside the home.

Some educated women shunned marriage entirely, believing that only by remaining single could they play the roles they envisioned in the public world. Single women were among the most prominent reformers of the time. Some of these women lived alone. Others lived with other women, often in long-term relationships—some of them secretly romantic—that were known at the time as "Boston marriages." The divorce rate also rose rapidly in the late nineteenth century, from one divorce for every twenty-one marriages in 1880 to one in nine by 1916; women initiated the majority of divorces.

THE CLUBWOMEN

Among the most visible signs of the increasing public roles of women in the late nineteenth and early twentieth centuries were the women's clubs, which proliferated rapidly beginning in the 1880s and 1890s and became the vanguard of many important reforms.

The women's clubs began largely as cultural organizations to provide middle- and upper-class women with an outlet for their intellectual energies. In 1892, when women formed the General Federation of Women's Clubs, there were more than 100,000 members in nearly 500 clubs. By 1917, there were over 1 million members.

Much of what the clubs did was uncontroversial: planting trees; supporting schools, libraries, and settlement houses; building hospitals and parks. But clubwomen were also an important force in winning passage of state (and ultimately federal) laws that regulated the conditions of woman and child labor. They established government inspection of workplaces, regulated the food and drug industries, reformed policies toward the Indian tribes, applied new standards to urban housing, and, perhaps most notably, outlawed the manufacture and sale of alcohol. They were instrumental in pressuring state legislatures in most states to provide "mothers' pensions" to widowed or abandoned mothers with small children—a system that ultimately became absorbed into the Social Security system. In 1912, they pressured Congress into establishing the Children's Bureau in the Labor Department, an agency directed to develop policies to protect children.

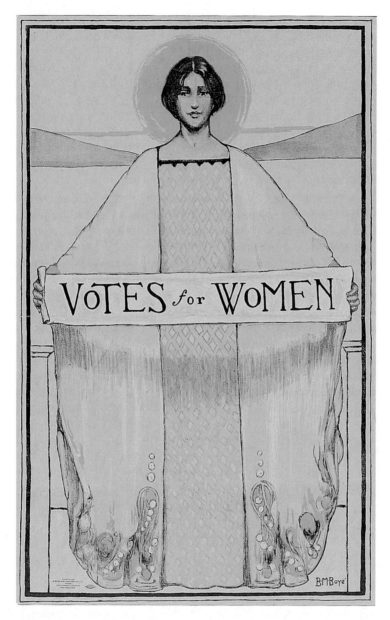

VOTES FOR WOMEN, BY B. M. BOYE This striking poster was the prize-winning entry in a 1911 contest sponsored by the College Equal Suffrage League of Northern California. (Schlesinger Library, Radcliffe Institute, Harvard University)

In many of these efforts, the clubwomen formed alliances with other women's groups, such as the Women's Trade Union League (WTUL), founded in 1903 by female union members and upper-class reformers and committed to persuading women to join unions. In addition to working on behalf of protective legislation for women, WTUL members held public meetings on behalf of female workers, raised money to support strikes, marched on picket lines, and bailed striking women out of jail.

Black women occasionally joined clubs dominated by whites. But most clubs excluded blacks, and so African Americans formed clubs of their own. Some of them affiliated with the General Federation, but most became part of the independent National Association of Colored Women. Some black clubs also took positions on issues of particular concern to African Americans, such as lynching and aspects of segregation.

Woman Suffrage

Perhaps the largest single reform movement of the progressive era, indeed one of the largest in American history, was the fight for woman suffrage.

It is sometimes difficult for today's Americans to understand why the suffrage issue could have become the source of such enormous controversy. But at the time, suffrage seemed to many of its critics a very radical demand. Throughout the late nineteenth century, many suffrage advocates argued that "natural rights" entitled them to the same rights as men—including, first and foremost, the right to vote. Elizabeth Cady Stanton, for example, wrote in 1892 of woman as "the arbiter of her own destiny . . . if we are to consider her as a citizen, as a member of a great nation, she must have the same rights as all other members." This was an argument that challenged the views of the many men and women who believed that society required a distinctive female "sphere," in which women would serve first and foremost as wives and mothers. And so a powerful antisuffrage movement emerged, dominated by men but with the active support of many women.

In the first years of the twentieth century, suffragists were becoming better organized and more politically sophisticated than their opponents. Under the leadership of Anna Howard Shaw, a Boston social worker, and Carrie Chapman Catt, a journalist from Iowa, membership in the National American Woman Suffrage Association (NAWSA) grew from about 13,000 in 1893 to over 2 million in 1917. The movement gained strength because many of its most prominent leaders began to justify suffrage in "safer," less threatening ways. Suffrage, some supporters began to argue, would not challenge the "separate sphere" in which women resided. Instead, they claimed that because women occupied a distinct sphere—because as mothers and wives and homemakers they had special experiences and special sensitivities to bring to public life—woman suffrage would make an important contribution to politics.

In particular, many suffragists argued that enfranchising women would help the temperance movement, by giving its largest group of supporters a political voice. Some suffrage advocates claimed that once women had the vote, war would become a thing of the past, since women would—by their calming, maternal influence—help curb the belligerence of men.

The principal triumphs of the suffrage movement began in 1910, when Washington became the first state in fourteen years to extend suffrage to women. California followed a year later, and four other western states in 1912. In 1913, Illinois became the first state east of the Mississippi to embrace woman suffrage. And in 1917 and 1918, New York and Michigan—two of the most populous states in the Union—gave women the vote. By 1919, thirty-nine states had granted women the right to vote in at least some elections; fifteen had allowed them full participation. In 1920, finally, suffragists won ratification of the Nineteenth Amendment, which guaranteed voting rights to women throughout the nation.

To some feminists, however, the victory seemed less than complete. Alice Paul, head of the militant National Woman's Party (founded in 1916), never accepted the relatively conservative "separate sphere" justification for suffrage. She argued that the Nineteenth

Amendment alone would not be sufficient to protect women's rights. Women needed more: a constitutional amendment that would provide full, legal protection for their rights and would prohibit all discrimination on the basis of gender. But Alice Paul's argument found limited favor even among many of the most important leaders of the recently triumphant suffrage crusade.

THE ASSAULT ON THE PARTIES

Sooner or later, most progressive goals required the involvement of government. Only government, reformers agreed, could effectively counter the many powerful private interests that threatened the nation. But American government at the dawn of the new century was poorly adapted to perform progressive demands. Before progressives could reform society effectively, they would have to reform government itself. Many reformers believed the first step must be an assault on the dominant role the political parties played in the life of the state.

EARLY ATTACKS

Attacks on party dominance had been frequent in the late nineteenth century. Greenbackism and Populism, for example, had been efforts to break the hammerlock with which the Republicans and Democrats controlled public life. The Independent Republicans (or mugwumps) had attempted to challenge the grip of partisanship.

The early assaults enjoyed some success. In the 1880s and 1890s, for example, most states adopted the secret ballot. Prior to that, the political parties themselves had printed ballots (or "tickets"), with the names of the party's candidates, and no others. They distributed the tickets to their supporters, who then simply went to the polls to deposit them in the ballot boxes. The old system had made it possible for bosses to monitor the voting behavior of their constituents. The new secret ballot—printed by the government and distributed at the polls to be filled out and deposited in secret—helped chip away at the power of the parties over the voters.

MUNICIPAL REFORM

Many progressives believed the impact of party rule was most damaging in the cities. Municipal government therefore became the first target of those working for political reform. The muckrakers were especially successful in arousing public outrage at corruption and incompetence in city politics. They struck a responsive chord among a powerful group of urban middle-class progressives, who set out to destroy the power of city bosses and their entrenched political organizations.

One of the first major successes in municipal reform came in Galveston, Texas, where the old city government proved completely unable to deal with the effects of a destructive tidal wave in 1900. Capitalizing on public dismay, reformers won approval of a new city charter that replaced the mayor and council with an elected, nonpartisan commission. In 1907, Des Moines, Iowa, adopted its own version of the commission plan, and other cities soon followed.

Another approach to municipal reform was the city manager plan, by which elected officials hired an outside expert—often a professionally trained business manager or engineer—to take

TOM JOHNSON   As sentiment for municipal reform grew in intensity in the late nineteenth century, it became possible for progressive mayors committed to ending "boss rule" to win election over machine candidates in some of America's largest cities. One of the most prominent was Tom Johnson, the reform mayor of Cleveland. Johnson made a fortune in the steel and streetcar business and then entered politics, partly as a result of reading Henry George's *Poverty and Progress*. He became mayor in 1901 and in his four terms waged strenuous battles against party bosses and corporate interests. He won many fights, but he lost what he considered his most important one: the struggle for municipal ownership of public utilities. (Western Reserve Historical Society, Cleveland, Ohio)

charge of the government. The city manager would presumably remain untainted by the corrupting influence of politics. By the end of the progressive era, almost 400 cities were operating under commissions, and another 45 employed city managers.

In most urban areas, reformers had to settle for less absolute victories. Some cities made the election of mayors nonpartisan (so that the parties could not choose the candidates) or moved them to years when no presidential or congressional races were in progress (to reduce the influence of the large turnouts that party organizations produced). Reformers tried to make city councilors run at large, to limit the influence of ward leaders and district bosses. They tried to strengthen the power of the mayor at the expense of the city council, on the assumption that reformers were more likely to succeed in getting a sympathetic mayor elected than they were to win control of the entire council.

Statehouse Progressivism

Other progressives turned to state government as an agent for reform. They looked with particular scorn on state legislatures, whose ill-paid, relatively undistinguished members, they believed, were generally incompetent, often corrupt, and totally controlled by party

SOCIAL DEMOCRACY

ENORMOUS energy, enthusiasm, and organization drove the reform efforts in America in the late nineteenth and early twentieth centuries, much of it a result of social crises and political movements in the United States. But the "age of reform," as some have called it, was not an American phenomenon alone. It was part of a wave of social experimentation that was occurring throughout much of the industrial world. "Progressivism" in other countries influenced the social movements in the United States. American reform, in turn, had significant influence elsewhere as well.

Several industrializing nations adopted the term "progressivism" for their efforts—not only the United States, but also England, Germany, and France. But the term that most broadly defined the new reform energies was "social democracy." Social democrats in many countries shared a belief in the betterment of society through the accumulation of knowledge. They favored improving the social condition of all people through reforms of the economy and government programs of social protection. And they believed that these goals could be achieved through peaceful political change, rather than through radicalism or revolution. Political parties committed to

these goals emerged in several countries: the Labour Party in Britain, social democratic parties in various European nations, and the short-lived Progressive Party in the United States. Intellectuals, academics, and government officials across the world shared the knowledge they were accumulating and observed one another's social programs. American reformers at the turn of the century spent much time visiting Germany, France, Britain, Belgium, and the Netherlands, observing the reforms in progress there; and Europeans, in turn, visited the United States. Reformers from both America and Europe were also fascinated by the advanced social experiments in Australia and, especially, New Zealand—which the American reformer Henry Demarest Lloyd once called "the political brain of the modern world." But New Zealand's dramatic experiments in factory regulation, woman suffrage, old-age pensions, progressive taxation, and labor arbitration gradually found counterparts in many other nations as well. William Allen White, a progressive journalist from Kansas, said of this time: "We were parts of one another, in the United States and Europe. Something was welding us into one social and economic whole with local political variations . . . [all] fighting a common cause."

bosses. Reformers began looking for ways to circumvent the boss-controlled legislatures by increasing the power of the electorate.

Two of the most important changes were proposed by Populists in the 1890s: the initiative and the referendum. The initiative allowed reformers to circumvent state legislatures by submitting new legislation directly to the voters in general elections. The referendum provided a method by which actions of the legislature could be returned to the electorate for approval. By 1918, more than twenty states had enacted one or both of these reforms.

Social democracy—or, as it was sometimes called in the United States and elsewhere, social justice or the social gospel—was responsible for many public programs. Germany began a system of social insurance for its citizens in the 1880s while simultaneously undertaking a massive study of society that produced over 140 volumes of "social investigation" of almost every aspect of the nation's life. French reformers pressed in the 1890s for factory regulation, assistance to the elderly, and progressive taxation. Britain pioneered the settlement houses in working-class areas of London—a movement that soon spread to the United States—and, like the United States, witnessed growing challenges to the power of monopolies at both the local and national levels.

In many countries, social democrats felt pressure from the rising worldwide labor movement and from the rise of socialist parties in many industrial countries as well. Strikes, sometimes violent, were common in France, Germany, Britain, and the United States in the late nineteenth century. The more militant workers became, the more unions seemed to grow. Social democrats did not always welcome the rise of militant labor movements, but they took them seriously and used them to support their own efforts at reform.

The politics of social democracy represented a great shift in the character of public life all over the industrial world. Instead of battles over the privileges of aristocrats or the power of monarchs, reformers now focused on the social problems of ordinary people and attempted to improve their lot.

FIGARO ILLUSTRÉ

(Archives Charmet/Bridgeman Art Library)

"The politics of the future are social politics," the British reformer Joseph Chamberlain said in the 1880s, referring to efforts to deal with the problems of ordinary citizens. That belief was fueling progressive efforts across the world in the years that Americans have come to call the "progressive era." •

UNDERSTAND, ANALYZE, & EVALUATE

1. What is social democracy? How does it differ from socialism?
2. What progressive era reforms in American social and political life can be seen in other nations as well?

The direct primary and the recall were other efforts to limit the power of party and improve the quality of elected officials. The primary election was an attempt to remove the selection of candidates from the bosses and give it to the people. In the South, it was also an effort to limit black voting—since primary voting, many white southerners believed, would be easier to control than general elections. The recall gave voters the right to remove a public official from office at a special election, which could be called after a sufficient number of citizens had signed a petition. By 1915, every state in the nation had instituted

CONSIDER THE SOURCE

KATHERINE PHILIPS EDSON BOASTS OF WOMEN'S INFLUENCE ON STATE LEGISLATION, 1913

NOW, what was woman's particular influence upon legislation? Women are supposed to have a moral influence on legislation. I know that is expected of us, and I think we made good. The bill we women were supposed to be greatly interested in, and in which we were, is the red-light abatement act. . . .

This measure is very revolutionary, but I think that it is an experiment worth the trial. Speaking about the influence of the women particularly when the time came to get that bill out of committee, all the committeemen were besieged with thousands of letters. It was done by the women of the W. C. T. U. [Women's Christian Temperance Union]—and they deserve credit for it because it was well done. When the time came for voting, I don't think any legislator had less than five hundred letters from constituents saying he had to vote for it. It was pitiable to see men get up and say, "I am entirely out of harmony with this bill, but my constituents say they wish me to do so, and therefore I vote aye." . . .

We have lots of law on the subject of prostitution . . . but this is . . . the first time in the history of the world that the punishment for prostitution has been taken away from the woman and put on property, and for that reason we think it is worth the trial.

Before I attended this session of the legislature, I never realized how strongly men felt on this question. The discussion on this and the health certificate for marriage brought it out, and when the question arose of making the age of consent eighteen instead of sixteen, the discussion was behind closed doors. The wives of some of the Senators and Assemblymen told us the discussion was positively unfit for us to hear.

Which all goes to show that what Bernard Shaw said is true, that many men are afraid of votes for women because they know that if women get power they will impose on men the same standards of sexual morality that men have imposed on women. Now, that is just exactly what we are going to do. If those standards are wrong for men, they are wrong for women. I don't know any better way to find out which is right than by enforcing the same standard for both.

The age of consent was raised to eighteen years and we have equal guardianship of our own children. We women have been fighting for that ten years and could not get it, and yet at this session there was not a man who voted against it. . . .

The bills of largest interest to me were those of great industrial importance: the minimum wage law, the extension of the eight hour law and many of the industrial bills having to do with the sanitation of work shops. My interest in those has been developed by my work in the Bureau of Labor.

The minimum wage legislation we feel proud of, and we believe we have the best bill in the United States. We have a law which is very advanced, from the economic standpoint. It gives the wage commission power, after an investigation lasting about a year, to fix wages if it deems it necessary. This commission may call into existence wage boards of employees and employers who may recommend to the commission standards of work, hours of work and the amount of the minimum wage. However, the commission is not under obligations to accept these. The commission itself has the fixing of the wages. The whole thing is, we have a flexible law in California that will give us an opportunity to go into a careful experiment and see if it is or is not the proper thing. . . .

We have been criticised because we have been anxious to extend the eight hour law. The only extensions made were apartment houses, public lodging houses and places of amusement, and student nurses in hospitals; and upon that part of the bill the battle raged. It was one of the most interesting fights in the whole session. The hospitals were there in force with their very powerful lobby. The women who were to be protected by the law, of course, could not have a lobby, and their work was carried on by Mr. Beach, of San Francisco, who did perfectly splendid work in presenting to the legislators their position.

I don't believe there is any class of women that need protection more than the student nurses. I know there have not been so many complaints brought to the Bureau of Labor from any other place as have come to me from the hospitals. I don't mean from the girls themselves, but the people who are in the hospitals. Patients have written me letters and telephoned me and come to me and complained of the lack of efficient care these girls have received and the long hours and overwork demanded of them. That being the case, it seems to me they should be given the protection of the law, just as women in the stores and places of that kind.

There was a great deal of hubbub about the "professional standing" of nurses. It was going to put them in the same class as labor unions. That is the sort of argument used against this bill. My only answer to that is this—that the young women who go into the nursing profession are the very finest we have. They are girls who have instilled in them the spirit of self-sacrifice; but that is no reason why they should be sacrificed. . . .

Then the cotton mills of Oakland made a hard fight on it. . . . I believe the cotton industry in Imperial is growing very rapidly, and it can't grow, it seems, unless women have longer hours. . . . [W]e asked why they did not run two eight hour shifts, if their machinery was so expensive that they would lose too much on their investment if they did not run longer, and they said they were working two shifts of fifteen hours-altogether fifteen hours and a half-and nobody understood why they didn't pay them the sixteen hours. Then, all of a sudden, it occurred to me. They said: "We don't work after 10 o'clock at night." I asked them: 'Is the reason because the majority of your employees are minors'; and they said: "Yes, madam, that is the reason." That means child labor and that is what is in the cotton mills; and we could not afford to let those children be exploited. . . .

It is by reason of such things we are interested in politics. . . .

Woman's business in politics is to keep alive the ideals and not to forget them.

UNDERSTAND, ANALYZE, & EVALUATE

1. Give some examples of laws that passed, according to Edson, thanks to women's political influence. Were these laws merely focused on the domestic sphere?
2. What seemed to distinguish women from men in their conduct of politics, according to Edson's examples?
3. In your view, how would Edson's political activism compare to the role of women in politics today?

Source: From Charles Farwell Edson, "Women's Influence on State Legislation," *The California Outlook,* 54, no. 24 (June 14, 1913): pp. 7–8, 19; located in: Sucheng Chan and Spencer Olin (eds.), *Major Problems in California History* (Boston: Houghton Mifflin Company, 1997), pp. 204–206.

primary elections for at least some offices. The recall encountered more strenuous opposition, but a few states (such as California) adopted it as well.

The most celebrated state-level reformer was Robert M. La Follette of Wisconsin. Elected governor in 1900, he helped turn his state into what reformers across the nation described as a "laboratory of progressivism." Under his leadership, Wisconsin progressives won approval of direct primaries, initiatives, and referendums. They regulated railroads and utilities. They passed laws to regulate the workplace and provide compensation for laborers injured on the job. They instituted graduated taxes on inherited fortunes, and they nearly doubled state levies on railroads and other corporate interests.

PARTIES AND INTEREST GROUPS

The reformers did not, of course, eliminate parties from American political life. But they did contribute to a decline in party influence. Evidence of their impact came from, among other things, the decline in voter turnout. In the late nineteenth century, up to 81 percent of eligible voters routinely turned out for national elections. In the early twentieth century, the figure declined markedly. In the presidential election of 1900, 73 percent of the electorate voted. By 1912, turnout had declined to about 59 percent. Never again has voter turnout reached as high as 70 percent.

Why did voter turnout decline in these years? The secret ballot was one reason. Party bosses had less ability to get voters to the polls. Illiterate voters had trouble reading the new ballots. Party bosses lost much of their authority and were unable to mobilize voters as successfully as they had in the past. But perhaps the most important reason for the decline of party rule (and voter turnout) was that other power centers were beginning to replace them. They have become known as "interest groups." Beginning late in the nineteenth century and accelerating rapidly in the twentieth century, new organizations emerged outside the party system: professional organizations, trade associations representing businesses and industries, labor organizations, farm lobbies, and many others. Social workers, the settlement house movements, women's clubs, and others learned to operate as interest groups to advance their demands without relying on parties.

SOURCES OF PROGRESSIVE REFORM

Middle-class reformers, most of them from the East, dominated the public image and much of the substance of progressivism in the late nineteenth and early twentieth centuries. But they were not alone in seeking to improve social conditions. Working-class Americans, African Americans, westerners, and even party bosses played crucial roles in advancing some of the important reforms of the era.

LABOR, THE MACHINE, AND REFORM

Although the American Federation of Labor, and its leader Samuel Gompers, remained largely aloof from many of the reform efforts of the time, some unions nevertheless played important roles in reform battles. Between 1911 and 1913, thanks to political pressure from labor groups such as the newly formed Union Labor Party, California passed a child labor law, a workmen's compensation law, and a limitation on working hours for women. Union pressures contributed to the passage of similar laws in many other states as well.

Party bosses sometimes allowed their machines to become vehicles of social reform. One example was New York's Tammany Hall, the nation's oldest and most notorious city machine. Its astute leader, Charles Francis Murphy, began in the early years of the twentieth century to fuse the techniques of boss rule with some of the concerns of social reformers. Tammany at times used its political power on behalf of legislation to improve working conditions, protect child laborers, and eliminate the worst abuses of the industrial economy.

In 1911, a terrible fire swept through the factory of the Triangle Shirtwaist Company in New York; 146 workers, most of them women, died. Many of them had been trapped inside the burning building because management had locked the emergency exits to prevent malingering. For the next three years, a state commission studied the disaster and the conditions of factories generally. In 1914, the commission issued a series of reports calling for major reforms in the conditions of modern labor. The report itself was a classic progressive document—based on the testimony of experts and filled with statistics and technical data. When its recommendations reached the New York legislature, its most effective supporters were two Tammany Democrats from working-class backgrounds: Senator Robert F. Wagner and Assemblyman Alfred E. Smith. With the support of Murphy and the backing of other Tammany legislators, they helped pass a series of pioneering labor laws that imposed strict regulations on factory owners and established effective mechanisms for enforcement.

WESTERN PROGRESSIVES

The American West produced some of the most notable progressive leaders of the time: Hiram Johnson of California, George Norris of Nebraska, William Borah of Idaho, and others—almost all of whom spent at least some of their political careers in the United States Senate. For western states, the most important target of reform was the federal government, which exercised a kind of authority in the West that it had never possessed in the East. Disputes over water, for example, almost always involved rivers and streams that crossed state lines. More significant, perhaps, the federal government exercised enormous power over the lands and resources of the western states and provided substantial subsidies to the region in the form of land grants and support for railroad and water projects. Huge areas of the West remained (and still remain) public lands, controlled by Washington. Much of the growth of the West was (and continues to be) a result of federally funded dams, water projects, and other infrastructure undertakings.

AFRICAN AMERICANS AND REFORM

Most white progressives paid little attention to race. But among African Americans themselves, the progressive era produced significant challenges to existing racial norms.

African Americans faced greater obstacles than any other group in seeking reform. So it was not surprising, perhaps, that so many African Americans embraced the message of Booker T. Washington in the late nineteenth century. Washington encouraged black men and women to work for immediate self-improvement rather than long-range social change. By the beginning of the twentieth century, however, a powerful challenge to the philosophy of Washington was emerging. The chief spokesman for this new approach was W. E. B. Du Bois, a sociologist and historian and one of the first African Americans to receive a degree from Harvard.

In *The Souls of Black Folk* (1903), Du Bois launched an open attack on the philosophy of Washington, accusing him of encouraging white efforts to sustain segregation and of limiting

THE CRISIS W. E. B. Du Bois founded *The Crisis*, the magazine of the NAACP, in 1910. Its object was to "show the danger of race prejudice, particularly as manifested today toward colored people." This picture shows the magazine's office. (© Underwood & Underwood/Corbis)

the aspirations of his race. Rather than content themselves with education at trade and agricultural schools, Du Bois encouraged talented blacks to accept nothing less than a full university education and aspire to the professions. They should, above all, fight for their civil rights, not simply wait for them to be granted as a reward for patient striving. In 1905, Du Bois and a group of his supporters met at Niagara Falls—on the Canadian side of the border because no hotel on the American side of the falls would have them—and launched what became known as the Niagara Movement. Four years later, they joined with sympathetic white progressives to form the National Association for the Advancement of Colored People (NAACP). In the years that followed, the new organization worked for equal rights.

Among the many issues that engaged the NAACP and other African American organizations was lynching in the South. The most determined opponents of lynching were southern women, and the most effective crusader was a black woman, Ida Wells Barnett, who worked both on her own (at great personal risk) and with such organizations as the National Association of Colored Women and the Women's Convention of the National Baptist Church to try to discredit lynching and challenge segregation.

CRUSADES FOR SOCIAL ORDER AND REFORM

Many reformers crusaded on behalf of what they considered moral issues—working to eliminate alcohol, curb prostitution, limit divorce, and restrict immigration.

THE TEMPERANCE CRUSADE

Many progressives considered the elimination of alcohol from American life a necessary step in restoring order to society. Scarce wages vanished as male workers spent hours in saloons. Drunkenness spawned violence, and occasionally murder, within urban families. Many working-class wives and mothers hoped through temperance to reform male behavior and thus improve women's lives. Employers, too, regarded alcohol as an impediment to industrial efficiency; workers often missed time on the job because of drunkenness or came to the factory intoxicated. Critics of economic privilege denounced the liquor industry as one of the nation's most sinister trusts. And political reformers, who (correctly) looked on the saloon as one of the central institutions of the urban machine, saw an attack on drinking as part of an attack on the bosses. Out of such sentiments emerged the temperance movement.

There had been a major temperance movement before the Civil War, mobilizing large numbers of people in a crusade with strong evangelical overtones. In 1873, the movement developed new strength. Temperance advocates formed the Women's Christian Temperance Union (WCTU), which was led after 1879 by Frances Willard. By 1911, it had 245,000 members and had become the single largest women's organization in American history to that point. In 1893, the Anti-Saloon League joined the temperance movement and, along with the WCTU, began to press for the legal abolition of saloons. Gradually, that demand grew to include the complete prohibition of the sale and manufacture of alcoholic beverages.

Pressure for prohibition grew steadily through the first decades of the new century. By 1916, nineteen states had passed prohibition laws. America's entry into World War I, and the moral fervor it unleashed, provided the last push to the advocates of prohibition. In 1917, with the support of rural fundamentalists who opposed alcohol on moral and religious grounds, progressive advocates of prohibition steered through Congress a constitutional amendment. Two years later, after ratification by every state in the nation except Connecticut and Rhode Island (with large populations of Catholic immigrants opposed to prohibition), the Eighteenth Amendment became law, to take effect in January 1920.

IMMIGRATION RESTRICTION

Virtually all reformers agreed that the growing immigrant population had created social problems, but there was wide disagreement on how best to respond. Some progressives believed that the proper approach was to help the new residents adapt to American society. Others argued that the only solution was to limit the flow of new arrivals.

In the first decades of the century, pressure grew to close the nation's gates. New scholarly theories argued that the introduction of immigrants into American society was polluting the nation's racial stock. Among the theories created to support this argument was eugenics. It began as the science of altering the reproductive processes of plants and animals to produce new hybrids or breeds. But in the late nineteenth century, eugenicists spread the spurious belief that human inequalities were hereditary and that immigration was contributing to the multiplication of the unfit. A special federal commission of "experts," chaired by Senator William P. Dillingham of Vermont, issued a study filled with statistics and scholarly testimony. It argued that the newer immigrant groups—largely southern and eastern Europeans—had proved themselves less assimilable than earlier immigrants. Immigration, the report implied, should be restricted by nationality. Even many people who rejected these racial arguments supported limiting immigration as a way to solve such urban problems as overcrowding, unemployment, strained social services, and social unrest.

PROGRESSIVISM

UNTIL the early 1950s, most historians seemed to agree on the central characteristics of early-twentieth-century progressivism. It was just what many progressives themselves had said it was: a movement by the "people" to curb the power of "special interests." More specifically, it was a protest by an aroused citizenry against the excessive power of urban bosses, corporate moguls, and corrupt elected officials.

In 1951, the historian George Mowry began challenging these assumptions by examining progressives in California and describing them as a small, privileged elite of business and professional figures: people who considered themselves the natural leaders of society and who were trying to recover their fading influence from the new capitalist institutions that had displaced them. Progressivism was not, in other words, a popular democratic movement but the effort of a displaced elite to restore its authority. Richard Hofstadter expanded on this idea in *The Age of Reform* (1955) by describing reformers as people afflicted by "status anxiety"—fading elites

suffering not from economic but from psychological discontent.

The Mowry-Hofstadter argument soon encountered a range of challenges. Gabriel Kolko, in *The Triumph of Conservatism* (1963), rejected both the older "democratic" view of progressivism and the newer "status-anxiety" view. Progressive reform, he argued, was not an effort to protect the people from the corporations; it was, rather, a vehicle through which corporate leaders used the government to protect themselves from competition.

A more moderate reinterpretation came from historians embracing what would later be called the "organizational" approach to twentieth-century American history. Samuel Hays, in *The Response to Industrialism* (1957), and Robert Wiebe, in *The Search for Order* (1967), portrayed progressivism as a broad effort by businessmen, professionals, and other middle-class people to bring order and efficiency to political and economic life. In the new industrial society, economic power was increasingly concentrated in large national organizations, while social

The combination of these concerns gradually won the support of some of the nation's leading progressives to limit immigration—among them former president Theodore Roosevelt. Powerful opponents—employers who saw immigration as a source of cheap labor, immigrants themselves, and their political representatives—managed to block the restriction movement for a time. But by the beginning of World War I, which itself effectively blocked immigration temporarily, the nativist tide was gaining strength.

THE DREAM OF SOCIALISM

Although never a force to rival or even seriously threaten the two major parties, the Socialist Party of America gained considerable strength during the early years of the and political life remained centered primarily in local communities. Progressivism, Wiebe argued, was the effort of a "new middle class"—a class tied to the emerging national economy—to stabilize and enhance its position in society by bringing those two worlds together.

In the 1970s and 1980s, much of the later scholarship on progressivism focused on discovering new groups among whom "progressive" ideas and efforts flourished. Historians found evidence of progressivism in the rising movement by consumers to define their interests; in the growth of reform movements among African Americans; in the changing nature of urban political machines; and in the political activism of working people and labor organizations.

Other scholars attempted to identify progressivism with broad changes in the structure and culture of politics. Richard McCormick, writing in 1981, argued that the crucial change in the progressive era was the decline of political parties and the corresponding rise of interest groups working for particular social and economic goals.

At the same time, many historians have focused on the role of women (and the vast network of voluntary associations they created in shaping and promoting progressive reform). Some progressive battles, historians such as Kathryn Sklar, Ruth Rosen, Elaine Tyler May, and Linda Gordon have argued, were part of an effort by women to protect their interests within the domestic sphere in the face of jarring challenges from the new industrial world. This protective urge drew women reformers to such issues as temperance, divorce, prostitution, and the regulation of female and child labor. Other women worked to expand their own roles in the public world, particularly through their support of suffrage. The gendered interests of women reformers are, many historians insist, critical to an understanding of progressivism.

More recently, a number of historians have sought to place progressivism in a broader context. Daniel Rodgers's *Atlantic Crossings* (1998) is an important study of how European reformers shaped the goals of many American progressives. Both Michael McGerr, in *A Fierce Discontent* (2003), and Alan Dawley, in *Changing the World* (2003), see progressivism as a fundamentally moral project—McGerr, as an effort by the middle class to create order and stability, and Dawley, as an effort by groups on the left to attack social injustice. Progressivism, they argue, was not just a political movement but an effort to remake society and reshape social relations.   •

UNDERSTAND, ANALYZE, & EVALUATE

1. What is the gendered view of progressive reform advanced by historians?
2. Was progressivism a "people's" movement?

twentieth century. In the election of 1900, it attracted the support of fewer than 100,000 voters; in 1912, its durable leader and perennial presidential candidate, Eugene V. Debs, received nearly 1 million ballots. Strongest in urban immigrant communities, particularly among Germans and Jews, it also attracted the loyalties of a substantial number of Protestant farmers in the South and the Midwest.

Virtually all socialists agreed on the need for basic structural changes in the economy, but they differed widely on the extent of those changes and the tactics necessary to achieve them. Some socialists endorsed the radical goals of European Marxists (a complete end to capitalism and private property); others envisioned more moderate reform that would allow small-scale private enterprise to survive but would nationalize major industries. Some believed in working for reform through electoral politics; others favored militant direct action. Among the militants was the radical labor union the Industrial Workers of the World (IWW), known to opponents as the "Wobblies." Under the leadership of William ("Big Bill") Haywood, the IWW advocated a single union for all workers and was one of the few labor organizations to champion the cause of unskilled workers. The Wobblies were widely believed to have been responsible for dynamiting railroad lines and power stations and committing other acts of terror in the first years of the twentieth century.

Moderate socialists who advocated peaceful change through political struggle dominated the Socialist Party. They emphasized a gradual education of the public to the need for change and patient efforts within the system to enact it. But the party refused to support the nation's war effort in World War I. The growing wave of antiradicalism during the war subjected the socialists to enormous harassment and persecution. It contributed to socialism's decline.

DECENTRALIZATION AND REGULATION

Most progressives retained faith in the possibilities of reform within a capitalist system. Rather than nationalize basic industries, many reformers hoped to restore the economy to a more human scale. They argued that the federal government should work to break up the largest combinations and enforce a balance between the need for bigness and the need for competition. This viewpoint came to be identified particularly closely with Louis D. Brandeis, a brilliant lawyer and, later, justice of the Supreme Court, who wrote widely (most notably in his 1913 book *Other People's Money*) about the "curse of bigness." Brandeis insisted that government must regulate competition in such a way as to ensure that large combinations did not emerge.

Other progressives were less enthusiastic about the virtues of competition. More important to them was efficiency. Government, they argued, should not fight "bigness" but rather should guard against abuses of power by large institutions. It should distinguish between "good trusts" and "bad trusts." Since economic consolidation was destined to remain a permanent feature of American society, continuing oversight by a strong, modernized government was essential. Thus, many progressives believed that government should play a more active role in regulating and planning economic life. One of those who came to endorse that position (although not fully until after 1910) was Theodore Roosevelt, who once said: "We should enter upon a course of supervision, control, and regulation of those great corporations." Roosevelt became, for a time, the most powerful symbol of the reform impulse at the national level.

THE CONSERVATIVE CRITIQUE OF PROGRESSIVISM

Not everyone, of course, was a champion of progressivism. Late-nineteenth- and early-twentieth-century conservatives made a case of their own that challenged the progressive tidal wave. Among them were some of the most distinguished figures of their time.

Henry Adams and Brooks Adams, brother and grandson of President John Quincy Adams, came to feel that they had no role in the rapidly changing world of the progressive era. They were hostile to the industrial and financial titans, who they believed were coarsening American life. Wealthy men through inheritance, they considered their vast riches and great power to be vulgar and dangerous. But they were equally concerned about the rapid changes in politics and society as the progressive era grew more and more powerful. Henry Adams, for example, wrote of his unhappiness with the modern society in his famous, conservative autobiography, *The Education of Henry Adams* (1907). He was a critic of the dynamic world of the early twentieth century, and he complained that the world was changing too fast. It was, he lamented, losing the greatness of the past. His brother Brooks Adams had similar complaints. "I am myself more than ever at odds with my time," he wrote. "I detest it, and everything that belongs to it, and live only in the wish to see the end of it."

Many other elite conservatives shared their view of a nation moving too quickly away from its traditions. Their love of the past included the greatness of the medieval gothic cathedrals, and they successfully worked to revive gothic architecture in the twentieth century—in churches, universities, libraries, and government buildings that mimicked the medieval world (buildings designed by the much-heralded architect Ralph Adams Cram, who was committed to reviving the great architecture of the past). The novelist Henry James, an American who as an adult lived mostly in Europe, decried the bold skyscrapers of New York. He missed "the authority of things of permanence or even of things of long duration." Even Theodore Roosevelt, a sometime champion of progressivism, was in many ways a conservative as well—in his aristocratic elitism, his hostility toward radicals, and his growing distaste for the rapidly growing population of immigrants.

Many elite conservatives of the turn of the century looked at the progress of their time and saw not a brave new world, but a kind of barbarism and immorality that was endangering a civilization that needed to be preserved.

THEODORE ROOSEVELT AND THE MODERN PRESIDENCY

To a generation of progressive reformers, Theodore Roosevelt was more than an admired public figure; he was an idol. No president before, and few since, attracted such attention and devotion. Yet for all his popularity among reformers, Roosevelt was in many respects decidedly conservative. He earned his extraordinary popularity less because of the extent of the reforms he championed than because he brought to his office a broad conception of its powers. He invested the presidency with something of its modern status as the center of national political life.

THE ACCIDENTAL PRESIDENT

When President William McKinley was assassinated in September 1901, Roosevelt, forty-two years old at the time, became the youngest man ever to assume the presidency. "I told William McKinley that it was a mistake to nominate that wild man at Philadelphia," party boss Mark Hanna was reported to have exclaimed. "Now look, that damned cowboy is President of the United States!"

As president, Roosevelt rarely openly rebelled against the leaders of his party. He became, rather, a champion of cautious, moderate change. Reform, he believed, was a vehicle less for remaking American society than for protecting it against more radical challenges.

Roosevelt allied himself with those progressives who urged regulation (but not destruction) of the trusts. At the heart of his policy was to give the government the power to investigate corporations and publicize the results.

Although Roosevelt was not a trustbuster at heart, he made a few highly publicized efforts to break up combinations. In 1902, he ordered the Justice Department to invoke the Sherman Antitrust Act against a great new railroad monopoly in the Northwest, the Northern Securities Company, a $400 million enterprise pieced together by J. P. Morgan and others. Roosevelt filed more than forty additional antitrust suits during the remainder of his presidency, but he had no serious commitment to reverse the prevailing trend toward economic concentration.

When a bitter 1902 strike by the United Mine Workers endangered coal supplies for the coming winter, Roosevelt asked both the operators and the miners to accept impartial federal arbitration. When the mine owners balked, Roosevelt threatened to send federal troops to seize the mines. The operators finally relented. Arbitrators awarded the strikers

THEODORE ROOSEVELT   This heroic portrait of Theodore Roosevelt, by the great American portraitist John Singer Sargent, hangs today in the White House. (White House Historical Association [White House Collection], 56)

a 10 percent wage increase and a nine-hour day, although no recognition of their union—less than the miners had wanted but more than they would likely have won without Roosevelt's intervention.

THE "SQUARE DEAL"

During the 1904 campaign for the presidency, Roosevelt boasted that he had worked in the anthracite coal strike to provide everyone with a "square deal." One of his first targets after winning the election was the powerful railroad industry. The Interstate Commerce Act of 1887, establishing the Interstate Commerce Commission (ICC), had been an early effort to regulate the industry, but over the years, the courts had sharply limited its influence. The Hepburn Railroad Regulation Act of 1906 sought to restore some regulatory authority to the government by giving the ICC the power to oversee railroad rates.

Roosevelt also pressured Congress to enact the Pure Food and Drug Act, which restricted the sale of dangerous or ineffective medicines. *The Jungle*, a powerful novel published by Upton Sinclair in 1906, included appalling descriptions of conditions in the meatpacking industry. Roosevelt pushed for passage of the Meat Inspection Act, which helped eliminate many diseases once transmitted in impure meat. Starting in 1907, he proposed even more stringent reforms: an eight-hour day for workers, broader compensation for victims of industrial accidents, inheritance and income taxes, and regulation of the stock market. Conservative opposition blocked much of his agenda, widening the gulf between the president and the conservative wing of his party.

BOYS IN THE MINES These young boys, covered in grime and no more than twelve years old, pose for the noted photographer Lewis Hine outside the coal mine in Pennsylvania where they worked as "breaker boys," crawling into newly blasted areas and breaking up the loose coal. The rugged conditions in the mines were one cause of the great strike of 1902, in which Theodore Roosevelt intervened. (Library of Congress)

ROOSEVELT AND THE ENVIRONMENT

Roosevelt's aggressive policies on behalf of conservation contributed to that gulf. Using executive powers, he restricted private development on millions of acres of undeveloped government land—most of it in the West—by adding them to the previously modest national forest system. When conservatives in Congress restricted his authority over public lands in 1907, Roosevelt and his chief forester, Gifford Pinchot, seized all the forests and many of the water power sites still in the public domain before the bill became law.

Roosevelt was the first president to take an active interest in the new and struggling American conservation movement. In the early twentieth century, many people who considered themselves "conservationists"—including Pinchot, the first director of the U.S. Forest Service (which he helped to create)—promoted policies to protect land for carefully managed development.

The Old Guard eagerly supported another important aspect of Roosevelt's natural resource policy: public reclamation and irrigation projects. In 1902, the president backed the National Reclamation Act, which provided federal funds for the construction of dams, reservoirs, and canals in the West—projects that would open new lands for cultivation and (years later) provide cheap electric power.

Despite his sympathy with Pinchot's vision of conservation, Roosevelt also shared some of the concerns of the naturalists—those committed to protecting the natural beauty of the land and the health of its wildlife from human intrusion. Early in his presidency, Roosevelt spent four days camping in the Sierras with John Muir, the nation's leading preservationist and the founder of the Sierra Club. Roosevelt also added significantly to the still-young National Park System, whose purpose was to protect public land from exploitation or development.

The contending views of the early conservation movement came to a head beginning in 1906 in a controversy over the Hetch Hetchy Valley in Yosemite National Park—a spectacular high-walled valley popular with naturalists. But many residents of San Francisco worried about finding enough water to serve their growing population. They saw Hetch Hetchy as an ideal place for a dam, which would create a large reservoir for the city.

In 1906, San Francisco suffered a devastating earthquake and fire. Widespread sympathy for the city strengthened the case for the dam, and Roosevelt turned the decision over to Pinchot, who approved its construction.

For over a decade, a battle raged between naturalists and the advocates of the dam, a battle that consumed the energies of John Muir for the rest of his life and that eventually, many believed, led him to an early death. To Pinchot, the needs of the city were more important than the claims of preservation. Muir helped place a referendum question on the ballot in 1908, certain that the residents of the city would oppose the project. Instead, San Franciscans approved the dam by a huge margin. Construction of the dam finally began after World War I.

This setback for the naturalists was not, however, a total defeat. The fight against Hetch Hetchy helped mobilize a new coalition of people committed to preservation of wilderness.

PANIC AND RETIREMENT

Despite the flurry of reforms Roosevelt was able to enact, the government still had relatively little control over the industrial economy. That became clear in 1907, when a serious panic and recession began. Conservatives blamed Roosevelt's "mad" economic policies for the disaster. And while the president naturally (and correctly) disagreed, he nevertheless acted quickly to reassure business leaders that he would not interfere with their recovery efforts.

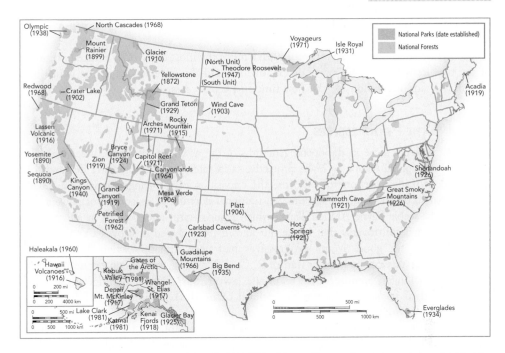

ESTABLISHMENT OF NATIONAL PARKS AND FORESTS   This map illustrates the steady growth throughout the late nineteenth and twentieth centuries of the systems of national parks and national forests in the United States. Although Theodore Roosevelt is widely and correctly remembered as a great champion of national parks and forests, the greatest expansions of these systems occurred after his presidency. Note, for example, how many new areas were added in the 1920s. • *What is the difference between national parks and national forests?*

The financier J. P. Morgan helped construct a pool of the assets of several important New York banks to prop up shaky financial institutions. The key to the arrangement, Morgan told the president, was a purchase by U.S. Steel of the shares of the Tennessee Coal and Iron Company, currently held by a threatened New York bank. Morgan insisted that he needed assurances that the purchase would not prompt antitrust action. Roosevelt tacitly agreed, and the Morgan plan proceeded. Whether or not as a result, the panic soon subsided.

Roosevelt loved being president, and many people assumed that he would run for reelection in 1908, despite the long-standing tradition of presidents serving no more than two terms. But the Panic of 1907 and Roosevelt's reform efforts so alienated conservatives in his own party that he might have had difficulty winning the Republican nomination. In 1904, moreover, he had made a public promise to step down four years later. And so in 1909, Roosevelt, fifty years old, retired from public life—briefly.

THE TROUBLED SUCCESSION

William Howard Taft, who assumed the presidency in 1909, had been Theodore Roosevelt's most trusted lieutenant and his hand-picked successor; progressive reformers believed him to be one of their own. But Taft was also a restrained and moderate jurist, a man with a punctilious regard for legal process; conservatives expected him to abandon Roosevelt's aggressive use of presidential powers. By seeming acceptable to almost everyone, Taft easily won election to the White House in 1908 over William Jennings Bryan, running for the Democrats for the third time.

Four years later, however, Taft would leave office the most decisively defeated president of the twentieth century, his party deeply divided and the government in the hands of a Democratic administration for the first time in twenty years.

TAFT AND THE PROGRESSIVES

Taft's first problem arose in the opening months of the new administration, when he called Congress into special session to lower protective tariff rates, an old progressive demand. But the president made no effort to overcome the opposition of the congressional Old Guard, arguing that to do so would violate the constitutional doctrine of separation of powers. The result was the feeble Payne-Aldrich Tariff, which reduced tariff rates scarcely at all.

A sensational controversy that broke out late in 1909 helped destroy Taft's popularity with reformers for good. Many progressives had been unhappy when Taft replaced Roosevelt's secretary of the interior, James R. Garfield, an aggressive conservationist, with Richard A. Ballinger, a conservative corporate lawyer. Suspicion of Ballinger grew when he attempted to invalidate Roosevelt's removal of nearly 1 million acres of forests and mineral reserves from private development.

In the midst of this mounting concern, Louis Glavis, an Interior Department investigator, charged Ballinger with having once connived to turn over valuable public coal lands in Alaska to a private syndicate for personal profit. Glavis took the evidence to Gifford Pinchot, still head of the U.S. Forest Service and a critic of Ballinger's policies. Pinchot took the charges to the president. Taft investigated them and decided they were groundless. Unsatisfied, Pinchot leaked the story to the press and asked Congress to investigate the scandal. The president discharged him for insubordination, and the congressional committee appointed to study the controversy, dominated by Old Guard Republicans, exonerated Ballinger. But progressives throughout the country supported Pinchot. The controversy aroused as much public passion as any dispute of its time. By the time it was over, Taft had alienated the supporters of Roosevelt completely—and, it seemed, irrevocably.

THE RETURN OF ROOSEVELT

During most of these controversies, Theodore Roosevelt was far away: on a long hunting safari in Africa and an extended tour of Europe. To the American public, however, Roosevelt remained a formidable presence. His return to New York in the spring of 1910 was a major public event. Roosevelt insisted that he had no plans to reenter politics, but within a month he announced that he would embark on a national speaking tour before the end of the summer. Furious with Taft, he was becoming convinced that he alone was capable of reuniting the Republican Party.

The real signal of Roosevelt's decision to assume leadership of Republican reformers came in a speech he gave on September 1, 1910, in Osawatomie, Kansas. In it he outlined a set of principles, which he labeled the "New Nationalism," that made clear he had moved a considerable way from the cautious conservatism of the years of his presidency. He argued that social justice was possible only through a strong federal government whose executive acted as the "steward of the public welfare." He supported graduated income and inheritance taxes, workers' compensation for industrial accidents, regulation of the labor of women and children, tariff revision, and firmer regulation of corporations.

SPREADING INSURGENCY

The congressional elections of 1910 provided further evidence of how far the progressive revolt had spread. In primary elections, conservative Republicans suffered defeat after defeat, while almost all the progressive incumbents were reelected. In the general election, the Democrats won control of the House of Representatives for the first time in sixteen years and gained strength in the Senate. But Roosevelt still denied any presidential ambitions and claimed that his real purpose was to pressure Taft to return to progressive policies. Two events, however, changed his mind. The first, on October 27, 1911, was the announcement by the administration of a suit against U.S. Steel, which charged, among other things, that the 1907 acquisition of the Tennessee Coal and Iron Company had been illegal. Roosevelt had approved that acquisition in the midst of the 1907 panic, and he was enraged by the implication that he had acted improperly.

Roosevelt was still reluctant to become a candidate for president because Senator Robert La Follette, the great Wisconsin progressive, had been working since 1911 to secure the presidential nomination for himself. But La Follette's candidacy stumbled in February 1912 when, exhausted and distraught over the illness of a daughter, he appeared to suffer a nervous breakdown during a speech in Philadelphia. Roosevelt announced his candidacy on February 22.

ROOSEVELT VERSUS TAFT

For all practical purposes, the campaign for the Republican nomination had now become a battle between Roosevelt and Taft. Roosevelt scored overwhelming victories in all thirteen presidential primaries. Taft, however, remained the choice of most party leaders, who controlled the nominating process.

The battle for the nomination at the Chicago convention revolved around an unusually large number of contested delegates: 254 in all. Roosevelt needed fewer than half the disputed seats to clinch the nomination. But the Republican National Committee, controlled by the Old Guard, awarded all but 19 of them to Taft. At a rally the night before the convention opened, Roosevelt addressed 5,000 cheering supporters. "We stand at Armageddon," he told the roaring crowd, "and we battle for the Lord." The next day, he led his supporters out of the convention, and out of the party. The convention then quietly nominated Taft on the first ballot.

Roosevelt summoned his supporters back to Chicago in August for another convention, this one to launch the new Progressive Party and to nominate himself as its presidential candidate. Roosevelt approached the battle feeling, as he put it, "fit as a bull moose" (thus giving his new party an enduring nickname). But Roosevelt was also aware that his cause was almost hopeless, partly because many of the insurgents who had supported him during the primaries refused to follow him out of the Republican Party. It was also because of the man the Democrats had nominated for president.

WOODROW WILSON AND THE NEW FREEDOM

The 1912 presidential contest was not simply one between conservatives and reformers. It was also one between two brands of progressivism. And it matched the two most important national leaders of the early twentieth century in an unequal contest.

WOODROW WILSON   Woodrow Wilson, the 28th President of the United States, was a Virginian (the first southerner to be elected president since before the Civil War), a professor of political science and later president of Princeton University, governor of New Jersey, and known as a brilliant progressive. His election to the presidency brought the first Democrat to the White House since 1896. (The Granger Collection, NYC)

WOODROW WILSON

Reform sentiment had been gaining strength within the Democratic Party as well as the Republican Party in the first years of the century. At the June 1912 Democratic Convention in Baltimore, Champ Clark, the conservative Speaker of the House, was unable to assemble the two-thirds majority necessary for nomination because of progressive opposition. Finally, on the forty-sixth ballot, Woodrow Wilson, the governor of New Jersey and the only genuinely progressive candidate in the race, emerged as the party's nominee.

Wilson had been a professor of political science at Princeton until 1902, when he was named president of the university. Elected governor of New Jersey in 1910, he quickly earned a national reputation for winning passage of progressive legislation. As a presidential candidate in 1912, Wilson presented a progressive program that came to be called the "New Freedom." Roosevelt's New Nationalism supported economic concentration and using government to regulate and control it. Wilson seemed to side with those who (like Louis Brandeis) believed that bigness was both unjust and inefficient, that the proper response to monopoly was not to regulate it but to destroy it.

The 1912 presidential campaign was an anticlimax. Taft, resigned to defeat, barely campaigned. Roosevelt campaigned energetically (until a gunshot wound from a would-be assassin forced him to the sidelines during the last weeks before the election), but he failed to draw any significant number of Democratic progressives away from Wilson. In November, Roosevelt and Taft split the Republican vote; Wilson held on to most

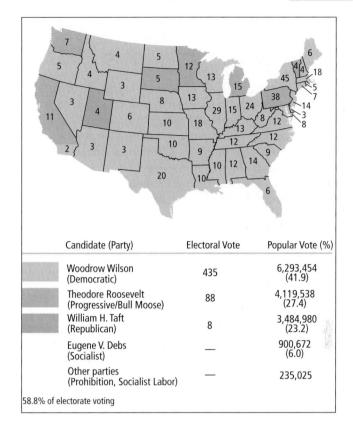

Candidate (Party)	Electoral Vote	Popular Vote (%)
Woodrow Wilson (Democratic)	435	6,293,454 (41.9)
Theodore Roosevelt (Progressive/Bull Moose)	88	4,119,538 (27.4)
William H. Taft (Republican)	8	3,484,980 (23.2)
Eugene V. Debs (Socialist)	—	900,672 (6.0)
Other parties (Prohibition, Socialist Labor)	—	235,025

58.8% of electorate voting

THE ELECTION OF 1912   The election of 1912 was one of the most unusual in American history because of the dramatic schism within the Republican Party. Two Republican presidents—William Howard Taft, the incumbent, and Theodore Roosevelt, his predecessor—ran against each other, opening the way for a victory by the Democratic candidate, Woodrow Wilson, who won with only 42 percent of the popular vote. A fourth candidate, the socialist Eugene V. Debs, received a significant 6 percent of the vote. • *What events caused the schism between Taft and Roosevelt?*

Democrats and won. He received only 42 percent of the popular vote, compared with 27 percent for Roosevelt, 23 percent for Taft, and 6 percent for the socialist Eugene Debs. But in the electoral college, Wilson won 435 of the 531 votes.

THE SCHOLAR AS PRESIDENT

Wilson was a bold and forceful president. He exerted firm control over his cabinet, and he delegated real authority only to those who were loyal to him. His most powerful adviser, Colonel Edward M. House, was an intelligent and ambitious Texan who held no office and whose only claim to authority was his personal intimacy with the president.

In legislative matters, Wilson skillfully welded together a coalition that would support his goals. Democratic majorities in both houses of Congress made his task easier. Wilson's first triumph as president was the fulfillment of an old Democratic (and progressive) goal: a substantial lowering of the protective tariff. The Underwood-Simmons Tariff provided cuts significant enough, progressives believed, to introduce real competition into American markets and thus to help break the power of trusts. To make up for the loss of revenue under the new tariff, Congress approved a graduated income tax, which the recently adopted Sixteenth Amendment to the Constitution now permitted. This first modern income tax imposed a 1 percent tax on individuals and corporations earning more than $4,000 a year, with rates ranging up to 6 percent on incomes over $500,000 annually.

Wilson held Congress in session through the summer to work on a major reform of the American banking system: the Federal Reserve Act, which Congress passed and the president signed on December 23, 1913. It created twelve regional banks, each to be owned and controlled by the individual banks of its district. The regional Federal Reserve banks would hold a certain percentage of the assets of their member banks in reserve; they would use those reserves to support loans to private banks at an interest (or "discount") rate that the Federal Reserve system would set; they would issue a new type of paper currency— Federal Reserve notes—that would become the nation's basic medium of trade and would be backed by the government. Most important, they would be able to shift funds quickly to troubled areas—to meet increased demands for credit or to protect imperiled banks. Supervising and regulating the entire system was a national Federal Reserve Board, whose members were appointed by the president.

In 1914, turning to the central issue of his 1912 campaign, Wilson proposed two measures to deal with the problem of monopoly, which took shape as the Federal Trade Commission Act and the Clayton Antitrust Act. The Federal Trade Commission Act created a regulatory agency that would help businesses determine in advance whether their actions would be acceptable to the government. The agency would also have authority to launch prosecutions against "unfair trade practices," and it would have wide power to investigate corporate behavior. Wilson signed the Federal Trade Commission Bill happily, but he seemed to lose interest in the Clayton Antitrust Bill, which proposed stronger measures to break up trusts. Wilson did little to protect it from conservative assaults, which greatly weakened it.

Retreat and Advance

By the fall of 1914, Wilson believed that the New Freedom program was essentially complete and that agitation for reform would now subside. He refused to support the movement for national woman suffrage. Deferring to southern Democrats, he condoned the reimposition of segregation in the agencies of the federal government (in contrast to Roosevelt, who had ordered the elimination of many such barriers). When congressional progressives attempted to enlist his support for new reform legislation, Wilson dismissed their proposals as unconstitutional or unnecessary.

The congressional elections of 1914, however, shattered the president's complacency. Democrats suffered major losses in Congress, and voters who in 1912 had supported the Progressive Party began returning to the Republicans. Wilson realized he would not be able to rely on a divided opposition when he ran for reelection in 1916. By the end of 1915, therefore, Wilson had begun to support a second flurry of reforms. In January 1916, he appointed Louis Brandeis to the Supreme Court, making him not only the first Jew but also the most advanced progressive to serve there. Later, he supported a measure to make it easier for farmers to receive credit, and another measure creating a system of workers' compensation for federal employees.

In 1916, Wilson supported the Keating-Owen Act, which prohibited the shipment of goods produced by underage children across state lines, thus giving an expanded importance to the constitutional clause assigning Congress the task of regulating interstate commerce. The president similarly supported measures that used federal taxing authority as a vehicle for legislating social change. After the Court struck down Keating-Owen, a new law attempted to achieve the same goal by imposing a heavy tax on the products of child labor. (The Court later struck down that law too.) The Smith-Lever Act of 1914 offered matching federal grants to support agricultural extension education. Over time, these innovative uses of government overcame most of the constitutional objections and became the foundation of a long-term growth in federal power over the economy.

CONCLUSION

The powerful surge of reform efforts in the last years of the nineteenth century and the first years of the twentieth century caused many Americans to identify themselves as "progressives." That label meant many different things to many different people, but at its core was a belief that human effort and government action could improve society. By the early twentieth century, progressivism had become a powerful, transformative force in American life.

This great surge of reform eventually reached the federal government and national politics, as progressives came to believe that success required the engagement of the federal government. Two national leaders, Theodore Roosevelt and Woodrow Wilson, contributed to a period of national reform that made the government in Washington a great center of power for the first time since the Civil War—a position it has never relinquished. Progressivism did not solve the nation's problems, but it gave movements, organizations, and governments new tools to deal with them.

RECALL AND REFLECT

1. What "moral" crusades did progressives undertake in their efforts to reform the social order?
2. How did W. E. B. Dubois's philosophy on race relations differ from that of Booker T. Washington?
3. What were some of the approaches progressives used to challenge the power and influence of capitalist corporate America?
4. What was the difference between Theodore Roosevelt's "New Nationalism" and Woodrow Wilson's "New Freedom"?

21 | AMERICA AND THE GREAT WAR

THE "BIG STICK": AMERICA AND THE WORLD,
   1901–1917
THE ROAD TO WAR
"WAR WITHOUT STINT"
THE SEARCH FOR A NEW WORLD ORDER
A SOCIETY IN TURMOIL

LOOKING AHEAD

1. What were the most important events that led up to the United States declaring war on Germany?
2. How did U.S. participation in the Great War affect the nation's economy and society, both during the war and after the conflict ended?
3. Why did the Great War fail to become the "war to end all wars"?

THE "GREAT WAR," AS IT was known to a generation unaware that another, greater war would soon follow, began quietly in August 1914 when Austria-Hungary invaded the tiny Balkan nation of Serbia. Within weeks, however, the conflict had grown into a conflagration engaging the armies of most of the major nations of Europe. Americans looked on with horror as the war became what many people claimed was the most savage in history. It dragged on, murderously and inconclusively, for over four years. Most Americans also believed at first that the conflict had little to do with them. They were wrong. After nearly three years of attempting to affect the outcome of the conflict without becoming embroiled in it, the United States formally entered the war in April 1917.

THE "BIG STICK": AMERICA AND THE WORLD, 1901–1917

To most of the American public, foreign affairs remained largely remote in the early twentieth century. But to Theodore Roosevelt and later presidents, that remoteness made foreign affairs appealing. Overseas, the president could act with less regard for Congress and the courts. The president could act unfettered and alone.

Roosevelt and "Civilization"

Theodore Roosevelt believed in using American power in the world (a conviction he once alluded to by citing the proverb, "Speak softly, and carry a big stick"). But he had two different standards for using that power.

Roosevelt believed that an important distinction existed between the "civilized" and "uncivilized" nations of the world. "Civilized" nations, as he defined them, were predominantly white and Anglo-Saxon or Teutonic; "uncivilized" nations were generally nonwhite, Latin, or Slavic. Civilized nations were also, by Roosevelt's definition, producers of industrial goods. Uncivilized nations were suppliers of raw materials and markets for industrial products. Roosevelt believed that a civilized society had the right and duty to intervene in the affairs of "backward nations" to preserve order and stability—for the sake of both nations. That belief, the obligation of a "civilized" nation to, in effect, police the world, was one important reason for Roosevelt's early support of the development of American sea power. By 1906, the American navy had attained a size and strength surpassed only by that of Great Britain.

TIME LINE

1914
World War I begins
Panama Canal opened

1915
U.S. troops in Haiti
Lusitania torpedoed
Wilson supports preparedness

1916
Wilson reelected
U.S. troops in Mexico

1917
German unrestricted submarine warfare
U.S. enters World War I
Selective Service Act
War Industries Board created

1918
Sedition Act
Wilson's Fourteen Points
Armistice ends war
Paris Peace Conference

1919
Senate rejects Treaty of Versailles
Race riots in Chicago and other cities
Steel strike and other labor actions

1920
Palmer raids and Red Scare
Harding elected president

1927
Sacco and Vanzetti executed

PROTECTING THE "OPEN DOOR" IN ASIA

In 1904, the Japanese staged a surprise attack on the Russian fleet at Port Arthur in southern Manchuria, a province of China that both Russia and Japan hoped to control. Roosevelt, hoping to prevent either nation from becoming dominant there, agreed to mediate an end to the conflict. Russia, faring badly in the war, had no choice but to agree. At a peace conference in Portsmouth, New Hampshire, in 1905, Roosevelt pressured the embattled Russians to accept Japan's territorial gains. The Japanese agreed to cease the fighting and expand no farther. At the same time, Roosevelt negotiated a secret agreement with the Japanese to ensure that the United States could continue to trade freely in the region. Roosevelt received the Nobel Peace Prize for his mediation of what became the Treaty of Portsmouth.

In the years that followed, relations between the United States and Japan steadily deteriorated. Japan, by then the preeminent naval power in the Pacific, began to exclude American trade from many of the territories it controlled. Roosevelt took no direct action against Japan, but to be sure the Japanese government recognized the power of the United States, he sent sixteen battleships of the new American navy (known as the "Great White Fleet" because the ships were temporarily painted white for the voyage) on an unprecedented journey around the world that included a call on Japan.

THE IRON-FISTED NEIGHBOR

Roosevelt took a particular interest in Latin America. Embarking on a series of ventures in the Caribbean and South America, he established a pattern of American intervention in the region that would long survive his presidency.

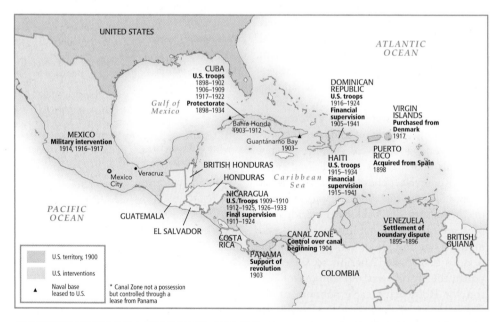

THE UNITED STATES AND LATIN AMERICA, 1895-1941 Except for Puerto Rico, the Virgin Islands, and the Canal Zone, the United States had no formal possessions in Latin America and the Caribbean in the late nineteenth century and the first half of the twentieth. But as this map reveals, the United States exercised considerable influence—both political and economic, augmented at times by military intervention—in these regions throughout this period. Note the particularly intrusive presence of the United States in the affairs of Cuba, Haiti, and the Dominican Republic—as well as the canal-related interventions in Colombia and Panama. • *What were some of the most frequent reasons for American intervention in Latin America?*

In 1902, the government of Venezuela began to renege on debts to European bankers. Naval forces of Britain, Italy, and Germany blockaded the Venezuelan coast in response. Then German ships began to bombard a Venezuelan port. Amid rumors that Germany planned to establish a permanent base in the region, Roosevelt used the threat of American naval power to pressure the German navy to withdraw.

The incident helped persuade Roosevelt that European intrusions into Latin America could result not only from aggression but also from instability or irresponsibility (such as defaulting on debts) within the Latin American nations themselves. As a result, in 1904 he announced what came to be known as the "Roosevelt Corollary" to the Monroe Doctrine. The United States, he claimed, had the right not only to oppose European intervention in the Western Hemisphere but also to intervene in the domestic affairs of its neighbors if those neighbors proved unable to maintain order and national sovereignty on their own.

The immediate motivation for the Roosevelt Corollary, and the first opportunity for using it, was a crisis in the Dominican Republic. A revolution had toppled its corrupt and bankrupt government in 1903, but the new regime proved no better able than the old to make good on the country's $22 million debts to European nations. Using the rationale provided by the Roosevelt Corollary, Roosevelt established, in effect, an American receivership, assuming control of Dominican customs and distributing 45 percent of the revenues to the Dominicans and the rest to foreign creditors. This arrangement lasted, in one form or another, for more than three decades.

THE PANAMA CANAL

The most celebrated foreign policy accomplishment of Roosevelt's presidency was the construction of the Panama Canal, which linked the Atlantic and the Pacific by creating a channel through Central America. At first, Roosevelt and many others favored a route across Nicaragua, which would permit a sea-level canal requiring no locks. But they soon turned instead to the narrow Isthmus of Panama (presently part of Colombia), the site of an earlier failed effort by a French company to construct a channel. Although the Panama route was not at sea level, it was shorter than the one in Nicaragua, and construction was already about 40 percent complete.

Roosevelt dispatched John Hay, his secretary of state, to negotiate an agreement with Colombian diplomats that would allow construction to begin without delay. Under heavy American pressure, the Colombian chargé d'affaires, Tomas Herrán, unwisely signed an agreement giving the United States perpetual rights to a six-mile-wide "Canal Zone" across Colombia; in return, the United States would pay Colombia $10 million and an annual rental of $250,000. The outraged Colombian senate refused to ratify the treaty. Colombia then sent a new representative to Washington with instructions to demand at least $20 million from the Americans plus a share of the payment to the French.

Roosevelt was furious and began to look for ways to circumvent the Colombian government. Philippe Bunau-Varilla, chief engineer of the French canal project, was a ready ally. In 1903, with the support of the United States, he helped organize and finance a revolution in Panama. Roosevelt landed troops from the U.S.S. *Nashville* there to "maintain order." Their presence prevented Colombian forces from suppressing the rebellion, and three days later Roosevelt recognized Panama as an independent nation. The new Panamanian government quickly agreed to the terms the Colombian senate had rejected. Work on the canal proceeded rapidly, and it opened in 1914.

OPENING THE PANAMA CANAL   The great Miraflores locks of the Panama Canal open in October 1914 to admit the first ship to pass through the channel. The construction of the canal was one of the great engineering feats of the early twentieth century. But the heavy-handed political efforts of Theodore Roosevelt were at least equally important to its completion. (© Corbis)

TAFT AND "DOLLAR DIPLOMACY"

Like his predecessor, William Howard Taft worked to advance the nation's economic interests in Latin America. But he showed little interest in Roosevelt's larger vision of world stability. Instead, Taft's secretary of state, Philander C. Knox, worked aggressively to extend American investments into less-developed regions. Critics called his policies "Dollar Diplomacy."

The policy was particularly visible in the Caribbean. When a revolution broke out in Nicaragua in 1909, the administration quickly sided with the insurgents and sent American troops into the country to seize the customs houses. As soon as peace was restored, Knox encouraged American bankers to offer substantial loans to the new government, thus increasing Washington's financial leverage over the country. When the new pro-American government faced an insurrection less than two years later, Taft again landed American troops in Nicaragua, this time to protect the existing regime. The troops remained there for more than a decade.

DIPLOMACY AND MORALITY

Woodrow Wilson entered the presidency with relatively little interest or experience in international affairs. Yet he faced international challenges of a scope and gravity unmatched by those of any president before him. In many respects, he continued—and even strengthened—the Roosevelt-Taft approach to foreign policy.

Having already seized control of the finances of the Dominican Republic in 1905, the United States established a military government there in 1916. The military occupation lasted eight years. In Haiti, Wilson landed marines in 1915 to quell a revolution during which a mob had murdered an unpopular president. American military forces remained in the country until 1934, and American officers drafted the new Haitian constitution adopted in 1918. When Wilson began to fear that the Danish West Indies might be about to fall into the hands of Germany, he bought the colony from Denmark and renamed it the Virgin Islands. He was concerned about the possibility of European influence in Nicaragua, and so he signed a treaty with that country's government. It ensured that no other nation would build a canal there, winning for the United States the right to intervene in Nicaragua to protect American interests.

But Wilson's view of America's role in the world was not entirely similar to the views of his predecessors, as became clear in his dealings with Mexico. For many years, under the friendly auspices of the corrupt dictator Porfirio Díaz, American businessmen had established an enormous economic presence in Mexico. In 1910, however, Díaz was overthrown by the popular leader Francisco Madero, who promised democratic reform and who also seemed hostile to American businesses in Mexico. The United States quietly encouraged a reactionary general, Victoriano Huerta, to depose Madero early in 1913, and the Taft administration, in its last weeks in office, prepared to recognize the new Huerta regime. Before it could do so, however, the new government murdered Madero, and Woodrow Wilson took office in Washington. The new president instantly announced that he would never recognize Huerta's "government of butchers."

At first, Wilson hoped that simply by refusing to recognize Huerta he could help topple the regime and bring to power the opposing constitutionalists, now led by Venustiano Carranza. But when Huerta, with the support of American business interests, established a full military dictatorship in October 1913, the president became more assertive. In April 1914, an officer in Huerta's army briefly arrested several American sailors from the U.S.S. *Dolphin* who had gone ashore in Tampico. The men were immediately released, but the American admiral—unsatisfied with the apology he received—demanded that the Huerta forces fire a twenty-one-gun salute to the American flag as a public display of penance. The Mexicans refused. Wilson used the trivial incident as a pretext for seizing the Mexican port of Veracruz.

Wilson had envisioned a bloodless action, but in a clash with Mexican troops, the Americans killed 126 of the defenders and suffered 19 casualties of their own. Now at the brink of war, Wilson began to look for a way out. His show of force, however, had helped strengthen the position of the Carranza faction, which captured Mexico City in August and forced Huerta to flee the country. At last, it seemed, the crisis might be over.

But Wilson was not yet satisfied. He reacted angrily when Carranza, whom he had previously supported, refused to accept American guidelines for the creation of a new government, and he briefly considered throwing his support to still another aspirant to leadership: Carranza's erstwhile lieutenant Pancho Villa, now staking his own claim to power. When Villa's military position deteriorated, however, Wilson abandoned him and finally, in October 1915, granted preliminary recognition to the Carranza government. By now, however, he had created yet another crisis. Villa, angry at what he considered an American betrayal, retaliated in January 1916 by shooting sixteen American mining engineers in northern Mexico. Two months later, he led his soldiers across the border into Columbus, New Mexico, where the Villa forces killed seventeen more Americans.

With the permission of the Carranza government, Wilson ordered General John J. Pershing to lead an American expeditionary force across the Mexican border in pursuit of Villa. The American troops never found Villa, but they did engage in two ugly skirmishes with Carranza's army, in which forty Mexicans and twelve Americans died. Again, the United States and Mexico stood at the brink of war. But at the last minute, Wilson

PANCHO VILLA AND HIS TROOPS   Pancho Villa (*fourth from left*) poses with some of the leaders of his army, whose members Americans came to consider bandits once they began staging raids across the U.S. border. He was a national hero in Mexico. (Brown Brothers)

drew back. He quietly withdrew American troops from Mexico and, in March 1917, finally granted formal recognition to the Carranza regime. By now, however, Wilson's attention was turning elsewhere—to the far greater international crisis engulfing the European continent and, ultimately, the United States as well.

THE ROAD TO WAR

By 1914, the European nations had created an unusually precarious international system. It careened into war very quickly on the basis of what seemed to be a minor series of provocations.

THE COLLAPSE OF THE EUROPEAN PEACE

The major powers of Europe were organized by 1914 in two great, competing alliances. The "Triple Entente," which during the war became known as the "Allies," linked Britain, France, and Russia. The "Triple Alliance," later called the "Central Powers," united Germany, the Austro-Hungarian Empire, and Italy (although when war began, Italy joined the Allies). The chief rivalry, however, was not between the two alliances but between the great powers that dominated them: Great Britain and Germany.

The conflict emerged most directly out of a controversy involving nationalist movements within the Austro-Hungarian Empire. On June 28, 1914, the Archduke Franz Ferdinand, heir to the throne of the tottering empire, was assassinated while paying a state visit to Sarajevo, the capital of Bosnia, then a province of Austria-Hungary. Slavic nationalists wished to annex Bosnia to neighboring Serbia. The archduke's assassin was a Serbian nationalist.

This local controversy quickly escalated through the complex system of alliances. Germany supported Austria-Hungary's decision to launch a punitive assault on Serbia. To help with their defense, the Serbians called on Russia, which began mobilizing its army on July 30. By August 3, Germany had declared war on both Russia and France and had invaded Belgium. On August 4, Great Britain—ostensibly to honor its alliance with France—declared war on Germany. (The British were attracted to war in the hopes of weakening Germany, which had become a powerful commercial rival.) Russia and the Austro-Hungarian Empire formally began hostilities on August 6. Within months, other smaller nations joined the fighting. By early 1915, virtually the entire European continent (and part of Asia) was embroiled in a major war.

Wilson's Neutrality

Wilson called on his fellow citizens in 1914 to remain "impartial in thought as well as deed." But that was impossible. Most Americans sympathized with Britain. Lurid reports of German atrocities in Belgium and France, skillfully exaggerated by British propagandists, strengthened the hostility of many Americans toward Germany.

Economic realities also made it impossible for the United States to deal with the belligerents on equal terms. The British had imposed a naval blockade on Germany to prevent munitions and supplies from reaching the enemy. As a neutral, the United States had the right, in theory, to trade with Germany, but the British blockade made that impossible. A truly neutral response to the blockade would have been to stop trading with Britain as well. But while the United States could survive an interruption of its relatively modest trade with the Central Powers, it could not easily weather an embargo on its much more extensive trade with the Allies. So America tacitly accepted the blockade of Germany and continued trading with Britain. By 1915, the United States had gradually transformed itself from a neutral power into the arsenal of the Allies.

The Germans, in the meantime, were resorting to a new and, in American eyes, barbaric tactic: submarine warfare. Unable to challenge British domination on the ocean's surface, the Germans announced early in 1915 that they would sink enemy vessels on sight. Months later, on May 7, a German submarine (or U-boat, a name derived from the German *Unterseeboot*) sank the British passenger liner *Lusitania* without warning, causing the deaths of 1,198 people, 128 of them Americans. The ship was carrying both passengers and munitions, but most Americans considered the attack an unprovoked act on civilians.

Wilson angrily demanded that Germany promise not to repeat such outrages, and the Germans reluctantly agreed. But early in 1916, in response to an announcement that the Allies were now arming merchant ships to sink submarines, Germany proclaimed that it would fire on such vessels without warning. A few weeks later, it attacked the unarmed French steamer *Sussex*, injuring several American passengers. Again, Wilson demanded that Germany abandon its "unlawful" tactics; again, the German government relented.

Preparedness versus Pacifism

Despite the president's increasing bellicosity in 1916, he was still far from ready to commit the United States to war. One obstacle was American domestic politics.

The question of whether America should make military and economic preparations for war sparked a heated debate between pacifists and interventionists. Wilson at first denounced the idea of an American military buildup as needless and provocative. In the fall of 1915, however, he endorsed an ambitious proposal by American military leaders for a large and rapid increase in the nation's armed forces.

Still, the peace faction wielded considerable political strength, as became clear at the Democratic Convention in the summer of 1916. The convention became especially enthusiastic

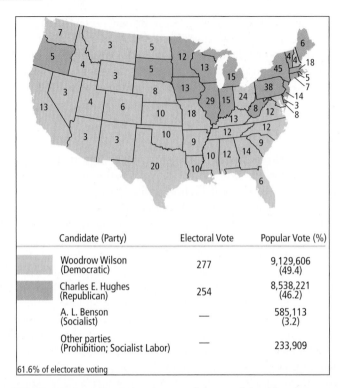

Candidate (Party)	Electoral Vote	Popular Vote (%)
Woodrow Wilson (Democratic)	277	9,129,606 (49.4)
Charles E. Hughes (Republican)	254	8,538,221 (46.2)
A. L. Benson (Socialist)	—	585,113 (3.2)
Other parties (Prohibition; Socialist Labor)	—	233,909

61.6% of electorate voting

THE ELECTION OF 1916 Woodrow Wilson had good reason to be concerned about his reelection prospects in 1916. He had won only about 42 percent of the vote in 1912, and the Republican Party—which had been divided four years earlier—was now reunited around the popular Charles Evans Hughes. In the end, Wilson won a narrow victory over Hughes with just under 50 percent of the vote and an even narrower margin in the electoral college. Note the striking regional character of his victory. • *How did Wilson use the war in Europe to bolster his election prospects?*

when the keynote speaker punctuated his list of the president's diplomatic achievements with the chant, "What did we do? What did we do? . . . We didn't go to war! We didn't go to war!" That speech helped produce one of the most prominent slogans of Wilson's reelection campaign: "He kept us out of war." During the campaign, Wilson did nothing to discourage those who argued that the Republican candidate, the progressive New York governor Charles Evans Hughes, was more likely than he to lead the nation into war. Wilson ultimately won reelection by fewer than 600,000 popular votes and only 23 electoral votes.

A War for Democracy

Tensions between the United States and Germany remained high. But Wilson still required a justification for American intervention that would unite public opinion. In the end, he created that rationale himself. The United States, Wilson insisted, was committed to constructing a new world order based on the same progressive ideals that had motivated a generation of progressive reform. In a speech before Congress in January 1917, he presented a plan for a postwar order in which a permanent league of nations would maintain the peace—a "peace without victory." These were, Wilson believed, goals worth fighting for if there was sufficient provocation.

In January, the military leaders of Germany decided on a dramatic gamble to achieve victory: unrestricted submarine warfare against American as well as Allied ships to cut Britain off from vital supplies. Then, on February 25, the British gave Wilson an intercepted telegram sent by the German foreign minister, Arthur Zimmermann, to the government of Mexico. It proposed that in the event of war between Germany and the United States, the Mexicans should join with Germany against the Americans in return for their "lost provinces" in the north when the war was over. Widely publicized by British propagandists and the American press, the Zimmermann telegram inflamed public opinion and helped build popular sentiment for war. In March 1917, a revolution in Russia toppled the reactionary czarist regime and replaced it with a new, republican government. The United States, it appeared, would now be spared the embarrassment of allying with a despotic monarchy.

On the rainy evening of April 2, two weeks after German submarines had torpedoed three American ships, Wilson appeared before a joint session of Congress and asked for a declaration of war. Even then, opposition remained. When the declaration of war finally passed on April 6, fifty representatives and six senators had voted against it.

"WAR WITHOUT STINT"

European armies on both sides of the conflict were decimated and exhausted by the time of Woodrow Wilson's declaration of war. The Allies looked desperately to the United States for help in breaking the stalemate.

AN APPEAL TO DUTY   This most famous of all American war posters, by the artist James Montgomery Flagg, shows a fierce-looking Uncle Sam requesting, almost demanding, that Americans join the army to fight in World War I. With the nation divided over the wisdom of entering the war, the Wilson administration believed it needed to persuade Americans not only to support the struggle but also—something unusual for Americans—to feel a sense of obligation to the government and its overseas commitments. (National Archives)

GEORGE M. COHAN, "OVER THERE," 1918

Johnnie, get your gun,
Get your gun, get your gun,
Take it on the run,
On the run, on the run.
Hear them calling, you and me,
Every son of liberty.
Hurry right away,
No delay, no delay,
Make your daddy glad
To have had such a lad.
Tell your sweetheart not to pine,
To be proud her boy's in line.

Chorus
Over there, over there
Send the word, send the word over there
That the Yanks are coming,
The Yanks are coming,
The drums rum-tumming
Ev'rywhere.
So prepare, say a pray'r,
Send the word, send the word to beware.
We'll be over, we're coming over,
And we won't come back till it's over
Over there.

Source: George M. Cohan, "Over There" (public domain).

Johnnie get your gun,
Get your gun, get your gun,
Johnnie show the Hun
Who's a son of a gun.
Hoist the flag and let her fly,
Yankee Doodle do or die.
Pack your little kit,
Show your grit, do your bit.
Yankee Doodle fill the ranks,
From the towns and the tanks.
Make your mother proud of you,
And the old Red, White and Blue.

(repeat chorus twice)

UNDERSTAND, ANALYZE, & EVALUATE

1. How did this song seek to motivate young men to join the army? What image of war did this song convey?
2. What relationship between the United States and Europe did the chorus imply?

THE MILITARY STRUGGLE

By the spring of 1917, Great Britain was suffering such vast losses from German submarines that its ability to receive vital supplies from across the Atlantic was in jeopardy. Within weeks of joining the war, the United States had begun to alter the balance. A fleet of American destroyers aided the British navy in attacking the U-boats and planting antisubmarine mines in the North Sea. The results were dramatic. Sinkings of Allied ships had totaled nearly 900,000 tons in the month of April 1917; the figure dropped to 350,000 by December 1917 and to 112,000 by October 1918.

Many Americans had hoped that providing naval assistance alone would be enough to end the war, but it quickly became clear that a major commitment of American ground forces would be necessary as well. Britain and France had few remaining reserves. After the Bolshevik Revolution in November 1917, a new communist government, led by V. I. Lenin, negotiated a hasty and costly peace between Russia and the Central Powers. That freed German troops to fight on the western front.

The United States did not have a large enough standing army to provide the necessary ground forces in 1917. Only a national draft could provide the needed men. Despite

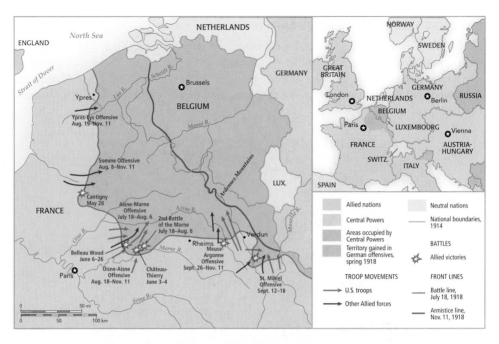

AMERICA IN WORLD WAR I: THE WESTERN FRONT, 1918 These maps show the principal battles in which the United States participated in the last year of World War I. The small map on the upper right helps locate the area of conflict within the larger European landscape. The larger map at left shows the long, snaking red line of the western front in France—stretching from the border between France and southwest Germany all the way to the northeast border between Belgium and France. Along that vast line, the two sides had been engaged in murderous, inconclusive warfare for over three years by the time the Americans arrived. Beginning in the spring and summer of 1918, bolstered by reinforcements from the United States, the Allies began to win a series of important victories that finally enabled them to begin pushing the Germans back. American troops, as this map makes clear, were decisive along the southern part of the front. • *At what point did the Germans begin to consider putting an end to the war?*

protests, Wilson won passage of the Selective Service Act in mid-May. The draft brought nearly 3 million men into the army. Another 2 million joined various branches of the armed services voluntarily.

The engagement of the American forces was brief but intense. Not until the spring of 1918 were significant numbers of American troops available for battle. Eight months later, the war was over. Under the command of General John J. Pershing, the American Expeditionary Force (AEF) joined Allied forces in turning back a series of new German assaults. In early June, the AEF assisted the French in repelling a bitter German offensive at Château-Thierry, near Paris. Six weeks later, Americans helped turn away another assault, at Rheims, farther south. By July 18, the German advance had been halted. On September 26, an American fighting force of over 1 million soldiers advanced against the Germans in the Argonne Forest. By the end of October, the AEF had helped push the Germans back toward their own border and had cut the enemy's major supply lines to the front.

Faced with an invasion of their own country, German military leaders now began to seek an armistice. Pershing wanted to drive on into Germany itself; but other Allied leaders, after first insisting on terms that made the agreement (in their eyes at least) little different from a surrender, accepted the German proposal. On November 11, 1918, more than four years after it began, the Great War shuddered to a close.

THE NEW TECHNOLOGY OF WARFARE

World War I was a proving ground for a range of new military technologies. The trench warfare that characterized the conflict was a result of the enormous destructive power of newly improved machine guns and higher-powered artillery. It was no longer feasible to send troops out into an open field. The new weaponry would slaughter them in an instant. Trenches sheltered troops while allowing limited, and usually inconclusive, fighting.

LIFE IN THE TRENCHES For most British, French, German, and, ultimately, American troops in France, the most debilitating part of World War I was the seeming endlessness of life in the trenches. Some young men lived in these cold, wet, muddy dugouts for months, even years, surrounded by filth, sharing their space with vermin, eating mostly rotten food. Occasional attacks to try to dislodge the enemy from its trenches usually ended in failure and became the scenes of terrible slaughter. (National Archives)

But technology overtook the trenches, too, as mobile weapons—tanks and flamethrowers—proved capable of piercing entrenched positions. Most terrible of all, perhaps, new chemical weapons—poisonous mustard gas, which required troops to carry gas masks at all times—made it possible to attack entrenched soldiers without direct combat.

The new forms of technological warfare required elaborate maintenance. Faster machine guns needed more ammunition. Motorized vehicles required fuel, spare parts, and mechanics capable of servicing them. The logistical difficulties of supply became a major factor in planning tactics and strategy. Late in the war, when the Allied armies were advancing toward Germany, they frequently had to stop for days at a time to wait for their equipment to catch up with them.

World War I was the first conflict in which airplanes played a significant role. The planes themselves were relatively simple and not very maneuverable; but antiaircraft technology was not yet highly developed either, so their effectiveness was still significant. Planes began to be constructed to serve various functions: bombers, fighters (planes that would engage in "dogfights" with other planes), and reconaissance aircraft.

The most "modern" part of the military during World War I was the navy. Battleships emerged that made use of new technologies such as turbine propulsion, hydraulic gun controls, electric light and power, wireless telegraphy, and advanced navigational aids. Submarines, which had made a brief appearance in the American Civil War, now became significant weapons (as the German U-boat campaign in 1915 and 1916 made clear). The new submarines were driven by diesel engines that were more compact than steam engines and used fuel that was less explosive than that of gasoline engines.

The new technologies were responsible for the most stunning and horrible characteristic of World War I—its appalling level of casualties, including the deaths of over 9 million people. A million men representing the British Empire (from Britain, Canada, Australia, India, and others) died. France lost 1.7 million men; Germany, 2 million; the former Austro-Hungarian Empire, 1.5 million; Italy, 460,000; and Russia, 1.7 million. The United States, which entered the war near its end and became engaged only in the last successful offensives, suffered 112,000 dead, half of them victims of influenza, not battle. But the American casualties were very high in the battles in which U.S. troops were centrally involved.

ORGANIZING THE ECONOMY FOR WAR

By the time the war ended, the federal government had appropriated $32 billion for war expenses—a staggering sum at the time. The entire federal budget had seldom exceeded $1 billion before 1915, and as recently as 1910 the nation's entire gross national product had been only $35 billion. To raise the money, the government relied on two devices. First, it launched a major drive to solicit loans from the American people by selling "Liberty Bonds" to the public. By 1920, the sale of bonds, accompanied by elaborate patriotic appeals, had produced $23 billion. At the same time, new taxes were bringing in an additional sum of nearly $10 billion—some of it coming from levies on the "excess profits" of corporations but much of it coming from new, steeply graduated income and inheritance taxes that ultimately rose as high as 70 percent in some brackets.

An even greater challenge was to organize the economy to meet war needs. In 1916, Wilson established the Council of National Defense, composed of members of his cabinet, and the Civilian Advisory Commission, which set up local defense councils in every state and locality. But this early administrative structure soon proved completely unworkable,

BILLY SUNDAY AND MODERN REVIVALISM

BILLY Sunday was a farm boy from Iowa who attended school only until the eighth grade, became a professional baseball player in his teens, and then, in 1886, at the age of twenty-four, experienced a conversion to evangelical Christianity. Over the next decade, he rose to become America's most successful revivalist of the early twentieth century.

The revivalism of that era was, among other things, an effort by conservative Christians to fight off the influence of Darwin and his theory of evolution. A great many American Protestants in the late nineteenth century had revised their faith to incorporate Darwin's teaching. In the process, they had discarded some beliefs from traditional Christianity: the literal truth of the Bible (including the story of Creation), faith in personal conversion, the factuality of miracles, a strong belief in the existence of heaven and hell, and many others. Faith in these religious "fundamentals" was important to conservatives (who began to be known as "fundamentalists"), because without them, they believed, religion would no longer be a vibrant, central presence in their lives.

Billy Sunday combined an instinctive feel for fundamentalist belief with a skillful understanding of modern techniques of marketing and publicity and a genius for making religion entertaining. He raised enormous sums of money and used most of it to publicize his revival meetings and build the elaborate, if temporary, "tabernacles" in which he spoke before up to 20,000 people at a time.

Part of Sunday's success was a result of his previous career as a baseball player, and part was a result of his flamboyant oratorical style. A natural showman, he had no inhibitions about using the techniques of entertainment to manipulate his audiences. But he was successful, too, because he combined fundamentalist religious themes with outspoken positions on social issues.

He was a highly effective advocate of prohibition and sometimes seemed to convert an entire community to temperance in a single stroke. He also spoke out about other reforms: cleaning up corrupt city governments, attacking the great trusts, fighting poverty. "I believe," he once said, "if society allows deserving men to stagger along with less than a living wage, . . . then society must share the responsibility if these people become criminals, thieves, cutthroats, drunkards, and prostitutes."

Yet he also insisted that individuals were not simply victims of society. Even the most degraded individuals, he argued, could save themselves through Christ. An active faith would not only give them spiritual peace; it would also help them rise in the world. Religion, as Sunday presented it, was a form of self-help in a time when many Americans

BILLY SUNDAY IN ILLINOIS, 1908 This photograph shows one of the many temporary tabernacles erected to house the enormous crowds—in this case over 5,000 people—whom Billy Sunday regularly attracted. He is shown here in Bloomington, Illinois, in January 1908, but the scene repeated itself in many places through the first decades of the twentieth century. (C. U. Williams, Bloomington, Illinois/Archives of the Billy Graham Center, Wheaton, Illinois)

were searching desperately for ways to gain control over their lives and their fates.

Sunday opposed American involvement in World War I in the first years of the fighting in Europe. But when the United States entered the fighting, he took second place to no one in the fervor of his support and the passion of his patriotism. By then, the surge of revivalism he had helped create had spread widely through America. The war increased the appetite for revivalism in many communities, and it brought Sunday a last great burst of success.

Sunday's popularity faded after 1920, as he became a harsh critic of "radicalism" and "foreignness" and as the popularity of revivals declined in the face of a beckoning new consumer culture. When he died in 1935, he was attracting crowds only in scattered, rural communities of deeply conservative views. But in his heyday, Sunday provided millions of Americans with a combination of dazzling entertainment and prescriptions for renewing their religious faith. •

UNDERSTAND, ANALYZE, & EVALUATE

1. Do you think Sunday's showmanship was a way of manipulating his audiences or of entertaining them? Is such showmanship necessarily manipulative?
2. Why would revivalism have peaked in the years around World War I? What social conditions of that era contributed to the success of revivalism? Can you think of other periods in American history when social change sparked a similar wave of religious fervor or revivalism?

and members of the council urged a more centralized approach. The administrative structure that slowly emerged was dominated by a series of "war boards," one to oversee the railroads, one to supervise fuel supplies (largely coal), another to handle food (a board that elevated to prominence the brilliant young engineer and business executive Herbert Hoover). The boards generally succeeded in meeting essential war needs without paralyzing the domestic economy.

The War Industries Board (WIB) was created in July 1917 to coordinate government purchases of military supplies. Casually organized at first, it stumbled badly until March 1918, when Wilson restructured it and placed it under the control of the Wall Street financier Bernard Baruch. Baruch decided which factories would convert to the production of which war materials, and he set prices for the goods they produced. When materials were scarce, Baruch decided to whom they should go. When corporations were competing for government contracts, he chose among them.

Baruch viewed himself, openly and explicitly, as a partner of business; and within the WIB, businessmen themselves—the so-called dollar-a-year men, who took paid leave from their corporate jobs and worked for the government for a token salary—supervised the affairs of the private economy.

The National War Labor Board, established in April 1918, served as the final mediator of labor disputes. It pressured industry to grant important concessions to workers: an eight-hour day, the maintenance of minimal living standards, equal pay for women doing equal work, recognition of the right of unions to organize and bargain collectively. In return, it insisted that workers forgo strikes and that employers not engage in lockouts.

THE SEARCH FOR SOCIAL UNITY

Government leaders were painfully aware that public sentiment about the war was sharply divided. The most conspicuous of its efforts to support the war was a vast propaganda campaign orchestrated by the Committee on Public Information (CPI), under the direction of the Denver journalist George Creel. The CPI supervised the distribution of over 75 million pieces of printed material and controlled much of the information available for newspapers and magazines. Creel encouraged journalists to exercise "self-censorship" when reporting war news, and most complied by covering the war largely as the government wished. By 1918, government-distributed posters and films were offering lurid (and exaggerated) portrayals of the savagery of the Germans.

The government also began efforts to suppress dissent. CPI-financed advertisements in magazines implored citizens to report to the authorities any evidence among their neighbors of disloyalty, pessimism, or yearning for peace. The Espionage Act of 1917 gave the government new tools with which to combat spying, sabotage, or obstruction of the war effort (crimes that were often broadly defined). The Sabotage Act and the Sedition Act, both passed in 1918, expanded the meaning of the Espionage Act to make illegal *any* public expression of opposition to the war; in practice, they allowed officials to prosecute anyone who criticized the president or the government.

The most frequent targets of the new legislation were anticapitalist groups such as the Socialist Party and the Industrial Workers of the World (IWW). Many Americans had favored the repression of socialists and radicals even before the war; the wartime policies now made it possible to move against them with full legal sanction. Eugene V. Debs, the humane leader of the Socialist Party and an opponent of the war, was sentenced to ten years in prison in 1918. (A pardon by President Warren G. Harding ultimately won his release in 1921.) Big Bill Haywood and members of the IWW were energetically prosecuted. Only by fleeing to the Soviet Union did Haywood avoid imprisonment. In all, more than 1,500 people were arrested in 1918 for the crime of criticizing the government or the war.

State and local governments, corporations, universities, and private citizens contributed as well to the climate of repression. A cluster of citizens' groups emerged to mobilize "respectable" members of communities to root out disloyalty. The greatest target of abuse was the German American community. Most German Americans supported the American war effort once it began, but public opinion still turned bitterly hostile. A campaign to purge society of all things German quickly gathered speed, at times assuming ludicrous forms. Performances of German music were frequently banned. German foods such as sauerkraut and bratwurst were renamed "liberty cabbage" and "liberty sausage." German books were removed from library shelves. Courses in the German language were dropped from school curricula. Germans were routinely fired from jobs in war industries, lest they "sabotage" important tasks.

THE SEARCH FOR A NEW WORLD ORDER

Woodrow Wilson had led the nation into war promising a just and stable peace at its conclusion. Even before the armistice, he was preparing to lead the fight for what he considered a democratic postwar settlement.

THE FOURTEEN POINTS

On January 8, 1918, Wilson appeared before Congress to present the principles for which he believed the nation was fighting. He grouped the war aims under fourteen headings, widely known as the "Fourteen Points." They fell into three broad categories. First, Wilson's proposals contained a series of eight specific recommendations for adjusting postwar boundaries and establishing new nations to replace the defunct Austro-Hungarian and Ottoman empires. Second, five general principles would govern international conduct in the future: freedom of the seas, open covenants instead of secret treaties, reductions in armaments, free trade, and impartial mediation of colonial claims. Finally, there was a proposal for a "League of Nations" that would help implement these new principles and territorial adjustments and resolve future controversies.

Wilson's international vision ultimately enchanted not only much of his own generation (in both America and Europe) but members of generations to come. It reflected his belief that the world was as capable of just and efficient government as were individual nations—that once the international community accepted certain basic principles of conduct and constructed modern institutions to implement them, the world could live in peace.

Despite Wilson's confidence, leaders of the Allied powers were preparing to resist him even before the armistice was signed. Britain and France, in particular, were in no mood for a benign and generous peace. At the same time, Wilson was encountering problems at home. In 1918, with the war almost over, Wilson unwisely tied support of his peace plans to the election of Democrats to Congress in November. Days later, the Republicans captured majorities in both houses. Domestic economic troubles, more than international issues, had been the most important factor in the voting; but the results damaged his ability to claim broad popular support for his peace plans. Wilson further antagonized the Republicans when he refused to appoint any important member of their party to the negotiating team that would attend the peace conference in Paris.

THE PARIS PEACE CONFERENCE

When Wilson entered Paris on December 13, 1918, he was greeted, some claimed, by the largest crowd in the history of France. The peace conference itself, however, proved less satisfying.

The principal figures in the negotiations were the leaders of the victorious Allied nations: David Lloyd George, the prime minister of Great Britain; Georges Clemenceau, the prime minister of France; Vittorio Orlando, the prime minister of Italy; and Wilson, who hoped to dominate them all.

From the beginning, the atmosphere of idealism Wilson had sought to create competed with a rival spirit of national self-interest and a fear of the unstable situation in eastern Europe and the threat of communism. Russia, whose new Bolshevik government was still fighting anti-Bolshevik counterrevolutionaries, was unrepresented in Paris; but the radical threat it seemed to pose to Western governments was never far from the minds of the delegates.

In this tense and often vindictive atmosphere, Wilson was unable to win approval of many of his broad principles or to prevent the other allies from imposing high reparations on the defeated Central Powers. Wilson did manage to win some important victories in Paris in setting boundaries and dealing with former colonies. But his most visible triumph, and the one most important to him, was the creation of a permanent international organization to oversee world affairs and prevent future wars. On January 25, 1919, the Allies voted to accept the "covenant" of the League of Nations.

THE RATIFICATION BATTLE

Wilson presented the Treaty of Versailles (so named for the palace outside Paris where the agreement was signed) to the Senate on July 10, 1919. But members of the Senate had many objections. Some—the so-called irreconcilables—believed that America should remain free of binding foreign entanglements. But many other opponents were principally concerned with constructing a winning issue for the Republicans in 1920. Most notable of these was Senator Henry Cabot Lodge of Massachusetts, the powerful chairman of the Foreign Relations Committee, who loathed the president and used every possible tactic to obstruct the treaty.

Public sentiment clearly favored ratification, so at first Lodge could do little more than play for time. Gradually, however, his opposition to the treaty crystallized into a series of "reservations"—amendments to the League covenant further limiting American obligations to the organization. Wilson might still have won approval at this point if he had agreed to some relatively minor changes in the language of the treaty. But the president refused to yield.

When he realized the Senate would not budge, Wilson decided to appeal to the public and embarked on a grueling, cross-country speaking tour to arouse public support for the treaty. For more than three weeks, he traveled over 8,000 miles by train, speaking as often as four times a day, resting hardly at all. Finally, he reached the end of his strength. After speaking at Pueblo, Colorado, on September 25, 1919, he collapsed with severe headaches.

Canceling the rest of his itinerary, he rushed back to Washington, where, a few days later, he suffered a major stroke. For two weeks, he was close to death; for six weeks more, he was so seriously ill that he was virtually unable to conduct public business. His wife and his doctor formed an almost impenetrable barrier around him, shielding the president from any official pressures that might impede his recovery.

Wilson ultimately recovered enough to resume a limited official schedule, but he was essentially an invalid for the remaining eighteen months of his presidency. His condition only intensified what had already been his strong tendency to view public issues in moral terms and to resist any attempts at compromise. When the Foreign Relations Committee finally sent the treaty to the Senate, recommending nearly fifty amendments and reservations, Wilson refused to consider any of them. The effort to win ratification failed.

In the aftermath of this defeat, Wilson became convinced that the 1920 national election would serve as a "solemn referendum" on the League. By now, however, public interest in the peace process had begun to fade as a series of other crises claimed attention.

A SOCIETY IN TURMOIL

Even during the Paris Peace Conference, many Americans were concerned less about international matters than about turbulent events at home. Some of this unease was a legacy of the almost hysterical social atmosphere of the war years; some of it was a response to issues that surfaced after the armistice.

THE UNSTABLE ECONOMY

The war ended sooner than almost anyone had anticipated. Without warning, without planning, the nation lurched into the difficult task of economic reconversion. At first, the boom continued, but accompanied by raging inflation. Through most of 1919 and 1920, prices rose at an average of more than 15 percent a year. Finally, late in 1920, the economic bubble burst as inflation began killing the market for consumer goods. Between 1920 and 1921, the gross national product declined nearly 10 percent; 100,000 businesses went bankrupt; and nearly 5 million Americans lost their jobs.

Well before this severe recession began, labor unrest increased dramatically. The raging inflation of 1919 wiped out the modest wage gains workers had achieved during the war; many laborers were worried about job security as veterans returned to the workforce; arduous working conditions continued to be a source of discontent. Employers aggravated the resentment by using the end of the war to rescind benefits they had been forced to concede to workers in 1917 and 1918—most notably, recognition of unions. The year 1919, therefore, saw an unprecedented strike wave. In January, a walkout by shipyard workers in Seattle, Washington, evolved into a general strike that brought the entire city to a virtual standstill. In September, the Boston police force struck to demand recognition of its union. With its police off the job, Boston erupted in violence and looting. Governor Calvin Coolidge called in the National Guard to restore order and attracted national acclaim by declaring, "There is no right to strike against the public safety."

Coolidge's statement tapped into a broad middle-class hostility to unions and strikes. His hostility played a part in defeating the greatest strike of 1919: a steel strike that began in September, when 350,000 steelworkers in several Midwestern cities demanded an eight-hour day and union recognition. The long and bitter steel strike climaxed in a riot in Gary, Indiana, in which eighteen strikers were killed. Steel executives managed to keep most plants running with nonunion labor, and public opinion was so hostile to the strikers that the American Federation of Labor timidly repudiated the strike. By January, the strike—like most of the others in 1919—had collapsed.

THE DEMANDS OF AFRICAN AMERICANS

Black World War I veterans (367,000 of them) came home in 1919 and marched down the main streets of cities with other returning troops. And then in New York and elsewhere they marched again through the streets of black neighborhoods such as Harlem, led by jazz bands and cheered by thousands of African Americans. They believed that the glory of black heroism in the war would make it impossible for white society ever again to treat African Americans as less than equal citizens.

As it turned out, the fact that black soldiers had fought in the war had almost no impact at all on white attitudes. But it profoundly affected black attitudes, accentuated African American bitterness, and increased the determination to fight for their rights. During the war, nearly half a million blacks had migrated from the rural South to industrial cities (often enticed by northern "labor agents," who offered free transportation) in search of the factory jobs the war was rapidly generating. This was the beginning of what became known as the "Great Migration." Suddenly, large black communities arose in northern cities, in some of which very few African Americans had lived in the past.

By 1919, the racial climate had become savage and murderous. In the South, lynchings suddenly increased; more than seventy blacks, some of them war veterans, died at the hands of white mobs in 1919 alone. In the North, black factory workers faced widespread layoffs as returning white veterans displaced them from their jobs. And as whites became convinced that black workers with lower wage demands were hurting them economically, animosity grew rapidly.

Wartime riots in East St. Louis and elsewhere were a prelude to a summer of much worse racial violence in 1919. In Chicago, a black teenager swimming in Lake Michigan on a hot July day happened to drift toward a white beach. Whites onshore allegedly stoned him unconscious; he sank and drowned. Angry African Americans gathered in crowds and marched into white neighborhoods to retaliate; whites formed even larger crowds and roamed into mostly black neighborhoods. For more than a week, Chicago was virtually at war. In the end, 38 people had died—15 whites and 23 blacks—and 537 were injured;

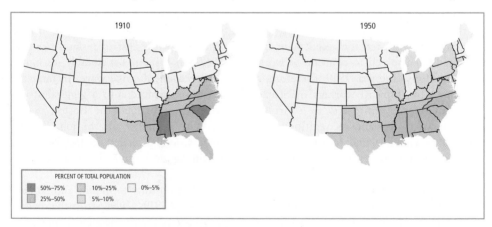

AFRICAN AMERICAN MIGRATION, 1910–1950 Two great waves of migration produced a dramatic redistribution of the African American population in the first half of the twentieth century—one around the time of World War I, the other during and after World War II. The map on the left shows the almost exclusive concentration of African Americans in the South as late as 1910. The map on the right shows both the tremendous increase of black populations in northern states by 1950, and the relative decline of black populations in parts of the South. Note in particular the changes in Mississippi and South Carolina. • *Why did the wars produce such significant migration out of the South?*

over 1,000 people were left homeless. The Chicago riot was the worst but not the only racial violence during the so-called red summer of 1919; in all, 120 people died in such racial outbreaks in little more than three months.

Racially motivated urban riots were not new. But the 1919 riots were different in one respect: they did not just involve white people attacking blacks, but also blacks fighting back. The NAACP signaled this change by urging blacks not just to demand government protection but also to defend themselves. The poet Claude McKay, one of the major figures of what would shortly be known as the Harlem Renaissance, wrote a poem after the Chicago riot called "If We Must Die":

> Like men we'll face the murderous cowardly pack.
> Pressed to the wall, dying, but fighting back.

At the same time, a black Jamaican, Marcus Garvey, began to attract a wide following in the United States with his ideology of black nationalism. Garvey encouraged African Americans to reject assimilation into white society and to develop pride in their own race and culture. His Universal Negro Improvement Association (UNIA) launched a chain of black-owned grocery stores and pressed for the creation of other black businesses. Eventually, Garvey began urging his supporters to leave America and return to Africa, where they could create a new society of their own. In the early 1920s, the Garvey movement experienced explosive growth for a time, but it began to decline after Garvey was indicted in 1923 on charges of business fraud. He was deported to Jamaica two years later. But the allure of black nationalism survived in black culture long after Garvey was gone.

THE RED SCARE

Many Americans regarded the industrial warfare and racial violence of 1919 as frightening omens of instability and radicalism. After the Russian Revolution of November 1917, communism was no longer simply a theory, but the basis of an important regime. Concerns about the communist threat grew in 1919 when the Soviet government announced the formation of the Communist International (or Comintern), whose purpose was to export revolution around the world.

In America, meanwhile, there was, in addition to the great number of imagined radicals, a modest number of real ones. These small groups of radicals were presumably responsible for a series of bombings in the spring of 1919. In April, the post office intercepted several dozen parcels addressed to leading businessmen and politicians that were triggered to explode when opened. Two months later, eight bombs exploded in eight cities within minutes of one another, suggesting a nationwide conspiracy.

In response to these and other provocations, what became known as the Red Scare began. Nearly thirty states enacted new peacetime sedition laws imposing harsh penalties on promoters of revolution. Spontaneous acts of violence against supposed radicals occurred in some communities, and universities and other institutions tried to expel radicals from their midst. But the greatest contribution to the Red Scare came from the federal government. On New Year's Day, 1920, Attorney General A. Mitchell Palmer and his ambitious young assistant, J. Edgar Hoover, orchestrated a series of raids on alleged radical centers throughout the country and arrested more than 6,000 people. Most of those arrested were ultimately released, but about 500 who were not American citizens were summarily deported. Later in 1920, a bomb exploded on Wall Street, killing thirty-eight people. No one was ever convicted of this bombing.

The ferocity of the Red Scare gradually abated, but its effects lingered well into the 1920s. In May 1920, two Italian immigrants, Nicola Sacco and Bartolomeo Vanzetti, were charged with the murder of a paymaster in South Braintree, Massachusetts. The case against them was weak and suffused with nativist prejudices and fears; but because both men were confessed anarchists, they faced a widespread public presumption of guilt. They were convicted and eventually sentenced to death. Over the next several years, public support for Sacco and Vanzetti grew to formidable proportions. But on August 23, 1927, amid widespread protests in the United States and around the world, Sacco and Vanzetti, still proclaiming their innocence, died in the electric chair.

REFUTING THE RED SCARE

An unexpected result of postwar turmoil was the emergence of a vigorous defense of civil liberties that not only discredited the Red Scare, but also helped give new force to the Bill of Rights. The heavy-handed actions of the federal government after the war created a powerful backlash. It destroyed the career of A. Mitchell Palmer. It almost nipped in the bud the ascent of J. Edgar Hoover. It damaged the Democratic Party. And it led to an organization committed to protecting civil liberties: the National Civil Liberties Bureau, launched in 1917, which in 1920 was renamed the American Civil Liberties Union (ACLU) and remains a prominent institution today. At the same time, members of the Supreme Court—most notably Justices Oliver Wendell Holmes and Louis Brandeis—gradually moved toward a strong position in defense of unpopular speech. The clash of "fighting faiths," Holmes wrote in a dissent in 1920, was best resolved "by free trade in ideas—that the best test of truth is . . . the competition of the market." This and other dissents eventually became law as other justices committed themselves to a robust defense of speech, however unpopular.

THE RETREAT FROM IDEALISM

On August 26, 1920, the Nineteenth Amendment, guaranteeing women the right to vote, became part of the Constitution. To the suffrage movement, this was the culmination of nearly a century of struggle. To many progressives, it seemed to promise new support for reform. Yet the Nineteenth Amendment marked not the beginning of a new era of progressive reform but the end of an earlier one.

Economic problems, labor unrest, racial tensions, and the intensity of the antiradicalism they helped create—all combined in the years immediately following the war to produce a general sense of disillusionment. That became particularly apparent in the election of 1920. Woodrow Wilson wanted the campaign to be a referendum on the League of Nations, and the Democratic candidates, Governor James M. Cox of Ohio and Assistant Secretary of the Navy Franklin D. Roosevelt, dutifully tried to keep Wilson's ideals alive. The Republican presidential nominee, Warren Gamaliel Harding, an obscure Ohio senator, offered a different vision. He embraced no soaring ideals, only a vague promise of a return, as he later phrased it, to "normalcy." He won in a landslide, with 61 percent of the popular vote and victories in every state outside the South. The party made major gains in Congress as well. To many Americans it seemed that, for better or worse, a new age had begun.

CONCLUSION

Presidents Roosevelt, Taft, and Wilson contributed to a continuation, and indeed an expansion, of America's active role in international affairs, in part as an effort to abet the growth of American capitalism and in part as an attempt to impose American ideas of morality and democracy on other parts of the world. Similar mixtures of ideals and self-interest soon guided the United States into a great world war.

For a time after the outbreak of war in Europe in 1914, most Americans—President Wilson among them—wanted nothing so much as to stay out of the conflict. But as the war dragged on and the tactics of Britain and Germany began to impinge on American trade and access to the seas, the United States found itself drawn into the conflict. In April 1917, Congress agreed to the president's request that the United States enter the war as an ally of Britain.

Within a few months of the arrival of American troops in Europe, Germany agreed to an armistice and the war shuddered to a close. American casualties, although not inconsiderable, were negligible compared to the millions suffered by the European combatants.

Wilson's bold and idealistic dream of a peace based on international cooperation suffered a painful death. The Treaty of Versailles, which he helped draft, contained a provision for a League of Nations, which Wilson believed could transform the international order. But the League quickly became controversial in the United States; and despite strenuous efforts by the president—efforts that hastened his own physical collapse—the treaty was defeated in the Senate. In the aftermath of that traumatic battle, the American people turned away from Wilson and his ideals and prepared for a very different era.

The social experience of the war in the United States was, on the whole, dismaying to reformers. Although the war enhanced some reform efforts—most notably prohibition and woman suffrage—it also introduced an atmosphere of intolerance and repression into American life. The aftermath of the war was even more disheartening to progressives, because of both a brief but highly destabilizing recession and a wave of repression directed against labor, radicals, African Americans, and immigrants.

RECALL AND REFLECT

1. Who opposed U.S. involvement in World War I and why?
2. How did the Wilson administration mobilize the nation for war?
3. What effect did the war have on race relations in the United States?
4. What were some of the ways that U.S. participation in the Great War changed American society?
5. Why did the battle over ratification of the Treaty of Versailles come to an impasse? Why did the Senate ultimately reject the treaty? What was the significance of that rejection?

22 | THE NEW ERA

THE NEW ECONOMY
THE NEW CULTURE
A CONFLICT OF CULTURES
REPUBLICAN GOVERNMENT

LOOKING AHEAD

1. How did the technological innovations of the early twentieth century affect industry and American social life of the 1920s?
2. What were some of the cultural conflicts of the 1920s, and what caused them?
3. Is the term the "New Era" a fitting description of the 1920s?

IN POPULAR CULTURE, THE 1920s are often remembered as an era of affluence, conservatism, and cultural frivolity. In reality, however, the decade was a time of significant, even dramatic social, economic, and political change. The American economy not only enjoyed spectacular growth but also developed new forms of organization. Many Americans reshaped themselves to reflect the increasingly urban, industrial, consumer-oriented society of the United States. And American government experimented with new approaches to public policy. That was why contemporaries liked to refer to the 1920s as the "New Era"—an age in which America was becoming a modern nation.

At the same time, however, the decade saw the rise of a series of spirited, and at times effective, rebellions against the transformations in American life. The intense cultural conflicts that characterized the 1920s were evidence of how much of American society remained unreconciled to the modernizing currents of the New Era.

THE NEW ECONOMY

After the recession of 1921–1922, the United States began a period of almost uninterrupted prosperity and economic expansion. Less visible at the time, but equally significant, was the survival (and even the growth) of inequalities and imbalances.

TECHNOLOGY, ORGANIZATION, AND ECONOMIC GROWTH

No one could deny the remarkable feats of the American economy in the 1920s. The nation's manufacturing output rose by more than 60 percent. Per capita income grew by a third. Inflation was negligible. A mild recession in 1923 briefly interrupted the pattern of growth; but when it subsided early in 1924, the economy expanded with even greater vigor.

The economic boom was a result of many things, but one of the most important was technology. As a result of the development of the assembly line and other innovations, automobiles now became one of the most important industries in the nation, stimulating growth in such related industries as steel, rubber, and glass, tool companies, oil corporations, and road construction. The increased mobility that the automobile made possible increased the demand for suburban housing, fueling a boom in the construction industry.

Radio contributed as well to the economic growth. Early radio had been able to broadcast little besides pulses, which meant that radio communication could occur only through the Morse code. But with the discovery of the theory of modulation, pioneered by the Canadian scientist Reginald Fessenden, it became possible to transmit speech and music. Many people built their own radio sets at home for very little money, benefiting from the discovery that inexpensive crystals could receive signals over long distances (but not very well over short ones). These "shortwave" radios, which allowed individual owners to establish contact with one another, marked the

TIME LINE

1914–1920
Great Migration of blacks to the North

1920
Prohibition begins

Harding elected president

1922
Lewis's *Babbitt*

1923
Harding dies; Coolidge becomes president

Harding administration scandals revealed

1924
National Origins Act passed

Coolidge elected president

Ku Klux Klan membership peaks

Leopold-Loeb trial

1925
Fitzgerald's *The Great Gatsby*

Scopes trial

1927
Lindbergh's solo transatlantic flight

First sound motion picture, *The Jazz Singer*

1928
Hoover elected president

beginning of what later became known as "ham radio." Once commercial broadcasting began, families flocked to buy more conventional radio sets powered by reliable vacuum tubes and capable of receiving high-quality signals over short and medium distances. By 1925, there were 2 million sets in American homes, and by the end of the 1920s, almost every family had one.

Commercial aviation developed slowly in the 1920s, beginning with the use of planes to deliver mail. On the whole, airplanes remained curiosities and sources of entertainment. But technological advances—the development of the radial engine and the creation of pressurized cabins—laid the groundwork for the great increase in commercial travel in the 1930s and beyond. Electronics, home appliances, plastics and synthetic fibers (such as nylon), aluminum, magnesium, oil, electric power, and other industries fueled by technological advances—all grew dramatically. Telephones continued to proliferate. By the late 1930s, there were approximately 25 million telephones in the United States, roughly one for every six people.

The seeds of future technological breakthroughs were also visible. In both England and America, scientists and engineers were working to transform primitive calculating machines into devices capable of performing more complicated tasks. By the early 1930s, researchers at MIT, led by Vannevar Bush, had created an instrument capable of performing a variety of complicated tasks—the first analog computer. A few years later, Howard Aiken, with financial assistance from Harvard and MIT, built a much more complex computer with memory, capable of multiplying eleven-digit numbers in three seconds.

Genetic research had begun in Austria in the mid-nineteenth century through the work of Gregor Mendel, a Catholic monk who performed experiments on the hybridization of vegetables in his monastery garden. His findings attracted little attention during his lifetime, but in the early twentieth century they were discovered by several investigators and helped shape modern genetic research. Among the American pioneers was Thomas Hunt Morgan of Columbia University and, later, Cal Tech, whose experiments with fruit flies revealed how several genes could be transmitted together. He also revealed the way in which genes were arranged along the chromosome. His work helped open the path to understanding how genes could recombine—a critical discovery that led to more advanced experiments in hybridization and genetics.

Large sectors of American business accelerated their drive toward national organization and consolidation. Certain industries—notably those dependent on large-scale mass production, such as steel and automobiles—seemed to move naturally toward concentrating production in a few large firms. Others—industries less dependent on technology and less susceptible to great economies of scale—proved more resistant to consolidation.

The strenuous efforts by industrialists throughout the economy to find ways to curb competition reflected a strong fear of overcapacity. Even in the booming 1920s, industrialists remembered how too-rapid expansion and overproduction had helped produce recessions in 1893, 1907, and 1920. The great unrealized dream of the New Era was to find a way to stabilize the economy so that such collapses would never occur again.

WORKERS IN AN AGE OF CAPITAL

Despite the remarkable economic growth, more than two-thirds of the American people in 1929 lived at no better than what one major study described as the "minimum comfort level." Half of those were at or below the level of "subsistence and poverty."

American labor experienced both the successes and the failures of the 1920s. On the one hand, most workers saw their standard of living rise during the decade. Some employers adopted paternalistic techniques that came to be known as "welfare capitalism." Henry Ford, for example, shortened the workweek, raised wages, and instituted paid vacations. By 1926,

THE STEAMFITTER Lewis Hine was among the first American photographers to recognize his craft as an art. In this carefully posed photograph from the mid-1920s, Hine made a point that many other artists were making in other media: the rise of the machine could serve human beings, but might also bend them to its own needs. (Image copyright © The Metropolitan Museum of Art/Art Resource, NY)

nearly 3 million industrial workers were eligible for at least modest pensions on retirement. When labor grievances surfaced despite these efforts, workers could voice them through the so-called company unions that emerged in many industries—workers' councils and shop committees, organized by the corporations themselves. But welfare capitalism, in the end, gave workers no real control over their own fates. Company unions were feeble vehicles. And welfare capitalism survived only as long as industry prospered. After 1929, with the economy in crisis, the entire system collapsed.

Welfare capitalism affected only a relatively small number of firms in any case. Most laborers worked for employers who were interested primarily in keeping their labor costs low. Workers as a whole, therefore, received wage increases that were proportionately far below the growth of the economy. At the end of the decade, the average annual income of a worker remained below $1,500 a year, when $1,800 was considered necessary to maintain a minimally decent standard of living. Only by relying on the combined earnings of several family members could many working-class families make ends meet.

The New Era was a bleak time for labor organization, in part because many unions themselves were relatively conservative and failed to adapt to the realities of the modern economy. The American Federation of Labor (AFL), led after Samuel Gompers's death by the cautious William Green, sought peaceful cooperation with employers and remained wedded to the concept of the craft union. In the meantime, the rapidly rising number of unskilled industrial workers received little attention from the craft unions.

But whatever the unions' weaknesses, the strength of the corporations was the principal reason for the absence of effective labor organization in the 1920s. After the turmoil of 1919, corporate leaders worked hard to spread the doctrine that a crucial element of democratic capitalism was the protection of the "open shop" (a shop in which no worker could be required to join a union). The crusade for the open shop, euphemistically titled the "American Plan," became a pretext for a harsh campaign of union-busting. As a result, union membership fell from more than 5 million in 1920 to under 3 million in 1929.

WOMEN AND MINORITIES IN THE WORKFORCE

A growing proportion of the workforce consisted of women, who were concentrated in what have since become known as "pink-collar" jobs—low-paying service occupations. Large numbers of women worked as secretaries, salesclerks, and telephone operators and in other nonmanual service capacities. Because, technically, such positions were not industrial jobs, the AFL and other labor organizations were uninterested in organizing these workers. Similarly, the half million African Americans who had migrated from the rural South into the cities during the Great Migration after 1914 had few opportunities for union representation. The skilled crafts represented in the AFL usually excluded black workers. Partly as a result of that exclusion, most blacks worked in jobs in which the AFL took no interest at all—as janitors, dishwashers, garbage collectors, and domestics and in other service capacities. A. Philip Randolph's Brotherhood of Sleeping Car Porters was one of the few important unions dominated and led by African Americans.

In the West and the Southwest, the ranks of the unskilled included considerable numbers of Asians and Hispanics. In the wake of the Chinese Exclusion Acts, Japanese immigrants increasingly replaced the Chinese in menial jobs in California. They worked on railroads, construction sites, farms, and in many other low-paying workplaces. Some Japanese managed to escape the ranks of the unskilled by forming their own small businesses or setting themselves up as truck farmers; and many of the Issei (Japanese immigrants) and Nisei (their American-born children) enjoyed significant economic success—so much so that California passed laws in 1913 and 1920 to make it more difficult for them to buy land. Other Asians—most notably Filipinos—also swelled the unskilled workforce and generated considerable hostility. Anti-Filipino riots in California beginning in 1929 helped produce legislation in 1934 virtually eliminating immigration from the Philippines.

Mexican immigrants formed a major part of the unskilled workforce throughout the Southwest and California. Nearly half a million Mexicans entered the United States in the 1920s. Most lived in California, Texas, Arizona, and New Mexico; and by 1930, most lived in cities. Large Mexican barrios grew up in Los Angeles, El Paso, San Antonio, Denver, and many other urban centers. Some of the residents found work locally in factories and shops; others traveled to mines or did migratory labor on farms but returned to the cities between jobs. Mexican workers, too, faced hostility and discrimination from the Anglo population of the region, but there were few efforts actually to exclude them. Employers in the relatively underpopulated West needed this ready pool of low-paid and unorganized workers.

AGRICULTURAL TECHNOLOGY AND THE PLIGHT OF THE FARMER

Like industry, American agriculture in the 1920s embraced new technologies. The number of tractors on American farms quadrupled during the 1920s, especially after they began to be powered by internal combustion engines (like automobiles) rather than by the cumbersome steam engines of the past. They helped to open 35 million new acres to cultivation. Increasingly sophisticated combines and harvesters proliferated, making it possible to produce more crops with fewer workers.

1900

1930

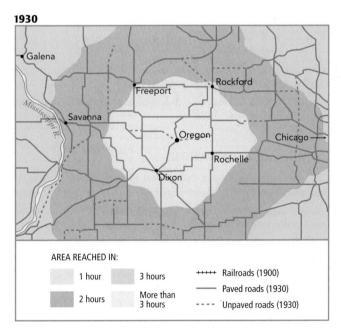

BREAKING DOWN RURAL ISOLATION: THE EXPANSION OF TRAVEL HORIZONS IN OREGON, ILLINOIS This map uses the small town of Oregon, Illinois—west of Chicago—to illustrate the way in which first railroads and then automobiles reduced the isolation of rural areas in the first decades of the twentieth century. The gold and purple areas of the two maps show the territory that residents of Oregon could reach within two hours. Note how small that area was in 1900 and how much larger it was in 1930, by which time an area of over 100 square miles had become easily accessible to the town. Note, too, the significant network of paved roads in the region by 1930, few of which had existed in 1900. • *Why did automobiles do so much more than railroads to expand the travel horizons of small towns?*

Agricultural researchers worked on other innovations: the invention of hybrid corn (made possible by advances in genetic research), which became available to farmers in 1921 but was not grown in great quantities for a decade or more; and the creation of chemical fertilizers and pesticides, which also had limited use in the 1920s but proliferated quickly in the 1930s and 1940s.

The new technologies greatly increased agricultural productivity, but the demand for agricultural goods was not rising as fast as production. As a result, there were substantial surpluses, a disastrous decline in food prices, and a severe drop in farmers' incomes beginning early in the 1920s. More than 3 million people left agriculture altogether in the course of the decade. Of those who remained, many lost ownership of their lands and had to rent instead from banks or other landlords.

In response, some farmers began to demand relief in the form of government price supports. One price-raising scheme in particular came to dominate agrarian demands: the idea of "parity." Parity was a complicated formula for setting an adequate price for farm goods and ensuring that farmers would earn back at least their production costs no matter how the national or world agricultural market might fluctuate. Champions of parity urged high tariffs against foreign agricultural goods and a government commitment to buy surplus domestic crops at parity and sell them abroad.

The legislative expression of the demand for parity was the McNary-Haugen Bill, which required the government to support prices at parity for grain, cotton, tobacco, and rice. It was introduced repeatedly between 1924 and 1928. In 1926 and again in 1928, Congress approved the bill. President Coolidge vetoed it both times.

THE NEW CULTURE

The urban and consumer-oriented culture of the 1920s helped Americans in all regions to live their lives and perceive their world in increasingly similar ways. That same culture exposed them to a new set of values. But different segments of American society experienced the new culture in different ways.

CONSUMERISM AND COMMUNICATIONS

The United States of the 1920s was a consumer society. More people than ever before could buy items not just because of need but for convenience and pleasure. Middle-class families purchased electric refrigerators, washing machines, and vacuum cleaners. People wore wristwatches and smoked cigarettes. Women purchased cosmetics and mass-produced fashions. Above all, Americans bought automobiles. By the end of the decade, there were more than 30 million cars on American roads.

No group was more aware of the emergence of consumerism (or more responsible for creating it) than the advertising industry. In the 1920s, partly as a result of techniques pioneered by wartime propaganda, advertising came of age. Publicists no longer simply conveyed information; they sought to identify products with a particular lifestyle. They also encouraged the public to absorb the values of promotion and salesmanship and to admire those who were effective "boosters" and publicists. One of the most successful books of the 1920s was *The Man Nobody Knows*, by the advertising executive Bruce Barton. It portrayed Jesus as not only a religious prophet but also a "super salesman." Barton's message, one in tune with the new spirit of the consumer culture, was that Jesus had been concerned with living a full and rewarding life in this world and that twentieth-century men and women should be concerned with doing the same.

The advertising industry made good use of new vehicles of communication. Newspapers were absorbed into national chains. Mass-circulation magazines attracted broad national audiences. Movies in the 1920s became an ever more popular and powerful form of mass communication. Over 100 million people saw films in 1930, as compared to 40 million in 1922. The addition of sound to motion pictures—beginning in 1927 with the first feature-length "talkie," *The Jazz Singer* starring Al Jolson—greatly enhanced film's appeal. A series of scandals in the early 1920s led to the creation of the new Motion Picture Association, which imposed much tighter controls over the content of films. The result was safer, more conventionally acceptable films, which may in fact have broadened the appeal of movies generally.

An equally important communications vehicle was the radio. The first commercial radio station in America, KDKA in Pittsburgh, began broadcasting in 1920, and the first national radio network, the National Broadcasting Company, was formed in 1927. That same year, Congress passed the Radio Act, which created a Federal Radio Commission to regulate the public airwaves used by private companies. (In 1935, it became the Federal Communications Commission, which survives today.)

WOMEN IN THE NEW ERA

College-educated women were no longer pioneers in the 1920s. There were now two and even three generations of graduates of women's or coeducational colleges and universities, and some were making their presence felt in professional areas that in the past women had rarely penetrated. The "new professional woman" was a vivid and widely publicized image in the 1920s. In reality, however, most employed women were still nonprofessional, lower-class workers. Middle-class women, in the meantime, remained largely in the home.

Yet the 1920s constituted a new era for middle-class women nonetheless. In particular, the decade saw a redefinition of motherhood. Shortly after World War I, John B. Watson and other behavioralists began to challenge the long-held assumption that women had an instinctive capacity for motherhood. Maternal affection was not, they claimed, sufficient preparation for child rearing. Instead, mothers should rely on the advice and assistance of experts and professionals: doctors, nurses, and trained educators.

For many middle-class women, these changes devalued what had been an important and consuming activity. Many attempted to compensate through what are often called "companionate marriages," the idea of devoting new attention to their roles as wives and companions. And many women now openly considered their sexual relationships with their husbands not simply as a means of procreation, as earlier generations had been taught, but as an important and pleasurable experience in its own right, the culmination of romantic love.

One result was growing interest in birth control. The pioneer of the American birth-control movement, Margaret Sanger, began her career as a promoter of the diaphragm and other birth-control devices out of a concern for working-class women; she believed that large families were among the major causes of poverty and distress in poor communities. By the 1920s, she was becoming more effective in persuading middle-class women to see the benefits of birth control. Nevertheless, some birth-control devices remained illegal in many states (and abortion remained illegal nearly everywhere).

To the consternation of many longtime women reformers and progressive suffragists, some women concluded that in the New Era it was no longer necessary to maintain a

THE CINEMA

THERE is probably no cultural or commercial product more closely identified with the United States than motion pictures—or, as they are known in much of the world, the cinema. Although the technology of cinema emerged from the work of inventors in England and France as well as the United States, the production and distribution of films has been dominated by Americans almost from the start. The United States was the first nation to create a film "industry," and it did so at a scale vaster than that of any other country. With 700 feature films a year in the 1920s, Hollywood produced ten times as many movies as any other nation; and even then, its films were dominating not only the vast American market but much of the world's market as well. Seventy percent of the films seen in France, 80 percent of those seen in Latin America, and 95 percent of the movies viewed in Canada and Great Britain were produced in the United States in the 1920s. As early as the 1930s, the penetration of other nations by American movies was already troubling many governments. The Soviet Union responded to the popularity of Walt Disney's Micky Mouse cartoons by inventing a cartoon hero of its own— a porcupine, designed to entertain in a way consistent with socialist values and not the capitalist ones that they believed Hollywood conveyed. During World War II, American films were banned in occupied France (prompting some antifascist dissidents to screen such American films as Frank Capra's *Mr. Smith Goes to Washington* in protest).

American dominance was a result in part of World War I and its aftermath, which debilitated European filmmaking just as movies were vigorously growing in the United States. By 1915, the United States had gained complete control of its own vast market and had so saturated it with movie theaters that by the end of World War I, half the theaters of the world were in America. Two decades later, after an extraordinary expansion of theaters in other nations, the United States continued to have over 40 percent of the world's cinemas. And while the spread of theaters through other areas of the world helped launch film industries in many other countries, it also increased the market (and the appetite) for American films and strengthened American supremacy in their production. "The sun, it now appears," the *Saturday Evening Post* commented in the mid-1920s, "never sets on the British Empire and the American motion picture." Movies were then, and perhaps remain still, America's most influential cultural export. Even American popular music, which has enormous global reach, faces more significant local competition than American movies do in most parts of the world.

Despite this American dominance, however, filmmaking has flourished—and continues to flourish—in many countries around the world. India's fabled "Bollywood," for example, produces an enormous number of movies for its domestic market—almost as many as the American industry creates— although few of them are widely exported. This global cinema has had a significant

VALENTINO The popularity of the film star Rudolph Valentino among American women was one of the most striking cultural phenomena of the 1920s. Valentino was slight and delicate, not at all like the conventional image of "manliness." But he developed an enormous following among women, in part—as this poster is obviously intended to suggest—by baring his body on screen. Valentino was Italian, which made him seem somehow strange and foreign to many older-stock Americans, and he was almost always cast in exotic roles, never as an American. His sudden death in 1926 (at the age of 31) created enormous outpourings of grief among many American women. (Photofest)

impact on American filmmaking, just as American films have influenced filmmakers abroad. The small British film industry had a strong early influence on American movies, partly because of the quality and originality of British films and partly because of the emigration of talented actors, directors, and screenwriters to the United States. The great Alfred Hitchcock, for example, made his first films in London before moving to Hollywood, where he spent the rest of his long career. After World War II, French "new wave" cinema helped spawn a new generation of highly individualistic directors in the United States. Asian cinema—especially the thriving film industry in Hong Kong with its gritty realism—helped lead to some of the powerfully violent American films of the 1980s and beyond, as well as the genre of martial-arts films that has become popular around the world. German, Italian, Swedish, Dutch, Japanese, Spanish, Australian, and Indian filmmakers also had enormous influence on Hollywood—and over time perhaps even greater influence on the large and growing "independent film" movement in the United States.

In recent decades, as new technologies and new styles have transformed films around the world, the American movie industry has continued to dominate global cinema. But national boundaries no longer adequately describe moviemaking in the twenty-first century. It is becoming a truly globalized enterprise in the same way that so many other commercial ventures are becoming. "American" films today are often produced abroad, often have non-American directors and actors, and are often paid for with international financing. Hollywood still dominates worldwide filmmaking, but Hollywood itself is now an increasingly global community. •

UNDERSTAND, ANALYZE, & EVALUATE

1. Did American movies, as the Soviet Union claimed in the 1930s, promote capitalism?
2. Why has the American movie industry continued to dominate global cinema?

rigid, Victorian female "respectability." They could smoke, drink, dance, wear seductive clothes and makeup, and attend lively parties. Those assumptions were reflected in the emergence of the "flapper"—the modern woman whose liberated lifestyle found expression in dress, hairstyle, speech, and behavior. The flapper lifestyle had a particular impact on lower-middle-class and working-class single women, who were filling new jobs in industry and the service sector. At night, such women flocked to clubs and dance halls in search of excitement and companionship. Many more affluent women soon began to copy the "flapper" style.

Despite all the changes, most women remained highly dependent on men and relatively powerless when men exploited that dependence. The National Woman's Party, under the leadership of Alice Paul, attempted to fight that powerlessness through its campaign for the Equal Rights Amendment, although it found little support in Congress. Responding to the suffrage victory, women organized the League of Women Voters and the women's auxiliaries of both the Democratic and Republican parties. Female-dominated consumer groups grew rapidly and increased the range and energy of their efforts.

Women activists won a brief triumph in 1921 when they helped secure passage of the Sheppard-Towner Act, which provided federal funds to states to establish prenatal and child health-care programs. From the start, however, the act produced controversy. Alice Paul and her supporters opposed the measure, complaining that it classified all women as mothers. More important, the American Medical Association fought Sheppard-Towner, warning that it would introduce untrained outsiders into the health-care field. In 1929, no longer worried about women voting as a bloc, Congress terminated the program.

THE DISENCHANTED

The generation that lived through (and in many cases fought in) the Great War quickly came to see the conflict as a useless waste of lives lost for no purpose. For many young people in the 1920s, disenchantment with the war contributed to a growing disenchantment with the United States. The newly prosperous and consumer-driven era they encountered seemed meaningless and vulgar to many artists and intellectuals in particular. As a result, they came to view their own culture with contempt. Rather than trying to influence and reform their society, they isolated themselves from it and embarked on a restless search for personal fulfillment. The American writer Gertrude Stein once referred to the young Americans emerging from World War I as a "Lost Generation."

Many artists and intellectuals coming of age in the 1920s experienced that fundamental disenchantment with modern America, reflected in a series of savage critiques of modern society by a wide range of writers, some of whom were known as the "debunkers." Among them was the Baltimore journalist H. L. Mencken, who delighted in ridiculing religion, politics, the arts, even democracy itself. Sinclair Lewis published a series of savage novels—*Main Street* (1920), *Babbitt* (1922), *Arrowsmith* (1925), and others—in which he lashed out at one aspect of modern bourgeois society after another. Intellectuals of the 1920s claimed to reject the "success ethic" that they believed dominated American life. The novelist F. Scott Fitzgerald, for example, attacked the American obsession with material success in *The Great Gatsby* (1925). The roster of important American writers active in the 1920s may have no equal in any other period. It included Fitzgerald, Lewis, Ernest Hemingway, Thomas Wolfe, John Dos Passos, Ezra Pound, T. S. Eliot, Gertrude Stein, Edna Ferber, William Faulkner, and Eugene O'Neill and a remarkable group of African American artists. In New York City, a new generation of African American

THE FLAPPER The "flapper"—with her short hair and cap pulled down low over the forehead, began as a working-class woman. By the later 1920s, affluent women began to dress like flappers. This woman stands on a cruise ship. (©Poodlesrock/Corbis)

intellectuals created a flourishing artistic life widely described as the "Harlem Renaissance." The Harlem poets, novelists, and artists drew heavily from their African roots in an effort to prove the richness of their own racial heritage, captured in a single sentence by the poet Langston Hughes: "I am a Negro—and beautiful." Other black writers in Harlem and elsewhere—James Weldon Johnson, Countee Cullen, Zora Neale Hurston, Claude McKay, Alain Locke—as well as black artists and musicians helped establish a thriving, and at times highly politicized, culture rooted in the historical legacy of race.

A CONFLICT OF CULTURES

The modern, secular culture of the 1920s did not go unchallenged. It grew up alongside an older, more traditional culture, with which it continually and often bitterly competed.

PROHIBITION

When the prohibition of the sale and manufacture of alcohol went into effect in January 1920, it had the support of most members of the middle class and most of those who considered themselves progressives. Within a year, however, it had become clear that the "noble experiment," as its defenders called it, was not working well. Prohibition did substantially reduce drinking in most parts of the country. But it also produced conspicuous and growing violations. Before long, it was almost as easy to acquire illegal alcohol in many parts of the country as it had once been to acquire legal alcohol. And since an enormous, lucrative industry was now barred to legitimate businessmen, organized crime took it over.

Many middle-class progressives who had originally supported prohibition soon soured on the experiment. But a large constituency of provincial, largely rural Protestant Americans continued vehemently to defend it. To them, prohibition represented the effort of an older America to protect traditional notions of morality. Drinking, which they associated with the modern city and Catholic immigrants, became a symbol of the new culture they believed was displacing them.

As the decade proceeded, opponents of prohibition (or "wets," as they came to be known) gained steadily in influence. Not until 1933, however, when the Great Depression added weight to their appeals, were they finally able to challenge the "drys" effectively and win repeal of the Eighteenth Amendment.

NATIVISM AND THE KLAN

Agitation for a curb on foreign immigration had begun in the nineteenth century and, as with prohibition, had gathered strength in the years before the war largely because of the support of middle-class progressives. In the years immediately following the war, when immigration began to be associated with radicalism, popular sentiment on behalf of restriction grew rapidly.

In 1921, Congress passed an emergency immigration act, establishing a quota system by which annual immigration from any country could not exceed 3 percent of the number of persons of that nationality who had been in the United States in 1910. The new law cut immigration from 800,000 to 300,000 in any single year, but the nativists remained unsatisfied. The National Origins Act of 1924 banned immigration from East Asia entirely and reduced the quota for Europeans from 3 to 2 percent. The quota would be based, moreover, not on the 1910 census but on the census of 1890, a year in which there had been far fewer southern and eastern Europeans in the country. What immigration there was, in other words, would heavily favor northwestern Europeans. Five years later, a further restriction set a rigid limit of 150,000 immigrants a year. In the years that followed, immigration officials seldom permitted even half that number actually to enter the country.

To defenders of an older, more provincial America, the growth of large communities of foreign peoples, alien in speech, habits, and values, came to seem a direct threat to their own embattled way of life. Among other things, this provincial nativism helped instigate the rebirth of the Ku Klux Klan as a major force in American society. The first Klan, founded during Reconstruction, had died in the 1870s. But in 1915, a new group of white southerners met on Stone Mountain near Atlanta and established a modern version of the society. Nativist passions had swelled in Georgia and elsewhere in response to the case of Leo Frank, a Jewish factory manager in Atlanta convicted in 1914 (on very flimsy evidence) of murdering a female employee; a mob stormed Frank's jail and lynched him. The premiere (also in Atlanta) of D. W. Griffith's film *The Birth of a Nation*, which glorified the early Klan, also helped inspire white southerners to form a new one.

At first the new Klan, like the old, was largely concerned with intimidating blacks. After World War I, however, concern about blacks gradually became secondary to concern about Catholics, Jews, and foreigners. At that point, membership in the Klan expanded rapidly and dramatically, not just in the small towns and rural areas of the South but in industrial cities in the North and Midwest. By 1924, there were reportedly 4 million members, including many women, organized in separate, parallel units. The largest state Klan was not in the South but in Indiana. Beginning in 1925, a series of scandals involving the organization's leaders precipitated a slow but steady decline in the Klan's influence.

Most Klan units (or "klaverns") tried to present their members as patriots and defenders of morality, and some did nothing more menacing than stage occasional parades and rallies. Often, however, the Klan also operated as a brutal, even violent, opponent of "alien" groups. Klansmen systematically terrorized blacks, Jews, Catholics, and foreigners. At times, they did so violently, through public whipping, tarring and feathering, arson, and lynching. What the Klan feared, however, was not simply "foreign" or "racially impure" groups, but anyone who posed a challenge to traditional values.

Religious Fundamentalism

Another cultural controversy of the 1920s was a conflict over the place of religion in contemporary society. By 1921, American Protestantism was already divided into two warring camps. On one side stood the modernists: mostly urban, middle-class people who were attempting to adapt religion to the teachings of modern science and to the realities of their modern, secular society. On the other side stood the fundamentalists: provincial, largely (although far from exclusively) rural men and women fighting to preserve traditional faith and to maintain the centrality of religion in American life. The fundamentalists insisted the Bible was to be interpreted literally. Above all, they opposed the teachings of Charles Darwin, whose theory of evolution had openly challenged the biblical story of the Creation.

By the mid-1920s, to the great alarm of modernists, fundamentalist demands to forbid the teaching of evolution in public schools were gaining political strength in some states. In Tennessee in March 1925, the legislature adopted a measure making it illegal for any public school teacher "to teach any theory that denies the story of the divine creation of man as taught in the Bible."

The Tennessee law caught the attention of the fledgling American Civil Liberties Union (ACLU), founded in 1917 to defend pacifists, radicals, and conscientious objectors during World War I. The ACLU offered free counsel to any Tennessee educator willing to defy the law and become the defendant in a test case. A twenty-four-year-old biology teacher in the town of Dayton, John T. Scopes, agreed to have himself arrested. And when the ACLU decided to send the famous attorney Clarence Darrow to defend Scopes, the aging William Jennings Bryan (now an important fundamentalist spokesman) announced that he would travel to Dayton to assist the prosecution. Journalists from across the country flocked to Tennessee to cover the trial. Scopes had, of course, clearly and deliberately violated the law; and a verdict of guilty was a foregone conclusion, especially when the judge refused to

CONSIDER THE SOURCE

BLACK SWAN RECORDS ADVERTISEMENT IN THE NEWSPAPER *CRISIS*, 1922

UNDERSTAND, ANALYZE, & EVALUATE

1. Explain what it means to "pass." Do you think this expression originally referred to Anglo-Americans?
2. What does the text of this ad suggest about African Americans in the consumer market in the 1920s?
3. Why, do you think, did the company choose that name? And what did this label— and this advertisement— suggest about the sense of self among African Americans in the 1920s?

Source: "Bert Williams," advertisement, *Crisis*, 24 (December 1922), 91.

---

permit "expert" testimony by evolution scholars. Scopes was fined $100, and the case was ultimately dismissed in a higher court because of a technicality. Nevertheless, Darrow scored an important victory for the modernists by calling Bryan himself to the stand to testify as an "expert on the Bible." In the course of the cross-examination, which was broadcast by radio to much of the nation, Darrow made Bryan's defense of biblical truths appear stubborn and foolish and finally maneuvered Bryan into admitting the possibility that not all religious dogma was subject to only one interpretation.

The Scopes trial put fundamentalists on the defensive. It discouraged many of them from participating openly in politics. But it did not resolve the conflict between fundamentalists and modernists, which continued to smolder.

DARROW AND BRYAN IN DAYTON Although the Scopes trial was chiefly significant for the issues it raised, it attracted national attention in 1925 at least as much because of its two celebrated attorneys: Clarence Darrow (*left*), the best-known defense attorney in America and a personification of the modern, skeptical, secular intellect; and William Jennings Bryan (*right*), the "Great Commoner," who had become, in the last years of his life, an ardent defender of Christian fundamentalism. (© Bettmann/Corbis)

The Democrats' Ordeal

The anguish of provincial Americans attempting to defend an embattled way of life proved particularly troubling to the Democratic Party during the 1920s. More than the Republicans, the Democrats consisted of a diverse coalition of interest groups, including prohibitionists, Klansmen, and fundamentalists on one side and Catholics, urban workers, and immigrants on the other.

At the 1924 Democratic National Convention in New York, a bitter conflict broke out over the platform when the party's urban wing attempted to win approval of planks calling for the repeal of prohibition and a denunciation of the Klan. Both planks narrowly failed. (The effort to condemn the Klan by name failed by one vote out of 1,085.) Even more damaging to the party was a deadlock in the balloting for a presidential candidate. Urban Democrats supported Alfred E. Smith, the Irish Catholic governor of New York; rural Democrats backed William McAdoo, Woodrow Wilson's Treasury secretary, who had skillfully positioned himself to win the support of southern and western delegates suspicious of modern urban life but whose reputation had been tarnished by a series of scandals resulting from his work as an attorney for an unsavory oil tycoon. For 103 ballots, the convention dragged on, with Smith supporters chanting "No oil on Al," until finally both Smith and McAdoo withdrew. The party settled on a compromise: the corporate lawyer John W. Davis, who lost decisively to Calvin Coolidge.

A similar schism plagued the Democrats again in 1928, when Al Smith finally secured his party's nomination for president. He was not, however, able to unite his divided party—in part because of widespread anti-Catholic sentiment, especially in the South. He was the first Democrat since the Civil War not to carry the entire South. Elsewhere, he carried no states at all except Massachusetts and Rhode Island. Smith's opponent, and the victor in the presidential election, was a man who perhaps more than any other personified the modern, prosperous, middle-class society of the New Era: Herbert Hoover.

REPUBLICAN GOVERNMENT

For twelve years, beginning in 1921, both the presidency and the Congress rested in the hands of the Republican Party. For most of those years, the federal government enjoyed a warm and supportive relationship with the American business community. Yet the government of the New Era was more than the passive, pliant instrument that critics often described. It attempted to serve in many respects as an agent of economic change.

HARDING AND COOLIDGE

Nothing seemed more clearly to illustrate the unadventurous nature of 1920s politics than the characters of the two men who served as president during most of the decade: Warren G. Harding and Calvin Coolidge.

Harding, who was elected to the presidency in 1920, was an undistinguished senator from Ohio. He had received the Republican presidential nomination as a result of an agreement among leaders of his party, who considered him, as one noted, a "good second-rater." Harding appointed distinguished men to some important cabinet offices, and he attempted to stabilize the nation's troubled foreign policy. But he seemed baffled by his responsibilities, as if he recognized his own unfitness. "I am a man of limited talents from a small town," he reportedly told friends on one occasion. "I don't seem to grasp that I am President." Harding's intellectual limits were compounded by personal weaknesses: his penchant for gambling, illegal alcohol, and attractive women.

Harding lacked the strength to abandon the party hacks who had helped create his political success. One of them, Ohio party boss Harry Daugherty, he appointed attorney general. Another, New Mexico Senator Albert B. Fall, he made secretary of the interior. Members of the so-called Ohio Gang filled important offices throughout the administration. Unknown to the public, Daugherty, Fall, and others were engaged in fraud and corruption. The most spectacular scandal involved the rich naval oil reserves at Teapot Dome, Wyoming, and Elk Hills, California. At the urging of Fall, Harding transferred control of those reserves from the Navy Department to the Interior Department. Fall then secretly leased them to two wealthy businessmen and received in return nearly half a million dollars in "loans" to ease his private financial troubles. Fall was ultimately convicted of bribery and sentenced to a year in prison; Harry Daugherty barely avoided a similar fate for his part in another scandal.

In the summer of 1923, only months before Senate investigations and press revelations brought the scandals to light, a tired and depressed Harding left Washington for a speaking tour in the West. In Seattle late in July, he complained of severe pain, which his doctors wrongly diagnosed as food poisoning. A few days later, in San Francisco, he died. He had suffered two major heart attacks.

In many ways, Calvin Coolidge, who succeeded Harding in the presidency, was utterly different from his predecessor. Where Harding was genial, garrulous, and debauched, Coolidge was dour, silent, even puritanical. In other ways, however, Harding and Coolidge were similar figures. Both took essentially passive approaches to their office.

Elected governor of Massachusetts in 1919, Coolidge had won national attention with his tough, if laconic, response to the Boston police strike that year. That was enough to make him his party's vice presidential nominee in 1920. Three years later, after Harding's death, he took the oath of office from his father, a justice of the peace, by the light of a kerosene lamp.

If anything, Coolidge was even less active as president than Harding, partly as a result of his conviction that government should interfere as little as possible in the life of the nation. In 1924, he received his party's presidential nomination virtually unopposed. Running against John W. Davis, he won a comfortable victory: 54 percent of the popular vote and 382 of the 531 electoral votes. Coolidge probably could have won renomination and reelection in 1928. Instead, in characteristically laconic fashion, he walked into a press room one day and handed each reporter a slip of paper containing a single sentence: "I do not choose to run for president in 1928."

GOVERNMENT AND BUSINESS

However passive the New Era presidents may have been, much of the federal government worked effectively and efficiently during the 1920s to adapt public policy to the widely accepted goal of the time: helping business and industry to operate with maximum efficiency and productivity. The close relationship between the private sector and the federal government forged during World War I continued. Secretary of the Treasury Andrew Mellon, a wealthy steel and aluminum tycoon, worked to achieve substantial reductions in taxes on corporate profits, personal incomes, and inheritances. Largely because of his efforts, Congress cut them all by more than half. Mellon also worked closely with President Coolidge after

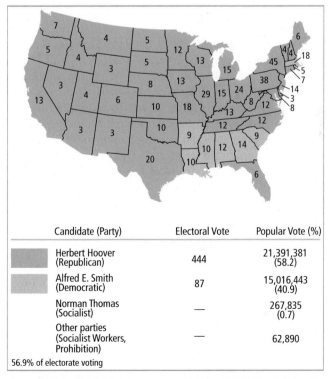

Candidate (Party)	Electoral Vote	Popular Vote (%)
Herbert Hoover (Republican)	444	21,391,381 (58.2)
Alfred E. Smith (Democratic)	87	15,016,443 (40.9)
Norman Thomas (Socialist)	—	267,835 (0.7)
Other parties (Socialist Workers, Prohibition)	—	62,890

56.9% of electorate voting

THE ELECTION OF 1928 The election of 1928 was, by almost any measure, highly one-sided. Herbert Hoover won over 58 percent of the popular vote to Alfred Smith's 41 percent. Smith carried only Massachusetts, Rhode Island, and some traditionally Democratic states in the South. • *Why did Smith do so poorly even in some of the South?*

1924 on a series of measures to trim dramatically the already modest federal budget, even managing to retire half the nation's World War I debt.

The most prominent member of the cabinet was Commerce Secretary Herbert Hoover. During his eight years in the Commerce Department, Hoover constantly encouraged voluntary cooperation in the private sector as the best avenue to stability. But the idea of voluntarism did not require that the government remain passive; on the contrary, public institutions, Hoover believed, had a duty to play an active role in creating the new, cooperative order. Above all, Hoover became the champion of the concept of business "associationalism"—a concept that envisioned the creation of national organizations of businessmen in particular industries. Through these trade associations, private entrepreneurs could, Hoover believed, stabilize their industries and promote efficiency in production and marketing.

Many progressives derived encouragement from the election of Herbert Hoover to the presidency in 1928. Hoover easily defeated Al Smith, the Democratic candidate. And he entered office promising bold new efforts to solve the nation's remaining economic problems. But Hoover had few opportunities to prove himself. Less than a year after his inauguration, the nation plunged into the severest and most prolonged economic crisis in its history—a crisis that brought many of the optimistic assumptions of the New Era crashing down and launched the nation into a period of unprecedented social innovation and reform.

CONCLUSION

The remarkable prosperity of the 1920s shaped much of what exuberant contemporaries liked to call the "New Era." In the years after World War I, America built a vibrant and extensive national culture. Its middle class moved increasingly into the embrace of the growing consumer culture. Its politics reorganized itself around the needs of a booming, interdependent industrial economy—rejecting many of the reform crusades of the previous generation but also creating new institutions to help promote economic growth and stability.

Beneath the glittering surface of the New Era, however, were great controversies and injustices. Although the prosperity of the 1920s was more widely spread than at any time in the nation's industrial history, more than half the population failed to achieve any real benefits from the growth. A new, optimistic, secular culture attracted millions of urban middle-class people. But many other Americans looked at it with alarm and fought against it with great fervor. The unprepossessing conservative presidents of the era suggested a time of stability, but in fact few eras in modern American history have seen so much political and cultural conflict.

The 1920s ended in a catastrophic economic crash that has colored the image of those years ever since. The crises of the 1930s should not obscure the real achievements of the New Era economy. Neither, however, should the prosperity of the 1920s obscure the inequity and instability in those years that helped produce the difficult years to come.

RECALL AND REFLECT

1. What was the impact of the automobile on American life?
2. How did labor fare during the 1920s? What particular problems did female, black, immigrant, and unskilled laborers face?
3. How did religion respond to the consumer culture of the 1920s?
4. What was the myth and what was the reality of the "new woman" of the 1920s?
5. What was the nature and extent of the nativism of the 1920s?

23

THE GREAT DEPRESSION

THE COMING OF THE DEPRESSION
THE AMERICAN PEOPLE IN HARD TIMES
THE DEPRESSION AND AMERICAN CULTURE
THE ORDEAL OF HERBERT HOOVER

LOOKING AHEAD

1. What were some of the causes of the Great Depression? What made it so severe, and why did it last so long?
2. What was the impact of the Depression on farmers, minorities, and women?
3. How did President Hoover and his administration try to deal with the Depression? What was the result of those efforts?

"WE IN AMERICA TODAY," Herbert Hoover proclaimed in August 1928, "are nearer to the final triumph over poverty than ever before in the history of any land." Only fifteen months later, those words would return to haunt him, as the nation plunged into the severest and most prolonged economic depression in its history—a depression that continued in one form or another for a full decade, not only in the United States but throughout much of the world.

TIME LINE

1929

Stock market crash; Great Depression begins

Agricultural Marketing Act

1930

Hawley-Smoot Tariff

Drought begins in Dust Bowl

1931

Scottsboro defendants arrested

1932

Reconstruction Finance Corporation established

Bonus Army in Washington

Franklin D. Roosevelt elected president

1934

Southern Tenant Farmers Union organized

1935

American Communist Party proclaims Popular Front

1936

Mitchell's *Gone with the Wind*

1939

Steinbeck's *The Grapes of Wrath*

1940

Wright's *Native Son*

THE COMING OF THE DEPRESSION

The sudden financial collapse in 1929 came as an especially severe shock because it followed so closely an era that appeared to offer economic miracles—miracles that seemed especially evident in the remarkable performance of the stock market.

In February 1928, stock prices began a steady ascent that continued, with only a few temporary lapses, for a year and a half. Between May 1928 and September 1929, the average price of stocks rose over 40 percent. Trading mushroomed from 2 or 3 million shares a day to over 5 million, and at times to as many as 10 or 12 million. In short, a widespread speculative fever grew steadily more intense, particularly once brokerage firms began encouraging the mania by offering absurdly easy credit to those buying stocks.

THE GREAT CRASH

In the autumn of 1929, the market began to fall apart. On October 29, "Black Tuesday," after a week of growing instability, all efforts to save the market failed. Sixteen million shares of stock were traded; the industrial index dropped 43 points (or nearly 10 percent), wiping out all the gains of the previous year; stocks in many companies became virtually worthless. Within a month, stocks had lost half their September value, and despite occasional, short-lived rallies, they continued to decline for several years after that.

Popular folklore has established the stock market crash as the beginning, and even the cause, of the Great Depression. But although October 1929 might have been the most visible early sign of the crisis, the Depression had earlier beginnings and other causes.

CAUSES OF THE DEPRESSION

Economists and historians have argued for decades about the causes of the Great Depression. But most agree on several things. They agree, first, that what is remarkable about the crisis is not that it occurred but that it was so severe and that it lasted so long, which most observers agree—even if they agree on little else—was the result of several factors.

One was a lack of diversification in the American economy in the 1920s. Prosperity had depended excessively on a few basic industries, notably construction and automobiles, which in the late 1920s began to decline. Expenditures on construction fell from $11 billion in 1926 to under $9 billion in 1929. Automobile sales fell by more than a third in the first nine months of 1929. Newer industries were emerging to take up the slack—among them petroleum, chemicals, electronics, and plastics—but none had yet developed enough strength to compensate for this decline.

A second important factor was the maldistribution of purchasing power and, as a result, a weakness in consumer demand. As industrial and agricultural production increased, the proportion of the profits going to potential consumers was too small to create an adequate market for the goods the economy was producing. Even in 1929, after nearly a decade of economic growth, more than half the families in America lived on the edge of or below the minimum subsistence level.

A third major problem was the credit structure of the economy. Farmers were deeply in debt, and crop prices were too low to allow them to pay off what they owed. Small banks were in constant trouble as their customers defaulted on loans; large banks were in trouble, too. Although most American bankers were very conservative, some of the nation's biggest banks were investing recklessly in the stock market or making unwise loans. When the market crashed and the loans went bad, some banks failed and others made the crisis worse by contracting already scarce credit and calling in loans that borrowers could not pay.

A fourth factor was America's position in international trade. Late in the 1920s, European demand for American goods began to decline, partly because European industry and agriculture were becoming more productive and partly because some European nations were having financial difficulties of their own. But it was also because the European economy was being destabilized by the international debt structure that had emerged in the aftermath of World War I.

This debt structure, therefore, was a fifth factor contributing to the Depression. When the war came to an end in 1918, all the European nations that had been allied with the United States owed large sums of money to American banks, sums much too large to be repaid out of their shattered economies, which is partly why the Allies had insisted on reparation payments from Germany and Austria. Reparations, they believed, would provide them with a way to pay off their own debts. But Germany and Austria were no more able to pay the reparations than the Allies were able to pay their debts.

The American government refused to forgive or reduce the debts. Instead, American banks began making large loans to European governments, which used them to pay off their earlier loans. Thus debts (and reparations) were being paid only by piling up new and greater debts. At the same time, American protective tariffs were making it difficult for Europeans to sell their goods in American markets. Without any source of foreign exchange with which to repay their loans, they began to default. The collapse of the international credit structure was one of the reasons the Depression spread to Europe after 1931.

CAUSES OF THE GREAT DEPRESSION

WHAT were the causes of the Great Depression? Economists and historians have debated this question since the economic collapse began and still have not reached anything close to agreement on it. In the process, however, they have illustrated several very different theories about how a modern economy works.

During the Depression itself, different groups offered interpretations of the crisis that fit comfortably with their own self-interests. Some corporate leaders claimed that the Depression was the result of a lack of "business confidence," that businessmen were reluctant to invest because they feared government regulation and high taxes. The Hoover administration blamed international economic forces and sought, therefore, to stabilize world currencies and debt structures. New Dealers, determined to find a domestic solution to the crisis, argued that the Depression was a crisis of "underconsumption"—that low wages and high prices had made it too difficult to buy the products of the industrial economy and that a lack of demand had led to the economic collapse.

Scholars in the years since the Great Depression have also created interpretations that fit their view of how the economy works. One of the first important postwar interpretations came from the economists Milton Friedman and Anna Schwartz, in their *Monetary History of the United States* (1963). In a chapter titled "The Great Contraction," they argued for what has become known as the "monetary" interpretation. The Depression, they claimed, was a result of a drastic contraction of the currency (a result of mistaken decisions by the Federal Reserve Board, which raised interest rates when it should have lowered them). These deflationary measures turned an ordinary recession into the Great Depression. The monetary argument fit comfortably with the ideas that Milton Friedman, in particular, advocated for many years: that sound monetary policy is the best way to solve economic problems—as opposed to fiscal policies, such as taxation and spending.

A second, very different argument is known as the "spending" interpretation, an interpretation supported by many liberal, Keynesian economists. It is identified with, among others, the economist Peter Temin and his book *Did Monetary Forces Cause the Great Depression?* (1976). Temin's answer to his own question is no. The cause of the crisis

PROGRESS OF THE DEPRESSION

The stock market crash of 1929 did not so much cause the Depression, then, as help trigger a chain of events that exposed larger weaknesses in the American economy. During the next three years, the crisis grew steadily worse.

The most serious problem at first was the collapse of much of the banking system. Between 1930 and 1933, over 9,000 American banks either went bankrupt or closed their doors to avoid bankruptcy. Partly as a result of these banking closures, the nation's money was not monetary contraction (although the contraction made it worse) but rather a drop in investment and consumer spending, which preceded the decline in the money supply and helped to cause it. Here again, there are obvious political implications. If a decline in spending was the cause of the Depression, then the proper response was an effort to stimulate demand—raising government spending, increasing purchasing power, redistributing wealth. The New Deal never ended the Depression because it did not spend enough. World War II did end it because it pumped so much public money into the economy.

Another important explanation comes from the historian Michael Bernstein. In *The Great Depression* (1987) he avoids trying to explain why the economic downturn occurred and asks, instead, why it lasted so long. The reason the recession of 1929 became the Depression of the 1930s, he argues, was the timing of the collapse. The recession began as an ordinary cyclical downturn. Had it begun a few years earlier, the basic strength of the automobile and construction industries in the 1920s would have led to a reasonably speedy recovery. Had it begun a few years later, a group of newer, emerging industries—aviation, petrochemicals and plastics, aluminum, and others—would have helped produce a recovery in a reasonably short time. But the recession began in 1929, too late for the automobile and construction industries to help and too soon for emerging new industries to help, since they were still in their infancies.

The political implications of this argument are less obvious than those of some other interpretations. But one possible conclusion is that if economic growth depends on the successful development of new industries to replace declining ones, then the most sensible economic policy for government is to target investment and other policies toward the growth of new economic sectors. One of the reasons World War II was so important to the long-term recovery of the U.S. economy, Bernstein's argument suggests, was not just that it pumped money into the economy but that much of that money contributed to developing new industries. This is, in other words, an explanation of the Depression that seems to support some of the economic ideas that became popular in the 1980s and 1990s calling for a more direct government role in stimulating the growth of new industries.

In the end, however, no single explanation of the Great Depression has ever seemed adequate to most scholars. The event, the economist Robert Lucas once argued, is simply "inexplicable" by any rational calculation. There is no one, wholly persuasive answer to the question of what caused it.   •

UNDERSTAND, ANALYZE, & EVALUATE

1. How do the "monetary" and "spending" arguments about the causes of the Great Depression differ from each other?
2. Why have there been such widespread and long-standing differences on the question of the causes of the Depression?

supply shrank by perhaps a third or more between 1930 and 1933, which caused a decline in purchasing power and thus deflation. Manufacturers and merchants began reducing prices, cutting back on production, and laying off workers. Some economists argue that a severe depression could have been avoided if the Federal Reserve system had acted responsibly. But late in 1931, in a misguided effort to build international confidence in the dollar, it raised interest rates, which contracted the money supply even further.

The American gross national product plummeted from over $104 billion in 1929 to $76.4 billion in 1932—a 25 percent decline in three years. By 1932, according to the

THE UNEMPLOYED, 1930   Thousands of unemployed men wait to be fed outside the Municipal Lodgers House in New York City. (Library of Congress)

relatively crude estimates of the time, 25 percent of the American workforce was unemployed. (Some argue that the figure was even higher.) For the rest of the decade, unemployment averaged nearly 20 percent, never dropping below 15 percent. Up to another one-third of the workforce was "underemployed"—experiencing major reductions in wages, hours, or both.

THE AMERICAN PEOPLE IN HARD TIMES

Someone asked the British economist John Maynard Keynes in the 1930s whether he was aware of any historical era comparable to the Great Depression. "Yes," Keynes replied. "It was called the Dark Ages, and it lasted 400 years." The Depression did not last 400 years. It did, however, bring unprecedented economic despair to the United States and much of the Western world.

UNEMPLOYMENT AND RELIEF

In the industrial Northeast and Midwest, cities were virtually paralyzed by unemployment. Cleveland, Ohio, for example, had an unemployment rate of 50 percent in 1932; Akron, 60 percent; Toledo, 80 percent. Unemployed workers walked through the streets day after day looking for jobs that did not exist. An increasing number of families turned to state and local public relief systems, just to be able to eat. But those systems, which in the 1920s had served only a small number of indigents, were totally unequipped to handle the heavy new demands.

In many cities, therefore, relief simply collapsed. Private charities attempted to supplement the public relief efforts, but the problem was far beyond their capabilities as well.

In rural areas, conditions were in many ways worse. Farm income declined by 60 percent between 1929 and 1932. A third of all American farmers lost their land. In addition, a large area of agricultural settlement in the Great Plains suffered from a catastrophic natural disaster: one of the worst droughts in the history of the nation. Beginning in 1930, the region that came to be known as the "Dust Bowl," which stretched north from Texas into the Dakotas, experienced a steady decline in rainfall and an accompanying increase in heat. The drought continued for a decade, turning what had once been fertile farm regions into virtual deserts.

Many farmers, like many urban unemployed, left their homes in search of work. In the South, in particular, many dispossessed farmers—black and white—simply wandered from town to town, hoping to find jobs or handouts. Hundreds of thousands of families from the Dust Bowl (often known as "Okies," since many came from Oklahoma) traveled to California and other states, where they found conditions little better than those they had left. Many worked as agricultural migrants, traveling from farm to farm, picking fruit and other crops at starvation wages.

AFRICAN AMERICANS AND THE DEPRESSION

Most African Americans had not shared very much in the prosperity of the previous decade. But they did share in the hardships of the Great Depression.

As the Depression began, over half of all black Americans still lived in the South. Most were farmers. The collapse of prices for cotton and other staple crops left some with no income at all. Many left the land altogether—either by choice or because they had been evicted by landlords who no longer found sharecropping profitable. Some migrated to

BLACK MIGRANTS The Great Migration of blacks from the rural South into the cities had begun before World War I. But in the 1930s and 1940s the movement accelerated. Jacob Lawrence, an eminent African American artist, created a series of paintings titled, collectively, *The Migration of the Negro*, to illustrate this major event in the history of African Americans. (© 2013 The Jacob and Gwendolyn Lawrence Foundation, Seattle/Artists Rights Society (ARS), New York)

THE GLOBAL DEPRESSION

THE Great Depression began in the United States. But it did not end there. The American economy was the largest in the world, and its collapse sent shock waves across the globe. By 1931, the American depression had become a world depression, with important implications for the course of global history.

The origins of the worldwide depression lay in the pattern of debts that had emerged during and after World War I, when the United States loaned billions of dollars to European nations. In 1931, with American banks staggering and in many cases collapsing, large banks in New York began desperately calling in their loans from Germany and Austria. That precipitated the collapse of one of Austria's largest banks, which in turn created panic through much of central Europe. The economic collapse in Germany and Austria meant that those nations could not continue paying reparations to Britain and France (required by the Treaty of Versailles of 1919), which meant in turn that Britain and France could not continue paying off their loans to the United States. This spreading financial crisis was accompanied by a dramatic contraction of international trade, precipitated in part by the Hawley-Smoot Tariff in the United States, which established the highest import duties in history and stifled much global commerce. Depressed agricultural prices—a result of worldwide overproduction—also contributed to the downturn. By 1932, worldwide industrial production had declined by more than one-third, and world trade had plummeted by nearly two-thirds. By 1933,

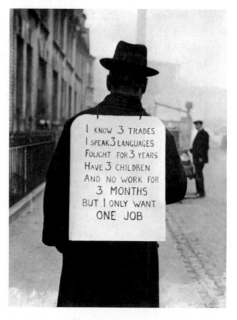

LOOKING FOR WORK IN LONDON, 1935 An unemployed London man wears a sign that seems designed to convince passersby that he is an educated, respectable person despite his present circumstances. (General Photographic Agency/Hulton Archive/Getty Images)

30 million people in industrial nations were unemployed, five times the number of four years before.

But the Depression was not confined to industrial nations. Imperialism and industrialization had drawn almost all regions of the world into the international industrial economy. Colonies and nations in Africa, Asia, and South America—critically dependent on exporting raw materials and agricultural goods to industrial countries—experienced a collapse in demand for their products and thus rising levels of poverty and unemployment. Some nations—among them the

Soviet Union and China—remained relatively unconnected to the global economy and suffered relatively little from the Great Depression. But in most parts of the world, the Depression caused tremendous social and economic hardship.

It also created political turmoil. Among the countries hardest hit by the Depression was Germany, where industrial production declined by 50 percent and unemployment reached 35 percent in the early 1930s. The desperate economic conditions there contributed greatly to the rise of the Nazi party and its leader Adolf Hitler, who became chancellor in 1933. Japan suffered greatly as well, dependent as it was on world trade to sustain its growing industrial economy and purchase essential commodities for its needs at home. And in Japan, as in Germany, economic troubles produced political turmoil and aided the rise of a new militaristic regime. In Italy, the fascist government of Benito Mussolini, which had first taken power in the 1920s, also saw militarization and territorial expansion as a way out of economic difficulties.

In other nations, governments sought solutions to the Depression through reform of their domestic economies. The most prominent example was the New Deal in the United States. But there were important experiments in other nations as well. Among the most common responses to the Depression around the world was substantial government investment in public works, such as roads, bridges, dams, public buildings, and other large projects. Among the nations that adopted this approach—in addition to the United States—were Britain, France, Germany, Italy, and the Soviet Union. Another response was the expansion of government-funded relief for the unemployed. All the industrial countries of the world experimented with various forms of relief, often borrowing ideas from one another in the process. And the Depression helped create new approaches to economics, in the face of the apparent failure of classical models of economic behavior to explain, or provide solutions to, the crisis. The great British economist John Maynard Keynes revolutionized economic thought in much of the world. His 1936 book *The General Theory of Employment, Interest, and Money*, despite its bland title, created a sensation by arguing that the Depression was a result not of declining production but of inadequate consumer demand. Governments, he said, could stimulate their economies by increasing the money supply and creating investment—through a combination of lowering interest rates and public spending. Keynesianism, as Keynes's theories became known, began to have an impact in the United States in 1938, and in much of the rest of the world in subsequent years.

The Great Depression was an important turning point not only in American history but in the history of the twentieth-century world. It transformed ideas of public policy and economics in many nations. It toppled old regimes and created new ones. And perhaps above all, it was a major factor—maybe the single most important factor—in the coming of World War II. •

UNDERSTAND, ANALYZE, & EVALUATE

1. How did the 1919 Treaty of Versailles and the Hawley-Smoot Tariff contribute to the global depression of the 1930s?
2. How did the governments of European nations respond to the Depression?
3. What effect did the global depression have on economic theory? Why was Keynes's economic theory so revolutionary?

southern cities. But there, unemployed whites believed they had first claim to what work there was, and some now began to take positions as janitors, street cleaners, and domestic servants, displacing the African Americans who formerly occupied those jobs. By 1932, over half the blacks in the South were unemployed.

Unsurprisingly, therefore, many black southerners—perhaps 400,000 in all—left the South in the 1930s and journeyed to the cities of the North. But conditions there were little better. In New York, black unemployment was nearly 50 percent. In other cities, it was higher. Two million African Americans—half the total black population of the country—were on some form of relief by 1932.

Traditional patterns of segregation and disenfranchisement in the South survived the Depression largely unchallenged. But a few particularly notorious examples of racism did attract the attention of the nation. The most celebrated was the Scottsboro case. In March 1931, nine black teenagers were taken off a freight train in northern Alabama (in a small town near Scottsboro) and were arrested for vagrancy and disorder. Later, two white women who had also been riding the train accused them of rape. In fact, there was overwhelming evidence, medical and otherwise, that the women had not been raped at all; they may have made their accusations out of fear of being arrested themselves. Nevertheless, an all-white jury in Alabama quickly convicted all nine of the "Scottsboro boys" (as they were known to both friends and foes) and sentenced eight of them to death.

The Supreme Court overturned the convictions in 1932, and a series of new trials began. The International Labor Defense, an organization associated with the Communist Party, came to the aid of the accused youths and began to publicize the case. Although the white southern juries who sat on the case never acquitted any of the defendants, all of the accused eventually gained their freedom—although the last of the Scottsboro defendants did not leave prison until 1950.

HISPANICS AND ASIANS IN DEPRESSION AMERICA

Similar patterns of discrimination confronted many Mexicans and Mexican Americans. The Hispanic population of the United States had been growing steadily since early in the century, largely in California and other areas of the Southwest. Chicanos (as Mexican Americans are sometimes known) filled many of the same menial jobs there that blacks had traditionally filled in other regions. Some farmed small, marginal tracts; others became agricultural migrants. It had always been a precarious existence, and the Depression made things significantly worse. Unemployed whites in the Southwest demanded jobs held by Hispanics, jobs that whites had previously considered beneath them. Thus Mexican unemployment rose quickly to levels far higher than those for whites. Some officials arbitrarily removed Mexicans from relief rolls or simply rounded them up and transported them across the border. Perhaps half a million Chicanos left the United States for Mexico in the first years of the Depression.

There were occasional signs of organized resistance by Mexican Americans themselves, most notably in California, where some formed a union of migrant farmworkers. But harsh repression by local growers and the public authorities allied with them prevented such organizations from having much impact. As a result, many Hispanics began to migrate to cities such as Los Angeles, where they lived in poverty comparable to that of urban blacks in the South and Northeast.

For Asian Americans, too, the Depression reinforced long-standing patterns of discrimination and economic marginalization. In California, where the largest Japanese American and Chinese American populations were, educated Asians had always found it difficult, if not impossible, to move into mainstream professions. Japanese American college graduates often found themselves working in family fruit stands. For those who found jobs in the industrial or service economy, employment was precarious; like blacks and Hispanics, Asians often lost jobs to white Americans desperate for work. Japanese farmworkers, like Chicano farmworkers, suffered from the increasing competition for even these low-paying jobs from white migrants from the Great Plains.

Chinese Americans fared no better. The overwhelming majority worked, as they had for many years, in Chinese-owned laundries and restaurants. Those who moved outside the Asian community could rarely find jobs above the entry level. Chinese women, for example, might find work as stock girls in department stores but almost never as salesclerks. Educated Chinese men and women could hope for virtually no professional opportunities outside the world of the Chinatowns.

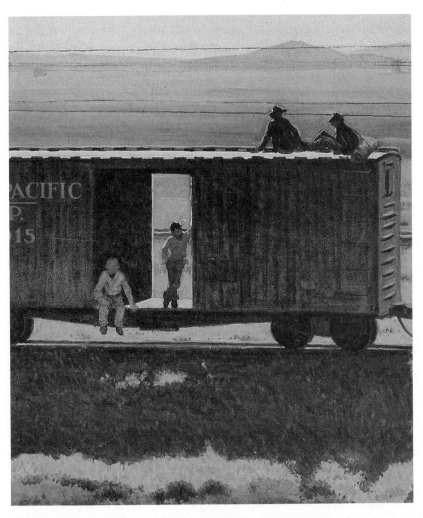

DETAIL FROM *PRIVATE CAR* (1932), BY LECONTE STEWART Thousands of men (and some women) left their homes during the Great Depression and traveled from city to city looking for work, often hopping freight trains for a free, if **illegal, ride.** (Museum of Church History & Art, Salt Lake City, Utah)

MR. TARVER REMEMBERS THE GREAT DEPRESSION IN A 1940 INTERVIEW WITH THE FEDERAL WRITERS' PROJECT

YES, I really went through the depression. [. . .] "There were thousands who went down during the panic—lost fortunes, homes, business, and in fact everything. Some have survived, and many never will. A great many were too old to begin building up again. In the kind of work I'm in I have been in position to know some of the devastating effects of it, and it certainly gets on your sympathy.

"I guess you would say I am recovering from it. When I say that though, I'm not boasting, but I'm deeply grateful for the good fortunes that have came my way. Then, too, I feel under everlasting obligations to some of my friends who have helped me to get where I am.

"I had not accumulated a great deal at the time of the panic, but I did have some savings and a good job. That was the trouble, my savings and my job went at the same time. Now that was real trouble. Nobody but my wife and I knew just what we did go through. [. . .]

I was making a fine salary, had a growing savings account, and a host of friends, and no serious troubles to worry about. My wife is just the smartest, thriftiest person you have ever seen. To her I owe a lot of my successes. She is fine with her needle and crocheting, and you never saw her idle. She made all her spending money that way. Even now since we have been in Washington she keeps it up. And her fruit cake! People here rave about it. She cooks an enormous amount of it every Christmas and sells it for a big profit. She can't fill all the orders she gets. She is very resourceful and right now, if I were to die and not leave her a thing, she would manage some way. One of my hobbies was gardening and it proved to be a profitable one too. This place we rented had a fine garden spot, the finest in Dublin, so every one said. I worked in it early every morning and in the afternoon after banking hours. I sold lots of vegetables, and realized a lot on them—especially the early variety that brought a good price." [. . .]

"One morning we three were at the breakfast table when the phone rang. It was one of the fellows who worked at the bank.

"'Tarver, he said, 'have you heard the news?'

"'What news? No, I haven't heard any news,' said I. What's it all about?'

WOMEN AND FAMILIES IN THE GREAT DEPRESSION

The economic crisis strengthened the widespread belief that a woman's proper place was in the home. Many men and women believed that with employment so scarce, what work there was should go to men and that no woman whose husband was employed should accept a job. Indeed, from 1932 until 1937, it was illegal for more than one member of a family to hold a federal civil service job.

But the widespread assumption that married women, at least, should not work outside the home did not stop them from doing so. Both single and married women worked in the 1930s because they or their families needed the money. By the end of the Depression, 25 percent more women were working than had been doing so at the beginning, despite considerable obstacles. Professional opportunities for women declined because unemployed men began moving into professions that had previously been considered women's fields. Female industrial workers were more likely to be laid off or to experience wage reductions than their male

"Well,' he said, "hurry on down and see.'

"If you will excuse the expression, when he said that, the seat of my britches almost dropped out. I felt like it meant trouble of some kind. I had had a terrible feeling of uneasiness over the bank for some time. Banks had been closing all over the country. There had been a run on our bank some time previous to that, but we tided that over, and since then it had seemed stronger than ever.

"I hurried down and, sure enough, in front of the bank, there stood a crowd of employees, as blank expressions on their faces as I've ever seen. They were too dumbfounded to be excited even.

"The bank was closed and a notice to that effect on the door. We stood there just looking at each other until finally one said, 'Well, boys, guess we had better go on the inside and see if we can find out what it's all about. I guess there goes our jobs.'

[. . .] "Just as I was getting in the dumps about a regular job, I was notified to report at once, to act as assistant receiver for a defunct bank in Florida. They were feeling the depression there even more than we were in Georgia, and banks were closing every day.

[. . .] "Banks were still closing until it was hard to get enough receivers for them. Oh, we did work. Banks in neighboring towns were added to our work until we were liquidating six banks at one time, all in different places. I had to have another car then but was lucky to pick up a good used car almost at my own price. People had lost their cars as well as their homes, so it was no trouble to buy a good used one. Sometimes I would ride to all six of these banks in one day and when night came I would be completely given out. I couldn't stop even then, for there was scarcely a night that we didn't work. [. . .]

UNDERSTAND, ANALYZE, & EVALUATE

1. Why was Mr. Tarver doubly affected by the banking crisis of the Great Depression? How did Mr. and Mrs. Tarver compensate for their losses in the job market?
2. How might the Great Depression have shaped the outlook of Mr. and Mrs. Tarver on work, leisure, and consumption for years, if not decades, to come?

Source: Mr. W. W. Tarver (White), Finance Officer in U.S. Treasury (Bank Conservator), 5001 Nebraska Ave., N.W., Washington, D.C., interviewed by Bradley. Library of Congress, *American Life Histories: Manuscripts from the Federal Writers' Project, 1936–1940.* http://memory.loc.gov/cgi-bin/query/r?ammem/wpa:@field%28DOCID+@lit%28wpa112060215%29%29

counterparts. But white women also had certain advantages in the workplace. The nonprofessional jobs that women traditionally held—salesclerks, stenographers, and other service positions—were less likely to disappear than the predominantly male jobs in heavy industry.

Black women suffered massive unemployment, particularly in the South, because of a great reduction of domestic service jobs. As many as half of all black working women lost their jobs in the 1930s. Even so, at the end of the 1930s, 38 percent of black women were employed, as compared with 24 percent of white women. That was so because black women—both married and unmarried—had always been more likely to work than white women, less out of preference than out of economic necessity.

The Depression also worked to erode the strength of many family units. There was a decline in the divorce rate, but largely because divorce was now too expensive for some. More common was the informal breakup of families, particularly the desertion of families by unemployed men trying to escape the humiliation of being unable to earn a living. The marriage rate and the birth rate both declined for the first time since the early nineteenth century.

THE DEPRESSION AND AMERICAN CULTURE

The Great Depression was a traumatic experience for millions of Americans. Out of the crisis emerged probing criticisms of American life. But the Depression also produced powerful confirmations of more traditional values and reinforced many traditional goals. There was not one Depression culture, but many.

DEPRESSION VALUES

Prosperity and industrial growth had done much to shape American values in the 1920s. But hard times had profound effects on the nation's social values. In general, however, American social values seemed to change relatively little in response to the Depression. Instead, many people responded to hard times by redoubling their commitment to familiar ideas and goals. The Depression did not destroy the success ethic.

The survival of the ideals of work and individual responsibility was evident in many ways, not least in the reactions of those most traumatized by the Depression: people who suddenly found themselves without employment. Some expressed anger and struck out at the economic system. Many, however, seemed to blame themselves. At the same time, millions responded eagerly to reassurances that they could, through their own efforts, restore themselves to prosperity and success. Dale Carnegie's *How to Win Friends and Influence People* (1936), a self-help manual preaching individual initiative, was one of the best-selling books of the decade. The most popular were cultural products of the 1930s that diverted attention away from the Depression. And they came to Americans primarily through the two most powerful instruments of popular culture in the 1930s—radio and the movies.

RADIO

Almost every American family had a radio in the 1930s. In cities and towns, radio consoles were as familiar a part of the furnishing of homes as tables and chairs. Even in remote rural areas without access to electricity, many families purchased radios and hooked them up to car batteries when they wished to listen.

Radio was often a community experience. Young people would place radios on their front porches and invite friends by to sit, talk, or dance. In poor urban neighborhoods, people would gather on a street or in a backyard to listen to sporting events or concerts. Within families, the radio often drew parents and children together to listen to favorite programs.

What did Americans hear on the radio? Although radio stations occasionally carried provocative programs, the staple of broadcasting was escapism: comedies such as *Amos 'n' Andy* (with its humorous, if demeaning, picture of urban blacks); adventures such as *Superman, Dick Tracy,* and *The Lone Ranger*; and other entertainment programs. Radio brought a new kind of comedy to a wide audience. Jack Benny, George Burns and Gracie Allen, and other masters of elaborately timed repartee began to develop broad followings. Enormously popular, especially among women who were alone in the house during the day, were soap operas (so named because they were generally sponsored by soap companies, whose advertising was targeted at women).

Radio provided Americans with their first direct access to important public events. Radio news and sports divisions grew rapidly to meet the demand. Some of the most dramatic moments of the 1930s were a result of radio coverage of celebrated events: the World Series, the Academy Awards, political conventions. When the German dirigible *Hindenburg* crashed in flames in Lakehurst, New Jersey, in 1937, it produced an enormous national reaction largely because of the live radio account by a broadcaster, overcome with emotion, who cried out, as he watched the terrible crash, "Oh the humanity! Oh the humanity!" The actor-director Orson Welles created another memorable event on Halloween night, 1938, when he broadcast a radio play about aliens landing in central New Jersey who had set off toward New York armed with terrible weapons. The play took the form of a news broadcast, and it created panic among millions of people who believed for a while that the events it described were real.

THE MOVIES

In the first years of the Depression, movie attendance dropped significantly. By the mid-1930s, however, most Americans had resumed their moviegoing habits in part because the movies (now with sound and, by the end of the decade, many of them in color) were becoming more appealing.

Hollywood continued to exercise tight control over its products in the 1930s through its resilient censor Will Hays, who ensured that most movies carried no sensational or controversial messages. The studio system—through which a few large movie companies exercised iron control over actors, writers, and directors—also worked to ensure that Hollywood films avoided controversy.

Neither the censor nor the studio system, however, could (or wished to) completely prevent films from exploring social questions. There were many serious films that portrayed the problems of the Depression—for example, King Vidor's *Our Daily Bread* (1932) and John Ford's adaptation of *The Grapes of Wrath* (1940). Gangster movies such as *Little Caesar* (1930) and *The Public Enemy* (1931) portrayed a dark, gritty, violent world with which few Americans were familiar, but their desperate stories were popular nevertheless with those engaged in their own difficult struggles.

But the most effective presentation of a social message came from the brilliant Italian-born director Frank Capra. Capra had a deep and somewhat romanticized love for his adopted country, and he translated that love into a vaguely populistic admiration for ordinary people. He contrasted the decency of small-town America and the common man with what he considered the grasping opportunism of the city and the greedy capitalist marketplace. In *Mr. Deeds Goes to Town* (1936), a simple man from a small town inherits a large fortune, moves to the city, and—not liking the greed and dishonesty he finds there—gives the money away and moves back home. In *Mr. Smith Goes to Washington* (1939), a decent man from a western state is elected to the United States Senate, refuses to join in the self-interested politics of Washington, and dramatically exposes the corruption and selfishness of his colleagues. Capra's films, outstandingly popular in the 1930s, helped audiences find solace in a vision of an imagined American past—in the warmth and goodness of idealized small towns and the decency of ordinary people.

More often, however, the commercial films of the 1930s, like most radio programs, were deliberately and explicitly escapist: lavish musicals such as *Gold Diggers of 1933*, "screwball" comedies (such as Capra's *It Happened One Night*), or the many films of the Marx Brothers—films designed to divert audiences from their troubles and, often, indulge their fantasies about quick and easy wealth.

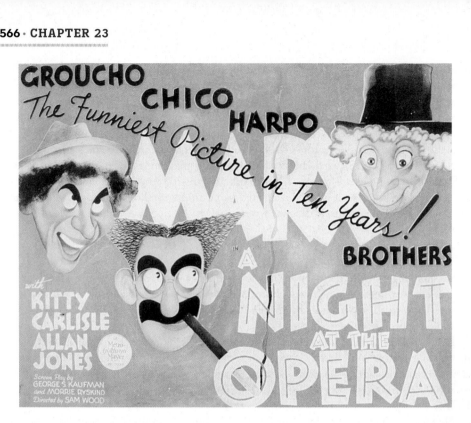

A NIGHT AT THE OPERA The antic comedy of the Marx Brothers provided a popular and welcome escape from the rigors of the Great Depression. The Marx Brothers, shown here in a poster for one of their most famous films, effectively lampooned dilemmas that many Americans faced in their ceaseless, and usually unsuccessful, efforts to find an easy route to wealth and comfort. (Everett Collection)

The 1930s were the first years of Walt Disney's long reign as the champion of animation and children's entertainment. After producing cartoon shorts for theaters in the late 1920s, many of them starring the newly created character Mickey Mouse, Disney began to produce feature-length animated films, starting in 1937 with *Snow White.* Other enormously popular films of the 1930s were adaptations of popular novels, such as *The Wizard of Oz* and *Gone with the Wind,* both released in 1939.

Hollywood did little to challenge the conventions of popular culture on issues of gender and race. Women in movies were portrayed overwhelmingly as wives and mothers, or if not, as sexually attractive flirts. Mae West portrayed herself in a series of successful films as an overtly sexual woman manipulating men through her attractiveness. Few films included important African American characters. Most of the black men and women who did appear in movies were portrayed as servants or farmhands or entertainers.

POPULAR LITERATURE AND JOURNALISM

Much literature and journalism in the 1930s dealt directly or indirectly with the tremendous disillusionment, and the increasing radicalism, of the time.

Not all literature, of course, was challenging or controversial. The most popular books and magazines of the 1930s, in fact, were as escapist and romantic as the most popular radio shows and movies. Two of the bestselling novels of the decade were romantic sagas set in earlier eras: Margaret Mitchell's *Gone with the Wind* (1936) and Hervey Allen's

Anthony Adverse (1933). Leading magazines focused more on fashions, stunts, scenery, and the arts than on the social conditions of the nation. The new and enormously popular photographic journal *Life*, first published in 1936, had the largest readership of any publication in the United States (with the exception of the *Reader's Digest*). It devoted some attention to politics and to the economic conditions of the Depression, but it was best known for stunning photographs of sporting and theater events, natural landscapes, and impressive public projects. One of its most popular features was "*Life* Goes to a Party," which took the chatty social columns of daily newspapers and turned them into glossy photographic glimpses of the rich and famous, but also ordinary people enjoying less lavish parties.

Other Depression writing, however, was frankly and openly challenging to the dominant values of American popular culture. Some of the most significant literature offered corrosive portraits of the harshness and emptiness of American life: John Dos Passos's *U.S.A.* trilogy (1930–1936), which attacked what he considered the materialistic madness of American culture; Nathanael West's *Miss Lonelyhearts* (1933), the story of an advice columnist overwhelmed by the sadness he encounters in the lives of those who consult him; Jack Conroy's *The Disinherited* (1933), a harsh portrait of the lives of coal miners; and James T. Farrell's *Studs Lonigan* (1932), a portrait of a lost, hardened working-class youth.

THE POPULAR FRONT AND THE LEFT

The Communist Party, a relatively small organization in the early twentieth century, flourished during the Great Depression. It had long been a harsh and unrelenting critic of American capitalism, largely hidden from the public world. But the Depression brought the communists into the light. They created what came to be called the "Popular Front," a broad coalition of "antifascist" groups on the left. Not all members of the Popular Front considered themselves communists, but communism was its driving force. The Popular Front presented itself as an American organization, but it was in fact largely controlled by the Soviet Union. Over time, Stalin and the Communist Party softened their attitude toward Franklin Roosevelt, hoping that he would become an ally against Nazi Germany. To that end, the Popular Front formed loose alliances with "progressive groups," and it praised even some strong anticommunists such as the labor leader John L. Lewis. In its heyday, the Popular Front did much to enhance the reputation and influence of the Communist Party. It also helped mobilize writers, artists, and intellectuals behind a critical, democratic sensibility.

The Spanish Civil War of the mid-1930s was a good example of how the left helped give meaning and purpose to individual lives. The war in Spain pitted the forces supporting Francisco Franco (who received support from Hitler and Mussolini and was thus allied with fascism) against the existing republican government. A substantial group of young Americans—more than 3,000 in all—formed the Abraham Lincoln Brigade and traveled to Spain to join in what they considered a fight against the fascists. The American Communist Party was instrumental in creating the Lincoln Brigade, and directed many of its activities.

The party was active as well in organizing the unemployed in the early 1930s and staged a hunger march in Washington, D.C., in 1931. Party members were among the most effective union organizers in some industries. And the party was virtually alone among political organizations in taking a firm stand in favor of racial justice; its active defense of the Scottsboro defendants was but one example of its efforts to ally itself with the aspirations of African Americans.

The American Communist Party was not, however, the open, patriotic organization it tried to appear. It was always under the close and rigid supervision of the Soviet Union. The subordination of the party leadership to the Soviet Union was most clearly demonstrated in 1939, when Stalin signed a nonaggression pact with Nazi Germany. Moscow sent orders to the American Communist Party to abandon the Popular Front and return to its old stance of harsh criticism of American liberals. Communist Party leaders in the United States immediately obeyed—although thousands of disillusioned members left the party as a result.

The Socialist Party of America, under the leadership of Norman Thomas, also cited the economic crisis as evidence of the failure of capitalism and sought vigorously to win public support for its own political program. Among other things, it attempted to mobilize support among the rural poor. The Southern Tenant Farmers Union (STFU), supported by the party and organized by a young socialist, H. L. Mitchell, attempted to create a biracial coalition of sharecroppers, tenant farmers, and others to demand economic reform. Neither the STFU nor the party itself, however, made any real progress toward establishing socialism as a major force in American politics.

Antiradicalism was a powerful force in the 1930s. Hostility toward the Communist Party, in particular, was intense at many levels of government. Congressional committees chaired by Hamilton Fish of New York and Martin Dies of Texas investigated communist influence wherever they could find (or imagine) it. White southerners tried to drive communist organizers out of the countryside, just as growers in California and elsewhere tried (unsuccessfully) to keep communists from organizing Mexican American and other workers.

At few times before (and few since) in American history did being part of the left seem so respectable and even conventional among workers, intellectuals, and others. The 1930s witnessed an impressive, if temporary, widening of the ideological range of mainstream art and politics. The New Deal, for example, sponsored artistic work through the Works Projects Administration that was frankly challenging to the capitalist norms of the 1920s. The filmmaker Pare Lorentz, with funding from New Deal agencies, made two powerful documentaries—*The Plow That Broke the Plains* (1936) and *The River* (1937)—that combined a celebration of New Deal programs with a harsh critique of the exploitation of people and the environment that industrial capitalism had produced.

Other New Deal–sponsored artists also sought to reveal the harshness of poverty and the human cost of social neglect. Notable among them were numerous documentary photographers, many of them employed by the Farm Security Administration, who traveled through rural areas recording the ravaged nature of agricultural life. They included some of the great photographers of their era—Dorothea Lange, Margaret Bourke-White, Arthur Rothstein, Russell Lee, Walker Evans, Ben Shahn, and others. Writers, too, devoted themselves to exposing social injustice, some of them working through the New Deal's Federal Writers' Project and Federal Art Project.

Perhaps the most successful chronicler of social conditions in the 1930s was the novelist John Steinbeck, particularly in his celebrated novel *The Grapes of Wrath*, published in 1939. In telling the story of the Joad family, migrants from the Dust Bowl to California who encounter an unending string of calamities and failures, he offered a harsh portrait of the exploitive features of agrarian life in the West, as well as a tribute to the endurance of his main characters—and to the spirit of community they represent.

THE ORDEAL OF HERBERT HOOVER

Herbert Hoover began his presidency in March 1929 believing, like most Americans, that the nation faced a bright and prosperous future. For the first six months of his administration, he attempted to expand the associational policies he had advocated during his eight years as secretary of commerce. The economic crisis that began before the year was out forced Hoover to deal with a new set of problems. But for most of the rest of his term, he continued to rely on the principles that had always governed his public life.

The Hoover Program

Hoover first responded to the Depression by attempting to restore public confidence in the economy. "The fundamental business of this country, that is, production and distribution of commodities," he said in 1930, "is on a sound and prosperous basis." He then summoned leaders of business, labor, and agriculture to the White House and urged them to adopt a program of voluntary cooperation for recovery. He implored businessmen not to cut production or lay off workers; he talked labor leaders into forgoing demands for higher wages or better hours. But by mid-1931, economic conditions had deteriorated so much that the structure of voluntary cooperation had collapsed.

Hoover also attempted to use government spending as a tool for fighting the Depression. The president proposed to Congress an increase of $423 million—a significant sum by the standards of the time—in federal public works programs, and he encouraged state and local governments to fund public construction. But the spending was not nearly enough in the face of such devastating problems. And when economic conditions worsened, he became less willing to increase spending, worrying instead about keeping the budget balanced.

Even before the stock market crash, Hoover had begun to construct a program to assist the troubled agricultural economy. In April 1929, he proposed the Agricultural Marketing Act, which established the first major government program to help farmers maintain prices. A federally sponsored Farm Board would make loans to national marketing cooperatives or establish corporations to buy surpluses and thus raise prices. At the same time, Hoover attempted to protect American farmers from international competition by raising agricultural tariffs. The Hawley-Smoot Tariff of 1930 increased protection on seventy-five farm products. But neither the Agricultural Marketing Act nor the Hawley-Smoot Tariff ultimately helped American farmers significantly. Agricultural surpluses, combined with declining consumption, kept the farm economy in crisis.

By the spring of 1931, Herbert Hoover's political position had deteriorated considerably. In the 1930 congressional elections, Democrats won control of the House and made substantial inroads in the Senate. Many Americans blamed the president personally for the crisis and began calling the shantytowns that unemployed people established on the outskirts of cities "Hoovervilles." Democrats urged the president to support more vigorous programs of relief and public spending. Hoover, instead, seized on a slight improvement in economic conditions early in 1931 as proof that his policies were working. The international financial panic of the spring of 1931 destroyed the illusion that the economic crisis was coming to an end.

By the time Congress convened in December 1931, conditions had grown so desperate that Hoover supported a series of measures designed to keep endangered banks afloat and protect homeowners from foreclosure on their mortgages. Most important was a bill passed in January 1932 establishing the Reconstruction Finance Corporation (RFC), a government agency to provide federal loans to troubled banks, railroads, and other businesses. Unlike some earlier Hoover programs, the RFC operated on a large scale. In 1932, it had a budget of $1.5 billion for public works alone.

Nevertheless, the new agency failed to deal directly or forcefully enough with the real problems of the economy to produce any significant recovery. The RFC lent funds only to financial institutions with sufficient collateral; much of its money went to large banks and corporations. At Hoover's insistence, it helped finance only those public works projects that promised ultimately to pay for themselves (toll bridges, public housing, and others). Above all, the RFC did not have enough money to make any real impact on the Depression, and it did not even spend all the money it had.

POPULAR PROTEST

For the first several years of the Depression, most Americans were either too stunned or too confused to raise much effective protest. By the middle of 1932, however, dissident voices began to be heard.

In the summer of 1932, a group of unhappy farm owners gathered in Des Moines, Iowa, to establish a new organization: the Farmers' Holiday Association, which endorsed the withholding of farm products from the market—in effect a farmers' strike. The strike began in August in western Iowa, spread briefly to a few neighboring areas, and succeeded in blockading several markets; but in the end, it dissolved in failure.

A more celebrated protest movement emerged from American veterans. In 1924, Congress had approved the payment of a $1,000 bonus to all those who had served in World War I, the money to be paid beginning in 1945. By 1932, however, many veterans were demanding that the bonus be paid immediately. Hoover, concerned about balancing the budget, rejected their appeal. In June, more than 20,000 veterans, members of the self-proclaimed Bonus Expeditionary Force, or "Bonus Army," marched into Washington, built crude camps around the city, and promised to stay until Congress approved legislation to pay the bonus. Some of the veterans departed in July, after Congress had voted down their proposal. Many, however, remained in Washington.

Their continued presence in Washington embarrassed President Hoover. Finally, in mid-July, he ordered police to clear the marchers out of several abandoned federal buildings in which they had been staying. A few marchers threw rocks at the police, and someone opened fire; two veterans fell dead. Hoover called the incident evidence of uncontrolled violence and radicalism, and he ordered the United States Army to assist the police in clearing out the buildings.

General Douglas MacArthur, the army chief of staff, carried out the mission himself and greatly exceeded the president's orders. He led the Third Cavalry, two infantry regiments, a machine-gun detachment, and six tanks down Pennsylvania Avenue in pursuit of the Bonus Army. The veterans fled in terror. MacArthur followed them across the Anacostia River, where he ordered the soldiers to burn their tent city to the ground. More than 100 marchers were injured.

The incident was another serious blow to Hoover's already battered political standing. The "Great Engineer," the personification of the optimistic days of the 1920s, had become a symbol of the nation's failure to deal effectively with its startling reversal of fortune.

THE BONUS EXPEDITIONARY FORCE, 1932   A crowd of approximately 15,000 World War I veterans gather in front of the U.S. Capitol demanding the bonus promised to them in 1945. In the face of the Great Depression, the marchers wanted the bonus right away. Congress supported their efforts, but President Hoover vetoed it. (© Corbis)

THE ELECTION OF 1932

As the 1932 presidential election approached, few people doubted the outcome. The Republican Party dutifully renominated Herbert Hoover for a second term of office, but few delegates believed he could win. The Democrats, in the meantime, gathered jubilantly in Chicago to nominate the governor of New York, Franklin Delano Roosevelt.

Roosevelt had been a well-known figure in the party for many years already. A Hudson Valley aristocrat, a distant cousin of Theodore Roosevelt, and a handsome, charming young man, he progressed rapidly: from a seat in the New York State legislature to a position as assistant secretary of the navy during World War I to his party's vice presidential nomination in 1920 on the ill-fated ticket with James M. Cox. Less than a year later, he was stricken with polio. Although he never regained use of his legs (and could walk only by using crutches and braces), he built up sufficient physical strength to return to politics in 1928. When Al Smith received the Democratic nomination for president that year, Roosevelt was elected to succeed him as governor. In 1930, he easily won reelection.

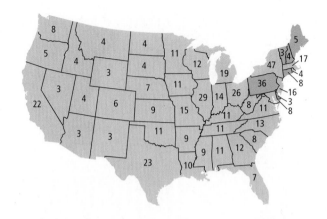

Candidate (Party)		Electoral Vote	Popular Vote (%)
	Franklin D. Roosevelt (Democratic)	472	22,821,857 (57.4)
	Herbert Hoover (Republican)	59	15,761,841 (39.7)
	Norman Thomas (Socialist)	—	881,951 (2.2)
	Other candidates (Communist, Prohibition, Socialist Labor, Liberty)	—	271,355

56.9% of electorate voting

THE ELECTION OF 1932 Like the election of 1928, the election of 1932 was exceptionally one-sided. But this time, the landslide favored the Democratic candidate, Franklin Roosevelt, who overwhelmed Herbert Hoover in all regions of the country except New England. Roosevelt obviously benefited primarily from popular disillusionment with Hoover's response to the Great Depression. • *But what characteristics of Roosevelt himself contributed to his victory?*

Roosevelt worked no miracles in New York, but he did initiate enough programs of government assistance to be able to present himself as a more energetic and imaginative leader than Hoover. In national politics, he avoided divisive cultural issues and emphasized the economic grievances that most Democrats shared. As a result, he was able to assemble a broad coalition within the party and win his party's nomination. In a dramatic break with tradition, he flew to Chicago to address the convention in person and accept the nomination. In the course of his acceptance speech, Roosevelt aroused the delegates with his ringing promise: "I pledge you, I pledge myself, to a new deal for the American people." Neither then nor in the subsequent campaign did Roosevelt give much indication of what that program would be. But Herbert Hoover's unpopularity virtually ensured Roosevelt's election.

Roosevelt won by a landslide, receiving 57.4 percent of the popular vote to Hoover's 39.7, and carried every state except Delaware, Pennsylvania, Connecticut, Vermont, New Hampshire, and Maine. Democrats won large majorities in both houses of Congress. It was a convincing mandate, but it was not yet clear what Roosevelt intended to do with it.

THE "INTERREGNUM"

The period between the election and the inauguration (which in the early 1930s lasted more than four months) was a season of growing economic crisis. Presidents-elect traditionally

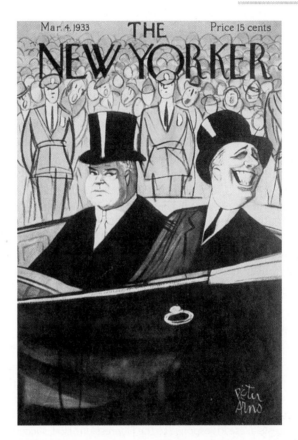

Mar. 4. 1933 THE Price 15 cents

THE NEW YORKER

THE CHANGING OF THE GUARD Long before the event actually occurred, Peter Arno of the *New Yorker* magazine drew this image of Franklin D. Roosevelt and Herbert Hoover traveling together to the Capitol for Roosevelt's inauguration. It predicted with remarkable accuracy the mood of the uncomfortable ride—Hoover glum and uncommunicative, Roosevelt buoyant and smiling. This was to have been the magazine's cover for the week of the inauguration, but after an attempted assassination of the president-elect several weeks earlier in Florida (in which the mayor of Chicago was killed), the editors decided to substitute a more subdued drawing. (Franklin Delano Roosevelt Library)

do not involve themselves directly in government. But in a series of brittle exchanges with Roosevelt, Hoover tried to exact a pledge from the president-elect to maintain policies of economic orthodoxy. Roosevelt genially refused.

In February, only a month before the inauguration, a new crisis developed when the collapse of the American banking system suddenly and rapidly accelerated. Depositors withdrew their money in panic; and one bank after another closed its doors and declared bankruptcy. Hoover again asked Roosevelt to give prompt public assurances that there would be no tinkering with the currency, no heavy borrowing, no unbalancing of the budget. Roosevelt again refused.

March 4, 1933, was, therefore, a day of both economic crisis and considerable personal bitterness. On that morning, Herbert Hoover rode glumly down Pennsylvania Avenue with a beaming, buoyant Franklin Roosevelt, who would shortly be sworn in as the thirty-second president of the United States.

CONCLUSION

The Great Depression changed many things in American life. It created unemployment on a scale never before experienced in the nation's history. It put enormous pressures on families, on communities, on state and local governments, and ultimately on Washington. The innovative but ultimately failed presidency of Herbert Hoover was unable to produce policies capable of dealing effectively with the crisis. In the nation's politics and culture, there were strong currents of radicalism and protest; and many middle-class Americans came to fear that a revolution might be approaching.

In reality, while the Great Depression shook much of American society and culture, it actually toppled very little. The capitalist system survived, damaged for a time but never truly threatened. The values of materialism and personal responsibility were shaken but never overturned. The American people in the 1930s were more receptive than they had been in the 1920s to evocations of community, generosity, and the dignity of common people. They were more open to experiments in government and business and even private lives than they had been in earlier years. But for most Americans, belief in the "American way of life" remained strong throughout the long years of economic despair.

RECALL AND REFLECT

1. Was the 1929 stock market crash the cause of the Depression? Why or why not?
2. How did farmers fare during the Depression? What environmental conditions contributed to their plight?
3. How did radio affect both social life and the life of the family?
4. What popular protests arose in response to the Depression? How successful were these protests?
5. How did Hoover's political beliefs affect his attempt to deal with the economic crisis of the Depression?

24 THE NEW DEAL

LAUNCHING THE NEW DEAL
THE NEW DEAL IN TRANSITION
THE NEW DEAL IN DISARRAY
LIMITS AND LEGACIES OF THE NEW DEAL

LOOKING AHEAD

1. What emergency measures did Franklin Delano Roosevelt (FDR) take in his first hundred days as president?
2. Who were the major critics of FDR's New Deal, and how did their criticisms influence FDR's "Second New Deal"?
3. What were the principal achievements of the "Second New Deal" in 1945?

DURING HIS TWELVE YEARS IN office, Franklin Roosevelt became more central to the life of the nation than any president had ever been. More importantly, his administration constructed a series of programs that fundamentally altered the federal government and its relationship to society. By the end of the 1930s, the New Deal (as the Roosevelt administration was called) had not ended the Great Depression; only World War II did that. But it had created many of the broad outlines of the political world we know today.

LAUNCHING THE NEW DEAL

Roosevelt's first task upon taking office was to alleviate the panic that was creating the chaos in the financial system. He did so in part by force of personality and in part by rapidly constructing an ambitious and diverse program of legislation.

RESTORING CONFIDENCE

Much of Roosevelt's early success was a result of his ebullient personality. He was the first president to make regular use of the radio; and his friendly "fireside chats," during which he explained in simple terms his programs and plans to the people, helped build public confidence in the administration. But Roosevelt could not rely on image alone. On March 6, two days after taking office, he issued a proclamation closing all American banks for four days until Congress could meet in special session to consider banking reform legislation. So great was the panic about bank failures that the "bank holiday," as the president euphemistically described it, created a general sense of relief and hope.

Three days later, Roosevelt sent to Congress the Emergency Banking Act, a generally conservative bill designed primarily to protect the larger banks from being dragged down by the weakness of smaller ones. The bill provided for Treasury Department inspection of all banks before they would be allowed to reopen. It also provided federal assistance to some troubled institutions and a thorough reorganization of those banks in the greatest difficulty. Congress passed the bill within a few hours of its introduction. Whatever else the new law accomplished, it helped dispel the panic. Three-quarters of the banks in the Federal Reserve system reopened within the next three days, and $1 billion in hoarded currency and gold flowed back into them within a month. The immediate banking crisis was over.

On the morning after passage of the Emergency Banking Act, Roosevelt sent to Congress another measure—the Economy Act—designed to convince the public (and especially the business community) that the federal government was in safe, responsible hands. The act proposed to balance the federal budget by cutting the salaries of government employees and reducing pensions to veterans by as much as 15 percent. Like the banking bill, this one passed through Congress almost instantly, even though the cost cutting reduced the growth of the economy. Later that spring, Roosevelt signed the Glass-Steagall Act of June 1933, which gave the government authority to curb irresponsible speculation by banks. More important, perhaps, it established the Federal Deposit Insurance Corporation (FDIC), which guaranteed all bank deposits up to $2,500. Even if a bank should fail, small depositors would be able to recover their money.

To restore confidence in the stock market, Congress passed the so-called Truth in Securities Act of 1933, requiring corporations issuing new securities to provide full and accurate information about them to the public. In June 1934, another act established the Securities and Exchange Commission (SEC) to police the stock market. Roosevelt also signed a bill to legalize the manufacture and sale of beer with a 3.2 percent alcohol content—an interim measure pending the repeal of prohibition, for which a constitutional amendment (the Twenty-first) was already in process. The amendment was ratified later in 1933.

Agricultural Adjustment

These initial actions were largely stopgaps, to buy time for more comprehensive programs. The first was the Agricultural Adjustment Act, which Congress passed in May 1933. Under the provisions of the act, producers of seven basic commodities (wheat, cotton, corn, hogs, rice, tobacco, and dairy products) would impose production limits on their crops. The government, through the Agricultural Adjustment Administration (AAA), would then tell individual farmers how much they should produce and would pay them subsidies for leaving some of their land idle. A tax on food processing (for example, the milling of wheat) would provide the funds for the new payments. Farm prices were to be subsidized up to the point of parity.

The AAA helped bring about a rise in prices for farm commodities in the years after 1933. Gross farm income increased by half in the first three years of the New Deal, and the agricultural economy as a whole emerged from the 1930s more stable and prosperous than it had been in many years. The AAA did, however, favor larger farmers over smaller ones. By distributing payments to landowners, not those who worked the land, the government allowed planters to reduce their acreage, evict tenants and sharecroppers, and fire field hands.

In January 1936, the Supreme Court struck down the crucial provisions of the AAA, arguing that the government had no constitutional authority to require farmers to limit production. But within a few weeks, the administration had secured passage of new legislation (the Soil Conservation and Domestic Allotment Act), which permitted the government to pay farmers to reduce production so as to "conserve soil," prevent erosion, and accomplish other secondary goals.

The administration launched several efforts to assist poor farmers as well. The Resettlement Administration, established in 1935, and its successor, the Farm Security Administration, created in 1937, provided loans to help farmers cultivating submarginal soil to relocate to better lands. But the programs moved no more than a few thousand farmers. More effective was the Rural Electrification Administration, created in 1935, which worked to make electric power available for the first time to thousands of farmers through utility cooperatives.

INDUSTRIAL RECOVERY

Since 1931, leaders of the United States Chamber of Commerce and many others had been urging the government to adopt an antideflation program that would permit trade associations to cooperate in stabilizing prices within their industries. Existing antitrust laws clearly forbade such practices, and Herbert Hoover had refused to endorse suspension of the laws. The Roosevelt administration was more receptive. In exchange for relaxing antitrust provisions, however, New Dealers insisted on other provisions. Business leaders would have to recognize the workers' right to bargain collectively through unions and to ensure that the incomes of workers would rise along with prices. And to help create jobs and increase consumer buying power, the administration added a major program of public works spending. The result of these and many other impulses was the National Industrial Recovery Act, which Congress passed in June 1933.

At its center was a new federal agency, the National Recovery Administration (NRA), under the direction of the flamboyant and energetic Hugh S. Johnson. Johnson called on every business establishment in the nation to accept a temporary "blanket code": a minimum wage of between 30 and 40 cents an hour, a maximum workweek of thirty-five to forty hours, and the abolition of child labor. At the same time, Johnson negotiated another, more specific set of codes with leaders of the nation's major industries. These industrial codes set floors below which no company would lower prices or wages in its search for a competitive advantage, and they included provisions for maintaining employment and production. He quickly won agreements from almost every major industry in the country.

SALUTING THE BLUE EAGLE   Several thousand San Francisco schoolchildren assembled on a baseball field in 1933 to form the symbol of the National Recovery Administration: an eagle clutching a cogwheel (to symbolize industry) and a thunderbolt (to symbolize energy). This display is evidence of the widespread (if brief) popular enthusiasm the NRA produced. NRA administrators drew from their memories of World War I Liberty Loan drives and tried to establish the Blue Eagle as a symbol of patriotic commitment to recovery. (© Bettmann/Corbis)

From the beginning, however, the NRA stumbled. The codes themselves were hastily and often poorly written. Large producers consistently dominated the code-writing process and ensured that the new regulations would work to their advantage and to the disadvantage of smaller firms. And the codes at times did more than simply set floors under prices; they actively and artificially raised them—sometimes to levels higher than the market could sustain.

Other NRA goals also worked against recovery. Section 7(a) of the National Industrial Recovery Act promised workers the right to form unions and engage in collective bargaining and encouraged many workers to join unions for the first time. But Section 7(a) contained no enforcement mechanisms. The Public Works Administration (PWA), established to administer the National Industrial Recovery Act's spending programs, only gradually allowed the $3.3 billion in public works funds to trickle out.

Perhaps the clearest evidence of the NRA's failure was that industrial production actually declined in the months after the agency's establishment, despite the rise in prices that the codes had helped to create. The NRA failed to increase the buying power for consumers, which made the higher prices an obstacle to growth. By the spring of 1934, the NRA was besieged by criticism. That fall, Roosevelt pressured Johnson to resign and established a new board of directors to oversee the NRA.

Then in 1935, the Supreme Court intervened with a case involving alleged NRA code violations by the Schechter brothers, who operated a wholesale poultry business confined to Brooklyn, New York. The Court ruled unanimously that the Schechters were not engaged in interstate commerce (and thus not subject to federal regulation) and, further, that Congress had unconstitutionally delegated legislative power to the president to draft the NRA codes. The justices struck down the legislation establishing the agency. Roosevelt denounced the justices for their "horse-and-buggy" interpretation of the interstate commerce clause. He was rightly concerned, for the reasoning in the Schechter case threatened many other New Deal programs as well. But many New Dealers—and many others—welcomed the NRA's devise.

Regional Planning

The AAA and the NRA largely reflected the beliefs of New Dealers who favored economic planning but wanted private interests (farmers or business leaders) to dominate the planning process. But other reformers believed that the government itself should be the chief planning agent in the economy. Their most conspicuous success was an unprecedented experiment in regional planning: the Tennessee Valley Authority (TVA).

Progressive reformers had agitated for years for public development of the nation's water resources as a source of cheap electric power. In particular, they had urged completion of a great dam at Muscle Shoals on the Tennessee River in Alabama—a dam begun during World War I but left unfinished when the war ended. But opposition from the utilities companies had blocked further progress on the dam.

In 1932, however, one of the great utility empires—that of the electricity magnate Samuel Insull—collapsed spectacularly, amid widely publicized exposés of corruption. Hostility to the utilities soon grew so intense that the companies were no longer able to block the public power movement. The result was legislation, supported by the president and enacted by Congress in May 1933, creating the Tennessee Valley Authority. The TVA was authorized to complete the dam at Muscle Shoals and build other dams in the region, and to generate and sell electricity from them to the public at reasonable rates. It was also

THE TENNESSEE VALLEY AUTHORITY The Tennessee Valley Authority was one of the largest experiments in government-funded public works and regional planning in American history to that point. The federal government had helped fund many projects in its history—canals, turnpikes, railroads, bridges, dams, and others. But never before had it undertaken a project of such great scope, and never before had it maintained such close control and ownership over the public works it helped create. This map illustrates the broad reach of the TVA within the Tennessee Valley region, which spanned seven states. TVA dams throughout the region helped control floods and also provided a source of hydroelectric power, which the government sold to consumers. Note the dam near Muscle Shoals, Alabama, in the bottom left of the map. It was begun during World War I, and efforts to revive it in the 1920s helped create the momentum that produced the TVA. • *Why were progressives so eager to see the government enter the business of hydroelectric power in the 1920s?*

intended to create a comprehensive redevelopment of the entire region: encouraging the growth of local industries, supervising a substantial program of reforestation, and helping farmers improve productivity.

Opposition by conservatives ultimately blocked many of the ambitious social planning projects proposed by the more visionary TVA administrators, but the Authority revitalized the region in numerous ways. It improved water transportation, virtually eliminated flooding in the region, and provided electricity to thousands who had never before had it. Throughout the country, largely because of the "yardstick" provided by the TVA's cheap production of electricity, private power rates declined. Even so, the Tennessee Valley remained a generally impoverished region despite the TVA's efforts.

THE GROWTH OF FEDERAL RELIEF

The Roosevelt administration did not consider relief to the unemployed its most important task, but it recognized the necessity of doing something to help impoverished Americans survive until the government could revive the economy to the point where relief might not be necessary. Among Roosevelt's first acts as president was the establishment of the Federal Emergency Relief Administration (FERA), which provided cash grants to states to prop up bankrupt relief agencies. To administer the program, he chose the director of the New York State relief agency, Harry Hopkins. Both Hopkins and Roosevelt had misgivings about establishing a government "dole," but they felt somewhat more comfortable with another form of government assistance: work relief. Thus when it became clear

ARRIVAL AT A CCC CAMP A group of boys from Idaho arrive for work in Andersonville, Tennessee, in October 1933, only months after the creation of the Civilian Conservation Corps. They were there to reforest a watershed above the Clinch River in the area of the Tennessee Valley Authority, another newly established New Deal agency. (National Archives)

that the FERA grants were not enough, the administration established a second program: the Civil Works Administration (CWA), which put more than 4 million people to work on temporary projects between November 1933 and April 1934. Some of the projects were of lasting value, such as the construction of roads, schools, and parks; others were little more than make-work. To Hopkins, however, the important things were pumping money into the economy and providing assistance to people with nowhere else to turn.

Roosevelt's favorite relief project was the Civilian Conservation Corps (CCC). The CCC created camps in national parks and forests and in other rural and wilderness settings. There, young unemployed men from the cities worked in a semimilitary environment on such projects as planting trees, building reservoirs, developing parks, and improving agricultural irrigation.

Mortgage relief was a pressing need for millions of farm owners and homeowners. The Farm Credit Administration, which within two years refinanced one-fifth of all farm mortgages in the United States, was one response to that problem. The Frazier-Lemke Farm Bankruptcy Act of 1933 was another. It enabled some farmers to regain their land even after the foreclosure of their mortgages. Despite such efforts, however, 25 percent of all American farm owners had lost their land by 1934. Homeowners were similarly troubled, and in June 1933 the administration established the Home Owners' Loan Corporation, which by 1936 had refinanced the mortgages of more than 1 million householders. A year later, Congress established the Federal Housing Administration to insure mortgages for new construction and home repairs.

THE NEW DEAL IN TRANSITION

Seldom has an American president enjoyed such remarkable popularity as Franklin Roosevelt did during his first two years in office. But by early 1935, the New Deal found itself the target of fierce public criticism. In the spring of 1935, partly in response to these growing attacks, Roosevelt launched an ambitious new program of legislation that has often been called the "Second New Deal."

THE CONSERVATIVE CRITICISM OF THE NEW DEAL

Despite his great popularity, Franklin Roosevelt had many conservative critics. Some of them detested him so bitterly that they would refuse to say his name—calling him "that man." Those critics included businessmen, financiers, wealthy families, and members of aristocratic society.

Roosevelt himself was among the most aristocratic presidents in American history. But he became the enemy of the very world that he came from. He was an alumnus of Harvard University, but the university treated him with icy distaste. When he came to Harvard to give a speech, the university president barely spoke to him. He was, as many members of the American elite called him, a "traitor to his class." But even greater hatred came from conservative businessmen and financiers, who correctly saw in the New Deal that the government was making the business and financial world abide by new regulations. His critics were also infuriated by new taxes imposed by Roosevelt, even though high taxation reached only a few wealthy people.

The hatred of Roosevelt from conservatives took many forms. In 1935, a "whispering campaign" emerged from a New Deal effort to regulate the public utility industry. Among the stories that abounded in response was that the president was a drug addict, that he was insane, and that he was surrounded by psychiatrists at all times. Hamilton Fish, Jr., a highly conservative member of Congress, said on the floor of the House of Representatives that "Whom the gods would destroy, they make first mad."

Not all critics were as virulent in their hatred of the president. Walter Lippmann, a revered columnist, complained that Roosevelt was moving away from the nation's traditions. "We belong to a generation that has lost its way," he wrote. "Unable to develop the great truths which it inherited from the emancipators, it has returned to the heresies of absolutism, authority, and the domination of men by men." He added that the "enormous concentration of power in the hands of appointed officials . . . can lead only to waste, confusion, bureaucratic rigidity, and the loss of personal liberty." He charged that Roosevelt had become attracted to fascism and communism, instead of protecting the freedom of individuals. And there were elements of the New Deal for a time that did have similarities to fascism and socialism.

Lewis Douglas, Roosevelt's first budget director, resigned in response to the president's determination to spend deficit funds to help provide relief to the unemployed. Al Smith, the former New York governor and twice the Democratic candidate, also turned against the president—partly because of jealousy, but also because he considered the New Deal much too far to the left. But for the most part, the New Deal was without a clear ideology, and instead experimented in many ways, some that conservatives found offensive.

Conservative business leaders were the most committed leaders of the attack on the New Deal. They formed a new organization called the Liberty League, led by the Du Pont family (owners of the nation's largest chemical company). Its goal was to arouse public opposition to what its members called the "dictatorial" policies of the New Deal and to what they considered its attacks on free enterprise. It was led by John Jacob Raskob (a former head of the Democratic National Committee, a former director of General Motors, and a trustee of Du Pont), who had abandoned the Democratic Party and joined the League. Within a year of its founding in 1934, there were more than 35,000 members of the League, reaching a peak of 125,000 in 1936. It also recruited college students from 345 institutions, gaining over 10,000 members. Almost all of the members were from Northeast industrialists. The league described itself as a "nonpartisan organization founded to defend the Constitution and defend the rights and liberties guaranteed by that Constitution." Its purpose was

> . . . to teach the necessity of respect for the rights of persons and property as fundamental to every form of government . . . to teach the duty of government, to encourage and protect individual and group initiative and enterprise, to foster the right to work, earn, save and acquire property, and to preserve the ownership and lawful use of property when acquired.

The Liberty League attracted considerable attention, but it had relatively little impact on the New Deal. Its leaders tried to remain nonpartisan, even though its members were staunchly anti-Roosevelt. But in the end it had very little impact on the New Deal and the Democratic Party and became a target for the president's campaign. After Roosevelt's landslide reelection, the League soon dissolved. Hatred of Roosevelt did not disappear, but there was little organized opposition after 1936.

THE POPULIST CRITICISM OF THE NEW DEAL

Roosevelt's critics on the far left also managed to produce alarm among some supporters of the administration, but like the conservatives, they proved to have only limited strength. The Communist Party, the Socialist Party, and other radical and semiradical organizations were at times harshly critical of the New Deal. But they, too, failed ever to attract genuine mass support.

More menacing to the New Deal than either the far right or the far left was a group of dissident political movements that defied easy ideological classification. Some gained substantial public support within particular states and regions. And three men succeeded in mobilizing genuinely national followings. Dr. Francis E. Townsend, an elderly California physician, rose from obscurity to lead a movement of more than 5 million members with his plan for federal pensions for the elderly. According to the Townsend Plan, all Americans over the age of sixty would receive monthly government pensions of $200, provided they retired (thus freeing jobs for younger, unemployed Americans) and spent the money in full each month (which would pump needed funds into the economy). By 1935, the Townsend Plan had attracted the support of many older men and women.

Father Charles E. Coughlin, a Catholic priest in the Detroit suburb of Royal Oak, Michigan, achieved even greater renown through his weekly nationally broadcast radio sermons. He proposed a series of monetary reforms—remonetization of silver, issuing of greenbacks, and nationalization of the banking system—that he insisted would restore prosperity and ensure economic justice. At first a warm supporter of Roosevelt, Coughlin had become disheartened by late 1934 by what he claimed was the president's failure to deal harshly enough with the "money powers." In the spring of 1935, he established his own political organization, the National Union for Social Justice.

Most alarming to the administration was the growing national popularity of Senator Huey P. Long of Louisiana. Long had risen to power in his home state through his strident attacks on the banks, oil companies, and utilities and on the conservative political oligarchy allied with them. Elected governor in 1928, he launched an assault on his opponents so thorough and forceful that they were soon left with virtually no political power. But he also maintained the overwhelming support of the Louisiana electorate, in part because of his flamboyant personality and in part because of his solid record of conventional progressive accomplishments: building roads, schools, and hospitals; revising the tax codes; distributing free textbooks; lowering utility rates. Barred by law from succeeding himself as governor, he ran in 1930 for a seat in the United States Senate and won easily.

Long, like Coughlin, supported Franklin Roosevelt for president in 1932. But within six months of Roosevelt's inauguration, Long had broken with the president. As an alternative to the New Deal, he advocated a drastic program of wealth redistribution, a program he ultimately named the Share-Our-Wealth Plan. The government, he claimed, could end the Depression easily by using the tax system to confiscate the surplus riches of the wealthiest men and women in America and distribute these surpluses to the rest of the population. That would, he claimed, allow the government to guarantee every family a minimum "homestead" of $5,000 and an annual wage of $2,500. In 1934, Long established his own national organization: the Share-Our-Wealth Society, which soon attracted a large following through much of the nation. A poll by the Democratic National Committee in the spring of 1935 disclosed that Long might attract more than 10 percent of the vote if he ran as a third-party candidate, possibly enough to tip a close election to the Republicans.

Members of the Roosevelt administration considered dissident movements—and the broad popular discontent they represented—a genuine threat to the president. An increasing number of advisers were warning Roosevelt that he would have to do something dramatic to counter their strength.

THE "SECOND NEW DEAL"

Roosevelt launched the so-called Second New Deal in the spring of 1935 in response both to growing political pressures and to the continuing economic crisis. The new proposals represented a shift in the emphasis of New Deal policy. Perhaps the most conspicuous change was in the administration's attitude toward big business. Symbolically at least, the president was now willing to attack corporate interests openly. In March, for example, he proposed to Congress an act designed to break up the great utility holding companies. The Holding Company Act of 1935 was the result, although furious lobbying by the utilities led to amendments that sharply limited its effects.

Equally alarming to affluent Americans was a series of tax reforms proposed by the president in 1935. Apparently designed to undercut the appeal of Huey Long's Share-Our-Wealth Plan, the Roosevelt proposals called for establishing the highest and most progressive peacetime tax rates in history—although the actual impact of these rates was limited.

The Supreme Court decision in 1935 to strike down the National Industrial Recovery Act also invalidated Section 7(a) of the act, which had guaranteed workers the right to organize and bargain collectively. A group of progressives in Congress, led by Senator Robert E. Wagner of New York, introduced what became the National Labor Relations Act of 1935. The new law, popularly known as the Wagner Act, provided workers with a crucial enforcement mechanism missing from the 1933 law: the National Labor Relations Board (NLRB), which would have power to compel employers to recognize and bargain

"AN ATTACK ON THE NEW DEAL" This cartoon by William Gropper appeared in *Vanity Fair* in 1935 to illustrate a long excerpt from an anti–New Deal editorial that had appeared a few weeks before in a Republican newspaper, the New York *Herald Tribune*. The cartoon echoes the newspaper's references to Jonathan Swift's famous satire *Gulliver's Travels*. In this case, Gulliver is Uncle Sam, and the Lilliputians who tie him down with a thousand tiny cords are New Deal agencies and laws. "Here is a giant if there ever was one," the *Herald Tribune* wrote, "the most powerful nation the world has ever seen. It has the makings of good times, [but] it does not make them. Why? Because the Lilliputians of the New Deal will not let it. These busy little folk cannot bear the thought of letting the great giant, America, escape." (The Granger Collection, NYC)

with legitimate unions. The president was not entirely happy with the bill, but he signed it anyway. That was in large part because American workers themselves had by 1935 become so important and vigorous a force that Roosevelt realized his own political future would depend in part on responding to their demands.

LABOR MILITANCY

The emergence of a powerful trade union movement in the 1930s occurred partly in response to government efforts to enhance the power of unions. It was also a result of the increased militancy of American workers. During the 1920s, most workers had displayed relatively little militancy. In the 1930s, however, the militancy revived. Business leaders and industrialists lost (at least temporarily) the ability to control government policies. Equally important, new and more powerful labor organizations emerged.

The American Federation of Labor (AFL) remained committed to the idea of the craft union: organizing workers on the basis of their skills. But that concept had little to offer unskilled laborers, who now constituted the bulk of the industrial workforce. During the 1930s, therefore, a newer concept of labor organization challenged the craft union ideal: industrial unionism. Advocates of this approach argued that all workers in a particular industry should be organized in a single union, regardless of what functions the workers performed. United in this way, workers would greatly increase their power.

Leaders of the AFL craft unions for the most part opposed the new concept. But industrial unionism found a number of important advocates, most prominent among them John L. Lewis, the leader of the United Mine Workers. At first, Lewis and his allies attempted to work within the AFL, but friction between the new industrial organizations Lewis was promoting and the older craft unions grew rapidly. At the 1935 AFL convention, Lewis became embroiled in a series of angry confrontations with craft union leaders before finally walking out. A few weeks later, he created the Committee on Industrial Organization. When the AFL expelled the new committee and all the industrial unions it represented, Lewis renamed the committee the Congress of Industrial Organizations (CIO) and became its first president.

The CIO expanded the constituency of the labor movement. It was more receptive to women and to African Americans than the AFL had been, in part because CIO organizing drives targeted previously unorganized industries (textiles, laundries, tobacco factories, and others) where women and minorities constituted much of the workforce. The CIO was also more militant than the AFL. By the time of the 1936 schism, it was already engaged in major organizing battles in the automobile and steel industries.

ORGANIZING BATTLES

The United Auto Workers (UAW) gradually emerged preeminent in the early and mid-1930s. But although it was gaining recruits, it was making little progress in winning recognition from the corporations. In December 1936, however, autoworkers employed a controversial and effective new technique for challenging corporate opposition: the sit-down strike. Employees in several General Motors plants in Detroit simply sat down inside the plants, refusing either to work or to leave, thus preventing the company from using strikebreakers. The tactic spread to other locations, and by February 1937, strikers had occupied seventeen GM plants. The strikers ignored court orders and local police efforts to force them to vacate the buildings. When Michigan's governor refused to call up the National Guard to clear out the strikers, and when the federal government also refused to intervene on behalf of employers, General Motors relented. In February 1937, it became the first major manufacturer to recognize the UAW. Other automobile companies soon did the same.

In the steel industry, the battle for unionization was less easily won. In 1936, the Steel Workers' Organizing Committee (SWOC), later the United Steelworkers of America, began a major organizing drive involving thousands of workers and frequent, at times bitter, strikes. In March 1937, to the surprise of almost everyone, United States Steel, the giant of the industry, recognized the union rather than risk a costly strike. But the smaller companies (known collectively as "Little Steel") were less accommodating. On Memorial Day 1937, a group of striking workers from Republic Steel gathered with their families for a picnic and demonstration in south Chicago. When they attempted to march peacefully (and legally) toward the steel plant, police opened fire on them. Ten demonstrators were killed; another ninety were wounded. Despite a public outcry against the "Memorial Day Massacre," the harsh tactics of Little Steel companies succeeded. The 1937 strike failed.

But the victory of Little Steel was among the last gasps of the kind of brutal strikebreaking that had proved so effective in the past. In 1937 alone, there were 4,720 strikes—over 80 percent of them settled in favor of the unions. By the end of the year, more than 8 million workers were members of unions recognized as official bargaining units by employers (as compared with

3 million in 1932). By 1941, that number had expanded to 10 million and included the workers of Little Steel, whose employers had finally recognized the SWOC.

SOCIAL SECURITY

From the first moments of the New Deal, important members of the administration had been lobbying for a system of federally sponsored social insurance for the elderly and the unemployed. In 1935, Roosevelt gave public support to what became the Social Security Act, which Congress passed the same year. It established several distinct programs. For the elderly, there were two types of assistance. Those who were presently destitute could receive up to $15 a month in federal assistance. More important for the future, many Americans presently working were incorporated into a pension system, to which they and their employers would contribute through a payroll tax; it would provide them with an income on retirement. Pension payments would provide only $10 to $85 a month to recipients. At first, payment was not to be distributed until 1942. But public pressure pushed the payment date back to 1937. Broad categories of workers (including domestic servants and agricultural laborers) were excluded from the program. But the act was a crucial first step in building the nation's most important social program for the elderly.

In addition, the Social Security Act created a system of unemployment insurance, which employers alone would finance. It also established a system of federal aid to people with disabilities and a program of aid to dependent children.

The framers of the Social Security Act wanted to create a system of "insurance," not "welfare." And the largest programs (old-age pensions and unemployment insurance) were in many ways similar to private insurance programs. But the act also provided considerable direct assistance based on need—to the elderly poor, to those with disabilities, to dependent children and their mothers. These groups were widely perceived to be small and genuinely unable to support themselves. But in later generations, the programs for these groups would expand until they assumed dimensions that the planners of Social Security had not foreseen.

NEW DIRECTIONS IN RELIEF

Social Security was designed primarily to fulfill long-range goals. But millions of unemployed Americans had immediate needs. To help them, the Roosevelt administration established in 1935 the Works Progress Administration (WPA). Like the Civil Works Administration and other earlier efforts, the WPA established a system of work relief for the unemployed. But it was much bigger than the earlier agencies.

Under the direction of Harry Hopkins, the WPA was responsible for building or renovating 110,000 public buildings and for constructing almost 600 airports, more than 500,000 miles of roads, and over 100,000 bridges. In the process, the WPA kept an average of 2.1 million workers employed and pumped needed money into the economy.

The WPA also displayed remarkable flexibility and imagination. The Federal Writers' Project of the WPA, for example, gave unemployed writers a chance to do their work and receive a government salary. The Federal Art Project, similarly, helped painters, sculptors, and others to continue their careers. The Federal Music Project and the Federal Theatre Project oversaw the production of concerts and plays, creating work for unemployed musicians, actors, and directors. Other relief agencies emerged alongside the WPA. The National Youth Administration (NYA) provided work and scholarship assistance to high-school- and college-age men and women. The Emergency Housing Division of the Public Works Administration began federal sponsorship of public housing.

NEW YORK PUBLIC LIBRARY

WPA MURAL ART The Federal Art Project of the Works Progress Administration commissioned an impressive series of public murals from the artists it employed. Many of these murals adorned post offices, libraries, and other public buildings constructed by the WPA. William Gropper's *Construction of a Dam*, a detail of which is seen here, is typical of much of the mural art of the 1930s in its celebration of the workingman. Workers are depicted in heroic poses, laboring in unison to complete a great public project. Most WPA iconography similarly portrayed workers as white men only. (Library of Congress)

The new welfare system dealt with men and women in very different ways. For men, the government concentrated mainly on work relief—on such programs as the CCC, the CWA, and the WPA. The principal government aid to women was not work relief but cash assistance—most notably through the Aid to Dependent Children program of Social Security, which was designed largely to assist single mothers. This disparity in treatment reflected a widespread assumption that men should constitute the bulk of the paid workforce. In fact, millions of women were already employed by the 1930s.

THE 1936 "REFERENDUM"

By the middle of 1936—with the economy visibly reviving—there could be little doubt that Roosevelt would win a second term. The Republican Party nominated the moderate governor of Kansas, Alf M. Landon, who waged a relatively dull campaign. Roosevelt's dissident challengers now appeared powerless. One reason was the assassination of their most effective leader, Huey Long, in Louisiana in September 1935. Another reason was the ill-fated alliance among Father Coughlin, Dr. Townsend, and Gerald L. K. Smith (an intemperate henchman of Huey Long), who joined forces that summer to establish a new political movement—the Union Party, which nominated an undistinguished North Dakota congressman, William Lemke.

The result was the greatest landslide in American history to that point. Roosevelt polled just under 61 percent of the vote to Landon's 36 percent and carried every state except Maine and Vermont. The Democrats increased their already large majorities in both houses of Congress.

The election results demonstrated the party realignment that the New Deal had produced. The Democrats now controlled a broad coalition of western and southern farmers, the urban working classes, the poor and unemployed, and the black communities of northern cities, as well as traditional progressives and committed new liberals—a coalition that constituted a substantial majority of the electorate. It would be decades before the Republican Party could again create a lasting majority coalition of its own.

THE NEW DEAL IN DISARRAY

Roosevelt emerged from the 1936 election at the zenith of his popularity. Within months, however, the New Deal was mired in serious new difficulties.

THE COURT FIGHT

The 1936 mandate, Franklin Roosevelt believed, made it possible for him to do something about the Supreme Court. No program of reform, he believed, could long survive the conservative justices, who had already struck down the NRA and the AAA.

In February 1937, Roosevelt sent a surprise message to Capitol Hill proposing an overhaul of the federal court system; included among the many provisions was one to add up to six new justices to the Supreme Court. The courts were "overworked," the president claimed, and needed additional manpower and younger blood to enable them to cope with their increasing burdens. But Roosevelt's real purpose was to give himself the opportunity to appoint new, liberal justices and change the ideological balance of the Court.

Conservatives were outraged at the "Court-packing plan," and even many Roosevelt supporters were disturbed by the plan. Still, Roosevelt might well have persuaded Congress to approve at least a compromise measure had not the Supreme Court itself intervened. Of the nine justices, three reliably supported the New Deal, and four reliably opposed it. Of the remaining two, Chief Justice Charles Evans Hughes often sided with the progressives, and Associate Justice Owen J. Roberts usually voted with the conservatives. On March 29, 1937, Roberts, Hughes, and the three progressive justices voted together to uphold a state minimum-wage law—in the case of *West Coast Hotel v. Parrish*—thus reversing a 5-to-4 decision of the previous year invalidating a similar law. Two weeks later, again by a 5-to-4 margin, the Court upheld the Wagner Act, and in May it validated the Social Security Act. Whatever the reasons for the decisions, the Court's newly moderate position made the Court-packing bill seem unnecessary. Congress ultimately defeated it.

On one level, Franklin Roosevelt had achieved a victory. The Court was no longer an obstacle to New Deal reforms. But the Court-packing episode did lasting political damage to the administration. From 1937 on, southern Democrats and other conservatives voted against Roosevelt's measures much more often than they had in the past.

RETRENCHMENT AND RECESSION

By the summer of 1937, the national income—which had dropped from $82 billion in 1929 to $40 billion in 1932—had risen to nearly $72 billion. Other economic indices also

THE GOLDEN AGE OF COMIC BOOKS

IN the troubled years of the Great Depression and World War II, many Americans sought release from their anxieties in fantasy. Movies, plays, books, radio shows, and other diversions drew people out of their own lives and into a safer or more glamorous or more exciting world. Beginning in 1938, one of the most popular forms of escape for many young Americans was the comic book.

In February 1935, Malcolm Wheeler-Nicholson founded the first comics magazine—what we now know as the "comic book"—titled *New Fun. New Fun* was not successful, but Wheeler founded a new company, Detective Comics. He began in 1937 to design a new magazine called *Action Comics.* Wheeler ran out of money before he could publish anything, but the company continued without him. In 1938, the first issue of *Action Comics* appeared with a startling and controversial cover—a powerful man in a skintight suit lifting a car over his head. His name was Superman, and he became the most popular cartoon character of all time.

Within a year, Superman had a comic book named after him, which was selling over 1.2 million copies each issue. By 1940, there was a popular Superman radio show—introduced by a breathless announcer crying, "It's a bird! It's a plane! It's . . . Superman!" Soon, other publishers began developing new "superheroes" (a term invented by the creators of Superman) to capitalize on this growing popular appetite. In 1939, a second great comic book publisher appeared—Marvel Comics.

By the early 1940s, Superman had been joined by other superheroes: the Human Torch, the Sub-Mariner, Batman, the Flash, and Wonder Woman, a character created in part to signal the importance of women to the war effort.

It is not hard to imagine why superheroes would be so appealing to Americans in the 1930s and 1940s—particularly to the teenage boys who were the largest single purchasers of comic books. Superman and other superheroes were idealized versions of the ideal boy—smart, good, "the perfect Boy Scout," as one fan put it. But they were also all-powerful, capable of righting wrong and preventing catastrophe. At a time when catastrophe was an ever-present possibility in the world, superheroes were a comforting escape from fear.

---

showed similar advances. Roosevelt seized on these improvements as a justification for trying to balance the federal budget. Between January and August 1937, for example, he cut the WPA in half, laying off 1.5 million relief workers. A few weeks later, the fragile boom collapsed. The index of industrial production dropped from 117 in August 1937 to 76 in May 1938. Four million additional workers lost their jobs. Economic conditions were soon almost as bad as they had been in the bleak days of 1932–1933.

The recession of 1937, known to the president's critics as the "Roosevelt recession," was a result of many factors. But to many observers at the time, it seemed to be a direct result

SUPERMAN The most popular action figure in the history of comic books was Superman, whose superhuman powers were particularly appealing fantasies to Americans suffering through the Depression and, later, World War II. (Hulton Archive/Getty Images)

Many of the early comic book writers were young Jewish men, conscious of their outsider status in an American culture not yet wholly open to them. Almost all the characters they created had alter egos, identities they used while living within the normal world. Superman was Clark Kent, a "mild-mannered reporter." Batman was Bruce Wayne, a wealthy heir. All were part of mainstream American society, and they expressed in part the outsider's dream of assimilation. The superheroes themselves were outsiders too—but outsiders endowed with special powers and abilities unavailable to ordinary people.

Even before America entered World War II, the comic superheroes were battling the Axis powers. Marvel's Human Torch and Sub-Mariner joined forces against the German navy. Superman fought spies and saboteurs at home. Captain America, a new character created in March 1941, was a frail young man rejected by the army who, after being given a secret serum by a military doctor, became extraordinarily powerful. The cover of the first issue of *Captain America* showed the title character punching Hitler in his headquarters in Germany.

The end of the war was also the end of this first golden age of American comic books. Many superhero magazines ceased publication as peacetime reduced the popular appetite for fantasy. In their place emerged new comic books, which emphasized romance, mild sexuality, and, over time, violence and cruelty. But comic books never surpassed the heights of popularity that the superhero comics attained during the Depression and World War II. •

UNDERSTAND, ANALYZE, & EVALUATE

1. What could comic books offer readers suffering through the crisis of the Great Depression?
2. How and why have comic book superheroes changed over time?

of the administration's unwise decision to reduce spending. And so in April 1938, the president asked Congress for an emergency appropriation of $5 billion for public works and relief programs, and government funds soon began pouring into the economy once again. Within a few months, another tentative recovery seemed to be under way.

At about the same time, Roosevelt sent a stinging message to Congress, vehemently denouncing what he called an "unjustifiable concentration of economic power" and asking for the creation of a commission to consider major reforms in the antitrust laws. In response, Congress established the Temporary National Economic Committee (TNEC),

CONSIDER THE SOURCE

FRANKLIN D. ROOSEVELT SPEAKS ON THE REORGANIZATION OF THE JUDICIARY, TUESDAY, MARCH 9, 1937

[. . .]Tonight, sitting at my desk in the White House, I make my first radio report to the people in my second term of office.

I am reminded of that evening in March, four years ago, when I made my first radio report to you. We were then in the midst of the great banking crisis.

Soon after, with the authority of the Congress, we asked the Nation to turn over all of its privately held gold, dollar for dollar, to the Government of the United States.

Today's recovery proves how right that policy was. [. . .]

In 1933 you and I knew that we must never let our economic system get completely out of joint again—that we could not afford to take the risk of another great depression.

We also became convinced that the only way to avoid a repetition of those dark days was to have a government with power to prevent and to cure the abuses and the inequalities which had thrown that system out of joint.

We then began a program of remedying those abuses and inequalities—to give balance and stability to our economic system—to make it bomb-proof against the causes of 1929.

Today we are only part-way through that program—and recovery is speeding up to a point where the dangers of 1929 are again becoming possible, not this week or month perhaps, but within a year or two.

National laws are needed to complete that program. Individual or local or state effort alone cannot protect us in 1937 any better than ten years ago.

It will take time—and plenty of time—to work out our remedies administratively even after legislation is passed. To complete our program of protection in time, therefore, we cannot delay one moment in making certain that our National Government has power to carry through.

Four years ago action did not come until the eleventh hour. It was almost too late.

If we learned anything from the depression we will not allow ourselves to run around in new circles of futile discussion and debate, always postponing the day of decision.

The American people have learned from the depression. For in the last three national elections an overwhelming majority of them voted a mandate that the Congress and the President begin the task of providing that protection—not after long years of debate, but now.

The Courts, however, have cast doubts on the ability of the elected Congress to protect us against catastrophe by meeting squarely our modern social and economic conditions.

We are at a crisis in our ability to proceed with that protection. It is a quiet crisis. There are no lines of depositors outside closed banks. But to the far-sighted it is far-reaching in its possibilities of injury to America.

I want to talk with you very simply about the need for present action in this crisis—the need to meet the unanswered challenge of one-third of a Nation ill-nourished, ill-clad, ill-housed.

Last Thursday I described the American form of Government as a three horse team whose members included representatives of both houses of Congress and officials from several executive agencies. Later in 1938, the administration successfully supported one of its most ambitious pieces of labor legislation, the Fair Labor Standards Act, which for the first time established a national minimum wage and a forty-hour workweek and which also placed strict limits on child labor.

provided by the Constitution to the American people so that their field might be plowed. The three horses are, of course, the three branches of government—the Congress, the Executive and the Courts. Two of the horses are pulling in unison today; the third is not. Those who have intimated that the President of the United States is trying to drive that team, overlook the simple fact that the President, as Chief Executive, is himself one of the three horses.

It is the American people themselves who are in the driver's seat.

It is the American people themselves who want the furrow plowed.

It is the American people themselves who expect the third horse to pull in unison with the other two.

[. . .] [S]ince the rise of the modern movement for social and economic progress through legislation, the Court has more and more often and more and more boldly asserted a power to veto laws passed by the Congress and State Legislatures [. . .].

In the last four years the sound rule of giving statutes the benefit of all reasonable doubt has been cast aside. The Court has been acting not as a judicial body, but as a policy-making body.

When the Congress has sought to stabilize national agriculture, to improve the conditions of labor, to safeguard business against unfair competition, to protect our national resources, and in many other ways, to serve our clearly national needs, the majority of the Court has been assuming the power to pass on the wisdom of these acts of the Congress— and to approve or disapprove the public policy written into these laws. [. . .]

We have, therefore, reached the point as a nation where we must take action to save the Constitution from the Court and the Court from itself. We must find a way to take an appeal from the Supreme Court to the Constitution itself. We want a Supreme Court which will do justice under the Constitution and not over it. In our courts we want a government of laws and not of men.

[. . .] What is my proposal? It is simply this: whenever a Judge or Justice of any Federal Court has reached the age of seventy and does not avail himself of the opportunity to retire on a pension, a new member shall be appointed by the President then in office, with the approval, as required by the Constitution, of the Senate of the United States. [. . .]

Those opposing this plan have sought to arouse prejudice and fear by crying that I am seeking to "pack" the Supreme Court and that a baneful precedent will be established.

What do they mean by the words "packing the Court"?

UNDERSTAND, ANALYZE, & EVALUATE

1. According to President Roosevelt, what had been most important for economic reform and recovery? How did he assess this recovery?
2. How were the three branches of government supposed to work, in the president's view?
3. What criticism did the president level against the courts? What solution did he offer? Was this conflict between the executive branch and the United States Supreme Court unique to the New Deal?

Source: On the Reorganization of the Judiciary, Tuesday, March 9, 1937 [35:28] WH, Fireside Chats of Franklin D. Roosevelt, Franklin D. Roosevelt Presidential Library, Hyde Park, New York.

Despite these achievements, however, by the end of 1938 the New Deal had essentially come to an end. Congressional opposition now made it difficult for the president to enact any major new programs. But more important, perhaps, the threat of world crisis hung heavy in the political atmosphere, and Roosevelt was gradually growing more concerned with persuading a reluctant nation to prepare for war than with pursuing new avenues of reform.

THE NEW DEAL

CONTEMPORARIES

of Franklin Roosevelt debated the impact of the New Deal with ferocious intensity. Conservatives complained of a menacing tyranny of the state. Liberals celebrated the New Deal's progressive achievements. Some people on the left charged that the reforms of the 1930s were largely cosmetic and ignored the nation's fundamental problems. Although the conservative critique found relatively little scholarly expression until many years after Roosevelt's death, the liberal and left positions continued for decades to shape the way historians described the Roosevelt administration.

The dominant view from the beginning was an approving liberal interpretation, and its most important early voice was that of Arthur M. Schlesinger, Jr. He argued in the three volumes of *The Age of Roosevelt* (1957–1960) that the New Deal marked a continuation of the long struggle between public power and private interests, a struggle Roosevelt had moved to a new level. Workers, farmers, consumers, and others now had much more protection than they had enjoyed in the past.

At almost the same time, however, other historians were offering more qualified assessments of the New Deal, although they remained securely within the liberal framework. Richard Hofstadter argued in 1955 that the New Deal gave American liberalism a "social-democratic tinge that had never before been present in American reform movements," but that its highly pragmatic approach lacked a central, guiding philosophy. James MacGregor Burns argued in 1956 that Roosevelt failed to make full use of his potential as a leader.

William Leuchtenburg's *Franklin D. Roosevelt and the New Deal* (1963) was the first systematic "revisionist" interpretation. Leuchtenburg challenged the views of earlier scholars who had proclaimed the New Deal a "revolution" in social policy. Leuchtenburg could muster only enough enthusiasm to call it a "halfway revolution," one that helped some previously disadvantaged groups (most notably farmers and workers) but that did little or nothing for many others (African Americans, sharecroppers, the urban poor).

Harsher criticisms soon emerged. Barton Bernstein in a 1968 essay concluded that the New Deal had saved capitalism, but

LIMITS AND LEGACIES OF THE NEW DEAL

The New Deal made major changes in American government, some of them still controversial today. It also left important problems unaddressed.

AFRICAN AMERICANS AND THE NEW DEAL

The New Deal was not hostile to black aspirations. Eleanor Roosevelt spoke throughout the 1930s on behalf of racial justice and put continuing pressure on her husband and others in the federal government to ease discrimination against blacks. The president himself at the expense of the least powerful. Ronald Radosh, Paul Conkin, and, later, Thomas Ferguson and Colin Gordon expanded on these criticisms. The New Deal, they contended, was part of the twentieth-century tradition of "corporate liberalism"—a tradition in which reform is closely wedded to the needs and interests of capitalism.

Most scholars in the 1980s and 1990s, however, seemed largely to have accepted the revised liberal view: that the New Deal was a significant and valuable chapter in the history of reform, but one that worked within rigid, occasionally crippling limits. Much of the later work on the New Deal, therefore, has focused on the constraints it faced. Some scholars (notably the sociologist Theda Skocpol) have emphasized the issue of "state capacity"—the absence of a government bureaucracy with sufficient strength and expertise to shape or administer many programs. James T. Patterson, Barry Karl, Mark Leff, and others have emphasized the political constraints the New Deal encountered—the conservative inhibitions about government that remained strong in Congress and among the public. Frank Freidel, Ellis Hawley, Herbert Stein, and many others point as well to the ideological constraints affecting Franklin Roosevelt and his supporters—the limits of their own understanding of their time. Alan Brinkley, in The End of Reform (1995), describes an ideological shift within New Deal liberalism that marginalized older concerns about wealth and monopoly power and replaced them with consumer-oriented Keynesianism. David Kennedy, in Freedom from Fear (1999), argues, by contrast, that the more aggressively anticapitalist measures of the early New Deal actually hampered recovery. Only when Roosevelt embraced the power of the market did prosperity begin to return.

The conservative attacks on the New Deal in the 2000s provided a newly powerful alternative view. A group of conservatives—among them Amity Schlaes and Burton Folsom—attacked the New Deal as a failure that created a vast bureaucracy and caused the Depression to last longer than it had to.

The phrase "New Deal liberalism" has come in the postwar era to seem synonymous with modern ideas of aggressive federal management of the economy, elaborate welfare systems, a powerful bureaucracy, and large-scale government spending. But many historians of the New Deal would argue that the modern idea of New Deal liberalism bears only a limited relationship to the ideas that New Dealers themselves embraced. •

UNDERSTAND, ANALYZE, & EVALUATE

1. How did the political atmosphere of the 1930s limit the New Deal?
2. Did the New Deal save capitalism? If so, how and why?

appointed a number of African Americans to significant second-level positions in his administration, creating an informal network of officeholders that became known as the "Black Cabinet." Eleanor Roosevelt, Interior secretary Harold Ickes, and WPA director Harry Hopkins all made efforts to ensure that New Deal relief programs did not exclude blacks, and by 1935 an estimated 30 percent of all African Americans were receiving some form of government assistance. One result was a historic change in black electoral behavior. As late as 1932, most American blacks were voting Republican, as they had been doing since the Civil War. By 1936, more than 90 percent were voting Democratic.

African Americans supported Franklin Roosevelt, but they had few illusions that the New Deal represented a major turning point in American race relations. The president

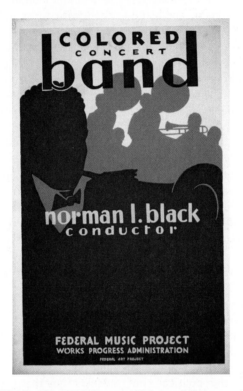

THE COLORED CONCERT BAND This 1936 WPA poster publicizes an all-black concert band—a reminder of how much segregation remained during the New Deal. (Library of Congress)

was, for example, never willing to risk losing the support of southern Democrats by supporting legislation to make lynching a federal crime or to ban the poll tax, one of the most potent tools by which white southerners kept blacks from voting.

New Deal relief agencies did not challenge, and indeed reinforced, existing patterns of discrimination. The CCC established separate black camps. The NRA codes tolerated paying blacks less than whites doing the same jobs. The WPA routinely relegated African Americans and Hispanic workers to the least-skilled and lowest-paying jobs; when funding ebbed, African Americans, like women, were among the first to be dismissed.

The New Deal was not hostile to African Americans, and it made some contributions to their progress. But it refused to make the issue of race a significant part of its agenda.

THE NEW DEAL AND THE "INDIAN PROBLEM"

New Deal policy toward the Indian tribes marked a significant break from earlier approaches, largely because of the efforts of the extraordinary commissioner of Indian affairs, John Collier. Collier was greatly influenced by the work of twentieth-century anthropologists who advanced the idea of cultural relativism—the theory that every culture should be accepted and respected on its own terms.

Collier wanted to reverse the pressures on Native Americans to assimilate and instead allow them to remain Indians. He effectively promoted legislation—which became the Indian Reorganization Act of 1934—that restored to the tribes the right to own land collectively and to elect tribal governments. In the thirteen years after passage of the 1934 bill, tribal land increased by nearly 4 million acres, and Indian agricultural income increased from under $2 million in 1934 to over $49 million in 1947. Even with the redistribution of lands under the 1934 act, however, Indians continued to possess, for the most part, only territory whites did not want—much of it arid, some of it desert. And as a group, they continued to constitute the poorest segment of the population.

WOMEN AND THE NEW DEAL

Symbolically at least, the New Deal marked a breakthrough in the role of women in public life. Roosevelt appointed the first female member of the cabinet in the nation's history: Secretary of Labor Frances Perkins. He also named more than 100 other women to positions at lower levels of the federal bureaucracy. But the administration was concerned not so much about achieving gender equality as about obtaining special protections for women.

The New Deal generally supported the widespread belief that in hard times women should withdraw from the workplace to open up more jobs for men. New Deal relief agencies offered relatively little employment for women. The Social Security program excluded domestic servants, waitresses, and other predominantly female occupations.

As with African Americans, so also with women: the New Deal was not actively hostile to feminist aspirations, but it accepted prevailing cultural norms. There was not yet sufficient political pressure from women themselves to persuade the administration to do otherwise. Indeed, some of the most important supporters of policies that reinforced traditional gender roles (such as Social Security) were themselves women.

THE NEW DEAL AND THE WEST

One part of American society that did receive special attention from the New Deal was the American West. The West received more government funds per capita through relief programs than any other region.

Except for TVA, the largest New Deal public works programs—the great dams and power stations—were mainly in the West, both because the best locations for such facilities were there and because the West had the greatest need for new sources of water and power. The Grand Coulee Dam on the Columbia River was the largest public works project in American history to that point, and it provided cheap electric power for much of the Northwest. Its construction, and that of other, smaller dams and water projects, created a basis for economic development in the region. Without this enormous public investment by the federal government, much of the economic growth that transformed the West after World War II would have been much more difficult, if not impossible, to achieve.

THE NEW DEAL, THE ECONOMY, AND POLITICS

The most frequent criticisms of the New Deal involve its failure to revive or reform the American economy. New Dealers never fully recognized the value of government spending as a vehicle for recovery. The economic boom sparked by World War II—not the New Deal—finally ended the crisis.

Nevertheless, the New Deal did have a number of important and lasting effects on the American economy. It helped elevate new groups—workers, farmers, and others—to positions from which they could at times challenge the power of the corporations. It increased the regulatory functions of the federal government in ways that helped stabilize previously troubled areas of the economy: the stock market, the banking system, and others. And the administration helped establish the basis for new forms of federal fiscal policy, which in the postwar years would give the government tools for promoting and regulating economic growth.

The New Deal also created the rudiments of the American welfare state through its many relief programs and, above all, through the Social Security system. The conservative inhibitions New Dealers brought to this task ensured that the welfare system that ultimately emerged would be limited in its impact, would reinforce some traditional patterns of gender and racial discrimination, and would be expensive and cumbersome to administer. But for all its limits, the new system marked a historic break with the nation's traditional reluctance to offer public assistance to its neediest citizens.

Finally, the New Deal had a dramatic effect on the character of American politics. It took a weak and divided Democratic Party, which had been a minority force in American politics for many decades, and turned it into a mighty coalition that would dominate national party competition for more than thirty years. It turned the attention of many voters away from some of the controversial cultural issues that had preoccupied them in the 1920s and awakened an interest in economic matters of direct importance to the lives of citizens.

CONCLUSION

From the time of Franklin Roosevelt's inauguration in 1933 to the beginning of World War II eight years later, the federal government engaged in a broad and diverse series of experiments designed to relieve the distress of unemployment and poverty; to reform the economy to prevent future crises; and to bring the Great Depression itself to an end. It had only partial success in all those efforts.

Unemployment and poverty remained high throughout the New Deal, although many federal programs provided assistance to millions of people who would otherwise have had none. The structure of the American economy remained essentially the same as it had been in earlier years, although there were by the end of the New Deal some important new regulatory agencies in Washington—and an important new role for organized labor. The New Deal failed to end the Great Depression. But some of its policies kept the Depression from getting worse; others helped alleviate the suffering of people caught in its grip; and still others pointed the way toward more effective economic policies in the future.

Perhaps the most important legacy of the New Deal was to create a sense of possibilities among many Americans. The New Deal persuaded many citizens that the fortunes of individuals need not be left entirely to chance or to the workings of an unregulated market. Many Americans emerged from the 1930s convinced that individuals deserved some protections from the unpredictability and instability of the modern economy. The New Deal—for all its limitations—had demonstrated the value of enlisting government in the effort to provide those protections.

RECALL AND REFLECT

1. What New Deal programs were aimed at agricultural and industrial recovery, and what was the effect of the programs in both areas?
2. What criticisms did critics on both the right and left level at the New Deal? How did FDR and his administration respond to these criticisms?
3. What gains did organized labor make during the 1930s?
4. What was the impact of the New Deal on women?

25 THE GLOBAL CRISIS, 1921–1941

THE DIPLOMACY OF THE NEW ERA
ISOLATIONISM AND INTERNATIONALISM
FROM NEUTRALITY TO INTERVENTION

LOOKING AHEAD

1. What are some of the views that Americans expressed as the world crises of the 1930s expanded?

2. How did the economic crisis of the worldwide Great Depression help create new political orders in many nations?

3. What was the sequence of events between 1939 and 1941 that brought the United States into military involvement in World War II?

HENRY CABOT LODGE OF MASSACHUSETTS, Republican chairman of the Senate Foreign Relations Committee, led the fight that defeated ratification of the Treaty of Versailles in 1919 and 1920. As a result, the United States declined to join the League of Nations. American foreign policy embarked instead on an independent course that for the next two decades would attempt, but ultimately fail, to expand American influence in the world without committing the United States to any lasting relationships with other nations.

Lodge was not an isolationist. He believed the United States should exert its influence internationally. But he believed, too, that the United States should remain unfettered by obligations to anyone else. He said in 1919:

> We are a great moral asset of Christian civilization. . . . How did we get there? By our own efforts. Nobody led us, nobody guided us, nobody controlled us. . . . I would keep America as she has been—not isolated, not prevent her from joining other nations for . . . great purposes—but I wish her to be master of her own fate.

In the end, the limited American internationalism of the interwar years proved insufficient to protect the interests of the United States, to create global stability, or to keep the nation from becoming involved in the most catastrophic war in human history.

1924
.... O
Dawes Plan

1928
O ....
Kellogg-Briand Pact

1931
.... O
Japan invades
Manchuria

1933
O ....
U.S. recognizes
Soviet Union

Good Neighbor Policy

1937
.... O
Roosevelt's
"quarantine" speech

1938
O ....
Munich Conference

1939
.... O
Nazi-Soviet
nonaggression pact

World War II begins

1940
O ....
Tripartite Pact

America First
Committee founded

1941
.... O
Lend-lease plan

Atlantic Charter

Roosevelt reelected

Destroyers-for-bases
deal

Japan attacks
Pearl Harbor

U.S. enters
World War II

THE DIPLOMACY OF THE NEW ERA

Critics in the 1920s often described American foreign policy with a single word: "isolationism." But in reality, the United States played a more active role in world affairs in the 1920s than it had at almost any previous time in its history.

REPLACING THE LEAGUE

By the time the Harding administration took office in 1921, American membership in the League of Nations was no longer a realistic possibility. But Secretary of State Charles Evans Hughes wanted to find a replacement for the League as a guarantor of world peace and stability.

The most important effort was the Washington Conference of 1921—an attempt to prevent a destabilizing naval armaments race among the United States, Britain, and Japan. Hughes proposed a plan for dramatic reductions in the fleets of all three nations and a ten-year moratorium on the construction of large warships. To the surprise of almost everyone, the conference ultimately agreed to accept most of Hughes's terms. The Five-Power Pact of February 1922 established limits for total naval tonnage and a ratio of armaments among the signatories. For every 5 tons of American and British warships, Japan would maintain 3 and France and Italy 1.75 each.

When the French foreign minister, Aristide Briand, asked the United States in 1927 to join an alliance against Germany, Secretary of State Frank Kellogg (who had replaced Hughes in 1925) proposed instead a multilateral treaty outlawing war as an instrument of national policy. Fourteen nations signed the agreement in Paris on August 27, 1928, amid wide international acclaim. Forty-eight other nations later joined the Kellogg-Briand Pact. It contained no instruments of enforcement.

Debts and Diplomacy

The first responsibility of diplomacy, Hughes, Kellogg, and others agreed, was to ensure that American overseas trade faced no obstacles. The Allied powers of Europe were struggling to repay $11 billion in loans they had contracted with the United States during and shortly after the war. At the same time, Germany was attempting to pay the reparations levied by the Allies. The United States stepped in with a solution.

Charles G. Dawes, an American banker who became vice president under Coolidge in 1925, negotiated an agreement in 1924 among France, Britain, Germany, and the United States. Under the Dawes Plan, American banks would provide enormous loans to Germany, which would use that money to pay reparations to France and Britain; Britain and France would agree to reduce the amount of those payments and, in turn, use those funds (as well as the large loans they themselves were receiving from American banks) to repay war debts to the United States. One historian said of the plan, "It would have made equal sense for the U.S. to have taken the money out of one drawer in the Treasury and put it into another." The flow of funds was able to continue only by virtue of the enormous debts the European nations were acquiring to American banks and corporations. The American economic involvement in Europe continued to expand until the worldwide depression shattered the system in 1931.

During the 1920s, American military forces maintained a presence in Nicaragua, Panama, and several other countries in the region, while United States investments in

THE KELLOGG-BRIAND PACT Leaders of the major countries gather at the Palais d'Orsay in Paris to sign the Kellogg-Briand Pact in Paris, which promised that there would be no further wars. Among those signing this unlikely pact were Frank Kellogg, the American Secretary of State, and Aristide Briand, the prime minister of France. (© Bettmann/Corbis)

Latin America more than doubled. American banks offered large loans to Latin American governments, just as in Europe; and as with the Europeans, the Latin Americans had difficulty earning the money to repay them in the face of the formidable United States tariff barrier.

HOOVER AND THE WORLD CRISIS

By 1931, the world financial crisis had produced a rising nationalism in Europe and Japan. It soon toppled some existing political leaders and replaced them with powerful, belligerent governments committed to expansion. Herbert Hoover thus confronted the beginning of a process that would ultimately lead to war.

In Latin America, Hoover tried to repair some of the damage earlier American policies had created. He made a ten-week goodwill tour through Latin America before his inauguration. Once in office, he generally abstained from intervening in the internal affairs of neighboring nations and moved to withdraw American troops from Nicaragua and Haiti. He also announced a new policy: America would grant diplomatic recognition to any sitting government in the region without questioning the means it had used to obtain power. He even repudiated the [Theodore] Roosevelt Corollary to the Monroe Doctrine by refusing to permit American intervention when several Latin American countries defaulted on debt obligations in October 1931.

In Europe, the administration enjoyed few successes. When Hoover's proposed moratorium on debts failed to produce financial stability, he refused to cancel all war debts to the United States as many economists advised him to do. Several European nations promptly went into default. Efforts to extend the 1921 limits on naval construction fell victim to French and British fears of German and Japanese militarism.

The ineffectiveness of American diplomacy in Europe was particularly troubling in light of the new governments on the Continent. Benito Mussolini's Fascist Party had been in control of Italy since the early 1920s and had become increasingly nationalistic and militaristic. Still more ominous was the growing power of the National Socialist (or Nazi) Party in Germany. By the late 1920s, the Weimar Republic, the nation's government since the end of World War I, had been largely discredited by, among other things, a ruinous inflation. Adolf Hitler, the leader of the Nazis, grew rapidly in popular favor and took power in 1933. He believed in, among other things, the genetic superiority of the Aryan (German) people and in extending German territory to provide *Lebensraum* (living space) for what he called the German "master race." He displayed a pathological anti-Semitism and a passionate militarism.

More immediately alarming to the Hoover administration was a major crisis in Asia— another early step toward World War II. The Japanese, suffering from an economic depression of their own, were concerned about the increasing power of the Soviet Union and about the insistence of the Chinese leader Chiang Kai-shek on expanding his government's power in Manchuria, officially a part of China but over which the Japanese had maintained informal economic control since 1905. In 1931, Japan's military leaders staged what was, in effect, a coup in Tokyo. Shortly after that, a railroad explosion in southern Manchuria, likely set by Japanese soldiers (and known as the "Mukden Incident"), served as a pretext for a Japanese invasion of northern Manchuria. They had conquered the region by the end of the year. Secretary of State Henry Stimson issued stern warnings to the Japanese but to no avail. Early in 1932, Japan moved farther into China, attacking the city of Shanghai and killing thousands of civilians.

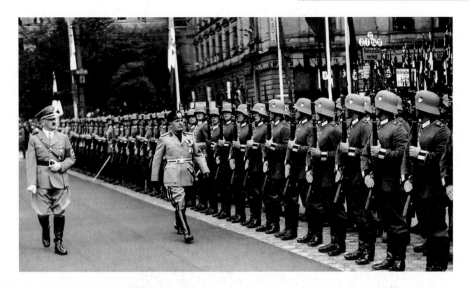

HITLER AND MUSSOLINI IN BERLIN   The German and Italian dictators (shown here reviewing Nazi troops in Berlin in the mid-1930s) acted publicly as if they were equals. Privately, Hitler treated Mussolini with contempt, and Mussolini complained constantly of being a junior partner in the relationship. (Photo by Instituto Nazionale Luce/Alinari/Getty Images)

ISOLATIONISM AND INTERNATIONALISM

The administration of Franklin Roosevelt faced a dual challenge as it entered office in 1933. It had to deal with the worst economic crisis in the nation's history, and it had to deal as well with the effects of a decaying international structure.

DEPRESSION DIPLOMACY

Perhaps Roosevelt's sharpest break with the policies of his predecessor was on the question of American economic relations with Europe. Hoover had argued that only by resolving the question of war debts and reinforcing the gold standard could the American economy hope to recover. He had, therefore, agreed to participate in the World Economic Conference, to be held in London in June 1933, to attempt to resolve these issues. By the time the conference assembled, however, Roosevelt had already become convinced that the gold value of the dollar had to be allowed to fall in order for American goods to compete in world markets. Shortly after the conference convened, he released what became known as the "bombshell message," repudiating the orthodox views of most of the delegates and rejecting any agreement on currency stabilization. The conference quickly dissolved.

At the same time, Roosevelt abandoned the commitments of the Hoover administration to settle the issue of war debts through international agreement. In April 1934, he signed a bill that prohibited American banks from making loans to any nation in default on its debts. The legislation ended the old, circular system by which debt payments continued only by virtue of increasing American loans. Within months, war-debt payments from every nation except Finland stopped for good.

Sixteen years after the Bolshevik Revolution of 1917, the American government still had not officially recognized the government of the Soviet Union. But a growing number of influential Americans were urging a change in policy—largely because the Soviet Union appeared to be a possible source of trade. The Russians, for their part, were hoping for American cooperation in containing Japan. In November 1933, the United States and the Soviet Union agreed to open formal diplomatic relations. Relations with the Soviet Union, however, soon soured. American trade failed to establish a foothold in Russia, disappointing hopes in the United States. The American government did little to reassure the Soviets that it was interested in stopping Japanese expansion in Asia, dousing expectations in Russia. By the end of 1934, the Soviet Union and the United States were once again viewing each other with considerable mistrust.

The Roosevelt administration was also taking a new approach toward Latin America, an approach that became known as the "Good Neighbor Policy" and that expanded on the changes the Hoover administration had made. At an Inter-American Conference in Montevideo, Uruguay, in December 1933, Secretary of State Cordell Hull signed a formal convention declaring: "No state has the right to intervene in the internal or external affairs of another."

THE RISE OF ISOLATIONISM

With the international system of the 1920s now beyond repair, the United States faced a choice between more active efforts to stabilize the world or more energetic attempts to isolate itself from it. Most Americans unhesitatingly chose isolation. Support for isolationism emerged from many quarters. Some Wilsonian internationalists had grown disillusioned with the League of Nations and its inability to stop Japanese aggression in Asia. Other Americans argued that the American role in World War I was a result of Wall Street and munitions makers. An investigation by a Senate committee chaired by Senator Gerald Nye of North Dakota claimed to have produced evidence of exorbitant profiteering and tax evasion by many corporations during the war, and it suggested that bankers had pressured Wilson to intervene in the war so as to protect their loans abroad. (Few historians now lend much credence to these charges.)

Roosevelt continued to hope for at least a modest American role in maintaining world peace. In 1935, he proposed to the Senate a treaty to make the United States a member of the World Court—a largely symbolic gesture. Isolationists led by Father Coughlin and William Randolph Hearst aroused popular opposition to the agreement, and the Senate voted it down.

In the summer of 1935, Mussolini's Italy was preparing to invade Ethiopia. Fearing the invasion would provoke a new European war, American legislators tried to prevent the United States from being dragged into the conflict. The Neutrality Act of 1935 established a mandatory arms embargo against both sides in any military conflict and warned American citizens against traveling on the ships of warring nations. Thus, isolationists believed, the "protection of neutral rights" could not again become an excuse for American intervention in war. A 1937 law established the so-called cash-and-carry policy, by which warring nations could purchase only nonmilitary goods from the United States and could do so only by paying cash and shipping their purchases themselves.

Isolationist sentiment showed its strength again in 1936–1937 in response to the civil war in Spain. The Falangists of General Francisco Franco, a group somewhat like the Italian fascists, revolted in July 1936 against the existing republican government. Hitler and Mussolini supported Franco, both vocally and with weapons and supplies. Some Americans traveled to Spain to assist the republican cause, but the United States government joined with Britain and France in an agreement to offer no assistance to either side.

In the summer of 1937, Japan intensified its six-year-old assault on Manchuria and attacked China's five northern provinces. In a speech in Chicago in October 1937, Roosevelt warned that Japanese and other aggressors should be "quarantined" by the international community to prevent the contagion of war from spreading. He was deliberately vague about what such a quarantine would mean. Even so, public response to the speech was hostile, and Roosevelt drew back. On December 12, 1937, Japanese aviators bombed and sank the United States gunboat *Panay*, almost certainly deliberately, as it sailed the Yangtze River in China. But so reluctant was the Roosevelt administration to antagonize the isolationists that the United States eagerly seized on Japanese claims that the bombing had been an accident, accepted Japan's apologies, and overlooked the attack.

THE FAILURE OF MUNICH

In 1936, Hitler had moved the revived German army into the Rhineland, rearming an area that had been off-limits to German troops since World War I. In March 1938, German forces marched without opposition into Austria, and Hitler proclaimed a union (or *Anschluss*) between Austria, his native land, and Germany, his adopted one. Neither in America nor in most of Europe was there much more than a murmur of opposition.

Germany had by now occupied territory surrounding three sides of western Czechoslovakia, a region Hitler dreamed of annexing. In September 1938, he demanded that Czechoslovakia cede him the Sudetenland, a part of Czechoslovakia in which many ethnic Germans lived. Although Czechoslovakia was prepared to fight to stop Hitler, it needed assistance from other nations. But most Western governments, including the United States, were willing to pay almost any price to settle the crisis peacefully. On September 29, Hitler met with the leaders of France and Great Britain at Munich in an effort to resolve the crisis. The French and British agreed to accept the German demands in Czechoslovakia in return for Hitler's promise to expand no farther.

The Munich agreement, which Roosevelt supported at the time, was the most prominent element of a policy that came to be known as "appeasement" and that came to be identified (not altogether fairly) with British Prime Minister Neville Chamberlain. Whoever was to blame, the policy was a failure. In March 1939, Hitler occupied the remaining areas of Czechoslovakia, violating the Munich agreement unashamedly. And in April, he began issuing threats against Poland.

At that point, both Britain and France assured the Polish government that they would come to its assistance in case of an invasion; they even tried, too late, to draw the Soviet Union into a mutual defense agreement. But Stalin, who had not even been invited to the Munich Conference, had decided he could expect no protection from the West. He signed a nonaggression pact with Hitler in August 1939, freeing the Germans, for a while, from the danger of a two-front war. Shortly after that, Hitler staged an incident on the Polish border to allow him to claim that Germany had been attacked, and on September 1, 1939, he launched a full-scale invasion of Poland. Britain and France, true to their pledges, declared war on Germany two days later. World War II, already underway in Asia, had begun in Europe.

FROM NEUTRALITY TO INTERVENTION

"This nation will remain a neutral nation," the president declared shortly after the hostilities began in Europe, "but I cannot ask that every American remain neutral in thought as well." There was never any question that both he and the majority of the American people favored Britain, France, and the other Allied nations in the contest. The question was how much the United States was prepared to do to assist them.

THE SINO-JAPANESE WAR, 1931–1941

LONG before Pearl Harbor, well before war broke out in Europe in 1939, the first shots of what would become World War II had been fired in the Pacific in a conflict between Japan and China.

Having lived in almost complete isolation from the world until the nineteenth century, Japan emerged from World War I as one of the world's great powers, with a proud and powerful military and growing global trade. But the Great Depression created severe economic problems for the Japanese; and as in other parts of the world, the crisis strengthened the political influence of highly nationalistic armed forces. Out of the Japanese military emerged dreams of a new empire in the Pacific. Such an empire would, its proponents believed, give the nation access to fuel, raw material, markets for its industries, as well as land for its agricultural needs and its rapidly increasing population. Such an empire, they also argued, would

free Asia from its exploitation by Europe and America and would create a "new world order based on moral principles."

During World War I, Japan had taken territory and economic concessions in China and had created a particularly strong presence in the northern Chinese region of Manchuria. There, in September 1931, a group of young, militant army officers seized on a railway explosion to justify a military campaign through which they conquered the entire province. Both the United States government and the League of Nations demanded that Japan evacuate Manchuria. The Japanese ignored them and for the next six years consolidated its control over the new territory.

On July 7, 1937, Japan began a wider war when it attacked Chinese troops at the Marco Polo Bridge outside Beijing. Over the next few weeks, Japanese forces overran a large part of southern China, including

NEUTRALITY TESTED

At the very least, Roosevelt believed, the United States should make armaments available to the Allied armies to counter the military advantage the large German munitions industry gave Hitler. In September 1939, he asked Congress to revise the Neutrality Acts and lift the arms embargo against any nation engaged in war. Congress maintained the prohibition on American ships entering war zones. But the 1939 law did permit belligerents to purchase arms on the same cash-and-carry basis that the earlier Neutrality Acts had established for the sale of nonmilitary materials.

After the German armies quickly subdued Poland, the war in Europe settled into a long, quiet lull that lasted through the winter and spring—a "phony war," some called it. But in the spring of 1940, Germany launched a massive invasion, known as the "blitzkrieg" (lightning war), to the west—first attacking Denmark and Norway, sweeping next across the Netherlands and Belgium, and driving finally deep into the heart of France. On June 10, Mussolini invaded France from the south as Hitler was attacking from the north. On most of the port cities, killing many Chinese soldiers and civilians in the process. Particularly notorious was the Japanese annihilation of many thousands of civilians in the city of Nanjing (the number has long been in dispute, but estimates range from 80,000 to over 300,000) in an event that became known in China and the West as the "Rape of Nanjing," or the Nanjing Massacre. The Chinese government fled to the mountains. As in 1931, the United States and the League of Nations protested in vain.

China was a nation in turmoil. It was engaged in a civil war of its own—between the so-called Kuomintang, a nationalist party led by Chiang Kai-shek, and the Chinese Communist Party, led by Mao Zedong; and this internal struggle weakened China's capacity to resist. But beginning in 1937, the two rivals agreed to an uneasy truce and began fighting the Japanese together, with some success—bogging the Japanese military down in a seemingly endless war and imposing great hardships on the Japanese people at home. The Japanese government and military, however, remained determined to continue the war against China, whatever the sacrifices.

One result of the costs of the war in China was a growing Japanese dependence on the United States for steel and oil to meet civilian and military needs. In July 1941, in an effort to pressure the Japanese to stop their expansion, the Roosevelt administration made it impossible for the Japanese to continue buying American oil. Japan now faced a choice between ending its war in China or finding other sources of fuel to keep its war effort (and its civilian economy) going. Japan chose to extend the war beyond China in a search for oil. The best available sources were in the Dutch East Indies. But the only way to secure that European colony, the Japanese believed, would be to neutralize the increasingly hostile United States in Asia. Visionary military planners in Japan began advocating a daring move to immobilize the Americans in the Pacific before expanding the war elsewhere—with an attack on the American naval base at Pearl Harbor. The first blow of World War II in America, therefore, was the culmination of more than a decade of Japanese efforts to conquer China. •

UNDERSTAND, ANALYZE, & EVALUATE

1. What were the goals of the Japanese militarists in the 1930s that led to the attacks on China?
2. Why was China unable to stop Japanese aggression in the 1930s?

June 22, France fell, and Nazi troops marched into Paris. A new French regime assembled in Vichy, largely controlled by the German occupiers; and in all Europe, only the shattered remnants of the British and French armies—daringly rescued from the beaches of Dunkirk by a hastily organized armada of English boats, trawlers, and yachts—remained to oppose the Axis forces.

On May 16, in the midst of the offensive, Roosevelt asked Congress for and quickly received an additional $1 billion for defense. That was one day after Winston Churchill, the new British prime minister, had sent Roosevelt the first of many long lists of requests for armaments, without which, he insisted, England could not long survive. Some Americans (including the ambassador to London, Joseph P. Kennedy) argued that the British plight was already hopeless, that any aid to the English was a wasted effort. But the president was determined to make war materials available to Britain. Roosevelt even circumvented the cash-and-carry provisions of the Neutrality Acts by giving England fifty American destroyers (most of them left over from World War I) in return for the right

THE BLITZ, LONDON   The German Luftwaffe terrorized London and other British cities in 1940–1941 and again late in the war by bombing civilian areas indiscriminately in an effort to break the spirit of the English people. The effort failed, and the fortitude of the British did much to arouse American support for their cause. (Brown Brothers)

to build American bases on British territory in the Caribbean. He also returned to the factories a number of new airplanes purchased by the American military so that the British could buy them instead.

Roosevelt was able to take such steps in part because of a major shift in American public opinion. By July 1940, more than 66 percent of the public (according to opinion polls) believed that Germany posed a direct threat to the United States. As a result, Congress was more willing to permit expanded American assistance to the Allies. Congress was also becoming more concerned about the need for preparations for war, and in September it approved the Burke-Wadsworth Act, inaugurating the first peacetime military draft in American history.

But a powerful new isolationist lobby—the America First Committee, whose members included such prominent Americans as Charles Lindbergh and Senators Gerald Nye and Burton Wheeler—joined the debate over American policy toward the war. The lobby had at least the indirect support of a large proportion of the Republican Party. Through the summer and fall of 1940, the debate was complicated by a presidential campaign.

THE CAMPAIGN OF 1940

The biggest political question of 1940 was whether Franklin Roosevelt would break with tradition and run for an unprecedented third term. The president himself did not reveal his own wishes. But by refusing to withdraw from the contest, he made it impossible for any rival Democrat to establish a claim to the nomination. And when, just before the

Democratic Convention in July, he let it be known that he would accept a "draft" from his party, the issue was virtually settled. The Democrats quickly renominated him and even reluctantly swallowed his choice for vice president: Agriculture Secretary Henry A. Wallace, a man too liberal and too controversial for the taste of many party leaders.

The Republicans nominated for president a politically inexperienced Indiana businessman, Wendell Willkie, who benefited from a powerful grassroots movement—as well as strong support from the Luce magazines—especially *Time* and *Life*. The Republicans took positions little different from Roosevelt's: they would keep the country out of war but would extend generous assistance to the Allies. Willkie was an appealing figure and a vigorous campaigner, and he managed to evoke more public enthusiasm than any Republican candidate in decades. But Roosevelt still won decisively. He received 55 percent of the popular vote to Willkie's 45 percent, and he won 449 electoral votes to Willkie's 82.

NEUTRALITY ABANDONED

In the last months of 1940, Roosevelt began to make subtle changes in the American role in the war. Great Britain was virtually bankrupt and could no longer meet the cash-and-carry requirements imposed by the Neutrality Acts. The president, therefore, proposed a new system for supplying Britain: "lend-lease." It would allow the federal government not only to sell but also to lend or lease armaments to any nation deemed "pivotal to the defense of the United States." In other words, America could funnel weapons to England on the basis of no more than Britain's promise to return them when the war was over. Congress enacted the bill by wide margins in March 1941.

Attacks by German submarines had made shipping lanes in the Atlantic extremely dangerous. The British navy was losing ships more rapidly than it could replace them and was finding it difficult to transport materials across the Atlantic from America. Roosevelt argued that the western Atlantic was a neutral zone and the responsibility of the American nations. By July 1941, therefore, American ships were patrolling the ocean as far east as Iceland.

At first, Germany did little to challenge these obviously hostile American actions. By September 1941, however, the situation had changed. Nazi forces had invaded the Soviet Union in June of that year. When the Soviets did not surrender, as many had predicted they would, Roosevelt persuaded Congress to extend lend-lease privileges to them. Now American industry was providing vital assistance to Hitler's foes on two fronts, and the American navy was protecting the flow of those goods to Europe. In September, Nazi submarines began a concerted torpedo campaign against American vessels. Roosevelt ordered American ships to fire on German submarines "on sight." In October, Nazi submarines hit two American destroyers and sank one of them, the *Reuben James,* killing many American sailors. Congress quickly voted to allow the United States to arm its merchant vessels and to sail all the way into belligerent ports. The United States had, in effect, launched a naval war against Germany.

In August 1941, Roosevelt met with Churchill aboard a British vessel off the coast of Newfoundland. The president made no military commitments, but he did join with the prime minister in releasing a document that became known as the Atlantic Charter, in which the two nations set out "certain common principles" on which to base "a better future for the world." It called openly for "the final destruction of the Nazi tyranny" and for a new world order in which every nation controlled its own destiny. It was, in effect, a statement of war aims.

THE QUESTION OF PEARL HARBOR

THE phrase "Remember Pearl Harbor!" became a rallying cry during World War II—reminding Americans of the surprise Japanese attack on the American naval base in Hawaii and arousing the nation to exact revenge. But within a few years of the end of hostilities, some Americans remembered Pearl Harbor for very different reasons. They began to challenge the official version of the attack on December 7, 1941, and their charges sparked a debate that has never fully subsided. Was the Japanese attack on Pearl Harbor unprovoked, and did it come without warning, as the Roosevelt administration claimed at the time? Or was it part of a deliberate plan by the president to make the Japanese force a reluctant United States into the war? Most controversial of all, did the administration know of the attack in advance? Did Roosevelt deliberately refrain from warning the commanders in Hawaii so that the air raid's effect on the American public would be more profound?

Among the first to challenge the official version of Pearl Harbor was the historian Charles A. Beard, who maintained in *President Roosevelt and the Coming of the War* (1948) that the United States had deliberately forced the Japanese into a position where they had no choice but to attack. By cutting off Japan's access to the raw materials it needed for its military adventure in China, and by stubbornly refusing to compromise, the United States ensured that the Japanese would strike out into the southwest Pacific to take the needed supplies by force—even at the risk of war with the United States. Not only was American policy provocative in effect, Beard suggested, it was deliberately provocative. More than that, the administration had some time before cracked the Japanese code. Beard insisted that Roosevelt must have known weeks in advance of Japan's plan to

attack—although he did not claim that officials knew the attack would come at Pearl Harbor. Beard supported his argument by citing Secretary of War Henry Stimson's comment in his diary: "The question was how we should maneuver them into the position of firing the first shot." This view has reappeared more recently in Thomas Fleming's *The New Dealers' War,* which also argues that Roosevelt deliberately (and duplicitously) maneuvered the United States into war with Japan.

A partial refutation of the Beard argument appeared in 1950 in Basil Rauch's *Roosevelt from Munich to Pearl Harbor.* The administration did not know of the planned attack on Pearl Harbor in advance, he argued. It did, however, expect an attack somewhere; and it made subtle efforts to "maneuver" Japan into firing the first shot in the conflict. But Richard N. Current, in *Secretary Stimson: A Study in Statecraft* (1954), offered an even stronger challenge to Beard. Stimson did indeed anticipate an attack, Current argued, but not an attack on American territory; rather, he anticipated an assault on British or Dutch possessions in the Pacific. The problem confronting the administration was not how to maneuver the Japanese into attacking the United States but how to find a way to make a Japanese attack on British or Dutch territory appear to be an attack on America. Only thus, Stimson believed, could Congress be persuaded to approve a declaration of war.

Roberta Wohlstetter took a different approach to the question in *Pearl Harbor: Warning and Decision* (1962), the most thorough scholarly study to appear to that point. Deemphasizing the question of whether the American government wanted a Japanese attack, she undertook to answer the question of whether the administration knew of the attack in advance. Wohlstetter concluded that the

PEARL HARBOR, DECEMBER 7, 1941 The destroyer U.S.S. *Shaw*, immobilized in a floating drydock in Pearl Harbor in December 1941, survived the first wave of Japanese bombers unscathed. But in the second attack, the Japanese scored a direct hit and produced this spectacular explosion, which blew off the ship's bow. Damage to the rest of the ship, however, was slight. Just a few months later, the *Shaw* was fitted with a new bow and rejoined the fleet. (U.S. Navy Photo)

enormous daring and great skill with which the Japanese orchestrated an ambitious operation that few Americans believed possible.

But the revisionist claims have not been laid to rest. John Toland revived the charges of a Roosevelt betrayal in 1982, in *Infamy: Pearl Harbor and Its Aftermath,* claiming to have discovered new evidence (the testi-

United States had ample warning of Japanese intentions and should have realized that the Pearl Harbor raid might be imminent. But government officials failed to interpret the evidence correctly, largely because their preconceptions about Japanese intentions were at odds with the evidence they confronted. Admiral Edwin T. Layton, who had been a staff officer at Pearl Harbor in 1941, also blamed political and bureaucratic failures for the absence of advance warning of the attack. In a 1985 memoir, *And I Was There,* he argued that the Japanese attack was a result not only of "audacious planning and skillful execution" by the Japanese, but of "a dramatic breakdown in our intelligence process . . . related directly to feuding among high-level naval officers in Washington."

The most thorough study of Pearl Harbor to date appeared in 1981: Gordon W. Prange's *At Dawn We Slept.* Like Wohlstetter, Prange concluded that the Roosevelt administration was guilty of a series of disastrous blunders in interpreting Japanese strategy; the American government had possession of enough information to predict the attack but failed to do so. But Prange dismissed the arguments of the "revisionists" (Beard and his successors) that the president had deliberately maneuvered the nation into the war by permitting the Japanese to attack. Instead, he emphasized the

mony of an unidentified seaman) that proves the navy knew at least five days in advance that Japanese aircraft carriers were heading toward Hawaii. From that, Toland concluded that Roosevelt must have known that an attack was forthcoming and that he allowed it to occur in the belief that a surprise attack would arouse the nation. But like the many previous writers who have made the same argument, Toland was unable to produce any direct evidence of Roosevelt's knowledge of the planned attack. Nor could he offer any plausible explanation of why an American leader would deliberately allow his nation to enter a war with its Pacific Fleet badly crippled and its navy humiliated.   ●

UNDERSTAND, ANALYZE, & EVALUATE

1. Some historians have argued that the United States provoked Japan into attacking Pearl Harbor. What is the basis for that argument?

2. Layton argued that the attack on Pearl Harbor resulted partially from a breakdown in the intelligence process. Other attacks on the United States have been attributed to a breakdown in intelligence. What evidence has been cited to support those claims? What arguments have been used to refute them?

JOINT STATEMENT BY PRESIDENT ROOSEVELT AND PRIME MINISTER CHURCHILL, AUGUST 14, 1941

THE President of the United States and the Prime Minister, Mr. Churchill, representing His Majesty's Government in the United Kingdom, have met at sea. [. . .]

They have considered the dangers to world civilization arising from the policies of military domination by conquest upon which the Hitlerite government of Germany and other governments associated therewith have embarked, and have made clear the stress which their countries are respectively taking for their safety in the face of these dangers.

They have agreed upon the following joint declaration:

Joint declaration of the President of the United States of America and the Prime Minister, Mr. Churchill, representing His Majesty's Government in the United Kingdom, being met together, deem it right to make known certain common principles in the national policies of their respective countries on which they base their hopes for a better future for the world.

First, their countries seek no aggrandizement, territorial or other;

Second, they desire to see no territorial changes that do not accord with the freely expressed wishes of the peoples concerned;

Third, they respect the right of all peoples to choose the form of government under which they will live; and they wish to see sovereign rights and self-government restored to those who have been forcibly deprived of them;

Fourth, they will endeavor, with due respect for their existing obligations, to further the enjoyment by all States, great or small, victor or vanquished, of access, on equal terms, to the trade and to the raw

THE ROAD TO PEARL HARBOR

Japan, in the meantime, was still extending its empire in the Pacific. In September 1940, the Japanese signed the Tripartite Pact, a loose defensive alliance with Germany and Italy (although in reality, the European Axis powers never developed a very strong relationship with Japan). In July 1941, Japanese troops moved into Indochina and seized the capital of Vietnam, a colony of France. The United States, having broken Japanese codes, knew Japan's next target was to be the oil-rich Dutch East Indies; and when Tokyo failed to respond to Roosevelt's stern warnings, the president froze all Japanese assets in the United States, severely limiting Japan's ability to purchase needed American supplies.

Tokyo now faced a choice. Either it would have to repair relations with the United States to restore the flow of oil and other supplies, or it would have to find those supplies elsewhere, most notably by seizing British and Dutch possessions in the Pacific. In October, militants in Tokyo forced the moderate prime minister out of office and replaced him with the leader of the war party, General Hideki Tojo.

By late November, the State Department had given up on the possibility of a peaceful settlement. American intelligence had decoded Japanese messages that made clear a Japanese attack was imminent. But Washington did not know where the attack would take place. Most officials continued to believe that the Japanese would not move first against American territory but against British or Dutch possessions to the south. A combination of confusion, miscalculation, and underestimation of the Japanese military materials of the world which are needed for their economic prosperity;

Fifth, they desire to bring about the fullest collaboration between all nations in the economic field with the objector securing, for all, improved labor standards, economic advancement and social security;

Sixth, after the final destruction of the Nazi tyranny, they hope to see established a peace which will afford to all nations the means of dwelling in safety within their own boundaries, and which will afford assurance that all the men in all the lands may live out their lives in freedom from fear and want;

Seventh, such a peace should enable all men to traverse the high seas and oceans without hindrance;

Eighth, they believe that all of the nations of the world, for realistic as well as spiritual reasons must come to the abandonment of the use of force. Since no future peace can be maintained if land, sea or air armaments continue to be employed by nations which threaten, or may threaten, aggression outside of their frontiers, they believe, pending the establishment of a wider and permanent system of general security, that the disarmament of such nations is essential. They will likewise aid and encourage all other practicable measures which will lighten for peace-loving peoples the crushing burden of armaments.

FRANKLIN D. ROOSEVELT
WINSTON S. CHURCHILL

UNDERSTAND, ANALYZE, & EVALUATE

1. What inspired this meeting between the United States and Great Britain in the Atlantic? What goals did the two nations set for future international diplomacy and the rights of nations?
2. Which mutual goals reflect the shared experience of the Great Depression? Which reflect the shared experience of World War I?

Source: The Atlantic Charter, published in Department of State Executive Agreement Series No. 236.

caused the government to overlook indications that Japan intended a direct attack on American forces.

At 7:55 A.M. on Sunday, December 7, 1941, a wave of Japanese bombers attacked the United States naval base at Pearl Harbor in Hawaii. A second wave came an hour later. Within two hours, the United States lost 8 battleships, 3 cruisers, 4 other vessels, 188 airplanes, and several vital shore installations. More than 2,400 soldiers and sailors died, and another 1,000 were injured. The Japanese suffered only light losses.

American forces were now greatly diminished in the Pacific (although by a fortunate accident, no American aircraft carriers—the heart of the Pacific Fleet—had been at Pearl Harbor on December 7). Nevertheless, the raid on Hawaii unified the American people behind war. On December 8, after a stirring speech by the president, the Senate voted unanimously and the House voted 388 to 1 to approve a declaration of war against Japan. Three days later, Germany and Italy, Japan's European allies, declared war on the United States; on the same day, December 11, Congress reciprocated without a dissenting vote.

CONCLUSION

American foreign policy in the years after World War I attempted something that ultimately proved impossible. Americans were determined to be a major power in the world. They were determined to extend the nation's trade broadly around the globe. And they were determined to influence other nations in ways that would be beneficial to America's, and the world's, interests. The United States was also determined to do nothing that would limit its own freedom of action. It would not join the League of Nations. It would not join the World Court. It would not form alliances with other nations. It would operate powerfully—and alone.

But ominous forces were at work in the world that would gradually push the United States into greater engagement with other nations. The economic disarray that the Great Depression created around the globe, the rise of totalitarian regimes, the expansionist ambitions of powerful new leaders—all worked to destroy the uneasy stability of the post–World War I international system. America's own interests, economic and otherwise, were now imperiled. And America's go-it-alone foreign policy seemed powerless to change the course of events.

Franklin Roosevelt tried throughout the later years of the 1930s to push the American people slowly into a greater involvement in international affairs. In particular, he tried to nudge the United States toward taking a more forceful stand against dictatorship and aggression. A powerful isolationist movement helped stymie him for a time, even after war broke out in Europe. Gradually, however, public opinion shifted toward support of the Allies (Britain, France, and the Soviet Union) and against the Axis (Germany, Italy, and Japan). The nation began to mobilize for war, to supply ships and munitions to Britain, even to engage in naval combat with German forces in the Atlantic. Finally, on December 7, 1941, the surprise Japanese attack on the American base at Pearl Harbor in Hawaii eliminated the last elements of uncertainty and drove the United States—now united behind the war effort—into the greatest and most terrible conflict in human history.

RECALL AND REFLECT

1. What diplomatic efforts and agreements of the 1920s and 1930s attempted to deal with the increasing global political crises of the era? Why were these efforts unsuccessful?
2. How did the goals of the Neutrality Acts change over the course of the 1930s? What was the reason for the change?
3. Why did Japan attack Pearl Harbor?

26 AMERICA IN A WORLD AT WAR

WAR ON TWO FRONTS

THE AMERICAN ECONOMY IN WARTIME

RACE AND GENDER IN WARTIME AMERICA

ANXIETY AND AFFLUENCE IN WARTIME CULTURE

THE DEFEAT OF THE AXIS

LOOKING AHEAD

1. What was the impact of the war on the U.S. economy?
2. How was the military experience of the United States in World War II different for Europe and the Pacific?
3. How did the war affect life on the home front, especially for women, organized labor, and minorities?

THE ATTACK ON PEARL HARBOR thrust the United States into the greatest and most terrible war in the history of humanity, a war that changed the world as profoundly as any event of the twentieth century. World War II also transformed the United States in profound, if not always readily visible, ways. The war forced the American people to accept an unprecedented level of government control over their everyday lives. It transformed the roles of many women, reshaped the nation's industrial landscape, and thrust the United States into a position of global leadership that it has maintained ever since.

TIME LINE

WAR ON TWO FRONTS

Whatever political disagreements and social tensions there may have been among the American people during World War II, there was striking unity of opinion about the conflict itself. But both unity and confidence faced severe tests in the first, troubled months of 1942.

CONTAINING THE JAPANESE

Ten hours after the strike at Pearl Harbor, Japanese airplanes attacked the American airfields at Manila in the Philippines, destroying much of America's remaining air power in the Pacific. Three days later, Guam, an American possession, fell. Wake Island and Hong Kong followed. The great British fortress of Singapore in Malaya surrendered in February 1942, the Dutch East Indies in March, and Burma in April. In the Philippines, exhausted Filipino and American troops gave up their defense of the islands on May 6. (The American commander, General Douglas MacArthur, vowed as he left, "I shall return.")

American strategists planned two broad offensives to turn the tide against the Japanese. One, under the command of MacArthur, would move north from Australia, through New Guinea, and eventually to the Philippines. The other, under Admiral Chester Nimitz, would move west from Hawaii toward major Japanese island outposts in the central Pacific. Ultimately, strategists predicted, the two offensives would come together to invade Japan itself.

The Allies achieved their first important victory in the Battle of the Coral Sea, just northwest of Australia, on May 7–8, 1942, when American forces turned back the previously unstoppable Japanese navy. An even more important turning point occurred a month later northwest of Hawaii, near the small American outpost at Midway Island. There, after an enormous four-day battle (June 3–6, 1942), the American navy, despite terrible losses, regained control of the central Pacific. Particularly significant was that the United States destroyed four Japanese aircraft carriers without losing one of its own.

The Americans took the offensive several months later in the southern Solomon Islands, to the east of New Guinea. In August 1942, American forces assaulted three of the islands: Gavutu, Tulagi, and Guadalcanal. A struggle of terrible ferocity continued at Guadalcanal for six months, inflicting heavy losses on both sides. In the end, however, the Japanese were forced to abandon the island—and with it their last chance of launching an effective

WINNER R. HOE & CO., INC. AWARD – NATIONAL WAR POSTER COMPETITION
HELD UNDER AUSPICES OF ARTISTS FOR VICTORY, INC. – COUNCIL FOR DEMOCRACY–MUSEUM OF MODERN ART

"SOMEONE TALKED" This World War II poster, created by the graphic artist Henry Koerner, was one of many stern reminders to Americans from the government of the dangers of disclosing military secrets. In particular, wartime leaders were worried about soldiers and their families talking loosely about troop and ship locations (hence the title of another such poster: "Loose Lips Sink Ships"). (© K.J. Historical/Corbis) offensive to the south. The Americans, with aid from the Australians and the New Zealanders, now began the slow, arduous process of moving toward the Philippines and Japan itself.

HOLDING OFF THE GERMANS

In the European war, the United States fought in cooperation with, among others, Britain and the exiled "Free French" forces in the west, and tried also to conciliate its new ally, the Soviet Union, which was now fighting Hitler in the east. The army chief of staff, General George C. Marshall, supported a plan for a major Allied invasion of France across the English Channel in the spring of 1943, and he placed a previously little-known general, Dwight D. Eisenhower, in charge of planning the operation. The Soviet Union, which was absorbing the brunt of the German war effort, wanted the Allied invasion to begin at the earliest possible moment. But the British wanted first to launch a series of Allied offensives around the edges of the Nazi empire—in northern Africa and southern Europe—before undertaking the invasion of France.

Roosevelt ultimately decided to support the British plan—in part because he was eager to get American forces into combat quickly and knew that a cross-Channel invasion would take a long time to prepare. At the end of October 1942, the British opened a counteroffensive against General Erwin Rommel and the Nazi forces in North Africa who were threatening the Suez Canal. In a major battle at El Alamein, they forced the Germans to retreat from Egypt. On November 8–10, Anglo-American forces landed at Oran and Algiers in Algeria and at Casablanca in Morocco—areas under the Nazi-controlled French government at Vichy—and began moving east toward Rommel. The Germans threw the full weight of their forces in Africa against the inexperienced Americans and inflicted a serious defeat on them at the Kasserine Pass in Tunisia. General George S. Patton, however, regrouped and began an effective counteroffensive. With the help of Allied air and naval power and of British forces attacking from the east under Field Marshall Bernard Montgomery (the hero of El Alamein), the American offensive finally drove the last Germans from Africa in May 1943.

The North African campaign had tied up a large proportion of Allied resources, postponing the planned May 1943 cross-Channel invasion of France, despite angry complaints from the Soviet Union. By now, however, the threat of a Soviet collapse seemed much diminished, for during the winter of 1942–1943, the Red Army had successfully held off a major German assault at Stalingrad in southern Russia. Hitler had committed such enormous forces to the battle, and had suffered such appalling losses, that he could not continue his eastern offensive.

The Soviet successes persuaded Roosevelt to agree, in a January 1943 meeting with Churchill in Casablanca, to a British plan for an Allied invasion of Sicily. Churchill argued that the operation in Sicily might knock Italy out of the war and tie up German divisions that would otherwise be stationed in France. On the night of July 9–10, 1943, American and British armies landed in southeast Sicily; thirty-eight days later, they had conquered the island and were moving onto the Italian mainland. In the face of these setbacks, Mussolini's government collapsed and the dictator himself fled north toward Germany. (He was later captured by Italian insurgents and hanged.) But Mussolini's successor, Pietro Badoglio, quickly committed Italy to the Allies. Germany moved eight divisions into Italy and established a powerful defensive line south of Rome. The Allied offensive, which began on September 3, 1943, met a strong German line below Rome

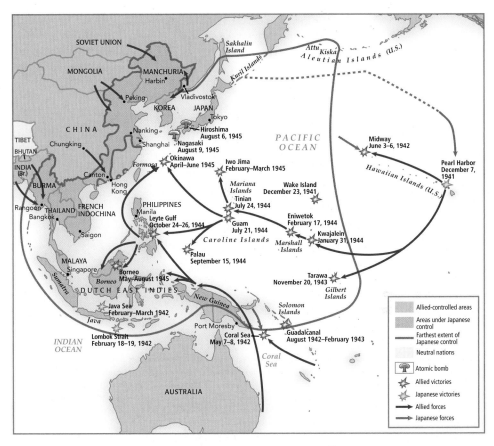

WORLD WAR II IN THE PACIFIC   This map illustrates the changing fortunes of the two combatants in the Pacific phase of World War II. The long red line stretching from Burma around to Manchuria represents the eastern boundary of the vast areas of the Pacific that had fallen under Japanese control by the summer of 1942. The blue lines illustrate the advance of American forces back into the Pacific beginning in May 1942 and accelerating in 1943 and after, which drove the Japanese forces back. The American advance was a result of two separate offensives—one in the central Pacific, under the command of Chester Nimitz, which moved west from Hawaii; and the other, under the command of Douglas MacArthur, which moved north from Australia. By the summer of 1945, American forces were approaching the Japanese mainland and were bombing Tokyo itself. The dropping of two American atomic bombs, on Hiroshima and Nagasaki, finally brought the war to an end. • *Why did the Soviet Union enter the Pacific war in August 1945, as shown in the upper left corner of the map?*

that kept the American forces bogged down. Not until May 1944 did the Allies break through the German defenses to resume their northward advance. On June 4, 1944, they captured Rome.

The invasion of Italy delayed the invasion of France by as much as a year, deeply embittering Stalin but also giving the Soviets time to begin moving toward the countries of eastern Europe.

AMERICA AND THE HOLOCAUST

In the midst of this intensive fighting, the leaders of the American government confronted one of history's great tragedies: the Nazi campaign to exterminate the Jews of Europe—which became known as the Holocaust. As early as 1942, high officials in

WORLD WAR II IN NORTH AFRICA AND ITALY: THE ALLIED COUNTEROFFENSIVE, 1942–1943 The United States and Great Britain understood from the beginning that an invasion of France across the English Channel would eventually be necessary for a victory in the European war. In the meantime, however, they began a campaign against Axis forces in North Africa, and in the spring of 1943 they began an invasion across the Mediterranean into Italy. This map shows the points along the coast of North Africa where Allied forces landed in 1942—with American forces moving east from Morocco and Algeria and British forces moving west from Egypt. The two armies met in Tunisia and moved into Italy from there. • *Why were America and Britain reluctant to launch the cross-Channel invasion in 1942 or 1943?*

Washington had incontrovertible evidence that Hitler's forces were rounding up Jews and others (including Poles, homosexuals, and communists) from all over Europe, transporting them to concentration camps in eastern Germany and Poland, and systematically murdering them. (The death toll would ultimately reach 6 million Jews and at least 4 million others.) News of the atrocities soon reached the public as well, and pressure began to build for an Allied effort to end the killing or at least to rescue some of the surviving Jews.

The American government consistently resisted almost all such demands. Although by mid-1944 Allied bombers were flying missions within a few miles of the most notorious death camp, at Auschwitz in Poland, the War Department argued that sending planes to destroy the crematoria was unfeasible. American officials also refused to destroy railroad lines leading to the camp. And the United States resisted pleas that it admit large numbers of Jewish refugees attempting to escape Europe.

More forceful action by the United States (and Britain, which was even less amenable to Jewish requests for assistance) might have saved at least some lives. That they did not take such action, it seems clear in retrospect, constituted a considerable moral failure. But policymakers justified their inaction by insisting that they needed to focus exclusively on the larger goal of winning the war. Any diversion of energy and attention to other purposes, they believed, would distract them from the overriding goal of victory.

THE ST. LOUIS Many people consider the fate of the German liner *St. Louis* to be a powerful symbol of the indifference of the United States and other nations to the fate of European Jews during the Holocaust, even though its forlorn journey preceded both the beginning of World War II and the beginning of systematic extermination of Jews by the Nazi regime. The *St. Louis* carried a group of over 900 Jews fleeing from Germany in 1939, carrying exit visas of dubious legality cynically sold to them by members of Hitler's Gestapo. It became a ship without a port as it sailed from country to country—Mexico, Paraguay, Argentina, Costa Rica, and Cuba—where its passengers were refused entry time and again. Most of the passengers were hoping for a haven in the United States, but the American State Department refused to allow the ship even to dock as it sailed up the American eastern seaboard. Eventually, the *St. Louis* returned to Europe and distributed its passengers among Britain, France, Holland, and Belgium (where this photograph was taken, showing refugees smiling and waving as they prepared to disembark in Antwerp in June 1939). Less than a year later, all those nations except Britain fell under Nazi control. (© Bettmann/Corbis)

THE AMERICAN ECONOMY IN WARTIME

Not since the Civil War had the United States been involved in so prolonged and consuming a military experience as World War II. American armed forces engaged in combat around the globe for nearly four years. American society, in the meantime, experienced changes that reached into every corner of the nation.

PROSPERITY AND THE RIGHTS OF LABOR

World War II had a profound impact on American domestic life by ending the Great Depression. By the middle of 1941, the economic problems of the 1930s—unemployment, deflation, industrial sluggishness—had vanished before the great wave of wartime industrial expansion.

The most important catalyst of the new prosperity was government spending, which after 1939 was pumping more money into the economy each year than had all the New Deal relief agencies combined. In 1939, the federal budget had been $9 billion, the highest in American peacetime history. By 1945, it had risen to $100 billion.

Largely as a result, the gross national product soared: from $91 billion in 1939 to $166 billion in 1945. Personal incomes in some regions grew by as much as 100 percent or more.

The West Coast, naturally, became the launching point for the war against Japan, and the government created large manufacturing facilities in California and elsewhere to serve the needs of the military. Altogether, the government made almost $40 billion worth of wartime capital investments (factories, military and transportation facilities, highways, power plants) in the West, more than in any other region. By the end of the war, the Pacific Coast had become the center of a growing American aircraft industry and an important shipbuilding center. Los Angeles, formerly a medium-sized city notable chiefly for its film industry, now became a major industrial center as well.

The war created a serious labor shortage. The armed forces took more than 15 million men and women out of the civilian workforce at the same time that the demand for labor was rising rapidly. Nevertheless, the supply of workers increased by almost 20 percent during the war—largely through the employment of many people previously considered inappropriate for the workforce: the very young, the elderly, minorities, and, most important, several million women.

The war gave a substantial boost to union membership, which rose from about 10.5 million in 1941 to over 13 million in 1945. That was in part a result of labor's "maintenance-of-membership" agreement with the government, which ensured that the thousands of new workers pouring into unionized defense plants would be automatically enrolled in the unions. But the government also managed to win two important concessions from union leaders. One was the "no-strike" pledge, by which unions agreed not to stop production in wartime. Another was the so-called Little Steel formula, which set a 15 percent limit on wage increases.

Despite the no-strike pledge, nearly 15,000 work stoppages took place during the war, mostly wildcat strikes (strikes not authorized by the union leadership). When the United Mine Workers defied the government by striking in May 1943, Congress reacted by passing, over Roosevelt's veto, the Smith-Connally Act (the War Labor Disputes Act), which required that unions wait thirty days before striking and which empowered the president to seize a struck war plant. In the meantime, public animosity toward labor rose rapidly, and some states passed laws to limit union power.

STABILIZING THE BOOM AND MOBILIZING PRODUCTION

The fear of deflation, the central concern of the 1930s, gave way during the war to a fear of inflation, particularly after prices rose 25 percent in the two years before Pearl Harbor. Fighting inflation was the task of the Office of Price Administration (OPA), led first by Leon Henderson and then by Chester Bowles. The OPA was successful enough that inflation was a much less serious problem than it had been during World War I. Even so, the agency was never popular. Black-marketing and overcharging grew in proportions far beyond OPA's policing capacity.

From 1941 to 1945, the federal government spent a total of $321 billion—twice as much as it had spent in the entire 150 years of its existence as a nation to that point, and ten times as much as the cost of World War I. The national debt rose from $49 billion in 1941 to $259 billion in 1945. The government borrowed about half the revenues it needed by selling $100 billion worth of bonds. Much of the rest it raised by radically increasing income-tax rates, through the Revenue Act of 1942. To simplify collection, Congress enacted a withholding system of payroll deductions in 1943.

In January 1942, the president responded to widespread criticism of earlier efforts to mobilize the economy for war by creating the War Production Board (WPB), under the direction of a former Sears Roebuck executive, Donald Nelson. Throughout its troubled history, the WPB was never able to win complete control over military purchases; the army and navy often circumvented the board. Nor was it able to satisfy the complaints of small business, which charged (correctly) that most contracts went to large corporations. Gradually, the president transferred much of the WPB's authority to a new office located within the White House: the Office of War Mobilization (OWM). But the OWM was only slightly more successful than the WPB.

Despite the administrative problems, however, the war economy managed to meet almost all of the nation's critical war needs. By the beginning of 1944, American factories were, in fact, producing more than the government needed. Their output was twice that of all the Axis countries combined.

WARTIME SCIENCE AND TECHNOLOGY

More than any previous American war, World War II was a watershed for technological and scientific innovation. That was so partly because the American government poured substantial funds into research and development beginning in 1940. In that year, the government created the National Defense Research Committee (which later became the Office of Scientific Research and Development). It was headed by the MIT scientist Vannevar Bush, a pioneer in the early development of the computer. By the end of the war, the new agency had spent more than $100 million on research, more than four times the amount spent by the government on military research and development in the previous forty years.

In the first years of the war, all the technological advantages seemed to lie with the Germans and Japanese. Germany had made great advances in tanks and other mechanized armor in the 1930s, particularly during the Spanish Civil War, when it had helped arm Franco's forces. It used its armor effectively during its blitzkrieg in Europe in 1940 and again in North Africa in 1942. German submarine technology was significantly advanced compared to British and American capabilities in 1940. Japan had developed extraordinary capacity in its naval-air technology, as indicated by the successful raid on Pearl Harbor.

But Britain and America had advantages of their own. American techniques of mass production—the great automotive assembly lines in particular—were converted efficiently to military production in 1941 and 1942 and soon began producing airplanes, ships, tanks, and other armaments in much greater numbers than could the Germans and Japanese. Allied scientists and engineers moved quickly as well to improve Anglo-American aviation and naval technology, particularly submarines and tanks. By late 1942, Allied weaponry was at least as advanced as, and more plentiful than, that of the enemy.

Each technological innovation by the enemy produced a corresponding innovation to limit the damage of the new techniques. American and British physicists made rapid advances in improving radar and sonar—taking advantage of advances in radio technology in the 1920s and beyond—which helped Allied naval forces decimate German U-boats in 1943 and virtually end their effectiveness in the war. Particularly important was the creation in 1940 of "centimetric radar." The narrow beams of short wavelength made radar more efficient and effective than ever before—as the British navy discovered in April 1941. The instruments on one of its ships detected a surfaced submarine ten miles away at night and, on another occasion, spotted a periscope at three-quarters of a mile range. These innovations put the Allies far in advance of Germany and Japan in radar technology. The Allies also learned early how to detect and disable German naval mines; and when the Germans tried to counter this progress by introducing an "acoustic" mine, which detonated when a ship came near, the Allies developed acoustical countermeasures of their own, which transmitted sounds through the water to detonate mines before ships came near them.

Anglo-American antiaircraft technology—both on land and on sea—also improved, but never to the point where it could defeat bombing raids altogether. Germany made substantial advances in the development of rocket technology in the early years of the war and managed to launch some rocket-propelled bombs (the V1s and V2s) across the English Channel, aimed at London. The psychological effects of the rockets on the British people were considerable. But the Germans were never able to create a production technology capable of building enough such rockets to make a real difference in the balance of military power.

Beginning in 1942, British and American forces seized the advantage in the air war by producing new and powerful four-engine bombers in great numbers—among them the British Lancaster B1 and the American Boeing B17F, capable of flying a bomb load of 6,000 pounds for 1,300 miles and reaching 37,500 feet. As a result, they were able to conduct extensive bombing missions over Germany (and, later, Japan) with much less danger of being shot down. But the success of the bombers rested heavily as well on new electronic guidance systems. The Gee navigation system used electronic pulses to help pilots plot their exact locations, something that in the past only highly skilled navigators could do, and then only in good weather. In March 1942, eighty Allied bombers fitted with Gee systems staged a devastatingly effective bombing raid on German industrial and military installations in the Ruhr Valley. In the past, studies had shown that nighttime bombing raids were at best 30 percent accurate. The Gee system doubled the accuracy rate. Also effective was the Oboe system, a radio device that sent a sonic message to airplanes to tell them when they were within 20 yards of their targets, first introduced in December 1942.

The area in which the Allies had perhaps the greatest advantage was the gathering of intelligence, much of it through Britain's top-secret Ultra project. Some of the advantages the Allies enjoyed came from the capture of German and Japanese intelligence devices. More important, however, were the efforts of cryptologists to puzzle out the enemy's systems, and advances in computer technology that helped the Allies decipher coded messages sent by the Japanese and the Germans. Much of Germany's coded communication made use of the so-called Enigma machine, which constantly changed the coding systems it used. In the first months of the war, Polish intelligence had developed an electromechanical computer. It was called the "Bombe," and it could decipher some Enigma messages. After the fall of Poland, British scientists, led by the brilliant computer pioneer Alan Turing, took the Bombe and greatly improved it. On April 15, 1940, the new, improved high-speed Bombe deciphered a series of German messages within hours (not days, as had previously been the case). A few weeks later, it began decrypting German messages at the rate of 1,000 a day, providing the British (and, later, the Americans) with a constant flow of information about enemy operations that continued—unknown to the Germans—until the end of the war. Later in the war, British scientists working for the intelligence services built the first real programmable, digital computer—the Colossus II, which became operational less than a week before the beginning of the Normandy invasion and which could decipher an enormous number of intercepted German messages almost instantly.

The United States also had some important intelligence breakthroughs, including, in 1941, a dramatic success by the American Magic operation (the counterpart to Ultra) in breaking a Japanese coding system not unlike the German Enigma. The result was that Americans had access to intercepted information that, if properly interpreted, could have alerted them to the Japanese raid on Pearl Harbor in December 1941. But because such a raid had seemed entirely inconceivable to most American officials, those who received the information failed to understand or disseminate it in time.

RACE AND GENDER IN WARTIME AMERICA

In many ways, the war loosened many traditional barriers that had restricted the lives of minorities and women. There was so much demand for fighting men, so much demand for labor, and so much fluidity and mobility that the social and cultural barriers could not survive intact.

AFRICAN AMERICANS AND THE WAR

In the summer of 1941, A. Philip Randolph, president of the mostly African American Brotherhood of Sleeping Car Porters Union, began to insist that the government require companies receiving defense contracts to integrate their workforces. To mobilize support for the demand, Randolph planned a massive march on Washington. Roosevelt finally persuaded Randolph to cancel the march in return for a promise to establish what became the Fair Employment Practices Commission (FEPC) to investigate discrimination against African Americans in war industries.

The need for labor in war plants greatly increased the migration of African Americans from the rural South into industrial cities. The migration improved the economic conditions of many African Americans. But it also created urban tensions and occasional violence. The most serious conflict occurred in Detroit in 1943, when racial friction produced a major riot in which thirty-four people died, twenty-five of them black, after tension grew between black and white citizens.

Despite such tensions, leading black organizations redoubled their efforts to challenge segregation. The Congress of Racial Equality (CORE), organized in 1942, mobilized mass popular resistance to discrimination in a way that the older, more conservative organizations had never done. Randolph, Bayard Rustin, James Farmer, and other, younger African American leaders helped organize sit-ins and demonstrations in segregated theaters and restaurants. CORE also organized "Freedom Rides" to desegregate buses and bus terminals. These efforts were mostly failures, but they contributed to the growth of racial equality.

Pressure for change also grew within the military. The armed forces maintained their traditional practice of limiting African Americans to the most menial assignments, keeping them in segregated training camps and units, and barring them entirely from the Marine Corps and the Army Air Force. But there were signs of change. By the end of the war, the number of black servicemen had increased sevenfold, to 700,000; some training camps were being at least partially integrated. African Americans were allowed to serve on ships with white sailors, and more black units were sent into combat. The changes did not come easily.

In some of the partially integrated army bases—Fort Dix, New Jersey, for example—riots broke out when black soldiers protested mistreatment at the hands of whites or having to serve in segregated divisions.

NATIVE AMERICANS AND THE WAR

Approximately 25,000 Indians served in the military during World War II. Many Native Americans saw combat. Others (mostly Navajo) became military "code-talkers," speaking their own language (which enemy forces would be unlikely to understand) over the radio and the telephones. The war had important effects on the Indians who served in the military. It brought them into intimate contact (often for the first time) with white society, and it awakened among some of them a taste for the material benefits of life in capitalist America that they would retain after the war. Some never returned to the reservations but chose to remain in the non-Indian world and assimilate to its ways.

The war had important effects, too, on the Native Americans who stayed on the reservations. Little war work reached the tribes. Government subsidies dwindled. Talented young people left the reservations to serve in the military or work in war production, creating workforce shortages in some tribes. The wartime emphasis on national unity undermined support for the revitalization of tribal autonomy that the Indian Reorganization Act of 1934 had launched. New pressures emerged to eliminate the reservation system and to require the tribes to assimilate into white society. The pressures were so severe that John Collier, the energetic director of the Bureau of Indian Affairs who had done so much to promote the reinvigoration of the reservations, resigned in 1945.

MEXICAN AMERICAN WAR WORKERS

Large numbers of Mexican workers entered the United States in response to wartime labor shortages on the Pacific Coast and in the Southwest. The American and Mexican governments agreed in 1942 to a program by which *braceros* (contract laborers) would be admitted to the United States for a limited time. Some worked as migrant farm laborers, but many Mexicans were able for the first time to find factory jobs. They formed the second-largest group of migrants (after African Americans) to U.S. cities in the 1940s. They concentrated mainly in the West but established significant Mexican communities in Chicago, Detroit, and other industrial cities.

The sudden expansion of Mexican American neighborhoods created tensions and occasional conflict in some American cities. Anglo residents of Los Angeles became alarmed at the activities of Mexican American teenagers, many of whom joined street gangs (*pachucos*). The Mexican American youths were particularly distinctive because of their style of dress. At a time when fabric had been rationed for the war effort, they wore long, loose jackets with padded shoulders, baggy pants tied at the ankles, long watch chains, broad-brimmed hats, and greased, ducktail hairstyles. The outfit was known as a "zoot suit." In June 1943, animosity toward the "zoot-suiters"—driven partly by ethnic prejudice and partly by the apparent disregard of rationing—produced a four-day riot in Los Angeles. Anglo sailors in Long Beach invaded Mexican American communities and attacked zoot-suiters (in response to alleged zoot-suiter attacks on servicemen). The police did little to restrain the sailors, who grabbed Hispanic teenagers, tore off and burned their clothes, cut off their ducktails, and beat them. When Mexicans tried to fight back, the police moved in and arrested them. In the aftermath of the "zoot-suit riots," Los Angeles passed a law prohibiting zoot suits.

YOUNG STREET, LOS ANGELES   Although the Anglo image of Mexican Americans in wartime southern California was dominated by the culture of the "zoot-suiters," there was a long-standing and thriving Mexican American middle class. Here two friends, Richard Garcia and John Urrea, pose in front of the Urrea home in the early 1940s. (SHADES OF L.A. ARCHIVES/ Los Angeles Public Library)

THE INTERNMENT OF JAPANESE AMERICANS

World War II, unlike World War I, produced little popular animosity toward Germans. But it created considerable animosity toward the Japanese. After the attack on Pearl Harbor, government propaganda and popular culture combined to create an image of the Japanese as a devious, malign, and savage people.

This racial animosity soon extended to Americans of Japanese descent. There were not many Japanese Americans in the United States—about 127,000, most of them concentrated in a few areas in California. About one-third were unnaturalized first-generation immigrants (Issei); two-thirds were naturalized or native-born citizens of the United States (Nisei). Because they generally kept to themselves and preserved traditional Japanese cultural patterns, it was easy for Anglo Americans to imagine that the Japanese Americans were engaged in conspiracies on behalf of their ancestral homeland. (There is no evidence that they actually were.)

In February 1942, in response to pressure from military officials and political leaders on the West Coast (including California Attorney General Earl Warren) and recommendations from the War Department, the president authorized the army to "intern" the Japanese Americans. More than 100,000 people (Issei and Nisei alike) were rounded up, told to dispose of their property however they could (which often meant simply abandoning it), and taken to what the government euphemistically called "relocation centers." In fact, they were facilities little different from prisons, many of them located in the western mountains and desert. A group of innocent people (many of them citizens of the United States) were forced to spend up to three years in grim, debilitating isolation, barred from lucrative employment, provided with only minimal medical care, and deprived of decent schools for their children. The Supreme Court upheld the evacuation in the 1944 *Korematsu* decision; and although most of the Japanese Americans were released later that year, they were unable to win any significant compensation for their losses until Congress finally acted in the late 1980s.

CHINESE AMERICANS AND THE WAR

At the same time that the war undermined the position of Japanese Americans, the American alliance with China during World War II significantly enhanced both the legal and social status of Chinese Americans. In 1943, partly to improve relations with the government of China, Congress repealed the Chinese Exclusion Acts, which had barred almost all Chinese immigration since 1892. The new quota for Chinese immigrants was minuscule (105 a year), but a substantial number of Chinese women managed to gain entry into the country through other provisions covering war brides and fiancées. Over 4,000 Chinese women entered the United States in the first three years after the war. Permanent residents of Chinese descent were finally permitted to become citizens.

Racial animosity toward the Chinese did not disappear, but it did decline—in part because government propaganda and popular culture both began presenting positive images of the Chinese (in some measure to contrast them with the Japanese) and in part because Chinese Americans (like African Americans and other previously marginal groups) began taking jobs in war plants and other booming areas suffering from labor shortages and hence moved out of the relatively isolated world of the Chinatowns. A higher proportion of Chinese Americans (22 percent of all adult males) was drafted than that of any other national group, and the entire Chinese community in most cities worked hard and conspicuously for the war effort.

WOMEN AND CHILDREN IN WARTIME

The number of women in the workforce increased by nearly 60 percent during the war, as many women replaced male industrial workers serving in the military. These wage-earning women were likely to be married and were, on the whole, older than most who had entered the workforce in the past.

Many factory owners continued to categorize jobs by gender, reserving the most lucrative positions for men. (Female work, like male work, was also categorized by race: black women were usually assigned more menial tasks, and paid at a lower rate, than their white counterparts.) But some women began to take on heavy industrial jobs that had long been considered "men's work." The famous wartime image of "Rosie the Riveter" symbolized the new importance of the female industrial worker. Women joined unions in substantial numbers and helped erode at least some of the prejudice, including the prejudice against mothers working, that had previously kept many of them from paid employment.

Most women workers during the war, however, were employed not in factories but in service-sector jobs. Above all, they worked for the government, whose bureaucratic needs expanded dramatically alongside its military and industrial needs. Even within the military,

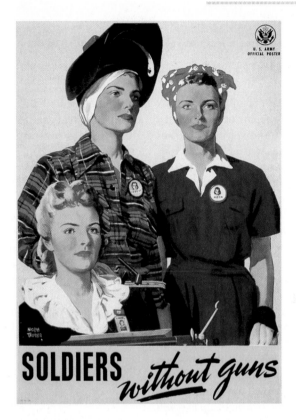

SOLDIERS *without guns*

WOMEN AT WAR Many American women enlisted in the army and navy women's corps during World War II, but an equally important contribution to the war effort was their work in factories and offices—often in jobs that would have been considered inappropriate for them in peacetime but that they were now encouraged to assume because of the absence of so many men. (Library of Congress)

which enlisted substantial numbers of women as WAACs (army) and WAVEs (navy), most female work was clerical.

Many mothers whose husbands were in the military had to combine work with child care. The scarcity of child-care facilities or other community services meant that some women had no choice but to leave young children—often known as "latchkey children" or "eight-hour orphans"—at home alone (or sometimes locked in cars in factory parking lots) or staying with relatives or neighbors while they worked.

Perhaps in part because of the family dislocations of the war, juvenile crime rose markedly in the war years. Young boys were arrested at increasing rates for car theft, burglary, vandalism, and vagrancy. For many children, however, the distinctive experience of the war years was not crime but work. More than a third of all teenagers between the ages of fourteen and eighteen were employed during the last years of the war, causing some reduction in high-school enrollments.

The return of prosperity helped increase the marriage rate and lower the age at which people married, but many marriages were unable to survive the pressures of wartime separation. The divorce rate rose rapidly. Even so, the rise in the birth rate that accompanied the increase in marriages was the first sign of what would become the great postwar "baby boom."

CONSIDER THE SOURCE

MARJORIE HASELTON WRITES HER HUSBAND RICHARD IN CHINA, AUGUST 15, 1945

YOU and I were brought up to think cynically of patriotism—not by our parents, but by the books, plays, movies and magazine features written by the bitter, realistic writers of the twenties and thirties. They called patriotism a tool of the demagogues, a spell binder to blind our eyes to the "real" truth. We thought they were right—at least, I know, I did. I hated everything in music, books, movies, etc. that stressed love of country. That was for the yokels. The uninitiated, but not for anyone who really was in the know. Maybe I was right—I don't know. One thing I AM sure of—a thing this war has taught me—I love my country and I'm not ashamed to admit it anymore. Perhaps I am only thinking along the lines the nation's propagandists want me to think. But I know I am proud of the men of my generation. Brought up like you and I, in false prosperity then degrading depression, they have overcome these handicaps. And shown the world that America has something the world can never take away from us—a determination to keep our way of life.

Underneath what the Jap [anese] and the Germans believe to be a "what-the-hell," decadent attitude—you boys proved that you had a fighting spirit and team work that couldn't be beaten. Call it Yankee ingenuity or whatever you will, it still is the one force that won the war—the thing the enemy never believed we had. That is why, tonight, I am proud to be an American, and married to one of its fighting men. None of you fellows wanted the deal life handed you—but just about every one of you gritted your teeth and hung on. "Do the job, get it over with, and get home again" was the by-word. You proved that Americans may look soft and easy going, "spoiled" by the highest standard of living in the world, yet when the hour of need came you showed them we could take it—and dish it out.

UNDERSTAND, ANALYZE, & EVALUATE

1. How did Marjorie Haselton describe her and possibly the nation's mood prior to the war?
2. Why did she feel so differently about herself and her country by the middle of August 1945? What events precipitated this letter earlier that month?
3. How did Haselton describe the character and attitude of American G.I.'s? How did this compare to enemy soldiers from Germany and Japan?

Origin: James H. Madison, *World War II: A History in Documents* (New York: Oxford University Press, 2010), p. 134.

ANXIETY AND AFFLUENCE IN WARTIME CULTURE

The war created considerable anxiety in American lives. Families worried about loved ones at the front, and as the war continued, many mourned relatives who had died in combat. Women struggled to support families in the absence of husbands and fathers. Businesses and communities struggled with shortages of goods and labor. People living on the two coasts, in particular, worried about enemy invasions and sabotage.

But the abundance of the war years also created a striking buoyancy in American life. Suddenly people had money to spend again and—despite the many shortages—at least some things to spend it on. In fact, consumerism became, as it had in the 1920s, one of the most powerful forces in American culture.

WARTIME ENTERTAINMENT AND LEISURE

The publishing, theater, and movie industries did record business during the war. Audiences equal to about half the nation's population attended movies each week. Magazines, particularly pictorial ones such as *Life*, reached the peak of their popularity by providing pictures of and stories about the war. Radio ownership and listenership also increased, for the same reason.

Fuel rationing and rubber shortages limited travel by car, but many people traveled nevertheless—by train or bus, or to places relatively close to their homes. Resort hotels, casinos, and racetracks were jammed with customers. More often, however, people sought entertainment in their own communities. Dance halls were packed with young people drawn to the seductive music of bands; soldiers and sailors home on leave, or awaiting shipment abroad, were especially attracted to the dances, which became to many of them a symbol of the life they were leaving and that they were fighting to defend.

The most popular music was the relatively new jazz form known as swing, which, like many other forms of popular music, had emerged from the African American musical world. During the heyday of swing, band leaders such as Benny Goodman, Duke Ellington, Tommy Dorsey, and Glenn Miller were among the most recognized and popular figures in American popular culture, rivaling movie stars in their celebrity. Swing became one of the first forms of popular music to challenge racial taboos. Benny Goodman hired the black pianist Teddy Wilson to play with his band in 1935; other white bandleaders followed.

WOMEN AND MEN IN THE ARMED SERVICES

For men at the front, the image of home was a powerful antidote to the rigors of wartime. They dreamed of music, food, movies, and other material comforts. Many also dreamed of women—wives and girlfriends, but also movie stars and others, who became the source of one of the most popular icons of the front: the pinup. Sailors pasted pinups inside their lockers. Infantrymen carried them (along with pictures of wives, mothers, and girlfriends) in their knapsacks. Fighter pilots gave their planes female names and painted bathing beauties on their nose cones.

For the servicemen who remained in America, and for soldiers and sailors in cities far from home in particular, the company of friendly, "wholesome" women was, the military believed, critical to sustaining morale. The branches of the United Service Organization (known as USOs) recruited thousands of young women to serve as hostesses in their clubs. They were expected to dress nicely, dance well, and chat happily with lonely men. Other women joined "dance brigades," traveling by bus to military bases for social evenings with servicemen. The "USO girls" and the members of the dance brigades were forbidden to have any contact with men except at parties at the clubs or during dances. Clearly, such regulations were often violated. The military took elaborate measures to root out gay men and lesbians from their ranks—vigilantly searching for evidence of homosexuality and unceremoniously dismissing gay people with undesirable discharges. The services quietly tolerated illicit heterosexual relationships, which they believed were both natural and, for many men, necessary.

WORLD WAR II IN EUROPE: THE ALLIED COUNTEROFFENSIVE, 1943–1945 This map illustrates the final, climactic movements in the war in Europe—the two great offensives against Germany that began in 1943 and culminated in 1945. From the east, the armies of the Soviet Union, having halted the Germans at Stalingrad and Moscow, swept across eastern Europe toward Germany. From the west and the south, American, British, and other Allied forces moved toward Germany through Italy and—after the Normandy invasion in June 1944—through France. The two offensives met in Berlin in May 1945. Note, too, the northern routes that America and Britain used to supply the Soviet Union during the war. • *What problems did the position of the Allied forces at the end of the war help to produce?*

As during World War I, the armed services virtually took over many American colleges and universities. Emptied of male students and professors (and many females as well), they turned themselves into training camps for military officers—helped by substantial funding from the federal government.

THE GROWTH OF WARTIME CONSERVATISM

Late in 1943, Franklin Roosevelt publicly suggested that "Dr. New Deal," as he called it, had served its purpose and should now give way to "Dr. Win-the-War." The statement reflected the president's own genuine shift in concern: victory was now more important than reform. But it reflected, too, the political reality that had emerged during the first two years of war.

The greatest assault on New Deal reforms came from conservatives in Congress, who seized on the war as a reason to do what many had wanted to do in peacetime: dismantle many of the achievements of the New Deal. They were assisted by the end of mass unemployment, which decreased the need for such relief programs as the Civilian Conservation Corps and the Works Progress Administration (both of which Congress abolished). They were assisted, too, by their own increasing numbers. In the congressional elections of 1942, Republicans gained 47 seats in the House and 10 in the Senate.

Republicans approached the 1944 election determined to exploit what they believed was resentment of wartime regimentation and unhappiness with Democratic reform. They nominated as their candidate the young and vigorous governor of New York, Thomas E. Dewey. Roosevelt was unopposed within his party, but Democratic leaders pressured him to abandon Vice President Henry Wallace, an advanced New Dealer and hero of the CIO. Roosevelt agreed to replace him with a more moderate figure, Senator Harry S. Truman of Missouri. Truman had won acclaim as chairman of the Senate War Investigating Committee (known as the Truman Committee), which compiled an impressive record uncovering waste and corruption in wartime production.

The election revolved around domestic economic issues and, indirectly, the president's health. The president was, in fact, gravely ill, suffering from, among other things, advanced arteriosclerosis. But the campaign seemed momentarily to revive him. He made several strenuous public appearances late in October, which dispelled popular doubts about his health and ensured his reelection. He captured 53.5 percent of the popular vote to Dewey's 46 percent, and 432 electoral votes to Dewey's 99. Democrats lost 1 seat in the Senate, gained 20 in the House, and maintained control of both.

THE DEFEAT OF THE AXIS

By the middle of 1943, America and its allies had succeeded in stopping the Axis advance in both Europe and the Pacific. In the next two years, the Allies themselves seized the offensive and launched a series of powerful drives that led the way to victory.

THE LIBERATION OF FRANCE

By early 1944, American and British bombers were attacking German industrial installations and other targets almost around the clock, drastically cutting production and impeding transportation. Especially devastating was the massive bombing of such German cities as Leipzig, Dresden, and Berlin. A February 1945 incendiary raid on Dresden created a great firestorm that destroyed three-fourths of the previously undamaged city and killed approximately 135,000 people, almost all civilians.

An enormous offensive force had been gathering in England for two years before the spring of 1944: almost 3 million troops and perhaps the greatest array of naval vessels and armaments ever assembled in one place. On the morning of June 6, 1944, this vast invasion force moved into action. The landing came not at the narrowest part of the English Channel, where the Germans had expected and prepared for it, but along sixty miles of the Cotentin Peninsula on the coast of Normandy. While airplanes and battleships offshore bombarded the Nazi defenses, 4,000 vessels landed American, British, Canadian, and other troops and supplies on the beaches. (Three divisions of paratroopers had been dropped chaotically behind the German lines the night before.) Fighting was intense along the beach, but the superior manpower and equipment of the Allied forces gradually prevailed. Within a week, the German forces had been dislodged from virtually the entire Normandy coast.

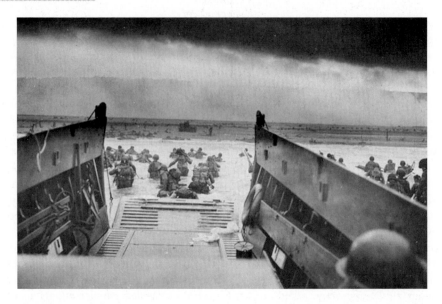

THE NORMANDY INVASION This photograph, taken from a landing craft, shows American troops wading ashore and onto the Normandy beaches, where one of the decisive battles of World War II was taking shape. The invasion was launched despite threatening weather and rough seas. (Robert Sargent/US Coast Guard/Time & Life Pictures/Getty Images)

For the next month, further progress remained slow. But in late July, in the Battle of Saint-Lô, General Omar Bradley's First Army smashed through the German lines. George S. Patton's Third Army, spearheaded by heavy tank attacks, then moved through the hole Bradley had created and began a drive into the heart of France. On August 25, Free French forces arrived in Paris and liberated the city from four years of German occupation. By mid-September the Allied armies had driven the Germans almost entirely out of France and Belgium.

The great Allied drive came to a halt, however, at the Rhine River against a firm line of Nazi defenses. In mid-December, German forces struck in desperation along fifty miles of front in the Ardennes Forest. In the Battle of the Bulge (named for a large bulge that appeared in the American lines as the Germans pressed forward), they drove fifty-five miles toward Antwerp before they were finally stopped at Bastogne. It was the last major battle on the western front.

While the western Allies fought their way through France, Soviet forces swept westward into central Europe and the Balkans. In late January 1945, the Russians launched a great offensive toward the Oder River, inside Germany. By early spring, they were ready to launch a final assault against Berlin. General Omar Bradley, in the meantime, was pushing toward the Rhine from the west. Early in March, Bradley's forces captured the city of Cologne, on the river's west bank. The next day, he discovered and seized an undamaged bridge over the river at Remagen; Allied troops were soon pouring across the Rhine. In the following weeks, the British commander Montgomery, with a million troops, pushed into Germany in the north while Bradley's army, sweeping through central Germany, completed the encirclement of 300,000 German soldiers in the Ruhr.

The German resistance was now broken on both fronts. American forces were moving eastward faster than they had anticipated and could have beaten the Russians to Berlin and Prague. The American and British high commands decided, instead, to halt the advance along the Elbe River in central Germany to await the Russians. That decision enabled the Soviets to occupy eastern Germany and Czechoslovakia.

On April 30, with Soviet forces on the outskirts of Berlin, Adolf Hitler killed himself in his bunker in the capital. And on May 8, 1945, the remaining German forces surrendered unconditionally.

THE PACIFIC OFFENSIVE

In February 1944, American naval forces under Admiral Chester Nimitz won a series of victories in the Marshall Islands and cracked the outer perimeter of the Japanese Empire. Within a month, the navy had destroyed other vital Japanese bastions. American submarines, in the meantime, were decimating Japanese shipping and crippling Japan's domestic economy.

America's principal ally in Asia was China, and the United States hoped that the Chinese forces would help defeat the Japanese. To assist them, the army sent General Joseph W. Stilwell to help provide critical supplies to China by a land route through India and across the Himalayas. It was a brutal task. The Japanese blocked them at several points, and Stilwell had to rely for a time on airlifts of supplies over the mountains. But finally in the fall of 1944, Stilwell's forces succeeded in constructing a road and pipelines across the mountains into China—a route that came to be known by several names: the Burma Road, the Ledo Road, and at times the Stilwell Road.

Japanese forces consistently threatened the Burma Road. More dangerously, the Japanese were also threatening the wartime capital of China in Chungking. Chiang Kai-shek, the Chinese premier, was reluctant to use his troops against the Japanese and seemed more concerned with attacking Chinese communists, who were also fighting the Japanese. This helped to create a famous feud between Stilwell and Chiang. Stilwell began to call Chiang—not entirely privately—the "peanut." The dispute continued for many months until Stilwell finally left China. Stilwell's successors had little more success in prodding Chiang to confront the Japanese.

The decisive battles of the Pacific war occurred not in China but at sea. In mid-June 1944, an enormous American armada struck the heavily fortified Mariana Islands and, after some of the bloodiest operations of the war, captured Tinian, Guam, and Saipan. In September, American forces landed on the western Carolines. And on October 20, General MacArthur's troops landed on Leyte Island in the Philippines. The Japanese now employed virtually their entire fleet against the Allied invaders in three major encounters—which together constituted the decisive Battle of Leyte Gulf, the largest naval engagement in history. American forces held off the Japanese onslaught and sank four Japanese carriers, all but destroying Japan's capacity to continue a serious naval war. In February 1945, American marines seized the tiny volcanic island of Iwo Jima, only 750 miles from Tokyo, but only after the costliest battle in the history of the Marine Corps.

The battle for Okinawa, an island only 370 miles south of Japan, gave evidence of the strength of the Japanese resistance in these last desperate days. Week after week, the Japanese sent kamikaze (suicide) planes against American and British ships, sacrificing 3,500 of them while inflicting great damage. Japanese troops on shore launched desperate nighttime attacks on the American lines. The United States and its allies suffered nearly 50,000 casualties before finally capturing Okinawa in late June 1945. Over 100,000 Japanese died in the siege.

It seemed likely that the same kind of bitter fighting would await the Americans when they invaded Japan. But there were also some signs early in 1945 that such an invasion

THE DECISION TO DROP THE ATOMIC BOMB

THERE has been continuing disagreement since 1945 among historians—and many others—about how to explain and evaluate President Truman's decision to use the atomic bomb against Japan.

Truman himself, both at the time and in his 1955 memoirs, insisted that the decision was a simple and straightforward one. The alternative to using atomic weapons, he claimed, was an American invasion of mainland Japan that might have cost as many as a million American lives. That view has received considerable support from historians. Herbert Feis argued in *The Atomic Bomb and the End of World War II* (1966) that Truman made his decision on purely military grounds—to ensure a speedy American victory. David McCullough, the author of a popular biography of Truman published in 1992, also accepted Truman's own account of his actions largely uncritically, as did Alonzo L. Hamby in *Man of the People* (1995), an important scholarly study of Truman. "One consideration weighed most heavily on Truman," Hamby concluded. "The longer the war lasted, the more Americans killed."

Others have strongly disagreed. As early as 1948, British physicist P. M. S. Blackett wrote in *Fear, War, and the Bomb* that the destruction of Hiroshima and Nagasaki was "not so much the last military act of the second World War as the first major operation of the cold diplomatic war with Russia." The most important critic of Truman's decision is the historian Gar Alperovitz, the author of two influential books on the subject: *Atomic Diplomacy: Hiroshima and Potsdam* (1965) and *The Decision to Use the Atomic Bomb* (1995). Alperovitz dismissed the argument that the bomb was used to shorten the war and save lives. Japan was likely to have surrendered soon even if the bomb had not been used, he claimed. Instead, he argued, the United States used the bomb less to influence Japan than to intimidate the Soviet Union, "to make Russia more manageable in Europe."

John W. Dower's *War Without Mercy* (1986) contributed, by implication at least, to another controversial explanation of the

might not be necessary. The Japanese had almost no ships or planes left with which to fight. The firebombing of Tokyo in March, in which American bombers dropped napalm on the city and created a firestorm in which over 80,000 people died, further weakened the Japanese will to resist. Moderate Japanese leaders, who had long since concluded the war was lost, were looking to end the fighting. But they continued to face powerful opposition from military leaders. Whether the moderates could ultimately have prevailed is a question historians continue to debate. In any case, their efforts became superfluous in August 1945, when the United States made use of a terrible new weapon it had been developing throughout the war.

THE RUINS OF NAGASAKI On August 9, 1945, an American plane dropped an atomic bomb on the city of Nagasaki in Japan, following a similar bomb dropped several weeks earlier in Hiroshima. Both cities were almost entirely destroyed, with enormous casualties. Shortly after these bombings, Japan surrendered. (Ingram Publishing)

American decision: racism. The Japanese, many Americans came to believe during the war, were almost a subhuman species. Even many of Truman's harshest critics, however, note that it is, as Alperovitz has written, "all but impossible to find specific evidence that racism was an important factor in the decision to attack Hiroshima and Nagasaki."

The debate over the decision to drop the atomic bomb is an unusually emotional one, and it has inspired bitter professional and personal attacks on advocates of almost every position. It illustrates clearly how history has often been, and remains, a powerful force in the way societies define themselves. •

UNDERSTAND, ANALYZE, & EVALUATE

1. The United States dropped two atomic bombs on Japan, one on Hiroshima and the other on Nagasaki. Was dropping the bomb on Hiroshima necessary? Was it justifiable? Do the reasons for dropping the bomb on Hiroshima apply equally to the bombing of Nagasaki?

2. How might the war in the Pacific have been different if the United States had decided not to drop the bombs?

THE MANHATTAN PROJECT AND ATOMIC WARFARE

Reports had reached the United States in 1939 that Nazi scientists had taken the first step toward the creation of an atomic bomb, a weapon more powerful than any previously devised. The United States and Britain immediately began a race to develop the weapon before the Germans did.

The search for the new weapon emerged from theories developed by atomic physicists, beginning early in the century, and particularly from some of the founding ideas of modern physics developed by Albert Einstein. Einstein's famous theory of relativity had revealed the relationships between mass and energy. More precisely, he had argued that, in theory at least, matter could be converted into a tremendous force of energy. Einstein himself, who by then had left his native Germany and was living in the United States, warned Franklin Roosevelt of German interest in atomic weapons. The effort to build atomic weapons centered on the use of uranium. Its atomic structure makes possible the creation of a nuclear chain reaction. A nuclear chain reaction occurs when the atomic nuclei in radioactive matter are split (a process known as nuclear fission) by neutrons. Each fission creates new neutrons that produce fissions in additional atoms at an ever-increasing and self-sustaining pace, creating a previously unknown power.

The construction of atomic weapons had become feasible by the 1940s because of Italian scientist Enrico Fermi's discovery of the radioactivity of uranium in the 1930s. In 1939, the great Danish physicist Niels Bohr sent news of German experiments in radioactivity to the United States, where new experiments began in many places. In 1940, scientists at Columbia University began chain-reaction experiments with uranium and produced persuasive evidence of the feasibility of using uranium as fuel for a weapon. In 1941, the work moved to Berkeley and the University of Chicago, where Enrico Fermi (who had emigrated to the United States in 1938) achieved the first controlled fission chain reaction in December 1942.

By then, the army had taken control of the research and appointed General Leslie Groves to reorganize the project—which soon became known as the Manhattan Project, because it was devised in the Manhattan Engineer District Office of the Army Corps of Engineers. Over the next three years, the government secretly poured nearly $2 billion into the Manhattan Project—a massive scientific and technological effort conducted at hidden laboratories in Oak Ridge, Tennessee; Los Alamos, New Mexico; Hanford, Washington; and other sites. Scientists in Oak Ridge, who were charged with finding a way to create a nuclear chain reaction that could be feasibly replicated within the confined space of a bomb, began experimenting with plutonium—a derivative of uranium first discovered by scientists at Berkeley. Plutonium proved capable of providing a practical fuel for the weapon. Scientists in Los Alamos, under the direction of J. Robert Oppenheimer, were charged with the construction of the actual atomic bomb.

By 1944, despite many unforeseen problems, the Manhattan Project scientists pushed ahead much faster than anyone had predicted. Even so, the war in Europe ended before they were ready to test the first weapon. Just before dawn on July 16, 1945, in the desert near Alamogordo, New Mexico, the scientists gathered to witness the first atomic explosion in history: the detonation of a plutonium-fueled bomb that scientists had named Trinity. The explosion—a blinding flash of light, perhaps brighter than any ever before seen on earth, followed by a huge, billowing mushroom cloud—created a vast crater in the barren desert. Watching the test, Oppenheimer was reminded of a passage from a Hindu scripture: "I am become death, the destroyer of worlds."

News of the explosion reached President Harry S. Truman (who had taken office in April on the death of Roosevelt) in Potsdam, Germany, where he was attending a conference of Allied leaders. He issued an ultimatum to the Japanese (signed jointly by the British), demanding that they surrender by August 3 or face utter devastation. When the Japanese failed to meet the deadline, Truman ordered the air force to use the new atomic weapons against Japan.

Controversy has continued for decades over whether Truman's decision to use the bombs was justified and what his motives were. Some have argued that the atomic attack was unnecessary—that had the United States agreed to the survival of the emperor before the bombs were used (which it ultimately did agree to after the bombings), or had it waited only a few more weeks, the Japanese would have surrendered. Others argue that nothing less than the atomic bombs could have persuaded the Japanese to surrender without a costly American invasion.

Most of nation's military and political leaders, however, seemed little concerned about such matters. Truman, who had not even known of the existence of the Manhattan Project until he became president, made what he apparently believed to be a simple military decision. A weapon was available that would end the war quickly; he could see no reason not to use it.

On August 6, 1945, an American B-29, the *Enola Gay*, dropped an atomic weapon on the Japanese industrial center at Hiroshima. With a single bomb, the United States completely incinerated a four-square-mile area at the center of the previously undamaged city. More than 80,000 civilians died, according to later American estimates. Many more suffered the crippling effects of radioactive fallout or passed those effects on to their children in the form of birth defects.

The Japanese government, stunned by the attack, was at first unable to agree on a response. Two days later, on August 8, the Soviet Union declared war on Japan. And the following day, another American plane dropped another atomic weapon—this time on the city of Nagasaki—inflicting 100,000 deaths and terrible damage on yet another unfortunate community. Finally, the emperor intervened to break the stalemate in the cabinet, and on August 14 the government announced that it was ready to give up. On September 2, 1945, on board the American battleship *Missouri*, anchored in Tokyo Bay, Japanese officials signed the articles of surrender.

The most destructive war in human history had come to an end, and the United States had emerged from it not only victorious but in a position of unprecedented power, influence, and prestige. It was a victory, however, that few could greet with unambiguous joy. Fourteen million combatants had died in the struggle. As many as 50 million or more civilians may have perished, making World War II by far the deadliest war in history. The United States had suffered only light casualties in comparison with some other nations (and particularly in comparison with Russia and Germany), but the cost had still been high: 322,000 dead, another 800,000 injured. And the world continued to face an uncertain future, menaced by the threat of nuclear warfare and by an emerging antagonism between the world's two strongest nations—the United States and the Soviet Union—that would darken the peace for many decades to come.

CONCLUSION

The United States played a critical, indeed decisive, role in the war against Germany and Italy. It defeated Imperial Japan in the Pacific largely alone. But America's contributions to and sacrifices in the war paled next to those of its most important allies. Britain, France, and, above all, the Soviet Union paid a staggering price—in lives, treasure, and social unity—that had no counterpart in the United States. Most American citizens in the United States experienced a booming prosperity and only modest privations during the four years of American involvement in the conflict. There were, of course, jarring social changes during the war that even prosperity could not entirely offset: shortages, restrictions, regulations, family dislocations, and, perhaps most of all, the absence of millions of men and considerable numbers of women, who went overseas to fight.

American fighting men and women, of course, had very different experiences from those of the people who remained at home. They endured tremendous hardships, substantial casualties, and much fear and loneliness. They fought effectively and bravely. They helped liberate North Africa and Italy from German occupation. And in June 1944, finally, they joined British, French, and other forces in a great and successful invasion of France. It led less than a year later to the destruction of the Nazi regime and the end of the European war. In the Pacific, Americans turned back the Japanese offensive through a series of difficult naval and land battles. Ultimately, however, it was not the American army and navy that brought the war against Japan to a close. It was the unleashing of the most destructive weapon ever created—the atomic bomb—on the people of Japan that finally persuaded the leaders of that nation to surrender.

RECALL AND REFLECT

1. List some of the measures that the federal government took to mobilize the nation's economy for the war effort.
2. How did advances in technology affect the course of the military conflict?
3. How did the United States contribute to the Allied victory in Europe? How important were America's allies? Which allies were most important?
4. How did the war affect U.S. society—women, workers, African Americans, Japanese Americans, and immigrants?
5. Why did the United States bomb civilians in Japan and Europe in the last years of the war?

27 | THE COLD WAR

ORIGINS OF THE COLD WAR
THE COLLAPSE OF THE PEACE
AMERICA AFTER THE WAR
THE KOREAN WAR
THE CRUSADE AGAINST SUBVERSION

LOOKING AHEAD

1. What made the growing tension between the United States and the Soviet Union evolve into the Cold War?
2. What is the theory of containment, and how did it drive U.S. foreign policy and foreign interventions in the postwar era?
3. Why did the U.S. government and the American people believe that there was a threat of internal communist subversion?

EVEN BEFORE WORLD WAR II ENDED, there were signs of tension between the United States and the Soviet Union. Once the fighting was over, those tensions grew to create what became known as the "Cold War"—a long and dangerous rivalry between the two former allies that would cast its shadow over international affairs and American domestic life for more than four decades.

The Cold War took shape gradually over a five-year period, during which the relationship between the United States and the Soviet Union deteriorated and the United States crafted a new structure for American foreign policy—known as "containment"—that sought to keep communism from expanding.

ORIGINS OF
THE COLD WAR

Few issues in twentieth-century American history have aroused more debate than the origins of the Cold War. Some have claimed that Soviet duplicity and expansionism created the international tensions; others, that American provocations and global ambitions were at least equally to blame.

SOURCES OF SOVIET-AMERICAN TENSION

At the heart of the rivalry between the United States and the Soviet Union in the 1940s was a fundamental difference in the ways the great powers envisioned the postwar world. One vision, first openly outlined in the Atlantic Charter in 1941, was a world in which nations abandoned their traditional beliefs in military alliances and spheres of influence and governed their relations with one another through democratic processes, with an international organization serving as the arbiter of disputes and the protector of every nation's right of self-determination. That vision appealed to many Americans, including Franklin Roosevelt.

The other vision was that of the Soviet Union and, to some extent, Great Britain. Both Stalin and Churchill had signed the Atlantic Charter. But Churchill had always been uneasy about the implications of self-determination for Britain's own enormous empire. And the Soviet Union was determined to create a secure sphere for itself in Central and Eastern Europe as protection against possible future aggression from the West. Both Churchill and Stalin, therefore, tended to envision a postwar structure vaguely similar to the traditional European balance of power, in which the great powers would control areas of strategic interest to them. Gradually, the differences between these two positions would turn the peacemaking process into a form of warfare.

WARTIME DIPLOMACY

Serious strains began to develop in the alliance with the Soviet Union in January 1943, when Roosevelt and Churchill met in Casablanca, Morocco, to discuss Allied strategy. The two leaders could not accept Stalin's most important demand—the immediate opening of a second front in Western Europe. But they tried to reassure Stalin by announcing that they would accept nothing less than the unconditional surrender of the Axis powers. They would not negotiate a separate peace with Hitler and leave the Soviets to fight on alone.

In November 1943, Roosevelt and Churchill traveled to Tehran, Iran, for their first meeting with Stalin. By now, however, Roosevelt's most effective bargaining tool—Stalin's need for American assistance against Germany—had been largely removed. The German advance against Russia had been halted; Soviet forces were now launching their own westward offensive. Nevertheless, the Tehran Conference seemed in most respects a success. Stalin agreed to an American request that the Soviet Union enter the war in the Pacific soon after the end of hostilities in Europe. Roosevelt, in turn, promised that an Anglo-American second front would be established within six months.

On other matters, however, the origins of future disagreements were already visible. Most important was the question of Poland. Roosevelt and Churchill were willing to agree to a movement of the Soviet border westward, allowing Stalin to annex some historically Polish territory. But they differed sharply on the nature of the postwar government in the portion of Poland that would remain independent. Roosevelt and Churchill supported the claims of the Polish government-in-exile that had been functioning in London since 1940; Stalin wished to install another, pro-communist exiled government that had spent the war in Lublin, in the Soviet Union. The three leaders left the Tehran Conference with the issue unresolved.

YALTA

More than a year later, in February 1945, Roosevelt joined Churchill and Stalin again, for a peace conference in the Soviet city of Yalta. In return for Stalin's renewed promise to enter the Pacific war, Roosevelt agreed that the Soviet Union should receive some of the Pacific territory that Russia had lost in the 1904–1905 Russo-Japanese War.

The negotiators also agreed to a plan for a new international organization, one that had been hammered out during the previous summer at a conference in Washington, D.C. The new United Nations would contain a General Assembly, in which every member would be represented, and a Security Council, with permanent representatives of the five major powers (the United States, Britain, France, the Soviet Union, and China), each of which would have veto power. The Security Council would also have temporary delegates from several other nations. These agreements became the basis of the United Nations charter, drafted at a conference of fifty nations beginning April 25, 1945, in San Francisco. In sharp contrast to the American rejection of the League of Nations a generation before, the United States Senate ratified the charter in July by a vote of 80 to 2. (It was, many internationalists believed, a "second chance" to create a stable world order.)

On other issues, however, the Yalta Conference produced no real accord. Basic disagreement remained about the postwar Polish government. Stalin, whose armies now occupied Poland, had already installed a government composed of the pro-communist "Lublin" Poles. Roosevelt and Churchill insisted that the pro-Western "London" Poles must be allowed a place in the Warsaw regime. Roosevelt envisioned a government based

YALTA, 1945 Churchill (*left*) and Stalin (*right*) were shocked at the physical appearance of Franklin Roosevelt (*center*) when he arrived for their critical meeting at Yalta. Roosevelt had enough energy to perform capably at the conference, but he was in fact gravely ill. Two months later, not long after he gave Congress what turned out to be an unrealistically optimistic report of the prospects for postwar peace, he died. (© Bettmann/Corbis)

on free, democratic elections—which both he and Stalin recognized the pro-Western forces would win. Stalin agreed only to a vague compromise by which an unspecified number of pro-Western Poles would be granted a place in the government. He said he would hold "free and unfettered elections" in Poland on an unspecified future date. They did not happen until 1989.

Nor was there agreement about Germany. Roosevelt seemed to want a reconstructed and reunited Germany. Stalin wanted to impose heavy reparations on Germany and to ensure a permanent dismemberment of the nation. The final agreement was, like the Polish accord, vague and unstable. The decision on reparations would be referred to a future commission. The United States, Great Britain, France, and the Soviet Union would each control its own "zone of occupation" in Germany—the zones to be determined by the position of troops at the end of the war. Berlin, the German capital, was already well inside the Soviet zone, but because of its symbolic importance, it would itself be divided into four occupied sectors. At an unspecified date, Germany would be reunited. As for the rest of Europe, the conference produced a murky accord on the establishment of governments "broadly representative of all democratic elements" and "responsible to the will of the people."

The Yalta accords, in other words, were less a settlement of postwar issues than a set of loose principles that sidestepped the most difficult questions. Roosevelt, Churchill, and Stalin returned home from the conference, each apparently convinced that he had signed an important agreement. But the Soviet interpretation of the accords differed so sharply from the Anglo-American interpretation that the illusion endured only briefly. In the weeks following the Yalta Conference, Roosevelt watched with growing alarm as the Soviet Union moved systematically to establish pro-communist governments in one Central or Eastern European nation after another and as Stalin refused to make the changes in Poland that the president believed Stalin had promised. Still believing the differences could be settled, Roosevelt left Washington early in the spring for a vacation at his retreat in Warm Springs, Georgia. There, on April 12, 1945, he suffered a sudden massive stroke and died.

THE COLLAPSE OF THE PEACE

The new president, Harry S. Truman, had almost no familiarity with international issues. Nor did he share Roosevelt's apparent faith in Soviet flexibility. Truman sided with the many people inside the government who considered the Soviet Union fundamentally untrustworthy and viewed Stalin himself with suspicion and even loathing.

THE FAILURE OF POTSDAM

Truman had been in office only a few days before he decided to "get tough" with the Soviet Union. On April 23, he met with Soviet Foreign Minister Molotov and sharply chastised him for violations of the Yalta accords. In fact, Truman had little leverage. Russian forces already occupied Poland and much of the rest of Central and Eastern Europe. Germany was already divided among the conquering nations. The United States was still engaged in a war in the Pacific and was neither able nor willing to enter into a second conflict in Europe. Truman insisted that the United States should be able to get "85 percent" of what it wanted, but he was ultimately forced to settle for much less.

He conceded first on Poland. When Stalin made a few minor concessions to the pro-Western exiles, Truman recognized the Warsaw government, hoping that noncommunist forces might gradually expand their influence there. (Until the 1980s, they did not.) To settle other questions, Truman met in July at Potsdam, in Russian-occupied Germany, with Churchill (who, after elections in Britain in the midst of the talks, was replaced as prime minister by Clement Attlee) and Stalin. Truman reluctantly accepted the adjustments of the Polish-German border that Stalin had long demanded; he refused, however, to permit the Russians to claim any reparations from the American, French, and British zones of Germany. This stance effectively confirmed that Germany would remain divided. The western zones ultimately united into one nation, friendly to the United States, and the Russian zone survived as another nation, with a pro-Soviet, communist government.

THE CHINA PROBLEM AND JAPAN

American hopes for an open, peaceful world "policed" by the great powers required a strong, independent China. But those hopes faced a major obstacle: the Chinese government of Chiang Kai-shek. Chiang was generally friendly to the United States, but his government was corrupt and incompetent, with feeble popular support. Ever since 1927, the nationalist government he headed had been engaged in a bitter rivalry with the communist armies of Mao Zedong. By 1945, Mao was in control of one-fourth of the population.

Some Americans urged the government to try to find a "third force" to support as an alternative to either Chiang or Mao. Truman, however, decided reluctantly that he had no choice but to continue supporting Chiang. For the next several years, the United States continued to pump money and weapons to Chiang, even as it was becoming clear that the cause was lost. But Truman was not prepared to intervene militarily to save the nationalist regime.

Instead, the American government began to consider an alternative to China as the strong, pro-Western force in Asia: a revived Japan. Abandoning the strict occupation policies of the first years after the war (when General Douglas MacArthur had governed the nation), the United States lifted restrictions on industrial development and encouraged rapid economic growth in Japan. The vision of an open, united world was giving way in Asia, as it was in Europe, to an acceptance of a divided world with a strong pro-American sphere of influence.

THE CONTAINMENT DOCTRINE

By the end of 1945, a new American foreign policy was slowly emerging. It became known as containment. Rather than attempting to create a unified, "open" world, the United States and its allies would work to "contain" the threat of further Soviet expansion.

The new doctrine emerged in part as a response to events in Europe in 1946. In Turkey, Stalin was trying to win control over the vital sea-lanes to the Mediterranean. In Greece, communist forces were threatening the pro-Western government; the British had announced they could no longer provide assistance. Faced with these challenges, Truman decided to enunciate a firm new policy. In doing so, he drew from the ideas of the American diplomat George F. Kennan, who had warned not long after the war that the only viable American response to Soviet power was "a long-term, patient but firm and vigilant containment of Russian expansive tendencies." On March 12, 1947, Truman appeared before Congress and used Kennan's warnings as the basis of what became known as the Truman Doctrine. "I believe," he argued, "that it must be the policy of the United States to support free peoples who are resisting attempted subjugation by armed minorities or by outside pressures." In the same speech, he requested $400 million for aid to Greece and Turkey, which Congress quickly approved.

The American commitment ultimately helped reduce Soviet pressure on Turkey and helped the Greek government defeat the communist insurgents and, in the process, establish containment as a basis for American policy that survived for more than forty years.

THE CONSERVATIVE OPPOSITION TO CONTAINMENT

The containment doctrine attracted broad, bipartisan support for dealing with the Cold War. But not everyone believed that containment was the right way to deal with communism. Some Americans on the left believed that containment was an unnecessarily belligerent approach to the Soviet Union, that the United States could have made peace with the Russians. Wider opposition to containment came from conservative Americans, who believed that containment was too weak a response to communism—that, indeed, it was a kind of appeasement.

Among the conservatives who disdained containment was an anticommunist organization known as the John Birch Society. Its leader was Robert Welch, a man so fearful of communism that he believed that some of the most important leaders of American government were trying to undermine the United States and collaborating with the Soviets. Welch presented his opposition in *The Blue Book of the John Birch Society*, in which he argued that much of the American government was riddled with treason. "For years," he wrote, "we have been taken steadily down the road to Communism by steps supposedly designed . . . as ways of *fighting* Communism." Instead, he argued, it was communist Americans themselves who were undermining the nation. "Both the U.S. and Soviet governments are controlled by the same furtive conspiratorial cabal of internationalists, greedy bankers, and corrupt politicians," Welch wrote. "If left unexposed, the traitors inside the U.S. government would betray the country's sovereignty to the United Nations for a collectivist New World Order, managed by a 'one-world' socialist government." Among the sources of treason, Welch claimed, was the creation of the United Nations and other international institutions.

Many Americans considered the John Birch Society an extremist organization, but the belief that communism was the greatest danger facing the United States was widely supported by many people who did not even know of the John Birch Society.

The opposition to containment reached some of the highest levels of the government. John Foster Dulles, who would soon become secretary of state in the Eisenhower administration, wrote the foreign policy plank in the Republican platform in 1952. "We charge that the leaders of the Administration in power lost the peace so dearly earned by World War II," Dulles charged. "They abandoned friendly nations such as Latvia, Lithuania, Estonia, Poland, and Czechoslovakia." Containment, they argued, was a policy of weakness that had allowed the communists to take over much of the world. Instead, those who opposed containment called for what was known as "rollback." Instead of containing communism, the United States should be pushing back the borders of communism, despite the possibility of another war. President Eisenhower, however, did not share Dulles's belief in rollback, and the government abided by the containment strategy throughout the 1950s and beyond—despite the fevered opposition to what some still considered to be treason.

THE MARSHALL PLAN

An integral part of the containment policy was a proposal to aid in the economic reconstruction of Western Europe. There were many motives: humanitarian concern for the European people; a fear that Europe would remain an economic drain on the United States if it could not quickly rebuild; and a desire for a strong European market for American goods. But above all, American policymakers believed that unless something could be done to strengthen the shaky pro-American governments in Western Europe, those governments might fall under the control of the growing domestic communist parties.

In June 1947, Secretary of State George C. Marshall announced a plan to provide economic assistance to all European nations (including the Soviet Union) that would join in drafting a program for recovery. Although Russia and its Eastern satellites predictably rejected the plan, sixteen Western European nations eagerly participated. Whatever isolationist opposition there was in the United States largely vanished after a sudden coup in Czechoslovakia in February 1948, which established a Soviet-dominated communist government. In April, Congress approved the creation of the Economic Cooperation Administration, the agency that would administer the Marshall Plan, as it became known. Over the next three years, the Marshall Plan channeled $13 billion of American aid into Europe, helping to spark a substantial economic revival. By the end of 1950, European industrial production had risen 64 percent, communist strength in the member nations had declined, and opportunities for American trade had revived.

MOBILIZATION AT HOME

In 1948, at the president's request, Congress approved a new military draft and revived the Selective Service System. In the meantime, the United States, having failed to reach agreement with the Soviet Union on international control of nuclear weapons, redoubled its own efforts in atomic research, elevating nuclear weaponry to a central place in its military arsenal. The Atomic Energy Commission, established in 1946, became the supervisory body charged with overseeing all nuclear research, civilian and military alike. And

DIVIDED EUROPE AFTER WORLD WAR II This map shows the sharp division that emerged in Europe after World War II between the area under the control of the Soviet Union and the area allied with the United States. In the east, Soviet control or influence extended into all the nations shaded brown—including the eastern half of Germany. In the west and south, the green-shaded nations were allied with the United States as members of the North Atlantic Treaty Organization (NATO). The countries shaded gold were aligned with neither of the two superpowers. The small map in the upper right shows the division of Berlin among the various occupying powers at the end of the war. Eventually, the American, British, and French sectors were combined to create West Berlin, a city governed by West Germany but entirely surrounded by communist East Germany. • *How did the West prevent East Germany from absorbing West Berlin?*

in 1950, the Truman administration approved the development of the new hydrogen bomb, a nuclear weapon far more powerful than those used in 1945.

The National Security Act of 1947 reshaped the nation's military and diplomatic institutions. A new Department of Defense would oversee all branches of the armed services, combining functions previously performed separately by the War and Navy departments. A National Security Council (NSC), operating out of the White House, would govern foreign and military policy. A Central Intelligence Agency (CIA) would replace the wartime Office of Strategic Services and would be responsible for collecting information through both open and covert methods; as the Cold War continued, the CIA would also engage in secret political and military operations on behalf of American interests. The National Security Act, in other words, gave the president expanded powers with which to pursue the nation's international goals.

The Road to NATO

The United States also moved to strengthen the military capabilities of Western Europe. Convinced that a reconstructed Germany was essential to the needs of the West, Truman reached an agreement with England and France to merge the three western zones of occupation into a new West German republic (which would include the three non-Soviet sectors of Berlin, even though that city lay within the Soviet zone). Stalin responded quickly. On June 24, 1948, he imposed a tight blockade around the western sectors of Berlin. If Germany was to be officially divided, Stalin was implying, then the country's Western government would have to abandon the capital city in the heart of the Soviet-controlled eastern zone. Truman refused to do so. Unwilling to risk war through a military challenge to the blockade, he ordered a massive airlift to supply the city with food, fuel, and other needed goods. The airlift continued for more than ten months, transporting nearly 2.5 million tons of food and other material, keeping a city of 2 million people alive. In the spring of 1949, Stalin lifted the now ineffective blockade. And in October, the division of Germany into two nations—the Federal Republic in the west (with its new capital in Bonn) and the Democratic Republic in the East (with its capital in East Berlin)—became official.

The crisis in Berlin accelerated the consolidation of what was already in effect an alliance among the United States and the countries of Western Europe. On April 4, 1949, twelve nations signed an agreement establishing the North Atlantic Treaty Organization (NATO)—declaring that an armed attack against one member would be considered an attack against all. The NATO countries would, moreover, maintain a standing military force in Europe to defend against what they believed was the threat of a Soviet invasion. The formation of NATO eventually spurred the Soviet Union to create an alliance of its own with the communist governments in Eastern Europe, as formalized in 1955 by the Warsaw Pact.

Reevaluating Cold War Policy

In September 1949, the Soviet Union successfully exploded its first atomic weapon. The Russian nuclear capacity came years earlier than predicted, shocking and frightening many Americans. So did the collapse of Chiang Kai-shek's nationalist government in China, which occurred with startling speed in the last months of 1949. Chiang fled with his political allies and the remnants of his army to the offshore island of Formosa (Taiwan), and the entire Chinese mainland came under the control of a communist government that many Americans believed to be an extension of the Soviet Union. The United States refused to recognize the new communist regime.

The fall of China to communism was one of the most traumatic events of the Cold War. It accelerated the fear of communism, and it persuaded many Americans that the defeat was a result of weakness, and even treason. As a result, American friends of China formed what came to be known as the China Lobby. Among its eminent leaders were members of Congress, high-level military figures, and powerful journalists. They believed that the United States had not done enough to prevent the communists from taking over mainland China. The failure persuaded many Americans that the government—particularly members of the State Department—were responsible.

In this atmosphere of escalating crisis, Truman called for a thorough review of American foreign policy. The result, a National Security Council report, issued in 1950

THE COLD WAR

FOR more than a decade after the beginning of the Cold War, few historians saw any reason to challenge the official American interpretation of its origins. The breakdown of relations between the United States and the Soviet Union was, most agreed, a direct result of Soviet expansionism and of Stalin's violation of the wartime agreements forged at Yalta and Potsdam. The Soviet imposition of communist regimes in Eastern Europe was part of a larger ideological design to spread communism throughout the world. American policy was the logical and necessary response: a firm commitment to oppose Soviet expansionism and to keep American forces in a continual state of readiness.

Disillusionment with the official justifications for the Cold War began to find expression even in the late 1950s, when anticommunist sentiment in America remained strong and pervasive. William Appleman Williams's *The Tragedy of American Diplomacy* (1959) insisted that the Cold War was simply the most recent version of a consistent American effort in the twentieth century to preserve an "open door" for American trade in world markets. The confrontation with the Soviet Union, he argued, was less a response to Soviet aggressive designs than an expression of the American belief in the necessity of capitalist expansion.

As the Vietnam War grew larger and more unpopular in the 1960s, the scholarly critique of the Cold War quickly gained intensity. Walter LaFeber's *America, Russia, and the Cold War,* first published in 1967, maintained that America's supposedly idealistic internationalism at the close of the war was in reality an effort to ensure a postwar order shaped in the American image—with every nation open to American influence (and to American trade). That was why the United States was so apt to misinterpret Soviet policy, much of which reflected a perfectly reasonable commitment to ensure the security of the Soviet Union itself, as part of a larger aggressive design.

The revisionist interpretations of the Cold War ultimately produced a reaction of their own: what has come to be known as "postrevisionist" scholarship. The most important work in this school attempted to

and commonly known as NSC-68, outlined a shift in the American position. The first statements of the containment doctrine—the writings of George Kennan, the Truman Doctrine speech—had made distinctions between areas of vital interest to the United States and areas of less importance to the nation's foreign policy. The containment doctrine also called for sharing the military burden of protecting the Western nations. But NSC-68 argued that the United States could no longer rely on other nations to take the initiative in resisting communism. It must move on its own to stop communist expansion virtually anywhere it occurred, regardless of the intrinsic strategic or economic value of the lands in question. Among other things, the report called for a acted in response to genuine, if not necessarily accurate, beliefs about the intentions of the other. "The United States and the Soviet Union were doomed to be antagonists," Ernest May wrote in 1984. "There probably was never any real possibility that the post-1945 relationship could be anything but hostility verging on conflict."

Since the fall of the Soviet Union in 1991, scholars have had access to newly released Russian archives that have enriched—although not fundamentally altered—the way historians view the Cold War. John Lewis Gaddis, in *We Now Know: Rethinking Cold War History* (1998) and *The Cold War* (2005), portrays a Cold War somewhat more dangerous than his own earlier studies, and those of many other scholars, had portrayed; and he argues that the strong anticommunist positions of Margaret Thatcher, Ronald Reagan, and Pope John Paul II had a larger impact on the weakening of the Soviet Union than was previously understood. Similarly assisted by newly released archives, Arne Westad, in *The Global Cold War* (2005), roots the origins of the dangerous instability in the so-called Third World in the frequent interventions of both the Soviet Union and the United States in the Cold War era. •

strike a balance between orthodoxy and revisionism and to identify areas of blame and patterns of misconceptions on both sides of the conflict. An important early statement of this approach was John Lewis Gaddis's *The United States and the Cold War, 1941–1947* (1972), which argued that "neither side can bear sole responsibility for the onset of the Cold War." Both sides had limited options, given their own political constraints and their own preconceptions. Other postrevisionist works—by Thomas G. Paterson, Melvyn Leffler, William Taubman, and others—have elaborated on ways in which the United States and the Soviet Union

UNDERSTAND, ANALYZE, & EVALUATE

1. What are the traditional and revisionist arguments concerning the origins of the Cold War?
2. Was the Cold War inevitable?

major expansion of American military power, with a defense budget almost four times the previously projected figure.

AMERICA AFTER THE WAR

The crises overseas were not the only frustrations the American people encountered after the war. The nation also faced serious, if short-lived, economic difficulties in adapting to peace. And it suffered from an exceptionally heated political climate that produced a new wave of insecurity and repression.

CONSIDER THE SOURCE

NATIONAL SECURITY COUNCIL PAPER NO. 68 (NSC-68) ARMS AMERICA, 1950

WITHIN the past thirty-five years the world has experienced two global wars of tremendous violence. It has witnessed two revolutions—the Russian and the Chinese—of extreme scope and intensity. It has also seen the collapse of five empires—the Ottoman, the Austro-Hungarian, German, Italian, and Japanese—and the drastic decline of two major imperial systems, the British and the French. During the span of one generation, the international distribution of power has been fundamentally altered. For several centuries it had proved impossible for any one nation to gain such preponderant strength that a coalition of other nations could not in time face it with greater strength. The international scene was marked by recurring periods of violence and war, but a system of sovereign and independent states was maintained, over which no state was able to achieve hegemony.

Two complex sets of factors have now basically altered this historical distribution of power. First, the defeat of Germany and Japan and the decline of the British and French Empires have interacted with the development of the United States and the Soviet Union in such a way that power has increasingly gravitated to these two centers. Second, the Soviet Union, unlike previous aspirants to hegemony, is animated by a new fanatic faith, antithetical to our own, and seeks to impose its absolute authority over the rest of the world. Conflict has, therefore, become endemic and is waged, on the part of the Soviet Union, by violent or nonviolent methods in accordance with the dictates of expediency. With the development of increasingly terrifying weapons of mass destruction, every individual faces the ever-present possibility of annihilation should the conflict enter the phase of total war. [. . .]

Our overall policy at the present time may be described as one designed to foster a world environment in which the American system can survive and flourish. It therefore rejects the concept of isolation and affirms the necessity of our positive participation in the world community.

This broad intention embraces two subsidiary policies. One is a policy which we would probably pursue even if there were no Soviet threat. It is a policy of attempting to develop a healthy international community. The other is the policy of "containing" the Soviet system. These two policies are closely interrelated and interact on one another. Nevertheless, the distinction between them is basically valid and contributes to a clearer understanding of what we are trying to do. . . .

UNDERSTAND, ANALYZE, & EVALUATE

1. What broader historical trends did the authors of this memorandum identify as precursors to global power relations after World War II?
2. How did Memorandum NSC-68 characterize the Soviet Union? How did it characterize the goals of the United States? How does this compare to the historical record presented to you in this text?

Source: U.S. Department of State, *Foreign Relations of the United States, 1950. National Security Affairs; Foreign Economic Policy* (Washington, D.C.: U.S. Government Printing Office, 1977), I, pp. 237, 252–253, 262–263, 264, 282, 290. Located in Elizabeth Cobbs Hoffman and Jon Gjerde (eds.), *Major Problems in American History. Volume II: Since 1865* (Boston: Houghton Mifflin Company, 2002), pp. 287–288.

THE PROBLEMS OF RECONVERSION

Despite widespread predictions that the end of the war would return America to depression conditions, economic growth continued after 1945. Pent-up consumer demand from workers who had accumulated substantial savings during the war helped spur the boom. So did a $6 billion tax cut. The Servicemen's Readjustment Act of 1944, better known as the GI Bill of Rights, provided housing, education, and job-training subsidies to veterans and increased spending even further.

The GI Bill expressed the progressive hopes of many Americans who wanted to see the government do more to assist its citizens. But it also expressed some of the enduring inequalities in American life. Few GI Bill benefits were available to women, even though many women had assisted the war effort in important ways. And while the GI Bill itself did not discriminate against African Americans, its provisions giving local governments jurisdiction allowed southern states, in particular, to deny or limit benefits to black veterans.

The flood of consumer demand contributed to more than two years of inflation, during which prices rose at annual rates of 14 to 15 percent. Compounding the economic difficulties was a sharp rise in labor unrest. By the end of 1945, major strikes had occurred in the automobile, electrical, and steel industries. In April 1946, John L. Lewis led the United Mine Workers out on strike, shutting down the coal fields for forty days. Truman finally forced coal production to resume by ordering government seizure of the mines. But in the process, he pressured mine owners to grant the union most of its demands. Almost simultaneously, the nation's railroads suffered a total shutdown—the first in the nation's history—as two major unions walked out on strike. By threatening to use the army to run the trains, Truman pressured the strikers back to work after only a few days.

Reconversion was particularly difficult for the millions of women and minorities who had entered the workforce during the war. With veterans returning home, employers tended to push women, African Americans, Hispanics, and others out of the plants to make room for white males. Some war workers, particularly women, left the workforce voluntarily, out of a desire to return to their former domestic lives. But as many as 80 percent of women workers, and virtually all black and Hispanic males, wanted to continue working. The postwar inflation, the pressure of a growing high-consumption society, the rising divorce rate (which left many women responsible for their own economic well-being)—all combined to create a high demand for paid employment among women. As women workers found themselves excluded from industrial jobs, therefore, they moved increasingly into other areas of the economy (above all, the service sector).

THE FAIR DEAL REJECTED

Days after the Japanese surrender, Truman submitted to Congress a twenty-one-point domestic program outlining what he later named the "Fair Deal." It called for an expansion of Social Security benefits, the raising of the legal minimum wage from 40 to 65 cents an hour, a program to ensure full employment through aggressive use of federal spending and investment, a permanent Fair Employment Practices Act, public housing and slum clearance, long-range environmental and public works planning, and government promotion of scientific research. Weeks later he added other proposals: federal aid to education, government health insurance and prepaid medical care, funding for the St. Lawrence Seaway, and nationalization of atomic energy.

But most of Truman's programs fell victim to the same public and congressional conservatism that had crippled the last years of the New Deal. Indeed, that conservatism seemed to be intensifying, as the November 1946 congressional elections suggested. Using the simple but devastating slogan "Had Enough?" the Republican Party won control of both houses of Congress, which quickly moved to reduce government spending and chip away at New Deal reforms. Its most notable action was its assault on the Wagner Act of 1935, in the form of the Labor-Management Relations Act of 1947, better known as the Taft-Hartley Act. It made illegal the closed shop (a workplace in which no one can be hired without first being a member of a union). And although it continued to permit the creation of union shops (in which workers must join a union after being hired), it permitted states to pass "right-to-work" laws prohibiting even that. The Taft-Hartley Act also empowered the president to call for a ten-week "cooling-off" period before a strike by issuing an injunction against any work stoppage that endangered national safety or health. Outraged workers and union leaders denounced the measure as a "slave labor bill." Truman vetoed it. But both houses easily overruled him the same day. The Taft-Hartley Act did not destroy the labor movement. But it did damage weaker unions in relatively lightly organized industries such as chemicals and textiles, and it made much more difficult the organizing of workers who had never been union members at all, especially in the South and the West.

THE ELECTION OF 1948

Truman and his advisers believed that the American public was not ready to abandon the achievements of the New Deal, despite the 1946 election results. As they planned their strategy for the 1948 campaign, therefore, they hoped to appeal to enduring Democratic loyalties. Throughout 1948, Truman proposed one reform measure after another (including, on February 2, the first major civil rights bill of the century). To no one's surprise, Congress ignored or defeated them all, but the president was building campaign issues for the fall.

There remained, however, the problems of Truman's personal unpopularity—the assumption among much of the electorate that he lacked stature and that his administration was weak and inept—and the deep divisions within the Democratic Party. At the Democratic Convention that summer, two factions abandoned the party altogether. Angered by Truman's proposed civil rights bill and by the approval at the convention of a civil rights plank in the platform (engineered by Hubert Humphrey, the reform mayor of Minneapolis), southern conservatives walked out and formed the States' Rights (or "Dixiecrat") Party, with Governor Strom Thurmond of South Carolina as its nominee. At the same time, some members of the party's left wing—contemptuous of what they considered Truman's ineffectual leadership and his excessively confrontational stance toward the Soviet Union—joined the new Progressive Party, whose candidate was Henry A. Wallace.

Many Democratic liberals who were unhappy with Truman were unwilling to leave the party. The Americans for Democratic Action (ADA), a coalition of anticommunist liberals, tried to entice Dwight D. Eisenhower, the popular war hero, to contest the nomination. Only after Eisenhower refused did liberals concede the nomination to Truman. The Republicans, in the meantime, once again nominated Governor Thomas E. Dewey of New York. Austere, dignified, and competent, he seemed to offer an unbeatable alternative to the president.

Only Truman seemed to believe he could win. As the campaign gathered momentum, he became more and more aggressive, turning the fire away from himself and toward Dewey and the "do-nothing, good-for-nothing" Republican Congress, which was, he told voters, responsible for fueling inflation and abandoning workers and common people. To dramatize his point, he called Congress into special session in July to give it a chance, he

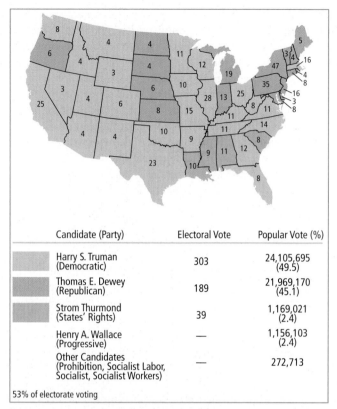

Candidate (Party)	Electoral Vote	Popular Vote (%)
Harry S. Truman (Democratic)	303	24,105,695 (49.5)
Thomas E. Dewey (Republican)	189	21,969,170 (45.1)
Strom Thurmond (States' Rights)	39	1,169,021 (2.4)
Henry A. Wallace (Progressive)	—	1,156,103 (2.4)
Other Candidates (Prohibition, Socialist Labor, Socialist, Socialist Workers)	—	272,713

53% of electorate voting

THE ELECTION OF 1948 Despite the widespread expectation that the Republican candidate, Thomas Dewey, would easily defeat Truman in 1948, the president in fact won a substantial reelection victory that year. This map shows the broad geographic reach of Truman's victory. Dewey swept most of the Northeast, but Truman dominated almost everywhere else. Strom Thurmond, the States' Rights candidate, carried four states in the South. • *What had prompted Thurmond to desert the Democratic Party and run for president on his own?*

said, to enact the liberal measures the Republicans had recently written into their platform. Congress met for two weeks and, predictably, managed to pass almost nothing.

On election night, to the surprise of almost everyone, Truman won a narrow but decisive and dramatic victory: 49.5 percent of the popular vote to Dewey's 45.1 percent (with the two splinter parties dividing the small remainder evenly between them), and an electoral margin of 303 to 189. Democrats regained both houses of Congress by substantial margins.

THE FAIR DEAL REVIVED

Despite the Democratic victories, the Eighty-first Congress was little more hospitable to Truman's Fair Deal reform. Truman did win some important victories. Congress raised the legal minimum wage from 40 cents to 75 cents an hour. It approved an important expansion of the Social Security system, increasing benefits by 75 percent and extending them to 10 million additional people. And it passed the National Housing Act of 1949, which provided for the construction of 810,000 units of low-income housing accompanied by long-term rent subsidies.

But on other issues—national health insurance and aid to education, among them—Truman made little progress. Nor was he able to persuade Congress to accept the civil rights legislation he proposed in 1949, legislation that would make lynching a federal crime, provide federal protection of black voting rights, abolish the poll tax, and establish a new Fair Employment Practices Commission to curb discrimination in hiring. Southern Democrats filibustered to kill the bill.

Undeterred, Truman proceeded on his own to battle several forms of racial discrimination. He ordered an end to discrimination in the hiring of government employees. He began to dismantle segregation within the armed forces. And he allowed the Justice Department to become actively involved in court battles against discriminatory statutes. The Supreme Court, in the meantime, signaled its own growing awareness of the issue by ruling, in *Shelley v. Kraemer* (1948), that courts could not be used to enforce private "covenants" meant to bar blacks from residential neighborhoods.

THE NUCLEAR AGE

Looming over the many struggles of the postwar years was the image of the great and terrible mushroom clouds that had risen over Alamogordo in July 1945 and over the ruined Japanese cities of Hiroshima and Nagasaki. Americans greeted these terrible new instruments of destruction with fear and awe, but also with expectation. Postwar culture was torn between a dark image of the nuclear war that many Americans feared would result from the rivalry with the Soviet Union, and the bright image of a dazzling technological future that atomic power might help to produce.

The fear of nuclear weapons appeared widely in popular culture, but it was often disguised. The late 1940s and early 1950s were the heyday of the *film noir*, a kind of filmmaking that originated in France and had been named for the dark lighting characteristic of the genre. American *film noir* portrayed the loneliness of individuals in an impersonal world—a staple of American culture for many decades—but also suggested the menacing character of the age, the looming possibility of vast destruction. Sometimes, popular fears addressed nuclear fear explicitly—for example, the celebrated television show of the 1950s and early 1960s, *The Twilight Zone*, which featured dramatic portrayals of the aftermath of nuclear war; or postwar comic books, which depicted powerful superheroes saving the world from destruction.

Such images resonated with the public because awareness of nuclear weapons was increasingly built into their daily lives. Schools and office buildings held regular air-raid drills to prepare people for the possibility of nuclear attack. Radio stations regularly tested the Emergency Broadcast System, which stood in readiness for war. Fallout shelters stocked with water and canned goods sprang up in public buildings and private homes. America was a nation filled with anxiety.

And yet, the United States was also an exuberant nation in these years, dazzled by its own prosperity and excited by the technological innovations transforming the nation, including nuclear power. The same scientific knowledge that could destroy the world, many believed, might also lead it into a dazzling future. The *New York Times*, only days after Hiroshima, expressed its own rosy view of the nuclear future: "This new knowledge . . . can bring to this earth not death but life, not tyranny and cruelty, but a divine freedom."

That kind of optimism soon became widespread. The "secret of the atom," many Americans predicted, would bring "prosperity and a more complete life." A public opinion poll late in 1948 revealed that approximately two-thirds of those questioned believed that, "in the long run," atomic energy would "do more good than harm." Nuclear power plants began to spring up in many areas of the country and were welcomed as the source of cheap and unlimited electricity, their potential dangers scarcely even discussed by those who celebrated their creation.

THE KOREAN WAR

On June 24, 1950, the armies of communist North Korea swept across their southern border and invaded the pro-Western half of the Korean peninsula. Within days, they had occupied much of South Korea, including Seoul, its capital. Almost immediately, the United States committed itself to the conflict.

THE DIVIDED PENINSULA

When World War II ended, both the United States and the Soviet Union had troops in Korea fighting the Japanese; neither army was willing to leave. Instead, they divided the nation, supposedly temporarily, along the 38th parallel. The Russians finally departed in

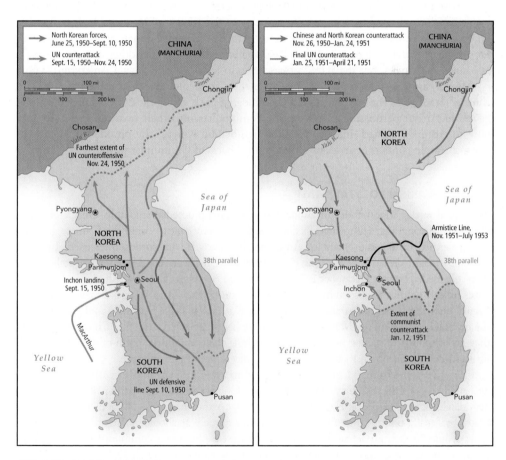

THE KOREAN WAR, 1950–1953   These two maps illustrate the changing fortunes of UN forces (which were mostly American) during the 1950–1953 Korean War. The map at the left shows the extent of the North Korean invasion of South Korea in 1950; communist forces for a time controlled all of Korea except a small area around Pusan in the southeast. On September 15, 1950, UN troops under Douglas MacArthur landed in force at Inchon and soon drove the North Koreans back across the border. MacArthur then pursued the North Koreans well into their own territory. The map at right shows the very different circumstances once the Chinese entered the war in November 1950. Chinese forces drove the UN army back below the 38th parallel and, briefly, deep into South Korea, below Seoul. The UN troops fought back to the prewar border between North and South Korea late in 1951, but the war then bogged down into a stalemate that continued for a year and a half. • *What impact did the Korean War have on American politics in the early 1950s?*

1949, leaving behind a communist government in the north with a strong, Soviet-equipped army. The Americans left a few months later, handing control to the pro-Western government of Syngman Rhee. Anticommunist but only nominally democratic, he used his relatively small military primarily to suppress internal opposition.

The relative weakness of the south offered a strong temptation to nationalists in the North Korean government who wanted to reunite the country, particularly after the American government implied that it did not consider South Korea within its own "defense perimeter." The Soviets and Chinese did not order the invasion, but they did not try to stop it. They supported the offensive once it began.

Almost immediately, on June 27, 1950, the president ordered limited American military assistance to South Korea, and on the same day he appealed to the United Nations to intervene. The Soviet Union was boycotting the Security Council at the time (to protest the council's refusal to recognize the new communist government of China) and was thus unable to exercise its veto power. As a result, American delegates were able to win UN agreement to a resolution calling for international assistance to the Rhee government. On June 30, the United States ordered its own ground forces into Korea, and Truman appointed General Douglas MacArthur to command the UN operations there. (Several other nations provided assistance and troops, but the "UN" armies were, in fact, overwhelmingly American.)

After a surprise American invasion at Inchon in September had routed the North Korean forces from the south and sent them fleeing back across the 38th parallel, Truman gave MacArthur permission to pursue the communists into their own territory. Hoping now to create "a unified, independent and democratic Korea," the president had moved beyond simple containment to an attempted rollback of communist power.

From Invasion to Stalemate

For several weeks, MacArthur's invasion of North Korea proceeded smoothly. On October 19, the capital, Pyongyang, fell to the UN forces. Victory seemed near—until the Chinese government, alarmed by the movement of American forces toward its border, intervened. In early November, eight divisions of the Chinese army entered the war. The UN offensive stalled and then collapsed. Through December 1950, outnumbered American forces were forced into a rapid, bitter retreat. Within weeks, communist forces had pushed the Americans back below the 38th parallel once again and had recaptured the South Korean capital of Seoul. By mid-January 1951 the rout had ceased; and by March the UN armies had managed to regain much of the territory they had recently lost, taking back Seoul and pushing the communists north of the 38th parallel for the second time. With that, the war turned into a protracted stalemate.

From the start, Truman had been determined to avoid a direct conflict with China, which he feared might lead to a new world war. Once China entered the war, he began seeking a negotiated solution to the struggle. But General MacArthur had ideas of his own. The United States was really fighting the Chinese, MacArthur argued. It should, therefore, attack China itself, if not through an actual invasion, then at least by bombing communist forces massing north of the Chinese border or even using atomic weapons. In March 1951, he indicated his unhappiness with Truman's reluctance to invade China. In a public letter to House Republican Leader Joseph W. Martin, he concluded: "There is no substitute for victory." His position had wide popular support. The release of the Martin letter struck the president as intolerable insubordination. On April 11, 1951, he relieved MacArthur of his command.

Sixty-nine percent of the American people supported MacArthur, a Gallup poll reported. When the general returned to the United States later in 1951, he was greeted with wild enthusiasm. Public criticism of Truman finally abated somewhat when a number of prominent military figures, including General Omar Bradley, publicly supported the president's decision. But substantial hostility toward Truman remained. In the meantime, the Korean stalemate continued. Negotiations between the opposing forces began at Panmunjom in July 1951, but the talks—and the war—dragged on until 1953.

LIMITED MOBILIZATION

The war in Korea produced only a limited American military commitment abroad. It also created only a limited economic mobilization at home.

Truman set up the Office of Defense Mobilization to fight inflation by holding down prices and discouraging high union wage demands. When these cautious regulatory efforts failed, the president took more drastic action. Railroad workers walked off the job in 1951, and Truman, who considered the workers' demands inflationary, ordered the government to seize control of the railroads. In 1952, during a nationwide steel strike, Truman seized the steel mills, citing his powers as commander in chief. But in a 6-to-3 decision, the Supreme Court ruled that the president had exceeded his authority, and Truman was forced to relent.

The Korean War significantly boosted economic growth by pumping new government funds into the economy at a point when many believed it was about to decline. But the war had other, less welcome effects. It came at a time of rising insecurity about America's position in the world and intensified anxiety about communism. As the long stalemate continued, producing 140,000 American dead and wounded, frustration turned to anger. The United States, which had recently won the greatest war in history, seemed unable to conclude what many Americans considered a minor border skirmish in a small country. Many began to believe that something must be deeply wrong—not only in Korea but within the United States as well. Such fears contributed to the rise of the second major campaign of the century against domestic communism.

THE CRUSADE AGAINST SUBVERSION

Why did the American people develop a growing fear of internal communist subversion—a fear that by the early 1950s had sometimes reached the point of near hysteria? There are many possible answers but no single definitive explanation.

One factor was obvious. Communism was not an imagined enemy. It had tangible shape, in Josef Stalin and the Soviet Union. Adding to the concern were the Korean stalemate, the "loss" of China, and the Soviet development of an atomic bomb. Searching for someone to blame, many began to believe that there was a communist conspiracy within American borders. But there were other factors as well, rooted in events in American domestic politics.

HUAC AND ALGER HISS

Much of the anticommunist furor emerged out of the search by Republicans for an issue with which to attack the Democrats, and out of the efforts of the Democrats to take that issue away from them. Beginning in 1947, the House Un-American Activities Committee (HUAC) held widely publicized investigations to prove that, under Democratic rule, the government had tolerated (if not actually encouraged) communist subversion. The committee turned first to the movie industry, arguing that communists had infiltrated Hollywood and tainted American films with propaganda. Writers and producers, some of them former communists, were called to testify; and when some of them (the "Hollywood Ten") refused to answer questions about their political beliefs and those of their colleagues, they were sent to jail for contempt. Others were barred from employment in the industry when Hollywood, attempting to protect its public image, adopted a "blacklist" of those of "suspicious loyalty."

More alarming to the public was HUAC's investigation into charges of disloyalty leveled against a former high-ranking member of the State Department: Alger Hiss. In 1948, Whittaker Chambers, a former communist agent, now a conservative editor at *Time* magazine, told the committee that Hiss had passed classified State Department documents to him in 1937 and 1938. When Hiss sued him for slander, Chambers produced microfilms of the documents (called the "pumpkin papers," because Chambers had kept them hidden in a pumpkin in his vegetable garden). Hiss could not be tried for espionage because of the statute of limitations (which protects individuals from prosecution for most crimes after seven years have passed). But largely because of the relentless efforts of Richard M. Nixon, a freshman congressman from California and a member of HUAC, Hiss was convicted of perjury and served several years in prison. The Hiss case not only discredited a prominent young diplomat; it cast suspicion on a generation of liberal Democrats. It also transformed Nixon into a national figure and helped him win a Senate seat in 1950.

THE FEDERAL LOYALTY PROGRAM AND THE ROSENBERG CASE

Partly to protect itself against Republican attacks and partly to encourage support for the president's foreign policy initiatives, the Truman administration in 1947 initiated a widely publicized program to review the "loyalty" of federal employees. By 1951, more than 2,000 government employees had resigned under pressure and 212 had been dismissed.

The Federal Employee Loyalty Program helped launch a major assault on subversion throughout the government—and beyond. The attorney general established a widely cited list of supposedly subversive organizations. The director of the Federal Bureau of Investigation (FBI), J. Edgar Hoover, investigated and harassed alleged radicals. In 1950, Congress passed the McCarran Internal Security Act, which, among other restrictions on "subversive" activity, required that all communist organizations register with the government and publish their records. Congress easily overrode Truman's veto of the bill.

The successful Soviet detonation of an atomic bomb in 1949, earlier than generally expected, suggested to some that there had been a conspiracy to pass American atomic secrets to the Russians. In 1950, Klaus Fuchs, a young British scientist, seemed to confirm those fears when he testified that he had delivered to the Russians details of the bomb's manufacture. The case ultimately moved to an obscure New York couple, Julius and Ethel Rosenberg, members of the Communist Party. The government claimed the Rosenbergs had received secret information from Ethel's brother, a machinist on the Manhattan Project in New Mexico, and had passed it on to the Soviet Union through other agents (including Fuchs). The Rosenbergs were convicted and, on April 5, 1951, sentenced to death. After two years of appeals and public protests, they died in the electric chair on June 19, 1953.

All these factors—the HUAC investigations, the Hiss trial, the loyalty investigations, the McCarran Act, the Rosenberg case—combined with other concerns by the early 1950s to create a fear of communist subversion that seemed to grip the entire country. State and local governments, the judiciary, schools and universities, labor unions—all sought to purge themselves of real or imagined subversives. It was a climate that made possible the rise of an extraordinary public figure.

McCarthyism

Joseph McCarthy was an undistinguished first-term Republican senator from Wisconsin until, in February 1950, in the midst of a speech in Wheeling, West Virginia, he lifted up a sheet of paper and claimed to "hold in my hand" a list of 205 known communists currently working in the American State Department. No person of comparable stature had ever made so bold a charge against the federal government. In the months to come, as McCarthy repeated and expanded on his accusations, he emerged as the nation's most prominent leader of the crusade against domestic subversion.

Within weeks of his charges against the State Department, McCarthy leveled accusations at other agencies. After 1952, with the Republicans in control of the Senate and McCarthy now the chairman of a special subcommittee, he conducted highly publicized investigations of alleged subversion in many areas of the government. McCarthy never produced conclusive evidence that any federal employee was a communist. But a growing constituency adored him nevertheless for his coarse, "fearless" assaults on a government establishment that many considered arrogant, effete, even traitorous. Republicans, in particular, rallied to his claims that the Democrats had been responsible for "twenty years of treason" and that only a change of parties could rid the country of subversion. McCarthy, in short, provided his followers with an issue into which they could channel a wide range of resentments: fear of communism, animosity toward the country's "eastern establishment," and frustrated partisan ambitions. For a time, McCarthy intimidated all but a few people from opposing him. Even the highly popular Dwight D. Eisenhower, running for president in 1952, did not speak out against him, although he disliked McCarthy's tactics and was outraged at, among other things, McCarthy's attacks on General George Marshall.

The Republican Revival

Public frustration over the stalemate in Korea and popular fears of internal subversion combined to make 1952 a bad year for the Democratic Party. Truman, now deeply unpopular, withdrew from the presidential contest. The party united instead behind Governor Adlai E. Stevenson of Illinois. Stevenson's dignity, wit, and eloquence made him a beloved figure to many liberals and intellectuals. But those same qualities seemed only to fuel Republican charges that Stevenson lacked the strength or the will to combat communism sufficiently.

Stevenson's greatest problem, however, was the Republican candidate opposing him. Rejecting the efforts of conservatives to nominate Robert Taft or Douglas MacArthur, the Republicans turned to a man who had no previous identification with the party: General Dwight D. Eisenhower—military hero, commander of NATO, president of Columbia University—who won nomination on the first ballot. He chose as his running mate the young California senator who had gained national prominence through his crusade against Alger Hiss: Richard M. Nixon.

In the fall campaign, Eisenhower attracted support through his geniality and his statesmanlike pledges to settle the Korean conflict. Nixon (after surviving early accusations of financial improprieties, which he effectively neutralized in a famous television address, the Checkers speech) exploited the issue of domestic anticommunism by attacking the Democrats for "cowardice" and "appeasement." The response at the polls was overwhelming. Eisenhower won both a popular and an electoral landslide: 55 percent of the popular vote to Stevenson's 44 percent, 442 electoral votes to Stevenson's 89. Republicans gained control of both houses of Congress for the first time since 1946.

McCARTHYISM

THE American Civil Liberties Union warned in the early 1950s, at the peak of what is now known as McCarthyism, that "the threat to civil liberties today is the most serious in the history of our country." It was expressing a view with which many Americans wholeheartedly agreed. But while there were unusually powerful challenges to freedom of speech and association in the late 1940s and early 1950s, there is wide disagreement about the causes and meaning of those challenges.

The simplest argument—and one that continues to attract scholarly support—is that the postwar Red Scare expressed real and legitimate concerns about communist subversion in the United States. William O'Neill, in *A Better World* (1982), and Richard Gid Powers, in *Not Without Honor* (1995), have both argued that anticommunism was a serious, intelligent, and patriotic movement, despite its excesses. The American Communist Party, according to this view, was an agent of Stalin and the Soviet Union within the United States, actively engaged in espionage and subversion. The effort to root communists out of public life was both understandable and justifiable—and the hysteria it sometimes produced was an unhappy but predictable by-product of an essentially rational and justifiable effort. "Anticommunism," Powers wrote, "expressed the essential American determination to stand against attacks on human freedom and foster the growth of democracy throughout the world. . . . To superimpose on this rich history the cartoon features of Joe McCarthy is to reject history for the easy comforts of moralism."

Most interpretations, however, have been less charitable. In the 1950s, in the midst of the Red Scare itself, an influential group of historians and social scientists began to portray the anticommunist fervor of their time as an expression of deep social maladjustment— an argument perhaps most closely associated with a famous essay by Richard Hofstadter, "The Paranoid Style in American Politics." There was, they argued, no logical connection between the modest power of actual communists in the United States and the hysterical form these scholars believed anticommunism was assuming. The explanation, therefore, had to lie in something other than reality, in a deeper set of social and cultural anxieties that had only an indirect connection with the political world as it existed. Extreme anticommunism, they claimed, was something close to a pathology; it expressed fear of and alienation from the modern world. A person afflicted with the "paranoid style," Hofstadter wrote:

> . . . believes himself to be living in a world in which he is spied upon, plotted against, betrayed, and very likely destined for total ruin. He feels that his liberties have been arbitrarily and outrageously invaded. He is opposed to almost everything that has happened in American politics in the past twenty years.

Other scholars, writing not long after the decline of McCarthyism, rejected the sociocultural arguments of Hofstadter and others but shared the belief that the crusade against subversion was a distortion of normal public life. They saw the anticommunist crusade as an example of party politics run amok. Richard Freeland, in *The Truman Doctrine and the Origins of McCarthyism* (1971), argued that the Democrats began the effort to purge the government of radicals to protect themselves from attacks by the

Republicans. Nelson Polsby, Robert Griffith, and others have noted how Republicans seized on the issue of communism in government in the late 1940s to reverse their nearly twenty-year exclusion from power. With each party trying to outdo the other in its effort to demonstrate its anticommunist credentials, it was hardly surprising that the crusade reached extraordinarily intense proportions.

Still other historians have emphasized the role of powerful government officials and agencies with a strong commitment to anticommunism—most notably J. Edgar Hoover and the FBI. Athan Theoharis and Kenneth O'Reilly introduced the idea of an anticommunist bureaucracy in work published in the 1970s and 1980s. Ellen Schrecker's *Many Are the Crimes* (1998) offers the fullest argument that the Red Scare was, at its heart, directed largely against communists (and not very often against people without any connection to the Communist Party) and that it was orchestrated by an interlocking cluster of official agencies with a deep commitment to the project.

Several scholars, finally, have presented an argument that does not so much challenge other interpretations as complement them. Anticommunist zealots were not alone to blame for the excesses of McCarthyism, they argue. It was also the fault of liberals—in politics, in academia, and, perhaps above all, in the media—who were so intimidated by the political climate, or so imprisoned within the conventions of their professions, that they found themselves unable to respond effectively to the distortions and excesses that they recognized around them. •

COMMUNIST-SOCIALIST PROPAGANDA IN AMERICAN SCHOOLS

VERNE · P · KAUB

THE COMMUNIST THREAT Verne P. Kaub, a retired journalist and head of the American Council of Christian Laymen, became—like many Americans—concerned about the dangers of communism in the years after World War II. This book, published in 1953, accused the National Education Association and its "self-styled progressive educators" of preparing the way for communism. "No technique of the propagandists for Communism-Socialism," he wrote, "is . . . more effective in preparing the minds of both adults and young people for acceptance of the Marxian ideology than the 'debunking' of American history." (Michael Barson Collection)

UNDERSTAND, ANALYZE, & EVALUATE

1. Why did the American public feel so threatened by communism? Who exploited the public's fears and why?
2. Was the public reaction to the Red Scare a logical response or disproportionate to the actual threat posed by communism?
3. How were party politics and McCarthyism connected? Do you find elements similar to McCarthyism in politics today?

CONCLUSION

Even during World War II, when the United States and the Soviet Union were allies, it was evident to leaders in both nations that America and Russia had quite different visions of what the postwar world should look like. Very quickly after the war ended, the once fruitful relationship between the world's greatest powers quickly soured. Americans came to believe that the Soviet Union was an expansionist tyranny little different from Hitler's Germany. Soviets came to believe that the United States was trying to protect its own dominance in the world by encircling the Soviet Union. The result of these tensions was what became known by the end of the 1940s as the Cold War.

In the early years of the Cold War, the United States constructed a series of policies designed to prevent both war and Soviet aggression. It helped rebuild the shattered economies of Western Europe through the Marshall Plan, to stabilize those nations and prevent them from becoming communist. America embraced a new foreign policy—known as containment—that committed it to keep the Soviet Union from expanding its influence further into the world. The United States and Western Europe formed a strong and enduring alliance, NATO, to defend Europe against possible Soviet advances.

In 1950, the armed forces of communist North Korea launched an invasion of noncommunist South Korea; and to most Americans, the conflict quickly came to be seen as a test of American resolve. The Korean War was long, costly, and unpopular, with many military setbacks and frustrations. In the end, however, the United States—working through the United Nations—managed to drive the North Koreans out of South Korea and stabilize the original division of the peninsula.

The Korean War hardened American foreign policy into a much more rigidly anticommunist form. It undermined the Truman administration, and the Democratic Party, and helped strengthen conservatives and Republicans. It greatly strengthened an already powerful crusade against communists, and those believed to be communists, within the United States—a crusade often known as McCarthyism, because of the notoriety of Senator Joseph McCarthy of Wisconsin, the most celebrated leader of the effort.

America after World War II was indisputably the wealthiest and most powerful nation in the world. But in the harsh climate of the Cold War, neither wealth nor power could dispel deep anxieties and bitter divisions.

RECALL AND REFLECT

1. How did American diplomats plan for the postwar world and settle postwar issues? How did opposing visions of the postwar world order thwart those efforts?
2. How did postwar economic problems affect American politics and society?
3. Why did the United States become involved in the war in Korea? What was the result of U.S. involvement in that war?
4. Why did the fear of communism at home reach such great proportions? What events helped fan that fear?

28 | THE AFFLUENT SOCIETY

LOOKING AHEAD

1. Why did the U.S. economy experience such a boom in the late 1950s and early 1960s? How did this boom affect American society?

2. Who constituted the "other America," who failed to share in the economic prosperity and affluence of the postwar era? Why were they left out?

3. What was the response to the Supreme Court decision in *Brown v. Board of Education*? How did the Court's decision affect African Americans and the early civil rights movement? How did it affect white southerners?

4. What policy guided foreign affairs under Eisenhower, and how was that policy implemented around the world?

IF AMERICA EXPERIENCED A GOLDEN age in the 1950s and early 1960s, as many Americans believed at the time and many continue to believe today, it was largely a result of two developments. One was a booming national prosperity, which profoundly altered the social, economic, and even physical landscape of the United States. The other was the continuing struggle against communism, a struggle that created considerable anxiety but that also encouraged many Americans to look even more approvingly at their own society. But if these powerful forces created a widespread sense of national purpose and self-satisfaction, they also helped blind many Americans to serious problems plaguing large groups of the population.

TIME LINE

THE ECONOMIC "MIRACLE"

Perhaps the most striking feature of American society in the 1950s and early 1960s was the booming economic growth that made even the heady 1920s seem pale by comparison. It was a better-balanced and more widely distributed prosperity than that of thirty years earlier. It was not, however, as universal as some Americans liked to believe.

ECONOMIC GROWTH

By 1949, despite the continuing problems of postwar reconversion, an economic expansion had begun that would continue with only brief interruptions for almost twenty years. Between 1945 and 1960, the gross national product grew by 250 percent, from $200 billion to over $500 billion. Unemployment remained at about 5 percent or lower throughout the 1950s and early 1960s. Inflation, in the meantime, hovered around 3 percent a year or less.

The causes of this growth were varied. Government spending, which had ended the Depression in the 1940s, continued to stimulate growth through public funding of schools, housing, veterans' benefits, welfare, interstate highways, and, above all, the military. Economic growth peaked during the first half of the 1950s, when military spending was highest because of the Korean War.

The national birth rate reversed a long pattern of decline with the so-called baby boom, which began during World War II and peaked in 1957. The nation's population rose almost 20 percent in the decade, from 150 million in 1950 to 179 million in 1960, which meant increased consumer demand and expanding economic growth.

Rapid suburban expansion—a 47 percent increase in the 1950s—helped stimulate growth in several important sectors of the economy. The number of privately owned

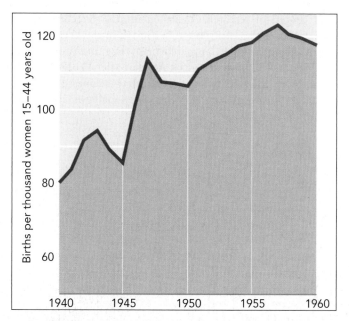

THE AMERICAN BIRTH RATE, 1940-1960   This chart shows how the American birth rate grew rapidly during and after World War II (following a long period of decline in the 1930s) to produce what became known as the "baby boom." At the peak of the baby boom, during the 1950s, the nation's population grew by 20 percent. • *What impact did the baby boom have on the nation's economy?*

cars more than doubled in a decade. Demand for new homes helped sustain a vigorous housing industry. The construction of roads stimulated the economy as well.

These and other forces helped the American economy grow nearly ten times as fast as the population in the thirty years after the war. And while that growth was far from equally distributed, the average American in 1960 had over 20 percent more purchasing power than in 1945 and more than twice as much as during the prosperous 1920s. The American people had achieved the highest standard of living of any society in the history of the world.

THE RISE OF THE MODERN WEST

No region experienced more dramatic changes than the American West. Its population expanded dramatically; its cities boomed; its industrial economy flourished. By the 1960s, some parts of the West were among the most important (and populous) industrial and cultural centers of the nation.

As during World War II, much of the growth of the West was a result of federal spending and investment—on the dams, power stations, highways, and other infrastructure projects that made economic development possible. Military contracts continued to flow disproportionately to factories in California and Texas, many built with government funds during the war. The growing number of automobiles created new demands for petroleum and contributed to the rapid growth of oil fields in Texas and Colorado and of the metropolitan centers, among them Houston, Dallas, and Denver. State governments in the West invested heavily in their universities. The University of Texas and University of California systems, in particular, became among the nation's largest and created important centers of research. They helped attract technology-intensive industries to the region. Climate also contributed to growth in the West. Southern California, Nevada, and Arizona, in particular, attracted many migrants from the East because of their warm, dry climates. The growth of Los Angeles after World War II was a remarkable phenomenon: more than 10 percent of all new businesses in the United States between 1945 and 1950 began in Los Angeles. Its population rose by over 50 percent between 1940 and 1960.

CAPITAL AND LABOR

Booming corporations were reluctant to allow strikes to interfere with their operations; and since the most important labor unions were now so large and entrenched that they could not easily be suppressed or intimidated, leaders of large businesses made important concessions to them. By the mid-1950s, factory wages in most industries had risen substantially, to an average of $80 per week. In December 1955, the American Federation of Labor and the Congress of Industrial Organizations ended their twenty-year rivalry and merged to create the AFL-CIO, under the leadership of George Meany.

But success also bred stagnation and corruption in some union bureaucracies. In 1957, the powerful Teamsters Union became the subject of a congressional investigation, and its president, David Beck, was charged with the misappropriation of union funds. Beck ultimately stepped down to be replaced by Jimmy Hoffa, whom government investigators pursued for nearly a decade before finally winning a conviction against him in 1967. The United Mine Workers, similarly, became tainted by violence and charges of corruption.

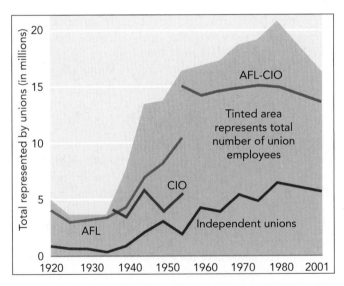

WORKERS REPRESENTED BY UNIONS, 1920–2001 This chart shows the number of workers represented by unions over an eighty-year period. Note the dramatic rise in the unionized workforce during the 1930s and 1940s, the slower but still significant rise in the 1960s and 1970s, and the steady decline that began in the 1980s. The chart, in fact, understates the decline of unionized labor in the postwar era, since it shows union membership in absolute numbers and not as a percentage of the rapidly growing workforce. • *Why did unions cease recruiting new members successfully in the 1970s, and why did they begin actually losing members in the 1980s?*

THE EXPLOSION OF SCIENCE AND TECHNOLOGY

In 1961, *Time* magazine selected as its "man of the year" not a specific person but "the American Scientist." The choice was an indication of the widespread fascination with which Americans in the age of atomic power viewed science and technology.

MEDICAL BREAKTHROUGHS

The twentieth century saw greater progress in the development of medical science than had occurred in all the centuries before it. A very large proportion of that progress occurred during and after World War II. Particularly important was the development of new anti-bacterial drugs capable of fighting infections that had once been all but untreatable.

The development of antibiotics originated in the discoveries of Louis Pasteur and Jules-Francois Joubert. Working in France in the 1870s, they produced the first conclusive evidence that virulent bacterial infections could be defeated by other, more ordinary bacteria. Using their discoveries, the English physician Joseph Lister revealed the value of antiseptic solutions in preventing infection during surgery.

But the practical use of antibacterial agents to combat disease did not begin until many decades later. In the 1930s, scientists in Germany, France, and England demonstrated the power of so-called sulfa drugs—drugs derived from an antibacterial agent known as sulfanilamide—which could be used effectively to treat streptococcal blood infections. New sulfa drugs were soon being developed at an astonishing rate and were frequently improved; they were enormously successful in treating what had once been a major cause of death.

In 1928, in the meantime, Alexander Fleming, an English medical researcher, accidentally discovered the antibacterial properties of an organism that he named penicillin. There was little progress in using penicillin to treat human illness, however, until a group of researchers at Oxford University, directed by Howard Florey and Ernest Chain, learned how to produce stable, potent penicillin in sizable enough quantities to make it a practical weapon against bacterial disease. The first human trials of the new drug, in 1941, were dramatically successful, but progress toward the mass availability of penicillin was stalled in England because of World War II. American laboratories further developed methods for the mass production and commercial distribution of penicillin, which became widely available to doctors and hospitals around the world by 1948. Since then, a wide range of new antibiotics of highly specific character have been developed so that bacterial infections are now among the most successfully treated of all human illnesses.

Immunization—the development of vaccines that can protect humans from contracting both bacterial and viral diseases—also progressed dramatically. The first great immunological triumph was the development of the smallpox vaccine by the English researcher Edward Jenner in the late eighteenth century. A vaccine effective against typhoid was developed by an English bacteriologist, Almorth Wright, in 1897 and was in wide use by World War I. Vaccination against tetanus became widespread just before and during World War II. Medical scientists also developed a vaccine, BCG, against another major killer, tuberculosis, in the 1920s; but controversy over its safety stalled its adoption, especially in the United States, for many years. It was not widely used in the United States until after World War II, when it largely eliminated tuberculosis until a limited recurrence began in the 1990s.

Viruses are much more difficult to prevent and treat than bacterial infections, and progress toward vaccines against viral infections—except for smallpox—was relatively slow. Not until the 1930s, when scientists discovered how to grow viruses in tissue cultures, could researchers study them with any real effectiveness. Gradually, they discovered how to produce forms of a virus capable of triggering antibodies that would protect vaccinated people from contracting disease. An effective vaccine against yellow fever was developed in the late 1930s, and one against influenza—one of the great killers of the early twentieth century—appeared in 1945.

A particularly dramatic postwar triumph was the development of a vaccine against polio. In 1954, the American scientist Jonas Salk introduced an effective vaccine against the disease that had killed or crippled thousands of children and adults (among them Franklin Roosevelt). It was provided free to the public by the federal government beginning in 1955. After 1960, an oral vaccine developed by Albert Sabin—usually administered in a sugar cube—made widespread vaccination even easier. By the early 1960s, these vaccines had virtually eliminated polio from American life and from much of the rest of the world.

As a result of these and many other medical advances, both infant mortality and the death rate among young children declined significantly in the first twenty-five years after the war (although not by as much as in Western Europe). Average life expectancy in that same period rose by five years, to seventy-one.

PESTICIDES

Scientists also developed new kinds of chemical pesticides to protect crops from destruction by insects and to protect humans from such insect-carried diseases as typhus and malaria. Perhaps the most famous of the new pesticides was dichlorodiphenyltrichloroethane, generally known as DDT, a compound discovered in 1939 by the Swiss chemist Paul Muller. He had discovered that although DDT seemed harmless to human beings and other mammals, it was extremely toxic to insects. American scientists learned of Muller's discovery in 1942, just as the army was grappling with the insect-borne tropical diseases—especially malaria and typhus—that threatened American soldiers.

DDT was first used on a large scale in Italy in 1943–1944 during a typhus outbreak, which it quickly helped end. Soon DDT was being sprayed in mosquito-infested areas of Pacific islands where American troops were fighting the Japanese. The incidence of malaria dropped precipitously. DDT quickly gained a reputation as a miraculous tool for controlling insects, and it undoubtedly saved thousands of lives. Only later did it become evident that DDT had long-term toxic effects on animals and humans.

POSTWAR ELECTRONIC RESEARCH

The 1940s and 1950s saw dramatic new developments in electronic technology. Researchers in the 1940s produced the first commercially viable televisions and created a technology that made it possible to broadcast programming over large areas. In the late 1950s, scientists at RCA's David Sarnoff Laboratories in New Jersey developed color television, which first became widely available in the early 1960s.

In 1948, Bell Labs, the research arm of AT&T, produced the first transistor, a solid-state device capable of amplifying electrical signals that was much smaller and more efficient than the cumbersome vacuum tubes that had powered most electronic equipment in the past. Transistors made possible the miniaturization of many devices (radios, televisions, audio equipment, hearing aids) and were also important in aviation, weaponry, and satellites. They contributed as well to another major breakthrough in electronics: the development of integrated circuitry in the late 1950s.

Integrated circuits combined a number of once-separate electronic elements (transistors, resistors, diodes, and others) and embedded them into a single, microscopically small device. They made it possible to create increasingly complex electronic devices requiring complicated circuitry that would have been impractical to produce through other means. Most of all, integrated circuits helped advance the development of the computer.

POSTWAR COMPUTER TECHNOLOGY

Prior to the 1950s, computers had been constructed mainly to perform complicated mathematical tasks, such as breaking military codes. In the 1950s, they began to perform commercial functions for the first time.

The first significant computer of the 1950s was the Universal Automatic Computer (or UNIVAC), which was developed initially for the U.S. Bureau of the Census by the Remington Rand Company. It was able to handle both alphabetical and numerical information easily. It used tape storage and could perform calculations and other functions much faster than its predecessor, the ENIAC. Searching for a larger market for its very expensive new device, Remington Rand arranged to use a UNIVAC to predict the results of the 1952 election for CBS television news. Analyzing early voting results, the UNIVAC accurately predicted an enormous landslide victory for Eisenhower over Stevenson. Few Americans had ever heard of a computer before that night, and the UNIVAC's television debut became a critical breakthrough in public awareness of computer technology.

Remington Rand had limited success in marketing the UNIVAC, but in the mid-1950s the International Business Machines Company (IBM) introduced its first major data-processing computers and marketed them among businesses in the United States and abroad. These early successes, combined with the enormous amount of money IBM invested in research and development, made the company the worldwide leader in computers for many years.

BOMBS, ROCKETS, AND MISSILES

In 1952, the United States successfully detonated the first hydrogen bomb. (The Soviet Union tested its first H-bomb a year later.) Unlike the plutonium and uranium bombs developed during World War II, the hydrogen bomb derives its vastly greater power not from fission (the splitting of atoms) but fusion (the joining together of lighter atomic elements with heavier ones).

The hydrogen bomb gave considerable impetus to a stalled scientific project in both the United States and the Soviet Union: the effort to develop unmanned rockets and missiles capable of carrying the new weapons—not suitable for delivery by airplanes—to their targets. Both nations began to put tremendous resources into their development. The United States benefited from the emigration to America of some of the German scientists who had helped develop rocketry for Germany during World War II.

In the United States, early missile research, conducted almost entirely by the air force, produced significant early successes in developing rockets capable of traveling several hundred miles. But American and Soviet leaders struggled to build longer-range missiles that were capable of traveling through space and across oceans and continents to reach distant targets: intercontinental ballistic missiles, or ICBMs. American scientists experimented in the 1950s first with the Atlas and then the Titan ICBM. Despite some early successes, the difficulty of massing sufficient stable fuel to provide the tremendous power needed to launch missiles beyond the atmosphere stymied progress. By 1958, however, scientists had created a solid fuel to replace the volatile liquid fuels of the early missiles. They had also produced miniaturized guidance systems capable of ensuring that missiles could travel to reasonably precise destinations. Within a few years, a new generation of missile capable of traveling several thousand miles, known as the Minuteman, became the basis of the American atomic weapons arsenal. American scientists also developed a nuclear missile capable of being carried and fired by submarines—the Polaris, which is launched from below the surface of the ocean by compressed air and fires its engines only once it is above the surface. A Polaris was first successfully fired from underwater in 1960.

THE SPACE PROGRAM

In the beginning, the American space program was a by-product of the rivalry with the Soviet Union. Its origins can be traced most directly to a dramatic event in 1957, when the Soviet Union announced that it had launched an earth-orbiting satellite—*Sputnik*—into outer space. The United States had yet to perform any similar feats, and the American government (and much of American society) reacted with alarm. Federal policy began encouraging (and funding) strenuous efforts to improve scientific education in the schools, to create more research laboratories, and, above all, to speed the development of America's own exploration of outer space. The United States launched its own first satellite, *Explorer I*, in January 1958.

The centerpiece of space exploration, however, soon became the manned space program, established in 1958 along with a new agency, the National Aeronautics and Space Administration (NASA). The first American space pilots, or "astronauts," quickly became revered heroes. On May 5, 1961, Alan Shepard became the first American launched into space. But his short suborbital flight came several months after a Soviet "cosmonaut," Yuri Gagarin, had made a flight in which he had actually orbited the earth. On February 2, 1962, John Glenn (later a United States senator) became the first American to orbit the globe. NASA later introduced the Gemini program, whose spacecraft could carry two astronauts at once.

These early successes led to the creation of the Apollo program, whose purpose was to land men on the moon. It suffered some catastrophic setbacks, most notably a fire in January 1967 that killed three astronauts during a training session. But on July 20, 1969, Neil Armstrong, Edwin "Buzz" Aldrin, and Michael Collins successfully traveled in a space capsule into orbit around the moon. Armstrong and Aldrin then detached a smaller craft from the capsule, landed on the surface of the moon, and became the first men to walk on a celestial body other than earth. Six more lunar missions followed, the last in 1972.

Eventually, the space program became a relatively modest effort to make travel in near-space easier and more practical through the development of the "space shuttle," an airplanelike device launched by a missile but capable both of navigating in space and landing on earth, much like a conventional aircraft. The first space shuttle was successfully launched in 1982. The explosion of one shuttle, *Challenger*, in January 1986 shortly after takeoff, killing all seven astronauts, stalled the program for two years. Missions resumed in the late 1980s, but problems remained, as illustrated by the explosion of the space shuttle

BACK TO EARTH   President Kennedy joins John Glenn at Cape Canaveral after he became the first American to orbit the earth. Kennedy considered the space program to be a signature of his presidency. (© Corbis)

Columbia during reentry in 2003. The space shuttle has been used to launch and repair communications satellites and to insert the Hubble Space Telescope into orbit in 1990 (and to repair its flawed lens on several occasions, including in 2009).

PEOPLE OF PLENTY

Among the most striking social developments of the postwar era was the rapid extension of a middle-class lifestyle and outlook to an expanding portion of the population. The historian David Potter published an influential examination of "economic abundance and American character" in 1954. He called it *People of Plenty*. For the American middle class in the 1950s, at least, it seemed an appropriate label.

The Consumer Culture

At the center of middle-class culture in the 1950s was a growing preoccupation with consumer goods—a result of increased prosperity, greater variety and availability of products, and the adeptness of advertisers in creating demand. It was also a result of the growth of consumer credit, which increased by 800 percent between 1945 and 1957 through the development of credit cards, revolving charge accounts, and easy-payment plans. Prosperity fueled such longtime consumer crazes as the automobile, and Detroit responded to the boom with ever-flashier styling and accessories. Consumers also responded eagerly to such new products as dishwashers, garbage disposals, television, hi-fis, and stereos.

Because consumer goods were so often marketed (and advertised) nationally, the 1950s were notable for the rapid spread of great national consumer crazes. For example, children, adolescents, and even some adults became entranced in the late 1950s with the hula hoop—a large plastic ring kept spinning around the waist. The popularity of the Walt Disney–produced children's television show *The Mickey Mouse Club* created a national demand for Mickey Mouse watches and hats and also contributed to the stunning success of Disneyland, an amusement park near Los Angeles that re-created many of the characters and events of Disney entertainment programs.

The Suburban Nation

A third of the nation's population lived in suburbs by 1960—a result not only of increased affluence but of important innovations in home building, which made single-family houses affordable to millions of new people. The most famous of the suburban developers, William Levitt, came to symbolize the new suburban growth with his use of mass-production techniques to construct large developments of houses, each selling for under $10,000. Many other relatively inexpensive suburban developments soon appeared throughout the country.

Why did so many Americans want to move to the suburbs? One reason was the enormous importance postwar Americans placed on family life after five years of war. Suburbs provided families with larger homes than they could find (or afford) in the cities and thus made it easier to raise larger numbers of children. The suburbs provided privacy and a sense of security from the noise and dangers of urban living. They offered space for new consumer goods—the appliances, cars, boats, outdoor furniture, and other products that many middle-class Americans craved.

Another factor motivating white Americans to move to the suburbs was race. Most suburbs were restricted to white inhabitants—both because relatively few African Americans could afford to live in them and because formal and informal barriers kept even prosperous blacks out of all but a few. In an era when the black population of most cities was rapidly growing, many white families fled to the suburbs to escape the integration of urban neighborhoods and schools.

The Suburban Family

For professional men (who tended to work in the city, at some distance from their homes), suburban life generally meant a rigid division between their working and personal worlds. For many middle-class women, it meant an increased isolation from the workplace. Many middle-class husbands considered it demeaning for their wives to be employed. And many women themselves shied away from the workplace when they could afford to, in part because of prevailing ideas about motherhood (popularized by such widely consulted books as Dr. Benjamin Spock's *Baby and Child Care*, first published in 1946) that advised women to stay at home with their children.

Some women, however, had to balance these pressures against other, contradictory ones. As expectations of material comfort rose, many middle-class families needed a second income to maintain the standard of living they desired. As a result, the number of married women working outside the home actually increased in the postwar years. By 1960, nearly a third of all married women were part of the paid workforce.

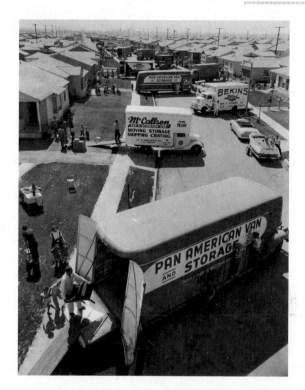

SUBURBAN LIFE   In the aftermath of World War II, suburban development experienced explosive growth—a result of the absence of housing construction during the war and the rapid population growth after it. This 1952 photograph, commissioned by *Life magazine*, shows a traffic jam of moving vans helping families settle in a new suburban development in Lakewood, California. (J.R. Eyerman/Time & Life Pictures/Getty Images)

THE BIRTH OF TELEVISION

Television was the result of a series of scientific and technological discoveries, but its impact was largely social and cultural. It quickly became perhaps the most powerful medium of mass communication in history. Experiments in broadcasting pictures (along with sound) had begun as early as the 1920s, but commercial television began only shortly after World War II. Its growth was phenomenally rapid. In 1946, there were only 17,000 sets in the country; by 1957, there were 40 million—almost as many television sets as there were families. More people had television sets, according to one report, than had refrigerators.

The television industry emerged directly out of the radio industry, and all three of the major networks—the National Broadcasting Company, the Columbia Broadcasting System, and the American Broadcasting Company—had started as radio companies. Like radio, the television business was driven by advertising. The need to attract advertisers determined most programming decisions; and in the early days of television, corporate sponsors often played a direct role in determining the content of programs. Many early television shows bore the names of the corporations that were paying for them: the *General Electric Theater*, the "Chrysler Theatre," the *Camel News Caravan*, and others. Some daytime serials (known as "soap operas," because their sponsors were almost always companies making household goods targeted at women) were actually written and produced by Procter & Gamble and other companies.

LUCY AND DESI

THE most popular show in the history of television began as an effort by a young comedian to strengthen her troubled marriage. In 1950, Lucille Ball was performing in a popular weekly CBS radio comedy, *My Favorite Husband,* in which she portrayed a slightly zany housewife who tangled frequently with her banker husband, played by Richard Denning. The network proposed to transfer the show from radio to television. Ball said she would do so only if she could replace Denning with her real-life husband of ten years, Desi Arnaz—a Cuban-born bandleader whose almost constant traveling was putting a strain on their marriage. Network officials tried in vain to talk her out of the idea. Arnaz had no acting experience, they told her. Ball herself recognized another reason for their reluctance: the radicalism of portraying an ethnically mixed marriage on the air. But she held her ground.

On Monday, October 15, 1951, the first episode of *I Love Lucy* was broadcast over CBS. Desi Arnaz played Ricky Ricardo, a Cuban bandleader and singer who spoke, at times, with a comically exaggerated Latin accent. Lucille Ball was Lucy Ricardo, his stagestruck and slightly dizzy wife. Performing with them were William Frawley and Vivian Vance, who played their neighbors and close friends, Fred and Ethel Mertz. In the premiere episode, "The Girls Want to Go to the Nightclub," Ricky and Fred want to go to a boxing match on the night of Fred and Ethel's anniversary, while the wives are arranging an evening at a nightclub.

The opening episode contained many of the elements that characterized the show throughout its long run and ensured its extraordinary success: the remarkable chemistry among the four principal actors, the unexpected comedic talent of Desi Arnaz, and, most of all, the brilliance of Lucille Ball. She was a master of physical comedy, and many of her funniest moments involved scenes of absurdly incongruous situations (Lucy working an assembly line, Lucy stomping grapes in Italy). Her characteristic yowl of frustration became one of the most familiar sounds in American culture. She was a beautiful woman, but she never hesitated to make herself look ridiculous. "She was everywoman," her longtime writer Jess Oppenheimer once wrote: "her little expressions and inflections stimulated the shock of recognition in the audience."

By the late 1950s, television news had replaced newspapers, magazines, and radios as the nation's most important vehicle of information. Television advertising helped create a vast market for new fashions and products. Televised athletic events gradually made college and professional sports one of the most important sources of entertainment (and one of the biggest businesses) in America. Television entertainment programming—almost all of it controlled by the three national networks and their corporate sponsors—replaced movies and radio as the principal source of diversion for American families.

Much of the programming of the 1950s and early 1960s created a common image of American life—an image that was predominantly white, middle class, and suburban. Television

LUCY AT HOME Although Lucy and Desi at first portrayed a childless, ethnically mixed couple living in a Manhattan apartment, many of the comic situations in the early years of the show were purely domestic. Here, Lucy, wearing an apron, deals with one of her many household predicaments with the extraordinary physical comedy that was part of her great success. Desi, watching skeptically, was a talented straight man to Lucy's zaniness. (Photofest)

In the first seasons, the fictional couples lived as neighbors, without children, in a Manhattan apartment building. Later, Lucy had a child and they all moved to the suburbs. (The show used Lucille Ball's real-life pregnancy on the air; and on January 19, 1953—only hours after Ball had given birth to her real son and second child—CBS aired a previously filmed episode of the fictional Lucy giving birth to a fictional son, "Little Ricky" Ricardo.)

Lucille Ball remained a major television star for nearly twenty years after *I Love Lucy* (and its successor, *The Lucy-Desi Comedy Hour*) left the air in 1960. Desi Arnaz, whom Ball divorced in 1960, remained for a time one of Hollywood's most powerful and successful studio executives as the head of Desilu Productions. And over sixty years after the first episode of *I Love Lucy* aired, the series remains extraordinarily popular all over the world. "People identified with the Ricardos," Lucille Ball once said, "because we had the same problems they had. We just took ordinary situations and exaggerated them." •

But it was not just the great talents of its cast that made *I Love Lucy* such a phenomenon. It was the skill of its writers in evoking some of the most common experiences and desires of television viewers in the 1950s. Lucy constantly engaged in zany and hilarious schemes to break into show business or somehow expand her world. The husbands wanted calm and conventional domestic lives—and time to themselves for conspicuously male activities: boxing, fishing, baseball.

UNDERSTAND, ANALYZE, & EVALUATE

1. In what ways did *I Love Lucy* reflect American society and family life of the 1950s?

2. How have television situation comedies since *I Love Lucy* copied the formula for success established by that program? Do you see elements of the *I Love Lucy* pattern in today's situation comedies?

was epitomized by the popular situation comedies, featuring families in which, as the title of one of the most popular shows put it, *Father Knows Best,* and in which most women were mothers and housewives striving to serve their children and please their husbands.

Yet television also could create conditions that could accentuate social conflict. Even those unable to share in the affluence of the era could, through television, acquire a vivid picture of how the rest of their society lived. While television was celebrating the white middle class, it was also showing the alienation and powerlessness of groups who felt excluded from the world it portrayed. And television news conveyed with unprecedented power the social upheavals that gradually spread beginning in the late 1950s.

Travel, Outdoor Recreation, and Environmentalism

Although the idea of a paid vacation for American workers, and the connection of that idea with travel, had entered American culture beginning in the 1920s, it was not until the postwar years that vacation travel became truly widespread among middle-income Americans. The construction of the interstate highway system contributed dramatically to the growth of travel. So did the increasing affluence of workers. Even in the 1950s, there was a healthy market for vacation vehicles—trailers and small vans. That market grew steadily larger in subsequent decades. But the urge to travel was also an expression of some of the same impulses that produced suburbs: a desire to escape the crowding and stress of densely populated areas and find a place where it was possible to experience the natural world.

Nowhere was this surge in travel and recreation more visible than in national parks, which experienced a long-term surge in attendance in the 1950s. People who traveled to national parks did so for many reasons—some to hike and camp, others to fish and hunt, and still others simply to see the extraordinary landscape. But whatever their motives, most visitors came in search of an experience in the wilderness. The importance of that search became clear in the early 1950s with the fight to preserve Echo Park.

Echo Park is a spectacular valley in the Dinosaur National Monument, on the border between Utah and Colorado and near the southern border of Wyoming. In the early 1950s, the federal government's Bureau of Reclamation—which encouraged irrigation, electric power, and water supplies—proposed building a dam across the Green River, which runs through Echo Valley, so as to create a lake for recreation and a source of hydroelectric power. The American environmental movement had been relatively quiet since its searing defeat early in the century in its effort to stop a similar dam in the Hetch Hetchy Valley at Yosemite National Park. (See p. 500.) But the Echo Park proposal helped rouse it from its slumber.

In 1950, Bernard DeVoto—a well-known writer and a great champion of the American West—published an essay in the *Saturday Evening Post* titled "Shall We Let Them Ruin Our National Parks?" It had a sensational impact, arousing opposition to the Echo Valley dam from many areas of the country. The Sierra Club, relatively obscure in previous decades, sprang into action. The controversy helped elevate a new and aggressive leader, David Brower, who eventually transformed the club into the nation's leading environmental organization. By the mid-1950s, a large coalition of environmentalists, naturalists, and wilderness vacationers had mobilized in opposition to the dam, and in 1956, Congress— bowing to public pressure—blocked the project and preserved Echo Park in its natural state. The controversy was a major victory for those who wished to preserve the sanctity of the national parks, and it was an important spur to the dawning environmental consciousness that would become so important a decade and more later.

Organized Society and Its Detractors

Large-scale organizations and bureaucracies increased their influence over American life in the postwar era, as they had been doing for many decades before. White-collar work- ers came to outnumber blue-collar laborers for the first time, and an increasing proportion of them worked in corporate settings with rigid hierarchical structures. Industrial workers also confronted large bureaucracies both in the workplace and in their own unions.

The debilitating impact of bureaucratic life on the individual became one of the central themes of popular and scholarly debate. William H. Whyte Jr. produced one of the most widely discussed books of the decade: *The Organization Man* (1956), which attempted to describe the special mentality of the worker in a large bureaucratic setting. Self-reliance, Whyte claimed, was losing place to conformity, to the ability to "get along" and "work as a team." The sociologist David Riesman made similar observations in *The Lonely Crowd* (1950), in which he argued that the traditional "inner-directed man," who judged himself on the basis of his own values and the esteem of his family, was giving way to a new "other-directed man," more concerned with winning the approval of the larger organization or community.

Novelists, too, expressed misgivings in their work about the impersonality of modern society. Saul Bellow produced a series of novels—*The Adventures of Augie March* (1953), *Seize the Day* (1956), *Herzog* (1964), and many others—that chronicled the difficulties of American Jewish men in finding fulfillment in modern urban America. J. D. Salinger wrote in *The Catcher in the Rye* (1951) of a prep-school student, Holden Caulfield, who is unable to find any area of society—school, family, friends, city—in which he can feel secure or committed.

The Beats and the Restless Culture of Youth

The most derisive critics of bureaucracy and middle-class society were a group of young poets, writers, and artists known as the "beats" (often called by disapproving critics "beat-niks"). They wrote harsh critiques of what they considered the sterility and conformity of American life, the meaninglessness of American politics, and the banality of popular culture. Allen Ginsberg's dark, bitter poem *Howl* (1955) decried the "Robot apartments! invincible suburbs! skeleton treasuries! blind capitals! demonic industries!" of modern life. Jack Kerouac produced the most popular document of the Beat Generation in his novel *On the Road* (1957), an account of a cross-country automobile trip that depicts the rootless, iconoclastic lifestyle of Kerouac and his friends.

The beats were the most visible evidence of a widespread restiveness among young Americans in the 1950s. The phenomenon of "juvenile delinquency" attracted tremendous public attention, and in both politics and popular culture, dire warnings surfaced about the growing criminality of American youth. The 1955 film *Blackboard Jungle*, for example, was a frightening depiction of crime and violence in city schools. Scholarly studies, presidential commissions, and journalistic exposés all contributed to the sense of alarm about the spread of delinquency—although in fact, youth crime did not dramatically increase in the 1950s.

The culture of alienation that the beats so vividly represented had counterparts even in ordinary middle-class behavior: teenage rebelliousness toward parents, youthful fascination with fast cars and motorcycles, and increasing sexual activity, assisted by the greater availability of birth-control devices. The popularity of James Dean, who starred in *Rebel Without a Cause* (1955), *East of Eden* (1955), and *Giant* (1956), was a particularly vivid sign of youth culture in the 1950s. Both in the roles he played (moody, alienated teenagers and young men with a streak of self-destructive violence) and in the way he lived his own life (he died in 1955, at the age of 24, in an automobile accident), Dean became an icon of the unfocused rebelliousness of American youth in his time.

Rock 'n' Roll

One of the most important cultural developments of the 1950s was the birth of rock 'n' roll—and the enormous popularity of the greatest early rock star, Elvis Presley. Presley became a symbol of a youthful determination to push at the borders of the conventional

ELVIS This early picture of Elvis Presley shows him relaxing outside. At this time, young female teenagers had an immediate and intense connection with him. Later in his career he performed for affluent and older men and women. (© Sunset Buulevard/Corbis)

and acceptable. His sultry good looks, his self-conscious effort to dress in the vaguely rebellious style of urban gangs (motorcycle jackets and slicked-back hair, even though Presley himself was a product of the rural South), and, most of all, the open sexuality of his music and his public performances—all made him wildly popular among young Americans in the 1950s. His first great hit, "Heartbreak Hotel," established him as a national phenomenon in 1956, and he remained a powerful figure in American popular culture well after his death in 1977.

Presley's music, like that of many early white rock musicians, drew heavily from black rhythm and blues traditions. Sam Phillips, a record promoter who had recorded some of the important black R&B musicians of his time, reportedly said in the early 1950s: "If I could find a white man with a Negro sound, I could make a billion dollars." Soon after that, he found Presley. But there were others as well—among them Buddy Holly and Bill Haley (whose 1955 song "Rock Around the Clock," used in the film *Blackboard Jungle,* announced the arrival of rock 'n' roll to millions of young people)—who were closely connected to African American musical traditions. Rock drew from other sources, too: from country western music (another strong influence on Presley), from gospel music, even from jazz.

The 1950s also saw African American bands and singers grow in popularity among both black and white audiences. Chuck Berry, Little Richard, B. B. King, Chubby Checker, the Temptations, the Miracles, the Supremes, and others—many of them recorded by the black producer Berry Gordy, the founder and president of Motown Records in Detroit—never rivaled Presley in their popularity among white youths but did develop significant multiracial audiences of their own.

The rapid rise of rock owed a great deal to innovations in radio and television programming. By the 1950s, radio stations no longer felt obliged to present mostly live programming—especially once television took over many of the entertainment functions radio had once performed. Instead, many radio stations devoted themselves almost entirely to playing recorded music. Early in the 1950s, a new breed of radio announcers, known as "disk jockeys," began to create programming aimed specifically at young fans of rock music; and when those programs became wildly successful, other stations followed suit. *American Bandstand,* which began airing in 1957, was a televised showcase for rock 'n' roll hits in which a live audience danced to recorded music. The program helped spread the popularity of rock—and made its host, Dick Clark, one of the best-known figures among young Americans.

Radio and television were important to the recording industry, of course, because they encouraged the rapidly increasing sale of records in the mid- and late 1950s, especially in the inexpensive and popular 45 rpm format—small disks that contained one song on each side. Also important were jukeboxes, which played individual songs on 45s and which proliferated in soda fountains, diners, bars, and other places where young people congregated. Sales of records increased from $182 million to $521 million between 1954 and 1960. So eager were record promoters to get their songs on the air that they routinely made secret payments to station owners and disk jockeys to encourage them to showcase their artists. These payments, which became known as "payola," produced a briefly sensational series of scandals when they were exposed in the late 1950s and early 1960s.

THE OTHER AMERICA

It was relatively easy for white middle-class Americans in the 1950s to believe that the world of economic growth, personal affluence, and cultural homogeneity was the world virtually all Americans knew, and that their values and assumptions were ones that most other Americans shared. But such beliefs were false. Large groups of Americans remained outside the circle of abundance and shared neither in the affluence of the middle class nor in many of its values.

ON THE MARGINS OF THE AFFLUENT SOCIETY

In 1962, the socialist writer Michael Harrington published a celebrated book called *The Other America,* which chronicled the continuing existence of poverty in the United States.

The great economic expansion of the postwar years reduced poverty dramatically but did not eliminate it. In 1960, at any given moment, more than a fifth of all American families (over 30 million people) continued to live below what the government defined as the poverty line (down from a third of all families fifteen years before). Many millions more lived just above the official poverty line, but with incomes that gave them little comfort and no security.

Most of the poor—up to 80 percent—experienced poverty intermittently and temporarily. But approximately 20 percent were people for whom poverty was a continuous, often inescapable reality. That included approximately half the nation's elderly and a significant proportion of African Americans and Hispanics. Native Americans constituted the single poorest group in the country.

This "hard-core" poverty rebuked the popular assumption that "a rising tide lifts all boats." It was a poverty that the growing prosperity of the postwar era seemed to affect hardly at all, a poverty, as Harrington observed, that appeared "impervious to hope."

RURAL POVERTY

Among those on the margins of the affluent society were many rural Americans. In 1948, farmers had received 8.9 percent of the national income; in 1956, they received only 4.1 percent. In part, this decline reflected the steadily shrinking farm population; in 1956 alone, nearly 10 percent of the rural population moved into or was absorbed by cities. But it also reflected declining farm prices. Because of enormous surpluses in basic staples, prices fell 33 percent in those years, even though national income as a whole rose 50 percent at the same time.

Sharecroppers and tenant farmers (most of them African American) continued to live at or below subsistence levels throughout the rural South—in part because of the mechanization of cotton picking after 1944, in part because of the development of synthetic fibers that reduced demand for cotton. (Two-thirds of the cotton acreage went out of production between 1930 and 1960.) Migrant farmworkers, a group concentrated especially in the West and Southwest and containing many Mexican American and Asian American workers, lived in similarly dire circumstances. In rural areas without much commercial agriculture—such as the Appalachian region in the East, where the decline of the coal economy reduced the one significant source of support for the region—whole communities lived in desperate poverty, increasingly cut off from the market economy. All these groups were vulnerable to malnutrition and even starvation.

THE INNER CITIES

As prospering white families moved from cities to suburbs in vast numbers, more and more inner-city neighborhoods became repositories for the poor, "ghettoes" from which there was no easy escape. The growth of these neighborhoods owed much to a vast migration of African Americans out of the countryside and into industrial cities. Not all these black migrants were poor, and many found in the city routes to economic progress similar to those of whites. But African Americans were substantially more likely to live in poverty than most other groups, in part because of the persistent patterns of discrimination that denied them any real opportunities.

More than 3 million black men and women moved from the South to northern cities between 1940 and 1960. Chicago, Detroit, Cleveland, New York, and other eastern and midwestern industrial cities experienced a major expansion of their black populations while many whites were leaving cities at the same time.

Similar migrations from Mexico and Puerto Rico expanded poor Hispanic neighborhoods in many American cities. Between 1940 and 1960, nearly a million Puerto Ricans moved into American cities, especially New York. Mexican workers crossed the borders into Texas and California and swelled the already substantial Latino communities of such cities as San Antonio, Houston, San Diego, and Los Angeles (which by 1960 had the largest Mexican American population of any city, approximately 500,000 people).

Inner cities filled up with poor minority residents at the same time that the unskilled industrial jobs they sought diminished. Employers were moving factories and mills from old industrial cities to new locations in suburban and rural areas, smaller cities, and even abroad—places where the costs of labor were lower. Even in the factories that remained, automation reduced the number of unskilled jobs. The economic opportunities that had helped earlier immigrant groups to rise up from poverty were unavailable to many of the postwar migrants. Racial discrimination in hiring, education, and housing doomed many members of these communities to continuing poverty.

THE RISE OF THE CIVIL RIGHTS MOVEMENT

After decades of skirmishes, an open battle began in the 1950s against racial segregation and discrimination, a battle that would prove to be one of the longest and most difficult social struggles of the twentieth century. White Americans ultimately played an important role in the civil rights movement. But pressure from African Americans themselves was the crucial element in raising the issue of race to prominence.

THE BROWN DECISION AND "MASSIVE RESISTANCE"

On May 17, 1954, the Supreme Court announced its decision in the case of *Brown v. Board of Education of Topeka*. In considering the legal segregation of a Kansas public school system, the Court rejected its own 1896 *Plessy v. Ferguson* decision, which had ruled that communities could provide African Americans with separate facilities as long as the facilities were equal to those of whites. The *Brown* decision declared that segregating public schools on the basis of race was unconstitutional. The justices argued that school segregation inflicted unacceptable damage on those it affected, regardless of the relative quality of the separate schools. Chief Justice Earl Warren explained the unanimous opinion of his colleagues: "We conclude that in the field of public education the doctrine of 'separate but equal' has no place. Separate educational facilities are inherently unequal." The following year, the Court issued another decision (known as *Brown II*) to provide rules for implementing the 1954 order. It ruled that communities must work to desegregate their schools "with all deliberate speed," but it set no timetable and left specific decisions up to lower courts.

Some communities, such as Washington, D.C., complied relatively quickly and quietly. More often, however, strong local opposition (what came to be known in the South as "massive resistance") produced long delays and bitter conflicts. More than 100 southern members of Congress signed a 1956 "manifesto" denouncing the *Brown* decision and urging their constituents to defy it. Southern governors, mayors, local school boards, and nongovernmental pressure groups (including hundreds of White Citizens' Councils) all worked to obstruct desegregation. By the fall of 1957, only 684 of 3,000 affected school districts in the South had even begun to desegregate their schools.

The Eisenhower administration was not eager to join the battle over desegregation. But in September 1957, it faced a case of direct state defiance of federal authority and felt compelled to act. Federal courts had ordered the desegregation of Central High School in Little Rock, Arkansas. An angry white mob tried to stop implementation of the order by blockading the entrances to the school. Governor Orval Faubus refused to do anything to stop the obstruction. President Eisenhower finally responded by sending federal troops to Little Rock to keep the peace and ensure that the court orders would be obeyed. Only then did Central High School admit its first black students.

LITTLE ROCK HIGH SCHOOL, 1957 Nine students in Little Rock, Arkansa become the first African Americans to enter the city's Central High School. This photograph shows some of the black students being escorted by the National Guard, sent to the city from President Eisenhower. (© Bettmann/Corbis)

THE EXPANDING MOVEMENT

The *Brown* decision helped spark a growing number of popular challenges to other forms of segregation in the South. On December 1, 1955, Rosa Parks, an African American woman, was arrested in Montgomery, Alabama, when she refused to give up her seat on a Montgomery bus to a white passenger (as required by the Jim Crow laws throughout most of the South). The arrest of this admired woman and local civil rights leader produced outrage in the city's African American community, which organized a boycott of the bus system to demand an end to segregated seating.

The boycott was almost completely effective. It put economic pressure not only on the bus company but on many Montgomery merchants, because the boycotters found it difficult to get to downtown stores and shopped instead in their own neighborhoods. Even so, the boycott might well have failed had it not been for a Supreme Court decision late in 1956, inspired in part by the protest, that declared segregation in public transportation to be illegal. The buses in Montgomery abandoned their discriminatory seating policies, and the boycott came to a close.

Among the most important accomplishments of the Montgomery boycott were the legitimization of a new form of racial protest and the elevation to prominence of a new figure in the civil rights movement. The man chosen to lead the boycott movement once it was launched was a local Baptist pastor, Martin Luther King Jr., the son of a prominent Atlanta minister, a powerful orator, and a gifted leader. King's approach to black protest was based on the doctrine of nonviolent resistance to injustice, even in the face of direct attack. And he produced an approach to racial struggle that captured the moral high ground for his supporters. For the next thirteen years—as leader of the Southern Christian Leadership Conference (SCLC), an interracial group he founded shortly after the boycott—he was the most influential and most widely admired black leader in the country. The popular movement he came to represent soon spread throughout the South and the country.

CAUSES OF THE CIVIL RIGHTS MOVEMENT

Several factors contributed to the rise of African American protest in these years. The legacy of World War II was one of the most important. Millions of black women and men had served in the military or worked in war plants during the war. They had derived from the experience a broader view of the world, and of their place in it.

Another factor was the growth of an urban black middle class, which had been developing for decades but which began to flourish after the war. Much of the impetus for the civil rights movement came from the leaders of urban black communities—ministers, educators, professionals. Much of it came as well from students at black colleges and universities, which had expanded significantly in the previous decades. Men and women with education were often more aware of the obstacles to their advancement than poorer and more oppressed people.

Television and other forms of popular culture also played a role in the rising consciousness of racism. More than any previous generation, postwar blacks had constant, vivid reminders of how the white majority lived—of the world from which they were effectively excluded. Television also conveyed the activities of demonstrators to a national audience, ensuring that activism in one community would inspire similar protests in others.

Other forces mobilized many white Americans to support the movement once it began. The Cold War made racial injustice an embarrassment to Americans trying to present their nation as a model to the world. Political mobilization of northern blacks created a substantial voting bloc within the Democratic Party. Politicians from northern industrial states could not ignore their views. Labor unions with substantial black memberships also played an important part in supporting (and funding) the civil rights movement.

This great and largely spontaneous social movement emerged as one of the most powerful forces in America.

EISENHOWER REPUBLICANISM

Dwight D. Eisenhower was the least experienced politician to serve in the White House in the twentieth century. He was also among the most popular and politically successful presidents of the postwar era. At home, he pursued essentially moderate policies, avoiding most new initiatives but accepting the work of earlier reformers. Abroad, he continued and even intensified American commitments to oppose communism but also brought a measure of restraint that his successors did not always match.

"WHAT WAS GOOD FOR . . . GENERAL MOTORS"

The first Republican administration in twenty years staffed itself with men drawn from the same quarter as those who had staffed Republican administrations in the 1920s: the business community. But by the 1950s, many business leaders had acquired a social and political outlook very different from that of their predecessors. Above all, many of the nation's leading business executives and financiers had reconciled themselves to at least the broad outlines of the Keynesian welfare state the New Deal had launched. Indeed, some corporate leaders had come to see it as something that actually benefited them—by helping maintain social order, by increasing mass purchasing power, and by stabilizing labor relations.

To his cabinet, Eisenhower appointed wealthy corporate lawyers and business executives who were unapologetic about their backgrounds. Charles Wilson, president of General Motors, assured senators considering his nomination for secretary of defense that "what was good for our country was good for General Motors, and vice versa."

Eisenhower encouraged private enterprise. He supported the private rather than public development of natural resources. To the chagrin of farmers, he lowered federal support for farm prices. He also removed the last limited wage and price controls maintained by the Truman administration, opposed the creation of new social service programs such as national health insurance, and strove constantly to reduce federal expenditures (even during the recession of 1958) and balance the budget. He ended 1960, his last full year in office, with a $1 billion budget surplus.

The Survival of the Welfare State

The president took few new initiatives in domestic policy, but he resisted conservative pressure to dismantle those welfare policies of the New Deal that had survived the assaults of the war years and after. Indeed, during his term, he agreed to extend the Social Security system to an additional 10 million people and unemployment compensation to an additional 4 million, and he approved an increase to the minimum hourly wage from 75 cents to $1. One of the most significant legislative accomplishments of the Eisenhower administration was the Federal Highway Act of 1956, which authorized $25 billion for a ten-year project that built over 40,000 miles of interstate highways—the largest public works project in American history to that point. The program was funded through a highway "trust fund," whose revenues would come from new taxes on the purchase of fuel, automobiles, trucks, and tires.

In 1956, Eisenhower ran for a second term, even though he had suffered a serious heart attack the previous year. With Adlai Stevenson opposing him once again, he won by another, even greater landslide, receiving 57.6 percent of the popular vote and 457 electoral votes to Stevenson's 73. Democrats retained control of both houses of Congress they had won back in 1954. In 1958—during a serious recession—they increased that control by substantial margins.

The Decline of McCarthyism

The Eisenhower administration did little in its first years in office to discourage the anti-communist furor that had gripped the nation. By 1954, however, what came to be known as McCarthyism began to become increasingly unpopular.

During the first year of the Eisenhower administration, McCarthy continued to operate with impunity. But in January 1954, he attacked Secretary of the Army Robert Stevens and the armed services in general, claiming that communists had intruded into the military. At that point, the administration and influential members of Congress organized a special investigation of the charges, the Army-McCarthy hearings, which were among the first congressional hearings to be nationally televised. Watching McCarthy in action—bullying witnesses, hurling groundless (and often cruel) accusations, evading issues—much of the public began to see him as a villain, and even a buffoon.

THE ARMY-MCCARTHY HEARINGS   Senator Joseph McCarthy confers with his aide, Roy Cohn, during a pause in the controversial hearings. (Byron Rollins/AP Images)

In December 1954, the Senate voted 67 to 22 to condemn him for "conduct unbecoming a senator." Three years later, he died—a victim, apparently, of complications arising from alcoholism. The Red Scare did not die with McCarthy, but its intensity soon began to decline.

EISENHOWER, DULLES, AND THE COLD WAR

The threat of nuclear war created a sense of high anxiety in international relations in the 1950s. But the nuclear threat also encouraged both superpowers to edge away from direct confrontations. The attention of both the United States and the Soviet Union began to turn instead to the rapidly growing instability in the Third World.

DULLES AND "MASSIVE RETALIATION"

Secretary of Slate John Foster Dulles was the most important figure in the Eisenhower administration next to the president himself. He was an aristocratic corporate lawyer with a stern moral revulsion to communism. He entered office denouncing the containment policies of the Truman years as excessively passive, arguing that the United States should pursue an active program of "liberation," which would lead to a "rollback" of communist expansion. Once in power, however, he had to defer to the more moderate views of the president himself.

The most prominent of Dulles's innovations was the policy of "massive retaliation," which he announced early in 1954. The United States would, he explained, respond to communist threats to its allies not by using conventional forces in local conflicts (a policy that had led to so much frustration in Korea) but by relying on "the deterrent of massive retaliatory power" (by which he clearly meant nuclear weapons). In part, the new doctrines reflected Dulles's inclination for tense confrontations, an approach he once defined as "brinksmanship"—pushing the Soviet Union to the brink of war in order to exact concessions. But the real force behind the massive-retaliation policy was economics. With pressure growing both in and out of government for a reduction in American military expenditures, an increasing reliance on atomic weapons seemed to promise, as some advocates put it, "more bang for the buck."

FRANCE, AMERICA, AND VIETNAM

On July 27, 1953, negotiators at Panmunjom finally signed an agreement ending the hostilities in Korea. Each antagonist was to withdraw its troops a mile and a half from the existing battle line, which ran roughly along the 38th parallel, the prewar border between North and South Korea. A conference in Geneva was to consider means by which to reunite the nation peacefully—although in fact that 1954 meeting produced no agreement and left the cease-fire line as the apparently permanent border between the two countries into the twenty-first century.

Almost simultaneously, however, the United States was being drawn into a long, bitter struggle in Southeast Asia. Ever since 1945, France had been attempting to restore its authority over Vietnam, its one-time colony, which it had been forced to abandon to the Japanese toward the end of World War II. Opposing the French, however, were the powerful nationalist forces of Ho Chi Minh, determined to win independence for their nation. Ho had hoped for American support in 1945, on the basis of the anticolonial rhetoric of the Atlantic Charter and Franklin Roosevelt's speeches, and also because he had received support from American intelligence forces during World War II while fighting the Japanese. He was, however, not only a committed nationalist but a committed communist. The Truman administration ignored him and supported the French, one of America's most important Cold War allies.

By 1954, Ho was receiving aid from communist China and the Soviet Union. America, in the meantime, had been paying most of the costs of France's ineffective military campaign in Vietnam since 1950. Early in 1954, 12,000 French troops became surrounded in a disastrous siege at the village of Dien Bien Phu. Only American intervention, it was clear, could prevent the total collapse of the French military effort. Yet despite the urgings of Secretary of State Dulles, Vice President Nixon, and others, Eisenhower refused to permit direct American military intervention in Vietnam, claiming that neither Congress nor America's other allies would support such action.

Without American aid, the French defense of Dien Bien Phu finally collapsed on May 7, 1954, and France quickly abandoned Vietnam. They agreed to a settlement of the conflict at the same international conference in Geneva that was considering the Korean settlement. The Geneva accords on Vietnam of July 1954, to a participant, established a supposedly temporary division of Vietnam along the 17th parallel. The north would be governed by Ho Chi Minh, the south by a pro-Western regime. Democratic elections would be the basis for uniting the nation in 1956. The agreement marked the end of the French commitment to Vietnam and the beginning of an expanded American presence there. The United States helped establish a pro-American government in the south, headed by Ngo Dinh Diem, a member of his country's Roman Catholic minority. Diem refused to permit the 1956 elections, which he knew he would lose. He felt secure in his refusal because the United States had promised to provide him with ample military assistance against any attack from the north.

COLD WAR CRISES

American foreign policy in the 1950s was challenged by both real and imagined crises in far-flung areas of the world. Among them were a series of crises in the Middle East, a region in which the United States had been little involved until after World War II.

On May 14, 1948, after years of Zionist efforts and a decision by the new United Nations, the nation of Israel proclaimed its independence. President Truman recognized the new Jewish homeland the next day. But the creation of Israel, while resolving some conflicts, created others. Palestinian Arabs, unwilling to accept being displaced from what they considered their own country, joined with Israel's Arab neighbors and fought determinedly against the new state in 1948—the first of several Arab-Israeli wars.

Committed as the American government was to Israel, it was also concerned about the stability and friendliness of the Arab regimes in the oil-rich Middle East, where American petroleum companies had major investments. Thus the United States reacted with alarm as it watched Mohammed Mossadegh, the nationalist prime minister of Iran, begin to resist the presence of Western corporations in his nation in the early 1950s. In 1953, the American CIA joined forces with conservative Iranian military leaders to engineer a coup that drove Mossadegh from office. To replace him, the CIA helped elevate the young shah of Iran, Mohammed Reza Pahlevi, from his position as token constitutional monarch to that of virtually absolute ruler. The shah remained closely tied to the United States for the next twenty-five years.

American policy was less effective in dealing with the nationalist government of Egypt, under the leadership of General Gamal Abdel Nasser. He began to develop a trade relationship with the Soviet Union in the early 1950s. In 1956, to punish Nasser for his friendliness toward the communists, Dulles withdrew American offers to assist in building the great Aswan Dam across the Nile. A week later, Nasser retaliated by seizing control of the Suez Canal from the British, saying that he would use the income from it to build the dam himself.

On October 29, 1956, Israeli forces attacked Egypt. The next day the British and French landed troops in the Suez to drive the Egyptians from the canal. Dulles and Eisenhower feared that the Suez crisis would drive the Arab states toward the Soviet Union and precipitate a new world war. By refusing to support the invasion, and by joining in a United Nations denunciation of it, the United States helped pressure the French and British to withdraw and persuaded Israel to agree to a truce with Egypt.

Cold War concerns affected American relations in Latin America as well. In 1954, the Eisenhower administration ordered the CIA to help topple the new, leftist government of Jacobo Arbenz Guzmán in Guatemala, a regime that Dulles (responding to the requests of the United Fruit Company, a major investor in Guatemala) argued was potentially communist.

No nation in the region had been more closely tied to America than Cuba. Its leader, Fulgencio Batista, had ruled as a military dictator since 1952, when American assistance helped him topple a more moderate government. Cuba's relatively prosperous economy had become a virtual colony of American corporations, which controlled almost all the island's natural resources and had cornered over half the vital sugar crop. American organized-crime syndicates controlled much of Havana's lucrative hotel and nightlife business. In 1957, a popular movement of resistance to the Batista regime began to gather strength under the leadership of Fidel Castro. On January 1, 1959, as Batista fled to exile in Spain, Castro marched into Havana and established a new government.

EISENHOWER WARNS OF THE MILITARY INDUSTRIAL COMPLEX IN HIS FAREWELL ADDRESS, JANUARY 17, 1961

GOOD evening, my fellow Americans. [. . .] This evening I come to you with a message of leave-taking and farewell, and to share a few final thoughts with you, my countrymen. Like every other citizen, I wish the new President, and all who will labor with him, Godspeed. I pray that the coming years will be blessed with peace and prosperity for all. [. . .]

America is today the strongest, the most influential, and most productive nation in the world. Understandably proud of this pre-eminence, we yet realize that America's leadership and prestige depend, not merely upon our unmatched material progress, riches and military strength, but on how we use our power in the interests of world peace and human betterment. [. . .]

A vital element in keeping the peace is our military establishment. Our arms must be mighty, ready for instant action, so that no potential aggressor may be tempted to risk his own destruction. Our military organization today bears little relation to that known by any of my predecessors in peacetime, or, indeed, by the fighting men of World War II or Korea. [. . .]

Now this conjunction of an immense military establishment and a large arms industry is new in the American experience. The total influence—economic, political, even spiritual—is felt in every city, every Statehouse, every office of the Federal government. We recognize the imperative need for this development. Yet we must not fail to comprehend its grave implications. Our toil, resources, and livelihood are all involved. So is the very structure of our society.

In the councils of government, we must guard against the acquisition of unwarranted influence, whether sought or unsought, by the military-industrial complex. The potential for the disastrous rise of misplaced power exists and will persist. We must never let the weight of this combination endanger our liberties or democratic processes. We should take nothing for granted. Only an alert and knowledgeable citizenry can compel the proper meshing of the huge industrial and military machinery of defense with our peaceful methods and goals, so that security and liberty may prosper together.

Akin to, and largely responsible for the sweeping changes in our industrial-military posture, has been the technological revolution during recent decades. In this revolution, research has become central, it also becomes more formalized, complex, and costly. A steadily increasing share is conducted for, by, or at the direction of the Federal government.

Today, the solitary inventor, tinkering in his shop, has been overshadowed by task forces of scientists in laboratories and testing fields. In the same fashion, the free university, historically the fountainhead of free ideas and scientific discovery, has

Castro soon began implementing drastic policies of land reform and expropriating foreign-owned businesses and resources. When Castro began accepting assistance from the Soviet Union in 1960, the United States cut back the "quota" by which Cuba could export sugar to America at a favored price. Early in 1961, as one of its last acts, the Eisenhower administration severed diplomatic relations with Castro. Isolated by the United States, Castro soon cemented an alliance with the Soviet Union.

experienced a revolution in the conduct of research. Partly because of the huge costs involved, a government contract becomes virtually a substitute for intellectual curiosity. For every old blackboard there are now hundreds of new electronic computers. The prospect of domination of the nation's scholars by Federal employment, project allocations, and the power of money is ever present—and is gravely to be regarded.

Yet, in holding scientific research and discovery in respect, as we should, we must also be alert to the equal and opposite danger that public policy could itself become the captive of a scientific-technological elite.

It is the task of statesmanship to mold, to balance, and to integrate these and other forces, new and old, within the principles of our democratic system—ever aiming toward the supreme goals of our free society.

. . . As we peer into society's future, we—you and I, and our government—must avoid the impulse to live only for today, plundering for our own ease and convenience the precious resources of tomorrow. We cannot mortgage the material assets of our grandchildren without risking the loss also of their political and spiritual heritage. We want democracy to survive for all generations to come, not to become the insolvent phantom of tomorrow. [. . .]

Disarmament, with mutual honor and confidence, is a continuing imperative. Together we must learn how to compose differences, not with arms, but with intellect and decent purpose. Because this need is so sharp and apparent, I confess that I lay down my official responsibilities in this field with a definite sense of disappointment. As one who has witnessed the horror and the lingering sadness of war, as one who knows that another war could utterly destroy this civilization which has been so slowly and painfully built over thousands of years, I wish I could say tonight that a lasting peace is in sight. [. . .]

You and I, my fellow citizens, need to be strong in our faith that all nations, under God, will reach the goal of peace with justice. May we be ever unswerving in devotion to principle, confident but humble with power, diligent in pursuit of the Nations' great goals. [. . .]

Now, on Friday noon, I am to become a private citizen. I am proud to do so. I look forward to it.

Thank you, and good night.

UNDERSTAND, ANALYZE, & EVALUATE

1. What specifically was the military-industrial complex, and how did it support American postwar prosperity? How did it change the relationship between knowledge, industrial production, and defense?
2. What dangers for American political traditions did Eisenhower foresee? What economic dangers did he envision for future generations of Americans?

Source: Farewell address by President Dwight D. Eisenhower, January 17, 1961; Final TV Talk 1/17/61 (1), Box 38, Speech Series, Papers of Dwight D. Eisenhower as President, 1953–61, Eisenhower Library; National Archives and Records Administration [Public Domain].

THE U-2 CRISIS

Although the problems of the Third World were moving slowly toward the center of American foreign policy, the direct relationship with the Soviet Union and the effort to resist communist expansion in Europe remained the principal concerns of the Eisenhower administration. Relations between the Soviet Union and the West soured further in 1956 in response to the

Hungarian Revolution. Hungarian dissidents had launched a popular uprising in November to demand democratic reforms. Before the month was out, Soviet tanks and troops entered Budapest to crush the uprising and restore an orthodox, pro-Soviet regime.

In November 1958, Nikita Khrushchev, who had become Soviet premier and Communist Party chief earlier that year, renewed the demands of his predecessors that the NATO powers abandon West Berlin. When the United States and its allies predictably refused, Khrushchev suggested that he and Eisenhower discuss the issue personally, both in visits to each other's countries and at a summit meeting in Paris in 1960. The United States agreed. Khrushchev's 1959 visit to America produced a cool but polite public response. Plans proceeded for the summit conference and for Eisenhower's visit to Moscow shortly thereafter. Only days before the Paris meeting, however, the Soviet Union announced that it had shot down an American U-2, a high-altitude spy plane, over Russian territory. Its pilot, Francis Gary Powers, was in captivity. Khrushchev lashed out angrily at the American incursion into Soviet airspace, breaking up the Paris summit almost before it could begin and withdrawing his invitation to Eisenhower to visit the Soviet Union.

After eight years in office, Eisenhower had failed to eliminate, and in some respects had actually increased, the tensions between the United States and the Soviet Union. Yet Eisenhower had also brought to the Cold War his own sense of the limits of American power. He had resisted military intervention in Vietnam. And he had placed a measure of restraint on those who urged the creation of an enormous American military establishment. In his farewell address in January 1961, he warned of the "unwarranted influence" of a vast "military-industrial complex." His caution, in both domestic and international affairs, stood in marked contrast to the attitudes of his successors, who argued that the United States must act more boldly and aggressively on behalf of its goals at home and abroad.

CONCLUSION

The booming economic growth of the 1950s—and the anxiety over the Cold War that formed a backdrop to it—shaped the politics and the culture of the decade. For most Americans, the 1950s were years of increasing personal prosperity. Sales of private homes increased dramatically; suburbs grew precipitously; young families had children at an astounding rate—creating what came to be known as the postwar "baby boom." After the end of the divisive Korean War, the nation's politics entered a period of relative calm, symbolized by the genial presence in the White House of Dwight D. Eisenhower, who provided moderate and undemanding leadership through most of the decade.

The nation's culture, too, helped create a broad sense of stability and calm. Television, which emerged in the 1950s as the most powerful medium of mass culture, presented largely uncontroversial programming dominated by middle-class images and traditional values. Movies, theater, popular magazines, and newspapers all contributed to a broad sense of well-being.

But the 1950s were not, in the end, as calm and contented as the politics and popular culture of the time suggested. A powerful youth culture emerged in these years, displaying a considerable level of restiveness and even disillusionment. African Americans began to escalate their protests against segregation and inequality. The continuing existence of widespread poverty among large groups of Americans attracted increasing attention as the decade progressed. These pulsing anxieties, combined with frustration over the continuing tensions of the Cold War, produced by the late 1950s a growing sense of impatience with the calm, placid public culture of the time. That was one reason for the growing desire for action and innovation as the 1960s began.

RECALL AND REFLECT

1. How did the economic boom of the postwar era change American lifestyles?
2. What were some of the significant scientific and technological breakthroughs, especially in medicine, chemistry, electronics, weaponry, and space exploration, of the 1950s and 1960s? How did these developments affect American life?
3. How did the increasing popularity of the automobile change the American landscape and American society?
4. How did the Cold War progress under Eisenhower?

29 CIVIL RIGHTS, VIETNAM, AND THE ORDEAL OF LIBERALISM

EXPANDING THE LIBERAL STATE
THE BATTLE FOR RACIAL EQUALITY
"FLEXIBLE RESPONSE" AND THE COLD WAR
THE AGONY OF VIETNAM
THE TRAUMAS OF 1968

LOOKING AHEAD

1. What was the domestic reform agenda of Kennedy's New Frontier, and how did Johnson's Great Society programs continue and expand on that agenda?
2. Why did the civil rights movement become increasingly assertive and militant over the course of the 1960s?
3. How did U.S. involvement in Vietnam escalate through the 1960s? What were the political and social consequences of that escalation, in both Vietnam and the United States?

BY THE LATE 1950s, a growing restlessness was bubbling beneath the apparently placid surface of American society. Ultimately, that restlessness would make the 1960s one of the most turbulent and divisive eras of the twentieth century. But at first, it contributed to a bold and confident effort by political leaders to attack social and international problems within the framework of conventional liberalism.

EXPANDING THE LIBERAL STATE

Those who yearned for a more active government in the late 1950s, and who accused the Eisenhower administration of allowing the nation to "drift," hoped for vigorous new leadership. The two men who served in the White House through most of the 1960s—John Kennedy and Lyndon Johnson—seemed for a time to embody these liberal hopes.

John Kennedy

The campaign of 1960 produced two young candidates who claimed to offer the nation active leadership. The Republican nomination went almost uncontested to Vice President Richard Nixon, who promised moderate reform. The Democrats, in the meantime, emerged from a spirited primary campaign united, somewhat uneasily, behind John Fitzgerald Kennedy, an attractive and articulate senator from Massachusetts who had narrowly missed being the party's vice presidential candidate in 1956.

John Kennedy was the young son of the wealthy, powerful, and highly controversial Joseph P. Kennedy, former American ambassador to Britain. He premised his campaign, he said, "on the single assumption that the American people are uneasy at the present drift in our national course." But his appealing public image was at least as important as his political positions in attracting popular support. He overcame doubts about his youth (he turned forty-three in 1960) and religion (he was Catholic) to win with a tiny plurality of the popular vote (49.7 percent to Nixon's 49.6 percent) and only a slightly more comfortable electoral majority (303 to 219).

Kennedy had campaigned promising a set of domestic reforms he described as the "New Frontier." But his thin popular mandate and a Congress dominated by a

1960
Kennedy elected president

1961
Freedom rides
Bay of Pigs
Berlin Wall erected

1962
Cuban missile crisis

1963
March on Washington
Kennedy assassinated; Johnson becomes president
Civil rights demonstrations in Birmingham

1964
Johnson launches war on poverty
Civil Rights Act
Gulf of Tonkin Resolution
Johnson elected president

1965
Malcolm X assassinated
Voting Rights Act
U.S. troops in Vietnam
Racial violence in Watts

1967
Antiwar movement grows
Racial violence in Detroit

1968
Tet offensive
Martin Luther King Jr. assassinated
Robert Kennedy assassinated
Nixon elected president

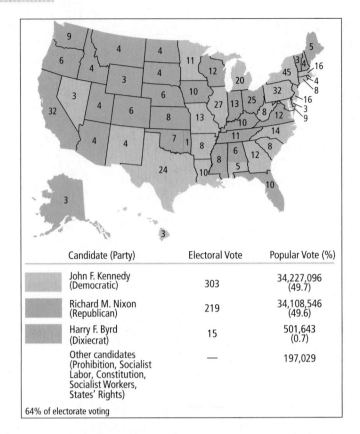

Candidate (Party)	Electoral Vote	Popular Vote (%)
John F. Kennedy (Democratic)	303	34,227,096 (49.7)
Richard M. Nixon (Republican)	219	34,108,546 (49.6)
Harry F. Byrd (Dixiecrat)	15	501,643 (0.7)
Other candidates (Prohibition, Socialist Labor, Constitution, Socialist Workers, States' Rights)	—	197,029

64% of electorate voting

THE ELECTION OF 1960   The election of 1960 was, in the popular vote at least, one of the closest in American history. John Kennedy's margin over Richard Nixon was less than one-third of 1 percent of the total national vote, but greater in the electoral college. Note the distribution of electoral strength of the two candidates. Kennedy was strong in the industrial Northeast and the largest industrial states of the Midwest, and he retained at least a portion of his party's traditional strength in the South and Southwest. But Nixon made significant inroads into the upper South, carried Florida, and swept most of the plains and mountain states. • *What was the significance of this distribution of strength to the future of the two parties?*

coalition of Republicans and conservative Democrats frustrated many of his hopes. Kennedy did manage to win approval of tariff reductions his administration had negotiated, and he began to build a legislative agenda—including a call for a significant tax cut to promote economic growth.

More than any other president of the century (except perhaps the two Roosevelts and, later, Ronald Reagan), Kennedy made his own personality an integral part of his presidency and a central focus of national attention. Nothing illustrated that more clearly than the popular reaction to the tragedy of November 22, 1963. In Texas with his wife and Vice President Lyndon Johnson for a series of political appearances, as the presidential motorcade rode slowly through the streets of Dallas, shots rang out. Two bullets struck the president—one in the throat, the other in the head. He was sped to a nearby hospital, where minutes later he was pronounced dead. Lee Harvey Oswald—a young man who had spent time in the Soviet Union and, later in Cuba—was arrested for the crime. Later that day he was mysteriously murdered by a Dallas nightclub owner, Jack Ruby, as he was being moved from one jail to another. Most Americans at the time accepted the

RETROACTIVE I, 1964   Within months of his death, John Kennedy had become a figure larger than life, a symbol of the nation's thwarted aspirations. The artist Robert Rauschenberg gave evidence of Kennedy's new mythological importance by making him the centerpiece of this evocation of contemporary American society. (Wadsworth Atheneum Museum of Art/Art Resource, NY/Art © Robert Rauschenberg Foundation/Licensed by VAGA, New York, NY)

conclusions of a federal commission appointed by President Johnson to investigate the assassination. The commission, chaired by Chief Justice Earl Warren, found that both Oswald and Ruby had acted alone, that there was no larger conspiracy. In later years, however, many Americans came to believe that the Warren Commission report had ignored evidence of a wider conspiracy behind the murders. Controversy over the assassination continues still.

LYNDON JOHNSON

The Kennedy assassination was a national trauma—a defining event for almost everyone old enough to be aware of it. At the time, however, much of the nation took comfort in the personality and performance of Kennedy's successor in the White House, Lyndon Baines Johnson. Johnson was a native of the poor "hill country" of west Texas and had risen to become majority leader of the U.S. Senate by dint of extraordinary, even obsessive, effort and ambition. Having failed to win the Democratic nomination for president in 1960, he surprised many who knew him by agreeing to accept the vice president nomination on the ticket with Kennedy. The events in Dallas thrust him into the White House.

Johnson's rough-edged, even crude, personality could hardly have been more different from Kennedy's. But like Kennedy, Johnson was a man who believed in the active use of power. Between 1963 and 1966, he compiled the most impressive legislative record of any president since Franklin Roosevelt. He was aided by the tidal wave of emotion that followed the death of Kennedy, which helped win support for many New Frontier proposals. But Johnson also constructed a remarkable reform program of his own, one that he ultimately labeled the "Great Society." And he won approval of much of it through the same sort of skillful lobbying in Congress that had made him an effective majority leader.

Johnson's first year in office was, by necessity, dominated by the campaign for reelection. There was little doubt that he would win—particularly after the Republican Party nominated the very conservative Senator Barry Goldwater of Arizona. In the November 1964 election, the president received a larger plurality, over 61 percent, than any candidate before or since. Goldwater managed to carry only his home state of Arizona and five states in the Deep South. Nevertheless, the failed Goldwater campaign mobilized many right-wing activists who would propel the growth of conservative political strength for decades to come. Record Democratic majorities in both houses of Congress, many of whose members had been swept into office only because of the margin of Johnson's victory, ensured that the president would be able to fulfill many of his goals.

THE ASSAULT ON POVERTY

For the first time since the New Deal, the federal government took steps in the 1960s to create important new social welfare programs. The most important of these, perhaps, was Medicare, which provides federal aid to the elderly for medical expenses. Its enactment in 1965 came at the end of a bitter twenty-year debate between those who believed in the concept of national health assistance and those who denounced it as "socialized medicine." But Medicare pacified many critics. For one thing, it avoided the stigma of "welfare" by making Medicare benefits available to all elderly Americans, regardless of need (just as Social Security had done with pensions). That created a large middle-class constituency for the program. It also defused the opposition of the medical community by allowing doctors serving Medicare patients to practice privately and (at first) to charge their normal fees; Medicare simply shifted responsibility for paying those fees from the patient to the government. In 1966, Johnson steered to passage the Medicaid program, which extended federal medical assistance to welfare recipients and other indigent people of all ages.

Medicare and Medicaid were early steps in a much larger assault on poverty—one that Kennedy had been planning in the last months of his life and that Johnson launched only weeks after taking office. The centerpiece of this "war on poverty," as Johnson called it, was the Office of Economic Opportunity (OEO), which created an array of new educational, employment, housing, and health-care programs. But the OEO was controversial from the start, in part because of its commitment to the idea of "Community Action."

Community Action was an effort to involve members of poor communities themselves in the planning and administration of the programs designed to help them. The Community Action programs provided jobs for many poor people and gave them valuable experience in administrative and political work. But despite its achievements, the Community Action approach proved impossible to sustain. Administrative failures damaged the program. So did the apparent excesses of a few agencies, which damaged the popular image of the Community Action programs and indeed the war on poverty as a whole.

The OEO spent nearly $3 billion during its first two years of existence, and it helped reduce poverty in some areas. But it fell far short of eliminating poverty altogether. That was in part because of the weaknesses of the programs themselves and in part because funding for them, inadequate from the beginning, dwindled as the years passed and a costly war in Southeast Asia became the nation's first priority.

Cities, Schools, and Immigration

Closely tied to the antipoverty program were federal efforts to promote the revitalization of decaying cities and to strengthen the nation's schools. The Housing Act of 1961 offered $4.9 billion in federal grants to cities for the preservation of open spaces, the development of mass-transit systems, and the subsidization of middle-income housing. In 1966, Johnson established a new cabinet agency, the Department of Housing and Urban Development (whose first secretary, Robert Weaver, was the first African American ever to serve in the cabinet). Johnson also inaugurated the Model Cities Program, which offered federal subsidies for urban redevelopment pilot programs.

Kennedy had fought for federal aid to public education, but he had failed to overcome two important obstacles. Many Americans feared that aid to education was the first step toward federal control of the schools, and Catholics insisted that federal assistance must extend to parochial as well as public schools. Johnson managed to circumvent both objections with the Elementary and Secondary Education Act of 1965 and a series of subsequent measures. The bills extended aid to both private and parochial schools and based the aid on the economic conditions of the students, not on the needs of the schools themselves.

The Johnson administration also supported the Immigration Act of 1965, one of the most important pieces of legislation of the 1960s. For decades since the 1920s, the law maintained a strict limit on the number of newcomers admitted to the country each year (170,000). But the 1965 act eliminated the "national origins" system established in the 1920s, which gave preference to immigrants from northern Europe over those from other parts of the world. It continued to restrict immigration from some parts of Latin America, but it allowed people from all parts of Europe, Asia, and Africa to enter the United States on an equal basis. By the early 1970s, the character of American immigration had changed dramatically. The numbers of immigrants grew significantly, with members of new national groups—and particularly large groups of Asians—entering the United States and transforming the character of the American population.

LEGACIES OF THE GREAT SOCIETY

Taken together, the Great Society reforms significantly increased federal spending. For a time, rising tax revenues from the growing economy nearly compensated for the new expenditures. In 1964, Johnson managed to win passage of the $11.5 billion tax cut that Kennedy had first proposed in 1962. The cut increased the federal deficit, but substantial economic growth over the next several years made up for much of the revenue initially lost. As Great Society programs began to multiply, however, and particularly as they began to compete with the escalating costs of America's military ventures, the federal budget rapidly outpaced increases in revenues. In 1961, the federal government had spent $94.4 billion. By 1970, that sum had risen to $196.6 billion.

The high costs of the Great Society, and the failures of much of it, weakened the popularity of the federal efforts to solve social problems. But the Great Society was also responsible for some significant achievements. It significantly reduced hunger in America. It made medical care available to millions of elderly and poor people who would otherwise have had great difficulty affording it. It contributed to the greatest reduction in poverty in American history. In 1959, according to the most widely accepted estimates, 21 percent of the American people lived below the officially established poverty line (a level that did not survive for very long). In 1969, only 12 percent remained below that line. Much of that progress was a result of economic growth, but some of it was a result of Great Society programs.

THE BATTLE FOR RACIAL EQUALITY

By the early 1960s, the effort to provide justice and equality was becoming impossible to avoid. African Americans themselves made sure of that.

EXPANDING PROTESTS

John Kennedy was sympathetic to the cause of racial justice, but he was hardly a committed crusader. Like presidents before him, he feared alienating southern voters and powerful southern Democrats in Congress. His administration hoped to contain the racial problem by enforcing existing laws and using executive orders—not proposing new legislation.

But the pressure for change was growing uncontainable even before Kennedy took office. Throughout the 1950s, African Americans in northern cities had grown increasingly active in opposing discrimination. They demanded progress in housing, jobs, and education. This restiveness soon spread to the South. In February 1960, black college students in Greensboro, North Carolina, staged a sit-in at a segregated Woolworth's lunch counter; and in the following months, such demonstrations spread throughout the South, forcing many merchants to integrate their facilities. In the fall of 1960, some of those who had participated in the sit-ins formed the Student Nonviolent Coordinating Committee (SNCC)—a student branch of Martin Luther King Jr.'s Southern Christian Leadership Conference; SNCC worked to keep the spirit of resistance alive.

In 1961, an interracial group of students, working with the Congress of Racial Equality (CORE), began what they called "freedom rides." Traveling by bus throughout the South, they tried to force the desegregation of bus stations. They were met in some places with such savage violence on the part of some white southerners that Attorney General Robert

Kennedy finally dispatched federal marshals to help keep the peace and ordered the integration of all bus and train stations.

Events in the Deep South in 1963 helped bring the growing movement to something of a climax. In April, Martin Luther King Jr. helped launch a series of nonviolent demonstrations in Birmingham, Alabama. Police Commissioner Eugene "Bull" Connor personally supervised a brutal effort to break up the peaceful marches, arresting hundreds of demonstrators and using attack dogs, tear gas, electric cattle prods, and fire hoses—at times even against small children—in full view of television cameras. Two months later, Governor George Wallace stood in the doorway of a building at the University of Alabama to prevent the court-ordered enrollment of several black students. Only after the arrival of federal marshals did he give way. The same night, NAACP official Medgar Evers was murdered in Mississippi. And in September, a bombing of a black church in Birmingham killed four African American children.

A National Commitment

The events in Alabama and Mississippi were a warning to the president that he could no longer avoid the issue of race. In an important television address the night of the University of Alabama confrontation, Kennedy spoke eloquently of the "moral issue" facing the nation. Days later, he introduced new legislative proposals prohibiting segregation

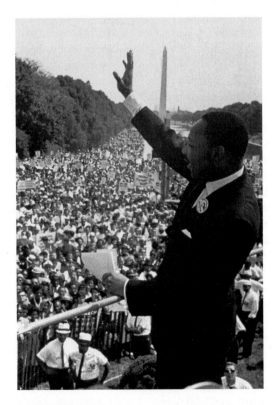

MARTIN LUTHER KING JR. IN WASHINGTON Moments after completing his memorable speech during the August 1963 March on Washington, King waves to the vast and enthusiastic crowd that had gathered in front of the Lincoln Memorial to demand "equality and jobs." (AP Images)

MARTIN LUTHER KING JR., "I HAVE A DREAM," DELIVERED AUGUST 28, 1963, AT THE LINCOLN MEMORIAL, WASHINGTON, D.C.

I am happy to join with you today in what will go down in history as the greatest demonstration for freedom in the history of our nation.

Five score years ago, a great American, in whose symbolic shadow we stand today, signed the Emancipation Proclamation. This momentous decree came as a great beacon light of hope to millions of Negro slaves who had been seared in the flames of withering injustice. It came as a joyous daybreak to end the long night of their captivity.

But one hundred years later, the Negro still is not free. One hundred years later, the life of the Negro is still sadly crippled by the manacles of segregation and the chains of discrimination. One hundred years later, the Negro lives on a lonely island of poverty in the midst of a vast ocean of material prosperity. One hundred years later, the Negro is still languished in the corners of American society and finds himself an exile in his own land. And so we've come here today to dramatize a shameful condition.

In a sense we've come to our nation's capital to cash a check. When the architects of our republic wrote the magnificent words of the Constitution and the Declaration of Independence, they were signing a promissory note to which every American was to fall heir. [. . .] Instead of honoring this sacred obligation, America has given the Negro people a bad check, a check which has come back marked "insufficient funds."

But we refuse to believe that the bank of justice is bankrupt. We refuse to believe that there are insufficient funds in the great vaults of opportunity of this nation. [. . .]

It would be fatal for the nation to overlook the urgency of the moment. This sweltering summer of the Negro's legitimate discontent will not pass until there is an invigorating autumn of freedom and equality. Nineteen sixty-three is not an end, but a beginning. And those who hope that the Negro needed to blow off steam and will now be content will have a rude awakening if the nation returns to business as usual. And there will be neither rest nor tranquility in America until the Negro is granted his citizenship rights. The whirlwinds of revolt will continue to shake the foundations of our nation until the bright day of justice emerges. [. . .]

The marvelous new militancy which has engulfed the Negro community must not lead us to a distrust of all white people, for many of our white brothers, as evidenced by their presence here today, have come to realize that their destiny is tied up with our destiny. And they have come to realize that their freedom is inextricably bound to our freedom.

We cannot walk alone.

And as we walk, we must make the pledge that we shall always march ahead.

We cannot turn back.

There are those who are asking the devotees of civil rights, "When will you be satisfied?" We can never be satisfied as long as the Negro is the victim of the unspeakable horrors of police brutality. We can never be satisfied as long as our bodies, heavy with the fatigue of travel, cannot gain lodging in the motels of the highways and the hotels of the cities. We cannot be satisfied as long as the negro's basic mobility is from a smaller ghetto to a larger one. We can never be satisfied as long as our children are stripped of their self-hood and robbed of their dignity by signs stating: "For Whites Only." We cannot be satisfied as long as a Negro in Mississippi cannot vote and a Negro in New York believes he has nothing for which to vote. No, no, we are not satisfied, and we will not be satisfied until "justice rolls down like waters, and righteousness like a mighty stream."

I am not unmindful that some of you have come here out of great trials and tribulations.

Some of you have come fresh from narrow jail cells. And some of you have come from areas where your quest—quest for freedom left you battered by the storms of persecution and staggered by the winds of police brutality. [. . .]

Let us not wallow in the valley of despair, I say to you today, my friends. [. . .]

And so even though we face the difficulties of today and tomorrow, I still have a dream. It is a dream deeply rooted in the American dream. I have a dream that one day this nation will rise up and live out the true meaning of its creed: "We hold these truths to be self-evident, that all men are created equal." I have a dream that one day on the red hills of Georgia, the sons of former slaves and the sons of former slave owners will be able to sit down together at the table of brotherhood. I have a dream that one day even the state of Mississippi, a state sweltering with the heat of injustice, sweltering with the heat of oppression, will be transformed into an oasis of freedom and justice. I have a dream that my four little children will one day live in a nation where they will not be judged by the color of their skin but by the content of their character.

I have a *dream* today!

I have a dream that one day, *down* in Alabama, with its vicious racists, with its governor having his lips dripping with the words of "interposition" and "nullification"— one day right there in Alabama little black boys and black girls will be able to join hands with little white boys and white girls as sisters and brothers.

I have a *dream* today!

I have a dream that one day every valley shall be exalted, and every hill and mountain shall be made low, the rough places will be made plain, and the crooked places will be made straight; "and the glory of the Lord shall be revealed and all flesh shall see it together."

This is our hope, and this is the faith that I go back to the South with. With this faith, we will be able to hew out of the mountain of despair a stone of hope. With this faith, we will be able to transform the jangling discords of our nation into a beautiful symphony of brotherhood. With this faith, we will be able to work together, to pray together, to struggle together, to go to jail together, to stand up for freedom together, knowing that we will be free one day. And this will be the day—this will be the day when all of God's children will be able to sing with new meaning: *My country 'tis of thee, sweet land of liberty, of thee I sing. Land where my fathers died, land of the Pilgrim's pride, From every mountainside, let freedom ring!*

And if America is to be a great nation, this must become true. And so let freedom ring from the prodigious hilltops of New Hampshire. Let freedom ring from the mighty mountains of New York. Let freedom ring from the heightening Alleghenies of Pennsylvania. Let freedom ring from the snow-capped Rockies of Colorado. Let freedom ring from the curvaceous slopes of California. But not only that: Let freedom ring from Stone Mountain of Georgia. Let freedom ring from Lookout Mountain of Tennessee. Let freedom ring from every hill and molehill of Mississippi. From every mountainside, let freedom ring. And when this happens, when we allow freedom to ring, when we let it ring from every village and every hamlet, from every state and every city, we will be able to speed up that day when *all* of God's children, black men and white men, Jews and Gentiles, Protestants and Catholics, will be able to join hands and sing in the words of the old Negro spiritual: *Free at last! Free at last! Thank God Almighty, we are free at last!*

UNDERSTAND, ANALYZE, & EVALUATE

1. What did Martin Luther King Jr. have to say about the history of African Americans in the nation's history since the Civil War?
2. King referenced a number of recent events in the civil rights movement. Can you identify them?
3. Based on this speech, what role did religious faith play for King?

Source: http://www.thekingcenter.org/archive/document/i-have-dream-1. Estate of Dr. Martin Luther King Jr., Intellectual Properties Management, One Freedom Plaza, 449 Auburn Avenue NE, Atlanta, GA 30312, fax: 404-526-8969.

THE CIVIL RIGHTS MOVEMENT

THE civil rights movement was one of the most important events in the modern history of the United States. It helped force the dismantling of legalized segregation and disenfranchisement of African Americans and also served as a model for other groups mobilizing to demand dignity and rights. And like all important events in history, it has produced scholarship that examines the movement in a number of different ways.

The early histories of the civil rights movement remain widely accepted. They rest on a heroic narrative of moral purpose and personal courage by which great men and women inspired ordinary people to rise up and struggle for their rights. This narrative generally begins with the *Brown* decision of 1954 and the Montgomery bus boycott of 1955, continues through the civil rights campaigns of the early 1960s, and culminates in the Civil Rights Acts of 1964 and 1965. Among the central events in this narrative are the March on Washington of 1963, with Martin Luther King Jr.'s famous "I have a dream" speech, and the assassination of King in 1968, which has often symbolized the end of the movement and the beginning of a different, more complicated period of the black freedom struggle. The key element of these narratives is the central importance to the movement of a few great leaders, most notably King himself. Among the best examples of this narrative are Taylor Branch's powerful studies of the life and struggles of King, *Parting the Waters* (1988), *Pillar of Fire* (1998), and *At Canaan's Edge* (2006), as well as David Garrow's important study, *Bearing the Cross* (1986).

Few historians would deny the importance of King and other leaders to the successes of the civil rights movement. But a number of scholars have argued that the leader-centered narrative obscures the vital contributions of ordinary people in communities throughout

the South, and the nation, to the struggle. John Dittmer's *Local People: The Struggle for Civil-Rights in Mississippi* (1994) and Charles Payne's *I've Got the Light of Freedom* (1995) both examine the day-to-day work of the movement's rank and file in the early 1960s and argue that their efforts were at least as important as those of King and other leaders. The national leadership helped bring visibility to these struggles, but King and his circle were usually present only briefly, if at all, for the actual work of communities in challenging segregation. Only by understanding the local origins of the movement, these and other scholars argue, can we understand its true character.

Scholars also disagree about the time frame of the movement. Rather than beginning the story in 1954 or 1955 (as in Robert Weisbrot's excellent 1991 synthesis *Freedom Bound* or in William Chafe's remarkable 1981 local study *Civilities and Civil Rights,* which examined the Greensboro sit-ins of 1961), a number of scholars have tried to move the story into both earlier periods and later ones. Robin Kelly's *Race Rebels* (1994) emphasizes the important contributions of working-class African Americans, some of them allied for a time with the Communist Party, to the undermining of racist assumptions starting in the 1930s. These activists organized some of the earliest civil rights demonstrations—sit-ins, marches, and other efforts to challenge segregation—well before the conventional dates for the beginning of the movement. Gail O'Brien's *The Color of the Law* (1999) examines a 1946 "race riot" in Columbia, Tennessee, arguing for its importance as a signal of the early growth of African American militancy and the movement of that militancy from the streets into the legal system.

Other scholars have looked beyond the 1960s and have incorporated events outside

BROWN V. BOARD OF EDUCATION This photograph, taken for an Atlanta newspaper, illustrated the long and dangerous walk that Linda Brown, one of the plaintiffs in the famous desegregation case that ultimately reached the Supreme Court, had to travel each day on her way to a segregated school in Topeka, Kansas. An all-white school was located close to her home, but to reach the black school she had to attend required a long walk and a long bus ride each day. Not only does the picture illustrate the difficulties segregation created for Linda Brown, it was also a part of a broad publicity campaign launched by the supporters of the case. (Photo by Carl Iwasaki/Time & Life Pictures/Getty Images)

the orbit of the formal "movement" to explain the history of the civil rights struggle. A growing literature on northern, urban, and relatively radical activists has suggested that focusing too much on mainstream leaders and the celebrated efforts in the South in the 1960s diverts our view from the equally important challenges facing northern African Americans and the very different tactics and strategies that they often chose to pursue their goals. The enormous attention historians have given to the life and legacy of Malcolm X—among them Alex Haley's influential *Autobiography of Malcolm X* (1965), Michael Eric Dyson's *Making Malcolm* (1996), and Marable Manning's important biography, *Malcolm X: A Life of Reinvention* (2012)—is an example of this, as is the increasing attention scholars have given to black radicalism in the late 1960s and beyond and to such militant groups as the Black Panthers. Other literature has extended the civil rights struggle even further, into the 1980s and beyond, and has brought into focus such issues as the highly disproportionate number of African Americans sentenced to death within the

criminal justice system. Randall Kennedy's *Race, Crime, and the Law* (1997) is a particularly important study of this issue.

Even *Brown v. Board of Education* (1954), the great landmark of the legal challenge to segregation, has been subject to reexamination. Richard Kluger's narrative history of the *Brown* decision, *Simple Justice* (1975), is a classic statement of the traditional view of *Brown* as a triumph over injustice. But others have been less certain of the dramatic success of the ruling. James T. Patterson's *Brown v. Board of Education: A Civil Rights Milestone and Its Troubled Legacy* (2001) argues that the *Brown* decision long preceded any national consensus on the need to end segregation and that its impact was far less decisive than earlier scholars have suggested. Michael Klarman's *From Jim Crow to Civil Rights* (2004) examines the role of the Supreme Court in advancing civil rights and suggests, among other things, that the *Brown* decision may actually have retarded racial progress in the South for a time because of the enormous backlash it created. Charles Ogletree's *All Deliberate Speed* (2004) and Derrick Bell's *Silent Covenants* (2004) both argue that the Court's decision did not provide an effective enforcement mechanism for desegregation and in many other ways failed to support measures that would have made school desegregation a reality. Stephen Tuck's *We Ain't What We Ought to Be: The Black Freedom Struggle from Emancipation to Obama* (2011) concludes his broad narrative of the road to racial equality by focusing on the continued activism of African Americans into the present.

As the literature on the African American freedom struggles of the twentieth century has grown, historians have begun to speak of civil rights *movements,* rather than a single, cohesive movement. •

UNDERSTAND, ANALYZE, & EVALUATE

1. If historians now speak of plural civil rights *movements,* what are these movements?
2. Why are the contributions of local grassroots workers so often overlooked, in studies of the civil rights movement as well as in accounts of other great events in American history?

in "public accommodations" (stores, restaurants, theaters, hotels), barring discrimination in employment, and increasing the power of the government to file suits on behalf of school integration.

To generate support for the legislation, and to dramatize the power of the growing movement, more than 200,000 demonstrators marched down the Mall in Washington, D.C., in August 1963 and gathered before the Lincoln Memorial for the largest civil rights demonstration in the nation's history to that point. Martin Luther King Jr., in one of the greatest speeches of his distinguished oratorical career, aroused the crowd with a litany of resonant American images prefaced again and again by the phrase "I have a dream."

The assassination of President Kennedy three months later gave new impetus to civil rights legislation. The ambitious measure that Kennedy had proposed in June 1963 was stalled in the Senate after having passed through the House of Representatives with relative ease. Early in 1964, after Lyndon Johnson had applied both public and private pressure, supporters of the measure finally mustered the two-thirds majority necessary to end a filibuster by southern senators; and the Senate passed the most important civil rights bill of the twentieth century.

THE BATTLE FOR VOTING RIGHTS

Having won a significant victory in one area, the civil rights movement shifted its focus to another: voting rights. During the summer of 1964, thousands of civil rights workers, black and white, northern and southern, spread throughout the South, but primarily into Mississippi, to work on behalf of black voter registration and participation. The campaign was known as "Freedom Summer," and it produced a violent response from some southern whites. Three of the first freedom workers to arrive in the South—two whites, Andrew Goodman and Michael Schwerner, and one African American, James Chaney—were murdered. Local law enforcement officials were involved in the crime.

The Freedom Summer also produced the Mississippi Freedom Democratic Party (MFDP), an integrated alternative to the regular state party organization. Under the leadership of Fannie Lou Hamer and others, the MFDP challenged the regular party's right to its seats at the Democratic National Convention that summer. President Johnson, with King's help, managed to broker a compromise by which members of the MFDP could be seated as observers, with promises of party reforms later on, while the regular party retained its official standing. Many MFDP members rejected the agreement and left the convention embittered.

A year later, in March 1965, King helped organize a major demonstration in Selma, Alabama, to press for the right of blacks to register to vote. Selma sheriff Jim Clark led local police in a brutal attack on the demonstrators, which was televised nationally. Two northern whites participating in the Selma march were murdered in the course of the effort there. The widespread national outrage that followed the events in Alabama helped push Lyndon Johnson to win passage of the Voting Rights Act of 1965, which provided federal protection to African Americans attempting to exercise their right to vote. But important as such gains were, they failed to satisfy the rapidly rising expectations of civil rights activists as the focus of the movement began to move from political to economic issues.

THE CHANGING MOVEMENT

By 1966, of African Americans 69 percent lived in metropolitan areas and 45 percent lived outside the South. Although the economic condition of most Americans was improving, in many poor urban black communities things were getting significantly worse. More than half of all nonwhite Americans lived in poverty at the beginning of the 1960s.

The great publicity of the southern movement intensified antidiscrimination efforts in northern cities. Those cities had no Jim Crow laws but much segregation. Many African American leaders (and their white supporters), having struggled in relative obscurity in the 1940s and 1950s, began to move the battle against job discrimination to a new level. They argued that the only way for employers to prove they were not discriminating against African Americans was to demonstrate that they were hiring minorities. If necessary, they should adopt positive measures to recruit minorities. Lyndon Johnson gave his support to the concept of "affirmative action" in 1965. Over the next decade, affirmative action guidelines gradually extended to virtually all institutions doing business with or receiving funds from the federal government (including schools and universities)—and to many others as well.

A symbol of the movement's new direction, and of the problems it would cause, was a major campaign in the summer of 1966 in Chicago, in which King played a prominent role. Organizers of the Chicago campaign hoped to direct national attention to housing and employment discrimination in northern industrial cities. But the Chicago campaign evoked vicious and at times violent opposition from white residents and failed to attract wide attention or support in the way events in the South had done.

URBAN VIOLENCE

Well before the Chicago campaign, the problem of urban poverty had thrust itself into national prominence when riots broke out in African American neighborhoods in major cities. There were disturbances in the summer of 1964, most notably in New York City's Harlem. The most serious race riot since the end of World War II occurred the following summer in the Watts section of Los Angeles. In the midst of a traffic arrest, a white police officer struck a protesting black bystander with his club. The incident triggered a storm of anger and a week of violence. Thirty-four people died during the uprising, which was eventually quelled by the National Guard. In the summer of 1966, forty-three additional outbreaks occurred, the most serious in Chicago and Cleveland. And in the summer of 1967, eight major disorders took place, including the largest of them all—a racial clash in Detroit in which forty-three people died.

Televised images of the violence alarmed millions of Americans and created both a new sense of urgency and a growing sense of doubt among some whites who had embraced the cause of racial justice only a few years before. A special Commission on Civil Disorders, ordered by the president in response to the riots, issued a celebrated report in the spring of 1968 recommending massive spending to eliminate the abysmal conditions of the ghettoes. To many white Americans, however, the riots exposed the need for stern measures to stop violence and lawlessness.

BLACK POWER

Disillusioned with the ideal of peaceful change through cooperation with whites, an increasing number of African Americans turned to a new approach to the racial issue: the philosophy of "black power." Black power meant many different things. But in all its forms, it suggested a shift away from the goals of assimilation and toward increased awareness of racial distinctiveness.

Perhaps the most enduring impact of the black-power ideology was a social and psychological one: instilling racial pride in African Americans. But black power took political forms as well, and it created a deep schism within the civil rights movement. Traditional black organizations that emphasized cooperation with sympathetic whites—groups such as the NAACP, the Urban League, and King's Southern Christian Leadership Conference—now faced competition from more radical groups. The Student Nonviolent Coordinating Committee and the Congress of Racial Equality had both begun as relatively moderate interracial organizations. By the mid-1960s, however, these and other groups were calling for more radical and occasionally even violent action against white racism and were openly rejecting the approaches of older, more established black leaders.

The most radical expressions of the black-power idea came from such revolutionary organizations as the Black Panthers, based in Oakland, California, and the separatist group the Nation of Islam, which denounced whites as "devils" and appealed to African Americans to embrace the Islamic faith and work for complete racial separation. The most celebrated of the Black Muslims, as whites often termed them, was Malcolm Little, who adopted the name Malcolm X ("X" to denote his lost African surname). He died in 1965 when gunmen, presumably under orders from rivals within the Nation of Islam, assassinated him. But he remained a major figure in many African American communities long after his death—almost as important to and revered by African Americans as Martin Luther King Jr.

"FLEXIBLE RESPONSE" AND THE COLD WAR

In international affairs as much as in domestic reform, the optimistic liberalism of the Kennedy and Johnson administrations dictated a more active and aggressive approach to dealing with the nation's problems than that of the 1950s.

DIVERSIFYING FOREIGN POLICY

The Kennedy administration entered office convinced that the United States needed to be able to counter communist aggression in more flexible ways than the atomic-weapons-oriented defense strategy of the Eisenhower years. In particular, Kennedy was unsatisfied with the nation's ability to meet communist threats in "emerging areas" of the Third World—the areas in which, Kennedy believed, the real struggle against communism would be waged in the future. He gave enthusiastic support to the expansion of the Special Forces (or "Green Berets," as they were soon known)—soldiers trained specifically to fight guerrilla conflicts and other limited wars.

Kennedy also favored expanding American influence through peaceful means. To repair the badly deteriorating relationship with Latin America, he proposed an "Alliance for Progress"—a series of projects for peaceful development and stabilization of the nations of that region. Kennedy also inaugurated the Agency for International Development (AID) to coordinate foreign aid. And he established what became one of his most popular innovations: the Peace Corps, which sent young American volunteers abroad to work in developing areas.

Among the first foreign policy ventures of the Kennedy administration was a disastrous assault on the Castro government in Cuba. The Eisenhower administration had started the project; and by the time Kennedy took office, the CIA had been working for months to train a small army of anti-Castro Cuban exiles. On April 17, 1961, with the approval of the new president, 2,000 of the armed exiles landed at the Bay of Pigs in Cuba, expecting first American air support and then a spontaneous uprising by the Cuban people on their behalf. They received neither. At the last minute, as it became clear that things were going badly, Kennedy withdrew the air support, fearful of involving the United States too directly in the invasion. Nor did the expected uprising occur. Instead, well-armed Castro forces easily crushed the invaders, and within two days the entire mission had collapsed.

CONFRONTATIONS WITH THE SOVIET UNION

In the grim aftermath of the Bay of Pigs, Kennedy traveled to Vienna in June 1961 for his first meeting with Soviet Premier Nikita Khrushchev. Their frosty exchange of views did little to reduce tensions between the two nations—nor did Khrushchev's veiled threat of war unless the United States ceased to support a noncommunist West Berlin in the heart of East Germany.

Khrushchev was particularly unhappy about the mass exodus of residents of East Germany to the West through the easily traversed border in the center of Berlin. But he ultimately found a method short of war to stop it. Before dawn on August 13, 1961, the East German government, complying with directives from Moscow, constructed a wall between East and West Berlin. Guards fired on those who continued to try to escape. For nearly thirty years, the Berlin Wall served as the most potent physical symbol of the conflict between the communist and noncommunist worlds.

The rising tensions culminated the following October in the most dangerous and dramatic crisis of the Cold War. During the summer of 1962, American intelligence agencies became aware of the arrival of a new wave of Soviet technicians and equipment in Cuba and of military construction in progress. On October 14, aerial reconnaissance photos produced clear evidence that the Soviets were constructing sites on the island for offensive nuclear weapons. To the Soviets, placing missiles in Cuba probably seemed a reasonable—and

THE UNITED STATES IN LATIN AMERICA, 1954–2006 The Cold War greatly increased the readiness of the United States to intervene in the affairs of its Latin American neighbors. This map presents the many times and ways in which Washington ordered interventions in Central America, the Caribbean, and the northern nations of South America. During much of this period, the interventions were driven by Cold War concerns—by fears that communists might take over nations near the United States as they had taken over Cuba in the early 1960s. • *What other interests motivated the United States to exert influence in Latin America even after the end of the Cold War?*

relatively inexpensive—way to counter the presence of American missiles in Turkey (and a way to deter any future American invasion of Cuba). But to Kennedy and most other Americans, the missile sites represented an act of aggression by the Soviets toward the United States. Almost immediately, the president—working with a special executive committee assembled to deal with the crisis—decided that the weapons could not be allowed to remain. On October 22, he ordered a naval and air blockade around Cuba, a "quarantine" against all offensive weapons. Preparations were under way for an American air attack on the missile sites when, late in the evening of October 26, Kennedy received a message from Khrushchev implying that the Soviet Union would remove the missile bases in exchange for an American pledge not to invade Cuba. Ignoring other, tougher Soviet messages, the president agreed. The crisis soon ended, paving the way for smoother American-Soviet relations and the Nuclear Test Ban Treaty of 1963, which banned atmospheric tests.

JOHNSON AND THE WORLD

Lyndon Johnson entered the presidency with little prior experience in international affairs. He was eager, therefore, not only to continue the policies of his predecessor but to prove quickly that he, too, was a strong and forceful leader.

An internal rebellion in the Dominican Republic gave him an opportunity to do so. A 1961 assassination had toppled the repressive dictatorship of General Rafael Trujillo, and for the next four years various factions in the country had struggled for dominance. In the spring of 1965, a conservative regime began to collapse in the face of a revolt by a broad range of groups on behalf of the left-wing nationalist Juan Bosch. Arguing (without any evidence) that Bosch planned to establish a pro-Castro communist regime, Johnson dispatched 30,000 American troops to quell the disorder. Only after a conservative candidate defeated Bosch in a 1966 election were the forces withdrawn.

From Johnson's first moments in office, however, his foreign policy was almost totally dominated by the bitter civil war in Vietnam and by the expanding involvement of the United States there.

THE AGONY OF VIETNAM

George Kennan, who helped devise the containment doctrine in the name of which America went to war in Vietnam, once called the conflict "the most disastrous of all America's undertakings over the whole 200 years of its history." Yet at first, the conflict in Vietnam seemed simply one more Third World struggle on the periphery of the Cold War.

AMERICA AND DIEM

Having thrown its support to the new leader of South Vietnam, Ngo Dinh Diem, in the aftermath of the 1954 Geneva accords, and having supported Diem in his refusal to hold the elections in 1956 that the accords had required, the United States found itself drawn steadily deeper into the unstable politics of this fractious new nation.

Although Diem was an aristocratic Catholic from central Vietnam and an outsider in the south, he was also a nationalist, uncontaminated by collaboration with the French.

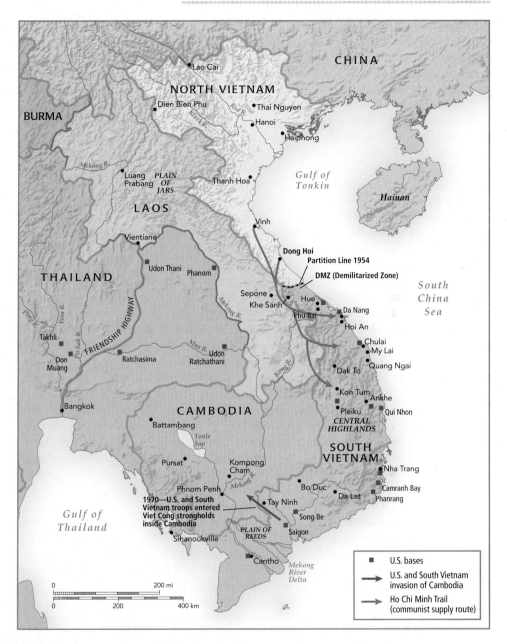

THE WAR IN VIETNAM AND INDOCHINA, 1964–1975 Much of the Vietnam War was fought in small engagements in widely scattered areas and did not conform to traditional notions of combat. But as this map shows, there were traditional battles and invasions and supply routes as well. The red arrows in the middle of the map show the general path of the Ho Chi Minh Trail, the main supply route by which North Vietnam supplied its troops and allies in the south. The blue arrow in southern South Vietnam indicates the point at which American troops invaded Cambodia in 1970. • *What is there in the geography of Indochina, as presented on this map, that helps to explain the great difficulty the American military had in securing South Vietnam against communist attacks?*

And he was, for a time, apparently successful. With the help of the American CIA, Diem waged an effective campaign against some of the powerful religious sects and the South Vietnamese mafia, which had challenged the authority of the central government. As a result, the United States came to regard Diem as a powerful and impressive alternative to Ho Chi Minh. America poured military and economic aid into South Vietnam.

Diem's early successes in suppressing sects led him in 1959 to begin a similar campaign to eliminate the supporters of Ho Chi Minh who had stayed behind in the south after the partition. That effort persuaded the Vietminh to resume the armed struggle for national unification. In 1959, the Vietminh cadres in the south created the National Liberation Front (NLF), known to many Americans as the Viet Cong—an organization closely allied with the North Vietnamese government. In 1960, under orders from Hanoi, and with both material and manpower support from North Vietnam, the NLF began military operations in the south. This marked the beginning of what Americans know as the Vietnam War.

By 1961, NLF forces had established effective control over many areas of the countryside. By then, Diem was also losing the support of many other groups in South Vietnam, including his own military. In 1963, the Diem regime precipitated a major crisis by trying to repress the South Vietnamese Buddhists in an effort to make Catholicism the dominant religion of the country. The Buddhists staged enormous antigovernment demonstrations, during which a monk doused himself with gasoline, sat cross-legged in downtown Saigon, and set himself on fire—in view of photographers and television cameras. Later, other Buddhists burned themselves in other areas.

Alarmed American officials pressured Diem to reform his now tottering government, but the president made no significant concessions. As a result, in the fall of 1963, Kennedy gave his approval to a plot by a group of South Vietnamese generals to topple Diem. In early November 1963, the generals staged the coup, assassinated Diem along with his brother Ngo Dinh Nhu (killings the United States had not wanted or expected), and established the first of a series of new governments, which were, for over three years, even less stable than the one they had overthrown. A few weeks after the coup, John Kennedy, too, was dead.

FROM AID TO INTERVENTION

Lyndon Johnson inherited what was already a substantial American commitment to the survival of an anticommunist South Vietnam. During his first months in office, he expanded the American involvement in Vietnam only slightly, sending an additional 5,000 military advisers there and preparing to send 5,000 more. Then, early in August 1964, the president announced that American destroyers on patrol in international waters in the Gulf of Tonkin had been attacked by North Vietnamese torpedo boats. Later information raised serious doubts as to whether the administration reported the attacks accurately. At the time, however, virtually no one questioned Johnson's portrayal of the incident as a serious act of aggression. By a vote of 416 to 0 in the House and 88 to 2 in the Senate, Congress hurriedly passed the Gulf of Tonkin Resolution, which authorized the president to "take all necessary measures" to protect American forces and "prevent further aggression" in Southeast Asia. The resolution became, in Johnson's view at least, an open-ended legal authorization for escalation of the conflict.

With the South Vietnamese leadership still in disarray and the communist military pressure growing stronger, more and more of the burden of opposition to the Viet Cong fell on the United States. In February 1965, after communist forces attacked an American military base at Pleiku, Johnson ordered American bombings of the north, in an attempt to destroy the depots and transportation lines responsible for the flow of North Vietnamese soldiers and supplies into South Vietnam. The bombing continued intermittently until 1972. A month later, in March 1965, two battalions of American marines landed at Da Nang in South Vietnam, bringing the total American troop strength to over 100,000.

Four months later, the president announced that American soldiers would now begin playing an active role in the conflict. By the end of the year, there were more than 180,000 American combat troops in Vietnam; in 1966, that number doubled; and by the end of 1967, over 500,000 American soldiers fought there. In the meantime, the air war intensified. By the spring of 1966, more than 4,000 Americans and an unknown number of Vietnamese had been killed.

The Quagmire

Central to the American war effort in Vietnam was a strategy known as "attrition," a strategy premised on the belief that the United States could inflict more damage on the enemy than the enemy could absorb. But the attrition strategy failed because the North Vietnamese, believing that they were fighting a war for national independence, were willing to commit many more soldiers and resources to the conflict than the United States had predicted.

The United States also failed in expecting its bombing of the north to eliminate the communists' war-making capacity. North Vietnam was not a modern industrial society, and it had relatively few of the sorts of targets against which bombing is effective. The North Vietnamese also responded to the bombing with great ingenuity. They created a network of underground tunnels, shops, and factories. The North Vietnamese also were provided substantial aid from the Soviet Union and China. They continually moved the Ho Chi Minh Trail to make it elusive to American bombers. Far from breaking the north's resolve, the bombing seemed actually to strengthen popular commitment to the war.

Another important part of the American strategy was the "pacification" program, whose purpose was to push the Viet Cong from particular regions and then "pacify" those regions by winning the "hearts and minds" of the people. Routing the Viet Cong was often possible, but the subsequent pacification was more difficult. Gradually, the pacification program gave way to a more heavy-handed relocation strategy, through which American troops uprooted villagers from their homes, sent them fleeing to refugee camps or into the cities (producing by 1967 more than 3 million refugees), and then destroyed the vacated villages and surrounding countryside. "It became necessary to destroy the village in order to save it," an American military official famously said of one such action, thus revealing the flawed assumptions of the pacification program.

As the war dragged on and victory remained elusive, some American officers and officials urged the president to expand the military efforts. But Johnson resisted—in part because he remembered the Korean War. He feared drawing China into the Vietnam War, and he was beginning to encounter obstacles and frustrations at home.

The War at Home

Few Americans, and even fewer influential ones, had protested the American involvement in Vietnam as late as the end of 1965. But as the war dragged on inconclusively, political support for it began to erode.

By the end of 1967, American students opposed to the war (and to the military draft) had become a significant political force. Enormous peace marches in New York, Washington, D.C., and other cities drew broad public attention to the antiwar movement. In the meantime, a growing number of journalists, particularly reporters who had spent

THE VIETNAM COMMITMENT

THE debate over why the United States became involved in the conflict in Vietnam (which is only one of many debates about the meaning of the war) has centered on two different, if related, questions. One is an effort to assess the broad objectives Americans believed they were pursuing in Vietnam. The other is an effort to explain how and why policymakers made the specific decisions that led the United States to a military commitment in Indochina.

Scholars and writers such as Norman Podhoretz, Guenter Lewy, and R. B. Smith, echoing elements of the "domino theory,"— the official government explanation of American intervention in the war in the 1960s—have argued that the communist aggression in Vietnam was part of a Chinese and Soviet design to spread revolution throughout Asia. America, therefore, was not only protecting Vietnam, although that was an important part of its mission; it was also defending the rest of Asia, which would soon be threatened by communism if Vietnam fell. The intervention in Vietnam was a rational and necessary expression of America's legitimate security interests and its belief in democracy.

Other scholars have been more skeptical. Historians on the left argue that America's intervention in Vietnam was a form of imperialism—part of a larger effort by the United States after World War II to impose a particular political and economic order on the world. "The Vietnam War," Gabriel Kolko wrote in 1985, "was for the United States the culmination of its frustrating postwar effort to merge its arms and politics to halt and reverse the emergence of states and social systems opposed to the international order Washington sought to establish." Others argued that the United States fought in Vietnam to serve the American economic interests that had a stake in the region or in the arms production the war stimulated. More moderate critics blame the Vietnam intervention on the myopia of a foreign policy elite unwilling to question its own unreflective commitment to containing communism everywhere and unable to distinguish between international aggression and domestic insurgency.

Those who have looked less at the nation's broad objectives than at the workings of the policymaking process have also produced competing explanations. David Halberstam's *The Best and the Brightest* (1972) argued that

> policymakers deluded themselves into thinking they could achieve their goals in Vietnam by ignoring, suppressing, or dismissing information that should have suggested that they

time in Vietnam, helped sustain the movement with their frank revelations about the brutality and apparent futility of the war.

Senator J. William Fulbright of Arkansas, chairman of the Senate Foreign Relations Committee, also turned against the war and in January 1966 began to stage highly publicized and occasionally televised congressional hearings to air criticisms of it. Other members of Congress joined Fulbright in opposing Johnson's policies—including, in 1967, committed troops to the war anyway because he feared that allowing Vietnam to fall would ruin him politically and destroy his hopes for building his Great Society at home. Leslie Gelb and Richard Betts made a related argument in 1979. Vietnam, they claimed, was the logical, perhaps inevitable, result of a political and bureaucratic order shaped by the ideology of the Cold War. However costly the intervention in Vietnam, policymakers concluded, the costs of allowing South Vietnam to fall always seemed higher. The war escalated in the 1960s not because American aims changed but because the situation in Vietnam deteriorated to the point where nothing short of intervention would prevent defeat. Only when the national and international political situation itself shifted in the late 1960s and early 1970s—only when it became clear that the political costs of staying in Vietnam were higher than the political costs of getting out—was it possible for the United States to begin disengaging. •

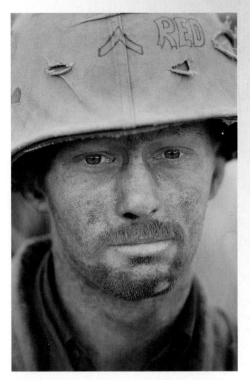

KHE SANH, VIETNAM, 1968 A beleaguered American soldier shows his exhaustion during the seventy-six-day siege of the American marine base at Khe Sanh, which began shortly before the 1968 Tet offensive in Vietnam. American forces sustained record casualties in the fierce fighting at Khe Sanh; the Vietnamese communist forces suffered far more. (Robert Ellison/Black Star/Stock Photo)

were wrong; because of arrogance or ideological rigidity, they simply refused to consider that victory was beyond their grasp.

Larry Berman, writing in 1982, offered a somewhat different view. Neither Johnson nor his advisers were unaware of the obstacles to success in Vietnam, almost everyone suspected that victory would be difficult, even impossible, to attain. The president was not misled or misinformed. But Johnson

UNDERSTAND, ANALYZE, & EVALUATE

1. What was the official government explanation for U.S. involvement in Vietnam?

2. Some scholars offer explanations that differ significantly from the government view. According to these scholars, why was the United States fighting in Vietnam?

3. What are the "lessons of Vietnam"? How have U.S. foreign affairs since Vietnam observed—or ignored—these lessons?

Robert F. Kennedy, brother of the slain president, now a senator from New York. Even within the administration, the consensus seemed to be crumbling. Robert McNamara, who had done much to help extend the American involvement in Vietnam, quietly left the government, disillusioned, in 1968. His successor as secretary of defense, Clark Clifford, became a quiet but powerful voice within the administration on behalf of a cautious scaling down of the commitment.

In the meantime, Johnson's commitment to fighting the war while continuing his Great Society reforms helped cause a rise in inflation, from the 2 percent level it had occupied through most of the early 1960s to 3 percent in 1967, 4 percent in 1968, and 6 percent in 1969. In August 1967, Johnson asked Congress for a tax increase to avoid even more ruinous inflation. In return, congressional conservatives demanded and received a $6 billion reduction in the funding for Great Society programs.

THE TRAUMAS OF 1968

By the end of 1967, the twin crises of the war in Vietnam and the deteriorating racial situation at home had produced great social and political tensions. In the course of 1968, those tensions burst to the surface and seemed to threaten national chaos.

THE TET OFFENSIVE

On January 31, 1968, the first day of the Vietnamese New Year (Tet), communist forces launched an enormous, concerted attack on American strongholds throughout South Vietnam. A few cities, most notably Hue, fell temporarily to the communists. But what made the Tet offensive so shocking to the American people, who saw vivid reports of it on television, was the sight of communist forces in the heart of Saigon, setting off bombs, shooting down South Vietnamese officials and troops, and holding down fortified areas (including, briefly, the American embassy). The Tet offensive also suggested to the American public something of the brutality of the fighting in Vietnam. In the midst of the fighting, television cameras recorded the sight of a South Vietnamese officer shooting a captured and defenseless young Viet Cong soldier in the head in the streets of Saigon.

American forces soon dislodged the Viet Cong from most of the positions they had seized. The Tet offensive inflicted enormous casualties on the communists and permanently depleted the ranks of the NLF, forcing North Vietnamese troops to take on a much larger share of the subsequent fighting. But after years of repeated assurances that the war was going well, all that had little impact on American opinion. Tet may have been a military victory for the United States, but it was a political defeat for the administration.

In the following weeks, opposition to the war grew substantially. Leading newspapers and magazines, television commentators, and mainstream politicians began taking public stands against the conflict. Public opposition to the war almost doubled. And Johnson's personal popularity rating had slid to 35 percent, the lowest of any president since Harry Truman.

THE POLITICAL CHALLENGE

Beginning in the summer of 1967, dissident Democrats tried to mobilize support behind an antiwar candidate who would challenge Lyndon Johnson in the 1968 primaries. When Robert Kennedy turned them down, they recruited Senator Eugene McCarthy of Minnesota. A brilliantly orchestrated campaign by young volunteers in the New Hampshire primary produced a startling showing by McCarthy in March; he nearly defeated the president.

A few days later, Robert Kennedy entered the campaign, embittering many McCarthy supporters but bringing his own substantial strength among minorities, poor people, and workers to the antiwar cause. Polls showed the president trailing badly in the next scheduled primary, in Wisconsin. On March 31, 1968, Johnson went on television to announce a limited halt in the bombing of North Vietnam—his first major concession to the antiwar forces—and, much more surprising, his withdrawal from the presidential contest.

Robert Kennedy quickly established himself as the champion of the Democratic primaries, winning one election after another. In the meantime, however, Vice President Hubert Humphrey, with the support of President Johnson, entered the contest and began to attract the support of party leaders and of the many delegations that were selected not by popular primaries but by state party organizations. He soon appeared to be the front-runner in the race.

Assassinations and Politics

On April 4, Martin Luther King Jr., who had traveled to Memphis, Tennessee, to lend his support to striking black sanitation workers in the city, was shot and killed while standing on the balcony of his motel. The assassin, James Earl Ray, who was captured two months later in London, had no apparent motive. Subsequent evidence suggested that he had been hired by others to do the killing, but he himself never revealed the identity of his employers.

King's tragic death produced a great outpouring of grief. Among African Americans, it also produced anger. In the days after the assassination, major riots broke out in more than sixty American cities. Forty-three people died.

Late in the night of June 6, Robert Kennedy appeared in the ballroom of a Los Angeles hotel to acknowledge his victory in that day's California primary. As he left the ballroom after his victory statement, Sirhan Sirhan, a young Palestinian apparently enraged by pro-Israeli remarks Kennedy had recently made, emerged from a crowd and shot him in the head. Early the next morning, Kennedy died. The shock of this second tragedy in two months—and only five years after the assassination of John Kennedy—cast a pall over the remainder of the presidential campaign.

When the Democrats finally gathered in Chicago in August, for a convention in which Hubert Humphrey was now the only real contender, even the most optimistic observers predicted turbulence. Inside the hall, delegates bitterly debated an antiwar plank in the party platform that both Kennedy and McCarthy supporters favored. Miles away, in a downtown park, thousands of antiwar protesters staged demonstrations. On the third night of the convention, as the delegates began their balloting on the now virtually inevitable nomination of Hubert Humphrey, demonstrators and police clashed in a bloody riot in the streets of Chicago. Hundreds of protesters were injured as police attempted to disperse them with tear gas and billy clubs. Aware that the violence was being televised to the nation, the demonstrators taunted the authorities with the chant, "The whole world is watching!" And Hubert Humphrey, who had spent years dreaming of becoming his party's candidate for president, received a nomination that night which appeared at the time to be almost worthless.

The Conservative Response

The turbulent events of 1968 persuaded some observers that American society was in the throes of revolutionary change. In fact, however, the response of most Americans to the turmoil was a conservative one.

The most visible sign of the conservative backlash was the surprising success of the campaign of George Wallace for the presidency. Wallace had been one of the leading

1968

THE year 1968 was one of the most turbulent in the postwar history of the United States. Much of what made it so traumatic were specifically American events—the growing controversy over the war in Vietnam, the assassinations of Martin Luther King Jr. and Robert Kennedy, racial unrest across the nation's cities, student protests on campuses throughout America. But the turmoil of 1968 was not confined to the United States. There were tremendous upheavals in many parts of the globe that year.

The most common form of turbulence around the world in 1968 was student unrest. In France, a student uprising in May far exceeded in size and ferocity anything that occurred in the United States. It attracted the support of French workers and briefly paralyzed Paris and other cities. It contributed to the downfall of the government of Charles de Gaulle a year later. In England, Ireland, Germany, Italy, the Netherlands, Mexico, Canada, Japan, and South Korea, students and other young people demonstrated in great numbers, and at times with violence, against governments,

universities, and other structures of authority. Elsewhere, there was more widespread protest, as in Czechoslovakia, where hundreds of thousands of citizens took to the streets in support of what became known as "Prague Spring." It caused a demand for greater democracy and a repudiation of many of the oppressive rules and structures imposed on the nation by its Soviet-dominated communist regimes. Russian tanks rolled into the city to crush the uprising.

Many people have tried to explain why so much instability emerged in so many nations at the same time. One factor that contributed to the worldwide turbulence of 1968 was simple numbers. The postwar baby boom had created a very large age cohort in many nations, and by the late 1960s it was coming of age. In the industrial West, the sheer size of the new generation produced a tripling of the number of people attending colleges and universities. In fewer than twenty years it also created a heightened sense of the power of youth. The long period of postwar prosperity and relative peace in which this generation had grown

spokesmen for the defense of segregation when, as governor of Alabama, he had attempted to block the admission of black students to the University of Alabama in 1963. In 1968, he became a third-party candidate for president, basing his campaign on a host of conservative grievances. He denounced the forced busing of students, the proliferation of government regulations and social programs, and the permissiveness of authorities toward crime, race riots, and antiwar demonstrations. There was never any serious chance that Wallace would win the election, but his standing in the polls rose at times to over 20 percent.

A more effective effort to mobilize the conservative middle in favor of order and stability was under way within the Republican Party. Richard Nixon, whose political career had seemed at an end after his losses in the presidential race of 1960 and a California gubernatorial campaign two years later, reemerged as the spokesman for what up contributed to heightened expectations of what the world should offer them—and a greater level of impatience than previous generations had demonstrated with the obstacles that stood in the way of their hopes. A new global youth culture emerged that was in many ways at odds with the dominant culture of older generations. It valued nonconformity, personal freedom, and even rebellion.

A second force contributing to the widespread turbulence of 1968 was the power of global media. Satellite communication introduced in the early 1960s made it possible to transmit live news across the world. Videotape technology and the creation of lightweight portable television cameras enabled media organizations to respond to events much more quickly and flexibly than in the past. The audience for these televised images was by now global and enormous, particularly in industrial nations but even in the poorest areas of the world. Protests in one country were suddenly capable of inspiring protests in others. Demonstrators in Paris, for example, spoke openly of how campus protests in the United States in 1968—for example, the student uprising at Columbia University in New York the previous month—had helped motivate French students to rise up as well. Just as American students were protesting against what they considered antiquated, paternalistic features of their universities, French students demanded an end to the rigid, autocratic character of their own academic world.

In most parts of the world, the 1968 uprisings came and went without fundamentally altering institutions and systems. But many changes came in the wake of these protests. Universities around the globe undertook significant reforms. Religious observance in mainstream churches and synagogues in the West declined dramatically after 1968. New concepts of personal freedom gained legitimacy, helping to inspire social movements in the years that followed—among them the dramatic growth of feminism in many parts of the world and the emergence of the gay and lesbian rights movement. The events of 1968 did not produce a revolution in the United States or in most of the rest of the world, but it did help launch a period of dramatic social, cultural, and political changes that affected the peoples of many nations. •

UNDERSTAND, ANALYZE, & EVALUATE

1. What factors combined to produce the turbulence that resulted in the uprisings of 1968?
2. Did the demonstrators of 1968 succeed or fail to achieve their objectives? What were the long-term effects of the 1968 uprisings?

he called the "silent majority." By offering a vision of stability, law and order, government retrenchment, and "peace with honor" in Vietnam, he easily captured the nomination of his party for the presidency. And despite a last-minute surge by Humphrey, Nixon hung on to eke out a victory almost as narrow as his defeat in 1960. He received 43.4 percent of the popular vote to Humphrey's 42.3 percent (a margin of only about 500,000 votes), and 301 electoral votes to Humphrey's 191. George Wallace, who like most third-party candidates faded in the last weeks of the campaign, still managed to poll 12.9 percent of the popular vote and to carry five southern states with a total of 46 electoral ballots. Nixon had hardly won a decisive personal mandate. But the election made clear that a majority of the American electorate was more interested in restoring stability than in promoting social change.

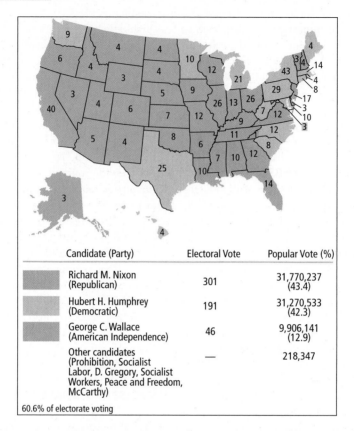

	Candidate (Party)	Electoral Vote	Popular Vote (%)
	Richard M. Nixon (Republican)	301	31,770,237 (43.4)
	Hubert H. Humphrey (Democratic)	191	31,270,533 (42.3)
	George C. Wallace (American Independence)	46	9,906,141 (12.9)
	Other candidates (Prohibition, Socialist Labor, D. Gregory, Socialist Workers, Peace and Freedom, McCarthy)	—	218,347

60.6% of electorate voting

THE ELECTION OF 1968 The 1968 presidential election, which Richard Nixon won, was almost as close as the election of 1960, which he lost. Nixon might have won a more substantial victory had it not been for the independent candidacy of Governor George C. Wallace, who attracted many of the same conservative voters to whom Nixon appealed. • *How does the distribution of Democratic and Republican strength in this election compare to that in 1960?*

CONCLUSION

Perhaps no decade of the twentieth century created more powerful and enduring images in America than the 1960s. It began with the election—and then the traumatic assassination—of an attractive and energetic young president, John Kennedy, who captured the imagination of millions and seemed to symbolize the rising idealism of the time. It produced a dramatic period of political innovation, led by President Lyndon Johnson, who greatly expanded the size and functions of the federal government and its responsibility for the welfare of the nation's citizens. He called it the Great Society. This time saw the emergence of a sustained and enormously powerful civil rights movement that won a series of important legal victories, including two major civil rights acts that dismantled the Jim Crow system constructed in the late nineteenth and early twentieth centuries.

The spirit of dynamism and optimism that made the early 1960s so productive also helped bring to the surface problems and grievances that had no easy solutions. The civil rights movement awakened expectations of social and economic equality that laws alone could not provide. The peaceful, interracial crusade of the early 1960s gradually turned into a much more militant, confrontational, and increasingly separatist movement toward the decade's end. The idealism among white youths that began the 1960s, and played an important role in the political success of John Kennedy, evolved into an angry rebellion against many aspects of American culture and politics and produced a large upsurge of student protest that rocked the nation at the decade's end. Perhaps most of all, a small and largely unnoticed Cold War commitment to defend South Vietnam against communist aggression from the north led to a large and disastrous war that destroyed the presidency of Lyndon Johnson, sent thousands of young men and women to their deaths, and showed no signs of producing a victory. A decade that began with high hopes and soaring ideals ended with division and deep disillusionment.

RECALL AND REFLECT

1. What were the political effects of John Kennedy's assassination?
2. How did increasing radicalism affect the successes and the setbacks of the civil rights movement?
3. What was the military strategy of the United States in Vietnam? What were the U.S. aims in that conflict? Why did the United States ultimately fail in Vietnam?
4. What accounted for growing opposition to the war in Vietnam?
5. What events made 1968 such a turbulent year both in the United States and elsewhere in the world? How did these events affect U.S. politics?

30 THE CRISIS OF AUTHORITY

THE YOUTH CULTURE
THE MOBILIZATION OF MINORITIES
THE NEW FEMINISM
ENVIRONMENTALISM IN A TURBULENT SOCIETY
NIXON, KISSINGER, AND THE VIETNAM WAR
NIXON, KISSINGER, AND THE WORLD
POLITICS AND ECONOMICS IN THE NIXON YEARS
THE WATERGATE CRISIS

LOOKING AHEAD

1. What were some of the characteristics of the social and cultural revolutions of the 1960s and 1970s?
2. How did the U.S. strategy in Vietnam change under Nixon? What was the result of the change in strategy?
3. What was the Watergate scandal and how did it affect the presidency?

THE ELECTION OF RICHARD NIXON in 1968 was the result of more than the unpopularity of Lyndon Johnson and the Vietnam War. It was the result, too, of a broad popular reaction against what many Americans considered an assault on the foundations of their society and culture. In Richard Nixon such Americans found a man who seemed to match their mood. A product of a hardworking, middle-class family, Nixon projected an image of stern dedication to traditional values. Yet the presidency of Richard Nixon, far from returning calm and stability to American politics, coincided with, and helped to produce, more years of crisis.

THE YOUTH CULTURE

Many conservatives in the 1960s and 1970s were alarmed by what they saw as a pattern of social and cultural anger by younger Americans. The protesters gave vent to two related impulses. One, emerging from the political left, was to create a great new community of "the people," which would rise up to break the power of elites and force the nation to end the war, pursue racial and economic justice, and transform its political life. The other, at least equally powerful impulse was the vision of personal "liberation." It found expression in part through the efforts of many groups—African Americans, Indians, Hispanics, women, gay people, and others—to define and assert themselves and make demands on the larger society. It also found expression through the efforts of individuals to create a new culture—one that would allow them to escape from what some considered the dehumanizing pressures of the modern "technocracy."

THE NEW LEFT

Among the products of the racial crisis and the war in Vietnam was a radicalization of many American students. In the course of the 1960s, they formed what became known as the New Left. In 1962, a group of students (most of them white and many of them from the University of Michigan) gathered in Michigan to form Students for a Democratic Society (SDS), which became the most prominent organization of the New Left. Their declaration of beliefs, the Port Huron Statement, expressed their disillusionment with the society they had inherited and their determination to build a new politics. In the following years, SDS became the leading organization of student radicalism.

Since most members of the New Left were students, much of their radicalism centered for a time on issues related to the

TIME LINE

1963
Friedan's *The Feminine Mystique*

1964
Free Speech Movement begins

1966
National Organization for Women formed

1968
Turmoil in universities

1969
Antiwar movement's Vietnam "moratoriums"

Rock concert in Woodstock, NY

1970
Cambodian incursion

1971
Nixon imposes wage-price controls

1972
Nixon visits China

SALT I

"Christmas bombing" of North Vietnam

Watergate burglary

Nixon reelected

1973
U.S. withdraws from Vietnam

Arab oil embargo

Agnew resigns

Supreme Court decides *Roe v. Wade*

1974
Nixon resigns; Ford becomes president

1975
South Vietnam falls

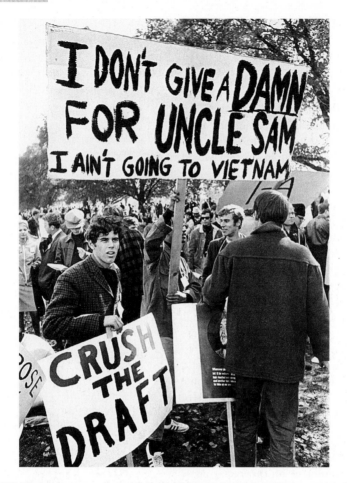

THE WAR AT HOME   Demonstrators gather on the Mall in Washington in the fall of 1967 for one of the first of the great antiwar demonstrations of the late 1960s. Over time, the antiwar movement helped erode the national consensus on the conflict in Vietnam. But the principal basis for opposing the war was never the moral or economic arguments of the left; it was simply the frustration among many Americans of seeing a war continuing too long and too inconclusively.   (Leif Skoogfors/Woodfin Camp & Associates)

modern university. A 1964 dispute at the University of California at Berkeley over the rights of students to engage in political activities on campus—the Free Speech Movement—was the first major outburst of what was to be nearly a decade of campus turmoil. The antiwar movement greatly inflamed and expanded the challenge to the universities; and beginning in 1968, campus demonstrations, riots, and building seizures became almost commonplace. At Columbia University in New York, students seized the offices of the president and others and occupied them for several days until local police forcibly ejected them. Over the next several years, hardly any major university was immune to some level of disruption. Small groups of especially dogmatic radicals—among them the "Weathermen," an offshoot of SDS—were responsible for a few cases of arson and bombing that destroyed campus buildings and claimed several lives.

Not many people accepted the radical political philosophy of the New Left. But many supported the position of SDS and other groups on particular issues, and above all on the

Vietnam War. Between 1967 and 1969, student activists organized some of the largest political demonstrations in American history to protest the war.

A related issue that helped fuel the antiwar movement was opposition to the military draft. The gradual abolition of many traditional deferments—for graduate students, teachers, husbands, fathers, and others—swelled the ranks of those faced with conscription (and thus likely to oppose it). Many draft-age Americans simply refused induction, accepting what were occasionally long terms in jail as a result. Thousands of others fled to Canada, Sweden, and elsewhere (where they were joined by deserters from the armed forces) to escape conscription.

THE COUNTERCULTURE

Closely related to the New Left was a new youth culture openly scornful of the values and conventions of middle-class society. The most visible characteristic of the counterculture, as it became known, was a change in personal styles. As if to display their contempt for conventional standards, young Americans flaunted long hair, shabby or flamboyant clothing, and a rebellious disdain for traditional speech and decorum. Also important to the counterculture was a new, more permissive view of sex and drugs.

Like the New Left, the counterculture challenged modern American society, attacking what it claimed were its banality, its hollowness, its artificiality, its isolation from nature. The most committed adherents of the counterculture—the hippies, who came to dominate the Haight-Ashbury neighborhood of San Francisco and other places, and the social dropouts, many of whom retreated to rural communes—rejected modern society altogether and attempted to find refuge in a simpler, more "natural" existence. But even those whose commitment to the counterculture was less intense shared the idea of personal fulfillment through rejecting the inhibitions and conventions of middle-class culture and giving fuller expression to personal instinct and desire.

The counterculture was only an exaggerated expression of impulses coursing through the larger society. Long hair and freakish clothing became the badge not only of hippies and radicals but of an entire generation. The widespread use of marijuana, the freer attitudes toward sex, the iconoclastic (and often obscene) language—all spread far beyond the true devotees of the counterculture.

One of the most powerful elements of the new youth society was rock music. Its growing influence in the 1960s was a result in part of the phenomenal popularity of the Beatles, the English group whose first visit to the United States in 1964 created a remarkable sensation. For a time, most rock musicians—like most popular musicians before them—concentrated largely on uncontroversial romantic themes. By the late 1960s, however, rock had begun to reflect many of the new iconoclastic values of its time. The Beatles, for example, abandoned their once simple and seemingly innocent style for a new, experimental, even mystical approach that reflected the growing popular fascination with drugs and Eastern religions. Other groups, such as the Rolling Stones, turned even more openly to themes of anger, frustration, and rebellion. Many popular musicians used their music to express explicit political radicalism as well—especially some of the leading folk singers of the era, such as Bob Dylan and Joan Baez. Rock's driving rhythms, its undisguised sensuality, its often harsh and angry tone—all made it an appropriate vehicle for expressing the themes of the social and political unrest of the late 1960s.

A powerful symbol of the fusion of rock music and the counterculture was the great music festival at Woodstock, New York, in the summer of 1969, where 400,000 people

CONSIDER THE SOURCE

DEMANDS OF THE NEW YORK HIGH SCHOOL STUDENT UNION, 1970

1—No suspensions, involuntary transfers, exclusion from classes, detention, harassment of students. Due process for students.

2—No cops in schools, no narcos, security guards, plain clothesmen, informers.

3—No program cards, hall checks, ID's, passes.

4—An end to commercial and general diplomas, one diploma for every student upon graduation.

5—Open admissions to colleges, a college education free for everyone who wants one.

6—Jobs and housing for every student who wants them on graduating, dropping out, or leaving home. The army is not a decent job.

7—No military recruiting in schools, no military assemblies, literature, no sending names to draft boards or recruiters. An immediate end to the draft.

8—Black and Latin departments controlled by Black and Latin students.

9—Community control of the schools and every other community facility. Students are part of the community.

10—POWER! Student control of curriculum, publications, assemblies, clubs, student government, dress, etc. The right to organize politically.

11—We support the fifteen points of the Black and Puerto Rican Citywide HS Council.

UNDERSTAND, ANALYZE, & EVALUATE

1. What might have inspired the students' demand for "due process"? And what other evidence of an anti-authoritarian sentiment can you detect here?

2. How did the civil rights and the black power movements shape this Student Union? One broad and significant rights movement of the late 1960s and early 1970s did not influence this student union at all. Can you determine which?

3. What role did the Vietnam War play for these students—what made this a possibly quite personal issue?

Source: *New York High School Free Press* (an underground newspaper), No. 8, reprinted in John Birmingham, *Our Time Is Now: Notes from the High School Underground* (New York: Praeger, 1970), p. 178.

---

gathered on a farm for nearly a week. Despite heavy rain, mud, inadequate facilities, and impossible crowding, the attendees remained peaceful and harmonious. Champions of the counterculture spoke rhapsodically at the time of how Woodstock represented the birth of a new youth culture, the "Woodstock nation." Four months later, however, another large rock concert—at the Altamont racetrack near San Francisco, featuring the Rolling Stones and attended by 300,000 people—exposed a darker side of the youth culture. Altamont became a brutal and violent event at which four people died, several accidentally or from drug overdoses but one because of injuries inflicted by members of a Hells Angels motorcycle gang, who were serving as security guards at the concert and who brutally beat and stabbed a number of people.

WOODSTOCK   The Woodstock Rock Festival near Bethel, New York in August 1969 attracted an enormous number of young people and a great many musicians. This was at the peak of the youth movement of the sixties, and Woodstock was in many ways its symbol. Here, many of the participants are covered with mud. (© Peter Menzel/HIP/The Image Works)

THE MOBILIZATION OF MINORITIES

The growth of African American protest encouraged other minorities to assert themselves and demand redress of their grievances. For Indians, Hispanic Americans, gay men and lesbians, and others, the late 1960s and 1970s were a time of growing self-expression and political activism.

SEEDS OF INDIAN MILITANCY

Few minorities had deeper or more justifiable grievances against the prevailing culture than did American Indians—or Native Americans, as they began defiantly to call themselves in the 1960s. Indians were the least prosperous, least healthy, and least stable ethnic group in the nation. And while African Americans attracted the attention (for good or for ill) of many whites, Indians for years had remained largely ignored.

For much of the postwar era, federal tribal policies tried to incorporate Indians into mainstream American society whether Indians wanted to assimilate or not. Two laws passed in 1953 established the basis of this policy, which became known as "termination."

Through termination, the federal government withdrew all official recognition of the tribes as legal entities; they were no longer administratively separate from state governments and were subject to the same local jurisdictions as non–Native American residents. At the same time, the government encouraged Indians to assimilate into the white world and worked to funnel Native Americans into cities, where, presumably, they would adapt themselves to the larger society and lose their cultural distinctiveness.

Despite some individual successes, the new policies were a disastrous failure on the whole. Indians themselves fought so bitterly against them that in 1958, the Eisenhower administration barred further terminations. In the meantime, the struggle against termination mobilized a new generation of Indian militants and breathed life into the principal Native American organization, the National Congress of American Indians, which had been created in 1944.

The Democratic administrations of the 1960s made no effort to revive termination. Instead, they made modest efforts to restore at least some degree of tribal autonomy such as funneling Office of Economic Opportunity money to tribal organizations through the Community Action program. In the meantime, the tribes themselves began to fight for self-determination. The new militancy benefited from the rapid increase in the Indian population, which was growing much faster than that of the rest of the nation (nearly doubling between 1950 and 1970 to a total of about 800,000).

THE INDIAN CIVIL RIGHTS MOVEMENT

In 1961, more than 400 members of 67 tribes gathered in Chicago and issued the Declaration of Indian Purpose, which stressed the "right to choose our own way of life" and the "responsibility of preserving our precious heritage." Another example of a growing Indian self-consciousness, the National Indian Youth Council, created in the aftermath of the 1961 Chicago meeting, promoted the idea of Indian nationalism and intertribal unity. In 1968, a group of young, militant Indians established the American Indian Movement (AIM), which drew support from urban areas and reservations alike.

The new activism produced results. In 1968, Congress passed the Indian Civil Rights Act. It guaranteed reservation Indians protections by the Bill of Rights, but also recognized the legitimacy of tribal laws within the reservations. In 1968, Indian fishermen, citing old treaty rights, clashed with Washington State officials on the Columbia River and in Puget Sound. The following year, members of several tribes occupied the abandoned federal prison on Alcatraz Island in San Francisco Bay, claiming the site "by right of discovery."

In response, the Nixon administration appointed Louis Bruce, a Mohawk-Sioux, as commissioner of Indian affairs in 1969; and in 1970, the president promised both increased tribal self-determination and an increase in federal aid. But the protests continued. In November 1972, nearly a thousand demonstrators, most of them Lakota Sioux, forcibly occupied the building of the Bureau of Indian Affairs in Washington, D.C., for six days. In February 1973, members of AIM seized the town of Wounded Knee, South Dakota, the site of the 1890 massacre of Sioux by federal troops. For two months, they occupied the town, demanding that the government honor its long-forgotten treaty obligations.

The Indian civil rights movement, like other civil rights movements of the same time, fell far short of winning full equality for Native Americans. But it helped the tribes win a series of new legal rights and protections that, together, gave them a stronger position than they had enjoyed at any previous time in the twentieth century.

LATINO ACTIVISM

The fastest-growing minority group in the United States in the 1970s was Latinos, or Hispanic Americans. Large numbers of Mexicans had entered the country during World War II in response to the wartime labor shortage, and many had remained in the cities of the Southwest and the Pacific Coast. By 1960, Los Angeles had a bigger Mexican population than any place except Mexico City.

But the greatest expansion in the Latino population of the United States was yet to come. In 1960, the census reported slightly more than 3 million Latinos living in the United States. By 1970, that number had grown to 9 million and by 2000 to 35 million. By 2010, the number passed 50 million. Hispanics constituted more than a third of all legal immigrants to the United States after 1960. There were also an uncounted but very large number of illegal Latino immigrants. Estimates in 2010 reached 12 million.

Large numbers of Puerto Ricans (who were entitled to American citizenship by birth) migrated to eastern urban areas, particularly New York City, where they formed one of the poorest communities in the city. South Florida's substantial Cuban population began with a wave of middle-class refugees fleeing the Castro regime in the early 1960s. These first Cuban migrants quickly established themselves as a successful and highly assimilated part of Miami's middle class. In 1980, a second, much poorer wave of Cuban immigrants—the so-called Marielitos, named for the port from which they left Cuba—arrived in Florida when Castro temporarily relaxed exit restrictions. Later in the 1980s, large numbers of immigrants (both legal and illegal) began to arrive from Central and South America—from Guatemala, Nicaragua, El Salvador, Peru, and other countries.

Like African Americans and Indians, many Latinos responded to the highly charged climate of the 1960s by strengthening their ethnic identification and by organizing for political and economic power. Affluent Hispanics in Miami filled influential positions in the professions and local government; in the Southwest, Latino voters elected Mexican Americans to seats in Congress and to governorships. A Mexican American political organization, La Raza Unida, exercised influence in southern California and elsewhere in the Southwest in the 1970s and beyond. One of the most visible efforts to organize Hispanics occurred in California, where an Arizona-born farmworker of Mexican descent, César Chávez, created an effective union of largely Mexican itinerant farmworkers: the United Farm Workers (UFW).

For most Latinos, however, the path to economic and political power was more difficult. Mexican Americans and others were slow to develop political influence in proportion to their numbers. In the meantime, Latinos formed one of the poorest segments of the United States population.

GAY LIBERATION

The last important liberation movement to emerge in the 1960s was the effort by gay men and lesbians to win political and economic rights and social acceptance. Homosexuality has been a generally unacknowledged reality throughout American history. Nonheterosexual men and women were forced for generations to suppress their sexual preferences, to exercise them surreptitiously, or to live within isolated and often persecuted communities. But by the late 1960s, the liberating impulses that had affected other groups helped mobilize gay men and lesbians to fight for their own rights.

On June 27, 1969, police officers raided the Stonewall Inn, a gay nightclub in New York City's Greenwich Village, and began arresting patrons simply for frequenting the place. The raid was not unusual, but the response was. Gay onlookers taunted the police and then attacked them. Someone started a blaze in the Stonewall Inn itself, almost trapping the policemen inside. Rioting continued throughout Greenwich Village (the center of New York's gay community) through much of the night.

The "Stonewall Riot" marked the growth of the gay liberation movement—one of the most controversial challenges to traditional values and assumptions of its time. New organizations—among them the Gay Liberation Front, founded in New York in 1969—sprang up around the country. Public discussion and media coverage of homosexuality, long subject to an unofficial taboo, quickly and dramatically increased. Gay activists had some success in challenging the long-standing assumption that homosexuality was aberrant behavior; many argued that no sexual preference was any more normal than another.

Most of all, however, the gay liberation movement transformed the outlook of many gay men and lesbians themselves. It helped them to "come out," to express their preferences openly and unapologetically, and to demand from society a recognition that gay relationships could be as significant and worthy of respect as heterosexual ones. By the early 1980s, the gay liberation movement had made remarkable strides. Even the ravages of the AIDS epidemic, which, in the beginning at least, affected the gay community more disastrously than any other group, failed to halt the growth of gay liberation. In many ways, it strengthened it.

By the early twenty-first century, gay men and lesbians had achieved many of the same milestones that other oppressed minorities had attained in earlier decades. Openly gay politicians won election to public office. Universities established gay and lesbian studies programs. Laws prohibiting discrimination on the basis of sexual preference made slow, halting progress at the state and local levels. But gay liberation produced a powerful backlash as well. President Bill Clinton's 1993 effort to end the ban on gay men and lesbians serving in the military met a storm of criticism from members of Congress and within the military itself. Conservative voters in some cities and states approved referendum questions on their ballots outlawing civil rights protections for gay men and lesbians, and, during a bitter debate over gay rights in the 2004 presidential campaign, voted state bans on gay marriage. And antigay violence continued periodically in communities around the country. At the same time, however, support for gay rights grew stronger in many parts of the country. In 2008 and 2009, the number of states legalizing gay marriage steadily increased. And in 2010, President Obama and the Congress repealed the "Don't Ask, Don't Tell" policy that forced people in the military to hide their homosexuality.

THE NEW FEMINISM

Women constitute over 50 percent of the United States population. But during the 1960s and 1970s, many women began to identify with minority groups as they renewed demands for a liberation of their own.

THE REBIRTH

The 1963 publication of Betty Friedan's *The Feminine Mystique* is often cited as one of the first events of contemporary women's liberation. A writer for women's magazines in the 1950s, Friedan traveled around the country interviewing women who had graduated with her from Smith College in 1947. Most of these women were living out the dream that

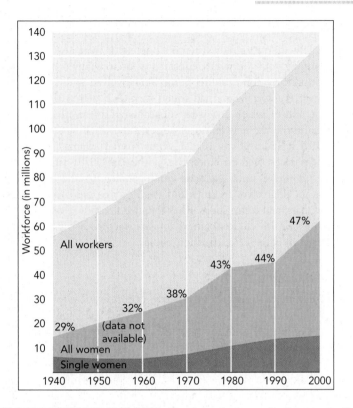

WOMEN IN THE PAID WORKFORCE, 1940-2000   The number of women working for wages steadily expanded from 1940 on, to the point that in 2000, they constituted just under half the total workforce. • *What role did this growing participation in the paid workforce have on the rise of feminism in the 1960s and beyond?*

postwar American society had created for them: they were affluent wives and mothers living in comfortable suburbs. And yet many of them were deeply frustrated and unhappy, with no outlets for their intelligence, talent, and education. Friedan's book did not so much cause the revival of feminism as help give voice to a movement that was already stirring.

By the time *The Feminine Mystique* appeared, President Kennedy had established the President's Commission on the Status of Women, which brought national attention to sexual discrimination. Also in 1963, the Kennedy administration helped win passage of the Equal Pay Act, which barred the pervasive practice of paying women less than men for the same work. A year later, Congress incorporated into the Civil Rights Act of 1964 an amendment—Title VII—that extended to women many of the same legal protections against discrimination that were being extended to African Americans and other minorities.

In 1966, Friedan joined with other feminists to create the National Organization for Women (NOW), which was to become the nation's largest and most influential feminist organization. NOW responded to the complaints of women by demanding greater educational opportunities for women and denouncing the domestic ideal and the traditional concept of marriage. But the heart of the movement was an effort to address the needs of women in the workplace.

WOMEN'S LIBERATION

By the late 1960s, new and more radical feminist demands were also attracting a large following, especially among younger, white, educated women. Many of them drew inspiration from the New Left and the counterculture. Some were involved in the civil rights movement; others, in the antiwar crusade. Many had found that even within those movements, they faced discrimination and exclusion and were subordinated to male leaders.

In its most radical form, the new feminism rejected the whole notion of marriage, family, and even heterosexual relationships (a vehicle, some women claimed, of male domination). Not many women embraced such extremes. But by the early 1970s, large numbers of women were coming to see themselves as an exploited group banding together against oppression and developing a culture of their own. In cities and towns across the country, feminists opened women's bookstores, bars, and coffee shops. They founded feminist newspapers and magazines. They created women's health clinics, centers to assist victims of rape and abuse, day-care centers, and, particularly after 1973, abortion clinics.

EXPANDING ACHIEVEMENTS

In 1971, the government extended its affirmative action guidelines to include women—linking sexism with racism as an officially acknowledged social problem. Women made rapid progress, in the meantime, in their efforts to move into the economic and political mainstream. The nation's all-male educational institutions began to open their doors to women. (Princeton and Yale did so in 1969, and many others soon did the same.) In 1972, Congress approved legislation (known as Title IX) requiring universities to support male and female athletic programs at equal levels.

Women were also becoming an important force in business and the professions. Nearly half of all married women held jobs by the mid-1970s, and almost 90 percent of all women with college degrees worked. The two-career family, in which both the husband and the wife maintained active professional lives, became a widely accepted middle-class norm. (It had been common within much of the working class for decades.) There were also important symbolic changes, such as the refusal of many women to adopt their husbands' surnames when they married and the use of the term "Ms." in place of "Mrs." or "Miss" to signal the irrelevance of a woman's marital status in the professional world.

By the mid-1980s, women were serving in both houses of Congress, on the Supreme Court, in numerous federal cabinet positions, as governors of several states, and in many other political positions. In 1981, Ronald Reagan named the first female Supreme Court justice, Sandra Day O'Connor; in 1993, Bill Clinton named the second, Ruth Bader Ginsburg. In 1984, the Democratic Party chose a woman, Representative Geraldine Ferraro of New York, as its vice presidential candidate. Madeleine Albright (under Clinton) and Condoleezza Rice (under George W. Bush) became the first women to serve as secretary of state. And in 2008, Hillary Clinton nearly became the Democratic candidate for president. She, too, became secretary of state in the Obama administration. In academia, women were expanding their presence in traditional scholarly fields; they were also creating new fields—women's and gender studies, which in the 1980s and 1990s were among the fastest-growing areas of American scholarship.

In 1972, Congress approved the Equal Rights Amendment (ERA) to the Constitution and sent it to the states. For a while, ratification seemed almost certain. By the late 1970s, however, the momentum behind the amendment had died because of a rising chorus of objections to it from people (including many antifeminist women) who feared that it would disrupt traditional social patterns. In 1982, the amendment finally died when the ten years allotted for ratification expired.

THE ABORTION ISSUE

A major goal of American feminism since the 1920s has been the effort by women to win greater control of their own sexual and reproductive lives. In its least controversial form, this impulse helped produce an increasing awareness beginning in the 1970s of the problems of rape, sexual abuse, and domestic abuse. The dissemination of contraceptives and birth-control information became more widespread and less controversial than it had been earlier in the century. A related issue, however, stimulated as much popular controversy as any question of its time: abortion.

Abortion had once been legal in much of the United States, but by the beginning of the twentieth century, it was banned by statute in most of the country and remained so into the 1960s (although many abortions continued to be performed quietly, and often dangerously, out of sight of the law). The women's movement created strong new pressures for the legalization of abortion. Several states had abandoned restrictions on abortion by the end of the 1960s. And in 1973, the Supreme Court's decision in *Roe v. Wade,* based on a new theory of a constitutional "right to privacy" first recognized by the Court only a few years earlier in *Griswold v. Connecticut,* invalidated all laws prohibiting abortion during the "first trimester"—the first three months of pregnancy. But even then, the issue remained far from settled.

ENVIRONMENTALISM IN A TURBULENT SOCIETY

Like feminism, environmentalism entered the 1960s with a long history and relatively little public support. Also like feminism, environmentalism profited from the turbulence of the era and emerged by the 1970s as a powerful force in American life. The rise of this new movement was in part a result of the environmental degradation in advanced industrial societies of the late twentieth century. It was a result, too, of the growth of ecology, a science that provided environmentalists with new and powerful arguments.

THE NEW SCIENCE OF ECOLOGY

Until the mid-twentieth century, most people who considered themselves environmentalists (or, to use the more traditional term, conservationists) based their commitment on aesthetic or moral grounds. They wanted to preserve nature because it was too beautiful to despoil, because it was a mark of divinity on the world, or because it permitted humans a spiritual experience that would otherwise be unavailable to them. In the course of the twentieth century, however, scientists in much of the world began to create a new rationale for environmentalism. They called it ecology.

Ecology is the science of the interrelatedness of the natural world. It addresses such problems as air and water pollution, the destruction of forests, the extinction of species, and toxic wastes, which are not separate, isolated problems. All elements of the earth's environment are intimately and delicately linked. Damaging any one of those elements, therefore, risks damaging all the others.

Among the early contributions to popular knowledge of ecology was the work of writer and naturalist Aldo Leopold. During a career in forest management, Leopold sought to apply the new scientific findings on ecology to his interactions with the natural world. And in 1949, he published a classic of environmental literature, *The Sand County Almanac*, in which he argued that humans had a responsibility to understand and maintain the balance of nature, that they should behave in the natural world according to a code that he called the "land ethic." By then, the science of ecology was spreading widely in the scientific community. Among the findings of ecologists were such now-common ideas as the "food chain," the "ecosystem," "biodiversity," and "endangered species." Rachel Carson's sensational 1962 book, *Silent Spring*, which revealed the dangers of pesticides, was based solidly on the ideas of ecologists and did at least as much as Leopold's work to introduce those ideas to a larger public.

ENVIRONMENTAL ADVOCACY

Among the major environmental organizations were the Wilderness Society, the Sierra Club, the National Audubon Society, the Nature Conservancy, the National Wildlife Federation, and the National Parks and Conservation Association. All of these organizations predated the rise of modern ecological science, but all of them entered the last decades of the twentieth century reenergized and committed to the new concepts of environmentalism. They found allies among such groups as the American Civil Liberties Union, the League of Women Voters, the National Council of Churches, and even the AFL-CIO.

Out of these organizations emerged a new generation of environmental activists able to contribute to the legal and political battles of the movement. Scientists provided the necessary data. Lawyers fought battles with government agencies and in the courts.

Many other forces contributed to what became the environmental movement. Lady Bird Johnson, the first lady, helped raise public awareness of the landscape with her energetic "beautification" campaign in the mid-1960s—a campaign unconnected to any ecological concepts, but one that reflected a growing popular dismay at the despoiling of the landscape by rapid economic growth. Members of the counterculture contributed to environmental awareness with their romanticization of the natural world and their repudiation of the "technocracy."

But perhaps the greatest force behind environmentalism was the condition of the environment itself. By the 1960s, the damage to the natural world from postwar population and economic growth was becoming hard to ignore. Water pollution—which had been a problem in some areas of the country for many decades—was becoming so widespread that almost every major city was dealing with the unpleasant sight and odor, as well as the health risks, of polluted rivers and lakes. In Cleveland, Ohio, for example, the Cuyahoga River actually burst into flame from time to time from the petroleum waste being dumped into it; the city declared the river an official fire hazard.

Perhaps more alarming was the growing awareness that the air itself was becoming unhealthy, that toxic fumes from factories, power plants, and, most of all, automobiles were poisoning the atmosphere. Weather forecasts and official atmospheric information began to refer to "smog" levels—using a relatively new word formed from a combination of "smoke" and "fog," which became an almost perpetual fact of daily life in such cities as Los Angeles and Denver. In 1969, a damaged oil-well platform off Santa Barbara, California, spewed hundreds of thousands of gallons of crude oil into the ocean just off the popular beaches of an affluent city. This oil spill had a tremendous impact on the environmental consciousness of millions of Americans. Another, much larger spill—indeed, the largest in American history—occurred off the coast of Alaska in 1989 when the giant tanker *Exxon Valdez* hit a reef in Prince William Sound. The damage it caused to the nearby shoreline and wildlife also greatly increased environmental consciousness. A much greater oil spill occurred in the Gulf of Mexico after an explosion on an offshore drilling platform in 2010.

Environmentalists brought to public attention many long-term dangers and helped create a broad and powerful movement.

EARTH DAY AND BEYOND

On April 22, 1970, people all over the United States participated in the first "Earth Day." Originally proposed by Wisconsin Senator Gaylord Nelson as a series of teach-ins on college campuses, Earth Day gradually took on a much larger life. Carefully managed by people who wanted to avoid associations with the radical left, it had a less threatening quality than antiwar demonstrations and civil rights rallies seemed to have. According to some estimates, over 20 million Americans participated in Earth Day observances, making Earth Day, possibly, the largest single demonstration in the nation's history.

The cautious, centrist character of Earth Day and related efforts to popularize environmentalism helped create a movement that was for a time less divisive than other, more controversial causes. Gradually, environmentalism became more than simply a series of demonstrations and protests. It became part of the consciousness of the vast majority of Americans—absorbed into popular culture, built into primary and secondary education, and endorsed by almost all politicians (even if many of them actually opposed some environmental goals).

It also became part of the fabric of public policy. In 1970, Congress passed and President Nixon signed the National Environmental Protection Act, which created a new agency—the Environmental Protection Agency—to enforce antipollution standards on businesses and consumers. The Clean Air Act, also passed in 1970, and the Clean Water Act, passed in 1972, became additional tools in the government's arsenal of weapons against environmental degradation.

Different administrations displayed varying levels of support for environmental goals, and new environmental problems continued to emerge even as older ones sometimes found solutions. Environmentalism became simultaneously a movement, a set of public policies, and a broad national ideal—and it was the combination of all those aspects that made it a powerful force in American life.

NIXON, KISSINGER, AND THE VIETNAM WAR

Richard Nixon assumed office in 1969 committed not only to restoring stability at home but to creating a new and more stable order in the world. Central to his hopes for international stability was a resolution of the stalemate in Vietnam. Yet the new president felt no freer than his predecessor to abandon the American commitment there.

VIETNAMIZATION

Despite Nixon's own deep interest in international affairs, he brought with him into government a man who at times seemed to overshadow the president himself in the conduct of diplomacy: Henry Kissinger, a Harvard professor whom Nixon appointed as his special assistant for national security affairs. Kissinger quickly established dominance over Secretary of State William Rogers and Secretary of Defense Melvin Laird. Together, Nixon and Kissinger set out to find an acceptable solution to the stalemate in Vietnam.

The new Vietnam policy moved along several fronts. One was the move to "Vietnamize" the conflict—that is, train and equip the South Vietnamese military to assume the burden of combat in place of American forces. In the fall of 1969, Nixon announced the withdrawal of 60,000 American ground troops from Vietnam. By the fall of 1972, relatively few American soldiers remained in Indochina. From a peak of more than 540,000 in 1969, the number had dwindled to about 60,000.

Vietnamization (and the decreased draft calls it produced) did help quiet domestic opposition to the war for a time. It did nothing, however, to break the stalemate in the negotiations with the North Vietnamese in Paris. The new administration decided that new military pressures would be necessary to do that.

ESCALATION

By the end of 1969, Nixon and Kissinger had decided that the most effective way to tip the military balance in America's favor was to destroy the bases in Cambodia and Laos. The American military believed the North Vietnamese were launching many of their attacks from these bases. Very early in his presidency, Nixon secretly ordered the air force to begin bombing Cambodian and Laotian territory to destroy the enemy sanctuaries. On April 30, 1970, the president announced that he was ordering American ground troops across the border into Cambodia to clean out enemy bases.

Literally overnight, the Cambodian invasion restored the dwindling antiwar movement to vigorous life. The first days of May saw widespread and vocal antiwar demonstrations. A mood of crisis was already mounting when, on May 4, four college students were killed and nine injured after members of the National Guard opened fire on antiwar demonstrators at Kent State University in Ohio. Ten days later, police killed two African American students at Jackson State University in Mississippi during a demonstration there.

The clamor against the war spread into the government and the press. Congress angrily repealed the Gulf of Tonkin Resolution in December. Then, in June 1971, first the *New York Times* and later other newspapers began publishing excerpts from a secret study of the war prepared by the Defense Department during the Johnson administration. The so-called Pentagon Papers were leaked to the press by former Defense official Daniel Ellsberg. They provided evidence that the government had been dishonest, both in reporting the military progress of the war and in explaining its own motives for American involvement. The administration went to court to suppress the documents, but the Supreme Court ruled that the press had the right to publish them.

Morale and discipline among American troops in Vietnam were rapidly deteriorating in the waning years of the war. In 1971 Lieutenant William Calley was tried and convicted of overseeing a massacre of more than 100 unarmed South Vietnamese civilians in 1968 near the village of My Lai. It attracted wide public attention to the dehumanizing impact of the war on those who fought it—both Americans and Vietnamese. Less publicized were other, more widespread problems among American troops in Vietnam: desertion, drug addiction, racism, refusal to obey orders, even the killing of unpopular officers by enlisted men.

By 1971, polls indicated that nearly two-thirds of Americans supported withdrawal from Vietnam. President Nixon, however, believed that a defeat in Vietnam would cause unacceptable damage to the nation's credibility. The FBI, the CIA, the White House itself,

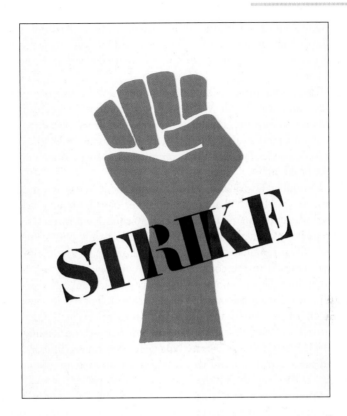

HARVARD ON STRIKE, 1969   This poster, one of several versions of the same image, was designed by architecture students at Harvard in the spring of 1969 during a strike that threw the university into turmoil. As at other universities, students occupied an administration building; police were called in to clear them out; and a crisis followed that at Harvard, as at Columbia the year before, led to the resignation of the president. Another version of this poster superimposed a list of reasons for the strike, among them: "Strike because you hate cops/strike because your roommate was clubbed . . . strike to seize control of your life/strike to become more human . . . /strike because there's no poetry in your lectures/strike because classes are a bore/strike for power/strike to smash the corporation/strike to make yourself free/ . . . strike because they are trying to squeeze the life out of you." (Courtesy of the Harvard University Archives, HUA 969.100.2 pf)

and other federal agencies increased their efforts to discredit and harass antiwar and radical groups, often through illegal means.

In Indochina, meanwhile, the fighting raged on. American bombing in Vietnam and Cambodia increased. In March 1972, the North Vietnamese mounted their biggest offensive since 1968 (the so-called Easter offensive). American and South Vietnamese forces managed to halt the communist advance, but it was clear that without American support, the South Vietnamese would not have succeeded. At the same time, Nixon ordered American planes to bomb targets near Hanoi, the capital of North Vietnam, and Haiphong, its principal port, and called for the mining of seven North Vietnamese harbors.

"Peace with Honor"

As the 1972 presidential election approached, the administration stepped up its effort to produce a breakthrough in negotiations with the North Vietnamese. In April, the president dropped his longtime insistence on the removal of North Vietnamese troops from the south before any American withdrawal. Meanwhile, Henry Kissinger met privately in Paris with the North Vietnamese foreign secretary, Le Duc Tho, to work out terms for a cease-fire. On October 26, only days before the presidential election, Kissinger announced that "peace is at hand."

Several weeks later (after the election), negotiations broke down once again. Although both the American and the North Vietnamese governments were ready to accept the Kissinger-Tho plan for a cease-fire, President Nguyen Van Thieu of South Vietnam balked, still insisting on a full withdrawal of North Vietnamese forces from the south. Kissinger tried to win additional concessions from the communists to meet Thieu's objections, but on December 16 talks broke off.

The next day, December 17, American B-52s began the heaviest and most destructive air raids of the entire war on Hanoi, Haiphong, and other North Vietnamese targets. Civilian casualties were high, and fifteen American B-52s were shot down by the North Vietnamese; in the entire war to that point, the United States had lost only one of the giant bombers. On December 30, Nixon terminated the "Christmas bombing." The United States and the North Vietnamese returned to the conference table; and on January 27, 1973, they signed an "agreement on ending the war and restoring peace in Vietnam." Nixon claimed that the Christmas bombing had forced the North Vietnamese to relent. At least equally important, however, was the enormous American pressure on Thieu to accept the cease-fire.

The terms of the Paris accords were little different from those Kissinger and Tho had accepted in principle a few months before. Nor were they much different from the peace plan Johnson had proposed in 1968. There would be an immediate cease-fire. The North Vietnamese would release several hundred American prisoners of war. The Thieu regime would survive for the moment, but North Vietnamese forces already in the south would remain there. An undefined committee would work out a permanent settlement.

DEFEAT IN INDOCHINA

American forces were hardly out of Indochina before the Paris accords began to collapse. In March 1975, the North Vietnamese launched a full-scale offensive against the now greatly weakened forces of South Vietnam. Thieu appealed to Washington for assistance. The president (now Gerald Ford) appealed to Congress for additional funding; Congress refused. Late in April 1975, communist forces marched into Saigon, shortly after officials of the Thieu regime and the staff of the American embassy had fled the country in humiliating disarray. The communist forces quickly occupied the capital, renamed it Ho Chi Minh City, and began the process of reuniting Vietnam under Hanoi. At about the same time, the Lon Nol regime in Cambodia fell to the murderous forces of the Khmer Rouge—whose brutal policies led to the death of more than a third of the country's people over the next several years.

Such were the dismal results of more than a decade of direct American military involvement in Vietnam. More than 1.2 million Vietnamese soldiers had died in combat, along with countless civilians throughout the region. A beautiful land had been ravaged, its agrarian economy left in ruins; until an economic revival began in the early 1990s, Vietnam remained for more than a decade one of the poorest nations in the world. The United States had paid a heavy price as well. The war had cost the nation almost $150 billion in direct costs and much more indirectly. It had resulted in the deaths of over 57,000 young Americans and the injury of 300,000 more. And the nation had suffered a blow to its confidence and self-esteem from which it did not soon recover.

EVACUATING SAIGON In the last weeks of April 1975, American forces evacuated Saigon and most of the rest of Vietnam as the Vietnam War shuddered to its end. This photograph shows the evacuation of soldiers, diplomats, and many Vietnamese working for the Americans climbing into helicopters to take them to American ships, which would bring them to the United States. A CIA officer organized the evacuation. (© Bettmann/Corbis)

NIXON, KISSINGER, AND THE WORLD

The continuing war in Vietnam provided an unhappy backdrop to what Nixon considered his larger mission in world affairs: the construction of a new international order. The president had become convinced that the old assumptions of a "bipolar" world—in which the United States and the Soviet Union were the only real great powers—were now obsolete. America must adapt to the new "multipolar" international structure, in which China, Japan, and Western Europe were becoming major, independent forces. Nixon had a considerable advantage over many other politicians in changing the assumptions behind American foreign policy. His long anticommunist record gave him credibility among many conservatives for his effort to transform American relations with communist China and the Soviet Union.

THE CHINA INITIATIVE AND SOVIET-AMERICAN DÉTENTE

For more than twenty years, ever since the fall of Chiang Kai-shek in 1949, the United States had treated China, the most populous nation on earth, as if it did not exist. Instead, America recognized the regime-in-exile on the small island of Taiwan as the legitimate government of China. Nixon and Kissinger wanted to forge a new relationship with the Chinese communists—in part to strengthen them as a counterbalance to the Soviet Union. The Chinese, for their part, were eager to end China's own isolation from the international arena.

In July 1971, Nixon sent Henry Kissinger on a secret mission to Beijing. When Kissinger returned, the president made the startling announcement that he would visit China himself within the next few months. That fall, with American approval, the United Nations admitted the communist government of China and expelled the representatives

DÉTENTE AT HIGH TIDE The visit of Soviet premier Leonid Brezhnev to Washington in 1973 was a high-water mark in the search for détente between the two nations. Here, Brezhnev and Nixon share friendly words on the White House balcony. (© Wally McNamee/Corbis)

of the Taiwan regime. Finally, in February 1972, Nixon paid a formal visit to China. It erased much of the deep animosity between the United States and the Chinese communists. Nixon did not yet formally recognize the communist regime, but in 1972 the United States and China began low-level diplomatic relations.

The initiatives in China coincided with an effort by the Nixon administration to improve relations with the Soviet Union, an initiative known by the French word "détente." In 1971, American and Soviet diplomats produced the first Strategic Arms Limitation Treaty (SALT I), which froze the arsenals of some nuclear missiles (ICBMs) on both sides at present levels. In May of that year, the president traveled to Moscow to sign the agreement. The next year, the Soviet premier, Leonid Brezhnev, visited Washington.

DEALING WITH THE THIRD WORLD

The policies of rapprochement with communist China and détente with the Soviet Union reflected Nixon's and Kissinger's belief in the importance of stable relationships among the great powers. But, as America's experience in Vietnam already illustrated, the so-called Third World remained the most volatile and dangerous source of international tension.

The Nixon-Kissinger policy toward the Third World tried to maintain the status quo without involving the United States too deeply in local disputes. In 1969 and 1970, the president described what became known as the Nixon Doctrine, by which the United States would "participate in the defense and development of allies and friends" but would leave the "basic responsibility" for the future of those "friends" to the nations themselves. In practice, the Nixon Doctrine meant a declining American interest in contributing to Third World development. There was a growing contempt for the United Nations, where underdeveloped nations were gaining influence through their sheer numbers. And there was increasing American support for authoritarian regimes attempting to withstand radical challenges from within.

In 1970, for example, the CIA poured substantial funds into Chile to help support the government against a communist challenge. When the Marxist candidate for president, Salvador Allende, came to power through an open election despite American efforts, the United States began funneling more money to opposition forces in Chile to help destabilize the new government. In 1973, a military junta seized power from Allende, who was subsequently murdered. The United States developed a friendly relationship with the new, repressive military government of General Augusto Pinochet.

In the Middle East, conditions grew more volatile in the aftermath of a 1967 war in which Israel had occupied substantial new territories, dislodging many Palestinian Arabs from their homes. The refugees were a source of considerable instability in Jordan, Lebanon, and the other surrounding countries into which they moved. In October 1973, on the Jewish high holy day of Yom Kippur, Egyptian and Syrian forces attacked Israel. For ten days, the Israelis struggled to recover from the surprise attack; finally, they launched an effective counteroffensive against Egyptian forces in the Sinai. At that point, the United States intervened, placing heavy pressure on Israel to accept a cease-fire rather than press its advantage.

The imposed settlement of the Yom Kippur War demonstrated the growing dependence of the United States and its allies on Arab oil. A brief but painful embargo by the Arab governments on the sale of oil to America in 1973 provided an ominous warning of the costs of losing access to the region's resources.

POLITICS AND ECONOMICS IN THE NIXON YEARS

Nixon ran for president in 1968, promising a return to more conservative social and economic policies and a restoration of law and order. Once he was in office, however, his domestic policies sometimes continued and even expanded the liberal initiatives of the previous two administrations.

DOMESTIC INITIATIVES

Many of Nixon's domestic policies were a response to what he believed to be the demands of his constituency—the "silent majority" of conservative, mostly middle-class people who, he believed, wanted to reduce federal interference in local affairs. He tried, unsuccessfully, to persuade Congress to pass legislation prohibiting school desegregation through the use of forced busing. He forbade the Department of Health, Education, and Welfare to cut off federal funds from school districts that had failed to comply with court orders to integrate. At the same time, he began to reduce or dismantle many of the social programs of the Great Society and the New Frontier. In 1973, he abolished the Office of Economic Opportunity—a centerpiece of the antipoverty program of the Johnson years.

Yet Nixon's domestic policies had progressive and creative elements as well. He signed legislation creating the Environmental Protection Agency and establishing the most stringent environmental regulations in the nation's history. He ordered the first affirmative action program for workers on federally funded projects. One of the administration's boldest efforts was an attempt to overhaul the nation's welfare system. Nixon proposed replacing the existing system with what he called the Family Assistance Plan (FAP). It

THE END OF COLONIALISM

ON July 4, 1946, less than a year after the close of World War II, a ceremony in Manila marked what Senator Millard Tydings of Maryland called "one of the most unprecedented, most idealistic, and most far-reaching events in all recorded history." On that day, the United States voluntarily ended nearly five decades of colonial control of the Philippines, which it had acquired as part of the spoils from the 1898 Spanish-American War. Philippine independence was only a small part of a dramatic change in the political structure of the world. The close of World War II marked not only the defeat of fascism in Germany, Italy, and Japan, but also the beginning of the end of the formal system of imperialism that European powers had maintained for centuries. The repudiation of colonialism was driven in part by the heightened belief in democracy and self-determination that the war helped to strengthen through much of the world. It was also driven by the weakness of the European powers after World War II and their inability to sustain control over their increasingly restive colonies. Like most great geopolitical changes, the drive for colonial independence was turbulent and often violent.

The United States had been a latecomer to the imperialist system. But even its peaceful divestiture of the Philippines reflected the challenges many imperial powers and post-colonial nations faced in renegotiating colonial relationships. America was not quite as ready to cede military presence and economic influence in the region as it was to give up political responsibility over the islands. Philippine independence came with important caveats: that the United States maintained control of Fillipino military bases and that required (through the Bell Trade Act, passed by Congress in 1946) that the Philippines not engage in any direct economic competition with the United States and that it revise its constitution to allow American interests free and unfettered access to the nation's natural resources. Many Filipinos argue that their nation did not achieve full independence until 1991, when the Philippine Senate refused to ratify a treaty that would have extended the American lease on the Subic Bay naval base (once the largest U.S. Navy installation in the Pacific). A year later, the United States closed the base and left, marking the first time in 400 years that the Philippines (once a Spanish possession) was not home to a foreign military power.

England's imperial holdings were the vastest in the world, and the existence of the British Empire was deeply embedded in England's economic life and national self-image. But it, too, withdrew from most of its colonies in the decades after World War II—beginning in 1947 with its largest and most important colony, India. The British Raj—as the colonial government was known—withdrew from South Asia in response to a growing independence movement on the subcontinent. As often happened as colonial rule ended, suppressed conflicts in the native population quickly emerged—in the case of India, between Hindus and Muslims. The price of Indian independence, therefore, was the partition of the country into India and Pakistan (and, several decades later, Bangladesh).

A year later, the British gave up its World War I mandate of Palestine (ceding the territory to the United Nations and allowing for the creation of Israel) as well as many of its holdings in Southeast Asia, including Burma and Ceylon. Malaya followed in 1957 and Singapore in 1965. In 1982, England passed the Canada Act, effectively severing Canada from the United Kingdom and culminating a move toward full Canadian self-government that had begun several decades earlier. In 1997, England returned one of its last important overseas territories, Hong Kong, to the control of China, bringing nearly to an end the era of the British Empire.

The dissolution of the British Empire did not always proceed smoothly. The Suez Crisis of 1956, in which the combined efforts of Britain, France, and Israel failed to halt Egypt's nationalization of the Suez Canal, dealt a decisive blow to England's status as a major power in the Middle East. In 1982, England's dispute over the tiny Falkland Islands erupted into war with Argentina, which claimed the islands (just off its coast) as its own. After the deaths of 258 English and 649 Argentine soldiers, England maintained its control of the Falklands, although Argentina continues to assert its right to the islands.

Despite these controversies, the dissolution of the British Empire proceeded relatively smoothly compared to the experience of the French, who became engaged in several major conflicts after 1945. In late 1946, Vietnamese nationalists rose up against the French colonial government that had recently reoccupied the region after the defeat of Japan in World War II. France's effort to return to Vietnam culminated ultimately in its defeat at Dien Bien Phu in 1954 and its subsequent withdrawal from Indochina. France also became embroiled in, and tried to suppress by force, a number of other violent colonial uprisings—in Madagascar, Cameroon, and, most notably, Algeria. The Algerian War (1954–1962) was a particularly bloody and costly conflict, taking on aspects of a civil war and involving guerrilla warfare, torture, acts of terrorism, and, eventually, the collapse of the French government in 1958. Algeria ultimately won its independence.

The end of the colonial system had its greatest impact on Africa. European powers had carved up almost all of sub-Saharan Africa in the nineteenth century. In the decades after World War II, almost all the African colonies won their independence, even if not always easily: Morocco (1956), Ghana (1957), the Congo (1960), Nigeria (1960), Uganda (1962), Kenya (1963), and Gambia (1965). African nationalism was troubled for decades by political instability and, in some countries, extreme poverty. The Caribbean also saw many new independent nations born in the postwar era, including Jamaica (1961), Trinidad and Tobago (1962), Barbados (1966), and Guyana (1966).

The most recent epicenter of independence movements has been in the lands that used to comprise the former Soviet Union. A long and costly war in Afghanistan began in the 1970s as the Soviet Union struggled to retain control of the nation in the face of powerful local insurgencies. The war was one of the principal factors in the unraveling of the Soviet Empire that began in 1991. Many of the former Soviet republics—which considered themselves colonies of Russia—soon separated from Russia and became independent nations. These included Estonia, Latvia, and Lithuania—the formerly independent Baltic nations seized by the Soviet Union during World War II. Other former Soviet possessions that became independent nations included Ukraine, Moldavia, Armenia, Georgia, Azerbaijan, Kazakhstan, Uzbekistan, Tajikistan, and Turkmenistan. Russia continues to deal with the problems of empire. A vicious conflict with Chechnya, an Islamic area of Russia insisting on independence, created terror and instability for years.

The end of colonialism was one of the most epochal global changes of the last several centuries—a change that brought to an end a system that was based on the assumption of European (and American) superiority over non-Western peoples. Despite the many problems new postcolonial nations have encountered since their independence, few, if any, such nations would choose to become colonies again. But although formal colonialism came to an end in the post–World War II era, other aspects of imperialism did not. Many former colonies, which comprise much of the nonindustrialized world, still struggle with the indirect exercise of economic power that wealthy Western nations continue to exert over them. •

UNDERSTAND, ANALYZE, & EVALUATE

1. How did the experience of World War II contribute to the end of colonialism?
2. What have been the effects of colonialism—and the end of colonialism—on Africa? Why have the effects been so pronounced on that continent, more so than in other areas of the world?

would, in effect, have created a guaranteed annual income for all Americans: $1,600 in federal grants, which could be supplemented by outside earnings up to $4,000. The FAP won approval in the House in 1970, but the bill failed in the Senate. Nixon also became the first president since Truman to propose a plan for national health insurance, which likewise made no progress in Congress.

FROM THE WARREN COURT TO THE NIXON COURT

Of all the liberal institutions that aroused the enmity of the conservative silent majority in the 1950s and 1960s, none evoked more anger and bitterness than the Supreme Court under Chief Justice Earl Warren. The Warren Court's rulings on racial matters disrupted traditional social patterns in both the North and the South. Its defense of civil liberties directly contributed to the increase in crime, disorder, and moral decay in the eyes of many Americans. In *Engel v. Vitale* (1962), the Court ruled that prayers in public schools were unconstitutional, sparking outrage among religious fundamentalists and others. In *Roth v. United States* (1957), the Court sharply limited the authority of local governments to curb pornography. In a series of other decisions, the Court greatly strengthened the civil rights of criminal defendants and, many Americans believed, greatly weakened the power of law enforcement officials to do their jobs. For example, in *Gideon v. Wainwright* (1963), the Court ruled that every felony defendant was entitled to a lawyer, regardless of his or her ability to pay. In *Escobedo v. Illinois* (1964), it ruled that a defendant must be allowed access to a lawyer before questioning by police. In *Miranda v. Arizona* (1966), the Court confirmed the obligation of authorities to inform a criminal suspect of his or her rights. By 1968, the Warren Court had become the target of Americans who felt the United States had shifted too far toward helping the poor, the dispossessed, and the criminal at the expense of the middle class.

Nixon promised to give the Court a more conservative cast. When Chief Justice Earl Warren retired early in 1969, Nixon replaced him with a federal appeals court judge of conservative leanings, Warren Burger. At about the same time, Associate Justice Abe Fortas resigned his seat after the disclosure of a series of alleged financial improprieties. To replace him, Nixon named Clement F. Haynsworth, a respected federal circuit court judge from South Carolina. But Haynsworth came under fire from Senate liberals, black organizations, and labor unions for his conservative record on civil rights. The Senate rejected him. Nixon's next choice was G. Harrold Carswell, a Florida federal appeals court judge of little distinction. He, too, was rejected.

Nixon angrily denounced the votes. But he was careful thereafter to choose men of standing within the legal community to fill vacancies on the Supreme Court: Harry Blackmun, a moderate jurist from Minnesota; Lewis F. Powell Jr., a respected lawyer from Virginia; and William Rehnquist, a member of the Nixon Justice Department.

The new Court, however, fell short of what the president and many conservatives had expected. Rather than retreating from its commitment to social reform, the Court in many areas actually moved further toward it. In *Swann v. Charlotte-Mecklenburg Board of Education* (1971), it ruled in favor of forced busing to achieve racial balance in schools. Despite intense and occasionally violent opposition of local communities as diverse as Boston and Louisville, Kentucky, the judicial commitment to integration was not overturned. In *Furman v. Georgia* (1972), the Court overturned existing capital punishment statutes and established strict new guidelines for such laws in the future. In *Roe v. Wade* (1973), one of the most controversial decisions in the Court's modern history, it struck down laws forbidding abortions in the first three months of pregnancy.

In other decisions, however, the Burger Court did demonstrate a more conservative temperament than the Warren Court had shown. Although the justices approved busing as a tool for achieving integration, they rejected, in *Milliken v. Bradley* (1974), a plan to transfer students across municipal lines (in this case, between Detroit and its suburbs) to achieve racial balance. While the Court upheld the principle of affirmative action in its celebrated 1978 decision, *Bakke v. Board of Regents of California*, it established restrictive new guidelines for such programs in the future. In *Stone v. Powell* (1976), the Court agreed to certain limits on the right of a defendant to appeal a state conviction to the federal judiciary.

THE 1972 LANDSLIDE

Nixon entered the presidential race in 1972 with substantial strength. His energetic reelection committee had collected enormous sums of money. The president himself used the powers of incumbency to strengthen his political standing in strategic areas. And Nixon's foreign policy successes, especially his trip to China, increased his stature in the eyes of the nation.

Nixon was most fortunate in 1972, however, in his opposition. George Wallace, partly at Nixon's urging, entered the Democratic primaries and helped divide the party until a would-be assassin shot the Alabama governor during a rally at a Maryland shopping center in May. Paralyzed from the waist down, Wallace was unable to continue campaigning. In the meantime, the most liberal factions of the party succeeded in establishing their candidate, Senator George S. McGovern of South Dakota, as the front-runner for the nomination. An outspoken critic of the war and a forceful advocate of liberal positions on many social and economic issues, McGovern profited greatly from party reforms (which he himself had helped to draft) that gave increased influence to women, minorities, and young people in the selection of the Democratic ticket. But in the process, the McGovern campaign came to be associated with aspects of the turbulent 1960s that many middle-class Americans were eager to reject.

On election day, Nixon won reelection by one of the largest margins in history: 60.7 percent of the popular vote to McGovern's 37.5 percent and an electoral margin of 520 to 17. The Democratic candidate carried only Massachusetts and the District of Columbia. But serious problems, some beyond the president's control and others of his own making, were already lurking in the wings.

THE TROUBLED ECONOMY

Although it was political scandal that would ultimately destroy the Nixon presidency, the most important issue of the early 1970s was the beginning of a long-term transformation of the American economy. For three decades, that economy had been the envy of the world. In fact, however, America's prosperity rested in part on several artificial conditions that were rapidly disappearing by the late 1960s.

The most immediate change was the end of the nation's easy access to cheap raw materials, a change that became a major cause of the serious inflation that plagued the economy through much of the 1970s. For many years, the Organization of Petroleum Exporting Countries (OPEC) had operated as an informal bargaining unit for the sale of oil by Third World nations but had seldom managed to exercise any real strength. But in the early 1970s, OPEC began to use its oil both as an economic tool and as a political weapon. In 1973, in the midst of the Yom Kippur War, Arab members of OPEC announced that they would no longer ship petroleum to nations supporting Israel—that is, to the United States and its allies in Western Europe. At about the same time, the OPEC nations agreed to raise their prices 500 percent (from $3 to $15 a barrel). These twin shocks produced momentary economic chaos in the West. The United States suffered its first fuel shortage since World War II. And although the crisis eased a few months later, the price of energy continued to rise.

Another, longer-term change in the American economy was the transformation of the nation's manufacturing sector. Ever since World War II, American industry had enjoyed relatively little competition from the rest of the world. By the end of the 1960s, however, both Western Europe and Japan had recovered from the damage their manufacturing sectors had absorbed during World War II. By the early 1970s, they were providing stiff competition to American firms in the sale of automobiles, steel, and many other products, both in world markets and within the United States. Some American corporations failed. Others restructured themselves to become more competitive again in world markets. In the process, they closed many older plants and eliminated hundreds of thousands of once-lucrative manufacturing jobs. The high-wage, high-employment industrial economy that had been a central fact of American life since the 1940s was gradually disappearing.

THE NIXON RESPONSE

Nixon's initial answer to these mounting economic problems was a conventional anti-inflationary one. He reduced spending and raised taxes, producing a modest budget surplus in 1969. But when those policies proved difficult to sustain, Nixon turned increasingly to control of the currency. Placing conservative economists at the head of the Federal Reserve Board, he ensured sharply higher interest rates and a contraction of the money supply. Even so, the cost of living rose a cumulative 15 percent during Nixon's first two and a half years in office. Economic growth, in the meantime, declined. The United States was encountering a new dilemma: "stagflation," a combination of rising prices and general economic stagnation.

In the summer of 1971, Nixon imposed a ninety-day freeze on all wages and prices at their existing levels. Then, in November, he launched the second phase of his economic plan: mandatory guidelines for some wage and price increases, to be administered by a federal

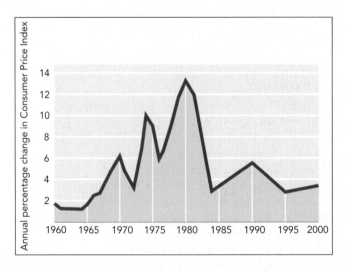

INFLATION, 1960–2000   Inflation was the biggest economic worry of most Americans in the 1970s and early 1980s, and this chart shows why. Having remained very low through the early 1960s, inflation rose slowly in the second half of the decade and then dramatically in the mid- and late 1970s, before beginning a long and steady decline in the early 1980s. • *What caused the great spike in inflation in the 1970s?*

agency. Inflation subsided temporarily, but the recession continued. Fearful that the recession would be more damaging than inflation in an election year, the administration reversed itself late in 1971: interest rates were allowed to drop sharply, and government spending increased—producing the largest budget deficit since World War II. The new tactics helped revive the economy in the short term, but inflation rose substantially. In 1973, prices rose 9 percent; in 1974, after the Arab oil embargo and the OPEC price increases, they rose 12 percent—the highest rate since shortly after World War II. The new energy crisis, in the meantime, was quickly becoming a national preoccupation. But while Nixon talked often about the need to achieve "energy independence," he offered few concrete proposals.

THE WATERGATE CRISIS

Although economic problems greatly concerned the American people in the 1970s, another stunning development preoccupied the nation beginning early in 1973: the fall of Richard Nixon. The president's demise was in part a result of the turbulent climate of the early 1970s. It was also a result of his own personality. The president believed the United States faced grave dangers from the radicals and dissidents who were challenging his policies.

THE SCANDALS

Early on the morning of June 17, 1972, police arrested five men who had broken into the headquarters of the Democratic National Committee in the Watergate office building in Washington, D.C. Two others were seized a short time later and charged with supervising the break-in. When reporters for the *Washington Post* began researching the backgrounds of the culprits, they discovered that among those involved in the burglary were former employees of the Committee for the Re-Election of the President (CRP). One of them had worked in the White House itself. They had, moreover, been paid for the break-in from a secret fund of the reelection committee, a fund controlled by, among others, members of the White House staff.

Public interest in the disclosures grew slowly in the last months of 1972. Early in 1973, however, the Watergate burglars went on trial; and under prodding from federal judge John J. Sirica, one of the defendants, James W. McCord, agreed to cooperate both with the grand jury and with a special Senate investigating committee recently established under Senator Sam J. Ervin of North Carolina. McCord's testimony opened a floodgate of confessions, and for months a parade of White House and campaign officials exposed one illegality after another. Foremost among them was a member of the inner circle of the White House, John Dean, counsel to the president, who had warned Nixon that the Watergate cover-up was a "cancer on the presidency" and who later leveled allegations against Nixon himself.

Two different sets of scandals emerged from the investigations. One was a general pattern of abuses of power involving both the White House and the Nixon campaign committee, which included, but was not limited to, the Watergate break-in. The other scandal, and the one that became the major focus of public attention for nearly two years, was the way in which the administration tried to manage the investigations of the Watergate break-in and other abuses—a pattern of behavior that became known as the "cover-up." There was never any conclusive evidence that the president had planned or approved the burglary in advance. But there was mounting evidence that he had been involved in illegal efforts to obstruct investigations of the episode.

WATERGATE

TWENTY-FIVE years after Watergate—one of the most famous political scandals in American history—historians and others continue to argue about its causes and significance. Their interpretations tend to fall into several broad categories.

One argument emphasizes the evolution of the institution of the presidency over time and sees Watergate as the result of a much larger pattern of presidential usurpations of power that stretched back at least several decades. Arthur M. Schlesinger Jr. helped develop this argument in his 1973 book *The Imperial Presidency,* which argues that ever since World War II, Americans have believed that the nation was in a state of permanent crisis—threatened from abroad by the menace of communism, threatened from within by the danger of insufficient will. A succession of presidents believed in the urgency of this crisis, and in their duty to take whatever measures might be necessary to combat it. That led them gradually to usurp more and

more power from Congress, from the courts, and from the public. Initially, this expansion of presidential power came in the realm of international affairs. It included covert and at times illegal activities overseas. Gradually, presidents began to look for ways to circumvent constraints in domestic matters as well. Nixon's actions in the Watergate crisis were, in other words, a culmination of this long and steady expansion of covert presidential power. Jonathan Schell, in *The Time of Illusion* (1975), offers a variation of this argument, tying the crisis of the presidency to the pressure that nuclear weapons place on presidents to protect the nation's—and their own—"credibility."

Another explanation of Watergate emphasizes the difficult social and political environment of the late 1960s and early 1970s. Nixon entered office, according to this view, facing an unprecedentedly radical opposition that would stop at nothing to discredit the war and destroy his authority. He found himself, therefore, drawn into taking similarly

Nixon accepted the departure of members of his administration implicated in the scandals. But the president continued to insist on his own innocence. There the matter might have rested had it not been for the disclosure during the Senate hearings of a White House taping system that had recorded virtually every conversation in the president's office during the period in question. All those investigating the scandals sought access to the tapes. Nixon, pleading "executive privilege," refused to release them. A special prosecutor appointed by the president to handle the Watergate cases, Harvard law professor Archibald Cox, took Nixon to court in October 1973 in an effort to force him to relinquish the recordings. Nixon fired Cox and suffered the humiliation of watching both Attorney General Elliot Richardson and his deputy resign in protest. This "Saturday night massacre," as it was called, made the president's predicament much worse. Not only did public pressure force him to appoint a new special prosecutor, Texas attorney Leon Jaworski, who proved just as determined as Cox to subpoena desperate measures of his own to defend himself. Nixon made this argument in his own 1975 memoirs:

> Now that this season of mindless terror has fortunately passed, it is difficult—perhaps impossible—to convey a sense of the pressures that were influencing my actions and reactions during this period, but it was this epidemic of unprecedented domestic terrorism that prompted our efforts to discover the best means by which to deal with this new phenomenon of highly organized and highly skilled revolutionaries dedicated to the violent destruction of our democratic system.*

The historian Herbert Parmet echoes parts of this argument in *Richard Nixon and His America* (1990). Stephen Ambrose offers a more muted version of the same view in *Richard Nixon* (1989).

Most of those who have written about Watergate, however, search for the explanation not in institutional or social forces but in the personalities of the people involved and, most notably, in the personality of Richard Nixon. Even many of those who have developed structural explanations (Schlesinger, Schell, and Ambrose, for example) return eventually to Nixon himself as the most important explanation for Watergate. Others begin there, perhaps most notably Stanley I. Kutler, in *The Wars of Watergate* (1990) and, later, *Abuse of Power* (1997), in which he presents extensive excerpts from conversations about Watergate taped in the Nixon White House. Kutler emphasizes Nixon's lifelong resort to vicious political tactics and his long-standing belief that he was a special target of unscrupulous enemies and had to "get" them before they got him. Watergate was rooted, Kutler argues, "in the personality and history of Nixon himself." A "corrosive hatred," he claims, "decisively shaped Nixon's own behavior, his career, and eventually his historical standing." •

UNDERSTAND, ANALYZE, & EVALUATE

1. For scholars who cite social and institutional forces as explanations for Watergate, what are these forces? How did they contribute to the Watergate scandal?

2. Most scholars see Nixon himself as the party most responsible for Watergate. How did Nixon's personality contribute to both his rise to power as president and his downfall as a result of Watergate?

3. What have been the lasting effects of Watergate on the public's perception of the presidency and the government?

the tapes; but the episode precipitated an investigation by the House of Representatives into the possibility of impeachment.

THE FALL OF RICHARD NIXON

Nixon's situation deteriorated further in the following months. Late in 1973, Vice President Spiro Agnew became embroiled in a scandal of his own when evidence surfaced that he had accepted bribes and kickbacks while serving as governor of Maryland and even as vice president. In return for a Justice Department agreement not to press the case, Agnew pleaded no contest to a lesser charge of income-tax evasion and resigned from the government. With the controversial Agnew no longer in line to succeed to the presidency, the prospect of removing Nixon from the White House became less worrisome to his

NIXON'S FAREWELL Only moments before, Nixon had been in tears, saying good-bye to his staff in the East Room of the White House. But as he boarded a helicopter to begin his trip home to California shortly after resigning as president, he flashed his trademark "victory" sign to the crowd on the White House lawn. (© Bettmann/Corbis)

opponents. The new vice president was House Minority Leader Gerald Ford, an amiable and popular Michigan congressman.

The impeachment investigation quickly gathered momentum. In April 1974, in an effort to head off further subpoenas of the tapes, the president released transcripts of a number of relevant conversations, claiming that they proved his innocence. Investigators and much of the public felt otherwise. Even these edited tapes seemed to suggest Nixon's complicity in the cover-up. In July, the crisis reached a climax. First the Supreme Court ruled unanimously, in *United States v. Richard M. Nixon*, that the president must relinquish the tapes to Special Prosecutor Jaworski. Days later, the House Judiciary Committee voted to recommend three articles of impeachment.

Even without additional evidence, Nixon might well have been impeached by the full House and convicted by the Senate. Early in August, however, he provided at last the "smoking gun"—the concrete proof of his guilt—that his defenders had long contended was missing from the case against him. Among the tapes that the Supreme Court compelled Nixon to relinquish were several that offered apparently incontrovertible evidence of his involvement in the Watergate cover-up. Only three days after the burglary, the recordings disclosed, the president had ordered the FBI to stop investigating the break-in. Impeachment and conviction now seemed inevitable.

For several days, Nixon cloistered himself in the White House. Finally, on August 8, 1974, he announced his resignation—the first president in American history ever to do so. At noon the next day, while Nixon and his family flew west to their home in California, Gerald Ford took the oath of office as president.

Many Americans expressed relief and exhilaration that, as the new president put it, "our long national nightmare is over." But the wave of good feeling could not obscure the deeper and more lasting damage of the Watergate crisis. In a society in which distrust of leaders and institutions of authority was already widespread, the fall of Richard Nixon confirmed for many Americans their most cynical assumptions about the character of American public life.

CONCLUSION

The victory of Richard Nixon in the 1968 presidential election represented a popular repudiation of turbulence and radicalism. It was a call for a restoration of order and stability. But order and stability were not the dominant characteristics of Nixon's troubled years in office. Nixon entered office when the left and the counterculture were approaching the peak of their influence. American culture and society in the late 1960s and early 1970s were shaped decisively by, and were deeply divided over, the challenges by young people to the prevailing social norms. These were also the years in which a host of new liberation movements joined the drive for racial equality and when, above all, women mobilized effectively to demand changes in the way society treated gender differences.

Nixon had run for office attacking the failure of his predecessor to end the war in Vietnam. But for four years under his presidency, the war—and the protests against it—continued and even in some respects escalated. The division of opinion over the war was as deep as any of the many other divisions in national life. It continued to poison the nation's politics and social fabric until the American role in the conflict finally shuddered to a close in 1973.

But much of the controversy and division in the 1970s was a product of the Nixon presidency itself. Nixon was in many ways a dynamic and even visionary leader, who proposed some important domestic reforms and who made important changes in American foreign policy, most notably making overtures to communist China and forging détente with the Soviet Union. He was also, however, a devious, secretive man whose White House became engaged in a series of covert activities that produced the most dramatic political scandal in American history. Watergate, as it was called, preoccupied much of the nation for nearly two years beginning in 1972; and ultimately, in the summer of 1974, the scandal forced Richard Nixon—who had been reelected to office only two years before by one of the largest majorities in modern history—to become the first president in American history to resign.

RECALL AND REFLECT

1. What was the New Left? How was it related to the counterculture?
2. How did ethnic minorities, especially Native Americans and Latinos, challenge the status quo in the 1970s?
3. What were the objectives of the new feminism of the 1970s? What gains did women achieve in this era? What setbacks did the feminist movement experience?
4. What was the "Nixon Doctrine"? How did this doctrine play out in foreign policy?
5. What was the effect of Nixon's policies on the U.S. economy? What was Nixon's response to escalating economic difficulties?

31

FROM "THE AGE OF LIMITS" TO THE AGE OF REAGAN

POLITICS AND DIPLOMACY AFTER WATERGATE
THE RISE OF THE NEW CONSERVATIVE MOVEMENT
THE "REAGAN REVOLUTION"
AMERICA AND THE WANING OF THE COLD WAR

LOOKING AHEAD

1. What economic and energy problems plagued the presidencies of Gerald Ford and Jimmy Carter? How did Ford and Carter attempt to deal with these problems?
2. What was the "New Right," and what effect did its rise have on American politics?
3. What was Reaganomics, and how did this policy affect the national economy?

THE FRUSTRATIONS OF THE EARLY 1970s—the defeat in Vietnam, the Watergate crisis, the decay of the American economy—inflicted damaging blows to the confident, optimistic nationalism that had characterized so much of the postwar era. Some Americans responded to these problems by announcing the arrival of an "age of limits," in which Americans would have to learn to live with increasingly constricted expectations. By the end of the decade, however, another response was gaining strength—one that combined a conservative retreat from some of the heady liberal visions of the 1960s with a reinforced commitment to the ideas of economic growth, international power, and American virtue.

POLITICS AND DIPLOMACY AFTER WATERGATE

In the aftermath of Richard Nixon's ignominious departure from office, many Americans wondered whether faith in the presidency, and in the government as a whole, could be restored. The administrations of the two presidents who succeeded Nixon did little to answer those questions.

THE FORD CUSTODIANSHIP

Gerald Ford inherited the presidency under unenviable circumstances. He had to try to rebuild confidence in government in the wake of the Watergate scandals and to restore prosperity in the face of major economic difficulties.

The new president's effort to establish himself as a symbol of political integrity suffered a setback only a month after he took office, when he granted Richard Nixon "a full, free, and absolute pardon" for any crimes he may have committed during his presidency. The pardon caused a decline in Ford's popularity from which he never fully recovered. Nevertheless, most Americans considered him a decent man; his honesty and amiability did much to reduce the bitterness and acrimony of the Watergate years.

The Ford administration enjoyed less success in its effort to solve the problems of the economy. To curb inflation, the president called for largely ineffective voluntary efforts. After supporting high interest rates, opposing increased federal spending (through liberal use of his veto power), and resisting pressures for a tax reduction, Ford had to deal with a serious recession in 1974 and 1975. Central to the economic problems was the continuing energy crisis. In the aftermath of the Arab oil embargo of 1973, the OPEC cartel raised the price of oil—by 400 percent in 1974 alone—one of the principal reasons why inflation reached 11 percent in 1976.

TIME LINE

1974
"Stagflation"
Ford pardons Nixon

1976
Carter elected president

1977
Panama Canal treaties signed
Apple introduces first personal computer

1978–1979
Camp David accords
American hostages in Iran
Soviet Union invades Afghanistan
U.S. and China restore relations
Three Mile Island nuclear accident

1980
U.S. boycotts Moscow Olympics
Reagan elected president

1981
American hostages in Iran released
Reagan wins tax and budget cuts
AIDS first reported in U.S.

1982
Severe recession

1983
U.S. invades Grenada

1984
Reagan reelected

1985
Reagan and Gorbachev meet

1986
Iran-contra scandal revealed

1988
George H. W. Bush elected president

1989
Berlin Wall dismantled
Communist regimes collapse
U.S. troops in Panama

1990
Iraq invades Kuwait

1991
Collapse of Soviet regime
Persian Gulf War

1992
Los Angeles race riots
Clinton elected president

Ford retained Henry Kissinger as secretary of state and continued the general policies of the Nixon years. Late in 1974, Ford met with Leonid Brezhnev at Vladivostok in Siberia and signed an arms control accord. Meanwhile, in the Middle East, Henry Kissinger helped produce a new accord by which Israel agreed to return large portions of the occupied Sinai to Egypt. The two nations pledged not to resolve future differences by force.

As the 1976 presidential election approached, Ford's policies were coming under attack from both the right and the left. In the Republican primary campaign, Ford faced a powerful challenge from former California governor Ronald Reagan, leader of the party's conservative wing, who spoke for many Americans on the right who opposed any agreements with communists. The president only barely survived the assault to win his party's nomination. The Democrats, in the meantime, were gradually uniting behind a new and until recently almost entirely unknown candidate: Jimmy Carter, a former governor of Georgia who appealed to the general unhappiness with Washington by offering honesty, piety, and an outsider's skepticism of the federal government. Unhappiness with the economy and a general disenchantment with Ford enabled the Democrat to win a narrow victory. Carter received 50 percent of the popular vote to Ford's 47.9 percent and 297 electoral votes to Ford's 240.

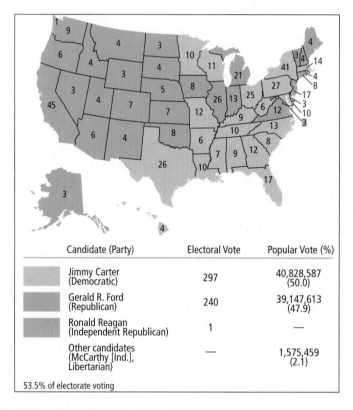

Candidate (Party)	Electoral Vote	Popular Vote (%)
Jimmy Carter (Democratic)	297	40,828,587 (50.0)
Gerald R. Ford (Republican)	240	39,147,613 (47.9)
Ronald Reagan (Independent Republican)	1	—
Other candidates (McCarthy [Ind.], Libertarian)	—	1,575,459 (2.1)

53.5% of electorate voting

THE ELECTION OF 1976 Jimmy Carter, a former governor of Georgia, swept the South in the 1976 election and carried enough of the industrial states of the Northeast and Midwest to win a narrow victory over President Gerald R. Ford. His showing indicated the importance to the Democratic Party of having a candidate capable of attracting support in the South, which was becoming increasingly Republican by the 1970s. • *What drove so many southerners into the Republican Party?*

THE TRIALS OF JIMMY CARTER

Like Ford, Jimmy Carter assumed the presidency at a moment when the nation faced problems of staggering complexity and difficulty. But Carter seemed at times to make his predicament worse by a style of leadership that many Americans considered self-righteous and inflexible.

Carter devoted much of his time to the problems of energy and the economy. Entering office in the midst of a recession, he moved first to reduce unemployment by raising public spending and cutting federal taxes. Unemployment declined, but inflation soared— mostly because of the continuing, sharp increases in energy prices by OPEC. During Carter's last two years in office, retail prices rose at over a 10 percent annual rate. Like Nixon and Ford before him, Carter responded with a combination of tight money and calls for voluntary restraint. Determined to stop inflation, he appointed conservative economists to head the Federal Reserve Board, which helped push interest rates to the highest levels in American history; at times, they exceeded 20 percent.

In the summer of 1979, instability in the Middle East produced a second major fuel shortage in the United States. In the midst of the crisis, OPEC announced another major price increase. Faced with increasing pressure to act, Carter went to Camp David, the presidential retreat in the Maryland mountains. Ten days later, he emerged to deliver a remarkable television address. It included a series of proposals for resolving the energy crisis. But it was most notable for Carter's bleak assessment of the national condition and his claim that there was a "crisis of confidence" that had struck "at the very heart and soul of our national will." The address became known as the "malaise" speech (although Carter himself had never used that word), and it helped fuel charges that the president was trying to blame his own problems on the American people. Carter's sudden firing of several members of his cabinet a few days later deepened his political dilemma.

HUMAN RIGHTS AND NATIONAL INTERESTS

Among Jimmy Carter's most frequent campaign promises was a new American foreign policy based on the defense of "human rights." Carter spoke out sharply about human rights violations in many countries (including, most prominently, the Soviet Union). But the administration also focused on more traditional concerns. Carter completed negotiations begun several years earlier on a pair of treaties to turn over control of the Panama Canal to the government of Panama. After an acrimonious debate, the Senate ratified the treaties by 68 to 32, only one vote more than the necessary two-thirds majority.

Carter's greatest success was in arranging a peace treaty between Egypt and Israel. Middle East negotiations had seemed hopelessly stalled when Egyptian president Anwar Sadat accepted an invitation in November 1977 from Prime Minister Menachem Begin to visit Israel. In Tel Aviv, he announced that Egypt was now willing to accept the state of Israel as a legitimate political entity.

When talks between Israeli and Egyptian negotiators stalled, Carter invited Sadat and Begin to a summit conference at Camp David in September 1978 and persuaded them to remain there for two weeks. On September 17, Carter escorted the two leaders into the White House to announce an agreement on a "framework" for an Egyptian-Israeli peace treaty. On March 26, 1979, Begin and Sadat returned together to the White House to sign a formal peace treaty between their two nations, known as the Camp David accords.

In the meantime, Carter continued trying to improve relations with China and the Soviet Union. He responded eagerly to the overtures of Deng Xiaoping, the new Chinese

SIGNING THE CAMP DAVID ACCORDS Jimmy Carter experienced many frustrations during his presidency, but his successful efforts in 1978 to negotiate a peace treaty between Israel and Egypt were undoubtedly his finest hour. Egyptian President Anwar Sadat and Israeli Prime Minister Menachem Begin join Carter here in the East Room of the White House in March 1979 to sign the accords they had begun to hammer out during two weeks at the president's retreat at Camp David several months before. (AP Images)

leader attempting to open his nation to the outside world. On December 15, 1978, Washington and Beijing announced the resumption of formal diplomatic relations. A few months later, Carter traveled to Vienna to meet with the aging and ailing Brezhnev to finish drafting the new SALT II arms control agreement, which set limits on the number of long-range missiles, bombers, and nuclear warheads on each side. Almost immediately, however, SALT II met with fierce conservative opposition in the United States Senate. The agreement was never ratified.

THE YEAR OF THE HOSTAGES

Ever since the early 1950s, the United States had provided political support and, more recently, massive military assistance to the government of the shah of Iran, hoping to make his nation a bulwark against Soviet expansion in the Middle East. By 1979, however, the shah was in deep trouble with his own people. Many Iranians resented the repressive, authoritarian tactics through which the shah had maintained his autocratic rule. At the same time, Islamic clergy (and much of the fiercely religious populace) opposed his efforts to modernize and westernize Iranian society. The combination of resentments produced a powerful revolutionary movement, which forced the shah to flee the country in January 1979.

By late 1979, power in Iran resided with a zealous religious leader, the Ayatollah Ruhollah Khomeini, who was fiercely anti-Western and anti-American. In late October 1979, the deposed shah arrived in New York to be treated for cancer. Days later, on November 4, an armed crowd invaded the American embassy in Tehran, seized the diplomats and military personnel inside, and demanded the return of the shah to Iran in exchange for their freedom. Fifty-three Americans remained hostages in the embassy for over a year.

Only weeks after the hostage seizure, on December 27, 1979, Soviet troops invaded Afghanistan, the mountainous Islamic nation lying between the USSR and Iran. The Soviet Union had been a power in Afghanistan for years and the dominant force since April 1978. But while some observers claimed that the Soviet invasion was a Russian attempt to secure the status quo, Carter claimed it was a Russian "stepping stone to their possible control over much of the world's oil supplies" and the "gravest threat to world peace since World War II." Carter angrily imposed a series of economic sanctions on the Russians, canceled American participation in the 1980 summer Olympic Games in Moscow, and announced the withdrawal of SALT II from Senate consideration.

THE RISE OF THE NEW CONSERVATIVE MOVEMENT

The jarring social and economic changes in American life in the 1960s and 1970s disillusioned many liberals, perplexed the already weakened left, and provided the right with its most important opportunity in generations to seize a position of authority in American life.

THE SUNBELT AND ITS POLITICS

One of the most widely discussed demographic phenomena of the 1970s was the rise of what became known as the "Sunbelt"—the states of the Southeast and the Southwest. By 1980, the population of the Sunbelt had risen to exceed that of the older industrial regions of the North and the East.

The strong populist traditions in the South and the West helped produce opposition to the growth of government and resentment of the proliferating regulations and restrictions of the liberal state. Many of those regulations and restrictions—environmental laws, land-use restrictions, and other laws—affected the West more than any other region.

The so-called Sagebrush Rebellion, which emerged in parts of the West in the late 1970s, mobilized conservative opposition to environmental laws and restrictions on development. It also sought to portray the West as a victim of government control. Its members demanded that the very large amounts of land the federal government owned in western states be opened for development.

Suburbanization also fueled the rise of the right. Not all suburbs bred conservative politics, of course; but the most militantly conservative communities in America—among them Orange County in southern California—were mostly suburbs. The seemingly tranquil life of the suburb contributed to a conservative view of the world.

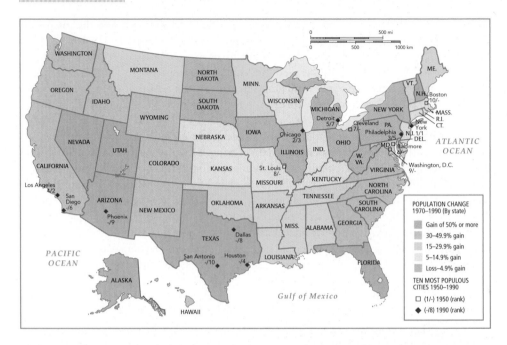

GROWTH OF THE SUNBELT, 1970-1990   One of the most important demographic changes of the last decades of the twentieth century was the shift of population out of traditional population centers in the Northeast and Midwest and toward the states of the so-called Sunbelt—most notably the Southwest and the Pacific Coast. This map gives a dramatic illustration of the changing concentration of population between 1970 and 1990. The orange states are those that lost population, while the purple and blue states are those that made significant gains (30 percent or more). • *What was the impact of this population shift on the politics of the 1980s?*

RELIGIOUS REVIVALISM

In the 1960s, traditional mainstream religion experienced a conspicuous decline. But in its place began a powerful religious revival. Some of the new religious enthusiasm found expression in the rise of various cults and unorthodox faiths: the Church of Scientology; the Unification Church of the Reverend Sun Myung Moon; even the tragic People's Temple, whose members committed mass suicide in their jungle retreat in Guyana in 1978. But the most important impulse of the religious revival was the growth of evangelical Christianity.

Evangelicals have in common a belief in personal conversion (being "born again" through direct communication with Jesus). Evangelical religion had been the dominant form of Christianity in America through much of its history. In its modern form, it became increasingly visible during the early 1950s, when evangelicals such as Billy Graham and Pentecostals such as Oral Roberts began to attract huge national (and international) followings for their energetic revivalism.

By the late 1970s, evangelical Christians had become more visible and more politically assertive. More than 70 million Americans now described themselves as born-again Christians. Christian evangelicals owned newspapers, magazines, radio stations, and television networks. They operated their own schools and universities. Three modern presidents—Jimmy Carter, Bill Clinton, and George W. Bush—have identified themselves as evangelicals.

Some evangelical Christians supported racial and economic justice and world peace. For many evangelicals, however, the message of evangelical religion was very different—but no less political. In the 1970s, may Christian evangelicals became active on the political and cultural right. Alarmed by what they considered the spread of immorality and disorder in American life, they were concerned about the way a secular culture was intruding into their communities, schools, and families. Many evangelical men and women feared that the growth of feminism posed a threat to the traditional family, and they resented the way in which government policies advanced the goals of the women's movement. Particularly alarming to them were Supreme Court decisions eliminating all religious observance from schools and, later, the decision guaranteeing women the right to an abortion.

By the late 1970s, the "Christian right" had become a powerful political force. Jerry Falwell, a fundamentalist minister in Virginia with a substantial television audience, launched a highly visible movement he called the Moral Majority. The Pentecostal minister Pat Robertson began a political movement of his own and, in the 1990s, launched an organization known as the Christian Coalition. These and other organizations of the Christian right opposed federal interference in local affairs; denounced abortion, divorce, feminism, and homosexuality; defended unrestricted free enterprise; and supported a strong American posture in the world. Some denied the scientific doctrine of evolution and instead urged the teaching in schools of the biblical story of the Creation or—beginning in the early twenty-first century—the idea of "intelligent design." Their goal was a new era in which Christian values once again dominated American life.

The role of religion in the growth of conservatism was not limited to evangelical Christians. In the 1970s, the Catholic Church began to make a strong case for tradition. The Church fought most zealously against abortion, thus joining the evangelical right in one of the most controversial issues of the time. Not all Catholics were or are conservatives; many priests and parishioners took strong liberal positions. But in the political world, Catholics became strong allies of the right, joining evangelicals in fighting for many conservative issues.

Mormons, too, began to emerge as an important element of the right. For many years, Mormons did not publicize their conservatism. But like Catholics, many Mormons began to take conservative stances in the 1970s on some of the controversial battles of the time. Some of these Mormons, wealthy and successful businessmen, became conservative political politicians in various parts of the country. (In 2012, two wealthy Mormons—Mitt Romney and Jon Huntsman, both former governors—were candidates for the presidency.)

THE EMERGENCE OF THE NEW RIGHT

Religious issues were only a part—although an important part—of what became known as the new right—a diverse but powerful movement that enjoyed rapid growth in the 1970s and early 1980s. It had begun to take shape after the 1964 election, in which Barry Goldwater had suffered his shattering defeat. Energetic organizers responded to that disaster by building a new and powerful set of right-wing institutions to help conservatives campaign more effectively in the future. Beginning in the 1970s, largely because of these organizational advances, conservatives found themselves almost always better funded and organized than their opponents. By the late 1970s, there were right-wing think tanks, consulting firms, lobbyists, foundations, and colleges and universities. Conservatives also succeeded in building mechanisms to raise money, mobilize activists, and project their

THE MALL

THE modern shopping mall is the direct descendant of an earlier retail innovation, the automobile-oriented shopping center, which strove to combine a number of different shops in a single structure, with parking for customers. The first modern shopping center, the Country Club Plaza, opened in Kansas City in 1924. By the mid-1950s, shopping centers—ranging from small "strips" to large integrated complexes—had proliferated throughout the country and were challenging traditional downtown shopping districts, which suffered from limited parking and from the movement of middle-class residents to the suburbs.

In 1956, the first enclosed, climate-controlled shopping mall—the Southdale Shopping Center—opened in Minneapolis, followed quickly by similar ventures in New York, New Jersey, Illinois, North Carolina, and Tennessee. As the malls spread, they grew larger and more elaborate. By the 1970s, vast "regional malls" were emerging—Tyson's Corner in Fairfax, Virginia; Roosevelt Field on Long Island; the Galleria in Houston; and many others—that drew customers from great distances and dazzled them not only with acres of varied retail space but also with restaurants, movie theaters, skating rinks, bowling alleys, hotels, video arcades, and large public spaces with fountains, benches, trees, gardens, and concert venues. "The more needs you fulfill, the longer people stay," one developer observed.

Malls became self-contained imitations of cities—but in a setting from which many of the troubling and abrasive features of downtowns had been eliminated. Malls were insulated from the elements. They were policed by private security forces, who (unlike real police) could and usually did keep "undesirable" customers off the premises. They were off-limits to beggars, vagrants, the homeless, and anyone else the managers considered unattractive to their customers. Malls set out to "perfect" urban space, recasting the city as a protected, controlled, and socially homogeneous site attractive to, and in many cases dominated by, white middle-class people.

Malls were designed with women, the principal consumers in most families, mainly in mind. "I wouldn't know how to design a center for a man," one architect said of the complexes he built. They catered to the concerns of mothers about their own and their children's safety, and they offered products of particular interest to them.

Malls also became important to young people, who flocked to them in the way that

ideas to a broad audience. Building from a list compiled by Richard Viguerie after the 1964 Goldwater campaign, the right built a direct-mail operation that ultimately reached millions of conservative voters. Evangelicals such as Pat Robertson used cable television to reach the conservative faithful. Conservative radio hosts such as Rush Limbaugh created shows that attracted a vast national audience.

Another factor in the revival of the right was the emergence in the late 1960s and early 1970s of Ronald Reagan. Once a moderately successful actor, he had moved into politics

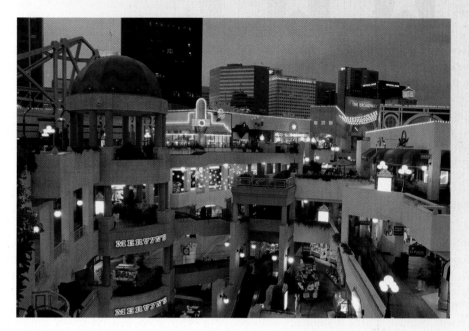

HORTON PLAZA SAN DIEGO This enormous shopping mall in 1985 is an example of the enormous growth of shopping and consumption. The malls also become places where groups of people—most of them young people—gather during the day. (© Richard Cummins/Corbis)

earlier generations had flocked to street corners and squares in traditional downtowns. The malls were places for teenagers to meet friends, go to movies, avoid parents, hang out. They were places to buy electronics, clothes, or personal items. And they were places to work. Low-paying retail jobs, plentiful in malls, were typical first working experiences for many teens.

The proliferation of malls has dismayed many people, who see in them a threat to the sense of community in America. By insulating people from the diversity and conflict of urban life, critics argue, malls divide groups from one another and erode the bonds that make it possible for those groups to understand one another. But malls, like the suburbs they serve, also create a kind of community. They are homogeneous and protected, to be sure, but they are also social gathering places in many areas where the alternative is not the rich, diverse life of the downtown but the even more isolated experience of shopping in isolated strips—or through catalogs, telephone, and the Internet. •

UNDERSTAND, ANALYZE, & EVALUATE

1. How did the shopping mall change suburban life?
2. Are malls a unifying influence on social life? In what ways are malls divisive?

in the early 1960s and in 1964 delivered a memorable television speech on behalf of Goldwater. After Goldwater's defeat, Reagan worked quickly to seize the leadership of the conservative wing of the party. In 1966, with the support of a group of wealthy conservatives, he won the first of two terms as governor of California.

The presidency of Gerald Ford also played an important role in the rise of conservatism. Ford, probably without realizing it, touched on some of the right's rawest nerves. He appointed as vice president Nelson Rockefeller, the liberal Republican governor of

New York and an heir to one of America's great fortunes; many conservatives had been demonizing Rockefeller and his family for more than twenty years. Ford proposed an amnesty program for draft resisters, embraced the hated Nixon-Kissinger policies of détente, presided over the fall of Vietnam, and agreed to cede the Panama Canal to Panama. When Reagan challenged Ford in the 1976 Republican primaries, the president survived, barely, only by dumping Nelson Rockefeller from the ticket and replacing him with Kansas Senator Robert Dole. He also agreed to a platform largely written by conservatives.

THE TAX REVOLT

At least equally important to the success of the new right was a new and potent conservative issue: the tax revolt. It had its public beginnings in 1978, when Howard Jarvis, a conservative activist in California, launched the first successful major citizens' tax revolt with Proposition 13, a referendum question on the state ballot rolling back property tax rates. Because property taxes were the most important source of funding for schools, Proposition 13 began the slow deterioration of much of the great California education system. Similar antitax movements soon began in other states and eventually spread to national politics.

In Proposition 13 and similar initiatives, members of the right succeeded in separating the issue of taxes from the issue of what taxes supported. Instead of attacking popular programs such as Social Security, they attacked taxes themselves and argued that much of the money government raised through taxes was wasted. Virtually no one liked to pay taxes, and as the economy grew weaker and the relative burden of paying taxes grew heavier, that resentment naturally rose.

THE CAMPAIGN OF 1980

By the time of the crises in Iran and Afghanistan, Jimmy Carter was in desperate political trouble—his standing in popularity polls lower than that of any president in history. Senator Edward Kennedy, younger brother of John and Robert Kennedy, challenged him in the primaries. And while Carter managed to withstand the confrontation and win his party's nomination, his campaign aroused little popular enthusiasm.

The Republican Party, in the meantime, rallied enthusiastically behind the man who, four years earlier, had nearly stolen the nomination from Gerald Ford. Ronald Reagan was a sharp critic of the excesses of the federal government. He linked his campaign to the spreading tax revolt by promising substantial tax cuts. He also championed a restoration of American "strength" and "pride" in the world.

On election day 1980, the anniversary of the seizure of the hostages in Iran, Reagan swept to victory, winning 51 percent of the vote to 41 percent for Jimmy Carter and 7 percent for John Anderson—a moderate Republican congressman from Illinois who had mounted an independent campaign. The Republican Party won control of the Senate for the first time since 1952; and although the Democrats retained a modest majority in the House, the lower chamber, too, seemed firmly in the hands of conservatives.

On the day of Reagan's inauguration, the American hostages in Iran were released after their 444-day ordeal. The government of Iran, desperate for funds to support its floundering war against neighboring Iraq, had ordered the hostages freed in return for a release of billions in Iranian assets that the Carter administration had frozen in American banks.

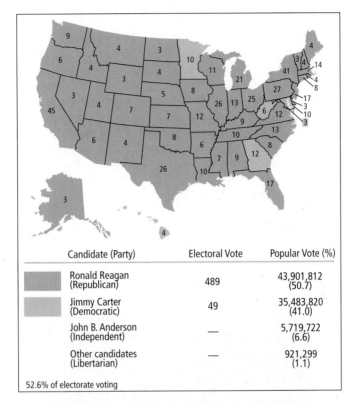

Candidate (Party)	Electoral Vote	Popular Vote (%)
Ronald Reagan (Republican)	489	43,901,812 (50.7)
Jimmy Carter (Democratic)	49	35,483,820 (41.0)
John B. Anderson (Independent)	—	5,719,722 (6.6)
Other candidates (Libertarian)	—	921,299 (1.1)

52.6% of electorate voting

THE ELECTION OF 1980 Although Ronald Reagan won only slightly more than half of the popular vote in the 1980 presidential election, his electoral majority was overwhelming—a reflection to a large degree of the deep unpopularity of President Jimmy Carter in 1980. • *What had made Carter so unpopular?*

Americans welcomed the hostages home with demonstrations of joy and patriotism seldom seen since the end of World War II. But while the celebration in 1945 had marked a great American triumph, the euphoria in 1981 marked something quite different—a troubled nation grasping for reassurance. Ronald Reagan set out to provide it.

THE "REAGAN REVOLUTION"

Ronald Reagan assumed the presidency in January 1981, promising a change in government more fundamental than any since the New Deal of fifty years before. While his eight years in office produced a significant shift in public policy, they brought nothing so fundamental as many of his supporters had hoped or his opponents had feared. But Reagan succeeded brilliantly in making his own engaging personality the central fact of American politics in the 1980s. He also benefited from the power of the diverse coalition that had united behind him.

THE REAGAN COALITION

The Reagan coalition included a relatively small but highly influential group of wealthy Americans firmly committed to unfettered capitalism. They believed that the market offered the best solutions to most problems, and they shared a deep hostility to most (although not all) government interference in markets. Central to this group's agenda in the 1980s was opposition to what it considered the "redistributive" politics of the government (and especially its highly progressive tax structure) and hostility to the rise of what they believed were "antibusiness" government regulations. Reagan courted these free-market conservatives carefully and effectively, and in the end it was their interests his administration most effectively served.

A second element of the Reagan coalition consisted of a small but influential group of intellectuals commonly known as "neoconservatives," who gave to the right something it had not had in many years—a firm base among "opinion leaders," people with access to the most influential public forums of ideas. Many of these people had once been liberals and, before that, socialists. But during the turmoil of the 1960s, they had become alarmed by what they considered a dangerous and destructive radicalism. Neoconservatives were sympathetic to the complaints and demands of capitalists, but their principal concern was to reassert legitimate authority and reaffirm Western democratic, anticommunist values and commitments. They considered themselves soldiers in a battle to "win back the culture"—from the crass, radical ideas that had polluted it.

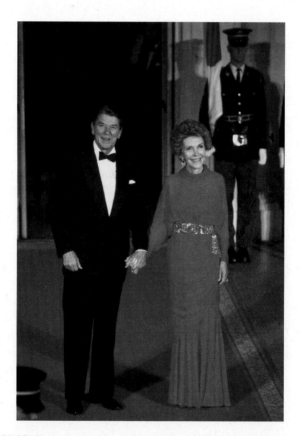

RONALD AND NANCY REAGAN The president and the first lady greet guests at a White House social event. Nancy Reagan was committed to making the White House, and her husband's presidency, seem more glamorous than those of most recent administrations. But she also played an important, if usually quiet, policy role in the administration. (Dirck Halstead/ Time & Life Pictures/Getty Images)

Neoconservatives also strongly dissented from the new foreign policy orthodoxies of liberals and the left in the aftermath of the Vietnam War. They rejected the idea that America should be a less interventionist nation, that it should work to ease tensions with the Soviet Union, and that it should tolerate radical regimes. Instead, they argued for an escalation of the Cold War as part of an effort to destabilize the Soviet Union. They insisted that the Vietnam War was an appropriate American commitment and that its abandonment was a terrible mistake. They believed that the United States had a special role to play in the world and should be willing to use military intervention. These ideas helped shape the foreign policy of the Reagan administration. The same ideas (and some of the same people) resurfaced in the early twenty-first century to help shape the international policies of the George W. Bush administration.

These groups formed an uneasy alliance with the broad grassroots conservative movement. This new right shared a fundamental distrust of the "eastern establishment": a suspicion of its motives and goals and a sense that it exercised a dangerous, secret power in American life. These populist conservatives expressed the kinds of concerns that outsiders—nonelites—have traditionally voiced in American society: an opposition to centralized power and influence and a fear of living in a world where distant, hostile forces are controlling society and threatening individual freedom and community autonomy. It was a testament to Ronald Reagan's political skills and personal charm that he was able to generate enthusiastic support from these populist conservatives while at the same time appealing to more elite conservative groups whose concerns were in many ways antithetical to those of the new right.

Reagan in the White House

Even many people who disagreed with Reagan's policies found themselves drawn to his attractive and carefully honed public image. He turned seventy years old a few weeks after taking office and was the oldest man ever to serve as president. But through most of his presidency, he appeared to be vigorous, resilient, even youthful. When wounded in an assassination attempt in 1981, he joked with doctors on his way into surgery and appeared to bounce back from the ordeal with remarkable speed. Even when things went wrong, as they often did, the blame seldom seemed to attach to Reagan himself (inspiring some Democrats to refer to him as the "Teflon president").

Reagan was not much involved in the day-to-day affairs of running the government; he surrounded himself with tough, energetic administrators who insulated him from many of the pressures of the office and who apparently relied on him largely for general guidance, not specific decisions. At times, the president revealed a startling ignorance about the nature of his own policies or the actions of his subordinates. But Reagan did make active use of his office to generate public support for his administration's programs.

"Supply-Side" Economics

Reagan's 1980 campaign for the presidency had promised to restore the economy to health by a bold experiment that became known as "supply-side"—or, to its critics, "trickle-down"—economics. Eventually, they were called "Reaganomics." Supply-side economics operated from the assumption that the woes of the American economy were in large part a result of excessive taxation, which left inadequate capital available to investors to stimulate growth.

CONSIDER THE SOURCE

EXCERPT FROM JAMES WATT, "DESPITE CRITICS, INTERIOR DEPT. MAKES RAPID PROGRESS," *HUMAN EVENTS*, 1982

Question: In a sense, Mr. Secretary, I only really have one question. What's all the fuss? You're probably the only Secretary of the Interior in history that wouldn't need an American Express card so that people would know who you are when you travel. What's the source of all this uproar?

Answer: I think that America is engaged in a great battle for its political liberty and spiritual freedom. And to take care of those two basic fundamentals, it is necessary that a people properly manage their human resources and their natural resources. The President, being the good conservative that he is, has focused his attention on human resource management and priorities. He has looked at the economic situation and social problems and he has focused his attention there. He has named me as the chief of natural resource management. Unless both resources are properly managed by the people, the country can never be great. In appointing me, he has picked a very conservative leader that shares his philosophies. The liberals who would seek to destroy our political liberty and our spiritual freedom because they believe in the institution of government rather than in the people and our fundamental

beliefs, recognize what President Reagan has done. He has put himself in charge of human resources and he's said, "Jim, take care of the natural resource issues." While we focus on the environment and on energy and the parks, those things are really not the issue. The issue is, "What type of government are we going to have?" The liberals have looked at my background and performance and have come to realize that they have met a guy who knows what the real battle is about. I don't get confused with a single park or a single oil well or that kind of thing. They have met a guy who is committed to an ideology and a set of principles that is fundamental to liberty and freedom. They are battling me on a philosophical war zone. That's why there is a vicious fight, because this is a battle of ideologies, not a battle over a park or anything else. Never before has anyone so clearly identified the human and natural resource issues of government and been able to lay it out and tell it like it is. And I don't compromise in what I say or what I believe. It makes good print and the print media have been captured by liberals who are not championing the causes of political liberty and spiritual freedom.

The solution, therefore, was to reduce taxes, with particularly generous benefits to corporations and wealthy individuals, in order to encourage new investments.

In its first months in office, the new administration hastily assembled a legislative program based on the supply-side idea. It proposed $40 billion in budget reductions and managed to win congressional approval of almost all of them. In addition, the president proposed a bold three-year, 30 percent reduction on both individual and corporate tax rates. In the summer of 1981, Congress passed it, too, after lowering the reductions to 25 percent. Reagan suceeded thanks to a disciplined Republican majority in the Senate and a Democratic majority in the House that was weak and riddled with defectors.

Question: If you want to put the question ideologically, a majority of Americans identify themselves as conservative. On the other hand, an overwhelming majority of those same Americans, now and throughout most of our history, have had strong conservationist feelings. America may have been the first country in the world to develop the idea of conserving natural resources systematically. And your critics are charging that you are going contrary to this idea, that you're going to allow America's public lands to be destroyed by mining and drilling and grazing.

Answer: It's true that that is what they say. But a real conservative is your best conservationist, because he believes in people and he manages the land for the present population, but also for future generations. The words "conservative" and "conservationist" come from the same root. We are the conservationists, we conservatives. The liberal has prostituted the word in an effort to achieve his political objectives.

Question: Which are?

Answer: Which are to institutionalize and centralize all social planning. So the battle, you see, is not over the environment. The facts are that our record as conservationists and environmentalists is second to none. We've brought massive change, as our annual report outlines. The Congress has supported us without exception on our major budget initiatives. There has not been one vote that would alter an initiative that we've taken. The governors of America have supported our massive change, with one exception: Jerry Brown of California. The state legislatures are with us. No man could present that record to you if he weren't being a good conservationist because the mood of America is to be a good environmentalist, to be a good steward, to take care of the land. But the point is that when we came in, the pendulum was so far out into left field we had to bring it down into the mainstream of the environmental movement in America. That is what we are doing and that is why we have the support of the Congress and the governors.

UNDERSTAND, ANALYZE, & EVALUATE

1. In Watt's view, what was at stake in the debate over environmental protection and conservation?
2. What attitude did Watt display toward his political opponents? How did he fit into broader trends among American conservatives?

Source: James G. Watt, "Despite Critics, Interior Dept. Makes Rapid Progress," *Human Events* 17, no. 27 (1982). Reprinted with permission by Human Events.

Reagan appointees fanned out through the executive branch of government, reducing the role of government in American economic life. "Deregulation," an idea many Democrats had begun to embrace in the Carter years, became almost a religion in the Reagan administration. Secretary of the Interior James Watt, a major figure in the antienvironmental Sagebrush Rebellion, opened up public lands and water to development. The Environmental Protection Agency (before some of its directors were indicted for corruption) relaxed or entirely eliminated enforcement of major environmental laws and regulations.

By early 1982, the nation had sunk into a severe recession. The Reagan economic program was not directly to blame for the problems, but neither did it offer a quick solution. During 1982, unemployment reached 11 percent, one of the highest levels since the

1930s. But before the recession could do great damage to Reagan, the economy recovered more rapidly and impressively than almost anyone had expected. By late 1983, unemployment had fallen to 8.2 percent, and it declined steadily for several years after that. The gross national product (GNP) grew 3.6 percent in a year, the largest increase since the mid-1970s. Inflation fell below 5 percent. The economy continued to grow, and both inflation and unemployment remained low through most of the decade.

The recovery was a result of many things. The years of tight money policies by the Federal Reserve Board had helped lower inflation; perhaps equally important, the Fed had lowered interest rates early in 1983 in response to the recession. A worldwide "energy glut" and the virtual collapse of the OPEC cartel had produced at least a temporary end to the inflationary pressures of spiraling fuel costs. And staggering federal budget deficits were pumping billions of dollars into the flagging economy. As a result, consumer spending and business investment both increased. The stock market rose up from its doldrums of the 1970s and began a sustained and historic boom. In August 1982, the Dow Jones Industrial Average stood at 777. Five years later it had passed 2,000. Despite a frightening crash in the fall of 1987, the market continued to grow for more than another decade. In the mid-2000s, the Dow Jones average briefly passed 14,000 in 2006.

The Fiscal Crisis

The economic revival did little at first to reduce the staggering, and to many Americans alarming, federal budget deficits (the gap between revenue and spending in a single year) or to slow the growth in the national debt (the debt the nation accumulates over time as a result of its annual deficits). By the mid-1980s, this growing fiscal crisis had become one of the central issues in American politics. Having entered office promising a balanced budget within four years, Reagan presided over record budget deficits and accumulated more debt in his eight years in office than the American government had accumulated in its entire previous history. Before the 1980s, the highest single-year budget deficit in American history had been $66 billion (in 1976). Throughout the 1980s, the annual budget deficit consistently exceeded $100 billion (and in 1991 peaked at $268 billion). The national debt rose from $907 billion in 1980 to nearly $3.5 trillion by 1991. Much larger deficits—and debt—were soon to come.

The enormous deficits had many causes. The budget suffered from enormous increases in the costs of "entitlement" programs (especially both Social Security and Medicare), a result of the aging of the population and dramatic increases in the cost of health care. The 1981 tax cuts, the largest in American history, also contributed to the deficit. The massive increase in military spending on which the Reagan administration insisted added much more to the federal budget than its cuts in domestic spending removed.

In the face of these deficits, the administration proposed further cuts in "discretionary" domestic spending, which included many programs aimed at the poorest (and politically weakest) Americans. By the end of Reagan's third year in office, funding for domestic programs had been cut nearly as far as Congress (and, apparently, the public) was willing to tolerate, and still no end to the rising deficit was in sight. By the late 1980s, many fiscal conservatives were calling for a constitutional amendment mandating a balanced budget—a provision the president himself claimed to support. But Congress never approved the amendment.

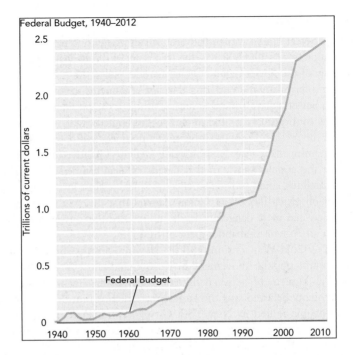

Federal Budget, 1940–2012

THE FEDERAL BUDGET For many years since the 1950s, the federal budget was close to being in balance. But beginning with the Bush tax cuts, the budget began to be in deficit and remained so since 2001. Adding to the deficits were the Iraq and Afghanistan Wars and the economic crisis. By 2012, the federal deficit was over $1.6 trillion dollars.

REAGAN AND THE WORLD

Relations with the Soviet Union, which had been steadily deteriorating in the last years of the Carter administration, grew still chillier in the first years of the Reagan presidency. The president spoke harshly of the Soviet regime (which he once called the "evil empire"), accusing it of sponsoring world terrorism and declaring that any armaments negotiations must be linked to negotiations on Soviet behavior in other areas. Although the president had long denounced the SALT II arms control treaty as unfavorable to the United States, he continued to honor its provisions. But the president proposed the most ambitious (and potentially most expensive) new military program in many years: the Strategic Defense Initiative (SDI), widely known as "Star Wars" (after the popular movie of that name). Reagan claimed that SDI, through the use of lasers and satellites, could provide an effective shield against incoming missiles and thus make nuclear war obsolete. The Soviet Union claimed that the new program would elevate the arms race to new and more dangerous levels and insisted that any arms control agreement should begin with an American abandonment of SDI.

The escalation of Cold War tensions and the slowing of arms control initiatives helped produce an important popular movement in Europe and the United States calling for a "nuclear freeze," an agreement between the two superpowers not to expand their atomic arsenals. In what many believed was the largest mass demonstration in American history, nearly a million people rallied in New York City's Central Park in 1982 to support the freeze. Perhaps partly in response to this growing pressure, the administration began tentative efforts to revive arms control negotiations in 1983.

The administration created a new policy known as the Reagan Doctrine, designed to help resist communism and anti-Americanism in the Third World. The United States sent soldiers and money to weaken or overturn anti-American countries—among them Grenada, El Salvador, and Nicaragua. But Reagan generally backed away from more serious warfare. In 1982, when the Israeli army invaded Lebanon, American peacekeeping forces entered Beirut to stabilize the nation. But when a terrorist bombing of a U.S. military barracks in Beirut led to the death of 241 marines, Reagan quickly withdrew the American forces. There were other terrorist events against America and other nations by attacking bombs, ships, and diplomatic buildings—the beginning of what would become a long battle against terrorism.

Reagan approached the campaign of 1984 at the head of a united Republican Party firmly committed to his candidacy. The Democrats nominated former vice president Walter Mondale. Mondale brought momentary excitement to the Democratic campaign by selecting a woman, Representative Geraldine Ferraro of New York, to be his running mate and the first female candidate ever to appear on a national ticket. But Reagan's triumphant campaign scarcely took note of his opponents and spoke instead of what he claimed was the remarkable revival of American fortunes and spirits under his leadership, or what he sometimes called "Morning in America." He won 59 percent of the vote and carried every state but Mondale's native Minnesota and the District of Columbia.

AMERICA AND THE WANING OF THE COLD WAR

Many factors contributed to the collapse of the Soviet Empire. The long, stalemated war in Afghanistan proved at least as disastrous to the Soviet Union as the Vietnam War had been to America. The government in Moscow failed to address a long-term economic decline in the

Soviet republics and the Eastern-bloc nations. Restiveness with the heavy-handed policies of communist police states was growing throughout much of the Soviet Empire. But the most visible factor at the time was the emergence of Mikhail Gorbachev, who succeeded to the leadership of the Soviet Union in 1985 and, to the surprise of almost everyone (probably including himself), very quickly became the most revolutionary figure in world politics in decades.

The Fall of the Soviet Union

Gorbachev transformed Soviet politics with two dramatic new initiatives: *glasnost* (openness), the dismantling of many of the repressive mechanisms that had been conspicuous features of Soviet life for over half a century, and *perestroika* (reform), an effort to restructure the rigid and unproductive Soviet economy by introducing, among other things, such elements of capitalism as private ownership and the profit motive. He also began to transform Soviet foreign policy.

The severe economic problems at home evidently convinced Gorbachev that the Soviet Union could no longer sustain its extended commitments around the world. As early as 1987, he began reducing the Soviet presence in Eastern Europe. And in 1989, in the space of a few months, every communist state in Europe—Poland, Hungary, Czechoslovakia, Bulgaria, Romania, East Germany, Yugoslavia, and Albania—either overthrew its government or forced it to transform itself into an essentially noncommunist (and in some cases, actively anticommunist) regime. Perhaps the most dramatic event of this extraordinary revolution was the tearing down of the infamous Berlin Wall.

In May 1989, students in China launched a mass movement calling for greater democratization. But in June, hard-line leaders seized control of the government and sent military

THE FALL OF THE BERLIN WALL   Thousands of Germans on both sides of the Berlin Wall swarm across the wall as it falls, marking the reunification of Germany and ending the Cold War. (© Caro/Alamy)

forces to crush the uprising. The result was a bloody massacre on June 3, 1989, in Tiananmen Square in Beijing, in which an unknown number of demonstrators died. The assault crushed the democracy movement and restored hard-liners to power. It did not, however, stop China's efforts to modernize and even westernize its economy.

But China was an exception to the widespread movement toward democratization. Early in 1990, the government of South Africa, long an international pariah for its rigid enforcement of "apartheid" (a system designed to protect white supremacy), legalized the chief black party in the nation, the African National Congress (ANC), which had been banned for decades. The government also released from prison the leader of the ANC, Nelson Mandela, who had been in jail for twenty-seven years. Over the next several years, the South African government repealed its apartheid laws. And in 1994, there were national elections in which all South Africans could participate. As a result, Nelson Mandela became the first black president of South Africa.

In 1991, communism began to collapse in the Soviet Union itself. An unsuccessful coup by hard-line Soviet leaders on August 19 precipitated a dramatic unraveling of communist power. Within days, the coup itself collapsed in the face of resistance from the public and crucial elements within the military. By the end of August, many of the republics of the Soviet Union had declared independence; the Soviet government was clearly powerless to stop the fragmentation. Gorbachev himself finally resigned as leader of the now virtually powerless Communist Party and Soviet government, and the Soviet Union ceased to exist.

The last years of the Reagan administration coincided with the first years of the Gorbachev regime; and while Reagan was skeptical of Gorbachev at first, he gradually became convinced that the Soviet leader was sincere in his desire for reform. In 1988, the two superpowers signed a treaty eliminating American and Soviet intermediate-range nuclear forces (INF) from Europe—the most significant arms control agreement of the nuclear age. At about the same time, Gorbachev ended the Soviet Union's long and frustrating military involvement in Afghanistan.

THE FADING OF THE REAGAN REVOLUTION

For a time, the dramatic changes around the world and Reagan's personal popularity deflected attention from a series of scandals that might well have destroyed another administration, including revelations of illegal and ethical lapses in the Environmental Protection Agency, the CIA, the Department of Defense, the Department of Labor, the Department of Justice, and the Department of Housing and Urban Development. A more serious scandal emerged within the savings and loan industry, which the Reagan administration had helped deregulate in the early 1980s. By the end of the decade, the industry was in chaos, and the government was forced to step in to prevent a complete collapse. The cost of the debacle to the public eventually ran to more than half a trillion dollars.

But the most politically damaging scandal of the Reagan years came to light in November 1986, when the White House conceded that it had sold weapons to the revolutionary government of Iran as part of a largely unsuccessful effort to secure the release of several Americans being held hostage. Even more damaging was the revelation that some of the money from the arms deal with Iran had been covertly and illegally funneled into a fund to aid the contras in Nicaragua.

In the months that followed, aggressive reporting and a series of congressional hearings exposed a widespread pattern of covert activities orchestrated by the White House and dedicated to advancing the administration's foreign policy aims through secret and at times

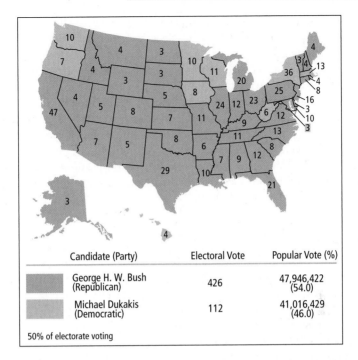

Candidate (Party)	Electoral Vote	Popular Vote (%)
George H. W. Bush (Republican)	426	47,946,422 (54.0)
Michael Dukakis (Democratic)	112	41,016,429 (46.0)

50% of electorate voting

THE ELECTION OF 1988 Democrats had high hopes going into the election of 1988, but Vice President George Bush won a decisive victory over Michael Dukakis, who did only slightly better than Walter Mondale had done four years earlier. • *What made it so difficult for a Democrat to challenge the Republicans in 1988 after eight years of a Republican administration?*

illegal means. The Iran-contra scandal, as it became known, did serious damage to the Reagan presidency—even though the investigations never tied the president himself to the most serious violations of the law.

THE FIRST BUSH PRESIDENCY

The fraying of the Reagan administration helped the Democrats regain control of the United States Senate in 1986 and fueled hopes in the party for a presidential victory in 1988. Michael Dukakis, a three-term governor of Massachusetts, eventually captured the nomination. Vice President George H. W. Bush was the largely unopposed Republican candidate. Neither candidate succeeded in creating public enthusiasm.

Beginning at the Republican Convention, Bush made his campaign a long, relentless attack on Dukakis, tying him to all the unpopular social and cultural stances Americans had come to identify with "liberals." Bush won a substantial victory in November: 54 percent of the popular vote to Dukakis's 46 percent, and 426 electoral votes to Dukakis's 112. But Bush carried few Republicans into office with him; the Democrats retained secure majorities in both houses of Congress. The broad popularity Bush enjoyed during much of his first three years in office was partly a result of his subdued, unthreatening public image. But it was primarily due to the wonder and excitement with which Americans viewed the dramatic events in the rest of the world. Bush moved cautiously at first in dealing with the changes in the Soviet Union. But like Reagan, he eventually cooperated with Gorbachev and reached a series of significant arms control agreements with the Soviet Union in its waning years.

On domestic issues, the Bush administration was less successful. His administration inherited a staggering burden of debt and a federal deficit that had been growing dramatically for nearly a decade. Constantly concerned about the right wing of his own party, Bush took divisive positions on such cultural issues as abortion and affirmative action that damaged his ability to work with the Democratic Congress.

Despite this political stalemate, Congress and the White House managed on occasion to agree on significant measures. In 1990, the president agreed to a significant tax increase as part of a multiyear "budget package" designed to reduce the deficit—thus violating his own 1988 campaign pledge of "no new taxes."

But the most serious domestic problem facing the Bush administration was one for which neither the president nor Congress had any answer: a recession that began late in 1990 and became more serious in 1991 and 1992.

THE GULF WAR

The fall of the Soviet Union left the United States in the unanticipated position of being the only real superpower in the world. The Bush administration, therefore, had to consider what to do with America's formidable political and military power in a world without another superpower.

The events of 1989–1991 suggested two possible answers. One was that the United States would reduce its military strength dramatically and concentrate its energies and resources on pressing domestic problems. The other was that America would continue to use its power actively, not to fight communism but to defend its regional and economic interests. The answer came quickly. In 1989, the administration ordered an invasion of Panama, which overthrew the unpopular military leader Manuel Noriega (under indictment in the United States for drug trafficking) and replaced him with an elected, pro-American regime. And in 1990, that same impulse drew the United States into the turbulent politics of the Middle East.

On August 2, 1990, the armed forces of Iraq invaded and quickly overwhelmed the emirate of Kuwait, the small oil-rich neighbor of Iraq. Saddam Hussein, the militaristic leader of Iraq, soon announced that he was annexing Kuwait. The Bush administration soon agreed to lead other nations in a campaign to force Iraq out of Kuwait—through the pressure of economic sanctions if possible, through military force if necessary. Within a few weeks, Bush had persuaded virtually every important government in the world, including the Soviet Union and almost all the Arab and Islamic states, to join in a United Nations–sanctioned trade embargo of Iraq.

At the same time, the United States and its allies (including the British, French, Egyptians, and Saudis) began deploying a large military force along the border between Kuwait and Saudi Arabia, a force that ultimately reached 690,000 troops (425,000 of them American). And on January 16, American and allied air forces began a massive bombardment of Iraqi troops in Kuwait and of military and industrial installations in Iraq itself.

The allied bombing continued for six weeks. On February 23, allied (primarily American) forces under the command of General Norman Schwarzkopf began a major ground offensive to the north of the Iraqi Forces. The allied armies encountered almost no resistance and suffered only light casualties (141 fatalities). Estimates of Iraqi deaths in the war were 100,000 or more. On February 28, Iraq announced its acceptance of allied terms for a cease-fire, and the brief Persian Gulf War came to an end.

THE ELECTION OF 1992

President Bush's popularity reached a record high in the immediate aftermath of the Gulf War. But the glow of that victory faded quickly as the recession worsened in late 1991. That gave Bill Clinton, the young five-term governor of Arkansas, an opportunity to emerge as the early front-runner. Clinton survived a bruising primary campaign and a series of damaging personal controversies to win his party's nomination.

Complicating the campaign was the emergence of Ross Perot, a blunt, forthright Texas billionaire who became an independent candidate by tapping popular resentment of the federal bureaucracy and by promising tough, uncompromising leadership to deal with the fiscal crisis. At several moments in the spring, Perot led both Bush and Clinton in public opinion polls. But in July, as he began to face hostile scrutiny from the media, he abruptly withdrew from the race. Early in October, he reentered and soon regained much (although never all) of his early support.

After a campaign in which the economy was the principal issue, Clinton won a clear, but hardly overwhelming, victory over Bush and Perot. He received 43 percent of the vote in the three-way race, to the president's 38 percent and Perot's 19 percent (the best showing for a third-party or independent candidate since Theodore Roosevelt in 1912). Clinton won 370 electoral votes to Bush's 168; Perot won none. Democrats retained control of both houses of Congress.

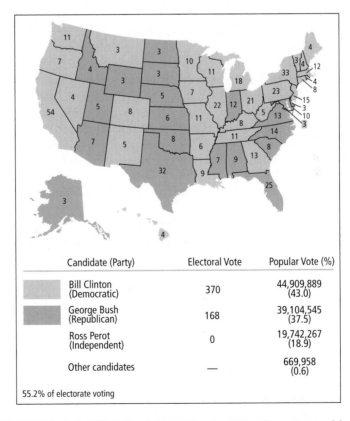

Candidate (Party)	Electoral Vote	Popular Vote (%)
Bill Clinton (Democratic)	370	44,909,889 (43.0)
George Bush (Republican)	168	39,104,545 (37.5)
Ross Perot (Independent)	0	19,742,267 (18.9)
Other candidates	—	669,958 (0.6)

55.2% of electorate voting

THE ELECTION OF 1992 In the 1992 election, for the first time since 1976, a Democrat captured the White House. And although the third-party candidacy of Ross Perot deprived Bill Clinton of an absolute majority, he nevertheless defeated George Bush by a decisive margin in both the popular and electoral votes. • *What factors had eroded President Bush's once-broad popularity by 1992? What explained the strong showing of Ross Perot?*

CONCLUSION

America in the late 1970s was, by the standards of its own recent history, an unusually troubled nation—numbed by the Watergate scandals, the fall of Vietnam, and perhaps most of all the nation's increasing economic difficulties. The unhappy presidencies of Gerald Ford and Jimmy Carter provided little relief from these accumulating problems and anxieties. Indeed, in the last year of the Carter presidency, the nation's prospects seemed particularly grim in light of severe economic problems, a traumatic seizure of American hostages in Iran, and a Soviet invasion of Afghanistan.

In the midst of these problems, American conservatives slowly and steadily prepared for an impressive revival. A coalition of disparate but impassioned groups on the right—including a large movement known as the "new right," with vaguely populist impulses—gained strength from the nation's troubles and from their own success in winning support for a broad-ranging revolt against taxes. Their efforts culminated in the election of 1980, when Ronald Reagan became the most conservative man in at least sixty years to be elected president of the United States.

Reagan's first term was a dramatic contrast to the troubled presidencies that had preceded it. He won substantial victories in Congress (cutting taxes, reducing spending on domestic programs, building up the military). Perhaps equally important, he made his own engaging personality one of the central political forces in national life. Easily reelected in 1984, he seemed to have solidified the conservative grip on national political life. In his second term, however, a series of scandals and misadventures—and the president's own declining energy—limited the administration's effectiveness. Nevertheless, Reagan's personal popularity remained high, and the economy continued to prosper—factors that helped his vice president, George H. W. Bush, to succeed him in 1989.

Bush's presidency was not as successful as Reagan's had been, and the perception of his disengagement with the nation's growing economic problems contributed to Bush's defeat in 1992. But a colossal historic event overshadowed most domestic concerns during Bush's term in office: the collapse of the Soviet Union and the fall of communist regimes all over Europe. The United States was to some degree a dazzled observer of this process. But the end of the Cold War also propelled the United States into the possession of unchallenged global preeminence—and drew it increasingly into the role of international arbiter and peacemaker. The Gulf War of 1991 was only the most dramatic example of the new global role the United States would now increasingly assume as the world's only true superpower.

RECALL AND REFLECT

1. Did the Ford and Carter presidencies fail to repair the damage done to the reputation of the presidency by the Watergate scandal and Nixon's resignation? If so, why?
2. Why did the American electorate become increasingly conservative during the 1970s and 1980s? What are some examples that testify to this increasing conservatism?
3. What philosophy guided foreign policy under Reagan? How did the rise of Mikhail Gorbachev alter Reagan's foreign policy toward the Soviet Union?

32 THE AGE OF GLOBALIZATION

A RESURGENCE OF PARTISANSHIP

THE ECONOMIC BOOM

SCIENCE AND TECHNOLOGY IN THE NEW ECONOMY

A CHANGING SOCIETY

A CONTESTED CULTURE

THE PERILS OF GLOBALIZATION

LOOKING AHEAD

1. How did increasing partisanship affect the presidential elections of the 1990s and 2000s, and what were the effects on the presidential administrations of those decades?

2. How did globalization account for the ups and downs of the national economy from the 1980s to the present?

3. How did the terrorist attacks of September 11, 2001, affect the American citizenry and American foreign policy?

AT 8:45 A.M. ON THE BRIGHT, sunny morning of September 11, 2001, a commercial airliner crashed into the side of one of the twin towers of the World Trade Center, the tallest buildings in New York, and exploded in flames. Less than half an hour later, another commercial airliner rammed into the companion tower, creating a second fireball. Little more than an hour after that, both towers—their steel girders buckling in response to the tremendous heat—collapsed. At about the same time, in Washington, another commercial airliner crashed into the Pentagon. And several hundred miles away, still another airplane crashed in a field not far from Pittsburgh, after passengers apparently seized the cockpit and prevented the hijackers from taking the plane to its unknown target. These four almost simultaneous catastrophes caused the deaths of nearly 3,000 people.

The events of September 11 and their aftermath produced significant changes in American life. And yet there was at least one great continuity between the world of the 1990s and the world that seemed to begin on September 11, 2001. The United States in the last years of the twentieth century and the first years of the twenty-first, more than at any other time in its history, was becoming more and more deeply entwined in a new age of globalism—an age that combined great promise with great peril.

TIME LINE

1993

NAFTA ratified

1994

Health-care reform fails

Republicans capture Congress

1995

Government shutdown

Crime rates decline

O. J. Simpson trial

1996

Welfare reform passed

Clinton reelected

1997

Microsoft antitrust suit begins

Balanced budget agreement

1998

Lewinsky scandal breaks

Democrats gain in congressional elections

Clinton impeached by House

1999

Clinton acquitted by Senate

2000

George W. Bush wins contested election

2001

9/11 attacks

U.S. defeats Taliban regime in Afghanistan

2002

Corporate scandals contribute to economic downturn

2003

U.S. invades Iraq

2004

Abu Ghraib scandal

Bush reelected

2005

Hurricane Katrina

2006

Democrats capture Congress

2007

Troop "surge" in Iraq

Mortgage crisis

2008

Obama elected nation's first African American president

A RESURGENCE OF PARTISANSHIP

Bill Clinton entered office in January 1993 as the first Democratic president since Jimmy Carter and the first self-proclaimed activist president since Lyndon Johnson. His domestic agenda was more ambitious than that of any president since the 1960s. But Clinton also had significant political weaknesses. Having won the votes of well under half the electorate, he had no powerful mandate. Democratic majorities in Congress were frail. The Republican leadership in Congress opposed the president with unusual unanimity on many issues. The president's tendency toward reckless personal behavior gave his many enemies repeated opportunities to discredit him. The Clinton years, therefore, became a time of intense and bitter partisan struggles.

LAUNCHING THE CLINTON PRESIDENCY

The new administration began with a series of missteps and misfortunes in its first months. The president's effort to end the longtime ban on gay men and women serving in the military met with ferocious resistance, and he was forced to settle for a compromise known as "don't ask, don't tell," which forbade recruiters to ask recruits about their sexual preferences but also forbade servicemen and servicewomen to reveal them. Several of his early appointments became so controversial he had to withdraw them. A longtime friend of the president, Vince Foster, serving in the office of the White House counsel, committed suicide in the summer of 1993, helping to spark an escalating inquiry into some banking and real estate ventures involving the president and his wife in the early 1980s, which became known as the Whitewater affair. An independent counsel began examining these issues in 1993. (The Clintons were ultimately cleared of wrongdoing in Whitewater in 2000.)

Despite its many problems, the Clinton administration had some significant achievements in its first year. The president narrowly won approval of a budget that marked a significant turn away from the policies of the Reagan-Bush years. It included a substantial tax increase on the wealthiest Americans, a significant reduction in many areas of government spending, and a major expansion of tax credits to low-income working people.

Clinton was a committed advocate of free trade. After a long and difficult battle against, among others, Ross Perot, the AFL-CIO, and many Democrats in Congress, he won approval of the North American Free Trade Agreement (or NAFTA), which eliminated most trade barriers among the United States, Canada, and Mexico. Later he won approval of other far-reaching trade agreements negotiated in the General Agreement on Trade and Tarriffs (or GATT).

The president's most important and ambitious initiative was a major reform of the nation's health-care system. Early in 1993, he appointed a task force, chaired by his wife, Hillary Rodham Clinton, which proposed a sweeping reform designed to guarantee coverage to every American and hold down the costs of medical care. But there was substantial opposition from those who believed the reform would transfer too much power to the government. Well-funded opposition doomed the plan.

The foreign policy of the Clinton administration was at first cautious and tentative. Yugoslavia, a nation created after World War I out of a group of small Balkan countries, dissolved again into several different countries in the wake of the 1989 collapse of its communist government. Bosnia was among the new nations, and it quickly became embroiled in a bloody civil war between its two major ethnic groups: one Muslim, the other Serbian and Christian, backed by the neighboring Serbian republic. All efforts by the other European nations and the United States to negotiate an end to the struggle failed until 1995, when the American negotiator Richard Holbrooke finally brought the warring parties together and crafted an agreement to partition Bosnia.

THE REPUBLICAN RESURGENCE

The trials of the Clinton administration, and the failure of health-care reform in particular, proved damaging to the Democratic Party as it faced the congressional elections of 1994. For the first time in over forty years, Republicans gained control of both houses of Congress.

Throughout 1995, the Republican Congress, under the aggressive leadership of House Speaker Newt Gingrich, worked at a sometimes feverish pace to construct what they called a "contract with America," an ambitious and even radical legislative program. The Republicans proposed a series of measures to transfer important powers from the federal government to the states; pushed for dramatic reductions in federal spending, including a major restructuring of the Medicare program, to reduce costs; and attempted to scale back a wide range of federal regulatory functions.

President Clinton responded to the 1994 election results by shifting his own agenda conspicuously to the center—announcing his own plan to cut taxes and balance the budget. But the presidential politics of 1996 made compromise between the president and Congress very difficult. In November 1995 and again in January 1996, the federal government literally shut down for several days because the president and Congress could not agree on a budget. Republican leaders refused to pass a "continuing resolution" (to allow government operations to continue during negotiations) in hopes of pressuring the president to agree to their terms. That proved to be an epic political blunder. Public opinion turned quickly and powerfully against the Republican leadership and against much of its agenda. Newt Gingrich quickly became one of the most unpopular political leaders in the nation, while President Clinton slowly improved his standing in the polls.

By the time the 1996 campaign began in earnest, President Clinton was in a commanding position to win reelection. Unopposed for the Democratic nomination, he faced a Republican opponent—Senator Robert Dole of Kansas—who inspired little enthusiasm even within his own party. Clinton benefited from the disastrous errors by congressional Republicans in 1995 and early 1996. But his greatest strength came from the remarkable success of the American economy and the marked reduction in the federal deficit. Like Reagan in 1984, he could campaign as the champion of peace, prosperity, and national well-being.

In a flurry of activity in the spring and summer of 1996, Congress passed several important bills. The most dramatic was a welfare reform bill that ended the fifty-year federal guarantee of assistance to families with dependent children and turned most of the responsibility for allocating federal welfare funds to the states. Most of all, it shifted the bulk of welfare benefits away from those without jobs and toward low-wage workers.

Clinton's buoyant campaign flagged slightly in the last weeks, but the president nevertheless received just over 49 percent of the popular vote to Dole's 41 percent; Ross Perot, running now as the candidate of what he called the Reform Party, received just over 8 percent of the vote. Clinton won 379 electoral votes to Dole's 159; Perot again won none. But the Democrats failed to regain either house of Congress.

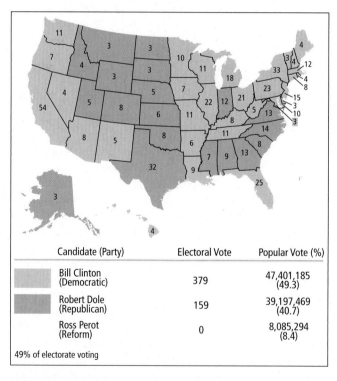

Candidate (Party)	Electoral Vote	Popular Vote (%)
Bill Clinton (Democratic)	379	47,401,185 (49.3)
Robert Dole (Republican)	159	39,197,469 (40.7)
Ross Perot (Reform)	0	8,085,294 (8.4)

49% of electorate voting

THE ELECTION OF 1996 Ross Perot did much less well in 1996 than he had in 1992, and President Clinton came much closer than he had four years earlier to winning a majority of the popular vote. Once again, Clinton defeated his Republican opponent, this time Robert Dole, by a decisive margin in both the popular and electoral votes. • *After the 1994 Republican landslide in the congressional elections, Bill Clinton had seemed permanently weakened. What explains his political revival?*

Clinton Triumphant and Embattled

The first Democratic president to win two terms as president since Franklin Roosevelt, Bill Clinton began his second administration with what appeared to be serene confidence. He proposed a relatively modest domestic agenda. He negotiated effectively with the Republican leadership on a plan for a balanced budget, which passed with much fanfare late in 1997. By the end of 1998, the federal budget was generating its first surplus in thirty years.

Clinton's renewed popularity was important to him in the turbulent year that followed, when the most serious crisis of his presidency suddenly erupted. Clinton had been the target of accusations of corruption and scandal since his first weeks in office: the investigation into Whitewater, charges of corruption against members of his cabinet and staff, accusations of illegalities in financing his 1996 campaign, and a civil suit for sexual harassment filed early in his first term by a former Arkansas state employee, Paula Jones.

In early 1998, inquiries associated with the Paula Jones case led to charges that the president had had a sexual relationship with a young White House intern, Monica Lewinsky. The most damaging charge was that he had lied about it in his deposition before Jones's attorneys. Those revelations produced a new investigation by the independent counsel in the Whitewater case, Kenneth Starr, a former judge and official in the Reagan Justice Department.

Clinton forcefully denied the charges, and a majority of the public strongly backed him. His popularity soared to record levels and remained high throughout the year that followed. In the meantime, a federal judge dismissed the Paula Jones case, which had launched the scandal.

But the scandal revived again with great force in August 1998, when Lewinsky struck a deal with the independent counsel and testified about her relationship with Clinton. Starr then subpoenaed Clinton himself, who—faced with the prospect of speaking to a grand jury—finally admitted that he and Lewinsky had had what he called an "improper relationship." A few weeks later, Starr submitted a lengthy and salacious report to Congress on the results of his investigation, recommending that Congress impeach the president.

Impeachment, Acquittal, and Resurgence

On December 19, 1998, the House, voting on strictly partisan lines, narrowly approved two counts of impeachment: lying to the grand jury and obstructing justice. The matter then moved to the Senate, where a trial of the president—the first since the trial of Andrew Johnson in 1868—began in early January. It ended with a decisive acquittal of the president. Neither of the charges attracted even a majority of the votes, let alone the two-thirds necessary for conviction.

The last two years of the Clinton presidency were relatively quiet. The president had no real hope of major domestic achievements in the face of a hostile Republican Congress. Overseas, however, he was more active.

In 1999, the president faced another crisis in the Balkans. This time, the conflict involved a province of Serbian-dominated Yugoslavia—Kosovo—most of whose residents were Albanian Muslims. A savage civil war erupted there in 1998 between Kosovo nationalists and Serbians. In May 1999, NATO forces—dominated and led by the United States—began a major bombing campaign against the Serbians, which after little more than a week led the leader of Yugoslavia, Slobodan Milosevic, to agree to a cease-fire. Serbian troops withdrew from Kosovo entirely, replaced by NATO peacekeeping forces. A precarious peace returned to the region.

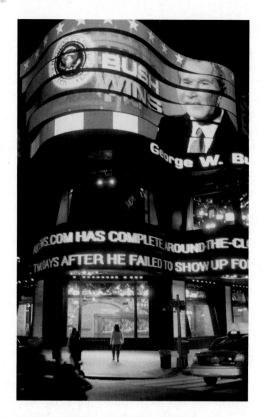

ELECTION NIGHT, 2000 The electronic billboard in New York City's Times Square, showing network coverage of the presidential contest, reports George Bush the winner of the 2000 presidential race late on election night. A few hours later, the networks retracted their projections because of continuing uncertainty over the results in Florida. Five weeks later, after the controversial intervention of the Supreme Court, Bush finally emerged the victor. (Chris Hondros/Getty Images)

Clinton finished his eight years in office with his popularity higher than it had been when he had begun. Indeed, public approval of Clinton's presidency—a presidency marked by remarkable prosperity and general world stability as well as persistent scandal—was consistently among the highest of any postwar president.

THE ELECTION OF 2000

The 2000 presidential election was one of the most extraordinary in American history—not because of the campaign that preceded it but because of the sensational controversy over its results, which preoccupied the nation for more than five weeks after the actual voting.

The two men who had been the front-runners for their parties' nominations a year before the election captured these nominations with only slight difficulty: Republican George W. Bush, son of the former president and a second-term governor of Texas, and Democrat Al Gore, former Tennessee senator and vice president under Clinton.

Both men ran cautious, centrist campaigns. In the congressional races, Republicans maintained control of the House of Representatives by a scant five seats, while the Senate split evenly between Democrats and Republicans. (Among the victors in the Senate races was First Lady Hillary Rodham Clinton, who won in New York.) In the presidential race, Gore won the national popular vote by the thin margin of about 540,000 votes out of

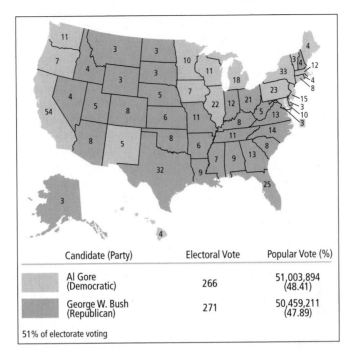

Candidate (Party)	Electoral Vote	Popular Vote (%)
Al Gore (Democratic)	266	51,003,894 (48.41)
George W. Bush (Republican)	271	50,459,211 (47.89)

51% of electorate voting

THE ELECTION OF 2000   The 2000 presidential election was one of the closest and most controversial in American history. It also starkly revealed a new pattern of party strength, which had been developing over the previous decade. Democrats swept the Northeast and most of the industrial Midwest and carried all the states of the Pacific Coast. Republicans swept the South, the plains states, and the mountain states (with the exception of New Mexico) and held on to a few traditional Republican strongholds in the Midwest.   •   *Compare this map to those of earlier elections, in particular the election of 1896. How did the pattern of party support change over the course of the twentieth century?*

about 100 million cast (or .5%). But on election night, both candidates remained short of the 270 electoral votes needed for victory because no one could determine who had won Florida.

After a mandatory recount over the next two days, Bush led Gore in the state by fewer than 300 votes. The technology of voting soon became central to the dispute. The Gore campaign asked for hand recounts in three critical counties, which the Florida Supreme Court unanimously supported.

The battle over the ballots continued until December 12, when the U.S. Supreme Court intervened. Voting 5 to 4, dividing sharply along party and ideological lines, the conservative majority overruled the Florida Supreme Court's order for a recount, insisted that any revised recount order be completed by December 12 (an obviously impossible demand, since the Court issued its ruling late at night on the 12th), and argued that the standards for evaluating punch-card ballots were too arbitrary and unfair to withstand constitutional scrutiny. Absent a recount, the certified Bush victory in Florida—and thus nationally—stood.

THE SECOND BUSH PRESIDENCY

George W. Bush assumed the presidency in January 2001 burdened by both the controversies surrounding his election and the widespread perception, even among some of his own supporters, that he was ill-prepared for the office. Nevertheless, Bush moved forcefully to enact an ambitious and controversial agenda.

Bush's principal campaign promise was to use the predicted budget surplus to finance a significant tax reduction. Bush relied on his own party's narrow control of Congress to win passage of the largest tax cut in American history—$1.35 trillion.

Having campaigned as a moderate, Bush spent his first term as president governing as a staunch conservative and relying on the most conservative members of his party for support. As the 2004 election approached, Karl Rove, the president's political adviser, encouraged the administration to take increasingly conservative positions to mobilize the party's conservative constituency in what almost everyone agreed was likely to be a very close election. A large part of the administration's strategy was to appeal to the large community of conservative, evangelical Christians and make them an active part of the Republican coalition.

The 2004 election revealed both the benefits and the costs of this strategy. Both Bush and his opponent, Massachusetts Senator John Kerry, campaigned with great intensity. The electorate was divided almost evenly throughout the campaign, and in the end turnout proved decisive. Although the Democrats turned out in much higher numbers than they had in 2000, the increase in the Republican vote was even larger. Bush won a narrow victory, with 51 percent of the popular vote and an electoral vote margin of 35.

Bush began his second term by claiming a significant popular mandate. But events soon put the administration on the defensive and reduced its ability to win congressional support for controversial measures. Bush's biggest problem was the increasing unpopularity of the Iraq War, which had begun in 2003 (see pp. 799–804). But domestic failures also contributed significantly to Bush's declining popular support, which by mid-2006 had dropped below 35 percent in major opinion polls.

A turning point in Bush's political fortunes—and a major national catastrophe in its own right—was the impact of Hurricane Katrina, a hurricane of tremendous force that struck the Gulf Coast of Louisiana and Mississippi in late August 2005. The storm did terrible damage to many communities along the coast, but the most severe impact was on the city

NEW ORLEANS, AUGUST 2005 In the aftermath of Hurricane Katrina, one of the most devastating storms in American history, New Orleans was almost entirely evacuated after the majority of the metropolitan area was flooded. The people at greatest risk were mostly poor African Americans, who—unlike the more affluent—did not own automobiles and had no easy way to escape. (Photo courtesy of U.S Army/U.S. Coast Guard photograph by Petty Officer 2nd Class Kyle Niemi)

of New Orleans. Some of the levees that protected the city failed, and massive flooding destroyed large areas of New Orleans. The entire population of the city was evacuated, and a slow process of rebuilding began.

The Bush administration suffered from Katrina because of its slow and halting response to the disaster. Only after widespread criticism did Bush visit the stricken city. The Federal Emergency Management Agency (FEMA)—which the Bush administration had staffed with inexperienced political allies—failed to handle the disaster effectively. To many Americans, the government's response to Katrina crystallized concerns about the competence and compassion of the Bush administration. A series of political scandals further tarnished Bush's presidency.

Bush managed some significant victories despite these setbacks. He won confirmation of two justices that he proposed for the Supreme Court: John Roberts, who succeeded William Rehnquist as chief justice; and Samuel Alito, who succeeded the retiring Sandra Day O'Connor. Both were staunch conservatives, inspiring hopes among some and fears among others that the Court would veer more sharply to the right.

THE ECONOMIC BOOM

The last two decades of the twentieth century and the first years of the twenty-first saw remarkable changes in American life. Some resulted from the end of the Cold War, others revealed the changing character of the American population, and still others reflected a rapidly evolving culture. But most of these changes were at least in part a product of the dramatic transformation of the American economy.

FROM "STAGFLATION" TO GROWTH

In the face of the sluggish growth and persistent inflation of the 1970s, many American corporations began making important changes in the way they ran their businesses. Those changes contributed both to the prosperity of the last decades of the twentieth century and to the growing inequality that accompanied it. Businesses invested heavily in new technology. Corporations began to pursue mergers to provide a more diversified basis for growth. Many enterprises created more energy-efficient plants and offices. American businesses sought to reduce their labor costs, which were among the highest in the world and which many believed had made the United States uncompetitive against economies that relied on low-wage workers.

Nonunion companies became more determined to stave off unionization drives. Companies already unionized won important concessions on wages and benefits in exchange for preserving jobs. Some firms moved their operations to areas of the country where unions were weak and wages low, and many others moved out of the United States entirely, to Latin America and Asia, where there were large available pools of cheap labor.

At the same time that many economic sectors were diminishing, new sectors were taking their place. The growth of digital technologies made possible an enormous range of new products and services that quickly became central to American economic life: computers, the Internet, cellular phones, digital music, video cameras, iPods, iPhones, iPads, and many others. The technology industries employed hundreds of thousands of people (many of them from outside the United States) and created new consumer needs and appetites.

For these and many other reasons, the American economy experienced robust growth in the last decades of the twentieth century. The gross national product (the total of goods and services produced by the United States) rose from $2.7 trillion in 1980 to over $9.8 trillion in 2000, almost quadrupling in twenty years. Inflation was low throughout these decades, never rising above 3 percent in any year and for a while in the late 1990s dropping below 2 percent. Stock prices soared to unprecedented levels, and with few interruptions, from the mid-1980s to the end of the century. The Dow Jones Industrial Average, the most common index of stock performance, stood at 1,000 in late 1980. Late in 1999, and again in 2007, it passed 14,000.

DOWNTURNS

Alan Greenspan, chairman of the Federal Reserve Board, warned in 1999 of the "irrational exuberance" with which Americans were pursuing profits in the stock market. A few months later, the market vindicated his concerns when, in April 2001, there was a sudden and disastrous collapse of the booming new "dot-com" sector of the economy—start-up companies and new, profitable businesses making use of the Internet.

At first, the bursting of the "tech bubble" seemed to have few effects on the larger economy. But by the beginning of 2001, the stock market—a great engine of growth over the previous decade—began a substantial decline, which continued for almost a year. In the fall of 2001, the economy as a whole slipped into a recession. The economy began to recover in 2002, but it did not grow at anything like the rates of the 1990s. And in 2008, a disastrous collapse of the home mortgage market drove both the stock market and the national economy into a deep recession.

SCIENCE AND TECHNOLOGY IN THE NEW ECONOMY

The "new economy" that emerged in the last decades of the twentieth century was driven by dramatic new scientific and technological discoveries that had profound effects on the way Americans—and people throughout the world—lived.

THE DIGITAL REVOLUTION

The dramatic growth in the use of computers and other digital devices was among the most significant innovations of the late twentieth century. The development of the microprocessor, first introduced in 1971 by Intel, represented a notable advance in the technology of integrated circuitry. A microprocessor miniaturized the central processing unit of a computer, making it possible for a small machine to perform calculations that in the past only very large machines could do. Considerable technological innovation was needed before the microprocessor could actually become the basis of what was first known as a "minicomputer" and then a personal computer. But in 1977, Apple launched its Apple II personal computer, the first such machine to be widely available to the public. Several years later, IBM entered the personal computer market with the first "PC." IBM had engaged a small software development company, Microsoft, to design an operating system for its new computer. No PC could operate without it. The PC, and its software, made

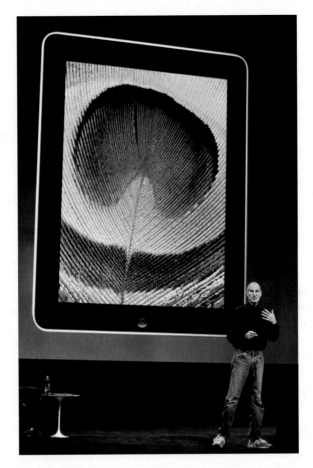

JOBS SHOWING IPADS. Steve Jobs, the long-time leader of Apple, presents the new iPad2 to a full auditorium in 2011. A few months later he died of pancreatic cancer. (Tony Avelar/Bloomberg via Getty Images)

its debut in August 1981 and immediately became enormously successful. Three years later, Apple introduced its Macintosh computer, which marked another major innovation in computer technology. For a time, Apple could not match IBM's marketing power. By the mid-1980s, the PC had established its dominance in the booming personal computer market. The computer revolution created thousands of new, lucrative businesses: computer manufacturers themselves, makers of the tiny silicon chips that ran the computers, and makers of software.

THE INTERNET

Out of the computer revolution emerged another dramatic source of information and communication: the Internet—a vast, geographically far-flung network of computers that allows people to communicate with others all over the world. It had its beginning in 1963, in the U.S. government's Advanced Research Projects Agency (ARPA), which funneled federal funds into scientific research projects. In the early 1960s, J. C. R. Licklider, the head of ARPA's Information Processing Techniques Office, launched a program to link together computers over large distances. It was known as ARPANET. For several years, ARPANET served mainly as a way for groups of people to exchange information and collaborate with one another through the remote use of a handful of computer networking facilities. Gradually, however, both the size and the uses of the network expanded.

This expansion was facilitated in part by two important new technologies. One was a system, developed in the early 1960s at the RAND Corporation in the United States and the National Physical Laboratory in England, known as "store-and-forward packet switching," which made possible the transmission of large quantities of data between computers without directly wiring the computers together.

By 1971, twenty-three computers were linked together in ARPANET, which served mostly research labs and universities. Gradually, interest in the system began to spread, and with it the number of computers connected to it. By 2012, there were well over a billion computers in use in the world (and many more now-obsolete ones). Virtually all of them are connected to the Internet. In the early 1980s, the Defense Department, an early partner in the development of ARPANET, withdrew from the project for security reasons. The network, soon renamed the Internet, was then free to develop independently. It did so rapidly, especially after the invention of technologies that made possible electronic mail (or e-mail) and the emergence of the personal computer, which vastly increased the number of potential users of the Internet. In 1989, Tim Berners-Lee, a British scientist working at a laboratory in Geneva, introduced the World Wide Web, which helped establish an orderly system for both the distribution and retrieval of electronic information.

BREAKTHROUGHS IN GENETICS

Computers helped create new scientific breakthroughs in genetics. Early discoveries in genetics by Gregor Mendel, Thomas Hunt Morgan, and others laid the groundwork for more dramatic breakthroughs—the discovery of DNA by the British scientists Oswald Avery, Colin MacLeod, and Maclyn McCarty in 1944; and in 1953, the dramatic discovery by the American biochemist James Watson and the British biophysicist Francis Crick of the double-helix structure of DNA, and thus of the key to identifying genetic codes. From these discoveries emerged the new science—and, ultimately, the new industry—of genetic engineering, through which new medical treatments and new techniques for hybridization of plants and animals have already become possible.

Scientists began to identify specific genes in humans and other living things. But the identification of genes was painfully slow; and in 1989, the federal government appropriated $3 billion to fund the National Center for the Human Genome, to accelerate the mapping of human genes. The Human Genome Project set out to identify all of the more than 100,000 genes by 2005.

But genetic research was (and continues to be) a source of great controversy. Many people were uneasy about predictions that the new science might alter aspects of human life that previously seemed beyond human control. Some critics feared genetic research on religious grounds, seeing it as an interference with God's plan. Others used moral arguments and expressed fears that it might allow parents, for example, to design their children. And a particularly heated controversy emerged over the way in which scientists obtained genetic material.

A CHANGING SOCIETY

The American population changed dramatically in the late twentieth and early twenty-first centuries. It grew larger, older, and more racially and ethnically diverse.

A SHIFTING POPULATION

Decreasing birth rates and growing life spans contributed to one of the most important characteristics of the American population in the early twenty-first century: its increasing agedness. The enormous "baby boom" generation—people born in the first ten years after World War II—drove the median age steadily upward (from 34 in 1996 to 37 in 2011 to a projected 39 by 2035). This growing population of aging Americans contributed to stresses on the Social Security and Medicare systems. It also had important implications for the workforce. In the last twenty years of the twentieth century, the number of people aged 25–54 (known statistically as the prime workforce) grew by over 26 million. In the first ten years of the twenty-first century, the number of American-born workers in that age group did not grow at all.

The slowing growth of the native-born population, and the workforce shortages it helped to create, was one reason for the rapid growth of immigration. In 2011, the number of foreign-born residents of the United States was the highest in American history—more than 40 million people, over 12 percent of the total population. These immigrants came from a wider variety of backgrounds than ever before, as a result of the 1965 Immigration Reform Act, which eliminated national origins as a criterion for admission. The growing presence of the foreign-born contributed to a significant drop in the percentage of white residents in the United States—from 90 percent in 1965 to 80 percent in 2008. (Non-Hispanic whites constituted just over 65 percent.) Latinos and Asians were by far the largest groups of immigrants in these years. But others came in significant numbers from Africa, the Middle East, Russia, and eastern Europe.

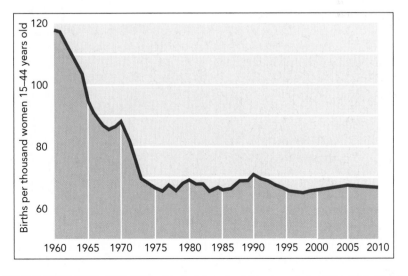

THE AMERICAN BIRTH RATE, 1960–2010 This chart shows the striking change in the pattern of the nation's birth rate beginning twenty years after 1940, which produced the great "baby boom." From 1960 onward, the nation's birth rate has declined steadily—in the 1960s and 1970s, dramatically so. • *What effect did this declining birth rate have on the age structure of the population?*

African Americans in the Post–Civil Rights Era

The civil rights movement and other liberal efforts of the 1960s had two very different effects on African Americans. On one hand, they increased opportunities for advancement to those in a position to take advantage of them. On the other hand, as the industrial economy declined and government services dwindled, there was a growing sense of help-lessness and despair among large groups of nonwhites who continued to find themselves barred from upward mobility.

By the early twenty-first century, the black middle class constituted over half of the African American population; progress was remarkable in the decades after the high point of the civil rights movement. Disparities between black and white professionals did not vanish, but they diminished substantially. African American families moved into more affluent urban communities and, in many cases, into suburbs—at times as neighbors of

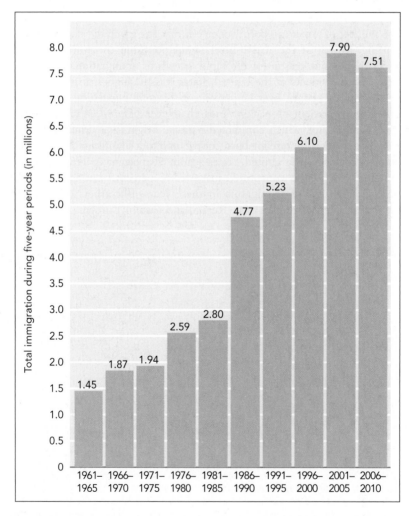

TOTAL IMMIGRATION, 1961-2010 This chart shows the tremendous increase in immigration to the United States in the decades since 1961. The immigration numbers between 1981 and 2010 were the highest since the late nineteenth century. • *What role did the Immigration Reform Act of 1965 have in increasing immigration levels?*

whites, more often into predominantly black communities. The percentage of black high-school graduates going on to college was virtually the same as that of white high-school graduates by the early twenty-first century (although a smaller proportion of blacks than whites managed to complete high school). And African Americans were making rapid strides in many professions. A generation earlier, they had been barred from many jobs because of segregation. Over half of all employed African Americans in the United States had skilled white-collar jobs in 2010. There were few areas of American life from which blacks were any longer entirely excluded.

But the rise of the black middle class also accentuated the increasingly desperate plight of other African Americans. Economic growth and the liberal programs of the 1960s and beyond had never reached them. A third of the nation's black population were categorized as impoverished, often described as the "underclass." As more success-ful blacks moved out of the inner cities, the poor were left behind in their decaying neighborhoods. Less than half of young inner-city blacks finished high school in 2010; more than 60 percent were unemployed. The black family structure suffered as well from the dislocations of urban poverty. There was a radical increase in the number of single-parent, female-headed black households. In 1970, 59 percent of all black children under eighteen years old lived with both their parents (already down from 70 percent a decade earlier). In 2010, only 35 percent of black children lived in such households, compared to 77 percent of non-Hispanic white children.

Nonwhites were disadvantaged by many factors in the changing social and economic climate of the late twentieth and early twenty-first centuries. Among them was a growing impatience with affirmative action and welfare programs for the poor. There was a steady decline in the number of unskilled jobs in the economy.

MODERN PLAGUES: DRUGS AND AIDS

Two new and deadly epidemics ravaged many American communities beginning in the 1980s. One was a dramatic increase in drug use, which penetrated nearly every community in the nation. The enormous demand for drugs, and particularly for "crack" cocaine in the late 1980s and early 1990s, spawned what was in effect a multibillion-dollar industry. Drug use declined significantly among middle-class people beginning in the late 1980s, but the epidemic declined much more slowly in the poor urban neighborhoods, where it was doing the most severe damage.

The drug epidemic was related to another scourge of the late twentieth and early twenty-first centuries: the epidemic spread of a new and lethal disease first documented in 1981 and soon named AIDS (acquired immune deficiency syndrome). AIDS is the product of the HIV virus, which is transmitted by the exchange of bodily fluids (blood or semen). The virus gradually destroys the body's immune system and makes its victims highly vul-nerable to a number of diseases (particularly to various forms of cancer and pneumonia) to which they would otherwise have a natural resistance. Those infected with the virus (that is, HIV-positive) can live for a long time without developing AIDS, but for many years those who became ill were almost certain to die. The first American victims of AIDS (and for many years the group among whom cases remained the most numerous) were homosexual men. But by the late 1980s, as the gay community began to take preventive measures, the most rapid increase in the spread of the disease occurred among hetero-sexuals, many of them intravenous drug users who spread the virus by sharing contaminated hypodermic needles.

"IGNORANCE = FEAR" The artist Keith Haring (whose work was inspired in large part by urban graffiti) created this striking poster in 1989, the year before he himself died of AIDS, to generate support for the battle against the disease. ACT UP, the organization that distributed it, was among the most militant groups in demanding more rapid efforts to search for a cure. (© The Keith Haring Foundation)

In 2010, there were an estimated 1.2 million Americans living with the AIDS virus. But the United States represented only a tiny proportion of the worldwide total of people afflicted with HIV, an estimated 34 million people in 2010. Over two-thirds of those cases were concentrated in Africa. Governments and private groups, in the meantime, began promoting AIDS awareness in increasingly visible and graphic ways—urging young people, in particular, to avoid "unsafe sex" through abstinence or the use of latex condoms.

In the mid-1990s, AIDS researchers, after years of frustration, began discovering effective treatments for the disease. By taking a combination of powerful drugs on a rigorous schedule, among them a group known as protease inhibitors, even people with advanced cases of AIDS experienced dramatic improvement—so much so that in many cases there were no measurable quantities of the virus left in their bloodstreams. The new drugs gave promise for the first time of dramatically extending the lives of people with HIV, perhaps to normal life spans. Poorer AIDS patients often could not obtain access to the drugs. They were especially scarce in Africa and other less affluent parts of the world where the epidemic was rampant. President George W. Bush provided $15 billion to fight AIDS in Africa.

A CONTESTED CULTURE

The 1980s and 1990s were a time of a profound redefinition of the roles of women. Those years also saw a mobilization of many minorities who fought to include themselves into mainstream culture. As a result, new controversies and new issues emerged.

Battles over Feminism and Abortion

Among the principal goals of the growing power of conservatism as it became more assertive in the late twentieth century was a challenge to feminism and its achievements. Leaders of the new right had campaigned successfully against the proposed Equal Rights Amendment to the Constitution. And they played a central role in the most divisive issue of the late 1980s and 1990s: abortion rights.

For women who choose to terminate unwanted pregnancies, the Supreme Court's decision in *Roe v. Wade* (1973) had seemed to settle the question. By the 1980s, abortion was the most commonly performed surgical procedure in the country. But at the same time, opposition to abortion was creating a powerful grassroots movement. The "right-to-life" movement, as it called itself, found its most fervent supporters among Catholics; and indeed, the Catholic Church itself lent its institutional authority to the battle against legalized abortion. Religious doctrine also motivated the antiabortion stance of Mormons, evangelical Christians, and other groups. The opposition of other antiabortion activists had less to do with religion than with their commitment to traditional notions of family and gender relations. To them, abortion was a particularly offensive part of a much larger assault by feminists on the role of women as wives and mothers. It was also, many foes contended, a form of murder. Fetuses, they claimed, were human beings who had a "right to life" from the moment of conception.

The right-to-life movement was persistent in its demand for a reversal of *Roe v. Wade*. It also attacked abortion in more limited ways, at its most vulnerable points. Starting in the 1970s, Congress and many state legislatures began barring the use of public funds to pay for abortions, thus making them inaccessible for many poor women. The Reagan and the two Bush administrations imposed further restrictions on federal funding. Right-to-life advocates began picketing. A few extremists bombed clinics performing abortions. Others killed doctors who performed abortions. Other physicians were subject to campaigns of terrorism and harassment. The changing composition of the Supreme Court between 1981 and 2009 (during which time new conservative justices were appointed to the Court) renewed the right-to-life movement's hopes for a reversal of *Roe v. Wade*.

The changing judicial climate of the late twentieth and early twenty-first centuries mobilized defenders of abortion. They called themselves the "pro-choice" movement, because they were defending not so much abortion itself as every woman's right to choose whether and when to bear a child. The pro-choice movement was in many parts of the country at least as strong as the right-to-life movement. With the election of President Clinton in 1992, a supporter of "choice," the immediate threat to *Roe v. Wade* seemed to fade. But abortion rights remained highly vulnerable. Clinton's successor, George W. Bush, openly opposed abortion, but Barack Obama was a mild supporter of choice.

The Growth of Environmentalism

The environmental movement continued to expand in the 1980s, 1990s, and 2000s. In the decades after the first Earth Day, environmental issues gained increasing attention and support. Although the federal government displayed only intermittent interest in the subject, environmentalists won a series of significant battles, mostly at the local level. They blocked the construction of roads, airports, and other projects that they claimed would be ecologically dangerous, taking advantage of new legislations protecting endangered species and environmentally fragile regions.

THE GLOBAL ENVIRONMENTAL MOVEMENT

AN international movement for well over a century, environmentalism has grown rapidly throughout the world in the late twentieth and early twenty-first centuries. What began as a series of localized efforts to preserve wilderness sites and to clean up air and water has evolved into a broad effort to deal with concerns that affect, and threaten, the entire globe.

During the 1960s, 1970s, and 1980s, while long-standing American environmental associations such as the Wilderness Society, the Sierra Club, and the National Audubon Society were becoming rejuvenated, organizations elsewhere in the world sought to create an international environmental movement. The World Wildlife Fund (WWF), created in Switzerland in 1961, eventually attracted more than 5 million supporters in over 90 countries and now claims to be the world's largest independent conservation organization. Greenpeace was founded in Canada in 1971 to oppose U.S. nuclear testing off the coast of Alaska. It, too, has grown into an international organization, with 2.9 million financial supporters worldwide and a presence in 42 nations.

Nongovernmental organizations (NGOs) such as Greenpeace and WWF were not the only institutions to recognize environmental concerns. In June 1972, the United Nations (UN) held its first Conference on the Human Environment in Stockholm, Sweden. Representatives of 113 countries attended the conference to discuss issues of global environmental importance—including the role of chlorofluorocarbons (CFCs), a chemical compound used in refrigerants and aerosol sprays, in depleting the ozone layer. After the conference, the UN created the United Nations Environment Programme (UNEP) to help coordinate international efforts for environmentalism and encourage sustainable development in poorer nations around the world.

The world's first "Green" parties—political parties explicitly devoted to environmental concerns (and often to other issues of social justice)—appeared in 1972, beginning in New Zealand (the Values Party) and Tasmania (the United Tasmania Group). Since then, Green parties have proliferated throughout the world, including in the United States. The most powerful Green party to date has been *Die Grünen* in Germany, founded in 1980. *Die Grünen* allied with the Social Democratic Party in a governing coalition from 1998, and in 2000, this coalition successfully passed the Nuclear Exit Law, which set a timetable of twenty years for Germany's eventual abandonment of nuclear power and a switch to renewable energy.

Large-scale ecological catastrophes have often helped galvanize the global environmental movement. Among the more significant of these events was the Bhopal disaster of 1984, in which a gas leak at a Union Carbide pesticide plant in Bhopal, India, resulted in the deaths of between

3,000 and 15,000 people. Two years later, a nuclear reactor accident in the Soviet city of Chernobyl, in Ukraine, caused 56 direct deaths, with predictions of many thousands more deaths to follow as a result of exposure. The area around Chernobyl itself is expected to be partially contaminated for 24,000 years, the radioactive half-life of plutonium-239. A less catastrophic nuclear accident at Three Mile Island, Pennsylvania, in 1979 heightened antinuclear sentiment in the United States. In 1989, the oil tanker *Exxon Valdez* ran aground on Bligh Reef in Prince William Sound, Alaska, and spilled approximately 10.9 million gallons of crude oil. Eventually covering thousands of square miles of ocean water (and 1,300 miles of Alaska shoreline) in oil, the spill killed hundreds of thousands of animals instantly and devastated the fragile ecosystem of the sound.

In developed, industrialized nations, environmental advocacy has largely focused on energy policy, conservation, clean technologies, and changing individual and social attitudes about consumption (as in the recycling movement). The growth of environmentalism is often linked to issues of human and democratic rights and freedom from First World exploitation. For example, the Green Belt Movement in Kenya, begun in 1977 by Wangari Maathai, encouraged Kenyan women to plant over 30 million trees across the nation to address the challenges of deforestation, soil erosion, and lack of water. The Green Belt Movement became an important human rights and women's rights organization, focused on reducing poverty and promoting peaceful democratic change through environmental conservation and protection. Maathai, winner of the 2004 Nobel Peace Prize, has since served as Kenya's assistant minister for environment and natural resources.

Over the past two decades, the environmental movement has grown even more global in scope, with multilateral environmental treaties and worldwide summits becoming the principal strategies of advocates. In 1997, an international effort to reduce global warming by mandating the lowering of greenhouse gas emissions culminated in the Kyoto Protocol, which as of June 2009 had been ratified by 185 nations (with the United States a conspicuous exception). While the George W. Bush administration rejected most efforts to limit carbon emissions, other leading Americans helped bring the issue of global warming to wide attention both in the United States and around the world. Perhaps most notable has been former vice president Al Gore, whose 2006 film *An Inconvenient Truth* may have done more to raise awareness of the threat of global warming than any other recent event—both in the United States and in many other nations. As a result of his efforts, Gore won the 2007 Nobel Peace Prize—an honor he shared with others, appropriately, given the global character of the movement he has championed. His cowinner was the Intergovernmental Panel on Climate Change, launched in Switzerland in 1988 and affiliated with the United Nations. •

UNDERSTAND, ANALYZE, & EVALUATE

1. Why are environmental movements in developing nations often linked to issues of human rights and protection from exploitation by developed nations? How do developed nations threaten the environment of developing nations?

2. How did the 2010 British Petroleum explosion and oil spill in the Gulf of Mexico affect the environment? What was the effect on the environmental movement?

In the late 1980s, the environmental movement began to mobilize around a new and ominous challenge—"global warming." It produced a steady rise in the earth's temperature as a result of emissions from the burning of fossil fuels (most notably coal and oil). Although considerable controversy continued for years over the pace, and even the reality, of global warming, by the early twenty-first century a growing consensus began to emerge—in part as a result of the efforts of significant public figures such as former vice president Al Gore, who won a Nobel Peace Prize in 2007 for his efforts, to draw attention to the problem. In 1997, representatives of the major industrial nations met in Kyoto, Japan, and agreed to a broad treaty establishing steps toward reducing carbon emissions and thus slowing or reversing global warming. But opposition to the treaty from Republicans in Congress prevented President Clinton from winning ratification of the treaty. In March 2001, President George W. Bush denounced the treaty for placing too great a burden on the United States and withdrew it from consideration.

THE PERILS OF GLOBALIZATION

The celebration of the beginning of a new millennium on January 1, 2000, was a notable moment not just because of the change in the calendar. It was a global event—a shared and, for the most part, joyous experience that united the world in its exuberance. But if the millennium celebrations suggested the bright promise of globalization, other events at the dawn of the new century suggested its dark perils.

OPPOSING THE "NEW WORLD ORDER"

In the United States and other industrial nations, opposition to globalization—or to what President George H. W. Bush once called "the new world order"—took several forms. To many Americans on both the left and the right, the nation's increasingly interventionist foreign policy was deeply troubling. Critics on the left charged that the United States was using military action to advance its economic interests—in the 1991 Gulf War and, above all, in the Iraq War that began in 2003. Critics on the right criticized humanitarian interventions in Somalia in 1993 and the Balkans in the late 1990s. Others complained that the United States was ceding its sovereignty to international organizations.

Labor unions insisted that the rapid expansion of free-trade agreements led to the export of jobs from advanced nations to less developed ones. Other groups attacked working conditions in new manufacturing countries on humanitarian grounds, arguing that the global economy was creating new classes of "slave laborers" working in conditions that few Western nations would tolerate. Environmentalists argued that globalization, in exporting industry to low-wage countries, also exported industrial pollution and toxic waste into nations that had no effective laws to control them, and contributed significantly to global warming. And still others opposed global economic arrangements on the grounds that they enriched and empowered large multinational corporations and threatened the freedom and autonomy of individuals and communities.

Varied opponents of globalization concurred on their discontent: not just free-trade agreements but also the multinational institutions that policed and advanced the global economy. Among them were the World Trade Organization, which monitored the enforcement of the General Agreement on Tariffs and Trade (GATT) treaties of the

1990s; the International Monetary Fund (IMF), which controlled international credit and exchange rates; and the World Bank, which made money available for development projects in many countries. In November 1999, when leaders of leading industrial nations gathered for their annual meeting in Seattle, Washington, tens of thousands protested—most of them peacefully. But some of them clashed with police, smashed store windows, and all but paralyzed the city. A few months later, a smaller but still substantial demonstration disrupted meetings of the IMF and the World Bank in Washington. And in July 2001, at a meeting of the same leaders in Genoa, Italy, an estimated 50,000 demonstrators clashed violently with police in a melee that left one protester dead and several hundred injured. The participants in the meeting responded to the demonstrations by pledging $1.2 billion to fight the AIDS epidemic in developing countries, and by deciding to hold future meetings in remote locations far from major cities.

DEFENDING ORTHODOXY

Outside the industrialized West, the impact of globalization created other controversies. Many citizens of nonindustrialized nations resented the way the world economy had left them in poverty. In their view, they were exploited and oppressed by the developed world. In some parts of the nonindustrialized world—particularly in some of the Islamic nations of the Middle East—the increasing reach of globalization created additional grievances, rooted not just in economics but also in religion and culture.

The Iranian Revolution of 1979, in which orthodox Muslims ousted a despotic government, was one of the first large and visible manifestations of a phenomenon that eventually reached across much of the Islamic world. It threatened the stability of the globe. Militants used isolated incidents of violence and mayhem, designed to disrupt societies and governments and to create fear among their peoples. Such tactics are known to the world as terrorism.

THE RISE OF TERRORISM

The term "terrorism" was used first during the French Revolution in the 1790s to describe the actions of radical Jacobins against the French government. It continued to be used intermittently throughout the nineteenth and early twentieth centuries to describe the use of violence as a form of intimidation against peoples and governments. But the widespread understanding of terrorism as an important fact of modern life is largely a product of the end of the twentieth century and the beginning of the twenty-first.

Acts of what came to be called terrorism have occurred in many parts of the world. Irish revolutionaries engaged in terrorism regularly against the English through much of the twentieth century. Jews used it in Palestine against the British before the creation of Israel, and Palestinians have used it frequently against Jews in Israel—particularly in the past several decades. Revolutionary groups in Italy, Germany, Japan, and France have engaged in terrorist acts intermittently over the past several decades.

The United States, too, has experienced terrorism for many years, much of it against American targets abroad—including the bombing of the Marine barracks in Beirut in 1983; the explosion that brought down an American airliner over Lockerbie, Scotland, in 1988; the bombing of American embassies in 1998; and the assault on the U.S. naval vessel *Cole* in 2000. Terrorist incidents were relatively rare, but not unknown, within the United States itself prior to September 11, 2001. Militants on the American left performed various acts of terror in the 1960s and early 1970s. In February 1993, a bomb exploded in the parking garage of the World Trade Center in New York, killing six people and causing serious, but not

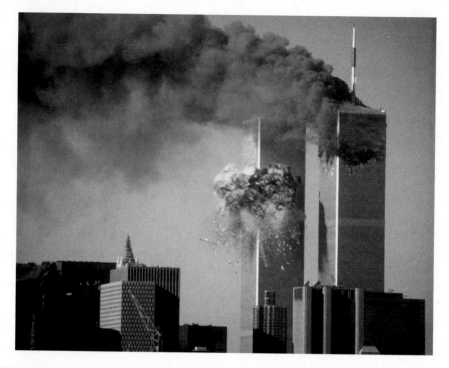

SEPTEMBER 11, 2001 A New York City symbol stands against a sky filled with the thick smoke from the destruction of another American symbol, New York City's World Trade Center towers, a few hours after terrorists crashed two planes into them. (© Sean Adair/Reuters/Corbis)

irreparable, structural damage to the towers. Several men connected with militant Islamic organizations were convicted of the crime. In April 1995, a van containing explosives blew up in front of a federal building in Oklahoma City, killing 168 people. Timothy McVeigh, a former Army soldier who had become part of a militant antigovernment movement of the American right, was convicted of the crime and eventually executed in 2001.

Most Americans, however, considered terrorism a problem that mainly plagued other nations. One of the many results of the terrible events of September 11, 2001, was to jolt the American people out of their complacency and alert them to the presence of continuing danger. That awareness increased in the years following September 11. New security measures changed the way in which Americans traveled. New government regulations altered immigration policies and affected the character of international banking. Warnings of possible new terrorist attacks created widespread tension and uneasiness.

THE WAR ON TERROR

In the aftermath of September 11 2001, the United States government launched what President Bush called a "war on terror." The attacks on the World Trade Center and the Pentagon, government intelligence indicated, had been planned and orchestrated by Middle Eastern agents of a powerful terrorist network known as Al Qaeda. Its leader, Osama Bin Laden—until 2001 little known outside the Arab world—quickly became one of the most notorious figures in the world. Convinced that the militant Taliban government of Afghanistan had sheltered and supported Bin Laden and his organization, the

United States began a sustained campaign of bombing against the regime and sent in ground troops. Afghanistan's Taliban regime quickly collapsed, and its leaders—along with the Al Qaeda fighters allied with them—fled the capital, Kabul. American and anti-Taliban Afghan troops pursued them into the mountains but failed to capture Bin Laden and the other leaders of his organization (until Navy Seals, under orders from President Obama, killed Bin Laden in his home in Pakistan on May 2, 2011).

American forces in Afghanistan rounded up several hundred people with suspected connections to the Taliban and Al Qaeda and moved these prisoners (and eventually others) to a facility at the American base in Guantánamo, Cuba. They were among the first suspected terrorists to be handled under new standards established by the federal government in dealing with terrorism after September 11, 2001. They were held for months, and in some cases years, without access to lawyers, without facing formal charges, and were subjected to intensive interrogation, and at times torture. Many critics denounced the dangers to basic civil liberties that they believed the war on terror had created. Others argued that the new tactics were necessary to protect Americans. President Obama, in his first month in the White House, pledged to close the prison at Guantánamo. But he soon found that the promise was difficult to keep.

THE IRAQ WAR

In his State of the Union address to Congress in January 2002, President Bush spoke of an "axis of evil," which included the nations of Iraq, Iran, and North Korea—all countries with anti-American regimes, all countries that either possessed or were thought to be trying to acquire nuclear weapons. Although Bush did not say so at the time, many

BAGHDAD, MARCH 21, 2003 At the beginning of the American invasion of Iraq in spring 2003, the United States military used techniques honed in the first Gulf War in Kuwait—the use of heavy bombing of Iraqi targets before deploying troops in the field. This photograph shows explosions in downtown Baghdad at the beginning of the war as American bombers tried to destroy strategic targets in the city. (Photo by Mirrorpix/Getty Images)

"KEEP FOREIGN TERRORISM FOREIGN,"
NEW YORK TIMES, 1993

THE latest arrests in New York and the Middle East in connection with the World Trade Center bombing add a bit more focus to the conspiracy that produced the worst terrorist attack in American history. Much still remains to be learned about the conspirators' motives and possible foreign involvement, though now investigators believe the five individuals arrested are members of a group called Liberation Army Fifth Battalion, which has threatened further terrorist acts aimed at reversing U.S. policies throughout the Middle East. The arrests also intensify interest in their spiritual mentor, Sheik Omar Abdel Rahman.

As well, they underscore the urgency of monitoring known terrorists' movements and tightening visa and deportation procedures accordingly.

Americans ought to be enraged at the laxness that allowed Mr. Abdel Rahman to enter and remain in the United States. On two separate occasions, U.S. officials granted him visas even though his name appeared on the State Department watch list of suspected terrorists.

More than a decade ago, Egyptian authorities charged that Mr. Abdel Rahman's fiery preaching led directly to the murder of Anwar Sadat. After his acquittal on that charge, the sheik re-emerged as the preeminent leader of the violent Islamic opposition to President Mubarak.

Today his followers in Egypt organize attacks on Coptic Christians and foreign tourists. Cairo now asks that he be returned to Egypt for prosecution, perhaps as a tacit quid pro quo for its cooperation in the arrest of Mahmud Abohalima, a Trade Center suspect flown back to the United States last week.

Earlier in his career, Mr. Abohalima fought in Afghanistan, on the side of U.S.-backed Islamic guerrillas opposed to the Communist Government there. And Mr. Abdel Rahman helped organize the supply network providing the Afghan fighters with volunteers, weapons and money. After he fled Egypt in 1990, he shifted his base of operations first to the Sudan, then to Pakistan and finally the U.S.

Late in 1990, one of the sheik's followers, El Sayyid A. Nosair, was accused of murdering

people around the world interpreted these words to mean that the United States would soon try to topple the government of Saddam Hussein in Iraq.

For over a year, the Bush administration slowly built a public case for invading Iraq. Much of that case rested on two claims. One was that Iraq was supporting terrorist groups that were hostile to the United States. The other, and eventually the more important, was that Iraq either had or was developing what came to be known as "weapons of mass destruction," which included nuclear weapons and agents of chemical and biological warfare. Less central to these arguments, at least in the United States, was the charge that the Hussein government was responsible for major violations of human rights. Except for the last, none of these claims turned out to be accurate.

In March 2003, American troops, with support from Great Britain and several other countries and partial authorization from the United Nations, invaded Iraq and quickly toppled the Hussein regime. Hussein himself went into hiding but was eventually captured in December 2003. He was executed in Iraq on December 30, 2006. In May 2003, shortly the Israeli demagogue Rabbi Meir Kahane, in a Manhattan hotel. Most of the trade center suspects regularly attended Mr. Nosair's trial and watching his acquittal of murder charges. Mr. Nosair's cousin, Ibrahim A. Elgabrowny, has also been arrested on charges related to the trade center blast.

At the time of the Kahane case, the authorities ruled out any conspiracy charges. But then, if not earlier, the group around Mr. Abdel Rahman came under official surveillance. Deportation charges against the sheik were begun last year.

Closer monitoring of the sheik may not necessarily have prevented the bombing. But it might have. Keeping him out of the country, or expelling him once his identity became clear, might have averted other violence linked to his preachings.

The official explanation for the Sudan visa is a misspelling of the sheik's name on the application form. But that's hard to accept. With one eyeball missing entirely, and the other disfigured, the sheik is hardly difficult to recognize.

Representative Tom Lantos of California wants to look more closely into the repeated slip-ups in the Abdel Rahman case. That's a good idea. Meanwhile, Representative Charles Schumer of New York has suggested closer cooperation between the F.B.I. and the Immigration and Naturalization Service and the stationing of I.N.S. agents in foreign capitals, both useful proposals. There also needs to be consideration of accelerated deportation procedures in cases with terrorist links.

Along with the search for accountability, America needs urgently to reinforce its safeguards against foreign terrorism. If incidents like the trade center bombing can't be completely prevented, they can and should be made extremely rare.

UNDERSTAND, ANALYZE, & EVALUATE

1. Were the terrorists involved in the first attack on the World Trade Center foreign or American? What do their records suggest about the connections between the United States and the Middle East?
2. What official failures did the New York Times lament? What solutions did the authors and politicians suggest in response?
3. What lessons could American officials and the public have learned from the 1993 bombing? Could these lessons have prevented the attacks of 9/11?

Source: "Keep Foreign Terrorism Foreign," New York Times, March 28, 1993, p. A1.

after the American capture of Baghdad, President Bush made a dramatic appearance on an aircraft carrier off the coast of California, where, standing in front of a large sign reading "Mission Accomplished," he declared victory in the Iraq War.

In the following months, events in Iraq suggested that the president's claim had been premature. Of the more than 4,000 American soldiers killed in Iraq as of mid-2009, over 3,600 of them died after the "mission accomplished" speech. And despite significant efforts by the United States and its allies to hand over authority to an Iraqi government and to restore order to the country, insurgents continued to disrupt the recovery with persistent attacks and terrorist actions throughout the fragile nation.

Support for the war in the United States steadily declined in the years after the first claim of victory. The failure of the occupiers to find evidence of the weapons of mass destruction, whose existence the president had claimed, was one blow to the war's credibility. Another blow came from reports of the torture and humiliation of Iraqi prisoners by American soldiers at the Abu Ghraib prison in Baghdad and other sites in Iraq and around the world.

CRISES IN THE MIDDLE EAST In the 1970s and beyond, the Middle East became one of the most turbulent regions of the world and one of the regions most vital to, and difficult for, the United States. The United States intervened in the Middle East frequently during the Cold War and beyond, in ways both large and small, as this map reveals. After the events of September 2001, those interventions increased. • *Why did the United States have so much at stake in the Middle East?*

EXPANSION OF ISRAEL

LEBANON
1958—U.S. intervention supports pro-West government
1981–1984—U.S. joins UN peacekeeping force, suffers series of violent attacks

ISRAEL
1993—Israel and PLO sign accords for Palestinian self-rule in Jericho and Gaza Strip
2002–2003—Escalating violence leads to erection of wall along border of West Bank

Israel, 1948		Territory occupied, 1982–1986	
Territory gained, 1949		Area of Israeli settlements	
Territory occupied, 1967		OPEC member nations	
Territory yielded, 1979–1982		▲ Major oil fields	

OPEC: Organization of Petroleum Exporting Countries
(Members not shown are Nigeria, Algeria, Gabon, Indonesia, Venezuela, and Ecuador)

PLO: Palestine Liberation Organization

The invasion of Iraq was the most visible evidence of a basic change in the structure of American foreign policy under the presidency of George W. Bush. Ever since the late 1940s, the containment policy had become the cornerstone of America's role in the world. The United States had worked to maintain stability in the world by containing, but not often directly threatening or attacking, its adversaries. Even after the Cold War ended, the United States continued to demonstrate a level of constraint, despite its now unchallenged military preeminence. In the administrations of George H. W. Bush and Bill Clinton, for example, American leaders worked closely with the United Nations and NATO to achieve U.S. international goals and resisted taking unilateral military action.

There had always been those who criticized these constraints. They believed that America should do more than maintain stability and should move actively to topple undemocratic regimes and destroy potential enemies of the United States. In the administration of George W. Bush, these critics took control of American foreign policy and began to reshape it. The legacy of containment was largely repudiated. Instead, the public stance of the American government was that the United States had the right and the responsibility to fight tyranny and spread freedom throughout the world—not just by exhortation and example but also, when necessary, by military force. In Latvia in May 2005, President Bush spoke of the decision at the end of World War II not to challenge Soviet domination of Eastern Europe. That decision had rested on the belief that such a challenge would lead the United States into another war. The controversial agreement negotiated at Yalta in 1945 by Roosevelt, Churchill, and Stalin, which failed to end the Soviet occupation of Poland and other Eastern European nations, was, the president said, part of an "unjust tradition" by which powerful governments sacrificed the interests of small nations. "This attempt to sacrifice freedom for the sake of stability," the president continued, "left a continent divided and unstable." The lesson, Bush suggested, was that the United States and other great powers should value stability less and freedom more, and should be willing to take greater risks in the world to end tyranny and oppression.

THE DECLINE OF THE BUSH PRESIDENCY

For most of the first three years of his presidency, George W. Bush enjoyed broad popularity. Although his domestic policies never had large public support, Bush was revered by many Americans because of his resolute stance against terrorism. Even the controversial Iraq War helped sustain his popularity for a time.

Bush's domestic policies did little to strengthen him politically. The massive tax cuts of 2001 went disproportionately to wealthy Americans, reflecting the view of White House economists that the best way to ensure growth was to put money into the hands of people most likely to invest. Other than the tax cuts, Bush's major accomplishment was an education reform bill, known as "No Child Left Behind," which tied federal funding in schools to the success of students in taking standardized tests. Seven years later, there was no clear agreement on whether the bill had markedly improved student performance. Still other proposals—an effort to privatize some aspects of the Social Security system, for example—never attracted significant support in Congress. In 2006, the Democrats regained control of the Congress. As a result, the Bush administration began to make much greater use of executive orders—laws and policies that did not require congressional approval.

The 2004 election was one of the last successful moments in the Bush administration. The unpopularity of the war in Iraq contributed to the rapidly declining approval ratings of the president himself—ratings that by mid-2008 had reached the lowest level of presidential approval in the history of polling. Perhaps even more damaging to Bush's popularity was the government's weak response to Hurricane Katrina. Scandals in the Justice Department, revelations of illegal violations of civil liberties, revulsion from tactics used against suspected terrorists, and declining economic prospects, culminating in a disastrous financial crisis beginning in early 2008—all reinforced the growing unpopularity of the president.

THE ELECTION OF 2008

The 2008 presidential election was the first since 1952 that did not include an incumbent president or vice president. Both parties began the campaign with large fields of candidates, but by the spring of 2008 the contest had narrowed considerably. Senator John McCain of Arizona emerged from the early primaries with his nomination ensured. In the Democratic race, the primaries quickly eliminated all but two candidates. They were Senator Hillary Clinton of New York, the former first lady, and Senator Barack Obama of Illinois, a young, charismatic politician and the son of an African father and a white American mother. As the first woman and the first African American to have a realistic chance of being elected president, Clinton and Obama attracted great enthusiasm. The passions driving both campaigns led to a primary contest that lasted much longer than usual. Not until the last primaries in June was it clear that Obama would be the nominee.

By the time of the party conventions in late August, Barack Obama was leading John McCain in the polls. Obama profited from the series of financial problems that began in mid-2007 and grew slowly worse until reaching crisis levels in the summer of 2008.

OBAMANIA Posters of and about Barack Obama were widely visible during the 2008 presidential campaign. In this photograph, a New Yorker walks past one example of the Obama street art that spread through many American cities—and, indeed, through cities around the world. Among the depictions of Obama were the works of artists who saw in him a figure of possibly historic significance. (Photo by Chris McGrath/Getty Images)

An important factor in the growth of the financial crisis was a significant downturn in the housing market, which in turn triggered a mortgage crisis. For years, financial institutions had been developing new credit instruments intended to make borrowing easier and cheaper, and which lured millions of people into taking on large mortgages—often much larger than would traditionally have seemed safe—on very low short-term rates, many of which escalated sharply after the first few years. Unable to pay their mortgages, which were often worth more than the market value of their homes, millions of homeowners had to default on their houses. At first, the defaults affected mostly companies that specialized in home mortgages, but since most mortgages were quickly sold and often resold several times, the bad debts spread throughout a widening swath of the financial world. Over the summer, some of the nation's most important economic institutions began to fail. Some were rescued (and effectively taken over) by the government. Others were bought up at very low prices by larger institutions, and a few—including Lehman Brothers, one of the oldest and most prestigious investment banks in America—collapsed altogether. By mid-September, the financial crisis showed signs of spiraling out of control. Secretary of the Treasury Henry Paulson proposed a massive appropriation of federal funds to help the government bail out the banks. Despite considerable opposition to the plan, the administration won congressional approval for a $750 billion package to be used to shore up tottering financial institutions. The bailout slowed the deterioration of financial institutions, but the credit markets remained constricted, and economic activity by both producers and consumers began to decline.

This extraordinary crisis formed the backdrop against which the two presidential candidates fought out the last two months of their campaign. Neither offered clear or convincing solutions to the crisis, but most voters came to believe that Obama would likely be a better

A PRESIDENTIAL PRESS CONFERENCE   President Obama gives a press conference in the White House rose garden in 2009, near the beginning of his presidency. (© Christy Bowe/Corbis)

steward of the economy than would McCain. Obama benefited both from the unpopularity of George W. Bush and from his success at persuading voters that McCain would continue Bush's policies. Obama held onto—and indeed increased—his lead through late September and October, helped by a heavily financed and highly disciplined campaign.

On November 4, 2008, Barack Obama won a decisive victory, winning the popular vote 53 percent to 46 percent and the electoral vote by an even larger margin. Obama became the first Democratic candidate since Lyndon Johnson to win so large a victory.

OBAMA AND HIS OPPONENTS

The global exuberance that Obama's election created in 2008 did not last for long. The first two years of his presidency coincided with the worst period of the economic crisis. But Obama was strengthened by large Democratic majorities in both houses of Congress. During those years, Obama passed a large stimulus package of $800 billion to support state and local budgets, public works, and other investments that he hoped would generate economic growth. He and his congressional colleagues also succeeded in passing significant financial regulations that were designed to avoid another crisis like the one that began in 2008. Even more important, he passed a broad health-care bill that would ensure that almost all Americans would have insurance, regardless of their means. But only one Republican congressman supported the health-care bill. For Obama, who had built much of his presidency around the idea of bipartisanship and conciliation, the polarization of the two parties was a significant setback. Many Republican state's attorneys sued to stop the health bill. Judges were divided as to whether the bill was constitutional, and its fate was settled by the Supreme Court in June 2012.

The 2010 midterm congressional campaigns were dominated by the emergence of a new social movement—the Tea Party movement, a conservative effort to reduce the national debt, lower taxes, and limit the role of government. This broad movement attracted mostly white men and women, largely middle-class. It had a large impact on the elections in November 2010. That election produced a large majority of Republicans in the House and reduced the majority of Democrats in the Senate. For the next two years, President Obama had great difficulty getting any proposals passed because he received the votes of almost no Republicans.

In 2011, another movement emerged—Occupy Wall Street (OWS). But this movement has goals very different from those of the Tea Party movement. The OWS goals were financial regulation, progressive taxation, stronger support for unions, more resources to reduce unemployment, assaults on economic inequality, and the end of what they believe are unnecessary and failed wars. They demonstrated their grievances by camping in a park in lower Manhattan. Soon after, similar demonstrations were seen in many other places in the United States and around the world.

Obama's efforts softened the turbulent crisis for a time, but the perils of the economy remained dangerous, especially because the crisis had spread through much of the world. By 2012, the economy was showing signs of growth. Unemployment in the United States, which had been over 10 percent in 2009, was reduced to approximately 8 percent. But the problems of the economy were far from over.

Obama, Clinton, and the World

Obama came into office with an ambitious plan for reshaping America's role in the world. The end of the American combat role in Iraq was already under way in the last year of the Bush administration. Obama brought it to an end in 2010. At the same time, he committed significant additional troops to the war in Afghanistan, where Americans had been fighting since 2001. Obama escalated the Afghan war in 2011. For almost ten years, a major goal of American foreign policy was to find Osama bin Laden, the head of Al Qaeda, the organization that had created the destruction of the Twin Towers in New York. In May 2011, Navy Seals found and killed bin Laden.

Obama had appointed Hillary Clinton as his secretary of state, and together they tried to create peace between Israel and Palestine—an effort that made little or no progress. Elsewhere they sought to improve relationships damaged by the Iraq War and to build new international trade opportunities as well. But increasing turmoil in the Middle East, and the growing power of China, created new challenges. The United States intervened in a civil war in Libya and helped end the regime of the longstanding leader Muammar Qadaffi. And in 2012, Obama and Clinton sought to stop Iran from creating nuclear weapons—an effort that remained unfinished.

The Election of 2012

The most expensive campaign in history put President Obama against Mitt Romney, a former governor of Massachusetts. The campaign was not only expensive, but raucous and at times quite angry. But as the election came near, the debates in October became the most important part of the campaign. In the first debate, most viewers saw President Obama to be tired and uninterested—a failure that gave a significant shift toward Romney. But in the next two presidential debates, Obama was more energetic and helped him rebuild his support.

For the last few weeks of the campaign, the polls were very close and remained so almost to the end—and the search for 270 electoral votes (the number for victory) continued almost to the end. But despite the closeness, the polls consistently showed Obama having a lead, even if by a small one. In the last few days of the campaign, Obama's lead grew. Enormous amounts of money and effort went into the few states that seemed to be close—among them Ohio, Virginia, Florida, Wisconsin, Iowa, New Hampshire, and several others. On election night, it became clear that the close states moved toward Obama in the last few days. He won one all of these close states. His victory was close in popular votes, but his electoral votes gave him a large lead of 332. The Democrats also won several new Senators, giving the Democrats a majority. The House of Representatives remained Republican, but their majority was smaller after the election.

As he entered his second term, Obama faced many problems—the turbulent Middle East, the rising debt, the high levels of unemployment, the fear of terrorism, the still stagnant economy. Obama's first term saw the economy grow and unemployment decline. But much more awaited him as he faced a troubled and divided nation.

CONCLUSION

America in the first decades of the twenty-first century was a nation beset by many problems and anxieties. American foreign policy after September 11, 2001, had not only divided the American people but also alienated much of the rest of the world, reinforcing a deep animus toward the United States that had been building slowly for decades. The American economy struggled to sustain even modest growth, with rapidly rising public and private debt, and increasing inequality of wealth and incomes.

These and other serious problems do not, however, provide a full picture of the United States in the early twenty-first century. America remains the wealthiest and most powerful nation in the world. It remains, as well, among the most idealistic—in the willingness of its people to contribute time, money, and effort to the solution of grave social problems at home and in the world, and in its commitment to principles of freedom and justice that, however contested, remain at the core of the nation's identity. Moving forward into an uncertain future, Americans are not only burdened by difficult challenges but also armed with the extraordinary energy and resilience that has allowed the nation—through its long and often turbulent history—to endure, to flourish, and continually to imagine and strive for a better future.

RECALL AND REFLECT

1. What challenges did Bill Clinton face upon his election to the presidency? What were the accomplishments of his administration? What were its setbacks and failures?
2. What led to the economic boom of the 1980s and 1990s? What setbacks to the economy occurred in those years?
3. How has America's relationship to the rest of the world changed as a result of the war on terrorism and U.S. involvement in Iraq and Afghanistan?
4. What have been Barack Obama's most important achievements in his first three years as president? What have been his principal failures?

APPENDICES

Documents & Tables

THE DECLARATION OF INDEPENDENCE

In Congress, July 4, 1776,

THE UNANIMOUS DECLARATION OF THE THIRTEEN UNITED STATES OF AMERICA

When, in the course of human events, it becomes necessary for one people to dissolve the political bands which have connected them with another, and to assume, among the powers of the earth, the separate and equal station to which the laws of nature and of nature's God entitle them, a decent respect to the opinions of mankind requires that they should declare the causes which impel them to the separation.

We hold these truths to be self-evident, that all men are created equal; that they are endowed by their Creator with certain unalienable rights; that among these, are life, liberty, and the pursuit of happiness. That, to secure these rights, governments are instituted among men, deriving their just powers from the consent of the governed; that, whenever any form of government becomes destructive of these ends, it is the right of the people to alter or to abolish it, and to institute a new government, laying its foundation on such principles, and organizing its powers in such form, as to them shall seem most likely to effect their safety and happiness. Prudence, indeed, will dictate that governments long established, should not be changed for light and transient causes; and, accordingly, all experience hath shown, that mankind are more disposed to suffer, while evils are sufferable, than to right themselves by abolishing the forms to which they are accustomed. But, when a long train of abuses and usurpations, pursuing invariably the same object, evinces a design to reduce them under absolute despotism, it is their right, it is their duty, to throw off such government and to provide new guards for their future security. Such has been the patient sufferance of these colonies, and such is now the necessity which constrains them to alter their former systems of government. The history of the present King of Great Britain is a history of repeated injuries and usurpations, all having, in direct object, the establishment of an absolute tyranny over these States. To prove this, let facts be submitted to a candid world:

He has refused his assent to laws the most wholesome and necessary for the public good.

He has forbidden his governors to pass laws of immediate and pressing importance, unless suspended in their operation till his assent should be obtained; and, when so suspended, he has utterly neglected to attend to them.

He has refused to pass other laws for the accommodation of large districts of people, unless those people would relinquish the right of representation in the legislature; a right inestimable to them, and formidable to tyrants only.

He has called together legislative bodies at places unusual, uncomfortable, and distant from the depository of their public records, for the sole purpose of fatiguing them into compliance with his measures.

He has dissolved representative houses repeatedly for opposing, with manly firmness, his invasions on the rights of the people.

He has refused, for a long time after such dissolutions, to cause others to be elected; whereby the legislative powers, incapable of annihilation, have returned to the people at large for their exercise; the state remaining, in the meantime, exposed to all the danger of invasion from without, and compulsions within.

He has endeavored to prevent the population of these States; for that purpose, obstructing the laws for naturalization of foreigners, refusing to pass others to encourage their migration hither, and raising the conditions of new appropriations of lands.

He has obstructed the administration of justice, by refusing his assent to laws for establishing judiciary powers.

He has made judges dependent on his will alone, for the tenure of their offices, and the amount and payment of their salaries.

He has erected a multitude of new offices, and sent hither swarms of officers to harass our people, and eat out their substance.

He has kept among us, in time of peace, standing armies, without the consent of our legislatures.

He has affected to render the military independent of, and superior to, the civil power.

He has combined, with others, to subject us to a jurisdiction foreign to our Constitution, and unacknowledged by our laws; giving his assent to their acts of pretended legislation:

For quartering large bodies of armed troops among us:

For protecting them by a mock trial, from punishment, for any murders which they should commit on the inhabitants of these States:

For cutting off our trade with all parts of the world:

For imposing taxes on us without our consent:

For depriving us, in many cases, of the benefit of trial by jury:

For transporting us beyond seas to be tried for pretended offences:

For abolishing the free system of English laws in a neighboring province, establishing therein an arbitrary government, and enlarging its boundaries, so as to render it at once an example and fit instrument for introducing the same absolute rule into these colonies:

For taking away our charters, abolishing our most valuable laws, and altering, fundamentally, the powers of our governments:

For suspending our own legislatures, and declaring themselves invested with power to legislate for us in all cases whatsoever.

He has abdicated government here, by declaring us out of his protection, and waging war against us.

He has plundered our seas, ravaged our coasts, burnt our towns, and destroyed the lives of our people.

He is, at this time, transporting large armies of foreign mercenaries to complete the works of death, desolation, and tyranny, already begun, with circumstances of cruelty and perfidy scarcely paralleled in the most barbarous ages, and totally unworthy the head of a civilized nation.

He has constrained our fellow citizens, taken captive on the high seas, to bear arms against their country, to become the executioners of their friends, and brethren, or to fall themselves by their hands.

He has excited domestic insurrections amongst us, and has endeavored to bring on the inhabitants of our frontiers, the merciless Indian savages, whose known rule of warfare is an undistinguished destruction of all ages, sexes, and conditions.

In every stage of these oppressions, we have petitioned for redress, in the most humble terms; our repeated petitions have been answered only by repeated injury. A prince, whose character is thus marked by every act which may define a tyrant, is unfit to be the ruler of a free people.

Nor have we been wanting in attention to our British brethren. We have warned them, from time to time, of attempts made by their legislature to extend an unwarrantable jurisdiction over us. We have reminded them of the circumstances of our emigration and settlement here. We have appealed to their native justice and magnanimity, and we have conjured them, by the ties of our common kindred, to disavow these usurpations, which would inevitably interrupt our connections and correspondence. They, too, have been deaf to the voice of justice and consanguinity. We must, therefore, acquiesce in the necessity which denounces our separation, and hold them as we hold the rest of mankind, enemies in war, in peace, friends.

We, therefore, the representatives of the United States of America, in general Congress assembled, appealing to the Supreme Judge of the world for the rectitude of our intentions, do, in the name, and by the authority of the good people of these colonies, solemnly publish and declare, that these united colonies are, and of right ought to be, free and independent states: that they are absolved from all allegiance to the British Crown, and that all political connection between them and the state of Great Britain is, and ought to be, totally dissolved; and that, as free and independent states, they have full power to levy war, conclude peace, contract alliances, establish commerce, and to do all other acts and things which independent states may of right do. And, for the support of this declaration, with a firm reliance on the protection of Divine Providence, we mutually pledge to each other our lives, our fortunes, and our sacred honor.

The foregoing Declaration was, by order of Congress, engrossed, and signed by the following members:

John Hancock

NEW HAMPSHIRE
Josiah Bartlett
William Whipple
Matthew Thornton

CONNECTICUT
Roger Sherman
Samuel Huntington
William Williams
Oliver Wolcott

NEW YORK
William Floyd
Philip Livingston
Francis Lewis
Lewis Morris

NEW JERSEY
Richard Stockton
John Witherspoon
Francis Hopkinson
John Hart
Abraham Clark

MASSACHUSETTS BAY
Samuel Adams
John Adams
Robert Treat Paine
Elbridge Gerry

PENNSYLVANIA
Robert Morris
Benjamin Rush
Benjamin Franklin
John Morton
George Clymer
James Smith
George Taylor
James Wilson
George Ross

DELAWARE
Caesar Rodney
George Read
Thomas M'Kean

MARYLAND
Samuel Chase
William Paca
Thomas Stone
Charles Carroll, of
   Carrollton

RHODE ISLAND
Stephen Hopkins
William Ellery

VIRGINIA
George Wythe
Richard Henry Lee
Thomas Jefferson
Benjamin Harrison
Thomas Nelson Jr.
Francis Lightfoot Lee
Carter Braxton

NORTH CAROLINA
William Hooper
Joseph Hewes
John Penn

SOUTH CAROLINA
Edward Rutledge
Thomas Heyward Jr.
Thomas Lynch Jr.
Arthur Middleton

GEORGIA
Button Gwinnett
Lyman Hall
George Walton

Resolved, That copies of the Declaration be sent to the several assemblies, conventions, and committees, or councils of safety, and to the several commanding officers of the continental troops; that it be proclaimed in each of the United States, at the head of the army.

THE CONSTITUTION OF THE UNITED STATES[1]

We the People of the United States, in Order to form a more perfect Union, establish Justice, insure domestic Tranquility, provide for the common defence, promote the general Welfare, and secure the Blessings of Liberty to ourselves and our Posterity, do ordain and establish this CONSTITUTION for the United States of America.

Article I

Section 1.
All legislative Powers herein granted shall be vested in a Congress of the United States, which shall consist of a Senate and House of Representatives.

Section 2.
The House of Representatives shall be composed of Members chosen every second Year by the People of the several States, and the Electors in each State shall have the Qualifications requisite for Electors of the most numerous Branch of the State Legislature.

No Person shall be a Representative who shall not have attained to the Age of twenty-five Years, and been seven Years a Citizen of the United States, and who shall not, when elected, be an Inhabitant of that State in which he shall be chosen.

[Representatives and direct Taxes[2] shall be apportioned among the several States which may be included within this Union, according to their respective Numbers, which shall be determined by adding to the whole Number of free Persons, including those bound to Service for a Term of Years, and excluding Indians not taxed, three fifths of all other Persons.][3] The actual Enumeration shall be made within three Years after the first Meeting of the Congress of the United States, and within every subsequent Term of ten Years, in such Manner as they shall by Law direct. The Number of Representatives shall not exceed one for every thirty Thousand, but each State shall have at Least one Representative; and until such enumeration shall be made, the State of New Hampshire shall be entitled to chuse three, Massachusetts eight, Rhode-Island and Providence Plantations one, Connecticut five, New York six, New Jersey four, Pennsylvania eight, Delaware one, Maryland six, Virginia ten, North Carolina five, South Carolina five, and Georgia three.

When vacancies happen in the Representation from any State, the Executive Authority thereof shall issue Writs of Election to fill such Vacancies.

The House of Representatives shall chuse their Speaker and other Officers; and shall have the sole Power of Impeachment.

Section 3.
The Senate of the United States shall be composed of two Senators from each State, chosen by the Legislature thereof, for six Years; and each Senator shall have one Vote.

Immediately after they shall be assembled in Consequence of the first Election, they shall be divided as equally as may be into three Classes. The Seats of the Senators of the first Class shall be vacated at the Expiration of the second Year, of the second Class at the Expiration of the fourth Year, and of the third Class at the Expiration of the sixth

---

[1]This version, which follows the original Constitution in capitalization and spelling, was published by the United States Department of the Interior, Office of Education, in 1935.
[2]Altered by the Sixteenth Amendment.
[3]Negated by the Fourteenth Amendment.

Year, so that one-third may be chosen every second Year; and if Vacancies happen by Resignation, or otherwise, during the Recess of the Legislature of any State, the Executive thereof may make temporary Appointments until the next Meeting of the Legislature, which shall then fill such Vacancies.

No Person shall be a Senator who shall not have attained to the Age of thirty Years, and been nine Years a Citizen of the United States, and who shall not, when elected, be an Inhabitant of that State for which he shall be chosen.

The Vice President of the United States shall be President of the Senate, but shall have no vote, unless they be equally divided.

The Senate shall chuse their other Officers, and also a President pro tempore, in the absence of the Vice President, or when he shall exercise the Office of President of the United States.

The Senate shall have the sole Power to try all Impeachments. When sitting for that purpose they shall be on Oath or Affirmation. When the President of the United States is tried, the Chief Justice shall preside: And no person shall be convicted without the Concurrence of two thirds of the Members present.

Judgment in Cases of Impeachment shall not extend further than to removal from Office, and disqualification to hold and enjoy any Office of honor, Trust, or Profit under the United States: but the Party convicted shall nevertheless be liable and subject to Indictment, Trial, Judgment, and Punishment, according to Law.

Section 4.
The Times, Places and Manner of holding Elections for Senators and Representatives, shall be prescribed in each State by the Legislature thereof; but the Congress may at any time by Law make or alter such Regulations, except as to the Places of Chusing Senators.

The Congress shall assemble at least once in every Year, and such Meeting shall be on the first Monday in December, unless they shall by Law appoint a different Day.

Section 5.
Each House shall be the Judge of the Elections, Returns and Qualifications of its own Members, and a Majority of each shall constitute a Quorum to do Business; but a smaller number may adjourn from day to day, and may be authorized to compel the Attendance of absent Members, in such Manner, and under such Penalties, as each House may provide.

Each House may determine the Rules of its Proceedings, punish its Members for disorderly Behaviour, and, with the Concurrence of two thirds, expel a Member.

Each House shall keep a Journal of its Proceedings, and from time to time publish the same, excepting such Parts as may in their Judgment require Secrecy; and the Yeas and Nays of the Members of either House on any question shall, at the Desire of one fifth of those Present, be entered on the Journal.

Neither House, during the Session of Congress, shall, without the Consent of the other, adjourn for more than three days, nor to any other Place than that in which the two Houses shall be sitting.

Section 6.
The Senators and Representatives shall receive a Compensation for their Services, to be ascertained by Law, and paid out of the Treasury of the United States. They shall in all Cases, except Treason, Felony, and Breach of the Peace, be privileged from Arrest during

their Attendance at the Session of their respective Houses, and in going to and returning from the same; and for any Speech or Debate in either House, they shall not be questioned in any other Place.

No Senator or Representative shall, during the Time for which he was elected, be appointed to any civil Office under the Authority of the United States, which shall have been created, or the Emoluments whereof shall have been increased, during such time; and no Person holding any Office under the United States shall be a Member of either House during his continuance in Office.

Section 7.
All Bills for raising Revenue shall originate in the House of Representatives; but the Senate may propose or concur with Amendments as on other bills.

Every Bill which shall have passed the House of Representatives and the Senate, shall, before it become a Law, be presented to the President of the United States; If he approve he shall sign it, but if not he shall return it, with his Objections, to that House in which it shall have originated, who shall enter the Objections at large on their Journal, and proceed to reconsider it. If after such Reconsideration two thirds of that House shall agree to pass the bill, it shall be sent, together with the objections, to the other House, by which it shall likewise be reconsidered, and if approved by two thirds of that House, it shall become a Law. But in all such Cases the Votes of both Houses shall be determined by Yeas and Nays, and the Names of the Persons voting for and against the Bill shall be entered on the Journal of each House respectively. If any Bill shall not be returned by the President within ten Days (Sundays excepted) after it shall have been presented to him, the Same shall be a Law, in like Manner as if he had signed it, unless the Congress by their Adjournment prevent its Return, in which Case it shall not be a Law.

Every Order, Resolution, or Vote to which the Concurrence of the Senate and House of Representatives may be necessary (except on a question of Adjournment) shall be presented to the President of the United States; and before the Same shall take Effect, shall be approved by him, or being disapproved by him, shall be repassed by two thirds of the Senate and House of Representatives, according to the Rules and Limitations prescribed in the Case of a Bill.

Section 8.
The Congress shall have Power To lay and collect Taxes, Duties, Imposts and Excises, to pay the Debts and provide for the common Defence and general Welfare of the United States; but all Duties, Imposts and Excises shall be uniform throughout the United States;

To borrow money on the credit of the United States;

To regulate Commerce with foreign Nations, and among the several States, and with the Indian Tribes;

To establish an uniform rule of Naturalization, and uniform Laws on the subject of Bankruptcies throughout the United States;

To coin Money, regulate the Value thereof, and of foreign Coin, and fix the Standard of Weights and Measures;

To provide for the Punishment of counterfeiting the Securities and current Coin of the United States;

To establish Post Offices and post Roads;

To promote the Progress of Science and useful Arts, by securing for limited Times to Authors and Inventors the exclusive Right to their respective Writings and Discoveries;

To constitute Tribunals inferior to the Supreme Court;

To define and punish Piracies and Felonies committed on the high Seas, and Offenses against the Law of Nations;

To declare War, grant Letters of Marque and Reprisal, and make Rules concerning Captures on Land and Water;

To raise and support Armies, but no Appropriation of Money to that Use shall be for a longer Term than two Years;

To provide and maintain a Navy;

To make Rules for the Government and Regulation of the land and naval forces;

To provide for calling forth the Militia to execute the Laws of the Union, suppress Insurrections and repel Invasions;

To provide for organizing, arming, and disciplining the Militia, and for governing such Part of them as may be employed in the Service of the United States, reserving to the States respectively, the Appointment of the Officers, and the Authority of training the Militia according to the discipline prescribed by Congress;

To exercise exclusive Legislation in all Cases whatsoever, over such District (not exceeding ten Miles square) as may, by Cession of particular States, and the acceptance of Congress, become the Seat of the Government of the United States, and to exercise like Authority over all Places purchased by the Consent of the Legislature of the State in which the Same shall be, for the Erection of Forts, Magazines, Arsenals, Dock-yards, and other needful Buildings;—And

To make all Laws which shall be necessary and proper for carrying into Execution the foregoing Powers, and all other Powers vested by this Constitution in the Government of the United States, or in any Department or Officer thereof.

Section 9.

The Migration or Importation of such Persons as any of the States now existing shall think proper to admit, shall not be prohibited by the Congress prior to the Year one thousand eight hundred and eight, but a tax or duty may be imposed on such Importation, not exceeding ten dollars for each Person.

The privilege of the Writ of Habeas Corpus shall not be suspended, unless when in Cases of Rebellion or Invasion the public Safety may require it.

No bill of Attainder or ex post facto Law shall be passed.

No capitation, or other direct, Tax shall be laid unless in Proportion to the Census or Enumeration herein before directed to be taken.

No Tax or Duty shall be laid on Articles exported from any State.

No Preference shall be given by any Regulation of Commerce or Revenue to the Ports of one State over those of another: nor shall Vessels bound to, or from, one State, be obliged to enter, clear, or pay Duties in another.

No Money shall be drawn from the Treasury, but in Consequence of Appropriations made by Law; and a regular Statement and Account of the Receipts and Expenditures of all public Money shall be published from time to time.

No Title of Nobility shall be granted by the United States: And no Person holding any Office of Profit or Trust under them, shall, without the Consent of the Congress, accept of any present, Emolument, Office, or Title, of any kind whatever, from any King, Prince, or foreign State.

Section 10.

No State shall enter into any Treaty, Alliance, or Confederation; grant Letters of Marque and Reprisal; coin Money; emit Bills of Credit; make any Thing but gold and silver Coin a Tender in Payment of Debts; pass any Bill of Attainder, ex post facto Law, or Law impairing the Obligation of Contracts, or grant any Title of Nobility.

No State shall, without the Consent of the Congress, lay any Imposts or Duties on Imports or Exports, except what may be absolutely necessary for executing its inspection Laws; and the net Produce of all Duties and Imposts, laid by any State on Imports or Exports, shall be for the use of the Treasury of the United States; and all such Laws shall be subject to the Revision and Control of the Congress.

No state shall, without the Consent of Congress, lay any duty of Tonnage, keep Troops, or Ships of War in time of Peace, enter into any Agreement or Compact with another State, or with a foreign Power, or engage in War, unless actually invaded, or in such imminent Danger as will not admit of delay.

Article II

Section 1.

The executive Power shall be vested in a President of the United States of America. He shall hold his Office during the Term of four years, and, together with the Vice President, chosen for the same Term, be elected, as follows:

Each State shall appoint, in such Manner as the Legislature thereof may direct, a Number of Electors, equal to the whole Number of Senators and Representatives to which the State may be entitled in the Congress: but no Senator or Representative, or Person holding an Office of Trust or Profit under the United States, shall be appointed an Elector.

[The Electors shall meet in their respective States, and vote by Ballot for two persons, of whom one at least shall not be an Inhabitant of the same State with themselves. And they shall make a List of all the Persons voted for, and of the Number of Votes for each; which List they shall sign and certify, and transmit sealed to the Seat of the Government of the United States, directed to the President of the Senate. The President of the Senate shall, in the Presence of the Senate and House of Representatives, open all the Certificates, and the Votes shall then be counted. The Person having the greatest Number of Votes shall be the President, if such Number be a Majority of the whole Number of Electors appointed; and if there be more than one who have such Majority, and have an equal Number of Votes, then the House of Representatives shall immediately chuse by Ballot one of them for President; and if no Person have a Majority, then from the five highest on the List the said House shall in like Manner chuse the President. But in chusing the President, the Votes shall be taken by States, the Representation from each State having one Vote; a quorum for this Purpose shall consist of a Member or Members from two-thirds of the States, and a Majority of all the States shall be necessary to a Choice. In every Case, after the Choice of the President, the Person having the greatest Number of Votes of the Electors shall be the Vice President. But if there should remain two or more who have equal votes, the Senate shall chuse from them by Ballot the Vice President.][4]

The Congress may determine the Time of chusing the Electors, and the Day on which they shall give their Votes; which Day shall be the same throughout the United States.

No person except a natural-born Citizen, or a Citizen of the United States, at the time of the Adoption of this Constitution, shall be eligible to the Office of President; neither shall any Person be eligible to that Office who shall not have attained to the Age of thirty-five years, and been fourteen Years a Resident within the United States.

In Case of the Removal of the President from Office, or of his Death, Resignation, or Inability to discharge the Powers and Duties of the said Office, the same shall devolve

[4]Revised by the Twelfth Amendment.

on the Vice President, and the Congress may by Law provide for the Case of Removal, Death, Resignation, or Inability, both of the President and Vice President, declaring what Officer shall then act as President, and such Officer shall act accordingly, until the disability be removed, or a President shall be elected.

The President shall, at stated Times, receive for his Services a Compensation, which shall neither be increased nor diminished during the Period for which he shall have been elected, and he shall not receive within that Period any other Emolument from the United States, or any of them.

Before he enter on the execution of his Office, he shall take the following Oath or Affirmation:—"I do solemnly swear (or affirm) that I will faithfully execute the Office of President of the United States, and will, to the best of my Ability, preserve, protect, and defend the Constitution of the United States."

Section 2.

The President shall be Commander in Chief of the Army and Navy of the United States, and of the Militia of the several States, when called into the actual Service of the United States; he may require the Opinion, in writing, of the principal Officer in each of the executive Departments, upon any subject relating to the Duties of their respective Offices, and he shall have Power to Grant Reprieves and Pardons for Offenses against the United States, except in Cases of Impeachment.

He shall have Power, by and with the Advice and Consent of the Senate, to make Treaties, provided two-thirds of the Senators present concur; and he shall nominate, and by and with the Advice and Consent of the Senate, shall appoint Ambassadors, other public Ministers and Consuls, Judges of the supreme Court, and all other Officers of the United States, whose Appointments are not herein otherwise provided for, and which shall be established by Law: but the Congress may by Law vest the Appointment of such inferior Officers, as they think proper, in the President alone, in the Courts of Law, or in the Heads of Departments.

The President shall have Power to fill up all Vacancies that may happen during the Recess of the Senate, by granting Commissions which shall expire at the End of their next Session.

Section 3.

He shall from time to time give to the Congress Information of the State of the Union, and recommend to their Consideration such Measures as he shall judge necessary and expedient; he may, on extraordinary occasions, convene both Houses, or either of them, and in Case of Disagreement between them, with respect to the Time of Adjournment, he may adjourn them to such Time as he shall think proper; he shall receive Ambassadors and other public Ministers; he shall take care that the Laws be faithfully executed, and shall Commission all the Officers of the United States.

Section 4.

The President, Vice President and all civil Officers of the United States, shall be removed from Office on Impeachment for, and Conviction of, Treason, Bribery, or other high Crimes and Misdemeanors.

Article III

Section 1.

The judicial Power of the United States, shall be vested in one supreme Court, and in such inferior Courts as the Congress may from time to time ordain and establish. The Judges, both of the supreme and inferior Courts, shall hold their Offices during good

Behaviour, and shall, at stated Times, receive for their Services, a Compensation, which shall not be diminished during their Continuance in Office.

Section 2.

The judicial Power shall extend to all Cases, in Law and Equity, arising under this Constitution, the Laws of the United States, and Treaties made, or which shall be made, under their Authority;—to all Cases affecting ambassadors, other public ministers and consuls;—to all cases of admiralty and maritime Jurisdiction;—to Controversies to which the United States shall be a Party;—to Controversies between two or more States;—between a State and Citizens of another State;[5]—between Citizens of different States—between Citizens of the same State claiming Lands under Grants of different States, and between a State, or the Citizens thereof, and foreign States, Citizens, or Subjects.

In all Cases affecting Ambassadors, other public Ministers and Consuls, and those in which a State shall be Party, the supreme Court shall have original Jurisdiction. In all the other Cases before mentioned, the supreme Court shall have appellate Jurisdiction, both as to Law and Fact, with such Exceptions, and under such Regulations as the Congress shall make.

The trial of all Crimes, except in Cases of Impeachment, shall be by Jury; and such Trial shall be held in the State where the said Crimes shall have been committed; but when not committed within any State, the Trial shall be at such Place or Places as the Congress may by Law have directed.

Section 3.

Treason against the United States, shall consist only in levying War against them, or in adhering to their Enemies, giving them Aid and Comfort. No Person shall be convicted of Treason unless on the Testimony of two Witnesses to the same overt Act, or on Confession in open Court.

The Congress shall have power to declare the Punishment of Treason, but no Attainder of Treason shall work Corruption of Blood, or Forfeiture except during the Life of the Person attained.

Article IV

Section 1.

Full Faith and Credit shall be given in each State to the public Acts, Records, and judicial Proceedings of every other State. And the Congress may by general Laws prescribe the Manner in which such Acts, Records and Proceedings shall be proved, and the Effect thereof.

Section 2.

The Citizens of each State shall be entitled to all Privileges and Immunities of Citizens in the several States.

A Person charged in any State with Treason, Felony, or other Crime, who shall flee from Justice, and be found in another State, shall on demand of the executive Authority of the State from which he fled, be delivered up, to be removed to the State having Jurisdiction of the crime.

---

[5]Qualified by the Eleventh Amendment.

No Person held to Service or Labour in one State, under the Laws thereof, escaping into another, shall, in Consequence of any Law or Regulation therein, be discharged from such Service or Labour, but shall be delivered up on Claim of the Party to whom such Service or Labour may be due.

Section 3.
New States may be admitted by the Congress into this Union; but no new State shall be formed or erected within the Jurisdiction of any other State; nor any State be formed by the Junction of two or more States, or parts of States, without the Consent of the Legislatures of the States concerned as well as of the Congress.

The Congress shall have Power to dispose of and make all needful Rules and Regulations respecting the Territory or other Property belonging to the United States; and nothing in this Constitution shall be so construed as to Prejudice any Claims of the United States, or of any particular State.

Section 4.
The United States shall guarantee to every State in this Union a Republican Form of Government, and shall protect each of them against Invasion; and on Application of the Legislature, or of the Executive (when the Legislature cannot be convened) against domestic Violence.

Article V

The Congress, whenever two-thirds of both Houses shall deem it necessary, shall propose Amendments to this Constitution, or, on the Application of the Legislatures of two-thirds of the several States, shall call a Convention for proposing Amendments, which, in either Case, shall be valid to all Intents and Purposes, as part of this Constitution, when ratified by the Legislatures of three-fourths of the several States, or by Conventions in three-fourths thereof, as the one or the other Mode of Ratification may be proposed by the Congress; Provided that no Amendment which may be made prior to the Year One thousand eight hundred and eight shall in any Manner affect the first and fourth Clauses in the Ninth Section of the first Article; and that no State, without its Consent, shall be deprived of its equal Suffrage in the Senate.

Article VI

All Debts contracted and Engagements entered into, before the Adoption of this Constitution, shall be as valid against the United States under this Constitution, as under the Confederation.

This Constitution, and the Laws of the United States which shall be made in Pursuance thereof; and all Treaties made, or which shall be made, under the Authority of the United States, shall be the supreme Law of the Land; and the Judges in every State shall be bound thereby, any Thing in the Constitution or Laws of any State to the Contrary notwithstanding.

The Senators and Representatives before mentioned, and the Members of the several State Legislatures, and all executive and judicial Officers, both of the United States and of the several States, shall be bound by Oath or Affirmation to support this Constitution; but no religious Tests shall ever be required as a qualification to any Office or public Trust under the United States.

Article VII

The Ratification of the Conventions of nine States shall be sufficient for the Establishment of this Constitution between the States so ratifying the same.

Done in Convention by the Unanimous Consent of the States present the Seventeenth Day of September in the Year of our Lord one thousand seven hundred and Eighty seven, and of the Independence of the United States of America the Twelfth. In Witness whereof We have hereunto subscribed our Names.[6]

George Washington
President and deputy from Virginia

NEW HAMPSHIRE
John Langdon
Nicholas Gilman

MASSACHUSETTS
Nathaniel Gorham
Rufus King

CONNECTICUT
William Samuel Johnson
Roger Sherman

NEW YORK
Alexander Hamilton

NEW JERSEY
William Livingston
David Brearley
William Paterson
Jonathan Dayton

PENNSYLVANIA
Benjamin Franklin
Thomas Mifflin
Robert Morris
George Clymer
Thomas FitzSimons
Jared Ingersoll
James Wilson
Gouverneur Morris

DELAWARE
George Read
Gunning Bedford Jr.
John Dickinson
Richard Bassett
Jacob Broom

MARYLAND
James McHenry
Daniel of St. Thomas Jenifer
Daniel Carroll

VIRGINIA
John Blair
James Madison Jr.

NORTH CAROLINA
William Blount
Richard Dobbs Spaight
Hugh Williamson

SOUTH CAROLINA
John Rutledge
Charles Coteswort Pinckney
Charles Pinckney
Pierce Butler

GEORGIA
William Few
Abraham Baldwin

Articles in Addition to, and Amendment of, the Constitution of the United States of America, Proposed by Congress, and Ratified by the Legislatures of the Several States, Pursuant to the Fifth Article of the Original Constitution.[7]

[Article I]

Congress shall make no law respecting an establishment of religion, or prohibiting the free exercise thereof; or abridging the freedom of speech, or of the press; or the right of the people peaceably to assemble, and to petition the Government for a redress of grievances.

[Article II]

A well regulated Militia, being necessary to the security of a free State, the right of the people to keep and bear Arms shall not be infringed.

[6]These are the full names of the signers, which in some cases are not the signatures on the document.
[7]This heading appears only in the joint resolution submitting the first ten amendments.

[Article III]

No Soldier shall, in time of peace, be quartered in any house, without the consent of the Owner, nor in time of war, but in a manner to be prescribed by law.

[Article IV]

The right of the people to be secure in their persons, houses, papers, and effects, against unreasonable searches and seizures, shall not be violated, and no Warrants shall issue, but upon probable cause, supported by Oath or affirmation, and particularly describing the place to be searched, and the persons or things to be seized.

[Article V]

No person shall be held to answer for a capital or otherwise infamous crime, unless on a presentment or indictment of a Grand Jury, except in cases arising in the land or naval forces, or in the Militia, when in actual service in time of War or public danger; nor shall any person be subject for the same offence to be twice put in jeopardy of life or limb; nor shall be compelled in any criminal case to be a witness against himself, nor be deprived of life, liberty, or property, without due process of law; nor shall private property be taken for public use, without just compensation.

[Article VI]

In all criminal prosecutions, the accused shall enjoy the right to a speedy and public trial, by an impartial jury of the State and district wherein the crime shall have been committed, which district shall have been previously ascertained by law, and to be informed of the nature and cause of the accusation; to be confronted with the witnesses against him; to have compulsory process for obtaining witnesses in his favour, and to have the Assistance of Counsel for his defense.

[Article VII]

In suits at common law, where the value in controversy shall exceed twenty dollars, the right of trial by jury shall be preserved, and no fact tried by a jury, shall be otherwise reexamined in any Court of the United States, than according to the rules of the common law.

[Article VIII]

Excessive bail shall not be required, nor excessive fines imposed, nor cruel and unusual punishments inflicted.

[Article IX]

The enumeration of the Constitution, of certain rights, shall not be construed to deny or disparage others retained by the people.

[Article X]

The powers not delegated to the United States by the Constitution, nor prohibited by it to the States, are reserved to the States respectively, or to the people.
[Amendments I–X, in force 1791.]

[Article XI][8]

The Judicial power of the United States shall not be construed to extend to any suit in law or equity, commenced or prosecuted against one of the United States by Citizens of another State, or by Citizens or Subjects of any Foreign State.

[Article XII][9]

The Electors shall meet in their respective States and vote by ballot for President and Vice-President, one of whom, at least, shall not be an inhabitant of the same State with themselves; they shall name in their ballots the person voted for as President, and in distinct ballots the person voted for as Vice-President, and they shall make distinct lists of all persons voted for as President, and of all persons voted for as Vice-President, and of the number of votes for each, which lists they shall sign and certify, and transmit sealed to the seat of the government of the United States, directed to the President of the Senate;—The President of the Senate shall, in the presence of the Senate and House of Representatives, open all the certificates and the votes shall then be counted;—The person having the greatest number of votes for President, shall be the President, if such number be a majority of the whole number of Electors appointed; and if no person have such majority, then from the persons having the highest numbers not exceeding three on the list of those voted for as President, the House of Representatives shall choose immediately, by ballot, the President. But in choosing the President, the votes shall be taken by states, the representation from each state having one vote; a quorum for this purpose shall consist of a member or members from two-thirds of the states, and a majority of all the states shall be necessary to a choice. And if the House of Representatives shall not choose a President whenever the right of choice shall devolve upon them, before the fourth day of March next following, then the Vice-President shall act as President, as in the case of the death or other constitutional disability of the President.—The person having the greatest number of votes as Vice-President, shall be the Vice-President, if such number be a majority of the whole number of Electors appointed, and if no person have a majority, then from the two highest numbers on the list, the Senate shall choose the Vice-President; a quorum for the purpose shall consist of two-thirds of the whole number of Senators, and a majority of the whole number shall be necessary to a choice. But no person constitutionally ineligible to the office of President shall be eligible to that of Vice-President of the United States.

[Article XIII][10]

Section 1.
Neither slavery nor involuntary servitude, except as a punishment for crime whereof the party shall have been duly convicted, shall exist within the United States, or any place subject to their jurisdiction.

Section 2.
Congress shall have power to enforce this article by appropriate legislation.

[8]Adopted in 1798.
[9]Adopted in 1804.
[10]Adopted in 1865.

[Article XIV][11]

Section 1.
All persons born or naturalized in the United States, and subject to the jurisdiction thereof, are citizens of the United States and of the State wherein they reside. No State shall make or enforce any law which shall abridge the privileges or immunities of citizens of the United States; nor shall any State deprive any person of life, liberty, or property, without due process of law; nor deny to any person within its jurisdiction the equal protection of the laws.

Section 2.
Representatives shall be apportioned among the several States according to their respective numbers, counting the whole number of persons in each State, excluding Indians not taxed. But when the right to vote at any election for the choice of electors for President and Vice-President of the United States, Representatives in Congress, the Executive and Judicial officers of a State, or the members of the Legislature thereof, is denied to any of the male inhabitants of such State, being twenty-one years of age, and citizens of the United States, or in any way abridged, except for participation in rebellion, or other crime, the basis of representation therein shall be reduced in the proportion which the number of such male citizens shall bear to the whole number of male citizens twenty-one years of age in such State.

Section 3.
No person shall be a Senator or Representative in Congress, or elector of President and Vice-President, or hold any office, civil or military, under the United States, or under any State, who, having previously taken an oath, as a member of Congress, or as an officer of the United States, or as a member of any State legislature, or as an executive or judicial officer of any State, to support the Constitution of the United States, shall have engaged in insurrection or rebellion against the same, or given aid or comfort to the enemies thereof. But Congress may by a vote of two-thirds of each House, remove such disability.

Section 4.
The validity of the public debt of the United States, authorized by law, including debts incurred for payment of pensions and bounties for services in suppressing insurrection or rebellion, shall not be questioned. But neither the United States nor any State shall assume or pay any debts or obligation incurred in aid of insurrection or rebellion against the United States, or any claim for the loss or emancipation of any slave; but all such debts, obligations, and claims shall be held illegal and void.

Section 5.
The Congress shall have the power to enforce, by appropriate legislation, the provisions of this article.

[Article XV][12]

Section 1.
The right of citizens of the United States to vote shall not be denied or abridged by the United States or by any State on account of race, color, or previous condition of servitude—

Section 2.
The Congress shall have power to enforce this article by appropriate legislation.

[11]Adopted in 1868.
[12]Adopted in 1870.

[Article XVI][13]

The Congress shall have power to lay and collect taxes on incomes, from whatever source derived, without apportionment among the several States, and without regard to any census or enumeration.

[Article XVII][14]

The Senate of the United States shall be composed of two Senators from each State, elected by the people thereof, for six years; and each Senator shall have one vote. The electors in each State shall have the qualifications requisite for electors of the most numerous branch of the State legislatures.

When vacancies happen in the representation of any State in the Senate, the executive authority of such State shall issue writs of election to fill such vacancies: *Provided*, That the legislature of any State may empower the executive thereof to make temporary appointments until the people fill the vacancies by election as the legislature may direct.

This amendment shall not be so construed as to affect the election or term of any Senator chosen before it becomes valid as part of the Constitution.

[Article XVIII][15]

Section 1.
After one year from the ratification of this article the manufacture, sale, or transportation of intoxicating liquors within, the importation thereof into, or the exportation thereof from the United States and all territory subject to the jurisdiction thereof for beverage purposes is hereby prohibited.

Section 2.
The Congress and the several States shall have concurrent power to enforce this article by appropriate legislation.

Section 3.
This article shall be inoperative unless it shall have been ratified as an amendment to the Constitution by the legislatures of the several States, as provided in the Constitution, within seven years from the date of the submission hereof to the States by the Congress.

[Article XIX][16]

The right of citizens of the United States to vote shall not be denied or abridged by the United States or by any State on account of sex.

Congress shall have power to enforce this article by appropriate legislation.

[Article XX][17]

Section 1.
The terms of the President and Vice-President shall end at noon on the 20th day of January, and the terms of Senators and Representatives at noon on the 3d day of January,

[13]Adopted in 1913.
[14]Adopted in 1913.
[15]Adopted in 1918.
[16]Adopted in 1920.
[17]Adopted in 1933.

of the years in which such terms would have ended if this article had not been ratified; and the terms of their successors shall then begin.

Section 2.
The Congress shall assemble at least once in every year, and such meeting shall begin at noon on the 3d day of January, unless they shall by law appoint a different day.

Section 3.
If, at the time fixed for the beginning of the term of the President, the President elect shall have died, the Vice-President elect shall become President. If a President shall not have been chosen before the time fixed for the beginning of his term or if the President elect shall have failed to qualify, then the Vice-President elect shall act as President until a President shall have qualified; and the Congress may by law provide for the case wherein neither a President elect nor a Vice-President elect shall have qualified, declaring who shall then act as President, or the manner in which one who is to act shall be selected, and such person shall act accordingly until a President or Vice-President shall have qualified.

Section 4.
The Congress may by law provide for the case of the death of any of the persons from whom the House of Representatives may choose a President whenever the right of choice shall have devolved upon them, and for the case of the death of any of the persons from whom the Senate may choose a Vice-President whenever the right of choice shall have devolved upon them.

Section 5.
Sections 1 and 2 shall take effect on the 15th day of October following the ratification of this article.

Section 6.
This article shall be inoperative unless it shall have been ratified as an amendment to the Constitution by the legislatures of three-fourths of the several States within seven years from the date of its submission.

[Article XXI][18]

Section 1.
The eighteenth article of amendment to the Constitution of the United States is hereby repealed.

Section 2.
The transportation or importation into any State, Territory, or possession of the United States for delivery or use therein of intoxicating liquors, in violation of the laws thereof, is hereby prohibited.

Section 3.
This article shall be inoperative unless it shall have been ratified as an amendment to the Constitution by conventions in the several States, as provided in the Constitution, within seven years from the date of the submission hereof to the States by the Congress.

---

[18]Adopted in 1933.

[Article XXII][19]

No person shall be elected to the office of the President more than twice, and no person who has held the office of President, or acted as President, for more than two years of a term to which some other person was elected President shall be elected to the office of the President more than once.

But this Article shall not apply to any person holding the office of President when this Article was proposed by the Congress, and shall not prevent any person who may be holding the office of President, or acting as President, during the term within which this Article becomes operative from holding the office of President or acting as President during the remainder of such term.

This article shall be inoperative unless it shall have been ratified as an amendment to the Constitution by the legislatures of three-fourths of the several states within seven years from the date of its submission to the states by the Congress.

[Article XXIII][20]

Section 1.

The District constituting the seat of Government of the United States shall appoint in such manner as the Congress may direct:

A number of electors of President and Vice-President equal to the whole number of Senators and Representatives in Congress to which the District would be entitled if it were a State, but in no event more than the least populous State; they shall be in addition to those appointed by the States, but they shall be considered, for the purposes of the election of President and Vice-President, to be electors appointed by a State; and they shall meet in the District and perform such duties as provided by the twelfth article of amendment.

Section 2.

The Congress shall have power to enforce this article by appropriate legislation.

[Article XXIV][21]

Section 1.

The right of citizens of the United States to vote in any primary or other election for President or Vice President, for electors for President or Vice President, or for Senator or Representative in Congress, shall not be denied or abridged by the United States or any state by reason of failure to pay any poll tax or other tax.

Section 2.

The Congress shall have the power to enforce this article by appropriate legislation.

[Article XXV][22]

Section 1.

In case of the removal of the President from office or of his death or resignation, the Vice President shall become President.

---

[19]Adopted in 1951.
[20]Adopted in 1961.
[21]Adopted in 1964.
[22]Adopted in 1967.

Section 2.

Whenever there is a vacancy in the office of the Vice President, the President shall nominate a Vice President who shall take office upon confirmation by a majority vote of both Houses of Congress.

Section 3.

Whenever the President transmits to the President Pro Tempore of the Senate and the Speaker of the House of Representatives his written declaration that he is unable to discharge the powers and duties of his office, and until he transmits to them a written declaration to the contrary, such powers and duties shall be discharged by the Vice President as Acting President.

Section 4.

Whenever the Vice President and a majority of either the principal officers of the executive departments or of such other body as Congress may by law provide, transmit to the President Pro Tempore of the Senate and the Speaker of the House of Representatives their written declaration that the President is unable to discharge the powers and duties of his office, the Vice President shall immediately assume the powers and duties of the office as Acting President.

Thereafter, when the President transmits to the President Pro Tempore of the Senate and the Speaker of the House of Representatives his written declaration that no inability exists, he shall resume the powers and duties of his office unless the Vice President and a majority of either the principal officers of the executive departments or of such other body as Congress may by law provide, transmit within four days to the President Pro Tempore of the Senate and the Speaker of the House of Representatives their written declaration that the President is unable to discharge the powers and duties of his office. Thereupon Congress shall decide the issue, assembling within forty-eight hours for that purpose if not in session. If the Congress, within twenty-one days after receipt of the latter written declaration, or, if Congress is not in session, within twenty-one days after Congress is required to assemble, determines by two-thirds vote of both Houses that the President is unable to discharge the powers and duties of his office, the Vice President shall continue to discharge the same as Acting President; otherwise, the President shall resume the powers and duties of his office.

[Article XXVI][23]

Section 1.

The right of citizens of the United States, who are eighteen years of age or older, to vote shall not be denied or abridged by the United States or by any State on account of age.

Section 2.

The Congress shall have power to enforce this article by appropriate legislation.

[Article XXVII][24]

No law varying the compensation for the services of the Senators and Representatives shall take effect until an election of Representatives shall have intervened.

[23]Adopted in 1971.
[24]Adopted in 1992.

PRESIDENTIAL ELECTIONS

Year	Candidates	Parties	Popular Vote	Percentage of Popular Vote	Electoral Vote	Percentage of Voter Participation
1789	**George Washington (Va.)***				69	
	John Adams				34	
	Others				35	
1792	**George Washington (Va.)**				132	
	John Adams				77	
	George Clinton				50	
	Others				5	
1796	**John Adams (Mass.)**	Federalist			71	
	Thomas Jefferson	Democratic-Republican			68	
	Thomas Pinckeny	Federalist			59	
	Aaron Burr	Fedearalist			30	
	Others	Dem.-Rep.			48	
1800	**Thomas Jefferson (Va.)**	Dem.-Rep.			73	
	Aaron Burr	Dem.-Rep.			73	
	John Adams	Federalist			65	
	C. C. Pinckney	Federalist			64	
	John Jay	Federalist			1	
1804	**Thomas Jefferson (Va.)**	Dem.-Rep.			162	
	C. C. Pinckney	Federalist			14	
1808	**James Madison (Va.)**	Dem.-Rep.			122	
	C.C. Pickney	Federalist			47	
	George Clinton	Dem.-Rep.			6	

*State of residence at time of election.

(continued)

Year	Candidates	Parties	Popular Vote	% of Popular Vote	Electoral Vote	% of Voter Participation
1812	James Madison (Va.)	Dem.-Rep.			128	
	De Witt Clinton	Federalist			89	
1816	James Monroe (Va.)	Dem.-Rep.			183	
	Rufus King	Federalist			34	
1820	James Monroe (Va.)	Dem.-Rep.			231	
	John Quincy Adams	Dem.-Rep.			1	
1824	John Q. Adams (Mass.)	Dem.-Rep.	108,740	30.5	84	26.9
	Andrew Jackson	Dem.-Rep.	153,544	43.1	99	
	William H. Crawford	Dem.-Rep.	46,618	13.1	41	
	Henry Clay	Dem.-Rep.	47,136	13.2	37	
1828	Andrew Jackson (Tenn.)	Democratic	647,286	56.0	178	57.6
	John Quincy Adams	National Republican	508,064	44.0	83	
1832	Andrew Jackson (Tenn.)	Democratic	687,502	55.0	219	55.4
	Henry Clay	National Republican	530,189	42.4	49	
	John Floyd	Independent			11	
	William Wirt	Anti-Mason	33,108	2.6	7	
1836	Martin Van Buren (N.Y.)	Democratic	765,483	50.9	170	57.8
	W. H. Harrison	Whig			73	
	Hugh L. White	Whig	739,765	49.1	26	
	Daniel Webster	Whig			14	
	W. P. Magnum	Independent			11	
1840	William H. Harrison (Ohio)	Whig	1,274,624	53.1	234	80.2
	Martin Van Buren	Democratic	1,127,781	46.9	60	
	J. G. Birney	Liberty	7,069		—	

Year	Candidates	Parties	Popular Vote	Percentage of Popular Vote	Electoral Vote	Percentage of Voter Participation
1844	James K. Polk (Tenn.)	Democratic	1,338,464	49.6	170	78.9
	Henry Clay	Whig	1,300,097	48.1	105	
	J. G. Birney	Liberty	62,300	2.3	—	
1848	Zachary Taylor (La.)	Whig	1,360,967	47.4	163	72.7
	Lewis Cass	Democratic	1,222,342	42.5	127	
	Martin Van Buren	Free-Soil	291,263	10.1	—	
1852	Franklin Pierce (N.H.)	Democratic	1,601,117	50.9	254	69.6
	Winfield Scott	Whig	1,385,453	44.1	42	
	John P. Hale	Free-Soil	155,825	5.0	—	
1856	James Buchanan (Pa.)	Democratic	1,832,955	45.3	174	78.9
	John C. Frémont	Republican	1,339,932	33.1	114	
	Millard Fillmore	American	871,731	21.6	8	
1860	Abraham Lincoln (Ill.)	Republican	1,865,593	39.9	180	81.2
	Stephen A. Douglas	Democratic	1,382,713	29.4	12	
	John C. Breckinridge	Democratic	848,356	18.1	72	
	John Bell	Union	592,906	12.6	39	
1864	Abraham Lincoln (Ill.)	Republican	2,213,655	55.0	212	73.8
	George B. McClellan	Democratic	1,805,237	45.0	21	
1868	Ulysses S. Grant (Ill.)	Republican	3,012,833	52.7	214	78.1
	Horatio Seymour	Democratic	2,703,249	47.3	80	
1872	Ulysses S. Grant (Ill.)	Republican	3,597,132	55.6	286	71.3
	Horace Greeley	Democratic; Liberal Republican	2,834,125	43.9	66	
1876	Rutherford B. Hayes (Ohio)	Republican	4,036,298	48.0	185	81.8
	Samuel J. Tilden	Democratic	4,300,590	51.0	184	
1880	James A. Garfield (Ohio)	Republican	4,454,416	48.5	214	79.4
	Winfield S. Hancock	Democratic	4,444,952	48.1	155	

Year	Candidates	Party	Popular Vote	%	Electoral Vote	% Voter Participation
1884	**Grover Cleveland (N.Y.)**	Democratic	4,874,986	48.5	219	77.5
	James G. Blaine	Republican	4,851,981	48.2	182	
1888	**Benjamin Harrison (Ind.)**	Republican	5,439,853	47.9	233	79.3
	Grover Cleveland	Democratic	5,540,309	48.6	168	
1892	**Grover Cleveland (N.Y.)**	Democratic	5,556,918	46.1	277	74.7
	Benjamin Harrison	Republican	5,176,108	43.0	145	
	James B. Weaver	People's	1,041,028	8.5	22	
1896	**William McKinley (Ohio)**	Republican	7,104,779	51.1	271	79.3
	William J. Bryan	Democratic People's	6,502,925	47.7	176	
1900	**William McKinley (Ohio)**	Republican	7,207,923	51.7	292	73.2
	William J. Bryan	Dem.-Populis	6,358,133	45.5	155	
1904	**Theodore Roosevelt (N.Y.)**	Republican	7,623,486	57.9	336	65.2
	Alton B. Parker	Democratic	5,077,911	37.6	140	
	Eugene V. Debs	Socialist	402,283	3.0	—	
1908	**William H. Taft (Ohio)**	Republican	7,678,908	51.6	321	65.4
	William J. Bryan	Democratic	6,409,104	43.1	162	
	Eugene V. Debs	Socialist	420,793	2.8	—	
1912	**Woodrow Wilson (N.J.)**	Democratic	6,293,454	41.9	435	58.8
	Theodore Roosevelt	Progressive	4,119,538	27.4	88	
	William H. Taft	Republican	3,484,980	23.2	8	
	Eugene V. Debs	Socialist	900,672	6.0	—	
1916	**Woodrow Wilson (N.J.)**	Democratic	9,129,606	49.4	277	61.6
	Charles E. Hughes	Republican	8,538,221	46.2	254	
	A. L. Benson	Socialist	585,113	3.2	—	

(continued)

Year	Candidates	Parties	Popular Vote	Percentage of Popular Vote	Electoral Vote	Percentage of Voter Participation
1920	**Warren G. Harding (Ohio)**	Republican	16,152,200	60.4	404	49.2
	James M. Cox	Democratic	9,147,353	34.2	127	
	Eugene V. Debs	Socialist	919,799	3.4	—	
1924	**Calvin Coolidge (Mass.)**	Republican	15,725,016	54.0	382	48.9
	John W. Davis	Democratic	8,386,503	28.8	136	
	Robert M. La Follette	Progressive	4,822,856	16.6	13	
1928	**Herbert Hoover (Calif.)**	Republican	21,391,381	58.2	444	56.9
	Alfred E. Smith	Democratic	15,016,443	40.9	87	
	Norman Thomas	Socialist	267,835	0.7	—	
1932	**Franklin D. Roosevelt (N.Y.)**	Democratic	22,821,857	57.4	472	56.9
	Herbert Hoover	Republican	15,761,841	39.7	59	
	Norman Thomas	Socialist	881,951	2.2	—	
1936	**Franklin D. Roosevelt (N.Y.)**	Democratic	27,751,597	60.8	523	61.0
	Alfred M. Landon	Republican	16,679,583	36.5	8	
	William Lemke	Union	882,479	1.9	—	
1940	**Franklin D. Roosevelt (N.Y.)**	Democratic	27,244,160	54.8	449	62.5
	Wendell L. Willkie	Republican	22,305,198	44.8	82	
1944	**Franklin D. Roosevelt (N.Y.)**	Democratic	25,602,504	53.5	432	55.9
	Thomas E. Dewey	Republican	22,006,285	46.0	99	
1948	**Harry S. Truman (Mo.)**	Democratic	24,105,695	49.5	303	53.0
	Thomas E. Dewey	Republican	21,969,170	45.1	189	
	J. Strom Thurmond	States' Rights Democratic	1,169,021	2.4	39	
	Henry A. Wallace	Progressive	1,156,103	2.4	—	
1952	**Dwight D. Eisenhower (N.Y.)**	Republican	33,936,252	55.1	442	63.3
	Adlai E. Stevenson	Democratic	27,314,992	44.4	89	

Year	Candidate	Party	Popular Vote	Percentage	Electoral Vote	Voter Participation
1956	Dwight D. Eisenhower (N.Y.)	Republican	35,575,420	57.6	457	60.6
	Adlai E. Stevenson	Democratic	26,033,066	42.1	73	
	Other	—			1	
1960	John F. Kennedy (Mass.)	Democratic	34,227,096	49.7	303	64.0
	Richard M. Nixon	Republican	34,108,546	49.6	219	
	Other	—			15	
1964	Lyndon B. Johnson (Tex.)	Democratic	43,126,506	61.1	486	61.7
	Barry M. Goldwater	Republican	27,176,799	38.5	52	
1968	Richard M. Nixon (N.Y.)	Republican	31,770,237	43.4	301	60.6
	Hubert H. Humphrey	Democratic	31,270,533	42.3	191	
	George Wallace	American Independent	9,906,141	12.9	46	
1972	Richard M. Nixon (N.Y.)	Republican	47,169,911	60.7	520	55.2
	George S. McGovern	Democratic	29,170,383	37.5	17	
	Other	—			1	
1976	Jimmy Carter (Ga.)	Democratic	40,828,587	50.0	297	53.5
	Gerald R. Ford	Republican	39,147,613	47.9	240	
	Other	—	1,575,459	2.1	1	
1980	Ronald Reagan (Calif.)	Republican	43,901,812	50.7	489	52.6
	Jimmy Carter	Democratic	35,483,820	41.0	49	
	John B. Anderson	Independent	5,719,722	6.6	—	
	Ed Clark	Libertarian	921,188	1.1	—	
1984	Ronald Reagan (Calif.)	Republican	54,455,075	59.0	525	53.3
	Walter Mondale	Democratic	37,577,185	41.0	13	
1988	George Bush (Tex.)	Republican	47,946,422	54.0	426	50.0
	Michael S. Dukakis	Democratic	41,016,429	46.0	112	
1992	William J. Clinton (Ark.)	Democratic	44,909,889	43.0	370	55.2
	George Bush	Republican	39,104,545	38.0	168	
	Ross Perot	Independent	19,742,267	19.0	0	

(continued)

Year	Candidates	Parties	Popular Vote	Percentage of Popular Vote	Electoral Vote	Percentage of Voter Participation
1996	William J. Clinton (Ark.)	Democratic	47,401,185	49.3	379	49.0
	Robert Dole	Republican	39,197,469	40.7	159	
	Ross Perot	Reform	8,085,294	8.4	—	
2000	George W. Bush (Tex.)	Republican	50,459,211	47.89	271	51.0
	Albert Gore Jr.	Democratic	51,003,894	48.41	266	
	Ralph Nader	Green	2,834,410	2.69	—	
2004	George W. Bush (Tex.)	Republican	62,028,285	50.73	286	60.0
	John Kerry	Democratic	59,028,109	48.27	251	
	Ralph Nader	Independent	463,647	0.38	0	
2008	Barack Obama (Ill.)	Democratic	65,070,489	53	364	61.7
	John McCain	Republican	57,154,810	46	174	

INDEX